GERMANY AND THE FRENCH REVOLUTION

GERMANY
AND THE
FRENCH REVOLUTION

G. P. GOOCH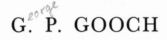

NEW YORK
RUSSELL & RUSSELL · INC
1966

FIRST PUBLISHED IN 1920
REISSUED, 1966, BY RUSSELL & RUSSELL, INC.
BY ARRANGEMENT WITH FRANK CASS & CO. LTD., LONDON
L.C. CATALOG CARD NO: 66-11636

Printed in Great Britain

PREFACE

WHILE the political history of the era of the French Revolution has been written by Sybel and Sorel and a crowd of lesser men, the influence of its ideas and of the moving drama of blood and tears on the mind and soul of the different countries of Europe has never been thoroughly explored. The universal significance of the upheaval was grasped at the outset both by actors and spectators. 'Your laws will be the laws of Europe, if you are worthy of them,' declared Mirabeau to the Constituent Assembly; 'so strong is the influence of great States, and, above all, of France.' 'Whoever regards this Revolution as exclusively French,' echoed Mallet du Pan, 'is incapable of pronouncing judgment upon it.' Friends and foes beyond the frontiers were at one in emphasising the power of its appeal; and men like Burke and Paine, Kant and de Maistre, who agreed in nothing else, were convinced that the problems which it raised concerned humanity as a whole. 'When France has a cold,' remarked Metternich bitterly, 'all Europe sneezes.' The verdict of contemporaries has been ratified by succeeding generations, and has now become an established commonplace.

The object of this book is to measure the repercussion of the French Revolution on the mind of Germany. The story of diplomacy and war in the closing decade of the eighteenth century has been told with ever-increasing knowledge by two generations of historians; and the atmospheric difference between the heated polemics of Häusser and the cool serenity of Heigel registers a welcome advance in the arts of interpretation. But no panoramic survey of the intellectual ferment has been attempted. It is scarcely necessary to remark that this chapter of German history, like every other, has been the theme of innumerable monographs; and to some learned specialists a synthetic treatment may appear to be premature. But the attempt is, at any rate, worth making; for few periods in the spiritual life of the modern world compare in interest with the Augustan Age of German literature, adorned

v

with the names of Goethe and Schiller, Wieland and Herder, Klopstock and the Romantics, Gentz and Humboldt, Kant and Fichte. To the friendly eyes of Madame de Staël Germany was a nation of thinkers and poets; and no one will contest the assertion of Chuquet, to whose writings every student of the period is deeply indebted, that of all Germans who used the pen there was not one whose works do not bear the mark of the Revolution. This rich field has been too little explored by British scholars, and large tracts of it are virtually unknown outside Germany. For this reason I have allowed my authors, as far as possible, to express their opinions in their own words. For most of the renderings of German poetry I am indebted to the kindness of Miss Dorothy Henkel.

While the main theme of the volume is the analysis of opinion, I have endeavoured in the later chapters to explain the influence of the cataclysm on the institutions of the Holy Roman Empire and on the internal development of the more important units of which it was composed. The earthquake in France was followed by a tidal wave, which swept away a mass of antiquated rubbish in the Rhineland and Central Europe, and cleared the ground for a limited number of States of tolerable size, governed on modern lines. The renaissance of Prussia falls outside my chronological limits; but I have briefly indicated the debt of the leading reformers to the principles and precedents of revolutionary France. Some illustrative passages have been taken from the dispatches of British Ministers at various German Courts, preserved in the Record Office; and it is scarcely necessary to add that the pleasure of working in the national archives has been enhanced by the ready kindness of Mr. Hubert Hall.

G. P. G.

76 CAMPDEN HILL ROAD, W. 8.
January, 1920.

CONTENTS

GERMANY AND THE FRENCH REVOLUTION

CHAPTER I

BEFORE THE REVOLUTION

I

DURING the years immediately preceding the French Revolution Germany presented a curious spectacle of political decrepitude and intellectual rejuvenescence. The Holy Roman Empire,[1] in regard to which Voltaire caustically inquired in what respect it was holy or Roman or an Empire, was afflicted with creeping paralysis. Its wheels continued to revolve; but the machinery was rusty and the output was small.

> The Holy Roman Empire,
> How does it hold together?

shouted Goethe's revellers in Auerbach's Keller. 'No Curtius,' remarked Justus Möser in 1781, 'leaps into the abyss for the preservation of the Imperial system'—a system which offered no security against foreign invasion or civil war, and which had long ceased to command the respect either of its own members or of the world. Germany, cried Friedrich Karl Moser in the bitterness of his heart, is a great but despised people. Every nation, he added, had a governing principle. In England it was liberty, in Holland trade, in France the honour of the King, while in Germany it was obedience. Many a pamphleteer lamented the anaemia of

---

[1] See Bryce, *The Holy Roman Empire*; Perthes, *Deutsches Staatsleben vor der Revolution*; Biedermann, *Deutschland im 18ten Jahrhundert*; Auerbach, *La France et le Saint Empire Germanique*; Häusser, *Deutsche Geschichte*, i. 64–132; Treitschke, *Germany*, vol. i.; Wenck, *Deutschland vor hundert Jahren*, vol. i.

the Fatherland; but not one of them could produce a restorative. The Imperial system was the consecration of anarchy, and Germany was racked by an incurable particularism. 'In my childhood,' wrote Wieland, 'I was told a great deal about duties; but there was so little about the duty of a German patriot that I cannot remember ever hearing the word German used with honour. There are Saxon, Bavarian, Frankfurt patriots; but German patriots, who love the Empire as their fatherland, where are they?' The Empire, in fact, was not even German. The King of England was a member as Elector of Hanover, the King of Denmark as Duke of Holstein, the King of Sweden as Lord of Pomerania, while Belgium participated as an appanage of the House of Hapsburg.

In theory the Imperial crown was elective; but in practice it was found impossible to override the traditional claims of the Hapsburgs, as Charles VII of Bavaria and his champions learned to their cost in the war of the Austrian Succession. The Empire appeared to revive for a moment in the coronation pageantry at Frankfurt, when the Emperor received the homage of the Estates on bended knee and the herald brandished his sword towards the four quarters of heaven in token that all Christendom was subject to his sway; but in the eighteenth century it was nothing but a picturesque survival. The Emperor was still the fount of honour; but, except for the grant of titles, his prerogatives had disappeared. As a German jurist aptly remarked: to prevent him from doing harm, he was prevented from doing anything. Such powers as he possessed he owed not to the crown of Charlemagne and Barbarossa, but to the territories and resources of the House of Hapsburg. The Golden Bull of Charles IV limited the Electors to seven, three of whom were the Archbishops of Mainz, Cologne, and Trier. The secular princes were the rulers of the Palatinate, Bohemia, Saxony, and Brandenburg, to which Bavaria and Hanover were added in the seventeenth century. The first in rank was the Elector of Mainz, the Arch-Chancellor of the Empire, who crowned the Emperor at Frankfurt. The legislative power was exercised by the Diet at Regensburg, to which ambassadors were accredited and from which the army of the Empire took its orders. Since 1663 it sat in permanence; but this change decreased instead of increasing its importance, as it was only attended by delegates—and most members of the Empire never troubled to be represented. It consisted of three Colleges, the Electors, the Princes (ecclesiastical and secular), and the Free Cities, sitting separately. If two Colleges agreed, and their wishes were sanctioned by the Emperor, the resolution became an Imperial law; but its execution depended on the separate decision of each separate unit, large or small, of which the Empire was composed. It was only at Regensburg that 'Germany' could be found; but the significance of the Diet had waned with the strength of the Empire, and its time was largely wasted in solemn trifling and hoary pedantries. While the Emperor resided at Vienna and the Diet sat at Regensburg, the Supreme Court of the Empire was moved in 1693 from Speyer to Wetzlar, a town which owes its later fame rather to Werther and Lotte than to its Imperial associations. The Court had earned an unenviable reputation for venality and procrastination ; and if a few petty tyrants were thwarted or punished by its decrees, it was too weak to strike at powerful offenders. Young jurists like Goethe spent a few months in the sleepy little town to learn the routine of the law of the Empire ; but its prestige was impaired by the fact that most of the important cases were reserved by the Emperor for the usurping Aulic Council at Vienna.

In addition to the Emperor, the Diet, and the Court of Appeal, the machinery of the Empire included ten Circles, or administrative districts, created to counteract the dangers of excessive particularism by the formation of large groups. Each Circle possessed a Diet and a Director, who commanded the troops, controlled the police, and provided for the execution of the Imperial laws. In the course of the centuries, however, great changes had occurred. The Circle of Burgundy had been swallowed up in France. Holland was free. Many territories, again, had become subject to members of the Empire—such as Hungary and the Polish provinces annexed by Austria and Prussia, which were not incorporated in the Empire. On the eve of the French Revolution there were nine Circles : Upper and Lower Saxony, Austria, Bohemia, Bavaria, Westphalia, the Upper Rhine, Swabia, Franconia. Differing widely in size and importance, they were alike in their invertebrate character. Prussia formed part of three Circles, while Swabia and Franconia presented a bewildering mosaic of petty principalities, ecclesiastical and secular. It was in these Circles of the lower and middle Rhine that the hundreds of Imperial Knights, who recognised no superior but the Emperor, exercised unfettered sway over their Liliputian territories. Western Germany was the classic land of duodecimo States, which afforded no foundation for healthy political life and offered a tempting prey to the sleepless ambitions of France.

Thus the Empire was a phantom, its machinery rotten and crumbling, its head a mere honorary president. Whatever shadowy sentiment of unity had survived the Wars of Religion and the Treaty of Westphalia, was destroyed in the prolonged duel of

Frederick the Great and Maria Theresa ; and the short but stormy reign of Joseph II showed that the Imperial dignity had sunk into the tool and plaything of the House of Hapsburg. Emperor and Empire were regarded as strangers, if not as enemies, in the larger States, especially in the Protestant North. So long as the Holy Roman Empire should continue to exist, Germany was condemned to remain a geographical expression.

Frederick the Great defined the Empire as a Republic of Princes with an elective head ; and the real political life of the country on the eve of the Revolution was in the States and principalities which composed it. Since the Peace of Westphalia, which accorded to them the right of making treaties with foreign Powers, the component States were independent in all but name ; and one of them climbed rapidly to a position from which it boldly challenged the overlordship of the Imperial house.[1] The Great Elector attracted the attention of Europe to Prussia by his victories and his diplomacy, and laid the foundations of the autocracy on which the Hohenzollerns reared one of the strongest political edifices of the modern world. His son Frederick I placed the crown upon his head, and his grandson, Frederick William I, created an administrative machine the ruthless efficiency of which surpassed the achievement of every State in Europe. Finding a well-trained army and an overflowing treasury on his accession in 1740, Frederick the Great seized Silesia and held it throughout two wars against the combined efforts of half Europe. Goethe has recorded in his Autobiography how the victories of the great King awoke Germany from her slumbers and gave a theme and an inspiration to poets, describing him as the pole-star round which Prussia, Germany, and indeed the world, seemed to revolve. ' His victories,' records Niebuhr, ' gave confidence and a sense of nationality to all Germans, not to Prussians and Protestants alone. The whole country felt that it had a prince whom Europe admired.' His prowess was sung in verse by Kleist and Gleim, and in prose by Archenholz. The Swabian Abbt was inspired by the disaster of Kunersdorf to write his ' Death for the Fatherland,' ' in order to stir up citizens to save the country, and fill them with noble patriotic sentiments, and above all to show my admiration for Frederick the Great.' But it was not only to the successful warrior that all eyes were turned, but to the exponent of a new theory and

---

[1] See Droysen, *Geschichte der Preussischen Politik* ; Ranke, *Zwölf Bucher Preussischer Geschichte* ; Koser, *König Friedrich der Grosse.* For more summary treatment, see Prutz, *Preussische Geschichte* ; Meinecke, *Die Hohenzollern* ; Treitschke, *Germany*, vol. i. ; Marriott and Robertson, *The Evolution of Prussia.*

practice of government. The contrast between the simple and laborious life of the King of Prussia and the idleness and dissolute extravagance of most of his contemporaries enhanced the prestige of the State. The Sovereign, declared the Crown Prince in his 'Anti-Machiavel,' far from being the absolute master of the people under his sceptre, is himself only their first servant. This celebrated sentence overthrew divine right and 'proprietary' monarchy by substituting the doctrine of service for the doctrine of property. Enlightened autocrats were to guide and govern their peoples as a wise father directs the steps of his children. Frederick was not the first philosophic despot; but his brilliant performance popularised the rôle, and founded a school of which the most eminent rulers of Germany and Europe were to be the disciples.

Frederick's State was so small and his energy so unflagging that for forty-six years he governed Prussia like no Hohenzollern before or after him. The Sovereign, he declared, was bound to act as if he had every moment to tender an account of his stewardship to his fellow-citizens.[1] He only slept for six hours; and when his doctor ordered the old man of sixty-nine to cancel a journey of inspection, the King replied, 'You have your duties and I have mine, and I will carry them out till my last breath.' But the burden of war and taxation was heavy, feudalism stood unchallenged, a short-sighted mercantilism kept the country poor, and the political education of the people was neglected. In the King's famous words, the arrangement was that his subjects should say what they liked and he should do what he liked. While Calas and La Barre were being tortured in France, the Philosopher of Sans Souci was declaring that in his dominions everyone might find his way to heaven in his own way. But this easy toleration was confined to religion, for which he cared nothing. He commenced his reign by allowing uncensored liberty to the Berlin papers; but the privilege was quickly revoked.[2] 'Do not talk to me of your liberty of thought and the press,' wrote Lessing from Hamburg to Nicolai in 1769. 'It reduces itself to the liberty to let off as many squibs against religion as one likes. Let somebody raise his voice for the rights of subjects or against exploitation and despotism, and you will soon see which is the most slavish land in Europe.' The general feeling was expressed by Wieland, who remarked that while he felt the greatest admiration for the

[1] 'Essais sur les formes de gouvernement et sur les devoirs des souverains'; Œuvres de Frédéric le Grand, vol. ix.
[2] See Consentius, Friedrich der Grosse und die Zeitungs-Zensur, Preussische Jahrbücher, Feb. 1904.

King of Prussia, he thanked heaven that he did not live under his stick or sceptre. Next to the King the army was supreme. ' In my State,' wrote Frederick, ' a lieutenant stands higher than a chamberlain.' The nobility, which he described as the incubator of officers, occupied almost all the higher posts in the army and the State, while the peasantry supplied the requisite cannon fodder. If Prussia was the best governed of the larger German States, her people, as Mirabeau argued at length in his massive study of ' The Prussian Monarchy,' were certainly neither the happiest nor the most prosperous ; for neither glory nor efficiency were substitutes for liberty and equality.

The springtime of Prussian greatness was merely the reflection of her ruler's dazzling personality ; and his successor had neither the power nor the will to stretch the bow of Ulysses.[1] ' The good King will never attain the terrible greatness of his uncle,' wrote Schlözer ; ' but in heart he leaves him far behind.' Mirabeau, who knew them both, described Frederick as all mind, and his nephew as all body ; and he uttered the prophetic words, ' I foretell nothing but weakness and confusion.' His Open Letter to the new King sketched out a bold programme of reform, including the over-throw of the privileges of the nobility, liberty of thought and the Press, and the abolition of monopolies ; but he had no expectation of its fulfilment. At first there was a sigh of relief at the removal of the iron hand which had governed with the inexorable rigidity of a machine. Frederick William II was affable and kind-hearted, and the temporary abolition of the hated monopoly of coffee and tobacco seemed to promise a less rigorous régime. But it was not long before the best minds in Prussia regretted the disap-pearance of the Master-Builder. While Frederick had scorned delights and lived laborious days dictating letters, reviewing his troops, and making tours of inspection throughout his dominions, his nephew filled Potsdam with loose women and dabblers in occultism, married first one and then another of his flames while his wife was still alive, wasted the treasure which his uncle had stored, and revoked the religious toleration which had been the brightest feature of the system of the royal philosopher. Thus, after a brief interval of relief and expectation, Prussia found herself less respected, less feared, and even less free than she had been under the sceptre of her greatest King.

The State most closely allied to Prussia by personal ties and community of political ideas was Brunswick. Charles William Ferdinand, the son of Frederick's sister, had won fame both in

[1] See Philippson, *Geschichte des deutschen Staatswesens*, vol. i. ; Heigel, *Deutsche Geschichte*, 1786–1806, vol. i. ch. 3.

the arts of war and peace.[1] He had distinguished himself in the Seven Years' War, had visited Voltaire at Ferney, and had studied Rome under the guidance of Winckelmann. On his accession to the Duchy in 1780, he proved himself a model ruler. Inheriting the debts incurred during the long reign of his extravagant father, he restored the financial equilibrium of his little State by rigorous public and private economy. He maintained a small army, improved the roads, humanised the poor law, encouraged Campe to reform education, and was only prevented by the clergy from introducing secular control of the schools. His wide culture and personal charm, his policy of toleration, which embraced the Jews, and the freedom which he granted to the Press, made him the second hero of the German Aufklärung. French travellers and savants visited his Court, and Mirabeau, who was never quite happy at Berlin, found the atmosphere of Brunswick exceptionally congenial. 'He delights greatly in France,' he reported, 'with which he is exceptionally well acquainted, and he likes everything which comes thence.' On the death of Frederick the Great the Duke succeeded to his position as the outstanding figure of Germany, and his victorious campaign in Holland in 1787 raised him to the pinnacle of military fame.

The Electorate of Hanover, on the other hand, lacked the amenities of a Court and the bracing initiative of a resident ruler.[2] But though the dominions of his ancestors were never visited by George III, who transferred the seat of government to London, the land was administered by an honest and reasonably efficient bureaucracy. Justice was pure, taxation was moderate, the Press was reasonably free, the dynasty was popular, and the nobility were not in exclusive control of the government. There was a higher respect for the rights of the subject, and, in the upper classes, a more widespread interest in the State than anywhere else in Germany. But though British influences were not wholly without effect, the country was none the less inert and sterile, and was described by Stein as the German China. The one splash of colour in a rather drab picture was supplied by the University of Göttingen, the child of Münchhausen, the enlightened minister of George II. The new school of learning quickly supplanted Halle as the leading German University; and young men destined for the service of the State flocked from every part of the country to

---

[1] See Fitzmaurice, *Charles William Ferdinand, Duke of Brunswick*. There is a good survey of the minor States in Heigel, *Deutsche Geschichte*, i. 79–116.

[2] See A. W. Ward, *Great Britain and Hanover*, Lecture VI.; and Treitschke, iv. 351–81.

its eminent teachers of law and history, economics, and political science.

An inferior variety of ' enlightened despotism ' was to be found in Saxony.[1] The Electors, Augustus II and III, aided and abetted by Count Brühl, the evil genius of the country, had overtaxed the resources of the State by their wars, their mad extravagance, and their endeavours to make Dresden the most brilliant capital in Europe after Paris. Though the Sistine Madonna was purchased, and Winckelmann was sent to Rome, the greater part of the money expended by the Court was wasted in riotous living. On the death of Augustus III in 1763, his grandson, Frederick Augustus, began his long reign at the age of thirteen, unencumbered by the burden of the Polish crown. A new spirit of order and economy was at once introduced. Debt was paid off, and the Court became a school of virtue. Torture was abolished, an Academy of Mines was founded at Freiberg which Werner made the first school of geology in Europe, and the book trade of Leipsic flourished during the generation of peace that succeeded the Seven Years' War. His subjects deservedly called him the Just ; but he was no statesman, and his conception of good government was abstinence from evil courses, not the introduction of reforms. While Frederick the Great and Ferdinand of Brunswick welcomed the rays of the Aufklärung, Frederick Augustus stood aloof from the cleansing and challenging currents of rationalism and humanitarianism that were beginning to surge through Europe. Even more remote from the sweep of modern ideas were the Mecklenburg Duchies, at that time, as to-day, politically the most backward of all German States. ' The home of the Mecklenburg noble who crushes his peasantry,' wrote Stein indignantly, ' seems to me to be like the lair of a wild beast, who ravages the neighbourhood and surrounds himself with the silence of the tomb.' The Dukes were as powerless as the peasants, and the feudal oligarchy reigned supreme.

The small States of central Germany revealed a similar variety of merit and defect. The Landgrave Frederick II of Hesse-Cassel shared the prevailing taste for French culture, transformed Cassel into an imposing city, enriched the picture-gallery, and summoned eminent scholars to the Collegium Carolinum ; but the Court was loose, and the sale of his subjects to England at £15 a head earned him the detestation of Europe. The plight of Hesse-Darmstadt, whose Landgrave, Ludwig IX, wasted his energy and resources on military antics, was no better. His son Ludwig X, who spent a long time at the Court of Berlin, shared Frederick's devotion to the Aufklärung, and counted Schiller and Goethe among his friends ;

[1] See Treitschke, iv. 289–329.

but his accession was quickly followed by the outbreak of war. Among the Duchies ruled by the Ernestine branches of the Saxon dynasty of Wettin, Saxe-Weimar stood out as the model of small principalities. The regency of Anna Amalia laid the foundations of the thrifty and enlightened administration which her son Karl August, with the aid of Goethe, practised throughout a reign of half a century. His maxims of government and intellectual interests were shared by Duke Ernest of Gotha and by Franz of Anhalt-Dessau, the patron of Basedow's Philanthropinum. A still more minute principality, that of Schaumburg-Lippe, had the good fortune to be ruled for a few years by Count Wilhelm, the friend of Abbt and Herder, a man who only needed a larger sphere of action to have written his name in conspicuous letters on the history of his country.

Among South German States the largest and the most stagnant was Bavaria.[1] The great outburst of energy in the Thirty Years' War had been followed by a rapid decline, which was accelerated by unsuccessful war and domestic misgovernment. A ray of light penetrated the darkness during the middle of the eighteenth century in the reign of Max Joseph, who founded the Academy of Sciences, waged war on the Jesuits, and encouraged Ickstatt to reform the system of education. But under his successor the country sank back into hopeless obscurantism, and was cruelly described by Frederick the Great as an earthly paradise inhabited by animals. Karl Theodor had ruled the Palatinate for thirty-five years before the failure of the direct line of the Wittelsbachs called him to Munich in 1777. The early years of his reign at Mannheim had not been wholly without distinction. His knightly bearing procured him the name of the First Cavalier of the Holy Roman Empire; his generosity to foreign scholars that of the German Maecenas. He founded an Academy of Science in Mannheim, enriched the galleries, and built the first Court theatre in Germany, soon to be the scene of the joint triumphs of Schiller and Iffland. But his faults increased with age, and his later years were disgraced by intolerance, immorality, and greed. Religious persecution drove thousands of his Protestant subjects to America, and he procured money for his mistresses and bastards by the sale of offices and the oppression of his people. The Elector exchanged Mannheim for Munich with a heavy heart, and saw in his new Electorate little but a means of supporting his illegitimate children. He disliked the heavy, boorish Bavarians, and was only prevented by Frederick the Great from

---

[1] See Döberl, *Entwickelungsgeschichte Bayerns*, vol. ii.; Temperley, *Frederick the Great* and *Kaiser Joseph*; Döllinger, *Studies in European History*; Kluckhohn, *Vorträge u. Aufsätze*; Kluckhohn, *Westenrieder*.

B

selling the country to Joseph II.   For a year or two he allowed the progressive tendencies of his predecessor full scope, and supported the reforms in agriculture and industry carried out by the gifted American adventurer, Benjamin Thompson, Count Rumford, still remembered at Munich as the creator of the ' English Garden.' But the discovery of the activities of the Illuminati frightened the ageing Elector into reaction, and the Court of Munich became a byword throughout the Empire for immorality and obscurantism. His confessor, Father Frank, reigned supreme, and the faith of the State was kept pure by a strenuous censorship while its mind slumbered.   The streets of the capital were filled with beggars, and the countryside was infested with robbers.   Munich was a city of churches, monasteries, and religious processions, while seventeen wonder-working relics competed for the patronage of the faithful. Bavaria deliberately and ostentatiously cut itself off from the rest of Germany, strangers were regarded as foreigners, and German was discouraged as the language of the Lutheran heresy.   Though the army shrunk to half its size there was a large annual deficit. A luxurious Court increased the sufferings of an impoverished people ; but the country suffered rather from anarchy than from tyranny.   Even greater were the misery and misrule of the Palatinate, over which the Elector continued to stretch his nerveless hand.

The position of Württemberg was in some respects more favourable than that of Bavaria.[1]   Alone among German principalities, its old constitution of Estates continued to possess at least the shadow of power ; and Fox once declared that the only countries in Europe which possessed constitutional government were England and Württemberg.   There was also far more civic spirit, and the land shared to the full in the intellectual revival of the eighteenth century.   But in other respects it was less favourably placed than its neighbour ; for its rulers were as extravagant as the Wittelsbachs and far more despotic.   For twenty years of the reign of Eberhard Ludwig the country was ruled by his mistress Wilhelmina von Grävenitz, whose monument is the vast palace of Ludwigsburg. But the sufferings of the State reached their height during the long reign of Karl Eugen, whose struggles with the Estates attracted the attention of Europe and whose tyranny drove Schiller abroad. The prince was educated at the Prussian Court, and Frederick the Great composed for his guidance his little tract ' Le Miroir des Princes.'   But the good advice was unheeded, and the young ruler became the scourge of his people.   He broke his oath to observe

[1] See Eugen Schneider, *Württembergische Geschichte* ; and Wohlwill *Weltbürgertum u. Vaterlandsliebe der Schwaben.*

the constitution of the country; and to a bold Senator, who protested in the name of the Fatherland, he replied, ' What is that ? I am the Fatherland.' The Estates found a champion in the great lawyer, J. J. Moser, the Coke of Württemberg, who set up the few surviving relics of primitive Germanic liberty as a breakwater against the flood of absolutism, and was punished by five years' imprisonment. The Standing Committee of the Estates presented protest after protest, and brought an action against the ruler in the Imperial Court, while the Courts of Prussia, England, and Denmark intervened with remonstrance and advice. The Duke's private life was no less detestable than his public activities. His fierce temper and ungovernable sensuality were the terror of his subjects, and his Court was modelled on that of Louis XV. The ruler of a poor and tiny duchy lived like an Oriental potentate, adding palace to palace, and passing his time at Ludwigsburg in balls and operas, hunting and gambling. Like his brother despots, he procured money for his pleasures by the sale of his subjects to foreign Powers and by putting up posts in the public service to auction. At length his mounting debts compelled him to seek a reconciliation with the Estates and to recognise the constitution, and in 1778 a message of repentance was read aloud in the churches on his fiftieth birthday. His extravagance was held in check, and his good resolutions were strengthened by his latest mistress, Franciska von Hohenheim, who became his second wife. His intellectual attainments were recognised by Schiller, and he posed as the friend of education by founding the Karlsschule at Stuttgart ; but though the closing years of his reign were very different from its opening, his yoke was never light, and he sent Schubart and other outspoken critics to rot for years in the gloomy dungeons of the Asperg.

Alone of South German States, on the eve of the Revolution, Baden was blessed with a ruler of capacity and conscience.[1] Karl Friedrich, the outstanding member of the House of Zähringen, ascended the throne as a boy, and his long reign witnessed the birth of a flourishing State. ' My neighbour of Württemberg,' he used to say in jest, ' does his utmost to ruin his land, and I do my utmost to raise mine ; but neither of us succeeds.' At any rate, he did all that could be done in a tiny State by a wise and unselfish ruler. Keenly interested in agriculture, he embraced the doctrines of the Physiocrats, corresponded with the elder Mirabeau and Dupont de Nemours, and himself wrote on political economy. He accepted and applied the famous maxim of Quesnay, ' Pauvres paysans,

---

[1] See Weech, *Badische Geschichte* ; Kleinschmidt, *Karl Friedrich von Baden* ; Windelband, *Die Verwaltung der Markgrafschaft Badens zur Zeit Karl Friedrichs* ; *Karl Friedrich's Brieflicher Verkehr mit Mirabeau u. Dupont.*

pauvre royaume ; pauvre royaume, pauvre roi.' But, though sharing the Physiocratic preference for agriculture, he did not overlook the claims of industry and trade. Burdensome taxes and tariffs were removed, justice fairly administered, and popular education provided. Himself a keen student of literature and a friend of Voltaire and Klopstock, Herder and Jung Stilling, he showed himself hospitable to all the enlightened ideas of his time. He grasped the manifold needs of a modern State, remarking that material well-being could never be firmly established where intellectual development was held in check. After a long sojourn at Karlsruhe, Klopstock described his host as ' a man with whom one could talk ' ; while Herder praised him as the only prince he knew without princely airs, and as perhaps the best German ruler alive in 1770. A still weightier tribute came from Frederick the Great, who at the end of his life remarked that he respected Karl Friedrich beyond all his princely contemporaries. He found an ideal colleague and counsellor in Edelsheim, one of the noblest political figures of the Aufklärung. Perfect harmony existed between ruler and people, and in 1783 a general expression of popular gratitude rewarded the abolition of serfdom. Though the Court was outwardly French, Karl Friedrich was thoroughly German at heart. He discussed the Fürstenbund with Karl August of Weimar and Franz of Dessau before Frederick the Great intervened ; and he instructed Herder to work out a plan for a ' Patriotic Institute for Germany,' which should emphasise and encourage the sense of national unity in intellectual pursuits. The union of Baden-Baden on the death of the last Margrave in 1771 with Karl Friedrich's own principality of Baden-Durlach joined lands which had been separated for more than two centuries, and afforded him the opportunity of showing that a pious Protestant ruler could respect the religion of his Catholic subjects.

If Karl Friedrich was the best of South-German rulers, Karl of Zweibrücken, the elder brother of the future King of Bavaria, was the worst. His consuming passion for the chase ruined the crops of his tiny principality, and his capricious cruelties were those of a madman. The scathing denunciations of Schlözer called the attention of the Empire to the insane freaks played beyond the Rhine, but were of no avail to rescue his subjects from the galling yoke. The Court was French, and the Duke received and squandered a French pension. Scarcely better was the plight of Ansbach-Baireuth, whose Margrave, Karl Alexander, nephew of Frederick the Great, dissipated the resources of his State first on the Parisian actress Clairon and then on Lady Craven ; sold his regiments to England for the American War ; and finally, at the bidding of his English mistress, sold his principality for hard cash to Prussia, and retired to England.[1] No more perfect illustration of the prevailing assumption that the State and its inhabitants were the private property of its ruler could be found than the disgraceful story of the closing years of the little principality.

The rule of the Electors of Mainz, Trier, and Cologne, which gave the Rhine the name of the Pfaffengasse or Parsons' Lane, was seldom tyrannical; but it was lifeless, enervating, and, as a rule, obscurantist.[2] The ecclesiastical States, of which the three Electorates were the most important, were highly unpopular in Protestant circles, and their shortcomings were fiercely denounced in 1787 by Friedrich Karl Moser. In Schlözer's journal the question was raised why people were less happy in the ecclesiastical principalities than elsewhere ; and the answer was that it was owing to the worldliness of the prelates. Secularisation was in the air, and even Pacca, the Nuncio, was conscious of an atmospheric change.

The first in importance was the Electorate of Mainz, which embraced large territories on the Rhine and the Main, and included the outlying dependency of Erfurt. As Chancellor of the Empire, President of the Electoral College, and Consecrator of the Emperor, the occupant of the See of Boniface could not fail to be an important figure in the life of Western Germany ; and the strength of one of the chief outposts of the Empire was a matter of importance to all its members. But since Schönborn, the friend and patron of Leibnitz, none of the Electors had been men of distinction ; and the frequent changes of ruler made continuity of policy impossible. The people were pious and conservative, and desired the cautious removal of abuses ; but their rulers oscillated between bold innovation and mindless reaction. Count Ostein (1743–63), a friend and admirer of Voltaire, was a child of the Aufklärung, reforming education and engaging in a sharp skirmish with the Jesuits ; but his subjects were frightened, and the Elector was forced to moderate his reforming zeal. His successor, Emmerich, continued the attempt to revive intellectual life by founding an *École normale* and summoning foreign scholars to replace Jesuit teachers at the University. But the clergy, backed by the ignorant masses, opposed the reform of education, attacked the Elector as a freethinker, and compelled him, like his predecessor, to compromise. The last of the Electors, Baron von Erthal, was chosen in 1774 as a champion of the old paths which his two predecessors had deserted.[3] His first step

[1] See Broadley and Melville, *The Beautiful Lady Craven.*
[2] See Perthes, *Politische Zustände u. Personen in Deutschland zur Zeit der französischen Herrschaft*; and Schultheiss, *Die Geistlichen Staaten beim Ausgang des alten Reichs.*
[3] See Herse, *Mainz vor der Revolution.*

was to remove freethinkers from the schools and to restore the strict observance of religious forms. But he quickly tired of the ascetic's rôle. 'He leads a purely worldly life,' reported Pacca, as he surveyed the brilliant scene, with its balls, its feasts, and its hunting parties. The candidate of the obscurantists finally blossomed out into an unblushing champion of the Aufklärung. He summoned Sömmerring, Dorsch, Wedekind, Blau, Metternich, Hofmann, and other 'freethinkers' to the University; appointed the Swiss Protestant, Johannes Müller, his Privy Councillor and Georg Forster his librarian. In the houses of some members of the Cathedral Chapter were seen busts of Voltaire and the philosophers, while works of classical art replaced statues of the Virgin and the Crucifix, and the writings of Helvétius and other French materialists lay on the table. At Court the Elector and his favourite, Countess Hatzfeld, listened without blushes to the licentious pages of 'Ardinghello' read aloud by Heinse, a brilliant Renaissance figure who preached the emancipation of the flesh and the religion of beauty to a master who compared himself with Leo X. Most leaders of thought and society in Mainz were real or pretended adherents of the Aufklärung, and Dalberg, the Coadjutor who held his Court in Erfurt, emulated his chief. But this 'enlightenment' was to a great extent a pose, and was never applied to the problems of government. Forster, who was both a scholar and a reformer, commented severely on the extravagance and self-indulgence of the nobles and higher clergy by whom the Electorate was governed. The old abuses and the old privileges remained. Materialism, thinly disguised under a veneer of culture, was supreme, and the graver tasks of administration and defence were neglected. The fortifications were turned into gardens under the control of the Court gardener. To those who had eyes to see it was obvious that when the tempest came the whole glittering edifice would topple over like a house of cards.

The Electorate of Trier showed similar variations during the eighteenth century, the general character of its rulers being that of benevolent inefficiency. The State was smaller and poorer than Mainz, and less in the public eye. While Erthal aped the fashions of Versailles at Mainz, Clemens Wenceslas, the last Elector of Trier, a lover of music and the domestic virtues, exercised a just and tolerant sway at Coblenz. Though an ex-officer in the Austrian army and a son of Augustus II of Saxony, the champion sinner of his age, the Elector won the testimony of the Nuncio to his irreproachable character. Pacca added that he had a weak will ; but he showed considerable vigour in his support of Hontheim, Bishop of Trier, better known by his *nom de plume* of Febronius, and of the anti-curial movement which convulsed Catholic Germany on the eve of the Revolution.[1] Though his ecclesiastical policy and the controversies to which it led were not to the taste of the mass of his subjects, the good-natured cleric was popular and respected ; but the old abuses lingered on, and no steps were taken to strengthen the State against the internal and external dangers which were soon to overwhelm it.

The most backward of the three Electorates was that of Cologne, whose rulers during the larger part of the seventeenth and eighteenth centuries were unworthy members of the Bavarian reigning house. Joseph Clemens refused to read mass or perform his episcopal duties if his confessor tried to separate him from his mistress, the mother of several children. His successor, Clemens August (1723-61), the last of the Wittelsbach Electors, observed the outward forms of religion, but led a life of wild dissipation, wasting the substance of his subjects on dancers and singers, balls, hunts, and palaces. The Count of Königseck ascended the Electoral throne with a good character ; but the vicious traditions of the Court at Bonn were too much for him. Not till the accession of the Archduke Max, youngest son of Maria Theresa, in 1784, did the Electorate possess an enlightened ruler whom it could respect and admire. The new Elector at once cleansed the Court and restored order to the finances ; but his main task was to assist his brother the Emperor Joseph in his crusade against Ultramontanism. He transformed the Academy, founded by his predecessor at Bonn, into a University, which was intended to render him independent of Cologne, from which the Electorate had hitherto drawn its officials and clergy. So bitter was the feud, indeed, that in 1789 the Elector decreed that in future no student from Cologne University should obtain any ecclesiastical or civil post in his dominions. Max was amply justified in desiring to emancipate his State from the paralysing embrace of obscurantism ; but his zeal outran his discretion. Though the nobles and officials were, as a rule, freethinkers or indifferentists, the bourgeoisie and the peasantry remained devout Catholics ; and they deeply resented the attacks on the Church, monasticism and pilgrimages launched by Eulogius Schneider, and other scoffers imported by the Elector. Not one of the three ecclesiastical Electorates possessed a ruler with the strength and resolution to sweep away the accumulated abuses of generations. The smaller ecclesiastical principalities, scattered at random over the west and south of Germany, reproduced the main features of the Rhine Electorates. Ecclesiastical only in name, their rulers were temporal princes whose worldly life vied with that of their secular

[1] See O. Meier, *Zur Geschichte der römisch-deutschen Frage*, vol. i.

neighbours. As a rule, their subjects suffered or vegetated in silence; but from time to time the curtain was lifted on some particularly gross scandal, and all Germany rang with the story of tyranny or caprice. Thus the rule of the Archbishop of Speier, the most forcible personality among the Prince-Bishops on the eve of the Revolution, was held up to the obloquy of Europe by the stinging pen of Schlözer.

The smallest members of the Empire were the Free Cities and the Imperial Knights. The former, once the pride of the Empire, differed in their size and vitality not less than the principalities. The Hansa towns in the north, Hamburg, Lubeck, and Bremen, were kept alive by their trade; and the largest of the three was the most cosmopolitan city in the Empire. Commercial intercourse with France and England brought liberal ideas to the Elbe, and the accumulated wealth of the merchant class provided an opportunity for culture which was eagerly seized. In no city in Germany was there such a free and vigorous intellectual life, such a number of well-informed men and women, such hospitality to new ideas. Klopstock made it his home in middle life; while Lessing rebuked theological obscurantism, and reformed the German theatre from its stage. The notes of Hamburg were energy, prosperity, and culture, political and religious liberalism. Next in wealth and superior in political prestige was Frankfurt, the Imperial city *par excellence*. The old town on the Main, with its cultivated bourgeoisie, makes a charming picture in the golden light of *Dichtung und Wahrheit*; but its pulse beat slower, and it was less liberal and ' modern ' than Hamburg. By far the greater number of the Free Cities had long fallen from their high estate and lived to themselves behind their crumbling walls. In many cases the population had shrunk since the Thirty Years' War almost to the dimensions of a rotten borough, and the government had become the hereditary monopoly of a tiny clique. Subject to the Emperor alone, they were at once independent republics and close corporations, and their vice was rather stagnation than tyranny. The magistrates were bound to summon the citizens or the Great Council on important occasions, and the newly elected officials had to swear fidelity to the Statutes. These forms in some degree helped to keep alive the tradition of law and liberty; but the little republics incurred the wrath and ridicule of the satirists. Wieland employed his recollections of his native Biberach in his ' Abderites.' Weckhrlin, who had crossed swords with the citizens of Augsburg and Nördlingen, denounced the cities as spiders' webs hanging on the Empire. Schubart spoke sternly of the moss-grown communities, ' in which inveterate abuses have deeper roots than the oldest oaks.' Towns with an even more illustrious pedigree than Hamburg and Frankfurt had sunk into objects of shame and derision. The old Imperial city of Aachen, the scene of coronations centuries before Frankfurt, had been ravaged by the contests of faction, and had fallen to political and economic ruin. Still more tragic was the fate of Cologne, which drew a cordon round her walls by the fourfold censorship of the University, the Archbishop, the Nuncio, and the Dominicans. No Protestant could own a house, hold office, or meet for service ; and the permission to build a church, reluctantly granted in 1787, was withdrawn in the following year. Whole streets fell into decay, and a battalion of beggars barred approach to the churches. Industry, trade, art, learning, politics, had fallen on evil days, and the once proud Roman Colonia was the abode of dirt, poverty, and superstition.

Like the Free Cities, the Imperial Knights had outlived their day. Subject to the Emperor alone and unrepresented in the Diet, they were undisputed lords of the tiny territory which they surveyed from their castle windows. Scattered by hundreds over the south and west of Germany, they were at best picturesque survivals of the Middle Ages, at worst the scene of petty tyranny when the patrimonial jurisdiction was exercised by men of boorish habits and vindictive temper. They, too, had few friends among the writers who voiced or created public opinion. 'If a place looks particularly derelict,' wrote Moser, 'we need not ask questions, for we know it to be the village of an Imperial Knight.' Of course, there were men like Stein who exercised their rights with restraint and took their duties seriously ; but the Reichsritter was an anachronism, and his possessions hindered the formation of larger and more healthy political units. At the first shock of the armed Revolution they were fated to disappear like bloodless spectres before the rising sun.

Such was the Holy Roman Empire in its last stages of decline, an object of scorn and derision to mankind. Few competent observers believed that it could be reformed, and an increasing number turned their eyes to Prussia as to a possible saviour. The Fürstenbund, the last creation of the mighty King, was hailed in certain quarters as the dawn of a new and better age.[1] In a pamphlet of 1787 Johannes Müller lauded it as a bulwark against the world-domination of the Emperor, a defence of the rights of every member of the Empire, and as a beneficent revolution from above. On the failure of Hapsburg ambitions, and the death of its founder, it fell to pieces ; and Johannes Müller again raised his

[1] See Ranke, *Die deutschen Mächte u. der Fürstenbund.*

voice in 1788. 'Without law or justice,' he cried in anguish, 'without security against capricious burdens, uncertain of maintaining our children, our liberties, our rights or our lives for a single day, the helpless prey of superior power, without national feeling— that is the *status quo* of our nation.' To stand still was to perish. The only alternative to revolution was reform of the Empire. 'I cannot understand,' he wrote, 'how we Germans have lost the courage and intelligence to advance from hoary pedantries to an effective Imperial constitution, to a true Imperial connection, to a common patriotism, so that we could at length say, We are a nation.' 'It is a rickety house,' echoed Thugut ; 'one must either leave it alone or pull it down and build another.' It was, indeed, past mending, and only waited for the *coup de grâce*. 'To say that Frederick the Great destroyed the Empire,' remarks Niebuhr, 'is to say that the person who buried the corpse killed the man.' If it had possessed real vitality, neither Frederick nor Napoleon could have destroyed it.

No less urgent was the need of reform in the majority of the component parts of the Empire. Nowhere in Europe was absolutism more crushing and repulsive than in the little Courts where Frederick's doctrine of 'service' had never penetrated, where mistresses ruled supreme, where venality placed the unfittest in office, where reckless ostentation stood out in glaring contrast to the poverty of the people. 'The peasant,' wrote a satirist grimly, 'is like a sack of meal. When emptied there is still some dust in it—it only needs to be beaten.' For the most part the victims suffered in silence ; but discontent was to find some interpreters, and the intellectual revival, aided by powerful external influences, began to wake the country from its slumbers. 'Who does not foresee great revolutions ?' asked the Hamburg Privy Councillor Creuz in 1767, after reviewing the evils of the time. The question was echoed by a growing chorus of voices in the next two decades ; and when the Rights of Man were proclaimed from the banks of the Seine, the German people was ready to welcome the new gospel.

II

While political life was thus backward and anaemic, a vigorous intellectual activity held out the promise of better days.[1] Wolff and Lessing, Moses Mendelssohn and Nicolai, the leaders of the

---

[1] See Julian Schmidt, *Geschichte der deutschen Litteratur* ; Hettner, *Deutsche Litteratur im 18ten Jahrhundert*, vols. iii.-iv. ; Scherer, *History of German Literature* ; Lévy-Bruhl, *L'Allemagne depuis Leibnitz* ; Erdmann, *History of Philosophy*, vol. ii. ; *Aufklärung* in *Realencl. f. Prot. Theologie*.

Aufklärung—a name derived from the frontispiece of one of Wolff's books, depicting the sun breaking through clouds—exhorted their countrymen to use their reason without fear; and deeper notes were struck by Kant and Herder, Hamann and Jacobi. The Augustan Age of German literature opened with Klopstock. Lessing and Wieland, Kleist and Gleim, Goethe and Schiller, Lenz and Klinger, Bürger and Voss, Thummel and Salzmann, Kotzebue and Iffland, poured forth a flood of poems, satires, novels, and dramas, which created and delighted a reading public. The new interest in things of the mind was stimulated by a crop of journals devoted to literature and philosophy, society and art. It was the thawing of the winter ice—an age of experiment, adventure, and rejuvenescence—when the arrows of criticism began to fly and the pent-up rills of emotion burst forth. The country was full of intellectual centres which offered a rich soil for the exchange and propagation of ideas. During the generation of peace following the Seven Years' War, Germany learned to read and to think, and began to ask questions. The critical spirit, once aroused, spread rapidly, finding nourishment in the rank evils which overspread the land. The ideas of reason and humanity, the starting-point and the goal of the Aufklärung, won almost uncontested supremacy over the mind of the educated bourgeoisie. Nicolai's organ, the ' Allgemeine Deutsche Bibliothek,' and the ' Berliner Monatschrift,' founded by Biester and Gedike in 1783, taught their readers to use their own judgment.[1] Though the roots of the Aufklärung were philosophic, not political, the revolt against authority spread to ever wider regions of discussion and remonstrance. Private citizens, carefully excluded from all share in government, felt no interest in the State, and saw only the individual and humanity, the august but invisible Church of which the humblest were members, and in comparison with which the State was a trifle. In an age of obscurantism and repression every leader of thought was on the side of the opposition. Hope was in the air, and there was a stirring in the stagnant waters. Everywhere there was an ideal of better conditions, without any clear idea as to the machinery by which they were to be secured.

The critical spirit which produced the Aufklärung assailed traditional religion before it grappled with political institutions.[2] As the sterile dogmatism of the century following Luther had been displaced by the pietism of Spener and Francke, so pietism in turn yielded in the first half of the eighteenth century to the rationalism

[1] See Hay, ' *Staat, Volk u. Weltbürgertum, in der Berlinischen Monatschrift.*'
[2] See Dorner, *History of Protestant Theology* ; Ritschl, *Geschichte des Pietismus*.

of Leibnitz and Wolff which reigned unchallenged till Hamann and Jacobi restated the case for the human heart.   A critical view of the New Testament was taught by Semler at Halle; and in the Wolfenbüttel Fragments Lessing offered to the world the radical negations of Reimarus half a century after his death.   Lessing himself, in his ' Education of the Human Race,' set forth a deeper view of the religious evolution of mankind than any of his predecessors or contemporaries; and in ' Nathan the Wise ' he immortalised his friend Moses Mendelssohn and embodied the ideal of religious toleration in imperishable literature.   The challenge to tradition could not draw rein at the frontiers of religion ; and, though the theological rebels lacked interest in politics, the habit of questioning authority and seeking grounds for beliefs spread through the educated bourgeoisie and encouraged it to bring secular ideas and institutions before the tribunal of the individual judgment.

An increasing interest in public affairs was displayed by men of letters and their readers.   ' It hardly occurred to anybody in my youth,' wrote Goethe in 1790, ' to envy the privileged class or grudge them their privileges.   But knights, robbers, an honest Tiers État, and an infamous nobility—such are the ingredients of our novels and plays during the last ten years.'   The arrogance and oppression to which it was necessary to bow during the day were denounced in the evening behind the footlights ; and the declamations of Figaro were as milk compared to the strong meat of ' Emilia Galotti ' and ' Love and Intrigue,' in which Lessing and Schiller depicted a society throttled by tyranny from which the only escape was death.   Wieland sketched both a model prince and a despot by divine right.   Kant declared that all history was a striving towards a just constitution for States and proper relations between them. Rousseau, Montesquieu, and Plutarch were read in every town, and Johannes Müller's dazzling picture of the struggles of the Cantons made the name of Switzerland a talisman of liberty. Even the gentle Claudius wrote :

> The King should be the better man,
> Else let the best be ruler.

Göcking regretted that Germany could not boast the execution of a monarch.   Young men quoted Karl Moor's cry ' Give me an army of men like myself, and Germany will become a Republic,' and Posa's outburst, ' Ich kann nicht Fürstendiener sein.'   Schiller pronounced the success of Fiesco at Berlin a sign that republican freedom was understood.   Friedrich Stolberg sang to liberty and the overthrow of tyrants.   Republicanism, of course, was purely academic ; but the bitter attacks on princes and the nobility were meant to hurt. Thümmel's 'Wilhelmine,' the most popular novel before 'Werther,' attacked the Courts, and Bürger launched a furious poem against the game which ravaged the harvest of the poor. Salzmann's vast didactic romance 'On Human Misery' saddled the State with responsibility for every evil, urged the overthrow of existing conditions, including the nobility and standing armies, and invited governments to secure the happiness and material well-being of their subjects.

There was no systematic thinking in Germany about the principles of politics before the French Revolution ; and the class which in France, Italy, and England reflected on the nature and duties of the State occupied itself with the machinery of the Empire and the practice of administration. From the middle of the sixteenth to the middle of the eighteenth century the stage is occupied by the Cameralists,[1] a succession of writers who accepted the Absolute State as an axiom and discussed how best to satisfy the fiscal needs of the ruler. In 'The German Princes' State,' published in 1655, Seckendorf produced a handbook of government and administration based on the practice of his master, Duke Ernst the Pious, of Gotha. Cameralism was the theory and practice of administration ; and though its exponents endeavoured to raise the standard of autocracy, they suggested no check more effective than religion and conscience. The State, not the people, was their starting-point, and its power and wealth were their aim ; whereas later thinkers were to start with the good of the people, and to work up to the government required to secure it. Cameralism was restated and brought up to date by Justi, whose writings reflect and idealise the theory and practice of benevolent despotism in the age of Frederick the Great. The common weal is presented as the goal of the State, and the happiness of the governed receives lip-homage ; but Justi assumes that absolute government secures it. Cameralism would have approved the convenient maxim of Bishop Horsley that the people have nothing to do with the laws except to obey them. As the contemporary of Montesquieu and Rousseau, he is aware of the growth of moral demands which form a standard for rulers ; but he never suggests that the people may enforce it. He urges that they should ' be something ' in every State, and appeals to the ruler to respect property and law, not to overtax his subjects and to refrain from war ; but they may not share in the making of laws or punish unjust rulers or ministers. Like all the Cameralists, he assumes the ruler to be wise and benevolent. Such teaching in such an age was less a sedative than a challenge ; for a bad government prompted the suffering subject to point out that the State

---

[1] See Albion Small, *The Cameralists.*

did not perform the duties which Justi declared that it should. The first breach in the system was announced in the writings of Sonnenfels, a German Jew who migrated to Austria and taught political science at the University of Vienna, of whom it has been said that he thought as an absolutist and felt as a democrat. He certainly tempered the rigidity of absolutism by philanthropic and sentimental ideas ; but he offered no challenge to the theory of autocracy, and he ranks rather as the last of the Cameralists than as a pioneer of democracy. Though the school passed away when the breeze of political criticism began to blow vigorously in the latter half of the eighteenth century, its influence remained. If Germany was the land of obedience, to borrow Herder's phrase, it was in part because for two centuries the Cameralists had preached without challenge the might and majesty of the State.

The political education of the German mind was seriously undertaken by a handful of courageous men who risked their liberty, if not their lives, in denouncing the evils under which the majority of their countrymen were groaning. The first of these brave tribunes of the people was Friedrich Karl Moser,[1] who inherited his reverence for law from his father, the champion of the Württemberg Estates. The treatise ' Der Herr und der Diener ' (Master and Servant) was published at Frankfurt in 1759, after a few years of official life. The book, truly described by the author as written with patriotic frankness, begins by reminding princes how easy it is to make their subjects happy and by lamenting how seldom they do so. ' The despotism of many of our German rulers, the harsh treatment of their subjects, the manifold breach of the most sacred promises to the Estates, the ignorance of most rulers of their duties, and many other signs of evil times, are usually due to the military character of government.' Rulers are brought up to be soldiers, not statesmen. A second and no less baneful mistake is the idea that a ruler is responsible to God alone. A capable ruler is a blessing ; but even in such a case several eyes are better than a single pair. Hopes are usually entertained of the heir, who indeed sometimes harbours the ambition to reform the State. ' But if one-tenth of these good resolutions were carried out, Germany would be living in the Golden Age.' The new ruler, for instance, is too often the slave of a favourite. ' If he has rioted in secret, he now declares his mistress, and presents himself to his land as an adulterer.' Others waste the substance of their subjects on building or hunting, the table or jewels ; and the prince is surrounded by those who chant the refrain, ' Your Highness has only to command.' A

---

[1] See Bluntschli, *Geschichte des Staatsrechts* ; and Rosenstein's two articles in *Preussische Jahrbücher*, vol. xv.

courtier will not shrink from exaggerating the wealth of the country
in order to secure the fulfilment of his selfish projects, and then even
a well-meaning prince becomes an extortioner. If he perceives
the evils of the State and the faults of his advisers, shall he dismiss
the whole band ? He can neither condemn them to ruin, nor
support both them and their successors. So the building is patched
up till it falls with a crash, when surprise is expressed that it has
stood so long. ' The great goal of all the motley throng at Court
is to win the favour of the ruler, who is like a beleaguered city and
is surrounded by spies and traitors. Even in small Courts you
will find a multitude of them. The fewer servants a ruler possesses,
the better is he served. If only the ruler possessed the secret
of securing real Christians for his councillors he would accomplish
marvels. There must always be a First ` Minister ; but what
mischief these men have done ! Certain things I dare not
mention,' he adds ominously, ' for we live in dangerous times.'

Ten thousand copies were printed of this memorable book, the
political classic of the German Aufklärung ; and French and Russian
translations appeared. Though it draws its historical examples
rather from France than Germany, it is in reality an audacious
transcript from the author's experience as Minister of the Landgrave,
Ludwig VIII, of Hesse-Darmstadt. The State had been reduced
by misgovernment to a pitiable condition and needed a firm hand.
' He got me out of the mud,' said the Prince ; but his tenure of
office was brief. Some years later he was recalled ; but, like Turgot,
he was too rapid and radical to remain long in power. His new
experiences were incorporated in his book ' Rulers and Ministers,'
published in 1784. It is the same message as that of ' Master and
Servant,' but with an added poignancy. What sinister memories
lurk behind the maxim that for the success of the Minister's plans
he needs not only the consent of the Prince but also of the ' Night
Ministry '—the wife, the mistress, the confessor, and the chamberlains ! Moser was a keen observer and an honest and capable
statesman ; but his writings are rather ethical than scientific. His
best thoughts, remarks Bluntschli, come from the heart. Though
interested in Rousseau and Montesquieu, he pronounced them too
theoretical. Nurtured on law and pietism he lacked the philosophic
background and the speculative sense. With passionate earnestness
he denounces the glaring faults of the ' Proprietary State ' ; but he
does not look beyond its reform. He finds the root of the mischief
in the evil education of princes, not in the principle of autocracy.
He sees only the Prince and his servants. The people, despite his
active sympathy, form only the background of the picture. The
supreme problem of government, as it presents itself to his eyes,

is to train a ruler to be worthy of his high calling.   And yet his
writings possess the honourable claim of being the only Mirror of
Princes fashioned in Germany during the eighteenth century.   He
was the first subject to demand that the official should be the servant
not of the Prince but of the State, and should oppose commands
which he considers to be wrong.   His ideal was that of Carmer and
the Prussian jurists who were to frame the Prussian Code.   In
theory the ruler was to remain absolute ; but in practice his power
was to be limited by the formulation of the law and the vigilance
of an honest and courageous bureaucracy.   ' Moser,' declared
Niebuhr many years later, ' was the first to raise the voice of political
liberty in Germany, the first to speak of the great evils of the country
and of some of its governments.   His books are hardly read now,
but they had then much influence, especially on officials.   But
the rulers were deaf.'   The appeal failed because he fired with blank
cartridge.   It was not enough to denounce evil rulers ; it was
necessary to frighten them.   By refusing to call the people to his
aid, Moser deprived himself of the only weapon by which he could
strike terror into the hearts of evil-doers in high places.

A less systematic but far more effective critic of public abuses
was Schlözer,[1] the earliest political journalist of Germany and
the first systematic political instructor of his fellow-countrymen.
With a pertinacious courage equal to that of Moser, he combined
an originality rare in an age of imitation.   He was an essentially
modern man, and no German publicist before the Revolution
could boast of such extended knowledge of foreign countries.
After leaving Göttingen he spent his early manhood in Sweden
and Russia, learning their languages, studying their institutions,
and writing their history.   Brief visits to France and Italy still
further enlarged his horizon, and laid the foundation of his
comprehensive interest in the politics of Europe.   Appointed
Professor at Göttingen after his return from Russia, he lectured
on history and the political sciences to large and eager audiences.
With the aid of Pütter, the oracle on constitutional law, Achen-
wall, the first of German statisticians, and Spittler, the most
brilliant historical teacher of his time, he made the young University the centre for political, legal, and diplomatic studies, and
the Mecca of aspirants from every part of the country to employment in the service of the State.   On reaching middle life, he
added to his labours as teacher and historian the foundation of a
political journal.   A visit to Paris in 1773, where he met d'Alem-

---

[1] See Schlözer's *Leben*, by his son ; Heeren, *Biographische und Literarische
Denkschriften* ; Bock, *Schlözer*; Frensdorff, ' *Von und über Schlözer*,' in *Abh.
d. Ges. d. Wissenschaften zu Göttingen*, 1909.

bert and other leading men, suggested his first journalistic venture, the 'Correspondence chiefly relating to Statistics.' Statistics and despotism, he used to maintain, could not co-exist. The journal failed after a year, but reappeared in 1776 as 'New Correspondence, Historical and Political.' This time it struck root, and quickly became the most powerful organ in central Europe. The editor's wide circle of friends in and beyond Germany secured an increasing flow of interesting communications. While in theory a purveyor of news, it owed its popularity and power to its criticisms. The editor wrote comparatively little ; but he added pungent comments to the communications of his contributors. Though no stylist, he was a master of sarcasm and knew how to plant his blows. The articles were as a rule anonymous, and full responsibility was taken by Schlözer, who was so careful of the safety of his contributors that in dangerous cases he copied the article with his own hand and destroyed the original. Thus writers were encouraged to tell all they knew, and readers learned to trust the accuracy of their informants.

The 'Correspondence,' which changed its name in 1782 to the 'Staatsanzeigen,' and gained a circulation of 4000, became the terror of evil-doers and the delight of their helpless victims. Niebuhr compared the paper to the lion's mouth at Venice, ever open to complaints. Duke Karl of Saxe-Meiningen offered his co-operation to foster enlightenment and toleration, to overthrow evil and folly. 'Your paper,' he wrote in 1781, 'is read everywhere. It is now the only one of its kind which is so universally useful and awakes so many good ideas in the bosom of a well-intentioned ruler. Oh, best of men, continue to enlighten us, and let nothing frighten you into abandoning your journal!' 'You, Herr Professor,' wrote his friend Count Schmettow, a Holstein diplomatist, in 1786, 'have benefited the world more than Luther himself. Believe me, bad ministers and princes are really afraid of you. Countless abominations have been prevented by you. You have made enemies, of course, just as no Monsignore or Abbé in Rome was Luther's friend ; but God and honest men must wish you well, and few or none of your contemporaries will be able on their deathbed to look back on so much good accomplished.' Its columns were studied by Maria Theresa and Joseph ; and the Empress would sometimes support her opinion in Council with the words, 'That will never do ; what would Schlözer say ?' The fearless editor knew the limits of his liberty, and was careful not to overstep them. As a Hanoverian subject, he had naturally to refrain from criticising the policy of his sovereign in the Electorate or beyond the seas ; and the long arm of Prussia and Austria

C

counselled circumspection in dealing with the dominions of the Hohenzollerns and the Hapsburgs. But he occupied a privileged position as the star of Göttingen and a favourite of the Hanoverian government. He once attacked the postal service of his own State, received a reprimand, and never repeated the offence ; but when remonstrances reached Hanover from other rulers the answer was that the Press was free. In his boisterous tournaments with all Germany looking on, he could count on the passive support of the only princes who had the power to silence or punish him. Jacob Grimm has complained that he had one pair of scales for the great Powers and another for the small ; but he had no real choice. Moreover, the petty tyrants were the worst offenders. One day he would attack the magistrates of a Free City, next an Imperial Knight who tyrannised over a village, following with a list of the mistresses of the Canons of Munster and anecdotes of the half-crazy Duke of Zweibrücken. None of his Homeric contests attracted more attention than the onslaught on the financial exactions of the Bishop of Speier. Though the incriminating article was not written by Schlözer, he as usual took full responsibility. The ruffled prince appealed to George III, but in vain. An angry demand for the mobilisation of the Empire against Hanover for tolerating the shameful audacity of its Professor was equally fruitless. Another controversy was of a more tragic character. A Zurich pastor, named Waser, was executed for his article in the paper, and his cruel fate increased the editor's detestation of oligarchical Republics. Not even the petty tyrants of Germany were more roughly handled than those of Zurich and Berne, of Holland and Venice. He was indeed born for conflict, and he rejoiced at the reverberation of his ringing blows. His strident tones broke the ban of secrecy, and compelled young men to interest themselves in public affairs.

Unlike Moser, Schlözer was far more than a critic of abuses. His creed was constitutional monarchy, and the two main planks in his programme were representative institutions and a free press. He was the child of Montesquieu, not of Rousseau, and shared his admiration for the British Constitution. The happiness of a prince, he declared, lay in ruling with his people, not over them. There should be a contract, so that if it was broken he might be deposed. He will hear nothing of divine right or patriarchal omnipotence ; for sovereignty resides in the people. His enemies complained that he could only talk of the duties of princes and of the rights of peoples ; but the sneer was undeserved. He detested mob-rule no less than the extravagances of ' personal government.' As a champion of the *juste milieu*, he was equally opposed to autocracy, oligarchy, and democracy. He scoffed at the ' Republiquettes ' of Greece, and maliciously dubbed aristocrats ' kakistocrats.' Freedom, he declared, was safer with a hereditary ruler than with two hundred hereditary or other councillors. He disapproved of the revolt of the American colonists, holding that the provocation was insufficient to justify rebellion. His ideal was ordered liberty, and he made its foes his own. ' His residence in Russia,' writes Heeren in his striking but somewhat unsympathetic portrait of his colleague, ' moulded his political and literary character. The classic land of despotism awakened the spirit of opposition in him. The foundation of his political creed was his hatred of despotic power ; and he hated it even more in republics than in monarchies.' The Cobbett of Germany naturally believed that the pen was mightier than the sword. Without a free press, liberty could be neither attained nor preserved. The deadliest enemy of despotism was publicity. Tyrants who were too strong to be overthrown must be intimidated, scandals dragged into the light of day, public indignation aroused, till the evil-doer was forced to ask himself whether the gratification of his whims and his lusts was worth the storm of obloquy. With the aid of a free and fearless press, politics became the hobby and responsibility of every citizen. From his safe anchorage in Hanover he denounced the concrete evils of his time—tyranny, privilege, exactions, the rule of mistresses, the hunting craze, intolerance, serfdom, torture ; and with every blow of the Rhadamanthus of Göttingen his fellow-countrymen became less submissive to oppression.

Though exerting a less extended influence than Schlözer, two Swabian publicists accomplished the same work of outspoken criticism in South Germany. Schubart's [1] fame owes as much to his ten years of imprisonment as to his journalism and his poems. His biographer, David Friedrich Strauss, has truly said that he had more blood than bones, more temperament than character, more sap than force. But though his ability was not of the highest order and his life was loose, he encouraged his countrymen to think and to dare. He was warmer and deeper in feeling than his Swabian rival Wieland, though less refined and less instructed. He was, indeed, a man of the people, as Wieland's temperament made him a man of the salon. Though the chief purpose of his ' Deutsche Chronik ' was to preach a vigorous nationalism, he strove with equal vigour to create a demand for internal reform. His sharpest darts were reserved for princes, and he regarded the nobility, ' which has prickles above as well as below,' as a

[1] See Strauss, *Schubart's Leben in Briefen.*

potentially useful bulwark against crowned tyrants. Editing his paper first in Augsburg and Ulm, he was enticed to Württemberg in 1777, and immured in the fortress of the Asperg, on the heights above Ludwigsburg. Freed in 1787 at the instance of Prussia, he emerged a broken man, a martyr to the cause of his country's political regeneration.

When Schubart was silenced, his mantle fell upon Weckhrlin,[1] his fellow Württemberger. There was nothing of the patriot about the man who spent nine years in Paris, worshipped Voltaire, loved France as the home and source of the Aufklärung and castigated the Holy Roman Empire; but in political criticism he was far more effective, and his biting wit quickly made him a power. Schlözer remarked that he rose like a comet over Germany. He edited a journal between 1778 and 1788 under three successive titles, in which he sharply attacked tyranny and obscurantism. Lacking the privileged position of Schlözer, he had to measure his words, and he preferred the rapier to the bludgeon. Tradition made no appeal to his sceptical mind; but he had a keen scent for the misdeeds of republics, and he attacked the mouldering Swiss oligarchies as vigorously as Schlözer himself. Yet he desired to retain the nobility as a separate Estate, and felt the scholar's contempt for the intelligence of the masses. His chief enemy was the Church, and with the Jesuits he waged a truceless war. Indeed, he cared less for political than for intellectual liberty. 'Give us our rights,' he exclaimed, 'freedom of thought, freedom of speech, freedom of the press, freedom of belief. With these four liberties any government will suffice.' But such privileges were not to be had in South Germany till a great conflagration had consumed a mass of antiquated tyrannies and dogmas in its purifying flame.

While most of the leading publicists of the time sought guidance in the dictates of reason, Justus Möser[2] detested the levelling rationalism of the Aufklärung and anticipated Savigny's demonstration of the utility of the existing and the traditional. 'This strong, rude German soul,' as Goethe named him, studied and wrote the history of his native Osnabrück, and based his political philosophy on his researches. A consistent and disinterested conservative, he rejected philosophic despotism and was no friend of aristocrats. Anchored in loving loyalty to the past, he supported the inherited rights and popular customs which sanctified the interests of common men. Entirely free from the sickly romanticism which loves or tolerates abuses for their antiquity, he tried

---

[1] See Ebeling, *Weckhrlin* ; and Böhm, *L. Weckhrlin*.
[2] See Hatzig, *Justus Möser*.

to revive the spirit of old institutions in order to save them ; and
he had no objection to cutting down dead trees. The backbone
of the State and the guarantee of continuity, he taught, was the
peasantry. While the liberal reformer looks to the townsman,
the conservative turns to the peasant, who alone can be trusted
to resist the seduction of new-fangled ideas. ' They do not walk
on all fours,' he remarked bitterly ; ' for they too are human
beings.' He deemed himself a friend of liberty ; but it was a
liberty founded on ancient rights and customs, not on an
imaginary social contract. A visit to England in middle life
strengthened his liberal conservatism. He regretted the decay
of the towns and the lack of the *Tiers État*. Though content with
the Estates, he recommends the German States to adopt some of
the English forms of government. ' He who is to act in common
must deliberate in common—that is the primeval formula of
Germanic law.' Liberty is only to be found in law ; but law is
the expression of the majority of qualified voices. Rights are the
correlative of property. Serfdom must be reformed, not abolished.
His ideal was a community of occupying owners. He sought his
golden age in primitive Germany, not in the Middle Ages when
the small man was strangled in the meshes of feudalism. Indeed,
his vision was so fascinated by the petty freeholder that it had no
room for the State. The State, with its rulers, its rigidity, and its
centralisation, seemed to him the enemy of liberty. ' The present
tendency to laws and regulations,' he declared in the ' Patriotische
Phantasien,' ' is dangerous to the common liberty. We are
deserting the true scheme of nature, which displays its richness
in variety, and thus smooths the way to despotism. Should not
each little town have its own constitution ? It is worth discussion
whether it would not produce a greater variety of virtues and a
stronger development of spiritual force, if each little social group
was more its own lawgiver and conformed less to the general type.'
But Möser's prescription was not what Germany required ; for the
patient was sick of the very particularism and traditionalism
which he exalted.

The widespread longing for a new and nobler age expressed
itself not only in the writings of publicists, but in the formation of
secret societies.[1] The founder of the Illuminati, Weishaupt, was
a curious mixture of a scamp and an idealist. Educated at a
Jesuit school in Ingoldstadt, the precocious boy reacted violently
against the clerical atmosphere and plunged into unbelief and

[1] See Kluckhohn, *Vorträge und Aufsätze, Die Illuminaten u. die Aufklärung in Bayern* ; Le Forestier, *Les Illuminés de Bavière* ; and Wolfram,
Die Illuminaten in Bayern.

materialism. On the suppression of the Society, he succeeded to
the chair of Canon Law in the University, which a Jesuit had
held ; and he also lectured on history and moral science. His
eloquence and audacity, which fascinated the students, scandalised
the partisans of the old order. He spoke with horror of the
mind-killing education of the Jesuits ; but he admired their iron
discipline, and resolved to create an organisation on similar lines
for the defence of the principles which they attacked. Masonry
had been imported from England in 1737, when the first lodge was
founded in Hamburg. Ferdinand of Brunswick threw himself
into the movement, and Frederick the Great joined the Brunswick
lodge shortly before his accession. Scores of lodges were quickly
formed in Protestant Germany by men of culture who desired
religious liberty. The better side of the movement was the
notion of a brotherhood of enlightenment, emancipated from
cramping local prejudices. But the love of the marvellous, never
more widespread than in the Age of Reason, led to the practice
of magic and alchemy ; and Masonry, the offspring of the
Aufklärung, became in many places associated with childish
superstition and obscurantism. It had already fallen from its
high estate when Weishaupt heard of it in 1774, and resolved
to borrow its outward forms for the new republic of his dreams.

Weishaupt's Order of Perfectibles—' a name which shows the
object of my foundation '—soon became the Order of the Illuminati. The first members were drawn from his Ingoldstadt pupils,
and instructions were issued to enrol clever young men in Munich
and other cities of Bavaria. Several grades were instituted,
elaborate processes of initiation were designed, and members were
sworn to secrecy and obedience. A cipher language was
constructed, and classical names were employed to heighten the
mystery and for purposes of concealment. Bavaria was Greece,
Munich was Athens, and the founder was Spartacus. ' My aim,'
declared Weishaupt, ' is to help reason to gain supremacy. The
ideal of the Order is to diffuse light. We are fighters
against darkness.' His creed was philosophic anarchism. The
existence of States and the subjection of man to man were only
temporary concessions to imperfection. The divine plan had
been to give liberty and equality ; but the leaders had turned
tyrants. The Aufklärung, or spread of reason, would render
princes and nations superfluous. The race would become a single
family, and the world the abode of reasonable beings. Nationalism,
like despotism, was the enemy of humanity. Patriotism meant
enlarging your country by force and fraud, the ruler sharing the
booty with a few of his subjects by a compact known as the

feudal system. Every evil arose from deserting cosmopolitanism, and every effort must be made by a new Order to return to it. A few princes, diplomatists, and scholars in Bavaria and other parts of Germany, became members, but only a handful joined in the first three years. The vague programme and childish ceremonies repelled more than they attracted ; and Weishaupt was no Loyola. His personal morality was lax, and his scanty following resented his autocratic ways. Spartacus was not a Mason ; but in 1778 one of his chief disciples joined a lodge, and the idea suggested itself that the Illuminati might present themselves as members of a higher grade of Masonry, which had long established its position. It was at this moment of critical transition that the second founder of the Illuminati was enrolled at Frankfurt by an itinerant recruiter.

Adolph, Freiherr von Knigge,[1] a member of an old Hanoverian family, had heard much in early youth of Masonry and occultism, and had dabbled in alchemy. At twenty he entered a Masonic lodge, half sceptical, half credulous. Like Weishaupt, he was part enthusiast and part impostor ; but he was superior to the Bavarian Professor in character and in knowledge of the world. The dream of founding a new Order had taken root in his mind ; but when he was told that such an Order was already in existence, he asked to be initiated, and brought a number of disillusioned Masons with him. Admitted at first only to the lower grade, Philo, as he was now called, desired to be seised of the mystery in its entirety. Weishaupt reluctantly confessed that the Order had no existence except in his head, and begged forgiveness for the fraud. Knigge rejoined that in that case the whole Masonic movement might be brought under their joint direction.. Philo taught his new associates the different Masonic systems, and was commissioned to work out a scheme for the higher mysteries of which the Illuminati were to be the guardians.

Knigge, who was no iconoclast, insisted on a promise of cautious steering in the danger zones of religion and politics. The highest ranks of the new Order, he argued, should be informed of its political and religious attitude, which he proceeded to elaborate. Like Weishaupt, he exalts the stateless condition of man, and foretells for the civilised man the privilege of liberty once enjoyed by the savage. When a nation reaches its majority, the need of tutelage ceases. ' Morality is the art which teaches man to enter on manhood and to do without princes. Morality alone can secure liberty.' Liberty and equality form the secret kernel of Christ's teaching, and Christianity is therefore the foundation

---

[1] See Gödeke, *Knigge*.

of the Illuminati. Religion and authority should be preserved and respected. The aim of the Order is not to overthrow the State and establish institutions by force, but to aid the natural processes of evolution, to keep monarchs from the path of evil, and to plant its members not only in the chief places of government, but in schools and bookshops. A corresponding Order should be formed by women. Under Knigge's bracing inspiration the Illuminati soon ranged from Paris to Warsaw, from Denmark to Italy. As public life offered few opportunities, secret societies became popular, and their cosmopolitan character gave their members a sense of release from the stifling influences of particularism. The prospects of the Order seemed bright ; but its strength was sapped by quarrels between its leaders. To Knigge, as the soul of the movement, its members turned for help and advice ; but he quickly discovered that there was no room for two heads ' An Order,' he wrote angrily, ' which tyrannises over men as Spartacus aspires to do, would be a heavier yoke than that of the Jesuits.' He therefore resigned, magnanimously declining to expose the founder ; and he determined never again to have dealings with secret societies, against which he uttered a warning in his ' Human Intercourse,' a popular though colourless treatise on social ethics.

Almost at the same moment clerical denunciations began to reach the Elector of Bavaria, though without naming the Order. Weishaupt vainly demanded an audience at Munich to demonstrate the innocence of his Order, omitting some dangerous points —such as the words, ' Parsons and evil princes stand in our way.' Utzschneider, Private Secretary of a Bavarian Duchess, left the fold, declaring membership inconsistent with his office. Other resignations followed, and on realising that the game was up the founder revealed the whole story to the Government. An edict was issued against Masons and Illuminati, Weishaupt was deprived of his chair, and documents were published revealing his character and activities. The Elector, now thoroughly alarmed and convinced that his throne and life had been in danger, imposed heavy penalties ; and when the French Revolution broke out, the Bavarian Government saw the spectre of its old enemy behind every bush. Rulers and conservatives were now everywhere on their guard. A great effect was produced in 1786 by an attack entitled ' The Unveiling of a Scheme for a World-Republic,' in which Göchhausen, a Prussian noble and officer, warned his countrymen that the Aufklärung was undermining society and morality, and called on rulers to combat irreligious cosmopolitanism by teaching religion and patriotism.[1] But the panic was

---

[1] See Wenck, i. 96-8.

groundless. The Order, even with better leadership, could only have been ephemeral ; but for a decade it exerted a subtle and potent influence. Their expulsion from Bavaria dispersed the Illuminati over the Empire, and the doctrine that Kings were out of date, and nobility the tool of despotism, was discussed with ardour behind closed doors and shuttered windows. ' If ever a secret society deserved admiration,' wrote Rebmann in 1796, ' it was this Order. It revealed much light and did so much for the victory of truth and right that if it did not succeed it was only on account of our slowness and cowardice. Far from desiring to support or create revolutions, it aimed rather at the philanthropic reformation which is the only safe defence against violent uprisings.' This was the testimony of a friend ; but there was a better foundation for his eulogy than for the panic-stricken paradoxes of Robison and the Abbé Barruel, who traced the harvest of the Revolution to the tares sown by Masons and Illuminati.

Liberal cosmopolitanism was not confined to the members of secret societies ; for the disunion and impotence of the country led inevitably to the philosophy which, though in other lands to some extent a pose, was in Germany the sincere conviction of many of the strongest and most generous minds. It was not, indeed, universal.[1] Klopstock's odes and dramatic epics endeavoured to revive interest and pride in primitive Germany. ' The cosmopolitan,' wrote Herder, ' is among citizens like the polyhistor among scholars. The one belongs to every State and does nothing for any one of them, while the other takes all knowledge for his province and achieves no result. The savage who loves his wife and child and burns with zeal for his tribe is a truer being than the educated shadow who is filled with zeal for his race, which, after all, is a mere name. The heart of a cosmopolitan is a shelter for nobody.' In his book, ' Death for the Fatherland,' Abbt denied that patriotism existed only in republics, and demanded an education in civic duties from which patriotism would result. In his ' National Spirit,' Friedrich Karl Moser deplored the pitiable state of the Fatherland, adding, ' My heart trembles at the sight of our chains.' If political unity was impossible, unity of feeling might at least be encouraged. In his ' Deutsche Chronik,' Schubart preached a virile nationalism and castigated the aping of Versailles. ' He who does not fling a curse across the frontier from the ruins of Heidelberg is no true German. And yet what is there that my countryman does not fetch from beyond the Rhine ? Fashions, cuisine, wine, and even the language. What he might learn from the Frenchman with advantage is

[1] See Meinecke, *Weltbürgertum u. Nationalstaat*, ch. ii.

patriotism.' He envies England her liberty, but finds her too commercial, and never loses hope of a better future for his country-men. 'Weep not,' he cries, 'over the flabbiness of thy people. The lions are waking, they hear the cry of the eagle. They rush forth and seize lands that the foreigner has torn away. A German Imperial throne will arise.'

The Nationalists, however, were voices crying in the wilderness. Particularism was the instinct of the masses, cosmopolitanism the creed of the *élite*. There was so little to be proud of in most German States that the eyes of their more reflective citizens turned abroad. Excluded from power and responsibility, men of liberal views felt themselves in closer association with reformers in other lands than with their own countrymen. 'German nationalism,' declared Nicolai bluntly, 'is a political monstrosity.' To such minds patriotism meant stagnation, a mulish antagonism to the stimulating challenge of foreign influences. 'I write as a citizen of the world who serves no prince,' remarked Schiller in 1784 ; 'I lost my Fatherland to exchange it for the great world.' Sonnenfels' 'Love of Fatherland' provoked Goethe in 1773 to a confession of unblushing cosmopolitanism. 'If we find a place where we can rest with our belongings, a field to support us, a house to shelter us, have we not a fatherland ? And do not thousands in every State possess it ? Wherefore, then, the vain striving for a feeling which we cannot and indeed do not desire to entertain, which is the result of special circumstances in certain peoples and at certain times ? '

The noblest cosmopolitan of his time has been described by Heine as ' our literary Arminius, who freed our theatre from the foreign yoke'; but in politics Lessing knew nothing of national boundaries.[1] ' In one of your poems,' he complains to Gleim, ' the patriot outcries the poet. Perhaps the patriot is not wholly over-laid in me, though to be praised as a zealous patriot is the last thing I crave—a patriot, that is, who would teach me to forget that I must be a citizen of the world. I have literally no conception of the love of the Fatherland (I am sorry to confess my shame), and it appears to me a heroic failing from which I am glad to be free.' ' Nathan the Wise,' ' The Education of the Human Race,' and ' Ernst and Falk,' his philosophic legacy, embody the author's dream of a grand association of men, regardless of religious and political differences, for the higher work of the world. His views on the State are contained in the three exquisite dialogues in which Ernst and Falk discuss the character and possibilities of Masonry.[2] Lessing,

---

[1] See Baumgarten, *Reden u. Aufsätze, War Lessing ein Deutscher Patriot ?*

[2] Cp. Erich Schmidt, *Lessing*, ii. 582-604.

himself a disillusioned Mason, speaking through Falk, declares that the highest duties of the Order can be fulfilled without being a member. The State is made for men, not men for the State ; and society also is nothing but a means. The duty of the individual is to develop his capacities, and to join hands with men who are engaged in the same task, whoever and wherever they be. The ideal Masonry would discard its childish tricks and work for the solidarity of mankind, offering itself as a counterpoise to the isolating influences of class and nation. 'Would that there were men in every State who knew exactly when patriotism ceases to be a virtue, who did not believe that only their own religion is good and wise, who rise above class ! What if the Masons made it part of their duty to reduce these barriers, which make people such strangers to one another, to the smallest dimensions ? ' There speaks the authentic voice of the Aufklärung, passionately convinced of the rationality of man, of the unity of civilisation, and of the fruitfulness of co-operative effort. Here was an alluring task for men of ability and good-will, a rich compensation for their exclusion from the tasks of government. Humanity was the religion of the eighteenth century, and Lessing was among the noblest of its prophets.

The political education of the German people was not more indebted to its own bolder spirits than to the kindling impact of foreign influences. The writings of Rousseau took the country by storm.[1] 'His influence was immense,' records Niebuhr, 'far greater than that of Voltaire. He was the hero of most clever people in my youth.' Lessing was among the earliest of his admirers. Kant declared that Rousseau first discovered the deep-hidden nature of men, and forgot his daily walk over a new volume. Herder fed on him. Klinger never freed himself from the spell. Schiller wrote an ode to him. Jacobi pronounced him the greatest genius who had written in French. Campe called him his patron saint. Arndt read 'Émile' with rapture at the age of fifteen, and Gentz pronounced parts of it to be sanctified for the whole human race. ' Rousseau, the friend of mankind and of virtue,' wrote Anselm Feuerbach, the Bavarian jurist, ' I thank thee for thy good services to my heart ; receive my gratitude in this holy resolve to love the good as thou lovedst it. I have warmed my heart at thy glow and strengthened myself to virtue through thy strength.' Lenz placed his statue beside Shakespeare. Adam Lux composed his own epitaph in the words ' Here lies a disciple of Jean Jacques Rousseau.' Nowhere did the teachings of ' Émile ' find disciples so earnest and practical

[1] See Fester, *Rousseau und die Deutsche Geschichtsphilosophie* ; Lévy-Bruhl, *L'Influence de Rousseau en Allemagne*, in *Annales de l'École libre des sciences politiques*, 1887.

as Basedow and Campe. The ' Contrat Social ' pronounced on some fundamental issues which no German thinker had dared to raise. While Montesquieu appealed forcibly to isolated students and thinkers, Jean Jacques became the guide, philosopher, and friend of men and women, young and old. The dramas and novels of the Romantic school from ' Werther ' to ' The Robbers ' were pure Rousseau, and Niebuhr attributed to the Swiss philosopher the appearance in German literature of ' the silly notion ' that virtue was only to be found in the lower classes. The doctrines of the sovereignty of the people and the social contract, a very charter of revolt, filtered in and encouraged the victims of misgovernment to criticise and to complain.

A second foreign influence of a stimulating character was the American War of Independence, in which the sympathy of almost every writer outside Hanover was unreservedly with the colonists, and every defeat of the British troops was hailed as a victory for liberty. Long extracts from the debates at Westminster and the speeches in Congress were circulated in the German papers, and even the Declaration of Independence was allowed to appear by princes who were not in the pay of the English King. Klopstock wrote an ode celebrating ' this war of noble heroes, the dawn of a great day to come,' and invited visitors to kiss his cane from Boston. Goethe testifies that Franklin and Washington were the names that shone in the German firmament. The revolt against oppression, the success of the daring adventure, and finally the establishment of a democratic republic, free from courts and armies, feudalism and poverty, leavened the fermenting thought of Europe. It was at once a warning to rulers that there was a limit to tyranny, and an inspiration to down-trodden peoples all over the world.

But Germany was far from being a mere spectator of the drama. Though no one of the stature of Lafayette or Kosciusko crossed the ocean to join in the crusade for liberty, Steuben, a Prussian noble, and other volunteers hurried to the standard of revolt. But for each German fighting of his own accord by the side of Washington there were hundreds fighting against him.[1] The traffic in human flesh carried on by German princes drew down fierce indignation on their heads and scarcely less on that of their British paymaster. That peaceable citizens were dragged from their homes and sold like cattle at so much a head to a foreign ruler engaged in trying to stamp out the liberties of small communities of his own children was the concrete argument which rallied German opinion in support of the colonists.   ' I cannot remember anybody in my father's circle or mine on the English side,' records Henriette Herz. ' The idea

[1] See Kapp, *Der Soldatenhandel deutscher Fürsten nach Amerika*.

of full equality before the law exerted perhaps an even greater spell then than now, and was embraced even by the young nobility in our circle. And the sale of Hessians and Brunswickers was felt as a disgrace to every German. Washington was the hero of the day.' Failing to obtain mercenaries in Holland and Russia, the King of England turned to the home of his race, and in spite of a few refusals succeeded in purchasing 29,000 soldiers at a price of £7,000,000, Of these no fewer than 17,000 were drawn from Hesse-Cassel, the rest being provided by the Duke of Brunswick, the Margrave of Anspach and one or two other petty rulers. The infamous traffic was denounced by German writers outside the borders of the States that were implicated, and by none more passionately than by the youthful Schiller, who wrote the scene in ' Love and Intrigue ' with the Anspach mutiny in his mind. The priceless necklace presented to Lady Milford has been bought with blood-money. ' Yesterday,' says the Chamberlain, ' seven thousand of our boys started for America, and I have two sons among them. They pay for all this.' ' None of them were forced to go ? ' queries the favourite. ' My God, no,' cries the stricken father in bitter irony, ' they are all volunteers.' But the most resounding protest was uttered by a foreign voice. In 1777 there appeared at Cleves an anonymous pamphlet entitled 'Avis aux Hessois et autres peuples de l'Allemagne, vendus par leurs Princes à l'Angleterre.' ' Will the brave Germans who defended their liberties against Rome now shed their blood in the interest of tyrants ? ' cried the author, who was none other than Mirabeau. The Landgrave of Hesse-Cassel bought up every copy of the stinging pamphlet on which he could lay hands, and issued a reply contending that it was his feudal right to sell his subjects. The anger of the people was increased by the knowledge that the blood-money was spent not on the needs of the State, but on the personal expenses of extravagant and degenerate rulers. But with indignation there was mingled another sentiment. As the surviving mercenaries drifted home, they brought stories of promise and opportunity, and Steuben wrote of the country where there were no kings or idle nobles, where all were happy and poverty was unknown. For a time academic republicanism was in the air. An anonymous professor published an ode on the United States in the ' Berliner Monatschrift ' in 1783, urging the establishment of republics in Europe. ' Alas ! my iron chain warns me that I am a German. Europe, raise thy head ; a day will come when thou, too, wilt be free and wilt expel thy princes.' The rising of Paoli was watched with sympathy, and the Corsican hero was fêted on his way to England.

Thus the lethargy which had weighed on Germany in the first

half of the eighteenth century was passing rapidly away. The personality and victories of Frederick the Great, the American War of Independence, the influence of Voltaire, Rousseau, and Montesquieu, the challenge of the Aufklärung, the radicalism of the dramatists, the arrows of Schlözer and Moser—these crowding and converging influences and experiences set the mind of the nation in a ferment. To borrow the words of Kant, written in 1784, it was not an enlightened age, but an age in process of enlightenment. Change was in the air, and the fragility of traditional institutions and ideas was widely recognised. 'The unconscious and largely innocent desire for ease and comfort which had followed the Seven Years' War was exhausted and had degenerated into slackness and sentimentality,' wrote Arndt in his Autobiography. 'In all directions, in social habits, art and science, theology and philosophy, there arose suddenly either new tendencies or the expectation of them.   There was a new political as well as a new philosophical striving abroad, and it was felt with immense rapidity and liveliness in the tremblings and shakings which it brought from the cottage to the palace.   Even in the narrow circle of our home, despite the conservative habits of my parents, this new epoch made its influence felt.   Political interest grew from year to year. I, too, took my share, and for several years I had not only read the papers aloud, but also to myself.' If such was the case in distant Pomerania, far greater was the tension in the centres of thought and discussion. In Germany, as in France, prophetic voices gave warning of the wrath to come. 'Europe,' wrote Georg Forster, who had seen more of the world than any German of his time, 'is on the threshold of a terrible revolution.   The mass is so corrupt that only the letting of blood can be effective.' 'Judging by every symptom,' pronounced Schubart in 1787, 'the political system of Europe is on the eve of a vast transformation.'   'I think it undesirable to marry,' wrote Johannes Müller to his brother in 1782, 'because, in the judgment of all great statesmen, Europe is preparing for revolutions ; and on such occasions it is better only to have to look after oneself.' In Germany, as in France, men of insight required no seismological indicators to inform them that the earth was trembling beneath their feet.

CHAPTER II

THE FIRST ECHOES

THE opening scenes of the French Revolution were watched with delight by the great majority of the spokesmen of German opinion, and its principles were hailed as a gospel of good tidings alike by old and young, the bourgeois and the artisan, the scholar and the peasant.[1] The Declaration of the Rights of Man put into words the muffled aspirations of the masses all over Europe, and gave to the humble and the disinherited a new sense of human dignity. When France in trumpet tones demanded the downfall of feudalism, proclaimed the equality of burdens, and declared every man possessed of certain inalienable rights, generous hearts were thrilled by the warmth and glory of the sunrise. Enthusiasm was intensified by the conviction of its universal significance. Condorcet's maxim, that a good law is good for all just as a true proposition is true for all, was generally accepted on both sides of the Rhine. ' If we succeed,' wrote André Chénier, ' the destiny of Europe will be changed. Men will regain their rights and the people their sovereignty. Kings, struck by the success of our labours and the example of the King of the French, may share their power with their peoples ; and perhaps the peoples, happier than we, may obtain a free and equitable constitution without passing through our troubles. Then the name of France will be blessed on earth.' The windows of the sunless prison-house seemed to fly open, and the light of liberty streamed in.

French politics became the main preoccupation of everyone who could read and write. ' I do not know where to turn,' wrote Caroline Böhmer to her sister, ' for the papers contain such

---

[1] See Wenck, *Deutschland vor hundert Jahren*, vol. ii. ; Heigel, *Deutsche Geschichte*, i. 273–326 ; Biedermann, *Deutschland im 18ten Jahrhundert*, iii. 1189–1223 ; Bruno Bauer, *Deutschland während der Französischen Revolution* ; Chuquet, '*Les Écrivains Allemands et la Révolution,*' in *Études d'histoire,* vol. vi. ; Hippolyte Carnot, '*Les Premiers échos de la Révolution au de là du Rhin,*' in *Séances de l'Académie des Sciences morales et politiques,* vol. cxxx.

great and splendid news that I am hot from reading.' Schlözer remarked that the angels must be singing Te Deums in heaven. Klopstock sighed for a hundred voices to hymn the triumphs of liberty. ' It is glorious,' cried Georg Forster, ' to see what philosophy has ripened in the brain and realised in the State.' Gentz proclaimed that mankind had awakened from its long sleep, and that the Revolution was the first practical triumph of philosophy. Wieland and Schubart, Bürger and Voss, Herder and the Stolbergs, Richter and Hölderlin, loudly expressed their joy. The journals of Archenholtz and Nicolai declared their approval, and in the crowded salons of Henriette Herz and Rahel Levin there was but one note. The weightiest vote in Germany, that of Immanuel Kant, was cast on the same side. In the wealthy city of Hamburg the leaders of culture and commerce sought relief for their emotions in odes and banquets. Prince Henry, the eldest surviving brother of Frederick the Great, announced that his life-long admiration for France was unchanged. In the schools and universities enthusiasm was universal. ' I love the Revolution,' wrote Schleiermacher to his father. Hegel and Schelling declaimed the principles of 1789 at Tübingen, while Georg Kerner burned his family's patent of nobility on the anniversary of the destruction of the Bastille. July 14 was the happiest day since the fall of the Roman Empire, wrote Johannes Müller, who was unaware that the sole inmates of the prison were four forgers, two madmen, and a notorious debauchee. ' The sun which has risen on the ruins of the Bastille,' wrote Hennings, ' has dispersed the clouds of prejudice and announced the return of the age of gold.' A pamphleteer prophesied that the French gospel of the abolition of serfdom and tithes would overflow neighbouring States even more rapidly than the Arabs with the Koran. ' Thrones are tottering and man is no longer a serf,' cried Jenisch, a Berlin pastor, in ecstatic verse. People struggled for the newspapers, and Bürger complained that almanacs of the revolution sold better than poetry. Germany was littered with pamphlets, articles, and odes, and French orators drew pictures of the two peoples embracing before dethroned tyrants and swearing on the standards of liberty to be brothers for ever.

> Bliss was it in that dawn to be alive,
> But to be young was very heaven.

I

The first consecutive account of the stupendous events in France was provided by Friedrich Schulz, a young Prussian novelist who had hurried to Paris as the curtain rose. The little volume of two hundred and sixty pages, entitled ' History of the Great Revolution in France,' was fought for in the bookshops, and gave to thousands of German readers their first clear notion of the character of the upheaval. The preface, dated from Paris on September 5, 1789, claims that the narrative is the record of an impartial eyewitness ; and the claim is not ill-founded. He sketches the *ancien régime* in dark colours, but makes no attempt to conceal the demented savagery of the mob. No nation, he declares, is subject to such intense emotions of joy, wrath, and fear. He sees Camille Desmoulins leap on a chair in the Palais Royal, shouting Death or Victory, and he watches the bloody heads borne through the streets after the fall of the Bastille. He records the throbbing excitement, the mushroom rumours, the surging tides of emotion which swept over the capital. He closes with the recall of Necker, and notes with pleasure the restoration of relative tranquillity. Troubles there had been and would be ; but they were less than might be expected. A great kingdom brought to the lowest depths of political and moral corruption could not be reformed in a day or a month. German readers were fortunate that a book so dispassionate and enlightening should fall into their hands at such an early stage of the portentous drama.

Equally vivid, but far less critical, was the picture painted by Campe, the celebrated Brunswick pedagogue.[1] Though admiringly described by Lessing as cool and steady, the Revolution went to his head like strong drink. Accompanied by his old pupil, Wilhelm von Humboldt, he set off in haste to the Mecca of liberty. His letters appeared in his own paper, ' The Brunswick Journal,' and in the following year were published in volume form.

' Is it really true,' begins the first letter, dated August 4, ' that I am in Paris ? That the new Greeks and Romans whom I see around me were only a few weeks ago Frenchmen ? That the great and wonderful drama which has been and is being performed is not a dream ? I left home with the hope that I should arrive in time to attend the funeral of French despotism ; and my hope is fulfilled. The mortal blow has been struck at the heart of the dragon, and I found the hydra lying in its blood ; but there is still life in its hundred heads, and it still writhes in the dust, unwilling to yield up its black spirit. But die it will and must, and I shall not return till I see it entombed. The day of its burial will be among the happiest of my life ; and for the oppressors to the ends of the world it will be one of the most instructive which history has ever displayed for their warning. Before we left Brabant, we heard of the terrible but splendid events of July 14 from the papers and from refugees.

[1] See Leyser, *J. H. Campe.*

D

The price was said to be 15,000 victims, and we were warned against venturing further. But we went forward with full confidence in the magnanimity of the nation. In Brabant we found autocracy at work, with soldiers and cannon in the streets—an excellent prelude to our visit to the land of freedom. On crossing the frontier, I cannot describe my emotions as we gazed at the symbol of liberty, the French cockade, on every head, and the proud and happy faces beneath them. I could have embraced the first people who met us. They seemed no longer French, and we had for the moment ceased to be Brandenburgers and Brunswickers. All national differences and prejudices melted away. They had regained their long-lost rights, and we felt that we were men. In Valenciennes, we were adorned with cockades. Laugh if you will! I felt as if the whole French nation had entered into brotherhood with me ; and if there had been a Bastille in the town to storm, who knows what I should have done? France is like a high-spirited horse which has thrown its clumsy rider and prances about bold, beautiful and strong, neighing with joy. It is impossible to witness a nobler or more touching spectacle. Even now, though the novelty is gone, I often stand for hours in the streets and watch the crowds, moved to tears of joy, observing in a thousand little traits the elevating effects of the new consciousness of liberty on the hearts and habits of men. But it is impossible to find German words for this spectacle never witnessed in Germany since the downfall of our primeval liberty.

' Even before we reached Paris, I often asked myself, Are these really the people we used to call and think of as French? Were the shrill chattering dandies, the arrogant and brainless swaggerers who used to cross the Rhine and turn up their noses at everything they saw in Germany—were they only the dregs and scum of a nation of which on our journey we have not seen a single example? Or has their whole character so changed with their revolution that the noble elements which were underneath have now come to the surface, and the vulgarity sunk out of sight? Both these explanations I believe to be correct. The Frenchman was always more of a fool abroad than at home ; and the cleansing of his national character in the purgatorial fires of liberty is a fact which has struck German and other observers who were here before the Revolution. The good qualities have remained—liveliness, wit, friendliness, politeness ; while frivolity seems to have disappeared, for the time if not for ever. In the towns through which we passed, the citizens seemed to be like one great family: the women in white, the men in brightly coloured clothes. Liberty and happiness were stamped on every face.'

Brutus and Cato, he added in the second letter, would not scorn to share in the new, rich life. ' The minds of the people, even in the lowest ranks, have torn off the fetters like cobwebs, and from hour to hour raise themselves to heights of thought and sentiment to which the blinking eyes of the foreigner can hardly follow them. One feels elevated and ennobled. If I do not return home strengthened in courage and in the sense of brotherhood, it will be my own fault. I never hear an angry word or witness a regrettable act. It is not the French that I am praising, but lofty human nature itself.'

He examined the ruins of the Bastille and attended a sitting at Versailles ; but he devotes most space to a pilgrimage to the house and grave of the author of ' Émile ' at Ermenonville. ' No other writer has ever affected me or affects me to-day like him. Tears filled my eyes. At every step on the holy ground the thought flamed up within me : On this very spot he stood. I should have liked to tread with bare feet.'

In the brilliant colours of his enthusiasm there are only one or two slight shadows. He regrets that the Assembly contains such a vast number of legislators, and he notes the apprehensions of certain onlookers that the night of August 4 exhibited too much ' patriotic intoxication.' But the ninth and closing letter, written on August 26, shows that his faith is undimmed :

' The more I see of it the more profoundly convinced am I that the French Revolution is the greatest and most wholesale blessing vouchsafed by Providence to mankind since Luther ; and all men, white and black, yellow and brown, ought to cry, Thank God for it.'

In publishing the collected letters in the autumn of 1790, the author added a preface, which shows that the temperature has begun to cool :

' I hereby raise a monument to the Government under which I have the happiness to live. Only in a land where despotism is unknown dare one write of despotism and liberty as I have done. At a time when every despot is trembling in his shoes, our ruler smiles down on his subjects like a father on his children, and gladly allows them to express their joy that other peoples will soon share the well-being of the happy Brunswicker.'

After this full-throated, but not wholly undeserved, paean to the Duke, he recalls the circumstances under which the letters were written. ' My readers will see that they were the first warm outpouring of a heart assailed by a throng of novel ideas and sensations crowded into a few short weeks. They will not forget that I was in France after the first series of excesses and before the second.

My letters are not a history, but the record of an observer who had the good fortune to witness the most favourable moments of the world-drama.'

The preface ends with a political confession : ' I believe that a people like the French must be brought to the extreme limit of oppression before it takes the bold step of breaking its chains by force. I believe that no revolution can be effected without horrors and inhumanities, even when the people is cultured and enlightened, and that seldom, if ever, does it enure to the happiness of the land which makes it, but rather of other countries and of posterity. I believe, therefore, that a community would be very foolish if it dared to take the dangerous step of altering its constitution by force unless impelled by the most urgent reasons. I believe that it is wiser to remain in an old, insecure and comfortless house than from an unwise love of innovation to pull away its foundations and let it collapse on one's head. I believe that Providence decrees events of this character from time to time in order to remind despots of the precarious nature of their power and to persuade them to act more mildly and justly. I believe that to those who have the high calling to be the watchdogs and counsellors of mankind, I mean the writers, falls the sacred task of fostering the beneficent designs of Providence on these occasions and of pleading for the rights of man. I believe that a brave writer must not allow himself to be deterred from his duty by fear of misunderstanding.'

A year after Campe's visit, the Oldenburg official, historian, and littérateur, Halem,[1] set out for the land of liberty. Taking the road through Switzerland, he sought out the haunts of Rousseau in a spirit of loving discipleship. ' Oh, why did not God spare him to witness the triumph of liberty ? ' he cries on the Île St. Pierre. ' He would now be journeying like a god through the fairest kingdom in Europe to the plaudits of millions.' ' We start to-morrow for France,' he wrote from Geneva. ' We have long heard the distant music of the cataract of Gallic liberty.' Among the statesmen of new France his hero was Mirabeau. ' To be a great Roman among Romans was nothing astonishing. But to display the greatness of a Roman among a people accustomed to slavery—that is what merits our admiration. For me, he is a planet whose orbit seems to many irregular on account of its great distance ; but time often reveals its course. To convince oneself that he is not a hypocrite one has only to listen to him.' Next to the famous Tribune, in the tràveller's estimation, stood Lafayette and Barnave. His favourite resorts were the Club Allemand, where he met his fellow-countrymen

---

[1] See Chuquet, *Paris en* 1790 ; *Voyage de Halem, Traduction, Introduction, et Notes.*

and read the German papers, and the Jacobin Club. 'My Jacobins always interest me, and I rarely miss their meetings, which are usually held thrice a week. The Club is not a faction ; for though there are a few factious members even they rarely depart from the principles of moderation. There is no idea of propaganda.' He witnessed the début of the future Louis Philippe, 'a beautiful and modest young man of about eighteen,' and saw the King and Queen on their way to mass. 'He looks so strong and well that one cannot believe he is unhappy. There is no grandeur about him ; but, beyond any doubt, he has the interests of his people at heart and he has less desire for absolute power than certain other kings. Besides, nearly every Frenchman loves him. The Queen I pity from the bottom of my heart. Prejudices against her are so inveterate that it will be difficult to uproot them. She should appear in public and go to the theatres as she used to do ; for I feel certain that she would thus touch the heart of the people.' The supreme experience was of course the pilgrimage to Ermenonville. 'A thrill passed through me as I read on a monument these words : Here rests the man of nature and truth. I was in presence of Rousseau's tomb.'

After a visit of two months, Halem left ' this dear Paris ' with a benediction. ' My profession of faith is liberty. Yes, liberty is the air in which all that is fair and good prefers to grow. What an absolute change confronts France now that the Revolution makes people understand and feel what liberty is and what it can achieve ! All the arts and sciences will spring to new life. I already notice how the most obscure individual regards the public weal as his private business and how marvellously liberty augments the force of all.' He admits that ' perhaps ' the reformers were going too far in the limitation of the royal power and sometimes in other things ; but he was not seriously concerned. ' What are all the scenes in the life of nations compared to the spectacle Gaul offers us to-day ? A hundred battles, victories, and alliances have changed nothing for the human race. The unique spectacle has been reserved for us of a nation choosing its representatives, profiting by its past experience, and founding a system of government which will lead it to the summit of happiness.' Only one momentary hesitation might mar the philosopher's satisfaction. Was the people sufficiently prepared for this great step ? No one doubted that the French were the most alert, the most civilised, the best informed, and the most open-minded of nations. Philosophy had recently lifted the veil from the truth. Many things would have gone better or been avoided, and passions would have been less unruly, if the representatives had not been disturbed in their deliberations by the Court. 'Who is there who does not regret the excesses ? But who provoked them ? Besides, the French were human like ourselves. They had drunk the cup of liberty. They became intoxicated and danced round the altar of the goddess like priests of Baal. It will be some time before they recover from their vertigo ; but peace will soon be restored when their fears are set at rest. The nation wishes to be free, and free it will be.' He concludes his survey by inquiring whether the rest of the world will profit by the Revolution. He replies that the peoples will bless it and wish it stability ; for is it not a mirror held up to the eyes of Europe ? 'As for us Germans, we are more cosmopolitan than any other nation. In the political sense, we have no German fatherland. And yet we are free enough as regards our person and property, and the spirit of justice reigns almost everywhere.' But this was the diplomacy imposed on the Oldenburg official by fear of the censorship ; for every page of his vivid narrative reveals his satisfaction that the dark spectres of the *ancien régime* have been chased away.

Even so late as January 1791 a mission to the French capital sent Goethe's friend Merck, the Darmstadt official, into transports. 'The transformation of the people is incredible,' he wrote to a friend.[1] 'Paris surpassed all expectation in thirst for truth, virtue, humanity. I saw " The Taking of the Bastille," a Shakespearian drama. I shed tears, not so much at the representation of events as at the interest of the public. It was as if I were at a feast where the father gave all he had in the house to the prodigal son. I felt like a guest in this great, great family. To-morrow the painter David, than whom there is no nobler or warmer heart, will propose me for the Jacobin Club, which contains every one of genius and warm heart. Here is the place where the foundation-stone of the well-being of the nation and perhaps of the world is being fashioned.'

II

The effect of the changing scenes of the Revolution on the Intellectuals of Germany is nowhere more clearly revealed than in the voluminous correspondence of Johannes Müller, the most learned man and the most celebrated historian of the age.[2] The young Swiss studied under Schlözer, and with the publication of his History of Switzerland he woke up to find himself famous. He desired to teach his countrymen to value their freedom by showing them how

[1] *Briefe von und an Merck*, pp. 278–9.
[2] See Henking, *Johannes von Müller* ; Wegele, *Geschichte der Deutschen Historiographie*. The correspondence is included in the *Sämmtliche Werke*, edited by his brother.

it had been won, and to strengthen national feeling, which had been largely submerged by the interests of canton and class. The book was full of warnings and exhortations, and opened the political eyes of innumerable readers not only in Switzerland, but in Germany. His Lectures on Universal History, delivered during his six years' residence at Geneva, in like manner became a popular favourite and a breviary of politicians. His views were those of a conservative eclectic. He defined his creed before the Revolution as reverence for democracy in Unterwalden, for aristocracy in Venice and Bern, for monarchy in all large States. He detested the doctrinaire radicalism of Rousseau, and in the constitutional struggles of Geneva, of which he was an eye-witness, his sympathies were on the side of the aristocrats and the old authority. Rejecting the fashionable rationalism of the Aufklärung, he based his political philosophy on history and experience like a loyal alumnus of Göttingen. When persuaded that the old order had perished beyond hope of resurrection, he was always ready to accept the new. Though a convinced Protestant, he claimed respect and gratitude for the Papacy as a great historic institution and a benefactor of Europe. In 1786 he gladly accepted an invitation to serve the Elector of Mainz, and in 1788 he became his secretary. Germany was henceforth his country, and no native scholar commanded greater respect.

Müller watched the approach of reform in France with delight. 'What a grand spectacle,' he wrote to a Swiss friend in September 1788 ; 'the throne of the great Louis crumbling to its foundations, and liberty renewing itself at the very moment it seemed to abandon Europe.' 'Everyone will remember the rights of humanity, the demand for which seemed to have become chimerical. J'aime bien la liberté.'[1] He saw in the Revolution a great act of national emancipation, and as such he hailed it with ecstasy. 'What a spectacle it is ! ' he wrote to Dohm,[2] August 6, 1789. 'Blessed be its influence on nations and rulers. I hope that many a Sultan in the Empire will have a salutary shiver, and many an oligarchy learn that things cannot be pushed too far. I am aware of the excesses ; but they are not too great a price to pay for a free constitution. Can there be any question that a clearing storm, even when it works some havoc, is better than the plague ? These seeds were sown by Montesquieu. So nothing is lost, and one has only to wait.' He wrote to his brother in the same exultant strain.[3] ' July 14 is the best day since the fall of the Roman Empire. Our century has copied French frivolity, but its successor will learn courage from them. Freedom has been cheaply purchased at the price of a few castles and a few heads, most of them guilty ones. It will

[1] *Werke*, xxxviii. 109, 116.   [2] *Ib.*, xvi. 380.   [3] *Ib.*, v. 269.

give them a terrible strength.   May they then fall, those who are
now trembling—unjust judges and intolerable tyrannies !   It is
quite right that kings and counsellors should learn that they, too,
are men.   Cancers cannot be healed with rose-water.'   A month
later he has become more critical.   'Doubtless you share my
regret that in the Assembly eloquence is more effective than good
sense, and you perhaps apprehend that owing to their wish to become
too free they will not become free at all.[1]   Yet there will always be
something to show, for these ideas are lodged in every heart and
permeate public opinion.   In our Empire we have wrapped up
German liberty in so many forms that it has become invisible, and
at bottom it is only the liberty of the princes to do what they like.
Such freedom amounts to less than nothing, and there is only a
certain public opinion which is beginning to grow and which these
Sultans are sometimes obliged to respect.   What prevents the
further spread of light is that in most parts of the country the
nobility, from whom the officers are usually drawn, do not read.
Besides, to be frank, what is occurring in France does not inspire
a desire for imitation ;   and people would rather retain the good or
even the tolerable than buy the better too dearly.   Yet at bottom
it is not the great who govern, but He who can each moment stretch
forth His omnipotent hand and overthrow the work of violence
and the deceit of fourteen centuries.'

A week later he unbosomed himself to his brother, who had
declined to share his enthusiasm.[2]   ' Good princes see that they are
but men, and that Providence is shaking them out of the slumber
in which the long-suffering of the nations has cradled them.   But
the rights of property and justice ought not to receive such injury.
They are both suffering to such an extent in France that I am
becoming. doubtful whether the work will stand.   It does not
resemble the revolution of 1688 when reason was in command.   In
the present case, we find only wit, systems, words.   Moreover,
universal experience shows that no free people can survive without
morals, nor morals without religion, which the Assembly regards
as folly.'   The effect of the Revolution on Germany was constantly
in his mind.   ' It is very natural,' he wrote on September 25, ' that
France's example should wake up her neighbours, and in some ways
certain of our German lands have more to grumble about than the
French.[3]   There is no danger of our vindicating the forgotten rights
of man with such savagery.   We have no St. Bartholomew in our
history.   Our people are more phlegmatic, the masses can do less,
our armies are more disciplined, and unfortunately our States are
too foreign to each other to make common cause in anything.   But

[1] *Werke*, xvi. 385.   [2] *Ib.*, v. 271.   [3] *Ib.*, xvi. 388.

I greatly wish the princes would take warning. Perhaps they could confer, and make some reasonable arrangement to meet these genuine grievances of the German nation. Human beings only put beneficial limitations on themselves when they are compelled. Few do good of their own accord ; but fear is a powerful stimulant, and in this way I hope much from the existing ferment. Our Empire is not without admirable qualities ; but everything is sleeping and weary, and any electric shock is a boon.' On October 9 he wrote to Jacobi, ' We sing chorus to your praise of Necker, who alone can reduce this Babel to sense. I approve neither the contempt for all the experience of other times and peoples, nor the violation of the most sacred rights of property. Not thus did the framers of the Bill of Rights act, for they were content to limit the prerogative.' [1]

Throughout the year 1790 Müller remained in this balancing mood—thrilled by the significance of the drama and angered by the clumsiness of the performers. ' What will happen in Brabant,' he wrote in February, ' only God knows.[2] Any other time one would have been safe to prophesy the triumph of liberty ; but the French caricature has upset people so much that the clergy and nobles can scarcely wish to be free for fear of being ruined. The unconscionable demands of the demagogues strengthen despotism where it exists and foster its return where it seemed to be banished.' Two months later he penned a remarkable confession of faith to his brother.[3] ' The common people is in a pretty ferment, owing to the all-pervading spirit of the renaissance of liberty. Hungary is still discontented, and now Bohemia and Austria are beginning to demand the restoration of their historic rights. Who would have dreamed of such scenes in the later years of Frederick the Great ? How far it will go and how it will end no human brain can forecast ; but I think there will be a balance of advantage for humanity. Many people hope or fear that the fall of the throne will mean the fall of the altar. For me, that would not be the greatest of misfortunes. In the message of Christ there are neither priests nor altars, and the religion of spirit and truth does not require so much scaffolding. Periodical revolutions must occur, for without them everything becomes lethargic and comatose. But we must remind the peoples who gain their freedom of the first laws of morality and order, so that they do not relapse into anarchy and thence into despotism.' On the anniversary of the destruction of the Bastille the historian was in a hopeful mood. ' To-day is the festival of liberty.[4] I sometimes think it

[1] *Werke*, xvi. 389.   [2] *Ib.*, v. 307.
[3] *Ib.*, v. 312–14.   [4] *Ib.*, v. 338.

will last. God seems to me to be in this work. He wishes for a
new order. The Reformation at first seemed unable to maintain
itself. The sense of liberty has penetrated the peoples too deeply
and widely, and their advantage from it is too clear to let it go.
The spirit will remain.' The same attitude prevailed throughout
1791, shrill cries of despair alternating with expressions of hope.
' If the French possessed religion, and founded their cause on God
and morality, I should believe in their success ; but now I say that
their building rests on sand, and a blast of the Lord will overthrow
it.' In the same week he wrote : ' I confess I find much good in
the Revolution. But the French are on a fatal road—abstract
theories are everything to them. But though I think their cause,
as it now is, bad, I desire not the restoration of despotism, but
a balanced system.' He accepted the Constitution of 1791 as
a transition. ' Heaven forbid that similar revolutions occur in
other lands ; but I do wish that it should serve as a mirror and
that its influence should be felt. And that it is doing.' [1]

No one was more profoundly convinced of the instability of
thrones and the fragility of the European system ; and the approach
of war filled the historian with dark apprehension. ' If the
French come,' he wrote early in 1792, ' they will certainly find
much support among the people, from hatred of the nobles, from
fear, and from love of novelty.[2] If hostilities break out, the flames
may well embrace all Europe, and the greatest conflict in history
will begin.' He had also to think of his own fate. On his return
to Mainz after an operation in the first winter of the Revolution
the Elector had received him with the greatest joy and paid his
doctor's bills ; and he was anxious to avoid all appearance of
disloyalty. ' People have told him,' he wrote in April 1792,
' though hitherto without effect, that I am a democrat and mixed
up with the enemies of princes. I am not. Every constitution
is good for some time or place ; though democracy is the most
imperfect, and despotism the most dangerous. These cabals are
a great worry to me.' [3] He was afflicted not only by the timidity
of the academic mind, but by a gnawing uncertainty as to the issue
of the coming struggle. To some of his radical friends he appeared
an apostate. ' The first edition of his history won my affection,'
wrote Reichardt at this time ; ' but since the Elector has ennobled
him, made him his Councillor, and called him to his table, he is as
zealous for the Émigrés and as hostile to the Constitution as he
was previously enthusiastic for liberty and the rights of man.'
Reichardt was unjust ; for Müller never became a reactionary.
He fully realised the strength of revolutionary France and the

[1] *Werke*, v. 369, 371, 380.   [2] *Ib.*, v. 382.   [3] *Ib.*, v. 384.

extent of the sympathies on which she could count beyond her frontiers. ' The well-to-do citizens,' he wrote in May, ' are apprehensive ; but the rest desire democracy. It seems impossible to destroy with bayonets the spirit that has been spreading over Europe for fifty years ; and were it possible it would be, perhaps, the greatest misfortune for mankind. I believe the Powers will win ; but, to be certain, I ought to know more exactly the extent of the enthusiasm of the French for the Constitution, a monarchy without a head, a Republic without a centre, religion or morals, a system of equality for twenty-five million passionate human beings. If their zeal for it equals the zeal of the early Arabs for the Koran, they will carry their gospel to the whole of Europe. If, however, many of them are only Jacobins to avoid lynching, if many would be content to resemble the free Britons, the Jacobins will be defeated and France and Europe will regain tranquillity.' [1]

In September the historian was summoned to Vienna by the Emperor, and on his return he found the French in occupation of Mainz. Custine was aware of the importance of securing the support of the most famous of its citizens, and did his best to win him. ' My conquest will be of greater pleasure to me if I can include you. Nothing would please me more than for you to be at the head of the new administration.' The invitation was politely declined. ' My writings prove that I love liberty, and I was born a republican ; but if I took part in affairs, I should seem to have contributed to them and should forfeit public esteem.' An interview followed, and Custine offered him place and honours ; but Müller again refused, and accepted a post at Vienna. He still, however, believed that the storm which was shaking the earth to its foundations would prove a blessing. ' God wishes to electrify the human race anew,' he wrote from Leipsic, ' and to purify our conceptions of politics and religion ; but this cannot be done without commotions. Years filled with revolutions are coming, till everything settles down into a better state.' [2]

Though the great scholar left the storm centre behind him, his troubles were not over, and from the şafe anchorage of the middle Danube he wrote in anger and alarm. ' Georg Forster has played me a dirty trick.[3] In a speech urging the Mainzers to sign the Red Book, he described me as at heart a friend of liberty and equality, and declared that I left as a legacy the advice to the citizens to swear to liberty and equality without hesitation. He omitted to state that my counsel was to be followed in the event of compulsion and in fear of the repetition of the scenes in Paris. Forster is a born enthusiast, who never sees more than one side.

[1] *Werke*, v. 384, 389.   [2] *Ib.*, v. 408.   [3] *Ib.*, v. 416.

Ten years ago he was very pious ; now he scoffs at the Bible. The greatest intolerance is found among the apostles of liberty. The whole world has to wear coats cut in the Jacobin Club. Patriotism, old customs, and local conditions are to be scrapped. What an uninteresting object mankind would become ! Europe will see either a total revolution or a notable modification of existing constitutions. I fear the first, though it is the latter that all wise heads desire.' His worst apprehensions were confirmed by the death of the King, which drove him, as it drove so many other writers and thinkers, into the camp of the counter-revolution. The horror entertained for the Revolution in Vienna increased his own.

'In every city of Europe,' he wrote in April, ' the people are against the Paris atheists. All mankind feels itself outraged in their deepest feelings by these Titans.[1] A correspondent who compared the French with the Romans received a sharp rebuke. The Romans were the most religious people in the world, while the French are scoffers. The Romans respected property, which the French have ceased to do. The Romans were the admiration as well as the masters of the world, while the French are becoming the nightmare of the human race.'[2] The Terror preyed upon his mind, and the death of Malesherbes gave him a sleepless night. He wrote to Speaker Abbott denouncing ' those madmen and monsters in France,' and he shared Burke's detestation of the regicide peace. ' I am all for evolution,' he wrote in 1796, ' never for revolution. But how blind are our contemporaries ! How prone to innovation our youth ! ' In Müller's mind, as in the case of most of the Intellectuals who had welcomed the Revolution, order had come to outweigh liberty.

III

A somewhat similar story is told by young Perthes, afterwards famous as a patriot and a publisher. ' Mankind is now entering a chaos from which it will emerge to make a great stride towards the ideal,' he wrote in 1792.[3] ' Mastery of oneself is the only true freedom ; and if all were free in this way, civic freedom would soon follow, as we should no longer need any executive authority. But the poor French could not wait for centuries and bear the burden which cried to heaven. They were quite right to throw it off. As a man and a cosmopolitan, I rejoice at the progress of the French arms ; but as a German, I weep ; and it will always be counted a

---

[1] *Werke*, v. 423.   [2] *Ib.*, xvi. 429.
[3] C. T. Perthes, *Perthes' Leben*, i. 26–8.

disgrace to have embraced the good cause only under compulsion. If the princes succeeded in vanquishing the peoples, a darkness like the Middle Ages would cover Europe ; but they will not. For every kind of knowledge is now shared by all classes, and the spirit of liberty and natural law has reached the hovels of beggars : and which of our rulers possesses the heroic courage which made the old tyrants so astonishing ? ' On the other hand, he had no illusions as to the virtues and capacities of his countrymen. ' I do not think we are good enough and clever enough to be capable of complete emancipation from despotism. The lower classes and the scholars scold the despots and the aristocrats ; but if one of them smiles, they forget their dignity and fawn upon him. And if one of themselves climbs higher, he becomes a wors aristocrat than he who is born to the position.'

His mood grew more and more sombre. ' The political world fills me with sadness,' he wrote early in 1793. ' In France, I see a wild and empty-headed people, and here, tyrants who break their promises. I always thought that even if the individual fell, the race would gradually rise ; but even that seems an illusion. The French are wonderful ; but with each success they grow more like other conquerors.'

The political education of numberless Germans had been commenced by the revolt of the American colonies, and it was to America that wistful hearts often turned when the old world was convulsed by war and revolution. Among them was Erhard,[1] the philosophic Nuremberg doctor, who counted Kant, Schiller, and Reinhold among his friends. ' I have thought much about the French Revolution,' he wrote to Reinhold in 1792. ' Civil society gives guarantees, not rights. A Constitution which challenges the Rights of Man destroys civil society, and should not be tolerated.' To friends he would say more than he really meant. ' He was sometimes a little too paradoxical,' wrote Baggesen after a visit in 1793. ' Thus he lamented the death of Marat, the brave and upright, and wondered that his murderess was not tortured.' This was, of course, mere paradox. ' He is far from being a revolutionary,' declared Sonnenfels. ' There is nothing in his " Rights of Revolution " that is dangerous except the title.' His radical ideas and the dangers of war filled him with yearning for a land of peace and liberty. A long letter to Washington, written in 1794, declared that he loved him like a father. ' From my earliest consciousness—that is, from the throwing of the tea into Boston harbour—my dearest wish has been to live in North America. My father gave me an education which fostered a free,

[1] See Varnhagen, *Biographische Denkmale*, vols. ix. and x.

republican mode of thought.' The letter is couched in exaggerated terms, and was probably never dispatched ; but it expressed a sentiment which must have been common enough in the years of trial. It was the same craving to live in a land of liberty that drove Bollmann to the United States, and Zschokke to exchange the Prussia of Wöllner's régime for the bracing air of Switzerland.

The honeymoon stage of the Revolution appealed to cultivated women of the bourgeoisie scarcely less than to their fathers, husbands, and sons. Johanna Schopenhauer, the mother of the philosopher, had visited Paris in 1787, where she had seen the King and Queen, *Égalité*, and many of the nobility ; and she was living in distant Danzig when the curtain rose on the drama.[1] ' The Assembly was to me what the Romans and the Americans had been to my childhood. I had always hated newspapers ; but now I could hardly wait for the " Hamburg Correspondent." I was standing one summer day at my window, waiting for the messenger to bring the paper, when my husband rode up. Only an occurrence of the utmost importance could have brought him. He had left his business to carry the news of the first triumph of freedom, the storming of the Bastille. From this moment a new life was awakened in me, with unheard-of hopes of a thorough change in the condition of the world. My contemporaries will remember the ardent love of liberty which burned in every young breast. Murders and excesses committed at the storming of the Bastille and on subsequent occasions were regarded as inevitable incidents in a time of excitement. My husband and all my friends sympathised in these emotions. The " Moniteur " with its eloquent harangues blinded us to its horrors.' In common with humane men and women all over the world, she abhorred the Terror and the Terrorists ; but when she visited Paris during the Consulate, she was still able ' to rejoice in the destruction of the horrid Bastille.'

Of the class which welcomed the opening scenes of the Revolution, but quickly lost faith and hope, the attractive figure of Jacobi [2] may serve as a type. While fully accepting the generous ideas of the Aufklärung, he was wholly free from the dry self-sufficiency and emotional poverty of many of its spokesmen. A man of business and substance, he combined the life of the world with study and reflection. Not long before the Revolution he explained his views of public affairs in a series of dissertations. The

[1] *Youthful Life*, ii. 73–81.
[2] See Zirngiebl, *Jacobi* ; Duntzer, *Freundesbilder aus Goethe's Leben*. His correspondence is printed in the *Werke*, the *Briefwechsel*, and the *Nachlass*.

essay ' On Right and Force ' attacked Wieland's contention that he who had the power had also the right, and argued that right was founded only on the moral law. He realised that the catastrophe was unavoidable, that it would lead to a new epoch, and that there was gold within the dross ; but his hopes were soon mingled with grave anxiety. ' God preserve us from that " fixed manner of government by reason " which Mirabeau desires for his own nation and then for the world,' he wrote to Forster in October 1789. ' Oh, the unfortunate Necker ! The soul of this noble man must suffer beyond words. The thought of him robs me of sleep and appetite.' ' French events,' he wrote to Reinhold a month later, ' are distracting me from work. The vast ambition of twelve hundred Lycurguses to frame a constitution inspired by reason has set all my ideas in revolt. I long to see the result of the endeavours of these philosophic Puritans.'

' I hardly like to begin about the Revolution,' he wrote in February 1790. ' I should never stop. I am doubly interested in its happy issue as a fiery lover of civic liberty and as a prophet. The zeal for liberty of which I boast needs no proof. For that very reason the gangs of evil men, the spirit of chaos, the deceit, the horrible mutinies in the Assembly make me furious. Think what would have happened without the wisdom, the almost supernatural serenity, the virtues of Necker. France would have been ruined. His lofty unselfishness shines through every word and deed. He is isolated to a degree almost without precedent. And soulless fellows doubted whether the most exalted of men was more than a great banker and accountant ! Good God, what hideous abortions are our leaders of the Aufklärung ! ' His balancing attitude was set forth in May in a long Open Letter to Laharpe. Nobody, he declared, could be more interested in the success of the French reformers. Necker was a paragon, and his master was worthy of him. ' What sovereign would have long deferred following the example of Louis XVI, the hero, not the martyr, of liberty ? Absolute power would have fled away into the darkness. But the Assembly was fanatical, and the Declaration of the Rights of Man was based on false premises.' When Necker was gone, he found consolation in the virtues of Lafayette and the genius of Mirabeau. He never ceased to believe that the people had a right to reasonable liberty and a share in power, and he complained that Goethe, in ' The Sons of Megaprazon,' gave no recognition to popular rights. He assured Heyne that there was nothing of the anti-revolutionary in him ; but his mood grew increasingly sombre. He found satisfaction in conservative writers alone. ' Burke's Reflections will delight you beyond words,' he wrote to Schlosser in 1791. 'Last summer I told you of an essay on the spirit of French legislation at which I was working. Many passages, I find, are almost verbally identical with Burke.' 'I received Burke's brochure and your latest essays,' he wrote later in the year to Rehberg. 'In reading Burke, I verily believed I was reading myself, just as I did in the Reflections. I admire your criticism of Paine. Last spring, I ordered the "Rights of Man," but stuck in the beginning.' On the eve of the fall of the Monarchy he had reached a condition of despair. 'My joy in the Revolution ceased in August 1789, and since then I have become ever more hopeless. I do not see how the human race is to be rescued. So I vote for the Last Judgment.'

The establishment and policy of the Republic filled him with horror. 'How Forster and his kind can hope that good will come to them from France is incomprehensible,' he wrote to Frau Schlosser at the end of 1792. 'I shudder at the excesses of this people abroad, while it shudders before a Marat and a Robespierre at home. I hardly see how the Franks will be able to remain people. All Europe must unite against them if it does not want a repetition of its experiences with the Goths, the Huns, and the Vandals.' But Jacobi, like other Germans of different schools, was disgusted by the conduct of the Émigrés. 'I am getting into their black books,' he wrote on the death of the King. 'There is no wisdom in the French princes or their counsellors. A Convention of these people, if it were to meet, would perpetrate even greater horrors than the Parisians. Ignorance, frivolity, coldness and corruption of heart and deep-seated immorality compose their character. One often hears the wish expressed that all libraries should be burned. To which I rejoin that all children not of noble birth should have their tongues cut out.' In this dark mood it was a peculiar satisfaction to receive a letter from Necker, accompanied by a copy of his works. 'For years I have lived in intimate connection with you,' replied Jacobi. 'I have read and re-read everything you now send me. Continue to enlighten Europe. I beg you, in the name of humanity, to explain the failure of the French to become free and happy.' A year later the advance of the enemy to the Rhine drove him from his comfortable Düsseldorf house.

If Marie Antoinette was hated in France as 'l'Autrichienne,' her Hapsburg blood increased the sympathy felt for her by those to whom the Empire was something more than a name. It is no exaggeration to say that the fate of the King and Queen caused more tears to flow in Germany than in France. Gagern,[1] the son

[1] *Mein Antheil an der Politik*, i. 52–5 ; cp. Treitschke, *Aufsätze*, vol. i.

of an Imperial Knight, believed in the Reich as the Guardian of little States such as his own Nassau-Weilburg. Though a life-long liberal, he was horrified by the excesses and above all by the death of the King.

'All men of feeling,' he writes in his Memoirs, 'were shocked by the sentence on Louis XVI, and the number of Republicans diminished. Marie Antoinette still pined in the Temple. I could not hear that the royal lady, daughter and granddaughter of my Emperors, had received an offer from any one to undertake her legal defence. She was German, and so I held it due to the honour of my nation to offer my services, regardless of danger. I not only wrote to her and to the Convention, but went to the Commissioners in Mainz. They received me at table, but spoke little. Merlin made a convulsive, melodramatic movement with his knife, stabbing his bread several times, and remarked that he could not be happy so long as one noble was alive. They took the letters, but I do not know if they were ever delivered.'

The missive was as follows : ' Louis XVI is on trial, and we fear your Majesty will have to face the same ordeal. If so, I offer to defend you, and I am here to demand the consent of the Convention through its deputies with the army of the Rhine. Your august consort has had three defenders accorded to him, and you cannot have less. Perhaps you will be glad to see in these moments of anxiety a good German among them. I am only twenty-six, and have never spoken in public. But you are a Queen, a beautiful woman, a German, and unfortunate, and the ardent desire to serve you will reinforce my talents.' On the same evening that he delivered the letters to the deputies he received warning that he would be arrested and sent to Paris. He at once fled across the Rhine and asked for a safe-conduct. ' What should I have done in Paris ? I wished to demand her back in the name of German youth. Probably I should have accompanied her to Germany, or to the scaffold.'

IV

The symphony of praise was broken at the outset by some discordant voices, even among those who had neither privileges to lose nor private interests to defend. Though a few elderly men like Kant and Klopstock were among its warmest admirers, the natural conservatism of age made other veterans shake their heads over the twilight of the gods. The aged Gleim,[1] the trumpeter of Frederick's victories and friend of princes and princesses, took

[1] See Körte, *Gleim's Leben*, pp. 256–410. No adequate biography exists.

E

down his rusty lyre from the wall and broke anew into song. His message, issued from his comfortable home at Halberstadt, was that men should live quietly under the laws ; and when his bourgeois ideals were upset, he believed that the world was dissolving into chaos. The Prussian Tyrtaeus saw nothing to admire and much to dread in the fierce struggles on the Seine, denounced the French as tigers, and excommunicated even moderates like Lafayette and Dumouriez. ' The new Romans must be vanquished like the old,' he exclaimed, ' or no German prince will sit safely on his throne.' He wrote a new series of ' Prussian Marching Songs,' and sent them to officers starting for the front in 1792. ' You must judge these Soldiers' Songs from the right standpoint,' he wrote to Wieland. ' The Old Grenadier is prejudiced in favour of his monarchy, his King and his constitution. The laws, not the monarch, rule in his fatherland. The King recognises the laws as the limits of his power, and every citizen is as free as the King himself—hence his love of country. The King has urged me to write these verses, and the soldiers sing them.' [1] These well-meant effusions were followed by ' Poems for the Time,' which he freely distributed as an antidote to the French virus. ' You ask what old Gleim is doing,' he wrote to Herder in May 1792. ' Verses, my dear Herder, verses. You shall soon see what songs of joy he has sung in this iron time, in which the French have turned into crocodiles and hyenas. He has composed as many as thirty in a week, so great is his enthusiasm.' [2] He could hardly fail to be aware that the poetic quality of his productions was no longer what it had been in the Seven Years' War. ' Old Gleim,' he wrote, ' was anxious to do his duty in preventing men becoming tigers. Whether his poetry is good or bad is another matter.' Here is a specimen of the doggerel in which he gave utterance to his political convictions :

> Be not astonished if you see
>   The thousand-headed beast
> Ascend the thrones of kings, and there
>   On royal bodies feast !
> You ask the cause ? It is not far
>   To seek : for, you must know,
> He came into the world a fool,
>   And men have left him so.

Despite his violent antipathy to France and the Revolution the old bard remained on friendly terms with younger and more

<hr />

[1] Pröhle, *Lessing, Wieland, Heinse*, pp. 246–7.
[2] *Von und an Herder*, i. 147–9.

radical friends ; and the affectionate correspondence with Franz von Kleist, a relative of Ewald, does credit to both.[1] The young diplomat, himself a budding poet, shared the prevailing enthusiasm for the new order, and frankly told Gleim in 1791 that he hoped before long everyone would be a democrat, The war against the Revolution filled him with indignation. ' Can there be anything more repulsive than to compel a King to be a tyrant against his will ? ' He urges Gleim not to champion the Émigrés and their evil cause, and pronounces Artois the greatest rascal under heaven. His appeal was unavailing, for the two men held different theories of citizenship. ' We can all contribute in some degree to the happy issue of great events,' came the reply. ' Be a patriot ! Make contented people in your State. In no other way can you be useful.' The progress of events, however, brought them nearer. Kleist was horrified by the overthrow of the Monarchy, described the city of the September massacres as a den of murder, and glorified in the death of Marat ; but he refused to condemn the whole nation for the crimes of a ' devilish sect.' While the younger man diverted his gaze from the Terror in disgust, the elder followed every move in the bloody game with strained attention. ' It is good that you hear, read, and see nothing of the tyrants in Paris,' he wrote early in 1794. ' I hear, read, and see (at any rate, in pictures) all the more. I congratulate you on being able to be indifferent to this unique event. In a thousand years, even the most credulous will refuse to believe that such tigers ever existed.' With Archenholtz, the old poet possessed the bond of a common worship of Frederick the Great. ' Do not doubt,' wrote the editor of ' Minerva,' in which several of Gleim's poems appeared, ' that I am a good Prussian. How could the historian of Prussian prowess lose his affection for the Prussian name ? ' ' There is no corner of the earth like Prussia for liberty and justice,' echoed the old man fervently. The successes of the hated Republic were a puzzle to his simple philosophy. ' Poor Matthisson,' he wrote to his brother-poet in 1794 ; ' so you have got the tooth-ache. If only the Paris tyrants had it ! At the end of this century of enlightenment the old gods seem to exist no longer. They used to punish evildoers with toothache and reward the good.' [2] Matthisson had graver troubles than toothache to face. When French citizenship was conferred on Madison, some ill-informed journalists confused the American statesman with the poet ; and the least political of German men of letters was denounced as a

---

[1] Kozlowski, *Die Stellung Gleims und seines Freundeskreises zu der franzosischen Revolution*, in *Euphorion*, vol. xi. 464–84 and 723–31.

[2] Matthisson, *Literarischer Nachlass*, iii. 33.

Jacobin until the mistake was corrected in Girtanner's widely read journal.[1]

It was not surprising that Justus Möser, perhaps the most conservative mind among the writers of Germany, should dislike the Revolution from the outset.[2] The life-long champion of tradition and historic right naturally disapproved a movement based on the appeal to reason and issuing in scenes of violence. He declared himself willing to recognise the French as the first people in the world if they were to bring to birth anything fruitful and lasting ; but he lacked belief in such a happy consummation. In an essay in the ' Berliner Monatschrift,' June 1790, ' On the Rights of Mankind, or the ground of the new French Constitution,' he obstinately based all rights on property. The State consisted of the owners of land and capital. In one of his last essays, ' When and how may a Nation alter its Constitution ? ' he contested the right of a people to give itself a new constitution, since it was not an integral being, but consisted of two classes—the old possessors and the new non-possessors. The State was like a company, which had the right to alter its rules only within certain limits. It was the outcome of conditions of property, existing before its creation. His view of the State, in fact, was legal rather than political. The prince and nobles own the State, as the landholders the land. The poor are born too late to have a share in a world already divided up.

In the household of Carsten Niebuhr in like manner the Revolution aroused hostility from the outset. On his return from the journey to Arabia and the Middle East which made him famous, the traveller settled in Holstein, and devoted himself to his studies and his children. ' He always felt an antipathy against the French as a nation,' records his son,[3] ' though he gratefully recalled many kindnesses in the East, and entertained the highest respect for their mathematicians and orientalists. When the Revolution broke out he watched it without faith or confidence and soon with marked aversion. The German belief that a golden age would arrive from France annoyed him greatly—not that his heart was drawn to the Court, the nobility, and the clergy. He saw in that nation our natural and hereditary enemy ; and I remember his satisfaction at the outbreak of war, not for the sake of the counter-revolution, but because he hoped that the German and Burgundian provinces torn away by France, which in teaching his children he always reckoned to Germany, might be regained. He became ever more hostile to the nation on account of its revolutions, its conquests

---

[1] Matthisson, *Literarischer Nachlass*, i. 313–15.
[2] See Kreyssig, *Justus Möser*.
[3] *Carsten Niebuhr's Leben*, in Niebuhr, *Kleine Schriften*, pp. 58–9.

so terrible to Germany, and the tyrannical government of Napoleon ; but when chosen Foreign Member of the French Institute, in 1802, he accepted the honour, recognising that no learned body could compare with it in celebrity and distinction.'

The great traveller's views were shared by his more celebrated son. Though only fourteen years old when the Revolution broke out, Barthold Niebuhr was never young, and his precocity was the amazement of every visitor. 'The French Revolution,' writes his sister-in-law, Dora Hensler, the editor of his ' Life and Letters,' ' excited a powerful interest in him from the beginning.[1] Its effect on his mind differed from that produced on most of the young and many of the elder people, who saw in it the promise of an era of glorious liberty, and many of whom carried their enthusiasm to such a height as to view the worst excesses as deplorable but inevitable steps in a transition to a higher development of the race. Hence arose a universal agitation which created estrangements between men of different views, and the arrogant tone of triumph which the enthusiasts assumed towards those whom they deemed the timorous and unenlightened. Niebuhr had studied history with an earnestness unusual at his age, and early recognised the workings and tendencies of democratic movements. The horror of anarchy and mob-rule filled him with deep sorrow and anxious misgivings for the fate of the rest of the world. He reverenced liberty when won through sacrifice and effort in conformity with the law ; and thus in later life he cherished respect for the Roman plebeians, who had conquered their rights by such means alone. But all that tended to lawlessness he detested from his earliest youth, because he saw therein the germs of barbarism. He would not have acquired these views so early nor held them throughout life with such unalterable tenacity, had they not received confirmation on so gigantic a scale from those great events. During these years he often grieved over the progress of affairs in France. The sense of horror almost disgusted him with Europe, and he and his sister often turned their thoughts towards America, hoping to find there, with a few friends, the repose which seemed to have forsaken the old world. Even then his mind was often visited by that anxiety about the retrogression of his contemporaries towards barbarism which darkened the last months of his life.'

In his Lectures on the Revolution, delivered in 1829, Niebuhr recalled the thronging memories of his early life. ' I have often taken pleasure in the thought of writing the history of the Revolution ; but I have found other tasks.[2] I began to read the papers

---

[1] *Life and Letters of B. G. Niebuhr*, i. 21–2.
[2] *Das Zeitalter der Revolution*, i. 38–40.

early. At the age of twenty, after meeting many of the Émigrés at Hamburg, I could talk with them about special circumstances in such a way that they thought I had lived in Paris, so vividly did the Revolution and its chief figures stand before my mind. I followed events with indescribable anguish. In England I met different classes of the Émigrés—those who supported the Revolution till October 6, 1789, and others—and I learned that I belonged to none of their parties.' He approved the crusade against the Revolution on the ground that the States of Europe formed a political family, each member of which was bound by an unwritten covenant to do its part in defence of the interests of civilisation. In his search for wisdom he looked with admiration to England, and plunged into the study of its history and literature. ' In four years,' he prophesied in 1794, ' a monarchical government will be re-established in France.[1] I find myself constantly confirmed in this opinion as I read English history. I have discovered in Algernon Sidney's Discourses very striking parallels. History grows dearer and dearer to me.' A week later he celebrates the anniversary of Sidney's death. ' In my eyes it is a consecrated day, especially as I have just been studying his noble life again. May God preserve me from a death like his ; yet even with such a death the virtue and holiness of his life would not be dearly purchased. And now he is almost forgotten throughout the world, and perhaps there are not fifty persons in all Germany who have taken the trouble to study his life and fortunes. Many may know his name, and many know him from his brilliant talents ; but they formed the least part of his true greatness.'[2]

When the Terror was over and North Germany was at peace, Niebuhr continued to follow events in France with undiminished interest, lamenting the successive failures of the more moderate groups. In 1796 he wrote ' a tremendously long letter to the French *chargé d'affaires* at Copenhagen about the revolution of Fructidor, setting forth the merits and innocence of the proscribed party and the black guilt and inexpiable crime of the triumphant faction. It is the only homage which a remote foreigner can bring to oppressed virtue.' Two years later he described his life in Copenhagen. ' In some houses politics are the all-important topic and swallow up everything else. One would think that there could be now but one voice on these questions, and that the Gallomaniacs must be silent ; but, unfortunately, it is quite the contrary. The former ignore all the excesses of the French Government and openly rejoice in its overweening power, while the latter are filled with undiscriminating anger. Thus it is impossible to agree with either side

---

[1] *Life and Letters*, i. 49.   [2] *Ib.*, i. 49–50.

and to avoid the dislike of both.'[1] He believed that political liberty needed constitutional government, and that it could only take root in a country where the soil was prepared by municipal and local autonomy. ' It was to Burke that he always directed me for political principles,' relates Lieber. He often said, ' It is the constitutional monarchy, as settled by the Whigs of 1688, that has saved England.'[2] And it was the British Constitution that he desired alike for France and for Germany.

In distant Pomerania, still under Swedish rule, Arndt watched the Revolution with less sympathy than most of his student contemporaries. Writing half a century later, he describes his attitude to the drama of 1789.[3] ' The beginning of the Revolution is rightly regarded as marking the transition from the sentimental and aesthetic to the philosophic and political epoch. Throughout, I have been a perhaps exaggerated royalist. As a Swedish subject, my hero was Gustavus Adolphus. How, then, could I fail to worship kings and place them above all Republics—those of Rome and Greece, of Plato and Fichte ? A Prussian friend of mine brought the worship of Frederick the Great into my home, and so another stream of royalism entered my heart. As a little boy, reading the newspapers aloud, I was always for England against America, when most of my elders were American partisans. And the French ? There, too, my political faith dated from the earliest years. The story of the arrogance, deceit, and devastations of Louis XIV filled me with distaste, even repulsion, for the whole people, and I felt towards them just like an Englishman. And now there broke forth the French Revolution, and with it a great emotional ferment in half Europe. It was hotly discussed in our house, where it had more friends than foes ; and, in spite of my dislike of the people, I often had to support it. For the misdeeds of the ministries of Louis XVI had been terrible, while many of the principles of the leaders were indisputably just and sacred, however much they were stained and dishonoured later. Yet I regretted every French victory, though my heart was rather Swedish than German.' This account, written in old age, makes Arndt more favourable to the Revolution than he had really been, as a letter of 1807 to his friend General Schwerin proves.[4] ' Few people in Europe have taken the Revolution more coolly. I might almost say that a dark foreboding led me, for, otherwise, I do not know why I did not catch fire, as every head and heart in those days was wild. Or was it that I understood the

---

[1] *Life and Letters*, i. 95–6.   [2] *Conversations with Niebuhr.*
[3] *Erinnerungen*, pp. 86–92.   Reclam edition.
[4] See Müsebeck, '*Arndt's Stellung zum fridericianischen Preussen und zur französischen Revolution.*' *Preussische Jahrbüscher*, August 1904.

people that promised to regenerate Europe ? I remember how, in the autumn of 1789, our Rector at Stralsund gave his newspaper course. He was no worse than others. Every one had to spout Aufklärung and liberty who did not want to be taken for a fool. One heard talk in every lecture-room of clericalism, the religion of reason, the rights of man, and many other inalienabilities which have become only too alienable. The good Rector related with devout enthusiasm the fetching of the King from Versailles, the splendid expression of the spirit of the people, and the inauguration of clubs and cockades. He even reproduced some of the speeches. He seemed really enthusiastic, which he seldom was, and this and his French way of speaking annoyed me. I laughed, and not only in jest. He saw it, and became more violent, and forced from me words in which I declared the French a vulgar people which would do nothing splendid, and I did not see how anyone could rejoice in childish tricks.'

<h2 style="text-align:center">V</h2>

Among the enemies of the Revolution it was accepted as an axiom that the Masons and the Illuminati had prepared the soil ; and the conviction was strengthened by the jubilations with which members of the secret societies greeted the overthrow of clericalism and autocracy. Their leaders were credited with an influence and a capacity for mischief which they were far from possessing. ' I have been reading a book containing the papers of the Illuminés seized in Bavaria,' wrote Prince Henry to Grimm.[1] ' Weishaupt is an eccentric genius. There are sublime ideas in the plan, but the methods are infamous. I shall not praise his heart, for he is a profound Machiavellian ; but his head is no common one. They wish sovereigns to tremble before them. There is an intimate relation between them and the Jacobins, as I have long believed. The head which has conceived this ambitious idea is even stronger than Catiline's. I am half inclined to visit Gotha and talk to this man.' Weishaupt was now an extinct volcano ; but his old colleague, Knigge, plunged fearlessly into the fray.[2] ' It is sometimes quite useful to say out loud,' he wrote in 1790, ' that those who rule and legislate owe their existence to the consent of the masses, so that the Sultans and Viziers do not forget that their crowns and wigs are not made from all eternity to sit on the heads of certain families. But equally one should not, through disparagement of rulers, among whom are so many wise and noble benefactors of humanity, teach every wry head to believe that a ruler can be made out of him.

---

[1] *Lettres de Grimm*, p. 531.   [2] Gödeke, *Knigge*, pp. 150–72.

Serious reform must begin from above. One must not draw up the populace to oneself, but bend down and approach the people. Princes and ministers, however, are merely the plenipotentiaries of the people. The people as a whole, and every individual composing it, have the fullest right to demand that they should not be led blindfold. The only safeguard against the abuse of power is publicity. The executive must explain any change in law; and, above all, the employment of public money must be subject to public supervision. Woe to the government which in twenty years' time will essay to gag the people and maintain the old system of secrecy and despotism. Soon no one will be found to believe that one man, perhaps the weakest of the nation, can possess an indefeasible right to control a hundred thousand wiser and nobler men than himself.'

The Hanoverian nobleman expressed his dislike of ' the sophist Burke ' and his admiration of Paine's ' Rights of Man,' and published his views on the Revolution in the ' History of the Enlightenment in Abyssinia,' 1791, a Voltairean satire on despotic German Courts, and ' The Papers of Herr von Schafskopf,' 1792. He returned to the charge in the same year in the ' Political Confession of Joseph von Wurmbrand, sometime Minister of Abyssinia.' He denies all connection between the Masons and the Jacobins, and defends himself and his friends from ' the childish charges' of Aloys Hofmann. He had never harboured the thought of suggesting or supporting a revolution in Germany. ' We cannot yet pronounce judgment on the Revolution ; but it was inevitable, and its excesses are not to be compared with the misdeeds of rulers.' He praises the Rights of Man, but leaves it to time to show whether the French nation is ripe for them. All the States of Europe, he adds, are approaching a transformation, and violence can only be avoided by rulers renouncing extravagance and chauvinism, by the grant of free speech, and by co-operating with representatives of the people. He strongly opposes the coming war. ' Why should we fight France ? To overthrow a constitution based on reason, right, and peace ? Too much is made of the excesses. If a prince sells thousands of his subjects, no outcry is raised ; but when now and then a few honest men are hung in company with a crowd of rascals there is a row. War would be not only unjust but dangerous ; for the French are not only better armed than the aristocrats admit, but war would weld them into a whole.' Two years later, his ' History of Gutmann ' registers a decline of democratic fervour. It is foolish, he declares, to wish to change a constitution all at once, and impossible to do so without violence. A limited monarchy is almost always preferable to a republic.

Though Knigge was mild enough in his views, the minds of

rulers and conservative thinkers all over Europe were agitated by visions of secret societies labouring stealthily for the overthrow of Church and State. The Revolution, it was argued, was only the first outcome of their unholy zeal, and worse would follow. The Duke of Orleans was at the head of the French Masons, and his association with the wilder spirits of the capital was fully established. ' Beware of all Masonic unions,' wrote Marie Antoinette to her brother, the Emperor Leopold, in 1790 ; ' in this way rascals in every country believe they can reach their goal. May God defend my fatherland and yourself from such disaster.' When Cagliostro was arrested in Rome, he testified to the Inquisition that the object of Masonry was the overthrow of despotism. The murder of Gustavus III was widely believed to be the beginning of organised tyrannicide.

The two chief literary alarmists were Zimmermann and Aloys Hofmann. The famous doctor [1] had begun life as a soldier in the army of the Aufklärung. ' We live in the twilight preceding a great revolution,' he had written in 1758, in his book on ' National Pride.' ' We find in Europe a second revolt in favour of sound thinking. The clouds of error and fear are dispersing. Tired of the long oppression, we cast off the fetters of prejudice in order to regain possession of the lost rights of reason and liberty.' But the meeting of the States-General found him old and sad, and he credited Germans no less than French with a desire to overthrow throne and altar. He traced the evil in large measure to the Aufklärung, to the presence of Illuminati, Masons, and Jacobins—whom he confounded together—in high place in Church and State. In the third volume of his ' Fragments on Frederick the Great,' published in 1790, he savagely attacked the Illuminati, and, above all, their representatives in Berlin. In 1791, at the suggestion of Aloys Hofmann, he repeated his charges in a pamphlet ' On the Madness of our Age,' in which he urged the Empire to suppress the Aufklärer by force. The pamphlet was dedicated to the Emperor, by whom the author was handsomely rewarded. These slashing attacks naturally produced a crop of replies, some of which treated him as senile or even insane. ' All the nests of democrats in Germany,' he wrote in 1792, ' are the echo of Knigge's principles, and Knigge himself is the echo of the American fanatic Paine.' Knigge at once sued his accuser for slander, and after a long trial won his case in 1795, by which time Zimmermann had become melancholy mad, largely owing to the French Revolution and to fear of similar events in Germany.

[1] See Bodemann, *J. G. Zimmermann* ; and Ischer, *Zimmermann's Leben u. Werke.*

The most eager and unrelenting enemy of the secret societies was Aloys Hofmann,[1] the indefatigable editor of the 'Wiener Zeitung,' which, though written and published in Vienna, was widely read in Germany, where it was regarded by friend and foe as the ablest of anti-revolutionary journals. Not content with attacking Sonnenfels, Alxinger, and other chiefs of the Illumination in Austria, he took all Germany for his province. Readers were informed of the editor's confidential relations with the great ones of the earth. The Emperor Leopold, for instance, had granted him an interview at Schönbrunn, discussed with him the foundation of a journal to combat the false Aufklärung, and thanked him for his efforts. The King of Prussia had invited him to chastise German and Prussian Aufklärer, and had thanked him for exposing their intrigues. The Elector of Bavaria is commended for compelling his officials to abjure membership of any secret society ; and the Hanoverian General, Freytag, is praised for his scheme of a military association to combat ' the little German Mirabeaus, Condorcets, and Brissots, who would gladly see Germany follow France into the furnace.' Hofmann proudly rejoiced at the counter-attacks to which he was exposed. ' I shall never cease to repeat that the Revolution has come from Masonry, and that it was made by writers and the Illuminati.' On the death of Leopold, the paper came to an end, and Hofmann lost his professorship ; but he continued his campaign against the ' workers for destruction.'

A third anti-Masonic gladiator was Göchhausen,[2] who pointed to the Revolution as proof of the soundness of his early warning that the intellectual anarchy of the Aufklärung led straight to political revolt. In Hofmann's paper, and in a new pamphlet, he raised the cry for coercion. ' Göchhausen seems to think that he was ordained by heaven to extirpate the Jacobins,' wrote the Duchess Luise of Weimar to Frau von Stein after a visit to Eisenach.[3] ' For this he makes every exertion, but I fear in vain. He maintains that the dead Bode is largely responsible for the French Revolution.' When the Terror was over, these charges were repeated in a crowd of pamphlets and amplified by the Abbé Barruel in his five volumes on the ' History of Jacobinism,' published in London in 1797. He traces the Revolution to the fusion of three great conspiracies—the Philosophes, the Masons, and the Illuminati. Weishaupt, he declares, brewed the poison, and Knigge sold it. Together they had infected the world, and they must be

[1] See Wenck, *Deutschland vor hundert Jahren*, vol. ii. ; Wurzbach, *Biographisches Lexikon*.

[2] Wenck, ii. 136–7.

[3] Duntzer, *Frau von Stein*, vol. ii., August 25, 1794.

numbered amongst the real authors of the cataclysm. The same
thesis was maintained by the Scottish Robison, who discovered in
the secret societies the organs of a general conspiracy against
monarchy and religion. The explanation of the Revolution by
the plots of little groups of Intellectuals was a mare's nest, the
result of the neurotic excitement of the age. A crushing reply
came in 1801 from Mounier,[1] who had been attacked by name,
and whose leading part in the drama of 1789 enabled him to speak
with authority. The Philosophes, he maintained, had done more
good than harm ; the connection between the Masons and the
Revolution was unproved ; and the Illuminati had been effectually
broken up by the Elector of Bavaria.   There was no mystery about
the Revolution, which was the result of concrete causes.   'Even if
there was not a Mason in the world, if rulers ruin their finances,
alienate their armies, reduce every part of the administration to
chaos, and summon a large crowd of deputies of the people to the
rescue, revolutions will be inevitable.'

VI

While the cultivated bourgeoisie loudly applauded the Revolution, and only finally withdrew their approval when the stage was
occupied by homicidal maniacs, the Courts and Cabinets of Germany
with few exceptions hissed the performance from the start, and
shared Rivarol's conviction that the Declaration of the Rights of
Man was a criminal preface to an impossible book. Not a few of
them were glad to register the progressive weakening of a formidable neighbour ; but their satisfaction was outweighed by their
fear that the conflagration might spread and involve them in
common ruin. Nor were their apprehensions wholly without
foundation ; for there was not a single principality whose laws and
administration did not infringe the new gospel of liberty and
equality. The Revolution in Liège, a member of the Empire, in
August 1789, and the expulsion of the Prince Bishop, sent a tremor
down the spine of many a petty potentate. During the early
months of the cataclysm there was considerable excitement among
the peasants in several parts of the country. 'The common people
are in a ferment from the all-pervading spirit of liberty,' wrote
Johannes Müller to his brother, from Mainz, in March 1790.
'Things look bad in Jülich, Cologne, and Trier.' Disturbances
occurred in Saxony and Silesia, in Mecklenburg, Trier, and Speyer.
The peasants demanded the revival of old rights to the woods,
whether real or imaginary, and refused feudal services. The

---

[1] His book is summarised by Lanzac de Laborie, *Mounier*, ch. 14.

Revolution merely intensified the chronic discontent, and the lords were often unable to prove the existence of the rights that they claimed to exercise. 'Our German princes have cause to wish that the French should not cross the Rhine,' wrote Reichardt from the seat of the Bishop of Speyer early in 1792.[1] 'The peasants of the Palatinate and Mainz say openly, Directly the French arrive, we shall join them. Here at Bruchsal the oppression of the people seems to be as severe as it was in France. At the beginning of the Revolution the game laws were less rigorously enforced, and the *corvées* were diminished; but they gradually returned to the old errors, encouraged by the rumour that the French princes were to receive aid from the Courts of Europe. If the French cross the Rhine, all the chances are in their favour—that is, assuming that they maintain strict discipline, abstain from molesting the cultivator, and pay for what they require. In the event of a revolution, the peasantry would doubtless obtain some alleviations at the expense of other classes; but they could easily arrive at the same result if they knew how to act like the Palatinate. When the Court resided at Mannheim, they had to furnish an immense quantity of wood for heating, and when the Court was transferred to Munich they continued to supply it. Last year, they announced that they would do so no longer. When threatened with the dispatch of troops, they replied, "We are not afraid. They are our children. When the officer says Fire, we will call out Hans, Michael, join us. And so they will." Since this little conference, the peasants no longer bring wood, and it is no longer demanded.'

Sporadic outbreaks also occurred in a few of the Free Cities. In one case the leaders of a petty revolt searched the city registers for the Red Book, which should tell them that they owed no services to their lords; but as no such book existed, their search was fruitless. Complaints were, indeed, almost always based on 'old right,' not on abstract declarations formulated in Paris. Thus in Dortmund, the opponents of the burgomaster based their action on the breach of ancient privileges, and denied that they were inspired by 'the blind intoxication of liberty.' In certain cases, the conflict between the Council and the citizens turned on the supply of food or some other equally concrete issue. Troubles occurred in Ulm, Augsburg, and Esslingen, and an authentic echo of the Revolution was heard at Reutlingen, where the gilds elected a Committee of twelve citizens in spite of the protests of the Magistracy. Not content with abolishing certain dues, the Committee decreed the commutation of serfdom, 'which dishonours humanity and which has therefore been abolished in many instances in our

[1] *Lettres*, pp. 38-40.

enlightened era, when the innate rights of man are being ever more respected.' Unable to reduce its critics to obedience, the Magistracy procured the suppression of the Committee by fiat of the Empire.

Some of the rulers took independent measures in view of the novel danger ; but there was a general demand for combined action. The opportunity arose when the death of the Emperor Joseph brought the Electors together, and the first discussions of the effect of the Revolution on the Empire were held. The Elector of Mainz proposed that ' no writing should be allowed incompatible with the Sacred Books or good morals, or which could contribute to the overthrow of the Constitution or a breach of public order.' Brunswick and Brandenburg contended that the matter lay within the competence of the individual ruler ; but the motion was carried, and the new Emperor Leopold was urged to issue a decree directed against the licence of the press. The fear of French ideas drove the majority of princes to sacrifice a portion of their power. Hertzberg instructed the representatives of Brandenburg to accept whatever was necessary for the tranquillity of the country, and to make inquiries from the Bavarian delegates in reference to the Illuminati. The Electoral College proceeded to prohibit a number of writings, on the ground that ' the spirit of unrest and opposition begins to be great and general,' and appealed to Leopold to take into consideration the dangers and losses of the small ecclesiastical princes. The subject was again discussed by the Diet in the spring of 1791. But the truth was hidden from nearly all who took part in these discussions, that the only effective cure for ' unrest ' was not the muzzling of opinion, but a radical transformation of the social and political system.

Though the early stages of the French Revolution aroused sympathy and even admiration in Germany, there was neither the desire nor the capacity to imitate it. Emotional effervescence, dissatisfaction with existing conditions, the craving for a juster society were very general, if not so universal as in France ; but certain factors that made for revolution in the one country were lacking in the other. France was a united and self-conscious nation, with a centralised government, while Germany was merely a bundle of States, loosely connected by the slender bonds of a common tongue and by membership of a decadent Empire. ' In Germany,' wrote Rebmann, ' there are three hundred Courts, two religions, and, instead of one suffering nation, many people separated by religion, customs, and institutions, some of them quite well governed, who could never keep in step.' ' We have no Paris, no centre, no common goal,' complained Brandes. ' The Swabian and the Saxon do not know each other. If the Mainzer stirs, the Hessian moves against him. Germans will always march to put down Germans.' A simultaneous and universal revolt was unthinkable, and local disturbances could be easily quelled by assistance from outside. The citizen thought first of his land and ruler, and only secondly, if at all, of the large and sprawling body of the Holy Roman Empire. In the intellectual sphere, moreover, there was no more unity than in the political. There was no capital to lead in rebellion, no central clearing-house of new ideas, no electric battery to send vitalising thrills and shocks throughout the nerve system of the country.

If Germany was saved from the danger of a revolution in the first place by particularism, of scarcely less importance was the difference in political character or temperament. ' The Germans,' wrote Madame de Staël, ' combine the greatest audacity of thought with the most obedient character.' Tradition was as strong in Germany as it was weak in France, where the Philosophes had undermined respect for the past and where democratic tendencies had often appeared. The political mind of the one country was anchored, while that of the other was on the wing. In addition to a greater respect for historic rights, Germany was far more subject to religious influences than her sceptical neighbour, despite the absence of Ultramontanism and the decay of the Lutheran Church. While there was scarcely a single French writer or thinker of note who retained the traditional belief, at least half the leaders of German thought abhorred impiety and professed and called themselves Christians. ' When all other nations have given up their respect for religion,' wrote Chateaubriand in 1797, ' it will find a haven among the Germans.' A fourth difference was that feudalism was on the whole less burdensome. Though the dues and services were heavy, and interference in private life often painful, there was more of the patriarchal relationship between lord and peasant; while in most States the *Tiers État* was less rigorously excluded from civil and military posts. Finally, the general level of government was higher, and in some States there was an honest efficiency unknown in the Bourbon monarchy. The enlightened despots had done good both by direct action and by their example ; and in certain cases gross tyranny could be thwarted by an appeal to a higher power. ' Owing to its being split up,' wrote Wieland, ' Germany enjoys a higher degree of human and civic liberty than any other great people. One estate of the Empire will also hold the other in check. The individual tyrant is always exposed to the abhorrence of the rest of the nation.'

For these reasons the great mass of German citizens were

actively or passively loyal to their rulers. If the reigning prince was hated, there was usually a welcome for his successor. In his pamphlet, ' A Word of Encouragement, dedicated to the Rulers and Princes of Germany,' Cranz distinguished between the bad and good governments : among the latter being Brunswick, Weimar, Gotha, Baden, Hesse-Homburg, Anhalt-Dessau, and the Electorate of Cologne. ' In these lands no revolt is to be feared, even with complete liberty of the press and opinion. If one broke out, the prince would have no need of soldiers, but would quell a whole crowd of peasants with a word and a stick. Revolution is equally impossible in Prussia, for no Prussian ruler has trampled on the laws.' The testimonial was not undeserved. Some deep furrows were ploughed in German life and some passing spasms were experienced ; but they awoke no elemental passions. ' Except for the Protestant part of the Palatinate,' wrote the democratic Reichardt in 1792, ' the German is not oppressed to the point of requiring a revolution. Besides, he is sufficiently enlightened to appreciate the ulterior advantages of a better constitution and to support with constancy the sacrifices which such a change would impose on the present generation. His temperament is not enthusiastic, and he would not shoulder burdens for the sake of his grandchildren. Moreover, the organisation of the Empire blocks the way to a general reform.' Thus partly from her political structure, partly from national temperament, and partly because on the whole the evils were less acute, Germany escaped an explosion and contented herself with gradual change. While in France the Revolution was embraced as a religion and championed with delirious zeal, there were but few Germans ready to don the Phrygian cap, to offer costly sacrifices to the Goddess of Liberty, or to follow her gleaming banner to death and glory.

CHAPTER III

THE HANOVERIAN WHIGS

THERE was perhaps less inflammatory material stored up in Hanover than in any other German State.[1] On the one hand there was little oppression, and on the other the leaders of opinion drew their inspiration rather from English than from French sources. The University of Göttingen, the brain of the Electorate, turned out young men by the hundred, trained in history and law, to whom concrete facts and institutions appealed more than speculation and ideals. Hanoverian opinion was neither liberal nor reactionary, but stood for a not wholly unprogressive conservatism. Hanover was, indeed, a sort of British *enclave* in Germany ; and Göttingen, with its library full of English political works, was the connecting link between English and German culture. ' We, here,' declared Spittler, ' are glad to be half Englishmen not only in clothes and fashions and habits, but also in character.' On such a solid and practical people the French Revolution was not likely to make much impression ; and the first reasoned opposition to what were called French principles came from this quarter. Rehberg and Brandes, who began writing before Burke's ' Reflections,' were voices crying in the wilderness when they attacked the philosophic foundation on which the Revolution rested. Their enemy was political rationalism, and their aim was to limit the claims of reason in politics as Kant had limited them in philosophy. The Hanoverian group consisted of real specialists—less popular, indeed, than the literary amateurs, but exerting a marked influence over the governing classes, and laying the foundation for the constitutional thought of the era of the Restoration.[2]

[1] See Heinemann, *Geschichte von Braunschweig u. Hannover*, iii. 379–94 ; and Ward, *England and Hanover*.

[2] See Rexius, *Studien zur Staatslehre der historischen Schule, Historische Zeitschrift*, vol. cvii. ; Wenck, vol. ii. ch. 8 ; and F. Braune, *Edmund Burke in Deutschland*, 1917.

F

I

The record of Schlözer, the Nestor of Hanoverian publicists, made it certain that he would welcome the downfall of despotism with open arms. For several years before the Revolution he had published full reports of events and tendencies in France from the Alsatian Pfeffel, the elder brother of the poet, who held a subordinate post in the French department of foreign affairs ; and he was well aware that a storm was brewing. The articles which appeared in his paper on the Diamond Necklace struck some of their readers as frankly revolutionary. ' Humanity,' he declared boldly, ' is ripe for a revolution. The burgher class demands its rights. It is most numerous and most enlightened in France, and it will succeed.' He hailed the approaching convocation of the States-General as ' the greatest event of our time,' and as a proof that the Estates, which for a thousand years had distinguished Europe from Asia and Africa, were no longer alive in England alone. On the recall of Necker, he inquires whether history can show any other example of a despotic Court exhibiting such deference to public opinion. He rejoices that the refreshing sleep of the Estates for 175 years has strengthened the mind and heart of the nation proper—the *Tiers État*. In France, unlike other nations, culture would, please God, climb from the middle classes to the higher nobility and clergy in the coming political reformation.

Unlike the younger generation of Hanoverian publicists, the rugged old Professor invariably expressed his opinions in strong language. All enlightened citizens of the world, he declared, congratulated the French nation on the achievement of July 14. If excesses occurred they were unavoidable in revolutions. Cancers could not be healed by rose-water, and the blood that had been shed—far less than the unjust wars of Louis XIV had caused to flow—was on the head of the despots and their infamous tools who made the Revolution inevitable. These events were lessons to oppressors in every country and in every class. ' One of the greatest nations in the world, the first in general culture, has thrown off the yoke of tyranny which it has borne for a hundred and fifty years. Doubtless the angels in heaven have sung a Te Deum. The Declaration of the Rights of Man, though not faultless, is a code for European humanity, which is approaching its majority. Before long, all its parts will be as free as England and France from the insolence of monarchs and aristocrats, torture-chambers, and similar relics of the past. And this will take place without recourse to the gallows. Every honourable German writer will agree that the Revolution has done good to the whole race. It has taught in practice what we Germans have long known in theory, that the Sovereign is responsible to his people. They will also agree that it was a necessity for France, where the government possessed no ears for the Rights of Man or the voice of the age ; and, further, that no such revolution is in store for Germany. Abuses will be abolished by reasonable inquiries, not by gunpowder. Mild governments, aided by a free press, should bring us the same results piecemeal. Let us preach from the housetops that the ruler is made for the people, not made by God, and that all citizens must be taxed. Then we need fear no revolution.'

This joyful mood was soon overcast. At the first news of the women's march to Versailles he declared that the horrors would not make him turn his back on the Revolution. ' I do not approve the cruelties,' wrote his friend Count Schmettow, the Danish Minister in Dresden, in November ; ' but they are nothing in comparison with the great benefits aimed at. Who can sow a field without a few seeds falling on stony places or being devoured by the birds ? No civil war in France has cost so little blood, and none has had such great and happy results for France and all Europe. Every king, every minister, will now think—*Veniet summa dies.*' The letter accurately expressed the sentiments of its recipient. The middle path would one day be found, wrote Schlözer, between the rule of metaphysicians, economists, and lawyers, and the detestable routine by which tyrannical, effeminate, and brainless Capetian kings, or rather their ministers, enchained the people. England had advanced through 1640 and 1660 to 1688, when she won her liberty, and salvation would ultimately come to France. On the other hand, the present state of the country was painted in darkening colours in the columns of his paper ; and he called for disciplinary action against the incendiary pamphlets which were tolerated in Germany. Early in 1790 he complained that a once great and happy kingdom had fallen a victim to an unrestrained ochlocracy. ' Twelve Cromwells and fifty rascals of the second class have dragged the crown into the mud.' A counter-revolution must rescue the monarch ; but he had no wish to restore the despotism which had held a great people in chains. He points his readers to England, which from William III onwards had been ' the happy home of free Britons.' A further article, ' Address to the Provinces of France,' angrily rebukes ' the heroes of the street '—Mirabeau, little Robespierre, loud-voiced Pétion, the greedy, drunken Orleans, the comical Barnave, and other scoundrels who achieve distinction as the executioners of France. He summons the provinces to redress the mischief of the capital by new elections, so that after the overthrow of the despotism of the throne France may not fall under the mindless tyranny of the mob.

The manifesto provoked a storm in the Gallophil ranks. Campe attacked the Göttingen weather-cock, and Wieland, though himself not much of an enthusiast, lamented the change. The editor replied that his constant wish was to provide material for an impartial judgment ; and he added a defence of his new position. He had not changed his view of the rights of States and of man, but only of their practice in Paris. Since the beginning of the troubles he had ceased to receive his accustomed correspondence from Paris, and was reduced to the newspapers. Direct information had now reached him that the destruction of the Bastille was the work of a cruel mob, and Mounier's pamphlet had revealed a connection between the apparently virtuous National Assembly and the rascals who threatened Versailles and burned the castles of the nobility. He still regarded monarchical and aristocratic despotism as a great evil, but not greater than ochlocracy. The overthrow of despotism, begun with cannibal fury in July, had, he declared, been continued with, if possible, even greater savagery. His conversion took place partly because he received better information than most of his compatriots, and partly because he lacked the power to rise above isolated events to a philosophic and historic vision. Spittler's guide and measure was the Reformation ; but Schlözer had always disbelieved in violent revolutions. ' I was an eyewitness of the great revolutions of 1756 and 1762 in Stockholm and St. Petersburg,' he used to remark, ' and since then I am not easily misled.' He had always held revolt as the last necessity, and he now discovered that the rising of July 1789 was not justified by necessity. Democracy, he wrote, was the happy mean between oligarchy and ochlocracy. But though nations had sought for it for thousands of years, not one had found it, and indeed it was unattainable in a large State. Despite his abhorrence of aristocratic arrogance, he considered hereditary aristocracy a corollary of monarchy. Monarchical democracy, at which the Assembly aimed, was a will-o'-the-wisp. Possessing no belief in the wisdom of the masses, he opposed the purely suspensive veto and demanded an Upper Chamber on the English model. The sovereignty of the people was as untenable as the infallibility of the Church.

Schlözer's new-born antagonism to the Revolution in no way softened his hostility towards despotism and misrule ; and he carried on a war on two fronts, as Luther had simultaneously assailed

Rome and the Anabaptists. On the outbreak of hostilities, he warned his readers that intervention would not stifle the hatred of France for the *ancien régime* which could never be restored without horrible bloodshed. ' If the Bastille and *lettres de cachet* are revived, it will be the heaviest stroke Europe ever had to bear.' He exalts 1789 as the year in which a rational public law appeared. He congratulates the Hungarians on the Emperor Leopold's restoration of the constitution, but blames the attempt of their nobility to limit the legitimate power of their King. Like other liberal German publicists, he welcomed and encouraged the effort of the patriotic Poles to save their State by reforming their constitution; but he deplored the omission to emancipate the serfs. When Poland was swallowed up a year or two later, he mingled with his regrets a hint that the nobles' neglect of the rights of the people had brought its Nemesis. In his own country, too, he steadily pursued the path on which he had entered long before 1789. Despite his waning confidence in the French Revolution, he shared Wieland's faith in a revolution to be produced by the operation of the power of truth, which no mercenary armies could resist. This peaceful re-acquisition of lost rights enjoyed the best prospects in Germany, owing to its loosely knit constitution. And where were there so many enlightened rulers ? But this transformation would probably be the work rather of writers than of Cabinets ; for the abuses and oppressions from which Germany, like other countries, suffered must be exposed and denounced by the pen, which, in the long run, was mightier than the sword.

Though his exposure of abuses was still a work of national importance, the tribunal of the Göttingen Rhadamanthus attracted less attention than of old ; for all eyes were turned to the greater battle that was raging on the Seine. Moreover, he had now no real following. He had a right to smile when he was denounced from opposing camps as a reactionary and a Jacobin. The friends of the Revolution could not forgive his philippics, while its enemies were angered by his onslaughts on the old régime in Germany. He was classed by the Brunswick Liberals with Schirach among the sophists, while Aloys Hofmann denounced him in the ' Wiener Zeitschrift ' as an iconoclast and sedition-monger. Though he attacked the Terror with his usual sledge-hammer blows, he was too outspoken for the gathering reaction. Hanover, like other States, began to be frightened, and in 1792 the Government authorised the Postmaster of Göttingen to open and withhold all printed matter from beyond the frontier. Schlözer was well aware of the new danger. For years, on the appearance of a new number, he would say, ' Perhaps that is the last.' The December issue of

1793 was indeed the last, for the sword fell in February 1794. The closing words summarised the teaching of a lifetime. ' We Germans need reforms. It is impossible always to stand in the old ways ; but keep us, good God, from revolutions ! We do not need them, and need not fear them. Everything that must come may be confidently awaited from gradual change. For where is there a land where true enlightenment is more advanced and more widely spread ? ' It was a fitting and characteristic epilogue from the lips of the old warrior who had never hesitated to express his opinion and was robustly indifferent to the praise and blame of men.

II

While Schlözer swung round from enthusiasm to detestation, Rehberg was from the first an uncompromising enemy of the principles on which the Revolution rested, and indeed the first important foe of French ideas in Germany.[1] The shrill voices of Girtanner and Schirach in Hamburg, Zimmermann in Hanover, and Aloys Hofmann in Vienna were raised in a chorus of denunciation ; but they carried little intellectual or moral weight. Rehberg grew up among the high-minded and conservative bureaucracy of Hanover to which his father belonged. At Göttingen he formed an intimate friendship with Stein, who declared in 1792 that they were in perfect agreement about politics. Both admired the English constitution and the English State, where they believed the only true freedom to exist. But while the Imperial Knight possessed a certain feeling for Germany and the Empire, the Hanoverian official was a particularist, devoted to his State and the Guelf dynasty and conscious of far closer allegiance to England than to Germany. He read the Parliamentary debates and drank gratefully at the fountain of Burke. Hating autocracy, he insisted that the monarch must be bound by representatives of the people. He was a realist, not an idealist ; and he tested institutions by their working, not by their conformity to abstract standards or principles. Next to the influence of England, he owed most to Justus Möser, under whom he worked at Osnabrück. The young man enjoyed the mellow wisdom of the old publicist, and his faith in limited monarchy was confirmed by residence in one of the few German States where autocracy had not crushed out the political life of the people. But he was a bureaucrat by tradition and temperament, and he never learned his master's sympathetic understanding for the lower classes. Möser, on the other hand, had no real system, but only a

[1] See the admirable monograph of K. Lessing, *Rehberg und die Französische Revolution.*

deep piety for the past. The mature Rehberg, in fact, was nearer Burke, whose view of the State was dynamic, while that of Möser was static.

It was improbable that the unimaginative Whig would be swept off his feet by the revolutionary flood. His shafts were aimed not at the excesses of the leaders, but at their metaphysics : above all, at the conception of the Law of Nature, which claimed to override existing conditions and historical rights. It was the standpoint of Burke, without Burke's emotional and almost neurotic temperament. He realised more fully than his English master the need of sweeping changes in France, where he desired to see a free constitution and a State system based on law ; but he believed that all necessary changes should be effected within the framework of existing institutions and imposed from above. A revolutionary body was bound to fail, both in its destructive and its constructive work. Unlike Gentz, who spoke to all who would listen, he addresses himself in measured tones to the governing classes. Invited to review the literature of the Revolution in a Jena journal, he contributed to its columns from 1790 to 1793. In 1792 he collected his articles into a book, ' Investigations into the French Revolution,' adding a survey of its history and a discussion of the constitution of 1791.

The preface, dated September 4, 1792, remarks that as the French constitution is the first instrument worked out from theory it must be tested solely by reason ; and that, if its principles are false, it loses all right to exist. The work opens with an attack on Rousseau—' whose splendid edifice rests on a foundation of soap-bubbles '—and on the doctrine of equality. Like Burke, he fixes on the Law of Nature as the kernel of the Revolution. ' Civic equality has taken possession of minds without number, who defend their ideal with passionate conviction. The citizen, however, must be wholly dissociated from the man in the sphere of politics. Only in the Christian Church and in the eyes of God are all men equal, and then only in relation to their Maker. Among themselves they are in no respect alike or equal. Citizenship and its rights do not spring from the universal qualities of human nature, and they have therefore nothing in common with the rights which man possesses by his nature.' The basis of civic rights is property. Rehberg declares open war on the disease of speculative politics. Metaphysics, he argues, have destroyed the monarchy and made the Revolution. There is no perfect or ideal instrument of government. ' Age, habit, and experience form the foundation of all political arrangements and all satisfactory administration.' Constitutions grow out of and are adapted to local and historical conditions. It is, for instance, impossible to transplant the English Constitution. To demand it is to demand that not only the present circumstances, but the past history of the people should resemble that of England. In the next place there is no excuse for upsetting a constitution unless the evil is intolerable and there is no other way of escape ; and this was certainly not the case with France. But even if there were greater justification, the nation would not benefit ; for only the lowest class, who possess nothing and have therefore no political rights, would gain. And this rough mob respects property as little as political rights, destroys the good with the evil, and compels the nation to retread the path to civilisation from the start.

The counsel for the prosecution now turns to the Constitution of 1791 and the Declaration of the Rights of Man. It is monstrous, he declares, to contend that men are born free and equal in rights ; for they are only equal before the judge. He complains that the sole reference to duties in the seventeen Articles is the command to the citizens to obey when summoned or arrested in the name of the law. The freedom of the press, again, is not a right but a danger ; for France is being ruined by pamphlets. The separation of powers is sound doctrine ; but the Constitution leaves the King no power at all against the legislature, since the suspensive veto is a broken reed. ' If it is contended that one man must defer to the will of the nation, I ask where is that will unambiguously expressed ? ' The monarchy, he concludes, was only retained because nobody knew what to do with the dynasty. ' The whole system is one of complete insubordination and anarchy.' The abolition of the old Estates was an error no less fatal than the suppression of the power of the throne. As a sturdy Protestant, Rehberg admits that the Roman Church had produced such terrible consequences that reasonable men naturally desired to make changes in the system ; and in France fanaticism had led to such evils that the Philosophes attacked not only the tyranny but Christianity itself. Despite the provocation, however, there was no excuse for the separation of Church and State or for the wholesale secularisation of ecclesiastical property ; for the Church is a great moral force and affords a make-weight to the aristocracy. The case against the abolition of the nobility is argued with much greater conviction. Sieyès's ' miserable pamphlet ' on the *Tiers État* is denounced for forgetting the services rendered by the nobility, which had defended the people against absolutism and sheltered the ruler from the mob. The French nobles, he contends, deserved a large influence in legislation as a body of wealthy and educated men. The only way to prevent the overthrow of the State and the inrush of the common people was to retain the *Noblesse* as a bulwark. The abolition of needless and degrading feudal services and of the exemption from the common burdens of taxation was perfectly right ; but to destroy the Estate itself was madness. Estates and classes should be retained ; but the individual should be allowed to rise from one class to another. Yet the Crown had also made grave mistakes, and to invite the presentation of the *Cahiers* was an unpardonable blunder. France required reform and a constitution ; but they should have emanated from the monarch himself. The author's opinions are further expressed in his reviews of the literature of the Revolution. His hero is Burke, whom he valiantly defends against bitter attack. ' If there is passion in his pages, it is only the passion for justice and virtue.' Tom Paine is dismissed as a rhapsodist, calling for mention merely because he was so widely read. Among French writers, Mounier finds most favour ; just as Mounier's party alone followed the path of wisdom in the Constituent Assembly. His plea for English models, however, had fallen on deaf ears. ' The English Constitution had become so hated that the French nation would have nothing to say to it ; for the aristocracy thinks it robs them of their power, and the democrats find it too aristocratic.' The whole question, however, had become academic, for when Rehberg wrote his preface the monarchy had fallen and the Constitution of 1791 was buried under its ruins.

The ' Investigations ' conclude with an analysis of German opinion on the Revolution. ' The first stages commanded almost universal approval ; for very few were sharp enough to scent the coming cataclysm in the first excesses of the mob. Most people saw only the great evils to be removed, and overlooked the vital question whether the methods employed could lead to good results. Antagonism to the aristocracy and the Court party was acute, and the lack of trustworthy information and of good literature on the side of the defeated party made many friends for the Revolution. Hope was as blind and as irrepressible as ever. When in a controversy ugly facts are admitted, but one is assured that a paradise is coming, one can only be silent. The Constitution found many admirers in Germany ; but how many people had read it, much less studied it ? Only experienced administrators were in a position to judge. Any other instrument would have received the same welcome ; for people rejoiced not at that particular constitution, but that there was one at all. A revolution is not to be feared in Germany ; but the spread of discontent among the reading classes constitutes a real danger. Little books, pamphlets, and newspapers are now the lever with which the world can be shifted from its axis. The primary need of political education both for individuals and nations is moderation and self-control ;

and the duty of rulers is to limit, not to enlarge, the freedom of the press.'

Rehberg firmly grasped the historical view of the State and its institutions ; but he failed to realise that the Revolution was also the result of historical factors, above all, of the instinctive striving of an educated bourgeoisie for political power. To him the great upheaval was mainly due to the spirit of criticism and the pitiful bungling of Ministers. His criticism of France was the weakest side of his achievement, the strength of which lay in his recognition of the necessity of organic growth. The conception and practice of State life, he taught, involved the recognition of existing institutions by each successive generation. This continuity was necessary both for order and for culture ; and the longer the chain of tradition, the more impossible it was to measure it by abstract standards. Society consisted not only of adult citizens, but of young men and maidens, and embraced the past and the future as well as the present. He turned the eyes of his readers from the idea of the State to its concrete embodiments, applying the teaching of Justus Möser directly to politics. Such minds are essentially conservative ; but Rehberg was never a reactionary. Fichte dubbed him a sophist for conceding the theoretical right of a people to provide itself with a new constitution, while forbidding them in practice to make use of the privilege ; but his criticisms of Haller proved that the historical school was sharply separated from patriarchal or theocratic absolutism. Like Stein he was no more and no less liberal at the end of the Revolution than at the beginning. His essay ' On the German Nobility,' published in 1803, urged the limitation of their rights ; but he never lost the contempt of the experienced official for the ignorant masses. He was not the first German publicist to sing the praises of the *juste milieu* ; but he was the first who boldly opposed organic development to theoretical discussion. The historical school of politics, which was to receive its charter a generation later from Savigny, traces its origin to Rehberg, who in turn derived his weapons from the armoury of Burke.

III

Brandes was wont to assert that he would never have ventured into print if Rehberg had resolved to write a book on the Revolution ; for their views were in almost every respect identical. Not only the opinions, but the careers, of the two men ran parallel. Ernst Brandes' father, a protégé and colleague of Münchhausen, had been officially responsible for the University of Göttingen, and had helped to secure to Schlözer the freedom he required for his journalistic activities. After a course at the University and a visit to France, the son spent some time in England in 1784-5, where he gained a minute acquaintance with English institutions and won the friendship of Burke, who thought so highly of his abilities that he wished to engage him as his Under-Secretary if he ever entered the Ministry. He was a man of wide culture and many interests, well versed in art and literature no less than in politics. We owe a picture of him to his brother-in-law, Heeren, the famous Göttingen Professor. ' Nature fitted my noble friend to rule. Though outwardly the picture of weakness, he was within all strength and energy, and in great issues resolute to boldness. In social intercourse he was caustic and sometimes unjust in his judgments, but highly conscientious in his actions. He was loved and hated by a few and avoided by many ; but he was respected even by those who disliked him.' [1]

In an article of 1787 Brandes asked, ' Is it expedient that the nobility possesses the first posts in the State ? ' and answered in the affirmative. ' Leave them their privileges, but control them, so that they do not go too far or allow themselves every sort of licence on the strength of their lineage. And you bourgeois, do not forget that, if they are noble, you are free.' Such a man would be neither intoxicated nor terrified by the Revolution, with which he dealt in two works of importance. In his ' Political Reflections,' published in 1790, he is far from an unreserved condemnation. He realises that the cataclysm found its justification in a certain necessity. He pronounces it reasonable that the Assembly should declare itself irremovable till its constitutional work has been accomplished, and dismisses a counter-revolution as improbable and undesirable. But in the debates of the Assembly, up till the time of writing in the summer of 1790, he finds grounds for alarm. He objects to a single legislature, to its loose connection with the executive, to the shadowy veto left to the King. Though influenced by his personal intercourse with Burke, he wrote before the appearance of the ' Reflections ' ; and his pages lack both the brilliant colouring and the searching invective of his master.

Two years later he published his second and more interesting book, ' On some Results of the French Revolution in Germany.' The tone is as measured as before ; but the attitude is more hostile. Burke's ' Reflections ' had bitten deep, and he recants the admission that the rebellion of 1789 was a necessity ; but there is no quiver of reaction in his voice. The effects of the earthquake in the large States—Prussia and Austria, Saxony and Hanover—are,

[1] Heeren, *Heyne*, pp. 326–31.

he declares, practically negligible. Such domestic troubles as have occurred arose from other causes, even if its example was not wholly without effect. The only benefit, so far registered in Germany, was the local alleviation of certain burdens. Its more general consequence was the stricter supervision of opinion; and for such precautions who will blame the rulers? Yet the muzzling of opinion can easily go too far. What can be said for a prince who opens the letters of his subjects and holds the landlord responsible for the table-talk of the travellers who gather in his inn? The reference is to Hesse-Cassel; but the author also deplores the article in the document presented to and accepted by the Emperor Francis on his election authorising the punishment of attacks on the books of Scripture and the constitutions of the German States. This weapon, he believes, will do no harm where the rulers are strong enough to resent interference; but it may produce disastrous results in the smaller principalities, as it offends against the fundamental principle of free inquiry. The danger of French influence is felt most in the ecclesiastical principalities; and not without reason. Liège was an object-lesson; and the spirit of the age was against them. The elective principle was bad, for each successive ruler thought merely of himself and his family; and there was nothing so stifling to the mind as a narrow Catholicism. But our impartial author states the credit as well as the debit side of ecclesiastical rule. An elected ruler is less harmful in a small State than in a great kingdom like Poland; and he is educated as a nobleman rather than as a priest. He usually serves as a member of the Chapter, which affords a better preparation for the cares of government than the customary military training. There is no great army to maintain, and mistresses are the exception. The Chapter is a bulwark against autocratic rule, and considerable progress has been made in some states—notably the Electorates of Cologne and Trier. The overthrow of ecclesiastical principalities, he concludes, though not improbable, would bring little lasting benefit to their inhabitants.

Brandes next discusses what he calls the preparatory ideas which have facilitated the spread of revolutionary influences. The first is the exaggerated notion of the perfectibility of the race and of constitutions. The campaign against traditional laws and customs has gone too far. For instance, the old criminal laws were harsh and cruel; but now philanthropy is in danger of letting off the offender too easily. Again the treatment of the Jews was indefensible; but the new demand for their complete enfranchisement overlooks the need of taking local circumstances into consideration. The race is progressing, and will progress still farther;

but the theoretical basis of the doctrine of perfectibility is false.
It is an error to imagine that more light involves a higher standard
of conduct ; for many who know perfectly well what is right are
too weak to do it.   Moreover, only the few are fitted by nature
for the effective development of their powers.   Enlightenment is
sufficient guide for the *élite* ; but authority will always remain
necessary for the crowd.   Let nothing therefore be done to weaken
authority and the force of habit and all that controls and directs
the common man, whose capacity is slender and whose will is weak.
Even the State can do but little for the education of the masses,
who must expend most of their energies in the struggle for their
daily bread.   In the same way, to expect perfection in constitutions
is as foolish as to demand it from the individual.   ' Improvements
are essential from time to time in every State ; but those who cry
loudest for them often forget how much caution is needed and how
necessary it is to choose the right moment for their inception.'
Another illusion is the superiority of republican institutions, the
vogue of which dates from the American War.   The author then
passes in review the critical and democratic influences of the years
preceding the Revolution—such as the attacks on despots and
aristocrats by poets and dramatists, the eager study of Rousseau,
the prodigious influence of Schlözer.   In most German States, he
concludes, there are great abuses ; and they are worst where no
representative body exists.   But writers usually contrast actual
conditions with the perfection that reason demands ; for they know
nothing of government, and tend to exaggerate the evils they
denounce.

   After thus mapping out the intellectual life of his country on
the eve of the Revolution, Brandes returns to the effect on Germany
of events in France.   In the first place they have fostered a tendency
to revolution in individual cases : few in any one State, but formidable when added together.   ' It would be monstrous to suggest that all
friends of the French Revolution desire a revolution in Germany, and
still more so to persecute them for mere opinions.   I know that many
of the strongest Francophils would be among the first to oppose
such a movement here.'   Moreover, the favourable impression left by
the opening scenes has been already weakened by events.   On the
other hand, the scribes have been busy—and they form an army
of over seven thousand.   The habit of reading has increased,
and writers love to flatter their readers.   They exaggerate the
abuses of their own country, and are sparing in criticism of
France.   The praise of the Revolution nourishes a revolutionary
tendency, and the terrible convulsions in France have not eradicated sympathy ; for the hope of the restoration of tranquillity

springs afresh every day, and reports of visitors increase the stock of goodwill towards the new France. Paine's ' Rights of Man' are widely studied and accepted ; the Émigrés are unwittingly effective champions of the Revolution ; and French propaganda, with its headquarters in Strasburg, is active. The second direct result is the fostering of the idea of equality. The dislike of the privileges of the nobles, formidable enough before 1789, has waxed ; and even among the nobility there are converts. The confiscation of Church lands, again, is widely approved, and it is forgotten that religion is one of the foundations of social stability. The conclusion of the inquiry is that disturbance of public order in Germany need not be anticipated, for no alarming symptoms are to be noted in the majority of States. Yet it is difficult to find traces of any great benefit. The Aufklärung has made giant strides for half a century. ' Look at its results, and say whether we needed such an example of anarchy to make liberty attractive and to direct its steps towards us. Assuredly, we should have arrived more certainly at the goal to which wisdom points without the Brissots and Condorcets.' Some princes and nobles have had a warning; but many have been turned against reform. If France, having secured her representative body, had gone wisely to work, what a blessing it would have been for herself and for Europe ! It is the familiar Whig doctrine of the *juste milieu*.

IV

Though born and bred in Württemberg, Spittler belongs to the Hanoverian school of political thought not only by prolonged residence in Göttingen, but by the quality of his mind and by his admiration for English models.[1] A friend of Lessing, he displayed his detestation of clericalism in his ' Church History.' An admirer of the Württemberg constitution, he was no friend of revolutions from above or below. He hated violence, and censured the reforming fury of Joseph II in the Netherlands. Filled with the historian's faith in the organic development of institutions, he desired the delicate poise between popular rights and princely power which English Whigs believed to have been attained in 1688. In his scholarly histories of Württemberg and Hanover he meted out equal condemnation to the attempts of rulers and Estates to monopolise power. Throughout life he preached moderation in thought and action, and in judging events of the past and present he seized with unerring instinct on the ruling tendency and the abiding result.

[1] See the essay of D. F. Strauss, *Gesammelte Schriften*, vol. ii.

The revolution in Liège secured his approval ; but such a cool and critical mind found it impossible to join in the hymn of praise which greeted the din and clatter on the Seine. He was well aware of the crimes and errors of French autocracy and desired to see France as free as England ; but her methods seemed to him inexcusable. He caustically remarked that the decrees of August 4 could never have been passed in broad daylight. Like Rehberg and Brandes, he blamed the Constituent Assembly for making a new constitution instead of amending the existing machinery. He condemns Campe's uncritical Letters from Paris, ' written when it was almost impossible to tell the truth, with an enthusiasm which is seldom without danger to historical truth.' He finds in Halem's description of his journey a new proof that for correct judgment much is needed besides having been on the spot. In an essay of 1790, on ' The Early Scenes of the French Revolution and its leading Actors,' he explained his position with perfect clearness.[1] As the jubilation was still in progress in most German papers, it was a duty to point out what had really occurred. ' I am not bound to praise the disgraceful means employed in the Revolution simply because the work of emancipation was highly desirable. I am a keen friend of culture and the Aufklärung ; but God preserve us from such illuminations.' His sympathies were reserved for the constitutional party of Mounier, ' one of the noblest and wisest men in the Assembly,' Lally-Tollendal, and other friends, who desired something like the British constitution. These able and unselfish men made the mistake of thinking people better than they were ; but the mistake of the government was far greater in refusing to work with them. ' By the monstrous folly of the Court party this honourable group, which really wished for liberty and a new and better constitution, was driven to join hands with the dishonourable Opposition.' Among those whom he most sharply castigated was Mirabeau, who was still a hero to the liberal bourgeoisie. The German public, he laments, talked and thought of leading events of the Revolution as they had done when the first news arrived, in spite of the fact that later information had thrown a different light on them : for instance, the murders committed in the assault on the Bastille. In his sketch of the history of European States he pays a tribute to Louis XVI, ' pious and diffident, deserted and alone. He sought for nothing but the common good, and he was the only man of whom that can be truly said.'[2]

Spittler's opinions were expressed in greater detail in reviews contributed to the ' Göttinger Gelehrte Anzeigen,' the famous periodical which still receives the erudite communications of the University

[1] In his *Werke*, vol. xiv. [2] *Ib.*, xiii. 243–8.

Professors.[1] In an analysis of three anonymous French pamphlets
he declares that, judging by the pamphlets reaching him, there were
more writers against the Revolution than for it.   This he interpreted
as a sign of a change of opinion which had begun in Paris and would
spread to the provinces.   Not that he ever voted for the counter-
revolution.   ' The old despotic régime will not be destroyed in a
hurry ; but it is time to lay the calumny that every honest man
who does not talk the language of the ochlocrats is an enemy of
his country and an aristocrat.'   Brandes' ' Political Reflections '
move the critic to admiration.   Nothing fairer or more penetrating,
he declared, had been written.   ' Our Gallicans will blame him for
making the English constitution something of a fetish ; but they
will find it difficult to rebut his criticisms of the new constitution.
The only possible reply to his strictures is that no great task in
which millions co-operate can be accomplished without a good dose
of dementia ; and this mixture not only comes from the mass which
is brought into ferment, but is necessary in order to set the mass in
motion.   Much that was said by Erasmus against the religious
revolt is equally applicable to the political revolution of to-day.
But that movement grew out of its childish ailments, and so will
this.   Brandes is right in saying that a constitution and a free press
are essential.'   The later work of Brandes is hailed as one of the
most useful of books and as meeting a real national need.   ' Whoever understands the sum total of the small but (in combination)
formidable causes now in operation has long shuddered at the
possibility of revolution in Germany.   The childish levity of some
of our most popular writers is indescribable—as if Germans were
not liable to seduction.   Many writers would have protested but
for fear of seeming to be apologists for the misdeeds of some
prince.   Happily, Brandes is beyond the reach of such a charge
of servility.' [2]

As a liberal conservative, Spittler has no praise to spare for the
uncompromising antagonists of French ideas.   While declaring
the ' Historical Description and Political Reflections on the French
Revolution ' the fullest and best German historical work on the
subject, he complains that Girtanner makes it his chief duty to
emphasise the shadows.   He lays too much stress on small mistakes,
which occur in all upheavals.   He exhorts the author to confess the
uselessness of trying to avoid revolutions by preventing enlightenment and by forcible repression of complaints.   As German princes
had begun to utilise the Revolution as an excuse for reaction, and
certain publicists were encouraging them, Spittler utters a solemn
warning.   ' Whoever hopes to obviate explosions by coercion is

[1] *Werke*, xiii.   [2] *Ib.*, xi. 710–16.

storing up terrible experiences for himself or his successors. When the slave breaks his chains, let his master beware.' He deprecates the censorious tone of Rehberg's 'Investigations.' Surveying the field of German opinion, he discovers no writer desirous of a revolution. 'From Germany's literary corps there is no influence hostile to tranquillity. Equally little need we fear popular movements. To take only one point : Where is there a State in Germany in which all religion is so despised and forgotten as it has been for decades in France ? Is it any wonder that the State fell into dissolution when all its members were literally rotten ? The German people is certainly clever enough not to expect a Republic of Plato and to value the advantages of the rulers and institutions it possesses.'

Spittler's historical writings were philosophy teaching by examples. His essay on the Danish Revolution of 1660, when the revolt of the bourgeoisie led to the establishment of monarchical absolutism, was intended as a warning to France. In his 'Sketch of the History of European States,' French mal-administration is depicted as making a revolution inevitable; while England is saved from a like fate by a political system which allows time for reflection and provides the machinery for rapid reform. His lectures on Political Science, which summarise the studies and experiences of his life, contain his final verdict on democracy. Its chief advantages are educational and spiritual. 'Every one takes part in everything. The feeling of liberty and equality intensifies the intellectual powers, and thus greatly aids the development of mankind. It is a joy to see people who are conscious of equality with their fellows. Among men whose lives have been passed in democracies, such as the Swiss, we notice a certain firm and manly bearing.' Real democracy, however, is only possible in very small communities—so small that they cannot effectively secure their defence against foreign enemies. Moreover, they are as a rule led by bad men ; for democratic States are notoriously the most subject to demagogy. Spittler, in fact, was by temperament and conviction a Trimmer, acutely conscious of the strength and weakness of every political system. He intervened in the controversy arising from the summoning of the Estates in his native country in 1796, and pointed out the changes necessary to avoid a revolution. A year later he was called to Stuttgart as Privy Councillor and quickly rose to the position of Minister of State. But the apostle of the *juste milieu* detested the brutal absolutism of Frederick, and entertained thoughts of retiring to England if the atmosphere of Württemberg became too oppressive. His political life was a failure ; for in South Germany there was little room for the Whig

G

who felt and expressed equal antagonism towards German autocracy and the doctrinaire radicalism of France. Fate should have cast his lot in the land of Halifax and Burke, where he would have found the *via media*, which he profoundly believed to be the last word in political doctrine and practice.

CHAPTER IV

GENTZ AND HUMBOLDT

I

THE most powerful and persistent literary opponents of the French Revolution were Burke, Joseph de Maistre, and Gentz.[1] But while the Irishman and the Savoyard abhorred it from the first, and repudiated the rationalism on which it was based, the appeal to authority and tradition played no part in the strategy of the sceptical and dissipated Prussian. The most brilliant of continental publicists fought his opponents with their own weapons ; and he alone of the prophets of the counter-revolution realised to the full the strength and seduction of the doctrines which he attacked. The peculiarity of his mental experience early revealed the gifts which were to make him the most celebrated German conversationalist of his time. After studying law at Königsberg, where he attended the lectures and made the acquaintance of Kant, he followed his father's footsteps by entering the Prussian civil service ; but his interest was less in his official work than in his books and friendships. He read and re-read Montesquieu, shared the prevailing enthusiasm for Rousseau's ' splendid writings,' and inwardly digested ' The Wealth of Nations.' He accepted the principles of the Aufklärung, with its unshakable belief in the power of reason and its airy contempt for the teachings of the past. He owed little of his political instruction to any German oracle but Garve, the Breslau Professor, whose essay ' On the Connection of Morals and Politics,' though not democratic enough for his taste, he studied with delight. ' To be taught by you,' he wrote gratefully, ' is my sole wish.' Garve felt a real admiration for his brilliant young friend ; but he was

---

[1] See Kircheisen, *Die Schriften von u. über Gentz. Mittheilungen des Instituts für Oesterreichische Geschichtsforschung*, vol. xxvii. The best book is by Guglia, *Friedrich von Gentz*. His correspondence has been admirably edited by Wittichen, whose early death interrupted the composition of a comprehensive biography. Valuable fragments are printed in *Forschungen zur Brand u. Preussischen Geschichte*, xix. 319–51, and *Hist. Vierteljahrschrift*, vol. xiv.

rather a moralist than a publicist, and his conservative and conventional thought exercised no enduring influence.   He held the form of government to be secondary, admiring both Frederick the Great and the English Constitution.   His treatise closes with an exhortation to a prince on ascending the throne.   ' The best stimulus to thy duties is to remember that there is a common ruler and father of all mankind.   All—even the least of thy subjects, even the inhabitants of other States—are of the same stock as thou and of a divine race.   Thou must enter into the divine plan and co-operate with the supreme spirit.'   A man thus rooted in the political philosophy of enlightened despotism could not be expected to wax lyrical over the Revolution.

Gentz, on the other hand, watched the dawn of the reforming movement in France with lively sympathy.   The assembly of the Notables filled him with enthusiasm, and Henriette Herz, of whose salon he was a leading ornament, depicts him as ' unforgettable in his noble love of liberty.'   ' I saw much of him at the beginning of the Revolution.   Never shall I forget how he, like many others, was carried away, and how he carried his hearers away with him. His power of speech far exceeded even his power of writing.'[1]   His zeal deeply impressed his Swedish friend Brinckmann, who wrote a poem expressing their common enthusiasm.   ' It is difficult to get the French papers,' he wrote in December 1790.   ' A few people of distinction have them.   A bookseller takes Mallet du Pan's " Mercure de France " for Ancillon and myself.'   At first he was more eager to learn than to teach.   Uncertain as yet of his own literary powers, he turned eagerly to his friend and master.   ' Let me solemnly urge you,' he wrote to Garve in March 1790, ' in the name of the age, of the increasing freedom and happiness of too long repressed humanity, and in the name of national pride which cannot allow our neighbours alone to be wise, to continue your work on politics, which would now be more fruitful than ever.   You have taught rulers their duties so admirably ; speak now to the peoples of their rights.   In your mouth things will sound wise, moderate, and true, which in another would perhaps be taken for the spirit of revolt.   You, who arouse no suspicion, should show the world that Germans know as well as other nations the meaning of law and right, slavery and liberty.   It is high time for humanity to wake from its long sleep.   I am young, and the universal striving for freedom inspires me with warm sympathy.   I myself dare not raise my voice, for I am only a pupil, whose productions would be dismissed as rhetorical exercises.   You, on the other hand, are an old prophet.'

[1] Fürst, *Henriette Herz*, pp. 139–40.

Garve refused to commit himself, and a year later his eager
young friend sadly confessed that the news from Paris was ' almost
wholly folly and chaos.' But he was in no way tempted to
doubt of ' the good cause.' ' I should regard the shipwreck of this
Revolution as one of the cruellest strokes that ever befell mankind.
It is the first practical triumph of philosophy, the first example of
a constitution based on definite principles and embodying a consistent system of ideas. It is our hope and comfort in face of so
many hoary evils under which mankind are sighing, and which,
if it failed, would return ten times more incurable. It would be
felt that men were only happy as slaves, and every tyrant, great
or small, would employ this confession to revenge himself for the
fright that the awakening of the French nation had given him. In
regard to the news from France there are two considerations to be
kept in mind—firstly the incredible stupidity and untrustworthi-
ness of our wretched press, and secondly the fact that we get most
of it from enemies of the Revolution. Those who supply us with
information are almost always compelled by fear of their governments to suppress any favourable features. Mallet du Pan, for
instance, is an extreme opponent. Though at first moderate and
even friendly, he grows more unjust and violent from number to
number. Yet I read the paper with pleasure because it is well
written and because it is the only French journal I can procure.
And I assure you that all his complaints and sarcasms do not in
the least prevent me from seeing that the Assembly is still acting
wisely, that the excesses and disorders are much exaggerated, that
the future is more hopeful than its enemy allows, and that, if no
unforeseen obstacles arise, a happy end will crown the greatest
work of history.'

Gentz's first book, ' The Origin and Principles of Right,'
written in 1790 and published in 1791, though dealing with the
abstract question of Natural Law, was directly inspired by the
Revolution. He was enraged by some essays in the ' Berliner
Monatschrift' by Justus Möser and Biester, in which the natural
rights of man were disparaged in a tone of intolerable indifference.
' I intend,' he explained to a friend, ' to establish Natural Right
by deduction from experience ; but I tremble at publicity.' He
follows the fashionable philosophy which derived right from reason,
not from God or history, and rejects the notion that political events
are merely the outcome of the play of elemental forces. Every
political question becomes for him a question of right as defined
by reason. ' Without the conception of right, man cannot be
thought of as an acting being.'

Throughout 1790 he maintained his Francophil faith. ' I have studied the speeches on the Assignats,' he wrote, ' but I find no decisive arguments against them.   Unless their value falls, which, thank God, seems unlikely, all the arguments against them collapse.'   The attack on the Church presented no difficulty to the convinced rationalist.   The last letter in which he appears as a supporter of the Revolution was written to Garve in April 1791, though he still continued to approve the action of certain of its leaders.   Like many of his countrymen, he felt the death of Mirabeau as a staggering blow, and censures Berlin for the grudging notice it took of the death of a man who would remain a benefactor of mankind even if the Revolution were to fail.   Various explanations of the change were subsequently given by his contemporaries. Henriette Herz, with a feminine disregard of dates, attributed it to the Austrian pension.   Ranke, who met him in old age, explains it on the ground that the Legislative Assembly ' separated itself from all the interests which bound France to Europe.'   One explanation is almost as fanciful as the other.   Like most of his friends, he changed when the Revolution itself changed and when the failure of the constitutional royalists had become patent.   He was also influenced by the serious study which he now undertook of its critics—Malouet, Mounier, Rivarol, and, above all, Burke. On studying the ' Reflections ' in April 1791, he remarked that the author deserved to be heard, and that he read the book with far greater pleasure than hundreds of superficial panegyrics.   ' You know the German writers on the Revolution.   Brandes does not satisfy me.   Girtanner disgusts me by his miserable reasoning— above all, by his refusal to recognise the Revolution as a great, new, unprecedented event, and by his comparison of it to an obscure rebellion under Vitellius.   I wonder people are not ashamed to write such books.'   He rejected both the principles and the conclusions of Burke.   But the book worked like a leaven and drove him to a comprehensive stock-taking.   He disliked its romantic conservatism, and condemned the prejudiced criticism of a movement still incomplete ; but the subsequent progress of events appeared to confirm and justify his apprehensions.   Like Necker, whose treatise on the Executive Power he read and admired, he saw no permanence in the Constitution of 1791, and he discovered in the Legislative Assembly the inexperience and other faults of the Constituent.   The tragic horrors of 1792 completed his conversion, and he determined to translate the work which he had read a year before with such qualified approval. His version appeared late in 1792, when France was a republic and the King and Queen prisoners in the Temple.[1]

[1] *Ausgewählte Schriften*, vol. i.

The Introduction was the first of the author's direct contributions to the European debate on the Revolution, and it defines the position from which he was never to depart. It is, moreover, one of the frankest as well as one of the most eloquent of his utterances. He has escaped from the Venusberg so recently that the spell of its seductions is still to some extent upon him, and he is aware how many victims he has left behind in the enchanted cave. The mood of France, he begins, does not surprise him ; but it is curious that a great part of Europe—indeed, the happiest part—sympathises with it. That is due, however, not only to the example or the propaganda of the French people, but also to human nature itself. ' For the eulogist of new systems always finds opinion on his side, while the defender of the old must appeal to reason. Political judgments and principles are dominated by emotions. As men are usually miserable and discontented, a secret longing for revolutions springs unquenchable in the human breast. No reasoning can banish the hope that a new order will bring better times. The disappointments of earlier upheavals produce no effect, and there are always men who see in violent change the chance of fame and power. The true life-principle of all great revolutions is in the combinations of these two classes, the poor and the ambitious.' The only reply is an appeal to cool reason. ' But what a task in a time like this ! The democrat can appeal to the instinct of independence, while all rule is limitation and all obedience a burden. The champion of revolutions praises a future good and attacks a present evil, while his opponent merely warns against a future evil and defends a present good. Peoples, like individuals, surge forward in the direction of change. Defenders of existing conditions are roughly asked, " In whose pay are you ? " A universal rage of revolution has seized Europe. It is the epidemic of our time.'

After this unflattering sketch of the human animal, Gentz turns to the treatise which he is introducing to German readers. ' He who will outcry the storm,' he explains apologetically, ' must speak with the voice of thunder.' Only from this standpoint can Burke's enterprise be judged. ' If his overwhelming book was written in a period when quiet criticism could secure a hearing, one would say that it is too muscular and rhetorical, and that he overreaches himself.' But he is fired not only by hatred of the French, but by love of the British Constitution and fears for European civilisation. The book lacks arrangement ; yet it is a rhapsody from which a complete system can be developed. If the translator criticises the manner of his author, he accepts his forecast without reserve. ' France will go from government to government, from catastrophe to catastrophe, as a warning to Europe against political frivolity and fanaticism.' Long before Gentz enlisted under his banner, the name of Burke was famous throughout Europe. The 'Reflections' had appeared in German dress, and his ideas were embodied in the writings of Rehberg and Brandes ; but his commanding influence in Germany dates from the appearance of this annotated translation.[1]

Now that Gentz had reached a definite standpoint, he poured out a torrent of eloquent denunciation and exhortation in a number of short dissertations tacked on to the translation.[2] The essay ' On Political Freedom ' describes the strength of the revolutionary appeal with the same horrified fascination which marked the Introduction to Burke. ' Where the silvery tones of Liberty are heard, every ear listens, every heart begins to beat. Peoples who possess this talisman look down on those who lack it, and it nerves them to undertakings that seemed far beyond their powers. With small bands they drive great armies before them. When deeply corrupted, peoples are seized by the passion of freedom ; one of the most terrible of diseases attacks them. Thrones topple down before their thunderous cries. The bonds which link citizen to citizen fall asunder. The whole edifice of social order collapses. Countries dissolve into chaos, humanity becomes a chimaera, vengeance rules supreme. The mind of the nation is darkened. Every feeling is stifled by the fanaticism of liberty.' After this thrilling impressionist sketch of France and her armies in the passionate exaltation of the early Republic, he passes on to define the nature of the goddess in whose name the world has been turned upside down. Freedom existed before States ; indeed, absolute freedom is only possible in a state of nature. Political freedom is limited freedom. States may have an excess of liberty or of rule ; but the former is the more dangerous, as the whole structure is overturned. The equilibrium is most nearly approached in England, whose constitution should be studied by every publicist but not copied wholesale ; for not every country is ripe for it. Tyranny is found where a low level of intellectual development prevails ; and that is largely the fault of the people, which to a great extent has the remedy in its own hands. ' When the French Revolution was in its first bloom and won the support of the best and wisest men, it was considered a crime to support any government, and such supporters were dismissed as flatterers and friends of despotism. This period is nearing its end. Reflection and observation have gradually opened our eyes, and we now realise that

[1] See F. Braune, *Edmund Burke in Deutschland*.

[2] *Ausgewählte Schriften*, vol. ii.

a little freedom combined with order is better than a great deal without it.' The tone of our author is still extremely moderate. His argument is rather that French principles have been exaggerated than that they were wrong, and bound to fail. His complaint is not that France has turned her back on tradition, but that she is blinded by passion to the teachings and warnings of reason.

Another essay of the same fruitful year deals with ' The Morality of Revolutions.' It would be impossible, he argues, to frame a formula, for it would inevitably grow into a shapeless mass of conditions and qualifications. Burke himself, the champion of 1688, never preached the absolute immunity of constitutions. He only attacked the principle that a people possesses the right to alter its constitution as often as it likes ; for that is a standing invitation to civil war. Gentz then proceeds to suggest not a formula, but a series of tests on which judgment should be based. An integral revolution is a movement on the moral as well as on the political plane. Only two such revolutions are known to the modern world, those of America and France ; for both the countries, disregarding the precedent of 1688, resolved on a wholly new set of institutions. But the example of the United States was the source of all the errors and illusions of France ; for a procedure which suited a young, simple and almost unanimous community in the New World was necessarily unsuited to an old and complex structure in Europe. The upshot of the argument is that a revolution is immoral unless it is practically unanimous, unless dictated by an extreme necessity, and unless a minimum of suffering is involved. These conditions virtually amount to the formula which he has just declared to be impracticable ; and they condemn not only the work of 1789, but that of 1776 and 1688. Its note of reaction struck every reader. ' The result of the essay,' complained Anselm Feuerbach, ' is that a revolution is only legitimate in the single case where the whole nation is unanimous ; otherwise it is immoral.'[1] Gentz was moving ever farther away from the generous liberalism which welcomed the principles, the aspirations, and the achievements of the Constituent Assembly.

A separate essay deals with the Declaration of the Rights of Man. The document which moved Burke to hysterical fury is treated in a very different spirit by the convinced believer in the Law of Nature and the Social Contract. He hails it as one of the most important utterances of the century, both in philosophy and politics ; a new gospel which has produced something like a revolution in the mind of Europe. ' That man, in being born, brings

[1] Ludwig Feuerbach, *Anselm Feuerbach's Leben*, i. 6.

with him rights of which nothing but his own will can deprive him,
nobody doubts; nor that he only surrenders a portion of those
rights on entering into society in order that the rest may be
guaranteed.' The principle, or as we now say the preamble,
of the Declaration is thus accepted ; but Gentz adds that such a
proclamation should not be drawn up or issued without prolonged
discussion.   In Germany, he complains, no two philosophers agree
on the meaning of the word Right ; and, if they did, it would be
a long journey to an agreed list.   In 1789 it rained Declarations
of Rights.   Every schoolboy flattered himself that he was an
oracle, and could settle questions which had baffled Locke and
Rousseau.   There was, moreover, no need for a Declaration in
France ; for such a manifesto is only needed when a new State is
called into existence.   It was also a colossal error to say nothing
of the duties of man, and it was both foolish and untrue to imply
that the source of evils lies outside man in institutions and political
machinery.   The articles are then dissected *seriatim*.   To the
governing clause, ' Men are born and remain free and equal in
rights,' he rejoins that no one is free, since each must surrender
part of his freedom to society.   ' It is a garish mixture,' he concludes, ' in which there is not a shadow of philosophical sequence
or precision, the work of a moment, an enthusiastic whim decked
out with the mask of philanthropy and patriotism.   Moreover,
never have human rights been trampled on as in these past three
years.'   In the same productive year he wrote a reply to Mackintosh.   He justly hails the ' Vindiciae Gallicae ' as a masterly work,
towering above all other answers to Burke, and gallantly adds that
the author must be admired and respected, even though he fails
in his attempt.

After thus firing off his own artillery, Gentz again became the
interpreter to his countrymen of the writings of distinguished
foreigners.   The days of balancing compromise are over, for the
Terror completed his conversion.   He invited Brinckmann, who
had shed his illusions at the same time, to write a satire on the
Revolution ; and the Swedish poet responded with a picture of
beautiful butterflies transformed into vultures.   In 1794 he
translated Mallet du Pan's essay on the Revolution and the
causes of its continuance.   ' I regard this work,' he writes in an
Introduction, ' as the weightiest and most powerful yet published.
It is worthy of the closest attention, because it surveys the movement as a whole.   Ignorance of its true course, and the resultant
inconsistency in the judgment of its various phases, has split up
the democratic and anti-democratic party in Germany and elsewhere into a large number of groups ; but one must be either for

or against the Revolution. There is no third way.' The translator associates himself with Mallet's appeal to all who disapprove of certain aspects of the Revolution to proclaim themselves its enemies and to combine for common action. A version of Mounier's book, ' On the Causes which prevented France from becoming Free,' quickly followed. In both cases the authors had welcomed the opening scenes of the drama, and Mounier had raised the banner of English constitutionalism in the States-General. For this reason their sponsor felt himself in much closer sympathy with their attitude than he had been with regard to Burke.

Like many other close students of the cataclysm, Gentz resolved to write its history. ' The only person with whom I have any interesting companionship is Gentz,' wrote Humboldt to Schiller in 1795. ' With extraordinary knowledge, and a very correct if not exactly fruitful mind, he combines a rare modesty. Of his writing I cannot judge so favourably. He is now more than ever buried in the history of the French Revolution.'[1] The author had no illusions as to the magnitude of the task. ' Nothing shall distract me from my great historical work,' he wrote in the same year ; ' but shall I ever complete it ? ' Two years later his friends were still awaiting the results of his labours. ' He is working at his history, for which he has collected the original documents at great expense,' wrote his old master, Garve, in 1797. But the book was never completed, and he was not the man to write it. His gifts were those of a publicist, not a historian, and he preferred to work directly on opinion by pamphlets and journalism. Though busied with his ambitious historical plan, he carried on an unceasing warfare with the enemy. In 1795 he accepted the invitation of Archenholz to contribute an article to ' Minerva ' on the speeches of Robespierre and St. Just, delivered shortly before Thermidor. ' The oligarchs have proved what till three years ago not even a madman would have dreamed—namely, that a state of revolution can be a form of government. This constitution has much more resemblance to a monarchy than to a republic, and approaches far closer to an autocracy than to the pure ochlocracy which Condorcet and other Brissotins desired.' He has no expectation of converting any of those whom a dark and unconquerable sentiment makes friends of the Revolution in its present form, and writes only for men who deal in reason and argument. In the same year he founded a short-lived review, mainly intended for political instruction. He opened the journal with a ' Survey of the Events of 1794,' and followed with political and historical articles. Next to his running fire against the Revolution, he gave most attention

[1] *Briefwechsel zw. Schiller u. Humboldt*, pp. 160-1.

to praise of the English Constitution, assuring his readers that England was the only country in Europe where real political liberty existed. He added warnings to the governments not to provoke their peoples to revolt by despotism and intolerable repression.

That the enemy of the Revolution was not wholly an enemy of liberty he proceeded to prove by his celebrated ' Open Letter to Frederick William III,' on his accession, in which he demanded unfettered freedom for the press.[1] The manifesto aroused the displeasure of Goethe, who ignorantly classed its author with the radical pamphleteers. He founded a new review in 1799, which lasted two years, and was almost entirely written by the editor. He warned his readers that they would find nothing of what some writers called impartiality or neutrality, which was nothing but a base surrender of sacred principles ; for impartiality merely demands that no facts should be suppressed, and political writing without a distinct standpoint is a monstrosity. Every page deals directly or indirectly with the Revolution, which is throughout conceived as a unity. The movement was ended neither by Thermidor, nor by the Directory, nor by Brumaire. The successive constitutions in France were all equally distant from the constitutional monarchy of his dreams, and France remained a danger to the world. An obituary of Washington reinforces the lesson that the Anglo-Saxons best understand how to secure and maintain their liberties.

With the rise of Napoleon the hostility of Gentz to France enters on a new phase. He becomes less of the political philosopher and more of a champion of the threatened independence of Europe. His remarkable book, ' The Origin and Character of the War against the Revolution,' published in 1801, surveys the great upheaval for the last time in large perspective, and discusses the conduct of the Powers in opposing it. His object is to combat what he describes as the general view that the Great War was the result of a deliberate combination against the Revolution. He begins by asking whether a Coalition is in itself justifiable, and answers the question in the affirmative. It is untrue that a nation has no title to intervene in the domestic affairs of a neighbour ; for Europe is a system of States. Though it is impossible to agree on a general formula, the French Revolution is assuredly one of the events which give every State the right to ask what is going on. As soon as anarchy and the overthrow of the legal basis of society are erected into a principle, they are under no obligation to respect the independence of the offender. Indeed, the Powers ought to have attacked France after the mob broke into the palace at Versailles. Moreover, France annexed Avignon, and threatened

[1] *Ausgewählte Schriften*, vol. v.

her neighbours. The duty of the Coalition was to stop the anarchy and to restore the Monarchy, not to dictate the exact constitution under which the country should live. But though it would have been perfectly justified in declaring war, the outbreak of hostilities was, in fact, the work of Brissot and his friends. The King of Prussia alone desired to attack, and the Declaration of Pillnitz was anything but a challenge to battle.

The second part of the book deals with the course, character, and results of the struggle. Having proved to his satisfaction that the war of the Allies was purely defensive, he argues that the Brunswick manifesto was not too strong. It was indeed the only language that murderers could understand; but after such a declaration it was necessary to conquer. For the failure of the Allied arms he supplied some remarkable reasons. Once again he frankly recognises the widespread sympathy with ' French ideas ' and with a nation rightly struggling to be free. ' In most countries the majority regarded the war as a capricious attack on the independence of a great nation and as contrary to the highest interests of mankind.' Among contributory causes were the military talent of the French generals and the lack of a commanding figure in the ranks of the Allies. The fight was still in progress and victory would not arrive till the Allies possessed the fixity of purpose,.the unity of direction, and the passionate enthusiasm which had made revolutionary France invincible. She had drawn her weapons from her own bosom, and Europe must do the same. Neutrality should not be tolerated, and Prussia must resume her place in the ranks. The future of Germany and Europe depended on the formation and maintenance of a Coalition far closer and stronger than had yet confronted France.

In entering the service of the Hapsburgs in 1802, Gentz was to continue his crusade against France; and he argued that to recognise the First Consul as Emperor would be to recognise the Revolution. But the struggle with Napoleon lacked the zest of the earlier campaigns. ' It is a misfortune to have been a political writer during the Revolution,' he confesses to Brinckmann; ' everything now seems utterly insipid, and I feel like an extinct volcano.' No German of his time had devoted himself to its study with such prolonged and passionate interest, and no one had proclaimed more insistently its epoch-making significance. ' The French Revolution,' he declared in 1794, ' is one of those events which belong to the whole human race. It is an event of such dimensions that it is hardly permissible to occupy oneself in its terrifying presence with any subordinate interest: of such magnitude that posterity will eagerly inquire how contemporaries of every country thought and felt about it, how they argued and how they acted.' Alone of his countrymen he followed not only the course of events, but their remotest reverberations throughout Europe. No book or pamphlet of importance published in France, England, or Germany escaped him, and he studied Price and Tom Paine as diligently as Burke and Mallet du Pan. He was by far the best informed of German writers on the greatest event of the age.

If we are to describe Gentz as the German Burke, it can only be on the ground that he was of all his countrymen the most brilliant and persistent foe of the Revolution ; for Burke's counterparts were the Hanoverians, Rehberg and Brandes. He grew to hate and fear the Revolution as much as the Tory philosopher ; but his temperament, training, and intellectual outlook were utterly different. Burke abhorred the rationalisation of politics, and found in the appeal to reason the source of antinomianism and national anarchy. Gentz, on the other hand, was born and died a rationalist, to whom the pieties of the past made little appeal. While many of his friends and pupils belonged to the Romantic movement and joined the Catholic Church, he remained a contented child of the eighteenth century.[1]   His heart was never his own ; but his head was always cool, and Metternich, the arch realist, testified that he always stood aloof from every sort of Romanticism. His complaint of the French reformers was not that they used their reason, but that they used it wrong.   Though he became secretary of the Congress of Vienna and the counsellor of Metternich, he retained a slight strain of liberalism. He always remained a champion of the American Revolution. He accepted the idea of contract as the foundation of the State ; but he rejected the sovereignty of the people as the claim of one of the contracting parties to tear it up. He never denied the rights of man, but contended that they had been merged in the rights of citizens. In forwarding a copy of his translation of Burke to the Emperor, he explained that he had attacked the champions of the Revolution with their own weapons—namely, those of philosophical reasoning ; and the claim was justified. Despite his affectionate admiration for his most brilliant disciple, Adam Müller, he was never impressed by the dead hand of authority whether in secular or ecclesiastical garb. He admitted the vigour of de Maistre's championship of Papal claims ; but the appreciation was purely aesthetic.   Friedrich Schlegel truly declared that he was never a conservative, and that he employed the old mechanical methods of the eighteenth

[1] This continuity of thought is emphasised by his latest biographer, Robinet de Cléry, 1917.

century. 'He was never a reactionary,' echoes his friend Varnhagen, himself an impenitent liberal, in his brilliant sketch ;[1]
' he never lost a certain instinct for liberty, a claim to independence,
a craving for inquiry, a recognition of the paramount rights of
reason. Those who took him for a defender of servility or despotism can never have known or understood him. He always felt
himself to be the equal of those in the highest stations.' Madame
de Staël met him on her tour in 1808, and pronounced him ' the most
interesting man in Germany.' He has no claim, however, to a
place in the front rank of political thinkers, for he lacked originality. ' I never invented anything,' he confessed to Rahel, ' but
I am all the more an incomparable conductor of electricity. My
receptivity is boundless.' It was, indeed, largely his eclectic mind
and his steady championship of the claims of reason which procured him his influence in Germany until political rationalism was
vanquished by the joint onslaught of the romanticists and the
historical school. ' We were all his pupils,' wrote Brinckmann in
1816 ; ' we all became anti-revolutionists and royalists.' Though
neither Gentz nor any German writer of the time could speak to
the masses like Paine or Cobbett, his exhortations to the governing
class and the bourgeoisie carried great weight, and after the death
of Burke he was beyond comparison the most influential publicist
in Europe.

II

While Gentz, like most of his cultured contemporaries, passed
from enthusiasm to detestation, his friend Humboldt contemplated
the whole pageant of, the Revolution in a spirit of philosophic
detachment.[2] Though a wealthy noble and the son of a high
Prussian official, he had no affinities with conservatism ; though
a disciple of the Aufklärung and standing on the threshold of manhood, he remained deaf to the siren voices from France. He was
never young and never old, never extravagantly excited and never
unduly depressed. The hot-blooded Görres pronounced him ' as
clear and frosty as the December sun.' More interested in the broad
tendencies of human society than in the excursions and alarums
of the moment, he judged the events of his time with passionless
impartiality. No German, and indeed no European thinker, possessed
his power of seeing things in the dry light recommended by Bacon.

[1] *Denkwürdigkeiten*, v. 1–37.
[2] See Haym, *W. v. Humboldt*; Gebhardt, *W. v. H. als Staatsmann*;
Otto Harnack, *W. v. Humboldt*; Challemel-Lacour, *La Philosophie Individu-
aliste : Étude sur Humboldt*; Varnhagen, *Denkwürdigkeiten*, v. 118–58 ;
Meinecke, *Weltbürgertum u. Nationalstaat*, ch. 3.

Far more than Goethe, he stands ' above the battle,' surveying the swaying masses of mortal men from the windless summits of Olympus.   In an age and country rich in outstanding personalities he occupies a place apart ; and the admiration of his friends was expressed in the words of Gentz : ' If there was no Humboldt, it would be necessary to invent him.'

Wilhelm, like his younger brother Alexander, was destined for the service of the State, and received the best private and public education that money could provide. His first tutor was Campe, whose personal influence was supplemented by his writings for children ; and particular branches of study were undertaken with the aid of Kunth, Dohm, Engel, and other specialists.   The training of the young man was further stimulated by intercourse with the leaders of the Aufklärung in Berlin, and by the delightful friendship of Henriette Herz.   At Göttingen he prepared himself for his official career ; but he derived greater pleasure from the lectures of Heyne, who described him as among the best philologists of his school.   His leisure hours were devoted to obtaining a thorough mastery of the Kantian philosophy.   In Heyne's house he met his daughter Therese and her husband Georg Forster, whom he visited at Mainz in the summer holidays of 1788, and with whom he remained on terms of friendship till the end, in spite of fundamental differences of temperament and opinion.   In the following summer the young noble accompanied his old tutor, Campe, to Paris, where the travellers spent the month of August.   The elder man discovered in the scenes around him the triumph of reason.   The younger, on the other hand, never lost his critical sense, and indeed felt little real interest in the drama.   The strangely assorted pair saw the sights of the city, attended the debates of the Assembly, and made a pilgrimage to Rousseau's grave at Ermenonville.   Only one letter from Paris has survived.   ' Do not expect a proper letter from me,' he wrote to his future wife on August 4, ' while I am living in this whirlpool. You know I am travelling with Campe, a good-natured, gentle, and merry fellow, though we can never enjoy an interesting talk.   I sit and think of you by the hour.   How long I shall stay, I do not know. He is only here for three weeks, and, unless I make some interesting acquaintances, I shall not stay longer.   What should I do in dirty Paris, in the monstrous throng of human beings ?   I have only been here two days, and I am already almost disgusted.   There is, however, one pleasant feature.   In the ceaseless noise, in the indescribable multitude, the individual disappears.   Nobody troubles about one ; indeed one is borne along in the stream like a drop in the ocean.   And that is what I like.'[1]   There are a few lines about

---

[1] *Wilhelm u. Caroline von Humboldt in Ihren Briefen*, i. 48–9.

pictures and churches, but not a word of the great issues with which the country was convulsed. It was this spirit which made Gentz impatiently declare that his friend ' despised equally kings and republics.'[1] He was the only German, and perhaps the only foreign visitor, who kept perfectly cool and felt neither terror nor hope. He was more interested in Mirabeau and other prominent individuals than in the masses, from whom his aristocratic individualism separated him by a yawning gulf. His convictions, however, though lukewarm, were liberal. ' Your Letters have given me pleasure,' he wrote to his travelling companion early in 1790. ' If anything noble is to be expected in Germany it can only come from such descriptions and such reasoning. It makes princes more ready to honour the rights of humanity and less able to trample on them ; and this alone can save Germany from the crisis to which despotism, sooner or later, leads, and from which France is now suffering like the scapegoat of mankind.'

On leaving the University, Humboldt entered the service of the State ; but after little more than a year in the courts, finding that his work interfered with the programme of self-realisation, which, like Goethe, he had set before himself, he resigned his post, married a rich and clever wife, and retired to the peace of the country. His ideal was set forth in a letter to Forster. ' To work on the character of mankind one has only to work on and for oneself. Be great, be something considerable, and men will take note and make use of it. The truly great, the intellectually and morally perfected man, operates more effectively than other people simply through his existence.' In a smaller mind, or a meaner soul, such words would suggest a selfish epicurean ; but to their writer they expressed a scheme of life which promised as much profit to the State as to the individual. He had shed the arid rationalism of Nicolai and his school without adopting the cloudy emotionalism of Jacobi and the intuitionists. He realised that the balance of mind and heart was essential for the highest humanity, and he believed that the production of a higher type of individual was at once more hopeful and more necessary than the construction or alteration of political machinery. It was from this standpoint of lofty individualism, which echoed the better teaching of Weishaupt and Knigge, that he judged the French Revolution.

The first use which he made of his leisure was to set forth his views on Constitutions, in a letter to Gentz, which was afterwards published with slight corrections. The letter was suggested by the completion of the French Constitution on which the Assembly had been at work for two years. Brief though it be, the essay, for

[1] Gentz, *Briefe*, ii. 9.

H

such it is, occupies a high place in the German literature of the
Revolution.[1] ' I am occupying myself in my solitude more with
political subjects than hitherto during my official life,' he writes.
' I read the papers more regularly ; and though I cannot say that
they arouse a very lively interest in me, events in France certainly
attract me most. My judgment, when I constrain myself to give
one, differs from that of every one else. That may indeed seem a
paradox—but you are used to my vagaries.' At this moment he
confided to a friend that his hopes of the Revolution were wrecked.
' But one must regard every event,' he concludes, ' as a useful and
edifying history, taking what is good and regarding the rest as
husks.'[2] Humboldt, indeed, as the essay was to prove, was not a
man of systems, but an eclectic.

' I have heard little but censure of the National Assembly and
its legislation,' he begins.   ' Sometimes it was accused of ignorance,
or prejudice, or fear of novelty ; but even 1200 sages are only men
after all. One cannot reach safe ground with mere blame or with
a verdict on particular measures. On the other hand, there is a
simple fact which contains all the data for comprehensive investigation of the whole enterprise. The Constituent Assembly had
set out to construct a wholly new edifice of State according to the
principles of reason. Yet no constitution can succeed which is
shaped by reason according to a plan fixed in advance, but only
that which issues from the conflict of circumstance with reason.
I accept for the moment this instrument as practicable, or, if you
will, as already in operation ; but I assert that it cannot flourish.
A new constitution must dovetail into its predecessor. From a
system which only thought of obtaining as much from the nation
for the satisfaction of the ambition and extravagance of a single
man as possible, there must emerge a system which aims at the
freedom, tranquillity, and happiness of every individual. Thus
two completely different sets of conditions follow each other ; and
where is the link which unites them ?   Who is skilful enough and
inventive enough to weave them together ?   If the work of man
is to succeed, it must spring from within him, not be imposed upon
him from without ; and what is a State but the sum of the forces
of working and suffering human beings ?   Every creation postulates
a corresponding power of acceptance or assimilation. But is the
French nation prepared to don its new garb ?   For a constitution
built on the pure principles of reason, a nation can never be ripe ;
since reason demands a co-operation of all forces—not only the
maximum of perfection in each, but intimacy and accuracy of

[1] In vol. i. of the *Gesammelte Schriften*, published by the Berlin Academy.
[2] Gebhardt, vol. i., *Einleitung*.

connection with one another. The wise legislator only modifies existing tendencies, and contents himself with drawing a little nearer to perfection. What must inevitably occur when the State has suddenly to seek not one advantage alone but all at once ? I answer, slackness and idleness. No one can work *con amore* who works with all forces at once equally on the strain.'

Search the history of constitutions as we will, we shall never find a high degree of perfection ; and yet in every one of them, however corrupt, we may discover some element of the ideal State. Humboldt traces the gradual development of liberty since the Middle Ages and the gradual decline of the power of the nobility, ' once a necessary and now an unnecessary evil.' As the State required more money, it encouraged the growth of industry. In this way the prosperity of the nation came to be necessary to the ambition of the government. The next stage was that writers contended that the well-being of the people was the end and the raising of revenue only the means. From time to time this notion found its way into the mind of a ruler, and thus arose the principle that the government must foster the happiness and the moral and physical welfare of the nation. From this principle, however, sprang the crassest and most oppressive despotism ; for men were fettered in their noblest powers, while believing themselves to be free. The Aufklärung enlightened men as to their rights, and once more aroused the longing for real freedom ; and it was precisely in the country where this longing was most powerful that the government most neglected its duties. It was therefore inevitable that the Revolution should start in France, and that no other system was possible than one of unlimited freedom. Men who had suffered from one extreme naturally sought salvation in the other. Will this constitution last ? History suggests a negative reply. ' But it will clarify ideas, stimulate virtues, and so spread its blessing far beyond the borders of France. It will confirm the general experience that the benefit is never operative in the place of its origin, but rather in the far distances of time and place. In every period there have been factors which, though bad in themselves, rescued some priceless treasure for mankind. What, for instance, kept freedom alive in the Middle Ages ? The system of fiefs. What preserved the sciences in the centuries of the barbarians ? Monasticism. In any given period only one spark of the lamp of humanity burns bright, while the rest glow dimly, awaiting their turn.'

It is difficult to believe that this mature and balanced utterance, with its firm lines and faultless perspective, was the work of a young man of twenty-four. But Humboldt, like Niebuhr, was a scholar and a thinker when his contemporaries were in the class-room. Though he had followed the welter of events with far less care than most of his friends, he displayed a juster insight into their character and a more accurate forecast of their outcome than any of his contemporaries. His analysis and conclusions are alike irrefragable. The Revolution, he declared, was an extreme provoked by another extreme. The Constitution of 1791 would not last ; for it had no roots in history, and continuity was the condition of success. The legislator's work, if it was to endure, must be a reform, not a revolution. Yet though the new edifice exhibited no marks of permanence, the effect of the Revolution on the life of the world had already been and would remain beneficial. What more can the historian say from his vantage-point of the twentieth century ? It is regrettable that the author never developed the idea of historic growth which forms the basis of his essay ; but even his brief indication of its importance entitles him to rank among the forerunners of Eichhorn and Savigny.

The pregnant little treatise, which cut right athwart party lines, aroused a good deal of attention and in some quarters antagonism. Dalberg, the Archbishop of Erfurt and Coadjutor of Mainz, who was not only a friend of the author but a relative of his wife, was nettled by the modest rôle assigned to legislation and by the emphasis on the impossibility of a State based on the principles of reason.[1] The man who was expecting at any moment to succeed the aged Elector repudiated the paradox that the care of government for the happiness and welfare, moral and physical, of a nation was the formula of the most oppressive despotism. The two men were soon deep in discussion. ' His society is the more agreeable,' wrote Humboldt to Forster, ' as our conversations are generally scientific and deal particularly with political philosophy, in which he is well versed. Theoretical principles are more interesting when their application lies so near at hand. I do not know, dear friend, if you have seen a little essay of mine—just a letter, written without thought of publication. Dalberg saw from this that I was occupied with ideas of this kind, and, a few days after my arrival, he urged me to set down my views on the proper limits of the authority of the State. I had prepared some materials and had more in my head, and it grew under my hands.'[2] In May 1792 his famous work, ' Thoughts on the Limitation of State Activity,' was ready. Portions were published in the ' Berliner Monatschrift ' and Schiller's ' Thalia ' at the time ; but the complete treatise only appeared long after the author's death. It is the German equivalent of Mill

[1] See Beaulieu-Marconnai, *Dalberg*, i. 190–200.
[2] Forster's *Briefwechsel*, ii. 824–30.

'On Liberty'; and Mill has expressed his indebtedness to his predecessor. The German nobleman of the era of the French Revolution and the Philosophic Radical of mid-Victorian England reach approximately the same conclusions ; and though the English manifesto enjoys the greater celebrity, Humboldt's volume remains one of the classics of political literature.[1]

The introductory chapter strikes the note of the book. There are two questions, he begins, involved in the attempt to create or transform a constitution. The first is, Who shall govern? The second relates to the sphere to which the government should extend its operations. The former problem was being discussed on all sides, while the latter, which was far more important, was almost entirely neglected. The greatest of all political issues are those which affect the private life of the citizen. The State exists for the man, not the man for the State. Every one must desire a fuller release of human forces ; but there is an essential condition to be fulfilled. ' The possibility of a higher degree of freedom presupposes a proportionate advance in civilisation, a decreasing necessity of acting in large masses, a richer variety of resources in the individual agents. If, then, the present age possesses this increased culture, freedom should unquestionably be accorded to it. If to behold a people breaking their fetters asunder, in the full consciousness of their rights as men and citizens, is an ennobling spectacle, still fairer and more hopeful must it be to witness a prince himself unloosing the bonds and granting liberty to his people—not as a gracious condescension, but in fulfilment of his imperative duty. For the freedom which a nation strives to obtain through the overthrow of existing institutions is but as hope to enjoyment, as preparation to perfection, in comparison with that which a State, once constituted, can bestow.' Without any overt reference to the Revolution, the writer thus exhorts the rulers of Germany to vouchsafe to their subjects all, and more than all, that the French were battling to secure.

Humboldt now proceeds to enunciate the major premiss of his argument. The true end of man, he affirms, is the harmonious development of his powers ; and reason demands a condition in which every man enjoys the most abundant opportunities of self-realisation. From this it follows that all obstacles to this evolution should be removed or diminished to the utmost extent. The care of the State for the positive welfare of the citizen, generally regarded as one of the main objects of government, is directly hurtful ; for it impedes the development of the individual. He agrees with the elder Mirabeau that ' the fury of governing ' is the most insidious

[1] *Ges. Schriften*, vol. i. A translation by Coulthard appeared in 1854.

malady of the modern State. ' A too anxious solicitude suppresses all spontaneity and active energy, and debases the moral character.' Whatever man does under, guidance or instruction fails to enter into his being and remains foreign to his deeper nature. State action is necessarily wholesale, and therefore can never be adapted to individual needs. Moreover, experience shows that few political measures respond to a vital demand ; and legislation involves an incredible number of functionaries. ' Every decade,' he complains in language of a strangely modern ring, ' the number of officials increases, while the liberty of the subject proportionately declines.' The activity of the State turns men into machines. ' It should not proceed a step farther than is necessary for the security and protection of citizens against foreign enemies ; and for no other object should it impose restrictions on freedom. It should abstain from all solicitude for their positive welfare. What cannot be done by the individual for himself is best accomplished by voluntary associations.' We might be listening to the plaintive cry of Herbert Spencer or Auberon Herbert.

After this introductory bombardment of government and legislation, the author carries on the siege in a series of chapters devoted to the ordinary activities of the State. Education, declares the future founder of Berlin University, should be wholly independent of the authorities. A national system turns out all its scholars on the same pattern, thereby repressing the vital energies of the nation. Where a people enjoys real freedom there will be no lack of educational facilities provided by private enterprise. Religion, in like manner, must have a free hand ; for an established Church, by encouraging certain opinions, gives a bias to the citizen and discourages freedom of thought. And freedom of thought is essential. ' When will someone arise to accomplish for legislation what Rousseau accomplished for education, and direct attention from mere external, physical results to the life and growth of the soul ? ' The choice of beliefs, the selection of ministers, and the nature of worship, should be left to individuals. ' Everything pertaining to religion is wholly beyond the sphere of the State.' It is a noble chapter, which might have been signed by Schleiermacher. In the next place, the State should have no more dealings with morality than with religion. Freedom is greater than morality, and true morality is only reached through freedom. ' A State in which the citizens were compelled to obey even the best of laws might be peaceable and prosperous ; but it would be a community of well-cared-for slaves rather than a nation of free and independent men.' The State must refrain from any attempt to operate directly or indirectly on the morals and character of the people—such as sumptuary laws or regulations against evil living. ' It is the man of virtue who feels every restriction most keenly, and it is precisely the cultivation of character and morals which gains its fairest results from freedom.' No serious consequences need be apprehended from the abuse of liberty. ' The State is merely a means to which man, the true end, must never be sacrificed.' The demand, in a word, is not for better government, but for less government. It is a modest request to address to a ruler, and can be granted without waiting for a revolution.

After thus ruling out vast tracts of governmental responsibility the author returns to the proper task of the executive. ' The duty of the State is the development of the powers of each of its citizens in his perfect individuality ; and it must therefore pursue no other object except that which alone they cannot procure themselves—namely, security.' Even here its activity must be strictly limited. Minors and idiots must of course be looked after, coercive contracts must be modified, and crime must be punished ; but the prevention of criminal actions is wholly beyond its scope. With so few duties to fulfil, the State will need but little money. It should not possess property, and all revenue should be derived from direct taxation, which requires the minimum of officials. A constitution is necessary to secure the power of the government and the freedom of the governed ; but to this momentous issue only a single page is devoted on the ground that the discussion of particular forms would be trenching on politics. It is the actions of the State with which he is concerned, and which, in his judgment, are alone of importance. Some publicists suggest the strengthening of the power of the executive, ' a plan somewhat perilous for freedom ' ; others desire a balance of forces. Without more precisely indicating his own preferences, the author merely remarks that the required constitution should exert the least possible pressure on the character of the citizens. It would be impossible to reveal more clearly his sense of the minor significance of the problem which filled the whole mental horizon of most contemporary thinkers. In the closing chapter, entitled ' The Practical Application,' the author approaches closer to realities. ' I have not attempted to prescribe rules for actual life or even to express disapproval of all that contradicts them in existing conditions. Without making definite changes, it is possible to work on the mind and character ; and it is this at which a wise man will aim. Two axioms of reform must always be borne in mind. Firstly, that theoretical principles must not be translated into reality till the situation offers no further obstacles to the manifestation of their consequences. Secondly, every reform should be allowed to proceed as far as possible from the minds of men.' Statesmanship is above all the recognition of opportunity, and the State is rather a spectator than an actor. ' A statesman must allow all restrictions on freedom to remain untouched so long as men do not show by unmistakable signs that they regard them as bonds and that they are ripe for freedom in those respects ; but as soon as such impatience is manifested, they must at once be removed. Finally, he must ripen men for an enlarged freedom by every possible means. This duty is at once most important and the easiest of fulfilment ; for by nothing is this ripeness for freedom so much promoted as by freedom itself. Let us remove the fetters one by one, and we shall hasten progress at every step.'

This earnest and eloquent work, the most perfect of his writings and the most original German political treatise of its time, assumes, like most other pleas for individualism, that human nature is on the whole good, just as Hobbes and other champions of ' resolute government ' assume that it is on the whole bad. ' Man,' declares the author cheerfully, ' is naturally more disposed to beneficent than to selfish actions. I have felt myself animated throughout by a sense of the deepest respect for the inherent dignity of man and for liberty.' But an even bolder assumption underlies his structure of argument and paradox. ' All my principles,' he confesses, ' assume men to be in full possession of their ripened powers of understanding.' But in reality they presuppose much more than that. He believes the world to be full of pure and noble beings like himself, possessing sufficient virtue and wisdom to be a law unto themselves and to make their life a thing of beauty without the guidance or intervention of authority. His State is only possible in a community of Humboldts ; and since such a community has never existed, the normal State will never become superfluous. Less than twenty years later the Prussian Minister of Education was to learn and to teach the value of a reforming government. In the eyes of the youthful Humboldt, however, constitutions are only machinery for ministering to the needs and developing the capacities of the individual. While France was demanding liberty for a nation, he pleads for liberty for himself. To the French and German champions of autocracy and democracy alike he replies that as civilisation advances there is less need of government, and its form becomes a matter of secondary importance. Thus friends and enemies of the Revolution are calmly informed that they are fighting about shadows and forgetting the substance. Such ethereal individualism looks doctrinaire enough ; but beneath the polished marble of his argument we catch his detestation of the cramping paternalism of the age of enlightened and unenlightened despots. If the origin of the treatise is to be found in the ferment of ideas produced by the Revolution, its main object was to protest against the practice of the State whose service he had recently resigned. Though brought up amid the influences of the Aufklärung, he uncompromisingly rejects its political doctrine : ' All for the people, nothing by the people.' He abhors the schoolmaster theory of government. No wonder the Prussian censor boggled at a book which held up the bureaucratic system to scorn, encouraged free inquiry, and summoned the State to take its hands off religion. No French or German idealist was more profoundly convinced than the cool-headed Prussian nobleman of the capacity of man to rise to undreamed of heights when the fetters of tyranny and custom should be struck off his limbs. Despite his exaggerated individualism, which sometimes anticipates the paradoxes of Max Stirner and Nietzsche, he remains an impressive figure ; and his teaching that a State must be judged not by its power and riches, but by the spiritual quality of its citizens, is a warning to the twentieth, not less than to the eighteenth, century.

Humboldt lived at a time when the moral contact of the individual with the State was broken, when autocracy needed neither the help nor the love of the people. In Germany the sentiment of the State and of the nation was lacking. The best a man had, his individuality, he felt to be hampered rather than fostered by the State ; but he never imagined that the individual was sufficient unto himself. This aspect of his thought, on which he might well have laid more stress, is emphasised in a remarkable explanatory letter to Forster. ' I flatter myself that you would agree with me on the whole. I have sought to counter-work the governing mania ; indeed, I go so far as to confine the ruler to the securing of safety. The citizen is best off where he is united to his fellow citizens by the greatest number of links, but chained to the government by as few as possible. For the individual in isolation can develop himself as little as he whose freedom is shackled.'[1] It is an interesting anticipation of the theory of quasi-independent corporations associated with the name of Gierke, and of the guild socialism which seeks a middle path between the impotence of individualism and the devouring activity of the State.

' I desired to print my essay in Berlin,' wrote the author to Schiller in October 1792, ' but the censor stopped it.' He therefore asked the poet to approach a publisher.[2] ' As it deals with politics, in which the public now seem to take special interest, Göschen ought to accept it. Caroline writes that some of my ideas interested you and that you are now occupying yourself more with these subjects.

[1] Forster's *Briefwechsel*, ii. 824–30.
[2] *Briefwechsel zwischen Schiller u. Humboldt*, pp. 44–6.

You half promised me once to send me some of your ideas. How would it be if you added something to my essay, in the form of a preface or appendix, with or without your name ? It would be interesting if a man of your intellect, without special study of these topics and therefore from a new and original standpoint, were to deal with these problems.' Schiller accepted the easier part of the commission, and wrote to Göschen, pointing out both its interest and its innocence. ' The essay contains very fruitful political hints and is built up on a sound philosophical basis. It is conceived and written with freedom ; but as the author remains on neutral ground there is nothing to fear at the hands of the aristocrats. Works composed in such a spirit are a need of our age, and I should think good business.'[1] Göschen, however, declined the book for the present. ' Perhaps it may appear in a year or two. There is no hurry, and I should have time to rewrite some portions. The subject is free from any relation to the events of the moment.' A day or two later Schiller wrote that he had found a publisher ; but the author no longer desired immediate publication. When the complete work appeared in 1851, Germany had long outgrown its ideal ; but in other countries it aroused interest and admiration. Mill's delight was shared by other Philosophic Radicals. ' It is written in a very excellent spirit,' pronounced Grote, ' and deserves every mark of esteem for the frankness with which it puts forward free individual development as an end, and also for the low comparative estimate it gives of passive imitation and submission.'[2] Laboulaye adopted its ideas in his ' L'État et ses Limites,' and Challemel-Lacour declared it specially valuable for France, which had always busied herself rather with the form than with the functions of the State. In Italy, Minghetti cited its authority in advocating ' A Free Church in a Free State.'

Humboldt's book might satisfy his literary friends ; but it failed to influence or even to remove the objections of Dalberg, its only begetter, with whom he had discussed the work in detail. If he complained of the little essay on Constitutions, how much more must he disapprove the audacious challenge to the whole theory and practice of government in which he had been brought up and had himself played an honourable part ! His anonymous counterblast, ' The true limits of the activity of the State in relation to its members,' appeared in 1793. The object of the State, he begins, is to secure the happiness of the people who created it with this very object by the union of their wills. It must awake the powers of men, which slumber till they are stirred to life. The best constitution is that which so fully occupies man that he has no time

---

[1] Schiller's *Briefe*, iii. 227.   [2] *Life of Grote*, p. 237.

to injure his fellows. The State should also strengthen its power by the hopes and fears of religion. Without these bonds or stimuli —religion, education, and police—men would become like beasts, and would be dominated by hunger and other purely animal instincts. On the other hand, Dalberg will hear nothing of the sovereign State, bound by no human or divine law. Every State is subordinate to the great organisation of mankind, and it must pledge its members to nothing contrary to the duties of a citizen of the world. Its authority is also limited by the claims of all animate life. Animals must not be tortured, nor plants disfigured, nor the beauties and treasures of the earth destroyed. It must support art and science, manufactures and agriculture, foster education and stimulate the idle. While religion must be closely associated with the State, there must be no coercion of conscience. The government must also labour to improve the morals of its citizens. It must perform not only all the tasks imposed by the constitution, but whatever is of moral value to the community. If the people are fettered by ignorance and prejudices, it must educate them till they are ripe for large reforms. Here was the very ideal against which Humboldt had written his book, and no amount of friendly controversy, public or private, could bridge the gulf. Starting from diametrically opposed views of the wisdom and capacity of rulers, it was impossible to reconcile enlightened autocracy and philosophic anarchy.

The antagonists remained friends ; for their judgments on current events differed far less than their theories of the State, and both took a cool and detached view of the Revolution. The news of Varennes reached Erfurt on Humboldt's wedding-day as the bridal pair and a number of friends were contemplating the moon and stars from a balcony of the palace. ' What are the events of this little earth in comparison with the boundless heavens ? ' cried the host sententiously, raising his eyes. ' A King and Queen fleeing from their kingdom—what is that to the world above us ? Everything seems small and transitory beside the changeless firmament.'[1] The fall of Mainz was of greater interest to them, both on private and public grounds. ' What say you to the events on the Rhine ? ' wrote Humboldt to Schiller. ' The Coadjutor assures me that they have moved, but not overwhelmed him. I, as a spectator, hardly know how it will end. Several considerations, among them my interest in the Coadjutor and the reflection that the Mainzers seem to me totally incapable of taking even a share in a free constitution, make me desire the recovery of the place. On the other hand, I do not at all like the prospect of the French being beaten. A noble enthusiasm has now seized the whole nation. It is no longer

[1] Beaulieu-Marconnai, *Dalberg*, i. 202–3.

the inclinations and prejudices of a few individuals, and the national energy must therefore increase enormously. It is this energy that I find lacking in recent centuries. In themselves free constitutions do not seem to me so important or valuable, and a limited monarchy usually imposes fewer fetters on the development of the individual ; but they certainly stretch the powers to a very high point and raise the stature of the whole man. And yet, in spite of my attachment to the Revolution, I cannot forgive Forster for suddenly and openly joining the French and entering their service.'[1] He was now for a time genuinely interested in the Revolution. ' Caroline tells me,' he writes to Schiller in the same letter, ' that you would like a journey to Paris. If there is peace and you would take us, we would gladly come. I should much like to see it again, in order to judge how the nation has altered since 1789.' His wish was one day to be realised ; but at this moment Paris was no place for a German nobleman. ' What do you say to the death of the King ? ' he wrote to Wolf. ' You see, my prophecy of evil has come true. The hideous trial and execution are a stain which cannot be wiped out.'[2]

While the Revolution was still in full swing, Humboldt began the systematic study of antiquity and aesthetics which was to claim the major part of his attention for many years. He turned with relief from the confused horror of the moment to the tranquil beauty of the classical world. ' Hardly ever were all the shibboleths of politics so ridiculous as to-day,' he wrote to his friend and master Wolf, in May 1793. ' The quiet writer, above all one so purely theoretical as myself, cannot expect to be understood. Whether I ever return to them is a question I should hesitate to answer in the affirmative. The Greeks absorb me wholly, or let me say the ancients.'[3] His friendship with Gentz, however, kept alive his interest at any rate in political theory. ' Try to look through Burke's Reflections,' he wrote to Wolf from Jena on receiving the work from Gentz. ' The translation is masterly, I am sure, and in the essays there is deep thought and fine observation. In this place, where I have more intercourse and better access to books, I have determined to resume some earlier studies and work out some ideas I have long had in mind. So I am returning to philosophy, political science, and aesthetics. Needless to say, the Greeks will not be neglected.'[4] ' I must confess to you that philosophy and political theory have again stolen a good deal of time from philology,' he confessed to Wolf a few weeks later ; ' but I do some Greek every day.' Gentz, however, was not greatly impressed by his

[1] *Briefwechsel zwischen Schiller u. Humboldt*, pp. 48–50.
[2] *Briefwechsel mit Wolf, Ges. Werke*, v. 34, edition of 1841.
[3] *Ib.*, v. 46.   [4] *Ib.*, v. 103.

friend's studies. ' I must tell you a divine piece of news about Humboldt,' he wrote to Brinckmann. ' Just imagine, he does not even know Algernon Sidney by name ! What would he say if we did not know of Xenophon or Hesiod ? '[1] The fault was soon corrected, and the notes on some classics of English political philosophy, made in 1795–6, were found among his papers.[2] Sidney's ' Discourses on Government ' are dismissed as a work of no scientific importance, though their zeal and virile strength are amply recognised. Harrington's ' Oceana ' is pronounced to possess little objective value, neither its reasoning nor psychology being above the average. Locke's Essays are described as on the whole rather mediocre, their chief value lying in the steady conviction that States only exist by consent and that power is revocable. These brief notes show no particular perspicacity ; but they reveal the mild liberalism which he never recanted. He disapproved violent changes of opinion, above all when they were induced by personal considerations. ' His family has suffered greatly, and his own prospects are uncertain,' he wrote in February 1794, after a long visit to Dalberg at Erfurt. ' He feels it all very much, but meets it with resolution. What delights me most is that he shares none of the passions which are now raging, that he judges all parties without partisanship. The deep interest which he necessarily feels in everything never disturbs his tranquil observation.' The moderation and disinterestedness which he admired in his friend were practised by himself. He was never either a democrat or an anti-Jacobin. He objected to the attacks on Forster in the ' Xenien ' ; but he also found parts of Kant's treatise on Perpetual Peace too democratic for his taste. In his critical essay on ' Hermann and Dorothea,' in which he finds a glorification of individuality, he agrees with Goethe's teaching that character is the best defence against the storms of life.[3]

In 1797 Humboldt's desire to revisit Paris was gratified ; but the political temperature was very different from that of 1789. It was now in his power to meet whomsoever he wished ; but he sought out authors, artists, and scientists rather than politicians. He learned a good deal about current events from Schlabrendorf ; but he preferred to study the France of the Directory in the theatre and the ballet rather than in the Chamber. He enjoyed the collection of monuments in the Musée des petits Augustins, whence Michelet was later to derive inspiration ; but he examined the faces rather as an anthropologist than a historian. In travelling, he declared, he desired ' to learn to know men and nations ' ; but he was at this time still too little interested in public affairs to be as competent a critic of nations as of individuals. His letters to

[1] Gentz, *Briefe*, ii. 37. [2] *Ges. Schriften*, vii. 571–80. [3] *Schriften*, vol. ii.

Goethe, Schiller, and Körner deal with philology, art, and society.
' As you know,' he wrote to Goethe, ' I do not take any notice
of politics.' He was never really enthusiastic about the modern
world. ' Beauty,' he wrote later, ' lies in the past. I try like
others, and more than others, to work for the present and the
future ; but our time and all modern times are an age of iron.'
He found his ideal in antiquity, above all in the harmonious
personalities of Athens ; and his duties as Prussian Minister in
Rome for six years left him ample time for the patient study of the
classical world.

It is a proof of Humboldt's greatness that in middle life he was
to win fame in the dusty arena of statesmanship, not inferior to that
which he already possessed as a scholar and a thinker. After Jena
Prussia needed the help of all her sons, and the arch-individualist
threw himself joyfully into the work of educational reform. His
years of creative achievement and diplomatic activity naturally
rendered him less hostile to the State ; but they never converted
him to the orthodox Prussian tradition. When a constitution was
under discussion in 1819, the Minister of the Interior worked out
a detailed plan, which embodied the compromise between the
philosopher and the statesman. It is still the old Humboldt
preferring the free activity of the individual to mechanical
guarantees of liberty. He supports a constitution not because it
is demanded, or on the ground of some imaginary ' right,' but
because in giving the people a direct share in affairs, it will increase
their energy, which is the only bulwark against external danger
and the only source of internal greatness. With the indefinite
postponement of constitutional reform, he withdrew to the quiet
beauty of Tegel, and resumed the profound linguistic studies to
which he owes no small portion of his undying renown.

CHAPTER V

KLOPSTOCK AND HIS SCHOOL

I

No spectator of the French drama applauded the performance
more frantically than the Nestor of German literature.[1] Klopstock had spent his life in singing the praises of his country and its
language, its art and its theology, and had resisted the seduction
of Gallic influence more than any of his prominent contemporaries
except Lessing; but, though an enemy of cosmopolitanism, he had
always been a friend to liberty. He had passionately encouraged
the revolt of the American Colonies, and his sojourn in Zurich had
taught him to admire the constitution of the Swiss cantons. He
shared the reverence for Brutus common to good republicans in
the eighteenth century, and sealed with the head of the noblest
Roman of them all. He maintained that as soon as a people was
agreed in wishing to be a Republic, their desire ought to be realised.
His love of liberty extended in a modified degree to the animal
world, for he kept his canaries on a string instead of in a cage.
His writings had proclaimed his faith in no faltering accents. In
the ' Messias,' evil kings are haled before the Almighty and lectured
like naughty schoolboys. ' You have dishonoured the most sacred
dignity of humanity. The theatre was large and the prize was
great. Heaven watched you, but turned away its eyes when it
saw your actions, your murderous wars, your vile favourites
oppressing the people, while virtue was left without recompense.'
But though the culprits are sent to expiate their crimes in hell,
the poet has no quarrel with enlightened princes, like his friends
and patrons Frederick V of Denmark, or Karl Friedrich of Baden.
Such rulers, however, were exceptional, and the love of battle was
the besetting sin of crowned heads. All wars that are not waged

---

[1] See Muncker's admirable biography; and Chuquet, *Klopstock et la
Révolution Française*, in his *Études d'histoire*, vol. ii. The best edition of the
Odes is by Muncker and Pawel.

solely for the defence of liberty are condemned; and Frederick the Great is contrasted with Arminius, the stainless hero of his cycle of epic dramas. His vision of a free and peaceful age was expressed in the ode ' Prophecy,' written in 1773. ' Oh, Germany, thou wilt be free! A century, and it is done. Reason will triumph over the sword.'

The world was not to wait a century for the great adventure. ' I began to display civism at the end of 1788 in my Ode to the States-General,' wrote the poet later to Roland. ' I foresaw the liberty of the French, and I said so with vivid joy and almost with tears in my eyes.'

LES ÉTATS-GÉNÉRAUX

Lo! the wise council of the sons of France
    Assembles now : a thrill, as of the dawn,
Hath pierced my heart. Revive us, glorious sun—
    Arise, undreamed-of messenger of morn!

Blest are these hoary hairs, and blest the strength
    That still endures, though three score years have passed ;
That guided me so far along life's road
    That I beheld this glorious day at last!

Forgive me, sons of France—my brothers now :
    Once, I exhorted Germany indeed
To turn aside, nor heed your clarion call ;
    But now I bid them follow where you lead.

When Frederick brandished Hercules' great club,
    I fondly mused, the century had known
No greater deed than thus to face the kings
    Of Europe—aye, and Europe's queens—alone.

Not thus I deem it now, France crowns herself
    With such a civic crown as none has worn,
Bedewed with blood, yet fairer than the wreath
    Of laurel by Olympian victor worn.

When the States-General assembled, Klopstock broke into rapturous paeans of praise. The old man became young again, and his voice rang out louder and more confident than that of any other poet in Europe. For the next six years his lyre was exclusively in the service of politics. His first ode, ' Louis XVI,' sings the praises of the wise and gentle King who, untempted by the bloody trophies of war, summons representatives of the people to assist him in lightening the burdens of his children. The next, ' Know thyself,' and ' The Prince and his Concubine,' appeared in a French translation by Meister in 1790, but were not published in Germany till 1798.   The former utters a passionate challenge to his countrymen. ' France has freed herself by the noblest deed of the century.   Are you so dull and blind that you do not recognise it ?   Search the annals of mankind and find if you can anything to approach it.   They are our brothers, the Franks. And we ?   You are silent, you Germans.   Is it eternal patience or weariness ?   Is it the calm before the storm ?   Everything is astir with love and joy, and the heavens look down smiling.'   The latter grimly pictures the attempts of a mistress to dispel the gloom of her lord.

Mistress : Why art thou so grave ?
Prince : Fill my glass with the golden wine.
Mistress : But thou drinkest not.
Prince : Sing me thy song.
Mistress : I sang, but thou heardest not.
Prince : Strew roses.
Mistress : But thou seest them not. Hark ! thy charger is neighing to carry thee to thy warriors. But thou art ever graver. What dost thou see ?   A spirit from the dead ?
Prince : Not a spirit from the dead, but the terrible spirit of liberty. Where is the magic that can hurl it back into the darkness of the dungeon whence it came ?   Who will dare wrestle with the giant of a hundred arms and a hundred eyes ?

The first year of the Revolution merely served to increase the poet's enthusiasm, and to fill him with shame that the resounding blow for liberty had not been struck by German arms.   The ode, ' You, not We,' written in June 1790 and dedicated to La Rochefoucauld, gives spirited utterance to the thoughts of many of his eager countrymen.

Had I a hundred voices—they would be scarcely sufficient
For the just praises of France : feeble indeed were my hymn !
What can she not accomplish, whose prowess has cast into fetters
War, the most hateful of all monsters that ravage the earth ?

Ah ! my country ! Life brings many griefs ; yet wounds are made easy
By Time's all-healing hand, so that their pain is assuaged.
Nevertheless, one wound is mine which can never be lessened,
Which, if my life ebbed away, still would continue to bleed :
Thou, my country, wast not the first to scale Liberty's summits :
Not from thee was the light shed on the rest of the world.

I

The ode was sent with an Open Letter, written in Latin to avoid the danger of mistakes in French.[1] He had met the Duke in Copenhagen, and he now expressed his admiration of his speeches and of the Revolution itself—this *novus saeculorum ordo* which placed France above all other nations. Had he sons and money he would leave Germany with them and become a French citizen. He hopes that France will be able to divert from the great river of liberty a few trickles of water to fertilise German soil.

The poet was the chief figure at the celebration of the anniversary of the fall of the Bastille given in Sieveking's hospitable house in Hamburg.[2] 'Klopstock read two odes on liberty,' wrote the host, ' which he does not intend to publish. He is wise ; for they are strong meat, and there are still despots at large.' The Odes were published in Paris, and the news of the fête spread throughout Europe. He followed every point in the game with eager attention, and wore mourning on the death of Mirabeau. He welcomed the Constitution of 1791, and in a letter to La Rochefoucauld declared his undying fidelity to it. The Duke told Matthisson that if Klopstock visited Paris, he would be welcomed like Voltaire. A report that he and Stolberg had started for France moved Schubart to ecstasy. 'The greatest of Germans comes with silver locks, rejuvenates himself in the blessed spectacle of an emancipated people, and pours his oil on the altar of the Fatherland.' The rumour was false ; but the poet was lavish with counsel and exhortation to his friends beyond the Rhine.

When war was declared, he made no secret of his wish for a speedy French triumph, and sat down to compose a passionate ode on 'The War of Liberty.' 'Humanity,' he cries, ' has created States, which are the condition of life ; for savages are like plants and animals. And now France has pushed forward beyond the mere artist's model till she has grown into something like a masterpiece of Raphael or Michelangelo. And this is the moment that the rulers of the nations call for the blood of the people which has forsworn wars of conquest, and desire to hurl it down from the giddy summits of liberty. Let them pause before they flesh their sword, for in their own lands the ashes are glowing. Ask not the courtier nor the aristocrat, but the common soldier, and you will learn what they see in the ashes. You despise them ; but war is a risky game, and mortals know not what God has in store for them.' The poet sent his ode to the Duke of Brunswick with an audacious letter urging, him to choose between true and false honour

---

[1] Lappenberg, *Briefe von und an Klopstock*, pp. 331–4.
[2] H. Sieveking, *G. H. Sieveking*, pp. 48–53.

and to withdraw from the command ; but his only answer was the Brunswick Manifesto.

In letters to his friends in Paris, Klopstock more than once expressed his desire to become a French citizen ; and his wishes were fulfilled on August 26, when he and seventeen other champions of liberty were accorded the highest distinction that France could bestow. The decree was signed by Roland as Minister of the Interior, to whom the poet addressed an expression of his gratitude. ' It is impossible to deserve the honour. The only thing which renders me in any sense worthy of it is my civism, which dates from before this unique and immortal rising.' He seized the occasion to advise the Republic to seek alliance with Denmark, whose Regent had freed the press, the serfs, and the negroes, and had declined to join the Coalition. Roland handed the letter to Brissot, by whom it was published. The new citizen watched the triumphs of French arms at Valmy with satisfaction and without surprise. ' He prophesies a general rising for liberty,' wrote Frau Reimarus to Hennings, ' if the princes are mad enough to venture on a second campaign. He has said much that is very strong and very fine ; but he dares not print it.' [1] The first shadows, however, were already falling. He demanded the punishment of the *Septembriseurs* not only because they deserved punishment, but in order to retain the sympathies of foreign friends of the Revolution. La Rochefoucauld was among the victims, and the fears evoked by the emergence of fierce and ruthless men found utterance in ' The Jacobins.' Free France, he declares, destroyed the corporations ; but a new corporation, the Jacobin Club, arose, its head in Paris and its arms embracing every part of France. ' If you do not drive this monstrous serpent back into his den and close up the entrance with rocks, it will trample liberty beneath its feet.' A further ode mournfully salutes the Manes of La Rochefoucauld.

Klopstock's zeal for the Revolution, which had been damped by the September massacres, was turned into loathing by the execution of the King. Stolberg reported that his friend manifested ' the most noble indignation ' ; and he denounced it in a Hamburg paper as a judicial murder. ' I hope you will now cease to attach any value to your French citizenship,' wrote Lavater.[2] ' O noble, great, influential man, speak noble, great, influential words to the representatives of a country that once thirsted for liberty, but is now drunk with anarchy.' He rejected the advice to return his diploma, alleging that the nation as a whole was

---

[1] *Sieveking's Leben*, p. 156.
[2] Lappenberg, *Briefe von und an Klopstock*, pp. 347–53.

guiltless of the hideous crime ; but he poured forth a flood of poetical recantation. ' My Mistake ' unburdens his sorrow.

> Now all my dreams of happiness depart,
> And vanished is the golden light of dawn ;
> And grief, the grief of love repulsed with scorn,
> Fills my aching heart.

Not only had France grown ferocious, but she had thrown to the winds her undertaking to renounce aggression. While she was resisting the invader, the poet's sympathies were with her ; but now she was carrying fire and sword far beyond her frontiers. This fresh disappointment found impassioned utterance in ' The War of Conquest.'

> Like as the lover is glad, when his beloved escapeth,
> Safe from the perilous wave, safely is brought to the shore,
> So I rejoiced when a great and powerful nation determined
> Never again to fight battles for conquest alone.

> Now, the monster, the horror of horrors, was lying in fetters !
> Verily, now was man exalted far over himself !
> But see to-day the same beings who tamed the horrible creature
> Breaking their glorious law, struggling for conquest alone.

Like most other German friends of the Revolution, he was deeply moved by the tragic fate of Charlotte Corday. He placed her portrait in his room and laid a poetical wreath on her bier.

THE TWO GRAVES

> Whose grave do I behold ?
> ' The grave of Rochefoucauld.'
> And this light-scattered mould ?
> ' Corday is laid beneath.'

> I will pluck flowers to strew
> On you with tender hand :
> You perished for your land !
> Nay, pluck them not.'

> Let weeping willows wave
> O'er your untimely grave,
> Who perished for your land !
> ' Nay, plant them not.

But, soon as thou canst weep,
  (Still from thine eyes, we know,
  Good friend, warm tears can flow)
Come back to where we sleep.

Return to us again,
  And let thy tears, thy tears of blood be shed
  On us, unhappy dead.
We perished for our land, but all in vain.

His hatred of the now dominant Jacobins found new expression in ' The Apparition,' which old Gleim joyfully pronounced to have restored Klopstock's honour. ' The Transformation ' relates how Liberty gave birth to a beautiful world, and how two Furies, Ambition and Rapacity, metamorphosed it. ' The Epochs ' declares that France should be called a State of executioners and slaves. In ' Hermann from Walhalla ' he sorrowfully accepts the war. ' Let it be war, then, since it must. But let it only be for defence. Let not the sword be reddened in the homeland of the Franks. Seek no laurels there.'

The fall of Robespierre was joyfully celebrated, and in the following autumn he wrote a letter to the President of the Convention which, however, he did not send. ' I have done my duty as a French citizen and told the truth about abominable deeds.' He then asks whether it is not treason in the representatives to forget the rights of man, and inquires how the defeat of the Jacobins at the next election can be secured. ' Nantes ' describes the *noyades* in the Loire, and in 1795 ' Retaliation ' celebrated Carrier's end with ferocious glee. Thus ended the cycle of Revolution odes in which the poet poured forth his joy and his sorrow. As literature they are too obscure and allusive to take high rank, and no one would dream of comparing them with the political verse of Milton or Dryden, Wordsworth or Victor Hugo. Matthisson considered the later odes equal to those of his prime ; but Wilhelm von Humboldt justly described ' Retaliation ' as of revolting crudity and terrible to the point of disgust. Their interest, indeed, lies rather on the political than on the literary plane, and their merit consists more in their courage than in their craftsmanship. ' In such an epoch of servility,' cried Friedrich Schlegel in admiration, ' to dare such odes was sublime.'

In spite of his great disappointment, Klopstock retained his faith in liberty, progress, and justice. In ' The Epochs,' he declared that he had no wish to become a misanthrope, and that he parted company with his French brethren in sorrow, not anger.

In certain moods he longs to forget politics, and in ' My Valley '
he pines for the waters of Lethe. But these were only passing
moods, and the poet could not long avert his eyes from the
absorbing spectacle. In 1797 he lamented to Herder his mistaken
judgment of the French, who ' have become demons ' ; to which
Herder discreetly replied that they had always been and would
always remain a potent leaven. ' The cock's crow offends the
ears ; but it awakens the sleeper.' ' The Directory represents
enslavement and robbery,' he wrote in 1799 to his old friend Cramer
in Paris.[1] ' As to the emergence of the principle of representation
at the end of the century, there is little difference between us,
except that I am a believer in things and you in words.' He was
never carried away by Bonaparte's victories, pronounced his head
and heart to be ' inflamed by the Jacobin pest,' and warned the
Rhine Republicans against France. In 1800 ' Conquerors and
Conquered ' denounced the invasion of Switzerland. France is
now ' the new Python,' springing on the peoples in order to drink
their blood. ' Happy England, saved by the sea and by her
courage ! ' He rejoiced at the news of Aboukir and welcomed
Nelson at Hamburg ; but when he learned of the fate of Caracciolo,
he turned against him in anger. In extreme old age, he wrote
some poetico-historical ' Memorials of the Revolution.' The
sketches were seen by Archenholtz, who described them as metrical
pictures of some of the great crises, equally remarkable for their
form and substance. But when French victories led to the Treaty
of Lunéville, the poet burned his manuscript in patriotic grief,
though it was ready for insertion in the complete edition of his
works. One of the first incidents of the peace was his nomination
as Foreign Associate of the Institut, a distinction which gave him
keen pleasure. He died with a kindly feeling for the great nation
whose bid for liberty had caused him the keenest joy of his life and
whose apostasy had turned his rejoicing into sorrow.

II

Among the poets of the Fatherland, in the years immediately
preceding the Revolution, a distinct place is held by the group
known as the Göttingen Bund, a body of old college friends living
for the most part in Holstein and united in loyal admiration of
Klopstock. Though Bürger alone possessed real poetic inspiration
they were all men of ability, and they all shared the eager interest
which the Revolution aroused in literary circles ; but the progress
of events accentuated the latent antagonism of temperament

[1] Lappenberg, *Von und an Klopstock*, pp. 390-1.

and opinion, and drove the leading members of the group into unconcealed hostility.

Voss, the eldest of the circle, was a man of critical and independent mind, on whom tradition weighed lightly.[1] As a student at Göttingen, he had been an enthusiast for liberty, and his residence in Eutin, near Hamburg, encouraged a liberal and cosmopolitan outlook. His passion for Greek antiquity, in which ' the Majesty of the People ' appeared to him to be the driving force, increased his impatience at the social inequalities and political lethargy of his country. He detested the nobility, in many cases rich and idle, and scorned hereditary privilege. Though a loyal servant of his prince, himself a friend of the Aufklärung, he was convinced that only a political earthquake could revive and regenerate Germany. Such a man naturally hailed the Revolution with delight, and bitterly complained when his friends passed with indecent haste into the hostile camp. Though sharing the heart-felt regret of all humane men at its excesses, he kept his eyes steadily fixed on the larger issues of the Revolution, and bluntly described the struggle as one between those who wished to advance and those who wished to retreat. He was one of the large number of Intellectuals who opposed an armed crusade against the Revolution, and his sympathies were with the foe. As a youth he had disliked the French ; but he now expressed his pity for the slavish Germans. The old political and social system, he considered, must be destroyed, if necessary by an enemy's sword, before a new Germany could arise. He failed to see the elements of value in existing institutions and the danger of a clean sweep. He spoke of ' Our Franks,' and openly rejoiced at their victories. After a visit to Klopstock, he said to him at parting, ' Great things have happened, but greater things are coming—the struggles of patricians and plebeians throughout Europe. After much misery, reason will triumph over the sword ; but we shall not live to see it.'

In the year which witnessed the outbreak of war Voss began to write a series of paeans to the new hope of the world.[2] The verse is hardly worthy of the translator of Homer ; but the message is clear enough. The ' Song of the New Franks,' to be chanted to the music of the Marseillaise, gives vigorous expression to his convictions at the opening of the conflict.

> To thee our joyful songs arise,
> To greet thee, glorious liberty,
> Whose hand confers all precious gifts
> And breaks the yoke of tyranny.

[1] See the full and excellent biography by Herbst.
[2] The political poems are in vols. iii. and iv. of the *Gedichte*.

O long-desired by thine elect,
From heav'n dost thou descend to earth
O tyrants, wherefore would your wrath
Restrain the gladness of new birth ?
  Arm, arm ye in the war
  For liberty and law !
Ye citizens, come forth : tremble, O hireling crew :
  Flee hence, death waits for you !

CHORUS.

We come, we come ! Tremble, O hireling crew :
  Flee hence, death waits for you !

None but the conqueror's pampered sons
Are honoured in your eyes : you shower
Your dignities on them, and though
They labour not, theirs is the power
Merit and talent are abused
By their vain show and pageantry :
The very name of citizen
Arouses scorn and obloquy.

E'en as a swarm of useless drones
Will snatch the spoils from labouring bees,
So is the welfare of the land
Abused by courtiers such as these.
The fruits of old iniquities,
Debt and taxation, now we reap,
Whilst toll and tithe accumulate,
And widows with the orphans weep.

The weight of countless armies—worse
Than foreign yoke—on them is laid ;
Born but to serve their conquerors,
They must abandon toil and trade.
They must endure wars waged by kings,
The prey of cunning and caprice,
And to an alien race, alas !
Their blood is sold by avarice.

Be but our father, conqueror,
And we like children will obey :
Hear but the counsels of the wise
Whom we have sent to thee to-day !
Let honour be ascribed alone
To virtue, mind, and industry !
But lo ! thou lov'st the proud in heart,
And heedest not thy people's cry.

A year later the gospel of hope was reiterated in ' The Song of the Germans.'

> Deep was the gloom of earth : our country
> Slumbered beneath the wings of night ;
> Then God arose, and, looking on us,
> Sent forth His word : ' Let there be Light ! '
> Then man, an inarticulate savage,
> Saw the dark shadows flee away,
> Gazed round, beheld the light, and welcomed
> The glory of the coming day.

CHORUS.

> All of us ! all of us !
> We lift up heart and hand :
> Let man and babe and woman cry :
> ' We greet thee, Liberty ! Hail, Fatherland ! '

> Reason, once overruled by tyrants,
> Grows ever bolder, and proclaims
> The rights of man, the civic union,
> Whereat all legislation aims.
> Wisdom's decrees, on magic pinions,
> Circle in thousands through the land,
> Win every heart, and soon establish
> Union of soul on every hand.

> Judges and priests no longer govern
> By formulas unknown before :
> The law of nations in its balance
> Weighs justice both for rich and poor.
> Custom no more replaces worship,
> Freely the truth pursues its way,
> And love unites e'en mosques and temples,
> Not only churches, 'neath its sway.

> Virtue alone, not birth, gives merit :
> None but the best gain dignities :
> Some rule in study and in council,
> Others in arts and industries.
> Some guard the people from oppression
> And from the foe's all-conquering lust,
> And hold their wealth, their lives, their honour,
> For fatherland in faithful trust.

> Fear not, O guardians of the nation !
> Man hath aspired to better things :
> Let but religion free from folly,
> Cleanse from abuse the thrones of kings.

> Vainly you strive to forge new fetters :
> God summons us to liberty,
> And, to aspiring souls, earth's triumphs
> Seem but a hollow mockery !

Neither the Terror nor the progress of French arms availed to overthrow the sturdy optimism of the poet, who in ' The Renewal of Humanity,' written in 1794, perhaps the finest of his odes, once more testified to his faith in the race.

> Dead and rigid the soul of mankind may seem
> Through the forces of hate and the tyrant's feud :
> Nevertheless, the conquering spirit of man
>> Rises to life renewed.

> True, it slept through the ages—a deadly sleep,
> Heavily chained, since liberty heavenward fled,
> Away from tyrants, away from idolatrous priests
>> By whom she was cursed as dead.

> Luther came : the slumbering spirit stirred,
> Gazed around, then sank into slumber again,
> Whilst from the ruins of Attic wisdom it heard
>> A faint and foreboding strain.

> Soon, as embers glow in the ash, as sparks,
> Fanned by the wind, burst forth into flames of fire,
> Giving out light and warmth, so the spirit of man
>> Rose from its sleep to aspire.

> And lo ! the fetters of ages were cast away,
> The altars of cursing fell, and the tyrant's towers,
> And beauty and strength and the will of the people sprang
>> To life, like the fairest flowers.

Voss opposed the war to the end, and continued to argue that the business of his countrymen was to set their own house in order, not to interfere with their neighbours.

> Sore misgivings filled our neighbour :
>> Times were bad he said :
> But his jolting brought the housetop
>> Down upon his head.
> Let us give him fellow feeling,
> Let us look to our own ceiling,
>> Floor and roof and wall,
>> Lest they crack and fall.

When the roof and rafters totter,
  Crushed by threatening blow,
Build the housetop more securely,
  Strengthen it below.
If some portions need repairs,
  Mend them—and discard your cares.
    He who seeks to mend
    Is no rascal, friend !

There was nothing of the revolutionary doctrinaire in this prosaic nature. His modest demands were for decent government, for the removal of the crying abuses of the feudal system, for impartial justice, and equality before the law. Had there been more men like him, North Germany would not have waited till 1806 to apply the lessons of the French Revolution.

III

In early life the brothers Stolberg shared the liberalism, but not the scepticism, of their friend and neighbour, Voss.[1] In 1775 Friedrich, in a ' Song of Liberty of the Twentieth Century,' foretold the French Revolution ;[2] and there was no more enthusiastic student of ' the divine Plutarch,' whose ' Lives,' he declared, ought to be read in every school. ' How happy will be the growing child when the sentiment of liberty colours his cheeks and when he learns to envy the Spartans at Thermopylae ! ' In a later ' Ode to Liberty,' he hails Tell, Hermann, Klopstock, Brutus, Timoleon, ' names graven on the heart of free men in letters of flame.'[3] On visiting Switzerland he celebrated ' the holy land of liberty.' Such a man, although a noble, naturally greeted the opening drama of 1789 with rapture. ' The glorious dawn of freedom in France gives me real joy,' he wrote to Voss on the fall of the Bastille.[4] ' The ground that has been won will be held ; for the soldier will never fire on the citizen. The capital may be forced to surrender for a few days ; but who could reduce France ? The Court may perhaps arrest the growth of the seeds of liberty, but it cannot obliterate them.' He had foreseen that despotism would fall, but not that the great plan of liberty would be so promptly and wisely carried out. The torrent of liberty would break the dykes of prejudice and overflow Europe. ' I never felt myself more cosmopolitan

---

[1] See Janssen, *Stolberg* ; and Chuquet, *Stolberg et la Révolution Française*, in his *Études d'histoire*, vol. vii.
[2] *Gedichte*, i. 65–74.   [3] *Ib.*, ii. 126–7.
[4] Stolberg's *Briefe an Voss*, p. 225.

than now,' he cried in delight.   At supper, in Berlin, he saluted
the dawn of a new age, and his companion, Nesselrode, forgot his
gout.

Stolberg's liberalism had no intellectual roots and after the
holocaust of privileges on August 4 the critical Voss detected in
him 'signs of nobility.'   He now became aware of the complexity
of the task.   'It is not a question of cutting one Gordian knot :
there are thousands of them to be patiently unravelled, if the
whole tissue is not to be torn to pieces.   I am watching, not without anguish, yet on the whole with confidence, that despotism is
for ever destroyed.'   All around he heard expressions of hope and
satisfaction.   'There is no land,' he wrote to Jacobi from Berlin,
in September, 'in which so many people applaud the French as
in our cosmopolitan Germany.   Even here the number of sympathisers is not so small as I should have expected, and the *servum
pecus* is beginning to venture on timid essays in approval.   But
it is our privilege to rejoice with our whole heart.   What we have
whispered and thought and felt now thunders forth as the utterance of the people, which is the voice of God, from the Pyrenees to
the Rhine, from the Channel to the Mediterranean.   It is no longer
the voice of one crying in the wilderness, but the accent of power
and consolation accompanied by signs and wonders.   I fear that many
Gallicisms, like those we have already experienced, will continue
to manifest themselves.   I give the French credit for courage and
zeal enough to raise themselves erect ; but they will not possess a
centre of gravity till liberty has made them wholly men.'[1]   During
the autumn and winter his fears gained ground.   'It is terrible
to see what confused ideas of liberty people have,' he wrote in
November.   In January 1790 he confessed his apprehensions to
his brother Christian, whose Gallophilism was somewhat more
robust.   'One thought mars my happiness—Are the people good
enough to be free ?   I fear we must look forward to the overthrow
of all constitutions if we cannot be sure of the great foundation—
religion.   Building a free constitution on frivolity and impiety is
like planting a Corinthian column on shifting sand.'   In March
he expressed surprise at the passionate zeal of his friend and
master, Klopstock.   He himself now saw in the Revolution only
'the spirit of the century,' and found little progress to record.
Perhaps no nation, he declared, was so unripe for liberty as the
French.   The people allowed their fetters to be struck off, but
were incapable of noble resolution and sacrifice.   Necker alone
rose above the throng of mediocrities, and France was a land of
convention and lies.

[1] *Aus Jacobi's Nachlass*, i. 113–14.

When Stolberg heard of the abolition of titles and armorial bearings, he remarked that he would gladly sacrifice his coat of arms, but that the decree was premature. Why offend the *noblesse* in such a crisis ? Ought a bourgeois majority to rob so many good folk of their ancient rights ? Could a monarchy exist without a nobility ? Two Houses would be better than one. At the end of 1790 he wrote to Voss in the same critical vein.[1] ' Things are going badly in France. I see nothing but little passions and little men.' The verdict becomes ever more severe. ' I was as zealous for the Revolution as a man could be. But the Assembly is a despot, for it claims both legislative and executive power, and the French are always the same. Paris, that nest of frivolities, that mother of immorality, may become a storm-centre, but not the shrine of sacred liberty.' There could be no liberty, he repeats, without morality and religion, and France has deluged all Europe with the poison of her immorality and irreligion. ' Is it not the riskiest of enterprises to rest on some political and metaphysical axioms, as on the point of a needle, the constitution of an extremely corrupt people ? A tyranny will come of which recent times have seen no example. An evil community cannot dispense with a tyrant.'

At the end of 1791 the news of the outbreak of war reached the poet in Italy ; and the intervention of the Powers appeared to him ' much more imprudent than unjust.' He described Brunswick's Manifesto as insensate ; but his contempt for the French increased day by day. On a visit to Jacobi, he found that the host, Princess Gallitzin, and other members of the circle, shared his hostility. On hearing of the September massacres, he called upon God to ' strike the French with His sceptre and break them in pieces like a potter's vessel.' He was angry that any German could still entertain sympathy with the Revolution. ' Can one confound the sanguinary rage of these monsters with the sentiment of liberty ? ' He denounces the nation of atheists, and dreaded that the plague of anarchy would invade Germany. The people had failed, and the best hope lay in the nobility. ' It seems clear that the lofty tower of the French political system will soon topple over,' he wrote to Jacobi. ' Like Babel it was built to defy heaven, and, like Babel, chaos has streamed forth from it over the whole earth.'[2] The death of the King was the last straw. ' The sins of the Caesars,' he cries fiercely, ' were only peccadillos beside the crimes of the French. Those who have hitherto excused their offences as the natural consequences of political effervescence now despair and

---

[1] Stolberg, *Briefe an Voss*, p. 240.
[2] Jacobi, *Briefwechsel*, ii. 119–20.

detest them.'[1] ' It has had an excellent effect on many people,'
he wrote to Jacobi. ' Like you, I see in it merely the fruit of four
years of folly and atheism. My brother has at last regained his
sight.'[2] The mere talk of peace with the regicides deprived him
of self-control. One day, when he was paying Voss a visit, another
visitor remarked : ' It looks as if we were to have peace.' At the
mention of peace with ' the cannibals,' Stolberg left the house
without a word. The friendship which had long shown signs of
wear and tear was at an end.[3]

The poet now vied with Klopstock in the violence of his
denunciations. ' I recognise the judgment of God,' he wrote to
Jacobi at the end of 1793, ' first in the blind stumbling towards
moral and political dissolution, secondly in the supernatural
indifference with which most men watch the horrors approach
with giant steps and the coolness with which they survey France's
abominations, which surpass everything in history.'[4] His ode,
' The Huns of the West,' was written in 1793, in his master's
pompous style, and breathed the same unmeasured fury.[5] ' By the
ashes of my mother, I will not suffer it ! Thou darest not name
the scum of mankind—Franks. Call those hordes rather the Huns
of the West—and even that is too good for them. Europe has
watched them put the poison to their lips, and, shameful to say,
some Germans, too, have longed to drink. Once swallowed, the
deadly draught makes black look white ; virtue and piety become
empty sounds, oaths a fleck of foam, obscenity wit, and folly
wisdom. Go to the desecrated temple, fling thyself in the dust
before the naked whore whom thou callest Reason, and pray her
to help thee in the hour of death.' An epigram of 1794 bitterly
complained that, after being promised the return of the Golden
Age by the sages of Gaul, their Kingdom of Saturn was nothing but
a Saturnalia. He deplored the disunion and lack of initiative
among his countrymen in face of ' this hydra.' The only way to
stop ' the infernal torrent ' was a *levée en masse*. ' What folly it
is of the Germans to let a raging hyena devour their children one
by one ! ' was his comment on the Peace of Basle. Like many other
counter-revolutionaries, he detected the hand of the Illuminati
in every disaster. ' He dreams of them,' wrote his old friend
Hennings disdainfully, ' and plasters with this label every one who
thinks differently from himself.' When Halem published an elegy
on the death of Knigge, the poet cried fiercely, ' There is plague in
the tomb and poison in the flowers.' His ode, ' Cassandra,' written
in 1795, denounced the secret society, suppressed but not abolished,

---

[1] Janssen, *Stolberg*, i. 312.   [2] Jacobi, *Briefwechsel*, ii. 128–9.
[3] Herbst, *Voss*, ii. 218.   [4] Jacobi, *Briefwechsel*, ii. 136.   [5] *Gedichte*, iii. 96.

with which the Convention had boasted its connection.[1] This passionate utterance aroused indignation among his old friends, and the poet defended himself in a letter to Frau Voss.[2] ' So long as I have breath in my body, I will attack the rascality of the secret fraternity which aims at anarchy and irreligion, and which is banded together for murder and poison. All our journals are in their hands. It is all proved by converted members of the sect. You and Voss must not think I am a Don Quixote tilting against windmills.' The ode, ' Expectation of Peace,' written in 1799, demanded death or victory, not peace with assassins, tigers, serpents, and cannibals.

The poet was now almost unhinged ; and he only regained his tranquillity when he was received into the Roman Church in the chapel of Princess Gallitzin, whose efforts had been seconded by the Marquise de Montagu, the sister of Madame Lafayette, whom Stolberg called his angel. Her story of the guillotining of her relatives, added to the virtues and piety of other Émigrés, revealed the heroic side of Catholicism, and brought him into the communion in which he recognised the most august embodiment of religion and the arch-enemy of the Revolution. His political and religious conversion provoked widespread contempt and anger, and was denounced with extraordinary bitterness by Voss. Goethe judged the event with his usual mildness, though the poet had figured among the victims of the Xenien.

> Once they wandered as Centaurs through woods and over the
>   mountains ;
> But the uncivilised race swiftly reversed its ideas.

The thrust was fully deserved ; for the liberalism of the brothers had been a house of cards, which toppled over almost at the first blast of the Revolution.

IV

Among the friends of Voss no face was more welcome than that of Boie, his neighbour and brother-in-law.[3] Though a member of the Göttingen Bund, his poetical vein was not very deep, and his attraction lay rather in his serene and affectionate temperament than in intellectual strength or originality. Like the rest of the Circle, he greeted the Revolution with satisfaction, recognising in

---

[1] *Gedichte*, iii. 97–101.
[2] Stolberg, *Briefe an Voss*, 289–90.
[3] See Weinhold, *H. C. Boie*.

it the inevitable result of concrete historical facts. 'The business in France,' he wrote to Voss, ' is the greatest thing we have seen, and it will have mighty consequences. Who would have expected to find in the French hotheads the gravity with which they are going to work ? That some outbreaks of mob passion occur is not surprising.' He shared the prevailing dislike of the nobility and their privileges. ' In studying the life of Richelieu one sees to what lengths the higher French nobility have gone, how the honour, the happiness—even the life of humble folk—meant nothing to them, and how the spirit of revenge must necessarily awake in these people.' He read Halem's narrative of his visit with pleasure, and congratulated the author. ' I have never been in France, and I do not read the " Moniteur " ; but I have long regarded events as you represent them.' He was, however, never carried away by emotion, and he was influenced by Burke's Reflections, which, he declared, admitted of no complete answer, though he did not agree with every page.

In the winter of 1791 Boie explained his new views with the moderation that distinguished him. ' I fear and hate the expansion of the French principles of liberty and equality, which are not calculated to secure the happiness of a State ; but the jealous ferreting out of opinions, and the punishment of every thoughtless utterance, is not the way to stop it. Indeed, nothing has made them more dangerous than the interference of German princes.' The Landgrave of Hesse-Cassel, for instance, opened the letters of his officials, and thus discovered the French sympathies of his librarian, whom he promptly dismissed. ' How little our princes know how to act !' he added regretfully. Shocked as he was by the death of Louis XVI, he refused to follow Stolberg into the camp of reaction. ' The only way I know of preventing revolutions,' he wrote, ' is to begin reforms oneself.' He had no superstitious reverence either for kings or crowds. ' Considering the slender capacity of the multitude, it is perhaps better that, as we poor creatures have to be governed, it should be done by one rather than by many.' Like Gentz and other disillusioned liberals, he continued to demand the freedom of the press ; but the cautious official always kept his opinions to himself, and he was never molested. He regretted the intervention in politics of friends like Claudius on one side and Cramer on the other. He was free from the craving to play a part on the political stage or even to influence the opinion of his fellows. Like so many of the cultured bourgeoisie, he was content to obey the law and to trust to the steady advance of the Aufklärung to secure the reforms which his country needed.

V

Matthias Claudius, the 'Wandsbeck Messenger,' possessed a non-political and rigidly conventional mind.[1] His early poems contained the usual academic commonplaces about flatterers and tyranny, and his couplet—

> The King should be the better man ;
> Else let the best be ruler,

was declaimed with animated gesture by hot-headed youths at the Universities. But he was perfectly satisfied with autocracy if the Prince recognised his duty to God and man. Till 1789 he gave little thought to politics, and cared only for the moral and spiritual development of mankind. Changes, he believed, should come from within. If they were imposed from without, it was like moving the hands of a clock in order to put the works right. Alone of the Klopstock Circle, he objected to the principle as well as to the excesses of the Revolution. In liberty and equality he saw the seeds of chaos ; in the abstract rights of man, a challenge to a divinely appointed order. His whole being revolted against godless cosmopolitanism, and custom meant more to him than law. He was unaware that absolutism was doomed and that he was watching the birthpangs of a new world. To adopt the image of Tom Paine, he pitied the plumage and forgot the dying bird.

Claudius sought the society of the Émigrés who found their way to Hamburg, and rejoiced at the conversion of the brothers Stolberg to 'a sound view of events in France.' His poem, 'Lamentation,' written in 1793, gives free rein to his boiling indignation. 'They thought themselves lords of all, they trampled order and custom underfoot, they arrogantly trod new paths remote from wisdom, they acted in the dark without a guiding-star, they wrought evil far and near. They murdered their King, they murder each other, they delight in murder, they dance round the scaffold. They wished to live without God in their wild sport. The seed of light and love which God planted in our breast, and which bears His stamp, is dead in them. They worship folly, and honour the devil.' A pamphlet of 1794, 'The New Policy,' is couched in milder terms, merely complaining that the change has been too precipitate. 'The cure must not be worse than the disease, and prejudice and affection for the old order are nobler than for the new.' His picture of an ideal ruler shows that his mind is still

---

[1] See Herbst, *Matthias Claudius*, pp. 405-56.

K

anchored in the doctrine of enlightened despotism. Even the liberty of the press excited his condemnation, and his fable, 'Brummelbär,' attacked the licence allowed in Denmark. In the animal world, he relates, the demand arose for perfect freedom of writing and speech. The King gave way, and the office of censor, held by the bear, was abolished. At once the nobler animals fell silent, while the vermin and the beasts of prey became vocal. Before long the bear was let loose again, to the general satisfaction. This naïve performance, like Stolberg's conversion, was too much for Voss, who issued a vigorous reply to its pusillanimous pleading. A further utterance in the same vein, 'Urian's News of the New Enlightenment,' attacked the talk of liberty and equality in mediocre verse ; and rejoinders by Reichardt, Hennings, and other liberals, left him unmoved. In no instance do we perceive more clearly the lack of political education and training, from which Germany was suffering, than in Claudius, who steered his course through the storms of the Revolution by the Bible and the Ten Commandments, blissfully unconscious that the old world, in which he had found fame and happiness, was crumbling beneath his feet.

VI

Among the disciples of Klopstock, Bürger holds a place apart ; for as a poet he towers above the rest of the Göttingen brotherhood, and as a man he falls far below them.[1]   The author of ' Lenore ' has his niche in the temple of fame ; but his loose life and matrimonial adventures wrecked his career and cut him off from many of the friends of his youth. In his radical views, his poetic genius, and his lack of self-control, he recalls the greater figure of Burns. Unlike most children of the ' Sturm und Drang ' period, he never outgrew it. Joining the Freemasons in early life, he found in their mysteries and vague humanitarianism the echo of his own romantic temperament. In fierce lines he describes the damage to crops by game preserved for the pleasure of the Prince, who is denounced as a robber and a tyrant. Such a man, filled with passionate pity for the weak and the disinherited, naturally embraced the Revolution with open arms ; and his conservative friends expected an outbreak. ' For heaven's sake,' wrote Gleim, ' do not join Klopstock's orchestra, and try to stop our fiery Bouterwek from doing so.'[2]   His views are contained in an address of 1790, entitled ' Encouragement to Liberty,' one

[1] See Bonet-Maury, *Bürger* ; and Würzbach, *Bürger*.
[2] *Briefe von und an Bürger*, iii. 293.

of his three Masonic discourses which survive. 'Do we not hear the beating of noble and powerful wings? It is the spirit of Humanity, bursting the bonds in which prejudice and superstition have imprisoned it. Shall we sit idly watching while it illumines the long-obscured Rights of Man with its celestial torch, so that we can distinctly read the words of the Tables of the Law? Shall not we, too, be kindled by the sacred flame which has stirred in Great Britain thousands of noble hearts to works for the emancipation of their black brothers of America? And the force which in Gaul has in the twinkling of an eye overturned the throne, raised aloft for centuries by despostism with its million slaves, this force which has been placed in our hearts by the Great Author of Nature—shall it for ever sleep the sleep of death? Where is there a heart which does not beat louder in presence of these events?'

In spite of his enthusiasm for France, Bürger wisely recommended his countrymen to adopt 'the Republic of England,' or the United States, as a model; and his knowledge of English institutions was revealed in a study of 'the English Republic.' But he ardently supported the right of the French people to work out their own salvation, and denounced the project of European intervention. 'The fury of proud tyrants menaces liberty with fire and sword,' he cried. 'Well! I will praise it all the same, and with undaunted heart. For since the Creation every sage has regarded liberty as the supreme good.' A poem on the causes for which men die showed where his sympathies lay when the clash of arms began.[1]

FORMS OF DEATH

He is a hero and redeems his race
Who dies for justice, liberty, and right;
For these none but the noblest sons of men
Have stained with their heart's blood their armour bright.

Truly they err who deem it great and good
To perish for the cause of kings alone.
So, cringing curs, though beaten, yet devour
The morsels from their master's table thrown.

His disappointment was all the keener when the French soldiers disgraced themselves at the first collision with the foe on the Belgian frontier.

[1] The *Gedichte* fill vol. i. of the *Sämmtliche Werke*.

A LAY OF CHIDING

Who cannot die for liberty
　　Is worthy of his fetters;
Let him be whipped on his own soil
　　By priests and by his betters.

O Frenchmen, all your mouthings wild
　　Awake my wrath and scorn.
Boast not your bravery, but show
　　How trials should be borne.

Not always can the victory
　　Be bought by blood and tears;
But I must chide you for your flight,
　　And for your craven fears.

By savage deeds you seek to hide
　　Your cowardice in vain;
Shame on you for the general
　　And captives you have slain!

Deceived by glitter, how the thought
　　Enflamed my eager heart
That I against the Teuton hordes
　　Might play Tyrtaeus' part!

I speed the arrow of my song
　　Towards you wrathfully,
And boldly welcome one and all
　　Who bring you slavery.

The French armies quickly redeemed their fame, and Bürger rejoiced at their prowess. The entrance of England into the war filled him with indignation. 'Thus speaks the Spirit of Prophecy —As the aristocratic despots of Great Britain prefer an unjust war to peace, they will lay a terrible democratic rod in pickle for their own backs.'[1] The poet eagerly discussed principles and events with his friends. 'We shall never agree about politics and metaphysics,' wrote Meyer in the summer of 1793. 'You dispose of everything *a priori*, while I go by experience. If all demagogues were like you, I should not mind seeing them at the helm. But just think of such miserable creatures as Böhmer and Wedekind ruling Mainz with a rod of iron. I salute in anticipation the dreams which you, aided by heaven and the guillotine, will bring to fruition;

[1] *Briefe von und an Bürger*, iv. 219.

but God grant that I am not there to see. I dare say the storm clears the air ; but I should not care to lash myself to the lightning-conductor.' [1] It was, however, becoming dangerous to give vent to Gallophil sentiments ; and in a brief poem of 1793, entitled ' Farewell to Politics,' he announced and explained his retirement from the arena of strife.

> Farewell, Dame Politics ! I charge thee to retire ;
> The censorship is passing strict to-day.
> How often it forbids what noble hearts desire !
> How seldom can a noble soul aspire
> To write that which he ought, or which he may !

Having himself made the great surrender, he exhorts his readers to find refuge in stoical resignation.

FREEDOM

> Freedom is thy desire, and yet with loud lamentations
> Thou bewailest its loss at cruel tyranny's hands ?
> Learn, O friend, to renounce ! Set grief and death at defiance :
> Then no Olympian god shall e'er be freer than thou.

We might be listening to Goethe ; but the fiery spirit was never really tamed, and such sentiments were little more than a literary pose. Bürger was a child of revolt, and it was his good fortune to die in 1794, before the counter-revolution reached its height.

[1] *Briefe*, iv. 225.

CHAPTER VI

WIELAND AND HERDER

I

OF all the great German writers,' remarked Crabb Robinson to Madame de Staël, ' Wieland is the most French.' ' I am aware of it,' she replied, ' and that is why I do not think much of him. I like a German to be a German.' [1] But though Wieland was never a star of the first magnitude, and might have belonged to any nation of western Europe, he occupies a prominent place in the intellectual history of his country.[2] He was not a great thinker, and his personality was undistinguished ; but he possessed a cool and observant mind, and his vast literary output accustomed his countrymen to turn to him for guidance in matters not only of literature and taste, but of life and politics. Lacking the moral depth of Lessing and Mendelssohn, and free from the arid pedantry of Nicolai, the German Voltaire was perhaps the most representative literary figure of the Aufklärung. For this reason the general effect of the Revolution on the cultured bourgeoisie can be best traced in the writings of their favourite author. With the single exception of Gentz, no German followed its changing scenes with such unflagging attention, and no one expressed his opinion so frequently and in such detail. Treitschke has pronounced him the only political head among the classical writers of Germany ; and, unlike Goethe and Schiller, he worked steadily at the formation of opinion. While the mercurial temperament of Gentz passed from enthusiasm to detestation, the cooler intellect of Wieland pursued a shorter and less adventurous course ; for by temperament and conviction he was an apostle of the *juste milieu*, hating extremes and distrusting emotion.

[1] Crabb Robinson, *Diary*, i. 96.
[2] See Gruber, *Wieland's Leben* ; Böttiger, *Literarische Zustände*, i. 139–264; Düntzer, *Freundesbilder aus Goethe's Kreise* ; Pröhle, *Lessing, Wieland, Heinse* ; Lord Goschen, *Life of G. J. Goschen* ; Wenck, *Deutschland vor hundert Jahren.* No adequate biography exists.

In his early manhood Wieland held republican views—in part due to a residence in Switzerland; but his admiration of the oligarchy of Bern shows that he was not a democrat. It was not till he neared middle age that he turned his pen to political problems. 'The Golden Mirror,' published in 1772, at the age of thirty-nine, belongs to the class of philosophical romances dear to the eighteenth century.[1] Though modelled on the 'Cyropaedia,' the story is strictly practical, and the author is as much in earnest in his appeal to princes as his rather frivolous temperament permitted him to be. The philosopher Danischmend is the very voice of the Aufklärung, the preacher of political and religious enlightenment. Tifan, the ruler, is modelled on Joseph II, and the book breathes the spirit of enlightened despotism which Wieland and most of his contemporaries accepted as the last word of political science. The story of an oriental monarchy, plunged by misrule into anarchy and finally rescued by a reforming genius, was at once a transcript from the common experience of France and Germany and an exhortation to their rulers. The story is lively enough; but it exhibits no special insight or originality. It is a vigorous plea for the kingship of Frederick the Great, which substituted the ideal of 'le premier domestique' for 'l'état, c'est moi,' and in which the author found a congenial compromise between the crude absolutism which he detested and the democracy which he never ceased to distrust. And such was the political condition of his country that the description of the 'Golden Mirror' constituted a rebuke to the lords of misrule. That he did not pitch his ideal beyond mortal achievement was shown by his confession in 1791—that he never expected his dream to be so nearly realised as in the person of Louis XVI. The interest of the book lies in the fact that it is his political confession, and contains the germ of the essays and dialogues of his later years. His reforming views found further expression in 'Schach Lolo,' a sharp condemnation of selfish despotism. Without laying claim to the title of a publicist, he exposed abuses with delicate skill and fostered the critical temper of the time. 'The author of the history of the Kings of Scheschian,' wrote Laukhard many years later, 'is the man who has taught us Germans the closer study of the course of politics. It is his merit to have called the attention of princes to their duties and of subjects to their rights.'

Wieland had hoped to win a Professorship at Vienna by the 'Golden Mirror,' as he had won the chair of philosophy at Erfurt by his philosophical autobiography, 'Agathon.' The enlightened Joseph read it 'with satisfaction'; but the call came not from the

[1] See Vogt, *Der Goldene Spiegel u. Wieland's Politische Ansichten.*

Danube, but from the Ilm. Anna Amalia, the widowed Duchess of Weimar, read the book with such delight that she invited the author to become the tutor of her sons Karl August and Constantine. The invitation was gratefully accepted, and the genial satirist had the satisfaction of watching his elder pupil develop into one of the model princes of his time. On settling in his new home, he founded the 'Deutsche Merkur,' which at once became the leading literary journal of Germany. Unlike Schlözer, whose organ was avowedly political and propagandist, the new monthly avoided the graver controversial issues of the time ; but the editor's influence was emphatically on the side of progress, and his rapier was in its own sphere as effective as Schlözer's bludgeon. He shared the dislike of his countrymen for the American policy of George III, and warmly welcomed the establishment of a transatlantic republic free from the dead hand of European traditionalism. He was conscious of Rousseau's spell without becoming a slavish disciple. He refused to believe in the happy innocence of primitive man, regarding him as a savage with an instinct for society. He rejected the social contract as unhistorical, and held the masses unripe for political power. If modern terminology is to be applied, he was a liberal, but not a democrat. He believed that every people had a right to decent government and rational liberty. 'Even if our forefathers were so stupid as formally to abdicate their rights to liberty,' he wrote in 1788, 'this renunciation would have no power to bind their descendants.' In the same year he exclaims that the time has arrived when nothing that is of merit needs to shun the light. 'At any rate, it has come for Germany. The free spirit of inquiry has never been less fettered in the happiest days of Greece, the source of all enlightenment.'

In 1788 Wieland announced the approach of a vast transformation, which he expected to be mild and gradual. 'Perhaps at the end of the nineteenth century much will be realised that may now be described as the dreams of a cosmopolitan in his dotage.' As a citizen of the world, he rejoiced in the progress of another country as much as if it had taken place among ' our honourable and—not to flatter them—rather stupid Germans.' He at once recognised the justification of the French Revolution. 'He has been asked to revise his " King of Scheschian," ' records Böttiger, ' and he is pleased to have it said that he enunciated almost all the ideas of popular right which the French nation are trying to realise in a novel written twenty years ago.' But he detested ' enthusiasm ' with all the fervour of the *saeculum rationalisticum,* and the apostle of the *juste milieu* soon found cause for apprehension. The ' Cosmopolitan Address to the Assembly by Eleutherius Filoceltes,' written

in October 1789, lacks nothing in frankness and decision.[1] ' I
am only a modest citizen of the world,' he begins, ' and I have much
the same views of the rights and duties of man as you. Your
patriotism inspired in me such passionate admiration that even
where I thought your measures overbold, I put it down to my
mistaken judgment, not to your lack of wisdom. But since August
I have not been able to stifle certain doubts as to your method of
commencing the rejuvenescence of the French monarchy.' He
then puts a series of searching questions. ' On what is the right
of the French thus to alter their constitution based ?   If on the
law of nature, does not every nation, every province, every town,
every village possess the same right to change, and to change as
often as it likes ?   But what would become of the tranquillity
and security of life and property ?   If you say that change is only
legitimate when conditions are intolerable, will not the people
concerned continually reply " They are " ?   The foundations of
the constitution will be insecure if every feeling of discomfort
and oppression entitles the people to shake off the laws and constitution and to punish those who are either satisfied or unwilling
to share in its overthrow. You are right to combat monarchical and
aristocratic despotism ; but one may be allowed to doubt whether
a kingdom, so long one of the mightiest of monarchies, can change
into a democracy without great disadvantages, and even whether
a great nation can flourish under a democratic constitution. If
you say that it is still a monarchy, I reply that monarchy has turned
into anarchy. The nation is suffering from liberty fever, which
makes the Parisians, the politest people in the world, thirst for the
blood of aristocrats. When the people, sooner or later, comes to
itself, will it not see that it is led by the nose by twelve hundred
petty tyrants instead of being governed by a King ?   You treat your
monarch as the Roman soldiers treated the Saviour—by putting
a crown of thorns on His head. Yet you cannot be more deeply
convinced than I that your nation was wrong to bear such
misgovernment so long ; that the best form of government is the
separation and equilibrium of the executive, legislature, and
judiciary ; that every people has an indefeasible right to as much
freedom as can coexist with order ; that the person and property of
every citizen must be secured against the caprices of power ; and
that each must be taxed in proportion to his income.' In a word,
French principles are sound enough, though they have been
unwisely applied.

[1] The *Aufsätze über die französische Revolution* are printed in vol. xxix.
of Göschen's edition of the works. A complete edition is in course of
publication by the Berlin Academy.

Wieland was far more of an anti-clerical than of a democrat, and the decree of the Assembly in 1790, abolishing monastic orders and vows, filled him with delight. He anticipated the best results for religion and education, agriculture, and the life of the State. He congratulates himself on living in a time ' when the most cultivated nation in Europe supplies an example of legislation which, founded solely on the rights of man, is in every sentence the clear expression of reason.' To construct the new edifice on a coherent plan the total demolition of the old ruin is essential, and, in view of the excellent conduct of the French, an enterprise of the greatest promise. He breaks a lance with Schlözer, who was beginning to attack the Revolution, and still more sharply castigates those who, like Burke, ' paint the grossest caricatures on the wall and then, pointer in hand, declaim the most horrible stories in the agonising tones of a singer at a fair.' He looks to the Assembly with the same feeling that he would watch an unfolding bud or an artist at work on what one feels with ever-growing certainty will emerge as a masterpiece. In May he writes : ' The world has never seen a great nation thus resist its oppressors and provide itself with a constitution which secures the ultimate end of society.' Despite the real or imaginary horrors of the mob, he adds in June : ' I am as much convinced as ever that the Revolution was a necessary and healthy work, or rather that it was the only means of rescuing the nation and making it, in all probability, happier than any nation has ever been.' Such authoritative support was warmly welcomed in France. At a Masonic meeting in Paris, in October 1790, the President announced that Wieland, ' one of the most celebrated of German authors,' who had at first written in a prejudiced manner of the Assembly, had now learned to know its principles better and had declared himself their admirer. ' The Circle demands a public homage to this great writer and friend of truth.' At these words the whole audience, estimated at five thousand, rose and applauded.[1]

When the new Constitution began to appear in outline, he complained that the English model was rejected. In ' Thoughts on the Abolition of Hereditary Nobility,' he denounces the decree, lamenting that his hope of a two-chamber system was gone for ever. ' From my cosmopolitan standpoint, there should have been a reform of the nobility as well as of the Court and the clergy. The hateful difference between the noble and the commoner should be abolished, and every post should be open to talent and services.' On the other hand, it was just and fitting for a magnanimous nation like the French to honour the services and virtues of noble ancestors

[1] Halem, *Paris en* 1790, ed. Chuquet, p. 290.

in their descendants. The English model of confining nobility to the eldest son should have been followed. As a disciple of Montesquieu he insisted on the separation of powers, and he sided with Mirabeau on the vexed question of the absolute veto. He believed in the honest representation of the people in the legislature, but he desired the executive to be strong and free. To his strictures on France he adds a hit at his own country, remarking that it would be waste of time to criticise its conditions, since Germany is not nearly advanced enough to discuss its common affairs with profit.

As the sky became more threatening, Wieland blamed the folly of those who were not prepared for the inevitable difficulties and stumblings in the execution of such a formidable enterprise. ' Is complaint made of the oppression of the royal power? I reply that a temporary supervision during the work on the Constitution is as natural as to divert the flow of water during the repair of a mill-wheel. Of course, too, future Assemblies will need to put many things straight; for no constitution or administration is so perfect that it does not need overhauling every half-century. Let Germans think not only of the twenty months of constitutional conflict in France, but of their own Thirty Years' War as the price of the constitution that emerged from the peace of Westphalia.' But with Mirabeau's death the feelings of Wieland underwent a decided change. He had blamed the demagogy and the bombast of the great tribune; but now the last hope of orderly progress seemed to vanish. ' Since his death and the gross excesses of the mob on April 18, which revealed the slavery of the King, it must be repugnant even to the most impartial spectator to spend another word on the Revolution. A people which desires to be free and has not learned in two years that, without unconditional obedience to the law, freedom is in theory a monster and in practice far worse than Asiatic slavery—a people which allows itself to be driven to acts which would disgrace cannibals—is, to put it mildly, unripe for freedom.' The outburst naturally aroused a good deal of attention. Halem lamented the loss of such a doughty champion; Voss pitied the poor fellow who was the sport of every passing breeze; and Herder and Gleim exchanged unfriendly comments on the time-server.[1] From the other camp came a bitter anonymous denunciation of the man who had now adopted the views which he had previously declared to be error and folly. But Wieland had only set one foot in the enemy's lines. A fanatical appeal to the princes of Europe to combine for the forcible extinction of the French conflagration provoked him to emphatic

[1] *Von und an Herder*, i. 152–3.

protest, which led Voss to exclaim with satisfaction that he had regained control of himself. He pronounces the Revolution not utterly beyond hope, and repudiates the contention that it is the common duty of kings to suppress it. One government may, indeed, support another against a revolt; but in this case it was the uprising of a nation.

In the October 'Mercury,' the Editor replied to Schubart, who had joined in the condemnation of the July manifesto. He explains that, though his fundamental convictions have undergone no change, his hopes for the victory of the nobler elements in France have steadily dwindled. He suggests that the new Constitution, now almost complete, should be rebuilt from its foundations by the Assembly and the King in the light of their experiences. Such a project indicates the straits to which he was reduced in the effort to blend his old and his new opinions. He had once spoken contemptuously of Burke and emphasised the necessity and splendour of the task of erecting a new edifice on the principles of reason; but he now quotes respectfully the Englishman's polemics against the right of peoples to alter their constitution at will. He explains his errors by his eager desire to see a great nation wisely using its power to construct a constitution on the basis of human rights. He held fast to the necessity of free discussion of the Revolution, continuing to allow articles of every colour to appear in the 'Mercury' and priding himself on his impartiality. 'Friends and foes (if such a harmless person can have foes) will, I hope, admit that all I have written about events in France breathes a certain spirit of dispassionate moderation. As I have not the honour to be related to the House of Capet, am neither a noble nor a prelate, and have as little to gain from the restoration of the *ancien régime* as to lose by a new constitution, I see nothing to prevent me being absolutely impartial; or, if that is beyond the power of man, from assuming such an attitude that neither Monarchists nor Jacobins can accuse me of unfairness. I have two simple maxims in judging of human affairs. Firstly, I never forget that men are neither more nor less than men; and thus I do not expect perfection. Secondly, I do not expect anything great to come to pass in a single throw, as one casts a metal statue. When the nation has no more to fear from the King's authority, he will recover as much power and prestige as the head of a free nation, or a monarchy, limited by laws to a purely beneficial activity, ought to possess. Mob outbreaks will cease; and correct conceptions of rights and duties will gradually filter down to the common man, and, with a better education of youth, will breed a generation to which this constitution is suited.'

In January 1792 Wieland delivered judgment on the constitution of 1791, which he describes as suited only to a small and simple community. The majority of Frenchmen disapproved it, and wise men disliked the omnipotence of the people and the paralysis of the executive. The reduction of the royal power to a shadow broke up the unity of the kingdom, and handed it over to the tender mercies of warring factions. But the French would be within their rights in championing it, despite its faults, with far more burning zeal against an attack by the enemies of all liberty, than their barbarian forefathers showed for the holy oriflamme. If only they would be content to remain on the defensive, their cause would be that of humanity, and any foreign power would be crazy to attack such a harmless and magnanimous nation. The Émigrés need not be considered, for they have lost the right to count. ' Inquire at Coblenz, Trier, and Mannheim, and you will wonder why the Assembly has not long ago instituted a national thanksgiving for their departure. It is difficult, even by biting one's lips, to keep back the reflections which surge up at the sight of all their misconduct on German soil.' It is no longer worth discussing whether the Revolution is right or wrong, just as it is no use discussing the morals of an earthquake or a tornado. No constitution is perfect, and too much must never be expected of mankind. ' Despite my distaste for democracy, and of important parts of the new system, I have not surrendered all hope of a happy issue.'

When the monarchy fell in blood and terror a few months later he wrote an essay on the change. ' So France is a Republic, and a second Revolution has occurred. They have begun badly. History knows no example of a great State, after centuries of monarchy, turning into a pure democracy.' It cannot be a true Republic, for the capital will dominate the country. Only a federation, as in Holland and America, would hold it together. It will be a despotism of force and caprice, for French democracy is a premature birth. The people once praised as the most civilised of nations is now denounced as a rash, excitable, untamable, and corrupt race, which, according even to its own writers, hides a terrible degree of physical and moral corruption beneath a brilliant exterior. He applies Schlözer's term, Kakistocracy, to the men who are about to emerge. He had been accused of describing the French as unripe ; perhaps he should have called them overripe. He neither hoped nor expected a successful resistance to the invaders. ' Men of the stamp of Carra and Cloots would now be omnipotent but that two of the greatest of monarchs are prepared to enter France with 200,000 men under the first General in Europe, to restore a system which the better part of the nation would at any rate prefer to the mob-rule of the moment.' He had hoped for the restoration of the monarchy in a purified form ; but the Brunswick Manifesto struck him like a thunderbolt. At this moment he contemplated the Jacobins and the Émigrés with impartial loathing.

In the very month of the King's execution Wieland issued a ringing challenge to the rising tide of reaction. For once he turns his eyes to his own country and attempts to measure the effects of the Revolution beyond the frontiers of France. Need we have been mixed up in the war ? he asks. Before it began, the opinion of the wisest men was that it would be best for the German Commonwealth of States to leave France to herself. In certain parts of the ' Reflections on the State of the Fatherland ' we might be listening to the resonant declamation of the youthful Fichte. It cannot be too often repeated, he begins, that in Europe, at any rate, the human race has attained its majority. It no longer permits itself to be lulled to sleep by tales and lullabies, and no longer respects prejudices merely because they are old. Even the lowest classes now discern their own interests and rights too clearly to be bewitched by magic enchantments. Abuses and tyrannies, once borne with sighs, are now felt to be intolerable because they are not inevitable. People begin to believe that they can help themselves. ' It was in this mood that a considerable part of the nation in our German fatherland found itself when the French Revolution broke out, and we gave it a warmer and more general sympathy than perhaps any other country.' This good-will was shared even in the highest circles. Had the rulers of Germany been the tyrants they were called by the French, they would have combined to stifle the Revolution in its cradle. On the contrary, convinced of the justice of the complaints of the French nation, they held their hands and only intervened after a series of insults, and on realising its necessity for the tranquillity of their own States.

He then sketches with rare insight the good and evil influences which had streamed across the Rhine. ' During the last four years many fallacies and half-truths have been thrown into circulation. But many truths of the highest importance, many wholesome doubts, many practical ideas on government, legislation, and the rights of man have also penetrated to the lower strata of society which were hitherto the esoteric doctrine of a little body of initiates, and which even they discussed *in camera*. Both the true and the false Aufklärung have increased more in these years than in the half-century preceding them.' Despotic measures cannot impede their progress. ' The kingdom of deception is at an end, and reason

alone can heal the wounds which its abuse has made.' In Germany
there is a party of hope and a party of fear, both observing events
with the eyes of passion, and therefore falsely. But Wieland is
never so happy as when he is trimming the balance, and he goes
on to pour scorn on the votaries of ' the new religion,' who worship
the goddesses of Liberty and Equality, and suffer no other. The
dictum of St. Just, ' Monarchy is a crime against nature,' and
other senseless maxims of the Jacobin Club and the Convention,
are now being spread abroad in Germany with apostolic zeal, and
in many parts are being greedily swallowed by youthful ignorance.
Even among those who would lose some privileges not a few have
the ambition to play a leading part in a state of liberty and equality.
In spite of the dangerous seduction of ' French principles,' the
Editor of the ' Mercury ' feels no more temptation to join the ' party
of fear,' than the ' party of hope.' ' If Germany was in the same
condition as France ; if we had not a constitution whose benefits
outweigh its disadvantages ; if we were not already in possession
of the larger part of the liberty which they had to win ; if we did
not enjoy for the most part a milder and more constitutional
government ; if our taxes were as crushing, our aristocracy as
intolerably arrogant and privileged, there is no doubt that the
example of France would have had very different effects, and the
German people would have been far more than a mere spectator.
The tranquillity we enjoy proves the respect both of rulers and
subjects for law, and exhibits the steadiness and good sense of
the nation which was not intoxicated by the triumph of liberty
and equality, and realised the immeasurable evils of anarchy.
It is not true that we are slaves. What people in Europe can
boast of greater enlightenment ? '

As the storm grew ever wilder, Wieland came to share more
fully the disbelief of his Weimar friends not only in revolutions,
but in political change. Four years of turmoil and the prospect
of an endless and indecisive war had induced a not unnatural
weariness, and he cries a plague on all disturbers of the peace. ' We
have had weather like Paradise,' he wrote to Göschen in July
1793.[1] ' Everything gives promise of a most splendid summer and
a most fruitful year. Why must rabid Republicans and sceptred
Cyclops mar the enjoyment of the boons of Mother Nature ? '
' Things look badly for the peace we all desire,' he wrote a few
weeks later, ' as the Jacobins and Sansculottes, who make up the
larger part of the French nation, are miles away from the thought
of surrender, and all the Powers together are incapable of over-
throwing so great a nation in which at least four millions of men,

[1] *Goschen's Life*, ii. 56.

capable of bearing arms, are determined to die sooner than submit to foreign dictation or allow their territory to be dismembered.' The essay, ' Words in Season,' published later in 1793, in the full flood of the Terror, expresses the author's hope, but not his expectation, of the fall of the Jacobins. ' One must just go on preaching, till men listen, that mankind can only grow happier by becoming more reasonable and more moral.' It is a mistake to accuse ' the great ' of every failing. When they deserve accusations it is not because they are ' great,' but because they are men. Ordinary people are no better nor more unselfish than their social superiors. Anti-royalism has brought more misery to France in four years than all her kings, from Clovis to Louis XVI. ' My eternal refrain is that reform must begin not with constitutions, but with the individual. The conditions of happiness are in our own hands.' It is the Weimar gospel, the message of Humboldt, Goethe, and Schiller, pointing us towards the political quietism of the Restoration era.

Though Wieland yielded to no one in his detestation of the bloody anarchy of France, he kept his head clear and refused to mutter the shibboleths of the counter-revolution. ' I am sure that my Gleim rejoices with me at the almost certain hope that the new campaign will bring us peace,' he wrote to the old poet in April 1793, ' and that Dumouriez's splendid resolve will rescue France from the abyss to which she has been brought by a crazy band of fools and knaves, and, with German and English aid, restore a well-ordered monarchy. The poor French have preached so much political and moral wisdom, to their own cost, that many decades will be needed to digest the teachings and warnings which their example has given to every class. The better part of the nation seems tired of the anarchical rule of the Jacobin Club ; but before order is restored, we shall see some more terrible scenes. My consolation is that the manifold good which the Revolution set in motion, despite the shocking excesses of aristocratic and democratic fanaticism, will not be lost to humanity, but gradually and peacefully bear fruit a thousandfold. For nothing that is good can be lost.' [1] In like manner, he refused to profess a patriotism which he did not feel. ' For some years I have heard such praise of German patriotism and patriots,' he wrote in May 1793, ' that I, too, should like to be one. But I cannot form a clear idea on the subject. It would be a moral and political miracle if a great State with heterogeneous and loosely connected parts were to be infused with a common patriotic spirit ; for we lack almost all factors which could produce it, and there are causes operating strongly

[1] *Ausgewählte Briefe*, iv. 28–9.

in the other direction. It is not patriotism, but the horrors in France and the resulting apprehensions that since the end of 1792, and still more since the death of the King, have so transformed our opinion of the Revolution. Provincial patriotism is the fruit of good government, which several parts of our country possess ; but, even if they all possessed it, there would still be no German patriotism.' An article on 'War and Peace,' written in 1794, reveals the same passionless serenity. Once again he sharply attacks the Émigrés. Every party to the Great War, he declares, believes himself to be fighting for right, and it is therefore useless to speak of peace. And yet force can do little against the fanaticism which animates the French. The evil can be most effectively dealt with by indirect methods—by removing the fuel which feeds the flame. The governing desire of France is to retain its unity and independence. If they are safe, the chief reason for the war would cease. It is nonsense to say that we cannot make peace with regicides. Peace must come some day, and it can only come by the recognition of the Republic. It is foolish as well as wrong to drive the nation to despair. He was answering by anticipation the arguments of Burke's 'Regicide Peace,' and preparing the ground for the approaching Treaty of Basle.

In addition to the articles in which he openly expresses his views of the changing scene, Wieland discussed the underlying principles of the Revolution in a series of 'Dialogues of the Gods,' written between 1790 and 1793, in the style of Lucian.[1] He chose the dialogue form as one in which he could present every aspect of a problem, rebuke extremes, and mingle idealism with his satire. His admiring friend and biographer, Gruber, pronounces them as good as Lucian. 'All you offer me of the fruits of your intellect,' wrote his friend and publisher, Göschen, in September 1790, ' is welcome. I accept at once and with infinite satisfaction the "Dialogues of the Gods." Make your own conditions. If the converse of the gods has such wit and reason, such nobility and delicacy of thought, who would not long to join them ? ' Göschen added that they could not be printed in Saxony, as the censor had just been instructed to let nothing pass which discussed the rights of man. They are, nevertheless, innocent enough. The preface to the volume in which they were collected, in 1796, claimed that they breathed a spirit of moderation and toleration which was no recommendation to any party at the time ; and the claim is not ill-founded.

In the first of the series, the tolerant and rather sceptical liberalism of the author is represented by Jupiter, while the

[1] *Werke*, vol. xxv.

L

royalist cause is stoutly championed by Juno. Their discussion may be summarised in the following extracts :—

Juno : I wish you would pay a little more attention to crowned heads.

Jupiter : You think I lean too much to the popular side ? Perhaps I do. In any case the present is not a favourable time for shepherds of the people ; it is the people's turn.

Juno : I cannot understand how the ruler of gods and men can be so indifferent and can look calmly on while his delegates are being turned into stage princes and paper kings.

Jupiter : But we cannot make men like Henry IV, or Frederick the Great, out of a paper king.

Juno : Of course such men are rare. But kings are only our representatives, and ordinary specimens are quite good enough if we only support them.

Jupiter : I will not fail them so long as they can stand on their own legs ; but let us never forget the great truth that kings are for peoples, not peoples for kings.

Juno : Kings are there to govern the people, who ought to let themselves be governed. As Homer said, Let there be one ruler.

Jupiter : That may have been true enough in primitive times ; but it is no longer the case with a people with sufficient experience and education to throw off the yoke of hoary prejudices. Nations are like individuals. They have their childhood, when they must be treated like children and blindly obey authority ; but they, too, put away childish things. It is a sin against nature to wish to keep them for ever in tutelage by force or fraud or both ; and it is a crime and a folly to treat them as children when they have come to manhood.

Juno : I agree that a higher civilisation needs a different system ; but, as all cannot govern, one ruler is still required.

Jupiter : But the people must see that the ruler and his favourites are prevented from evil-doing and wasting the resources of the State.

Juno : Of course, kings must remember that they hold their sceptre from Jupiter.

Jupiter : I pity the peoples if their kings have no one over them but me.

Juno : I admit they must rule by laws framed for the common good.

Jupiter : You are really too innocent ! Who is to give them their laws ? You are aware that I am able to look farther ahead than the rest of you. Everything is subject to the law of change. Our own monarchy is nearing its end, like the others. Nor does it matter, for it was only stucco.

Juno : You won't abdicate in favour of a National Assembly, will you ? Why should we not use all our strength to stifle the demon of revolt and the passion of power ? By all means let the 'peoples enjoy the privileges of liberty under a paternal government ; but they must not, and cannot, rule themselves. Equality is contrary to the nature of things. I have no intention of resigning my share in the government of the world, and you must promise not to thwart me.

Jupiter: Not so long as you are wise enough to hold yourself in check.

In the tenth and eleventh dialogues, St. Louis, Henri IV, and Louis XIV join the Immortals in a discussion of the Fête of Federation, which takes place in a cloud above the Champ de Mars.

Jupiter: Would you have thought that your Gallo-Franks would suddenly change from the most frivolous of peoples, as they were believed to be, to the wisest, and that they would set an example to the world which will inaugurate a new and better order? Has one ever heard of such a rapid leap from serfdom to liberty, of such energy and persistence?

St. Louis: The core of the nation was ever brave and sound. If my successors had followed my maxims, Louis XVI would not be playing his sad part to-day. My only mistake was the Crusades— my heart bleeds to think of them.

Jupiter (turning to Henri IV): If your successors had been men like you, Louis XVI would not have seen this day.

Henri IV: His difficulties are far greater than mine, and he has no good advisers. The representatives of the nation have laid the foundations of a good constitution, which has still to be erected. But much of their work has been hurried and partisan, and they have gone too far.

Jupiter: Remember that even the best and wisest are only men. When such an enlightened and sympathetic people has become free, be sure that it will have the strength to reach the goal. Everything has to be learned, including life. To live rightly is not easy, and to govern wisely is the hardest task of all.

Louis XIV: I deplore the abolition of classes. My people is returning to barbarism.

In the twelfth dialogue, Jupiter and Juno renew their controversy, Minerva joining in the defence of monarchical institutions. The discussion takes place on the day of the King's execution, and Juno pours out the vials of her wrath on ' the little gang of crazy scoundrels.'

Jupiter: I, too, regret the foibles of man ; but remember that he is half a beast. You can no more wash a Moor white than inoculate a man with the blessings of culture without adding a fault to every capacity, an error to every truth, a vice to every virtue. Have we not noticed that the highest refinement and the deepest depravity always coincide? Man can never follow the middle course. Who can wonder that such feeble creatures, confronted by a crisis of fate, go astray ? Do not let the injustices and violences inseparable from every great revolution blind you to the colossal evils which it has terminated and the immeasurable benefits it brings in its train. I am not taking the French Revolution under my wing—I am only observing. I wish well to mortals, but I am powerless against nature and necessity. When all the factors combine towards a world-event and reach maturity, as in the present case, your efforts and mine cannot prevent the fall of a single head ;, or poor Louis would not have laid his neck under the guillotine.

Juno : If you will do nothing, I will unite all peoples and princes for the extirpation of these enemies of gods and kings.

Jupiter : Not too fast ! One can easily turn a great evil into a greater. Leave the punishment of the regicides to a just and inexorable Nemesis. Take care that you do not spread the contagion all over Europe. Labour for the prestige of kings if you will ; but remember that idolatry injures them more than hate. If you wish them well, teach them to know their friends from their foes. Tell them that a throne resting on a constitution, on justice, and on the confidence of the people, cannot be overturned.

Juno : Things have gone no better since you turned moralist.

Jupiter (to Minerva) : What can we expect from mortals when even the gods talk such nonsense ?

The closing dialogue shows us the Council summoned by Juno in her capacity as patron of threatened thrones. Now that Jupiter favours democracy, declares the Queen of Olympus, she must act ; but first she will hear the opinions of the wisest and most experienced of her sex.

Semiramis : Monarchy is the best form of government, because it is the most natural. Its success depends on the ruler being a real father to his people. Even in time of revolutions it must be maintained ; for tyranny is better than anarchy and the oligarchy which follows it. Even now the peoples prefer monarchy when they are not seduced. Nothing is worse for a people than to know too much or to see too clear. Discussion must be kept within bounds. The wise should only tell the unwise what they can hear without danger.

Aspasia : It is true that in the East autocracy has prevailed from the beginning ; but Western communities have chosen their best hunter or warrior to rule. Thus Asia is slave and Europe free. I agree that the rule of one is the best; but he must really be the best, like Pericles, who was chosen by the people. Such men are difficult to find. Moreover, now that the inhabitants of Europe are like grown-up sons, the path of safety is to let the human mind have free play. To raise barriers is to invite revolutions.

Livia : The model for rulers is Augustus. A ruler unfit for his work should resign. Even a hereditary throne is usurped if it is not deserved.

Elizabeth : Nothing but a constitution, clearly defining the rights of all classes, can save a State from revolutions like France.

Juno : Quite right ; and why should not monarchs grant constitutions of their own free will ?

Elizabeth : Monarchs do not willingly part with power.

Juno : This very night I will send a dream to all the princes of the world. We will see first what my promptings are able to achieve.

When the crisis of the Revolution was past, and the Directory replaced Robespierre, Wieland returned to the problems of democracy and monarchy in a series of twelve dialogues entitled ' Tête-à-Tête.' [1] Though inferior in freshness and power to their predecessors, a few of them offer points of interest, and show that his opinions, like those of Kant, underwent little change from beginning to end of the stupendous drama. ' Germany seems to me in not much better case than in the Thirty Years' War,' he wrote to Göschen in 1796, ' and I confess that I have lost all confidence in the men among whom the sieve of destiny has dropped me.' [2] The author hoped, nevertheless, that they might fall under the eye of the new King of Prussia, as Queen Luise was among the subscribers to the ' Mercury.' His gospel was the necessity for mixed government, and he would encourage the young monarch to grant a constitution. But Frederick William III was no student, and it is unlikely that he ever read a line of these insipid exhortations. In the second and third dialogues, on the new oath of hatred to monarchy, Willibald and Heribert discuss the best form of government. The latter, a Frenchman, though no blind advocate of democracy, maintains that monarchy is far worse.

Willibald : A king can only reign by consent of his subjects ; for an individual cannot coerce a multitude.

Heribert : Your monarchy has never existed, and it was certainly not that of Louis XIII, XIV, XV, XVI.

Willibald : It is as senseless to swear hatred to monarchy as to religion or science, art or trade, or anything else which can be abused. An oath means nothing, and such coercion is tyrannical.

Heribert : I admit its absurdity ; but the Directory believes that it will strengthen the Republic, as the hatred of monarchy is beginning to cool.

Willibald : It will have no such effect. As you refuse a King, you will soon have a Dictator. Indeed, he is waiting for you. Bonaparte will restore the nation far more efficiently than a capricious democracy.

[1] Werke, vol. xxxi.   [2] Göschen's Life, i. 459.

Heribert : Even if Republicans are now in a minority, they alone are true Frenchmen, and they will never yield to a royalist majority.

Willibald : Then the people is not sovereign.

Heribert : We appeal from the people to the Nation, from its whim to its will.   The people must always allow a small body to act for it.

Willibald : If liberty is thus circumscribed in a Republic, why should you hate monarchy ?   For a Republic, especially one so large as yours, to flourish, virtue is the essential condition both in ruler and ruled.   Monarchy can, at need, get along with less.

The fourth and the sixth dialogues discuss the actual and potential effects of the Revolution beyond the frontiers of France.

Geron : It is sad to think of Germany, once so mighty, now clay in the hands of French demagogues, a mere footstool of France.   We are not a nation.

Heribert : Germany is like a Gothic castle with a few later additions; thoroughly unsafe and uncomfortable to live in, and now tottering from an earthquake.   Half the country is ruined by the war.   You cannot prolong the struggle.

Geron : I would rather surrender the left bank of the Rhine than see Germany democratised.

Heribert : Take comfort.   Nothing really good can be destroyed.

The sixth dialogue, entitled ' Universal Democracy,' offers a cure for the evils portrayed in the fourth.   There is one simple and unfailing method of preventing revolutions, declares the champion of France, and that is for the rulers of their own free will to introduce a constitution.   It should follow the English model, though not slavishly ; for the English Parliament is fettered by the influence of the Court, which neutralises almost all the strivings of the Opposition for the good of the nation.   The French Constitution of 1791, on the other hand, undermined the royal prestige to such an extent that the throne toppled over.   To make the British constitution as perfect as any work of man can be, only slight modifications are needed—fairer representation, shorter Parliaments, purer elections, and limitation of the royal prerogative to create peers.

The later dialogues betrayed all too plainly that Wieland's powers were beginning to flag, and they provoked the scoffing contempt of the Supreme Court of Literary Appeal at Weimar. ' I cannot keep to myself one of the funniest episodes of our time,' wrote Goethe to Schiller in 1798.[1]   ' Wieland is forbidden by a secret democratic tribunal to continue his dialogues in the

---

[1] *Goethe's Briefe*, xiii. 132–3.

" Mercury." The next number will show if the good old fellow
obeys. The poor author, who in his time told the strangest truths
to kings and rulers and who understood constitutions so well before
they existed, must now, when Gentz demands from the new King
unconditional freedom of the press, hide the nurselings of his old
age, the offspring of a silver wedding, as if they were illegitimates.
A fortnight ago he came to Weimar to garner some eulogies for these
productions. He read them aloud ; but they were received with
such indifference that he soon fled back to his country home. Meanwhile a council was held, and now, I hear, he has been told
to smother and bury these half-castes sprung from an aristo-
democratic wedlock.' Only six appeared in the ' Mercury,' the
remainder taking refuge in the collected works.

' The first years of the Consulate inspired great hopes in Germany
as well as in France,' wrote Wieland ; ' for we witnessed the return
of order and the consolidation of liberty.' But the old man had
almost ceased to influence opinion, and the ' Mercury ' was approaching its end. He was, however, still a celebrity, and every
visitor to Weimar paid his respects to the oracle. ' Our first call
was at the house of the aged Wieland,' wrote Crabb Robinson in
his Journal in 1801.[1] ' The course of my reading had not led me
to form terrifying ideas of his mental greatness, though he is not
less universally read and admired in Germany than was Voltaire
in France. He had already shrunk into the old man. His pale
and delicate countenance was plain and had something of the
satyr in it. He admitted that his hopes of any great improvement in mankind were faint. The best if not the only advantage
which might be expected from the French Revolution was the
promotion of the arts and sciences ; for he holds the French nation
absolutely incapable of forming a Republic. He vindicated the
administration of Bonaparte and did not censure the restoration
of the Roman Catholic Church. The Reformation, he asserted,
had been an evil and had retarded the progress of philosophy
for centuries. Luther ruined everything by making the people
a party to what ought to have been left to the scholars. Had he
not come forward with his furious knock-down attacks on the
Church, and excited a succession of horrible wars in Europe, liberty,
science, and humanity would have slowly made their way.
Melancthon and Erasmus were on the right road, but the violence
of the age was triumphant.'

Wieland was by temperament and conviction a Trimmer,
always praising and usually practising the ' golden mean.' He
hated violence and confusion in religion, politics, and literature.

[1] *Diary*, i. 58–9.

He never forsook the Aufklärung for romanticism.   He was sealed
of the tribe of Erasmus and Goethe, not of Luther and Fichte.
Though possessing nothing of the historic spirit and knowing little
of history, he instinctively recognised the superiority of tranquil
growth to spasmodic advances.   He shared the distrust of the
masses felt by most leaders of thought, and contended that the
Greek States had been wrecked by mob rule.   His ideal was the
British constitution as interpreted by Montesquieu and Delolme,
in which neither ruler nor people should have the power to tyrannise
over one another.   Monarchy was to him as natural as the relation
of father to children, and constitutional monarchy was the relation
of a father to his grown-up sons.   Autocracy was the despotism
of the father as the sovereignty of the people was the revolt of the
children.   In the course of a long life he denounced the hoary
abuses of the *ancien régime* in France and Germany, the blood-
stained anarchy of the Revolution, and the brutal despotism of
Napoleon ; but he changed less than most of his contemporaries.
From beginning to end of his literary career he was a preacher
of sweet reasonableness, a soldier in the army of enlightenment,
a peacemaker between the old world and the new.   The
reactionaries were bidden to advance, while the renovators were
warned to walk warily lest they should stumble and fall.

II

' Herder was not a star, but a constellation,' declared his friend
Jean Paul Richter.[1] ' He left no work behind him worthy of his
genius, but he was himself one of God's masterpieces.'   Though
a far greater man than Wieland, he was less of a politician.   Caring
nothing for the glories of the Seven Years' War or its hero, he left
Prussia as a young man with an abiding distaste for its bureaucratic and military atmosphere.   His interest in the life of the State
was aroused during his residence at Riga, which he described as a
sort of Geneva under the shadow of Russia—a Republic protected
by an Empire.   Something of the old free spirit of the Hansa
League survived in its corporate life, and the young theologian
rejoiced in the freedom which he found within its walls.   It was
personal and intellectual liberty which he prized ; and it was only
in later life that he realised that the best chance of obtaining it
lay in the advance of political liberty in its widest form.   From the
beginning to the end of his career, he detested the iron rule of

[1] See Caroline Herder, *Erinnerungen aus Herder's Leben* ; Haym's
monumental biography ; and Kühnemann, *Herder.* His writings have been
admirably edited by Suphan.

great military empires, the creation of force, and the enemies of individual self-realisation. Humanity was his religion, and he was its High Priest.

On leaving Riga, at the age of twenty-four, Herder took ship to Nantes, and spent some months of travel and study in France. He desired to escape from the library to the market-place, and spoke of observing everything from the standpoint of the State ; but the theorist peeps through the visor of the politician. The traveller's diary is at its best in dealing with literature ; and yet it is in France that he begins to feel himself a German. He is more impressed than pleased by the French, who strike him as an old nation on the point of collapse from excess of culture and exaggerated intellectualism. He is less attracted than repelled by Rousseau—'proud and arrogant, with his intolerable novelty and paradox.' The young student of eighteen had shared the ecstasy of his contemporaries ; but he regained his self-control at Riga, and spoke of his 'stomach overladen with the writings of Rousseau.' He learned from Hume to reject the notion of the state of nature ; and his love of history soon swept him beyond the reach of such appeals. He thankfully accepted the warning of 'Émile' not to hustle or coerce the budding character ; but he denied its author's claims to be an educator of society. While fully recognising his greatness, he maintained that his intellectual faults rendered him almost useless for a German. The final emancipation was facilitated by the growing reverence for the ripe and balanced intellect of Montesquieu, whose majestic survey of legislation and Roman civilisation fostered his passion for the philosophy of history. He calls him 'the great,' 'the incomparable,' with less of the false brilliancy of the French mind than any of his peers. He is already planning a great historico-philosophical work on humanity, and he resolves to learn and apply the method of the 'Esprit des Lois.' On the long journey from Nantes to Paris, Montesquieu is his only companion.

At the age of twenty-five Herder won the prize set by the Berlin Academy for an essay on the reciprocal influence of governments and the sciences. The best method by which the government can promote the intellectual life of a nation, he argues, is by granting liberty of thought, which he defines as 'the fresh air of heaven.' A State based on law, liberty, and well-being escapes the danger of being buffeted by the capricious breezes of opinion and pierced by the arrows of every vapid pamphleteer. He praises Republics, and states it as an axiom that 'the boldest thoughts of the human spirit are conceived and the fairest plans fulfilled in free States.' Next in merit comes legal and enlightened monarchy ; and he frankly prefers the ' fixed laws of a mild monarchy to the average republic.' Modern States are less brilliant but more permanent than those of antiquity. He sent a copy of his treatise to Joseph II, from whom, until the Fürstenbund, he hoped for national salvation. ' Oh! Emperor,' he cried in a poem of 1780, ' thou head of ninety-nine princes, give us what we all thirst for, a German fatherland, one law, one language, and true religion.'

The main occupation of the early years in Weimar, whither he was summoned at the instance of Goethe, was the ' Philosophy of History,' a panoramic study of the conditions and course of human development.   The second volume of his masterpiece sharply attacked Kant's newly published essay on Universal History for its emphasis on the State. A government, in Herder's eyes, is merely a machine.   His conception of the State, indeed, is so low and contemptuous that it can only be explained by his obsession with the excesses of autocracy. Only ' natural governments,' chosen for a special purpose and ending with its fulfilment, seemed to him to represent reason.   ' I do not know,' he wrote in a cancelled passage, ' if there is a greater absurdity than the right to rule in consequence of birth and the corresponding obligation to obey.' As hideous illustrations of ' rule by God's grace,' he cites the crazy cruelties of Morocco, Persia, and China.   The relations of family and friendship are natural instincts which render us happy.   The State, on the other hand, can give us only artificial tools, while it can easily rob us of something far more important—ourselves. He is torn between his conviction that it is a social necessity and his experience that it is almost always despotic ; and his antagonism renders the chapter on Governments, which he continually rewrote, the most confused in the book.   He misunderstands Kant's noble conception of the State as organised freedom, and cries ' What an evil principle it is that man is an animal who needs a master and looks for his happiness to one or more of them !   Let us turn the statement upside down and say, A man who needs a master is an animal ; as soon as he becomes a man he needs him no longer.' Equally abhorrent to him is Kant's contention that the goal of history is only to be attained in the race.   Misinterpreting this also, he asks what it can mean that the individual unfolds his spiritual powers in vain and that all the generations are sacrificed to the last, which will erect its throne on the scaffolding of the happiness of its predecessors.   His ultimate aim was as noble and his zeal for rational liberty as sincere as that of his old master ; but he was incapable of thinking out the construction of a better political system.

The fourth series of 'Scattered Leaves,' published in 1792, contained the miscellaneous writings of the preceding years, concluding with the philosophical sketch 'Tithonus and Aurora.' Not only individuals, he declares, grow old, but institutions, constitutions, estates, and corporations, the forces of religion, art, and science. During his prolonged Italian tour he had observed these survivals, 'which seem a compendium of all history and fill one with sadness.' They suggest the haunting question, How is rejuvenescence secured? Revolutions are useless, he replies, for they are the mark of barbarism, of arrogant power, of wild caprice. We must borrow the methods of Nature, the sovereign healer. A wise prince must regard himself as a steward, not as an antagonist of nature—the great mother who moves by the processes of evolution. In this a great example has been set by England, which has won the prize of a constitution destined to endure for centuries. To obviate 'those horrible attacks called revolutions,' the State must maintain or restore the free circulation of its vital sap and not struggle against the nature of things. Berkeley had expressed the hope that the scene of the fifth act of world-history would be laid in America. Herder, on the contrary, sees a new Aurora slumbering in the arms of the old Tithonus, Europa. 'Not four, hardly three acts of the great drama in our hemisphere are over, and who can say how often the old Tithonus of the human race may not renew his youth on our planet?'

'Tithonus and Aurora' reflected the glowing dawn of the French Revolution, to which the life-long student of the history of humanity naturally turned with fascinated gaze. He had carried away from Riga a vague radicalism which never left him; and in private conversation he would denounce the nobility as a monument of human folly, and thunder against the autocracies under which the world was groaning. To such a mind, though in principle an enemy of revolutions, the abolition of privileges and exemptions, the proclamation of the Rights of Man, and the establishment of a democratic constitution were like sparkling wine. His conversations and even his sermons became political, and the first ecclesiastical dignitary of Weimar was soon known as the leading radical of the little duchy. He was always angular in social intercourse, and the excitement of the times tempted him to passionate declamation. When Frau von Stein called on him, early in 1790, she found him closeted with Knebel and Wieland. 'They argued so hotly,' she records, 'that they were all shrieking when I entered.'[1] His devoted disciple, Georg Müller, the brother of the historian, wrote in May 1790 complaining of the effects of the Revolution in Switzerland,

[1] Düntzer, *Frau von Stein*, i. 341.

denouncing the Assembly as a band of fanatics, and scoffing at ' the great politician Wieland.' [1] As Herder made no reply, Müller urged him to read Burke's ' Reflections,' adding that he knew more of the chaos in France than his master in the middle of Germany ; but his remonstrance was unavailing. His views shocked the Duchess Luise, who hated the Revolution with a curious intensity. In a letter to Frau von Stein she mentions ' Herder's curious idea in a sermon admitting the necessity of differences in class, but reproaching those of high rank for their congenital prejudices, from which they can free themselves with difficulty.' ' The Duchess is more than ever set against France,' wrote Herder to Knebel in September 1790, ' and I have made a bond with myself no longer to offend with my tongue.' [2]

Though determined to avoid oral controversy, it was impossible for a teacher and thinker to keep silence in the greatest crisis of his life. The fourth part of the ' Philosophy of History,' describing the birth of modern Europe, was completed in 1788 and published in 1791 ; and he now resolved to write a fifth part, bringing the survey up to date. He soon became acutely conscious of the difficulties of his task, and, as usual, the seduction of a new scheme triumphed over the responsibilities of the old. He was too busy with official duties to grapple with the copious materials of a comprehensive work, and he had lost the power of concentration. It was easier, as well as more tempting, to apply the magic formula, ' Humanity,' to recent and current events. Thus arose in the spring of 1791 the idea of informal ' Letters on the Advances of Humanity,' in which, he told Gleim, he intended to embody the best offering of his head and heart, and which his wife described to the publisher as ' interesting for all classes.' ' The times forbid silence,' he explained ; ' they force one's mouth open.' [3]

The fulfilment of the scheme was postponed by illness, and in the summer of 1792 Herder spent three months in Aachen in search of convalescence. Here, on the border of France, he looked across the frontier into the seething cauldron, realising the strength of a nation thrilled by the cry of the Fatherland in danger, and resolved not only to defeat the invader, but to carry the gospel of liberty into neighbouring lands. His interest in the Revolution, always keen, now became intense. He read the Brunswick Manifesto with indignation, and attributed the September massacres in large measure to its impotent threats. The fact that Karl August and Goethe were among the invaders made no difference to his attitude,

---

[1] See the delightful essay, ' Herder u. Georg Müller,' in Baumgarten's Reden u. Aufsätze.

[2] Knebel, Nachlass, ii. 2.   [3] Von und an Herder, i. 151.

and his hopes were proof against the accumulating horrors of the summer and autumn. The overthrow of the Monarchy, indeed, aroused rather curiosity than repulsion. ' I cannot describe the impression that events have made on me,' he wrote to the sympathetic Knebel, ' here in Aachen, with the French in front of me, close to the Rhine. The few days we are to remain will teach us a great deal.' On his return to Weimar he kept his spirits, though not unmindful of the sufferings of his friends nor unmoved by the excesses of the foe. ' Herder has just left me,' wrote the Duchess Luise to Frau von Stein.[1] ' He seemed to have a special grudge against kings. He says the Brunswick Manifesto caused the horrors at Paris ; but he is wrong.' A week later she wrote to the same friend : ' It is quite right of your parson to pray for the French Royal Family. Herder would not do it.' Frau von Stein was no less indignant at her friend's radicalism. ' He has written to the Duchess,' she tells her son, ' defending the French, and saying that he loves not them, but reason. Is it possible to call the triumph of robbers the triumph of reason ? ' It was in these dark days that Prince August of Gotha secretly toasted him with the words ' La Salute della Liberta.' The collapse of the Mainz theocracy filled him with satisfaction, and he rejoiced at the advance of the troops in Belgium and on the Rhine with their war-cry, ' War on the palace, peace to the cottage.' ' What say you to these times and prospects ? ' he wrote to Gleim in November. ' Oh ! the honour and might of the Prussian cavalry, the money and the honour of the Prussian crown ! And the connection with deceitful Austria ! And Poland ! And the ambitions of Russia ! And the manifestoes of the French ! What does the Old Grenadier say to it all ? Are we not living in strange times, and must we not almost believe in the Apocalypse ? Whither is Providence leading us ? '[2] We hear the echo of his views in a letter of his wife to Jacobi, expressing her hope that the new turn of events may strengthen his belief in the Neo-Franks. ' The sun of liberty is rising ; you will render the homage that is due to this goddess, dear brother. In Germany we shall sit for some time longer in darkness, but the wind of the dawn is rising here and there.' The husband added a postscript, begging Jacobi not to misinterpret his wife's enthusiasm. ' She is not suffering from Liberty fever, but is a good German *in terra obedientiae*. Current events impel one to break silence. Thank God that a higher Providence is at work, which will bring peace from the storm and daylight out of darkness.'[3]

It was in this spirit of hopefulness that Herder embarked on

[1] Bojanowski, *Grossherzogin Luise*, pp. 225–6.
[2] *Von und an Herder*, i. 152. [3] *Aus Herder's Nachlass*, ii. 298.

the 'Letters on Humanity.'[1] They were to embody his political creed ; but nothing human was to be excluded, and the political reflections were only to appear as an application of his philosophy. He wrote not as a publicist or a journalist, but as a philosophic historian, surveying the development of affairs and the operations of Providence as from a lofty watch-tower. Fear of the censorship suggested the trick of expressing his views through the medium of an exchange of letters. 'These friends,' he wrote in the original preface, ' air their opinions, for none of which does the editor assume responsibility, and none of which need be accepted as the law and the gospel. If you disagree with a passage, read on till you find what you seek.' The plan was to weigh, to discuss, to illustrate, but not to decide. The advantage of this literary *genre*, wrote the author to Knebel with engaging candour, was that he could not be held responsible for any particular passage. He added the precaution of referring the letters to the opening months of the Revolution. 'A good many things would seem strange to you,' he wrote to Gleim, ' if they were said now ; but they were written years ago.' The lie was repeated in the original preface. ' If their writers had been able to forecast the march of events, they would perhaps have expressed themselves in many respects differently.' The discovery of a letter of Knebel, to whom Herder showed the manuscript, has revealed the fact that the ante-dating was a fiction ; and with Suphan's publication of the literary remains the mystery is solved. The original collection of ' Letters on the Advances of Humanity' consisted of twenty-four numbers, and was predominantly political. In these Letters Herder is filled with confidence in the irresistible power of the ' Spirit of the Age,' the spirit which vanquished clericalism at the Reformation and will disperse the darkness where it still prevails. The ' Zeitgeist ' also pronounces judgment on the political arrangements of Europe sprung from war and conquest—the old feudalism and the class privileges of blood which have outlived their time. ' There is only one Estate—namely, the People (not the mob), to which both king and peasant belong. Only the noblest, wisest, and best should be rulers : not aristocrats or democrats, but aristodemocrats—that is the mandate of the Spirit of the Time. Autocratic and hereditary rule is an abomination. In times of danger there must be leaders, but leaders designed by God and nature ; and the greatest benefactors transfer no rights to their descendants to burden the State for ever and ever. The folly of war—wars of religion, succession, and trade alike—should soon be recognised for the madness that it is.'

[1] The Letters, both in their original and their final form, are printed with full explanatory notes in vols. xvii. and xviii. of Suphan's edition.

Letters 16, 17, and 18 are devoted to the French Revolution.
' Tell me, my friends,' writes the supposititious author of Letter 16,
' whence comes your new, great hope of the perfecting of our conditions of life ? Is it the French Revolution—this terrible French
evil, so repulsive and at any rate so doubtful in its character ? If
so, how does the hope apply to us in Germany who do not desire
and will never attain a transformation by these methods ? And
tell me what France has gained so far by her revolution, since she
is now engulfed in chaos ? Since improvement in the civilisation
of the race can only be secured by better education, how can it be
expected from a revolution which abolishes the old educational
institutions and has no time to provide better ones, and which gives
rise to scenes of inhumanity, deceit, and disorder, the impressions
of which will perhaps for generations destroy all traces of humanity
in the minds of men ? What effect must this imposture of liberty
and the resultant bloody wars have on peoples and rulers, especially
on the sciences and arts, the organs of humanity ? Finally, is not
the whole conception of a continuous perfecting of the race a
mere dream, a sedative with which we toy ? What is the goal of
perfection ? Have the goodness, my friends, to answer me
these riddles.'

Letter 17 replies to these faint-hearted queries, and we may
take it as expressing the convictions of the writer. ' For myself,
I will not deny that the French Revolution occupies my mind more
than I like. I often wish that I had not lived through these times,
for I cannot confront them in a spirit of naïve and childlike joy.
Yet I am comforted by the thought that we live under a higher
superintendence which knows how to extract good from evil.
Nothing has happened to compare in importance with it since the
birth of Christianity and the *Völkerwanderung*,except the Renaissance
and the Reformation ; and so one has no choice but to reflect and
to weigh its consequences. It is impossible to exclude this mighty
event from the mind and the souls of men. And why should we
Germans wish to exclude it, since the character of the two nations
are as different as their constitutions and fortunes ? If it is true
that Germany has never suffered under these evils, that its governments are as humane as the French government was the reverse,
what German ruler would harbour fear or doubt ? That would be
an insult to a nation which for thousands of years has distinguished
itself by loyalty and, indeed, by almost blind obedience to its rulers.
We can watch the French Revolution as we watch a shipwreck at
sea from the safety of the shore, if our own evil genius does not hurl
us against our wishes into the flood. In an assembly of a thousand
men, many of them exceptional, the whole organisation of the nation

is discussed. These things closely concern every people in Europe, and indeed, in their results, the whole human race. What nation has not had a share in the corruption of France? Every petty ruler has aped Louis XIV, and the nobility have followed his evil example. The Constitution presents a problem without parallel, and, whether its enemies destroy it or not, does it not deserve the attention of all who are not mere animals? Since Providence has placed these events before our eyes, let us take heed that we learn their lesson. So it is lawful for us Germans to watch critically, to adopt what is good, and to reject what is evil. No German need shed a tear over the cleaning of the French throne, when the French after a thousand years determine to give it the washing of which it was sorely in need. That nation has done our country nothing but harm for centuries, and has much to make good. We wish to learn from France, but not to resemble her or to interfere in her concerns.'

Letter 18 deals with problems the solution of which the writer awaits with anxiety, but without undue apprehension. Once again it is clear that the ' Letter ' expresses the author's personal convictions, presented in tabular form.

(i.) What is the best constitution for France?—A constitutional monarchy or a republic—that is, a Commonwealth.

(ii.) Can such a Commonwealth exist in such a complex of territories as France?—I see no reason to the contrary; for the largest kingdoms have lived long, though unhappily, under the worst constitution, despotism, or even oligarchy.

(iii.) Can new France live in harmony with other European States? —Yes.

(iv.) How would France behave in case of opposition, in view of its principle of renouncing conquests?—A war of pure defence against foreign interference would provide the first example of a just and holy struggle. The Émigrés are deserters and traitors.

(v.) How will France divide her legislative, executive, and judicial powers?—No foreign State should interfere in the experiments of a free nation.

(vi.) How will it be with religion?—It is a question whether unbelief or superstition is the worst. We Protestants must not start crusading for the fallen altars, the secularised nunneries, and the perjured priests, or the Pope and the higher French clergy will laugh at us.

(vii.) How will it be with literature?—France will not become a Siberia, a land of monkeys, in two or three years; nor will its language decay. The Revolution will restore the republican and patriotic spirit of Greece and Rome, and with it the conditions of literary achievement will recur.

The same spirit of watchful interest and discriminating sympathy is inculcated in a later Letter (43) on the ' Gallomania of German Courts.' The writer speaks angrily of ' German France or French Germany,' a German body with a French heart ; but, while the nation must avoid becoming a hybrid, it must be ready to learn from France and her great political teachers, Rousseau and Montesquieu. ' Does a scientific investigation lose its value because it is the work of a Frenchman before or during the Revolution ? Does a truth become less true because it is written in French ? Let us follow the example of our great Leibnitz, who took the best from all nations and books. The Kingdom of Humanity is ruled neither by the smiles nor the frowns of Courts.' Though Herder thus boldly protests against the boycott which had succeeded the slavish worship of French models, he is no bloodless cosmopolitan. ' Self-defence the Root of all National Dignity ' is the title of Letter 116. How shall other nations, he cries, respect a people which does not respect itself ? A nation which cannot defend itself soon becomes like defenceless Italy, the object of universal contempt. Only a self-respecting nation which is able to defend itself and possesses a constitution adapted to the times is worthy of the name. Again, a nation which ceases to know and love its language has lost its tongue and brain. Further, a nation which has parted with its religion, or retains nothing but superstition, has lost the palladium of the constitution. ' If Germany is not to become a second Poland, we must foster in every individual the feeling that we are one people, one fatherland, one language.'

These intrepid Letters, full of hope and illusion, were written while Karl August was invading France. In returning them, shortly before Christmas, Knebel, who hated the war, expressed his lively satisfaction. ' Much has greatly delighted me, and I thank you for exposing so many of the sores of our fatherland.' [1] Goethe naturally delivered a very different verdict. ' You ought to thank God,' he wrote from Luxemburg, ' that He has not provided you and your friends with the opportunity of committing follies on a grand scale.' The rebuke was unmerited, for Herder never lost his head. The Letters, èven in their original form, are the work of a philosophic evolutionist, not of a dancing dervish. But Goethe's warnings were less effective than the news from Paris. The death of the King made it impossible for the first ecclesiastical dignitary of the duchy to publish the audacious passage on the cleansing of the French throne ; and his mood changed in a day from hopefulness to disgust. His impulsive wife kept pace with him, and wrote bitterly to Jacobi of the false

[1] *Von und an Herder*, ii. 89.

M

liberty of the Neo-Franks. His wishes, he told Gleim, were with Dumouriez, who, he hoped, would slay the Lernaean serpent and do more to restore tranquillity to France, and peace to Europe, than hostile armies could accomplish in years.[1] Though this hope was also frustrated, he informs Gleim of his conviction that some melody will finally issue from the clashing discords.

Under the altered circumstances the ' Letters ' were drastically revised, and appeared, with many omissions, in the spring of 1793. The essays on the Revolution could no longer be rendered palatable by the fiction that they were written in the early days of the great convulsion, and were quietly dropped. The provocative references to current events are replaced by an academic discussion of books and opinions, and the political manifesto shrinks into a literary causerie. ' Über Deutschland zu politisieren ist verboten,' he wrote bitterly. The programme is still a correspondence between friends on the progress or retrogression of Humanity ; but it is now a mere string of disconnected and somewhat colourless essays.

The most interesting is the sixth, which deals both critically and constructively with the state of Germany. In 1787, on the invitation of the noble Karl Friedrich of Baden, Herder had worked out the plan of a Patriotic Institute or Academy for the cultivation of national feeling, whose meetings should constitute a veritable Parliament, and whose reports should form a ' Year-book of German Nationalism.' The members, who were to be chosen by the princes, would report on their several States, and Herder naturally hoped that he would be the President. He exhorted the peoples and provinces to know each other in their best brains, to unite the forces of enlightenment, and to remove misunderstandings between the different States, ' so that one may belong to Germany wherever one is.' Among the first tasks would be the study of German history, and a crusade against the habitual use of French by the upper classes. ' Local sectarianism will die, for Germany has only one interest—the life and happiness of the whole people.' The project was shipwrecked by the timid provincialism in which the country was enmeshed, and Schlösser bluntly told Karl Friedrich that the different States were too diverse in culture and opinions to combine. The storms of the Revolution revived Herder's interest in the scheme, and strengthened his conviction of its necessity. ' Our fatherland is to be pitied that it has no place of assembly and no organ of expression. Everything is divided, and the division is maintained by religion, dialects, provinces, governments, laws, and customs. The churchyard is the only place of common

[1] *Von und an Herder*, i. 154.

recognition.' But his faith in his countrymen strengthened with their trials. 'The German name, which many now hold so cheap, will one day appear as perhaps the first in Europe.' Though he lacked political instinct, he was by no means deficient in patriotic feeling.

Goethe had watched the adventures of his friend with some apprehension, and he was not over pleased when he was asked to present the first two series of Letters to Karl August in his camp outside the beleaguered fortress of Mainz. He was therefore all the more delighted to find that the wild animal had been tamed. 'Go on with your collections,' he replied, 'and may they always be as beneficent as these.' The Duke's letter of acknowledgment invited Herder's assistance in the endeavour to keep 'French inhumanities' off German soil. If it was a hint, it was given in the most tactful manner. But he was now no longer tempted to return to the tone and temper of the autumn of 1792, for he watched the Terror with growing disgust. He was appalled by the execution of the Queen, and he threatened the French with the vengeance of the King of kings ; but he remained as critical as ever of the efforts of the counter-revolution. 'With Austrian pride confronting French brutality, one can only sigh in secret,' he wrote to a friend. 'In this war no laurels sprout, and no good will come of it.' He laments the folly of the combatants, and longs for peace. 'Goethe has helped to besiege and conquer Mainz,' he wrote to Jacobi. 'Would that all armies and Powers would now return to their dens ! They will not be able to suppress the anarchy in France.' [1] Letter 46, on 'the Madness of Men and Peoples,' attacks nationalist intolerance. 'In our days, we have seen how the words Rights, Liberty, Equality, have thrown an excitable people into confusion.' The world was out of joint, and the need of the time was moderation in thought and action.

Letter 57 propounds the question, 'Have we still the public and the fatherland of the Ancients ? ' The necessary unity, he replies, is lacking. Some people even use the French language. True patriotism is the self-dedication of the individual to the common weal. He pleads for light, a sense of community, a noble pride to be Germans on their own well-defended soil. It is like an anticipation of Arndt ; but he retains the horror of war common to the children of the Aufklärung. 'For fatherland to meet fatherland in bloody strife is the worst barbarism.' His longing for peace becomes a dream of perpetual peace ; the crime of intervention becomes the sin of attempting forcibly to mould the culture of other peoples. He calls standing armies ' this terrible burden of mankind,'

[1] *Aus Herder's Nachlass*, ii. 308.

and pronounces real elevation impossible where wars and conquest preoccupy the mind. Perpetual peace must come not from a federation of Courts and Cabinets, but from the purification of the human heart. The very word ' war ' should be hated like pestilence and famine. There should be less glorification of heroes. Deceitful statecraft should be condemned, and patriotism should be divorced from thoughts of conquest. Kindly feelings should be entertained towards other nations, and no claims for exclusive trade should be made. Such Platonic exhortations lag far behind the virile message of Kant ; but his detestation of war was equal to that of his old master. Though they had long since contrived to quarrel, they fought side by side under the banner of Liberty and Peace.

Herder aged rapidly, and his powers began to flag when he was fifty. ' I am broken and empty,' he wrote to Gleim in 1796. ' I work at Part X of the Letters,' he told his son, ' but with effort. I think I write too much. There is no echo to my voice.' He had, however, no reason to be ashamed of the quality or quantity of his work, and his enlightened ideas place him high among the teachers of Germany. ' When the French Revolution broke out,' wrote Caroline in her life of her husband,[1] ' and still more during the first unsuccessful campaign, certain people accused him of revolutionary principles, because he did not condemn it as passionately as they, and because, like Klopstock and many of the best men, he may at the beginning have harboured expectations which were not to be realised. His son Gottfried, too, was accused of taking part in a fête at Jena, when he was in fact at home. Herder scorned to defend himself against such suspicions ; but they embittered him.' He had not the makings of a revolutionary in him, and no German of his time was more thankful that the great experiment was carried out on the soil of another country. But he had quickly realised that it was the most important tide in the affairs of men since the Reformation, and he welcomed it as a no less decisive step towards freedom. The Reformation had thrown off the yoke of the Papacy, and the Revolution would liberate Europe from feudalism. Fetter after fetter must be struck off till man could unfold all his powers and grow to his full stature. He was as strong in his grasp of the principles of progress as he was weak in the sphere of politics ; and no member of the Weimar circle judged the greatest event of the age with such sanity and insight. He believed that the Revolution had braced the world, unfettered personality, and taught men to lay less stress on birth and station than on merit and character. His deepest convictions were expressed in his address at the confirmation of a prince in 1799. ' You live in times, and you must prepare

[1] *Erinnerungen*, iii. 12.

for times in which, as you yourself recognise, more is demanded of princes, and they are more exposed to blame than in olden days. As in previous ages they were flattered for their supernatural merits, the world is now inclined to overlook their real virtues. They can only vindicate themselves by striking deeds. Arm yourself not with contempt for your fellow men, but with free self-development and joyful many-sided training for your duties.' The gospel of the Revolution, *La carrière ouverte aux talents*, expressed his life-long convictions. Though a man of letters, not a man of action, he realised and taught that the secret of political no less than intellectual progress lay in the ever-widening measure of ordered liberty.

CHAPTER VII

GOETHE

THOUGH Goethe never displayed the slightest interest in political theory, the notion of Gervinus that he deliberately averted his gaze from the pageantry of events and buried himself in art, literature, and science, is without foundation.[1] No citizen of Frankfurt could fail to be vividly aware of the traditions and ceremonial of the Holy Roman Empire ; and during the Seven Years' War the lad followed with growing admiration the heroic struggles of the most famous of German sovereigns. In a well-known passage of his Autobiography he records how the victories of Frederick the Great gave poets an inspiration which they had hitherto lacked, and aroused respect for German prowess throughout the west and south hardly less than in the north. His study of law at Leipsic was followed by a sojourn at Wetzlar, the seat of the Imperial Court of Appeal. On his wanderings he paid close attention to social and economic conditions ; and his acquaintance with experienced administrators, like Karl Friedrich Moser and his brother-in-law Schlösser, enlarged his knowledge of public affairs and prepared him for the reforming activity which awaited him. In the very years when ' Werther ' and ' Götz ' were unfurling the banner of romantic revolt, and the young man was in the first flush of poetic inspiration, he found time to study the ' Patriotic Phantasies ' of Justus Möser. ' I take them with me everywhere,' he wrote at the age of twenty-five to the author's daughter ; ' wherever I open them, they do me good, and hundreds of wishes, hopes, and projects unfold themselves in my soul.' On his first meeting with Karl August, he spoke with such warmth of them and with such enthusiasm of the reformer's task that the young prince realised that the poet might become the counsellor as well as the ornament of the Court of Weimar.

[1] Gervinus, *Geschichte der deutschen Dichtung*, v. 435-49. The best biography is that of Bielschowsky, of which there is an English translation. For the pre-Weimar period, see Hume Brown, *The Youth of Goethe*. The writings, correspondence, and diaries must be studied in the Weimar edition.

When the brilliant Frankfurter settled in the little duchy in 1776, at the age of twenty-seven, he could already look back on years of intoxicating literary success; but for the next decade he subordinated poetical adventure to the prosaic tasks of government.[1] While Schiller fretted under the yoke of an extravagant despot, Goethe was privileged to co-operate with one of the most enlightened princes of the Empire. As the population of the duchy did not exceed 100,000, and the soil was poor, great results could not be expected; but the narrowness of the stage encouraged the actors to a conscientious study of their parts. In spite of the excesses and extravagances of youth which drew rebukes from Klopstock and other elderly friends, the poet and the prince resolved to make their territory a model principality. At this task Goethe laboured with unflagging zeal for ten years, and his master for half a century. On the birth of an heir in 1783, the Duke gave expression to his gratitude. ' Here is a hook on which I can hang my pictures,' he wrote to Merck. ' With the help of Goethe and good fortune, I will paint them in such a way that posterity will perhaps say *Ed egli fu pittore.*' The poet's influence and capacity were universally recognised. To Herder he was ' the Weimar factotum '; to Knebel, ' the backbone of affairs.' Though his more ambitious plans were never realised, he promoted the development of agriculture, industry, and mines, the reform of education and finance, the amelioration of the lot of the poor. But in 1786 the springs of Parnassus burst forth anew with uncontrollable force, and he hurried off to Italy. His public work was practically over; but it left deep traces in his life and thought. All that he had done and all that he had wished to do had been and could be accomplished by the will of a benevolent autocrat; and the elements of any political structure other than paternal government were absent. These impressions and convictions he carried with him to his grave, and they provided the compass by which he steered his course through the tempests of the revolutionary era. He knew too much of the realities of life to be satisfied with things as they were in Germany or anywhere else; but he was unalterably persuaded that reforms must come from above, that change must be gradual, and that order was more precious than liberty.

Goethe was not one of those whom the French Revolution caught unawares. ' As early as 1785,' he wrote long after in the 'Annals' of his life, ' the history of the Diamond Necklace had made an indelible impression on me. Out of the bottomless abyss here disclosed of immorality in city, Court, and State, there emerged, spectre-like, the most horrible apparitions. These long continued to haunt me, and indeed so affected my behaviour that the friends

[1] See the essay ' *Goethe als Staatsmann,*' in Schöll, *Goethe.*

with whom I was living when the news arrived, have confessed to me that I then appeared like one demented.' The figure of Cagliostro haunted him, and on his visit to Palermo in 1787 he sought out the family of the impostor. When the 'apparitions' assumed material form in anarchy and outrage, the first of his attempts to embody the event in dramatic form chose Cagliostro as its text. 'Hardly had I settled afresh into the life of Weimar,' adds the poet, 'than the French Revolution attracted the attention of the world; and I followed the development of the drama with close attention.' With attention indeed, but almost wholly without sympathy. The position reached by Schiller after storms and tribulations was occupied by his great rival from the first. He had long since convinced himself that order is heaven's first law. He was the subject and friend of a model prince. His administrative experience had impressed him with the value of reforms carried out from above. His recent sojourn in Italy strengthened his preference for classical harmony and measure. His scientific pursuits pointed to a gradual evolution governed by law. He had outgrown the fever of romanticism, and had reached the conviction that man must think with his brain, not with his emotions. Intellectual clearness, defined activity, discipline of mind and soul— such was his prescription alike for individuals and nations. *Natura non facit saltum.* His contempt for the political capacity of the masses was revealed in 'Egmont.' Though recognising to the full the justice of the punishment that fell on the monarchy and the privileged classes, he never for a moment expected any benefit to arise from the violent methods of the reformers; while the Declaration of the Rights of Man, which was music to some of his Weimar friends, was to him as meaningless, though not so repugnant, as to Burke.

'That the Revolution in France was also a revolution for me, you can well imagine,' wrote Goethe to Jacobi in March 1790.[1] There are, however, as few references to the early stages of the great drama in his correspondence as in that of Schiller; and he sometimes veiled the depth of his feelings beneath banter and wit. 'He joked a good deal,' wrote Salis-Seewis of a conversation on February 8, 1790, 'and he parodied the tone of the members of the National Assembly.'[2] The first literary expression of his views is to be found in the 'Venetian Epigrams,' written during his visit to Venice in the spring of 1790. In these spirited verses are revealed

---

[1] *Briefe.* ix. 184. The best summaries of his writings on the Revolution are in Dowden's *New Studies in Literature*, and Sir A. Ward's Presidential Address to the English Goethe Society, *Transactions*, vol. xiv.

[2] Goethe's *Gespräche*, ed. Biedermann, i. 173.

the principles, both critical and constructive, to which he was to give repeated utterance during the next decade.

50. I have been ever averse to all the apostles of freedom.
    After all, every one sought only for rule for himself.
    If thou desirest to liberate men, first venture to serve them.
    Is that a perilous task ?   Try, if thou seekest to know !

51. Kings desire the best for their subjects, and demagogues likewise,
    So it is said ; yet they err : they are but human like us.
    Never, we know, can the will of the people find fitting expression :
    Let that man lead the way who can decide for us all.

53. Let our rulers take warning betimes from France's misfortunes ;
    But, men of little degree, you should take warning still more.
    Great men go to destruction ; but who gives the people protection
    When the rough mob becomes tyrant over us all ?

55. Tell us now, are we not acting aright in deceiving the rabble ?
    Only consider what fools, savages, they have turned out !
    All who are victims of brutal deception are stupid and savage.
    Be but yourselves sincere : they will become more humane.

56. Princes so often impress their illustrious features on copper
    That has been scarce silvered o'er : long are the people deceived.
    Dreamers impress the seal of the mind on falsehood and folly :
    Those with no touchstone believe all to be genuine gold.

57. ' Those men are mad,' you remark, when we listen to passionate
       ranters
    Holding forth in the streets and market-places of France.
    I, too, consider them mad ; but fools who are free utter wisdom,
    Whilst the wise man, if enslaved, must remain silent perforce.

58. Long have our great ones conversed in the language of France,
       and accorded
    Scanty respect to the man who could not talk like themselves.
    Now all the mob is delighted to babble the tongue of the French-
       man :
    Mighty ones, be not enraged !   That which you asked for is gained.

Here are the strong, simple outlines of Goethe's unchanging political faith.   Since the masses cannot save themselves, it is the duty and the privilege of their rulers to save them.   To princes and people alike the Revolution brings a solemn warning.   For the prince to do too little and for the people to attempt too much is to court disaster.

The first of the series of plays inspired by the Revolution embodied the story of Cagliostro. ' In my usual way,' he writes in the ' Annals,' ' I transformed the whole event, under the title of " The Grand Cophta," into an opera, for which, perhaps, the subject was better adapted than for a play ; and Reichardt at once composed a good many airs for it.' In 1791 he resumed and recast the work in the form of a five-act drama, which he describes as a comedy. ' Lavater,' remarked the poet to Eckermann long after, ' believed in Cagliostro and his thaumaturgy. When the impostor was unmasked, he maintained that it was somebody else, since the miracle-worker was a holy man.' The sceptical Goethe was of course never deceived ; but he took the trouble to understand how the charlatan obtained his success. ' Cagliostro's pedigree and family history, which I learned in Palermo,' he wrote to Jacobi, ' I shall now reveal, so that no more doubt remains as to this good-for-nothing. I don't know if you have read the extract from his trial which has been printed in Rome. There is scarcely anything one did not know ; but how many people wished not to know ! It is pitiable to see how mankind gape for marvels in order to entrench themselves in their vulgar folly and to keep the rule of reason at arm's length.' [1] Deeply interested in the theme himself, he believed that it would prove of equal interest to his friends. ' Herewith the last two acts of " The Grand Cophta," ' wrote the author to Herder in September 1791. ' That is to be the name of the piece if you approve. If this title does not convey everything, it gives, at any rate, the greater part, and is both novel and romantic.'

The scene opens with a group of cultivated men and women dining in the house of a Count, but in his absence and without his knowledge. They are surprised by the arrival of the master, before whom the doors open of themselves. He orders the company to kneel ' not to me, but to the invisible powers who stand beside me.' Let them make themselves worthy to hasten the arrival and to see the face of the Grand Cophta. ' This great, glorious, and immortal man wanders in eternal youth over the face of the world. India and Egypt are his favourite sojourn. The hungry lion flies before his outstretched arm.' When the company departs, the Count, who is believed to fast for fourteen days, sits down to a good dinner. ' I seem to people a demi-god,' he slyly remarks, ' because I know how to conceal my needs.' In the second act several of the guests meet and exchange impressions. ' He is no common rogue,' says one, ' for there is as much reason as nonsense in his talk ; the purest truth and the greatest lie issue like twins

[1] *Briefe*, ix. 270.

from his lips.' 'One moment I suspect him,' says another, ' and
the next I am bound by the spell of his presence as if in chains.'
In the third act the stage is transformed into an Egyptian temple,
and music and incense fill the air.   In the middle sits a figure in
gorgeous robes, a white veil on his head, surrounded by kneeling
worshippers.   It is the Grand Cophta, whose coming the Count
has announced.   Impatient cries implore the holy one to reveal
himself.   He does so ; and it is the Count himself who stands before
them.   'Yes,' he cries, ' ye blind, ye hard of heart !   For a year
I have been with you, correcting your ignorance and awakening
your intelligence ; and not one of you saw that the man whom you
seek was in your midst, old as the priests of Egypt, wise as the sages
of India, above all human needs, one of a society of men spread over
the earth, for ever occupied in secret well-doing.' ' Is the circle of
these great ones closed ? ' asks a listener, ' or is there room for
others ? '   ' Many might enter, but few can do so, for the difficulties are too great.'   From this point the play incorporates the
world-famous history of the Diamond Necklace, the appearance
of the false Marie Antoinette, and the arrest of the Grand Cophta.

The drama is a powerful study of a corrupt and credulous
society. Cagliostro, the Count, is an impostor in the grand style,
an artist in deception, subtly mingling his appeals to the higher and
lower instincts of his dupes, and exploiting to the full the appetite
for delusion in an age when French society had drifted far from
its moorings. No one can read it and regard Goethe as the apolo-
gist of the *ancien régime*.   In externals it is not a political play ;
but, in dealing with some of the symptoms of the social and moral
decay, it embodies the author's conviction that monarchical France
was sick and in need of a physician.   Goethe always thought well
of this curious work. ' I am glad,' he wrote to Reichardt in 1792,
' that you have not lost your old liking for the " Cophta," and that
you enjoyed the performance in Lauchstädt.   I shall have it
played at least once a year as a symbol.   The other German theatres
will avoid it for more than one reason.   How easy it would be to
make an opera of it !   But where can one look for the courage for
such a task ?   Even if you devoted your energies to it, as with
" Erwin " and " Elmira " and with " Claudine," which are never
played, the political and personal obstacles which stand in the way
would equally apply to the opera, and we should once more have cast
a stone into the stream.' [1]   To the end it gave him pleasure to hear
it praised. ' I spoke of " The Grand Cophta," ' writes Eckermann
in his Diary on February 15, 1831.   I talked over the scenes one by
one and expressed a wish to see it on the stage.'   ' I am pleased,'

[1] *Briefe*, ix. 323.

replied the master, ' that you like that piece. It was no light labour to make a real fact first poetical and then dramatic. Schiller was also very partial to it, and we gave it once with brilliant effect. But it is not for the public in general ; the crimes of which it treats produce an uncomfortable feeling. It was a good subject, for it was not merely of moral but also of great historical significance. The Queen, through being implicated in that unlucky story of the Necklace, was no longer respected, and lost in the eyes of the people the ground where she was unassailable. It was, to a certain extent, the foundation of the French Revolution. Hate injures no one ; it is contempt that drags men down.' [1]

The author's favourable view was not generally shared in Weimar or beyond it. ' Goethe has sent me his " Grand Cophta," ' wrote Georg Forster to Jacobi.[2] ' As it was long since we had read a good book, we tore the pages open. But, oh, what a falling off ! This thing without savour, without a thought one can remember, without a character to interest one, this commonplace dialogue, these sordid pickpockets ! I will say no more.' Next day he wrote to Heyne in similar terms of almost angry vexation. ' Everything is missing which usually delights one in his works : no spark of wit, imagination, or aesthetic feeling. Can even Goethe have outlived himself ? It is a waste of printer's ink and paper.' Equally emphatic was the verdict of Caroline Böhmer, who at the moment was a visitor in Forster's house. Her host, she wrote, received a copy from the author and jumped up from his chair. ' For who would not expect a good thing ? But this trivial treatment, this waste of all the good situations ! Cagliostro appears as the barefaced impostor that he was, and that is perhaps a merit in the work. Goethe is a proud man, who cares nothing for the public and gives what he pleases. In the acting it went better. Tell me if you hear a different verdict.' To another friend she wrote : ' The piece was composed in his sleep. At any rate, his genius was not keeping watch.' [3] Wackenroder found in it ' a lot of good stuff,' but agreed with Tieck that it was below the usual standard of the author of ' Werther.' [4] Karl August, in a lengthy criticism, made proposals how it could be rendered more popular.[5]

When the war against the Revolution broke out, the poet accompanied his master to the front. ' Goethe with the army ! ' wrote

---

[1] Cp. the discussion of the play at the end of *The Campaign in France*.
[2] Forster's *Briefwechsel*, ii. 142–4.
[3] Caroline, *Briefe*, i. 260.
[4] *Briefe an Tieck*, iv. 197, 203.
[5] Karl August's *Briefwechsel mit Goethe*, i. 262–6.

Heyne to Sömmerring. 'What profanation!'[1] The invitation was indeed unexpected and not wholly welcome, for he was deep in the study of optics; but the Grand Duke was anxious for his company, and he promised himself an interesting experience. It was universally expected that the forces of the Coalition would reach Paris without much difficulty or delay; and, though no friend of the Revolution, he was anxious to see at close quarters the stage on which the drama was being played. With the aid of his letters, his diary, and 'The Campaign in France,' we can follow his movements almost from day to day. On his way he wrote half humorously, half ruefully to Jacobi from Frankfurt: 'I am going to the army. After home and bed and kitchen and cellar, life in a tent will indeed be a change, all the more as the death of aristocratic and democratic sinners leaves me absolutely cold.'[2] At Mainz he made his first acquaintance with the Émigrés—among them the Princess of Monaco, 'the pearl of Chantilly in happier days '—and visited Huber and the Forsters and other friends of the Revolution. 'We avoided politics,' he writes, ' as we knew we had to consider each other's feelings. For, while they did not altogether hide their republican opinions, I was on my way to join an army which was intended to put an extinguisher on all such ideas.'

Passing through Trier and Luxemburg, he reached the camp at Longwy on August 27. The weather had broken, and, as he wrote to a friend, everybody was complaining that Jupiter Pluvius had turned Jacobin. In spite of the rain, he found the Duke and the Higher Command in excellent spirits. 'The surrender of Longwy, the first French town, confirmed the assurances of the Émigrés that we should be welcomed everywhere with open arms, and there seemed no obstacle to the great design except the weather. The hatred and contempt of revolutionary France, expressed in the Duke of Brunswick's Manifesto, was universal with the Prussians, Austrians, and Émigrés.' On September 2, after a brief bombardment, Verdun capitulated, and he wrote cheerfully to Christiane: 'The pace is so hot that I shall soon be with you again, and I will bring you something from Paris.' A week later he is in a more chastened spirit. 'It is very interesting to be here where nothing of indifference can take place. To see the ways of war under so great a general, and to learn to know the French nation, affords even an idle spectator plenty of entertainment. What is to happen next, we are all wondering? The business is lengthening out. It is a stupendous enterprise, even with our great resources.' The news of the September massacres, while creating horror, appeared

[1] Forster's *Briefwechsel mit Sömmerring*, p. 596.
[2] The Campaign Letters are in *Briefe*, x. 6–40.

likely to facilitate the invasion. ' You will have heard of the mad events in Paris ; it all grows more and more crazy, so that at last both parties will thank the Powers which restore tranquillity, whatever the price.' His diagnosis was wrong, for French resistance stiffened into invincibility. A week later the battle of Valmy turned the tide. In the morning, he records in a celebrated passage, there was no thought but of annihilating the enemy ; and he shared the prevailing confidence in the army and its commander. In the evening the scene had changed. ' People avoided each other's glances. We could not even light a fire. Most of us were silent, and no one seemed capable of forming or expressing an opinion. After a time some one asked me what I thought, as I had often amused the circle with oracular utterances. On this occasion I remarked, "Here and to-day commences a new epoch of world-history, and you can boast you were present at its birth."'

The retreat began to the accompaniment of torrents of rain. Goethe was in better spirits than most of his companions, for he cared little for the objects of the expedition, and ' beguiled the tedium by my studies in the theory of optics.' However unsuccessful the invasion, it was at any rate a unique experience for a poet. ' In these four weeks,' he wrote to Knebel a few days after Valmy, ' I have learned much. I am glad indeed to have seen everything with my own eyes, and I can say of this historic epoch, *Quorum pars minima fui.*' A few days later he writes from Verdun to Christiane. ' You will know already that we are retreating ; the war is not going as it should. I have borne much, but my health and spirits are excellent.' His letters and diary, however, now begin to be filled with lamentations. ' Of the hindrance from weather and roads no one can form an idea who was not there. In six weeks we have borne and seen more misery and danger than in the rest of our lives. No pen and no tongue can describe the plight of the army. The roads are so bad and the weather so awful that I do not know how the men and carts will get out of France. This campaign will cut a sorry figure in history.' From this chamber of horrors he fled as quickly as possible. ' I hasten back to my fleshpots,' he wrote to the Herders, ' there to awake from a bad dream.' Hurrying eastwards through Trier and Coblenz, he reached a haven of rest under Jacobi's hospitable roof at Düsseldorf. ' I am enjoying the quiet,' he wrote to Christiane, ' while so many thousands, driven from house and home, are wandering about and know not where to go.' To Jacobi's critical glance he plainly bore the traces of his wild war-life.[1]

In addition to recording the experiences and impressions of the

[1] *Goethe's Gespräche*, i. 193.

moment, Goethe published a connected narrative after a lapse
of thirty years. 'The Campaign in France' is in some respects
a supplement to the 'Autobiography'; but it rests to a far greater
degree on contemporary material.[1] The author made use not
only of his own letters and diary, but of the Memoirs of Laukhard
and Massenbach on his own side, and of Dumouriez on the other.
The French General's life, he tells us, was carefully studied, 'in
order to master the epoch of his great deeds down to the smallest
and most secret detail.' The work naturally lacks the freshness
of the letters, but its scope is wider and we find more of the writer's
thought. The narrative is not without errors, and Ranke has
complained that it makes no contribution to history, since the
author was never in the confidence of Brunswick, the King of
Prussia, or the other leaders of the ill-starred enterprise. For
once, however, the Nestor of historians is too severe. 'Rarely
was a book written with greater loyalty to truth,' declares Hermann
Hüffer. 'The conception of conditions and the judgment of
opposing parties reveal a breadth of vision and an impartiality
which arouse admiration even in a book written long after the
events. The more we penetrate into the heart of the time, the
more apparent becomes the value of his observations.' His
authority was indeed confirmed in advance by Brunswick himself,
who expressed to the poet his satisfaction that one more trustworthy witness would testify that the invaders were defeated
by the elements, not by the foe. The atmosphere is rendered
with extraordinary power; and it is a testimony to its importance,
no less than to the writer's skill, that, alone of the narratives of
the Valmy campaign, it has secured a place in literature. The
man, no less than the author, emerges with credit. In theory a
mere onlooker, he bravely courted his baptism of fire, and remained
cheerful amid the horrors and disappointments of the campaign.
But the book shows that to bravery and serenity he added a clearness of vision to which few if any of his companions could lay claim.
The louder colours were deliberately softened after the lapse of
time; but the author was as free from passion when he lived through
his experiences as when he described them a generation later.
There is not a word of hate or recrimination in the letters or the
'Campaign.' He feels that aristocrats and democrats alike have
sinned, and that the French nation is the victim of its rulers, old
and new. His heart is filled with compassion for the victims
of war, for civilian sufferers as well as combatants. He was
constitutionally unfitted to fathom the heights and depths of the

---

[1] See Hüffer, *Zu Goethe's Campagne in Frankreich, Goethe-Jahrbuch*,
vol. iv.; and Chuquet, *Études de littérature Allemande*, vol. ii.

Revolution ; but he never shared the Émigré delusion that it was nothing but the outpouring of human wickedness or that it could be suppressed by the arm of flesh alone.   He returned home with a shuddering horror of war, more convinced than ever that wars and revolutions were not worth their price and that the highest duty of rulers was to render them unnecessary.   He never forgot these weeks of storm and stress, and constantly recurred to them in conversation.   ' It is very interesting,' wrote Böttiger in 1794, ' to hear him relate his adventures in the campaign.' [1]   His critical attitude had impressed his companions.   ' I spent many evenings with him during the campaign,' writes an *émigré* Marquis, ' though we did not always agree.   He seemed in politics, and even more in religion, to belong to the freethinkers.'   The same friend visited him later in Weimar.   ' We talked at length of the campaign,' he records.   ' In his political sentiments he seems to have improved, and he enunciated very conservative principles.' [2]

On his way home from the front, Goethe read to Jacobi and his friends at Düsseldorf the opening of a philosophic fable on the Revolution, in the style of Voltaire, of the origin of which we know nothing more than he tells us in 'The Campaign in France,' and which was not published till a century later.   ' I had begun a curious work in order to seek distraction from the monster.   It described a journey of six brothers, each serving the little group in his own way—a fairy-tale of adventure, half concealing its intention, a parable of our own condition.   I was asked to read it ; but I soon saw that nobody was edified, and I therefore left my family of wanderers in a harbour and proceeded no farther.'   Pantagruel's descendants, the six sons of Megaprazon, set sail for the islands discovered or described by their ancestors.   On landing in Papimany, the brothers learn of strange events in the neighbouring Monarchomany (France), one of the most renowned and beautiful islands of the archipelago.   The palaces of the King and the aristocracy were superb, the country fruitful, the peasantry industrious ; but an old law forbade the tillers of the field ever to satisfy their hunger.   The King could do,or thought he could do,what he pleased. This favoured spot, however, was subject to earth tremors, and contained boiling springs, while the lively character of the people matched the volcanic qualities of the soil.   In recent years earthquakes had been frequent,especially where the fields of the peasantry adjoined the heights occupied by the King and the nobles.   One night a great eruption took place—' we saw it all from our island' —the sky was aflame, the sea was disturbed.   Next morning the island had disappeared, split into three parts, each of which drifted

[1] *Gespräche*, i. 201.   [2] *Ib.*, i. 193.

over the ocean like a rudderless ship. The rocky promontory with the royal palace perched on its heights sailed away in one direction, and sailors brought word that another part, covered with stately dwellings, had been seen afar off. No one could tell what had become of the main body of the island.

To the picture of France in the throes of revolution the author adds a description of the effects of the upheaval on dwellers in other lands. During the voyage the brothers begin to quarrel violently about the story of a war between cranes and pygmies. When the altercation is at its height, a voice hails them from a passing boat, and the brothers ask its captain to act as arbiter. He replies, ' To-morrow,' and gives them medicine in the form of wine to calm their rage. Next day they are themselves again. ' Were we ill ? ' asks one of them. ' You have got it badly,' is the reply ; ' I found you in a violent crisis.' ' What sort of an illness was it ? ' ' It is the fever of the period—some call it the fever of the periodical.[1] It is a horrid, contagious disease which spreads itself through the air. I wager you caught it last night in the atmosphere of the floating islands.' ' What are its symptoms ? ' asks Alciphron. ' Melancholy. And, curiously enough, a man straightway becomes oblivious of his immediate surroundings and blind to his clearest interests, and sacrifices everything to an opinion which becomes his master passion. If no one hastens to his aid, the conviction fixes itself in his mind and becomes the axis on which the madness revolves. He then forgets the business which benefits those belonging to him and the State, and he sees father and mother, brothers and sisters no more.' It is a sombre little study of confusion and delusion ; but here, as elsewhere, the poet contrives to suggest that the Revolution was not without its cause. It is a pointed thrust that the peasantry were prevented by law from the full satisfaction of their hunger. On the other hand, the hit at newspaper fever was doubtless suggested by and intended for some of his Weimar friends.

The closing scenes of the tragedy of Louis XVI filled Goethe with sorrow and anger. ' Who was there who had not from childhood shuddered at the execution of Charles I,' he wrote in ' The Campaign in France,' ' and comforted himself with the hope that such scenes would never recur ? And now it was all repeated in a still more cruel form by the most civilised of nations as if before our eyes—day by day, step by step. Imagine the feelings throughout December and January of those who had marched forth to rescue the King and now were impotent to intervene in the trial

[1] *Zeitfieber, Zeitungsfieber.* I owe this rendering of the play on words to Mr. Bailey Saunders.

N

or to prevent the execution of the sentence ! It would be difficult to imagine any one at a distance from the scene of the tragedy more depressed. The world appeared to me bloodier and more bloodthirsty than before; and if the death of a King in battle counts like a thousand, it is of far greater significance in a constitutional struggle.'

In the spring following the campaign a sudden inspiration seized Goethe, and he threw off his brilliant little one-act play, ' The Citizen-General.' ' I hope you will like it,' he wrote to the Herders. ' Small pieces have the advantage that they are composed almost as rapidly as they are planned. It was scarcely three days from the moment of its conception to its completion. I hope I shall not regret yielding to my whim, either aesthetically or politically.' Further information was provided many years later in the ' Annals.' ' An active, productive mind, a patriotic man cultivating the literature of his country, may be excused if he feels alarmed at the overthrow of the established order, while lacking the expectation of anything better to take its place. Sympathy will not be denied to him if he laments that crazy and ignoble persons should seize the helm.'

The play is a light satire on the seduction of the quiet German peasantry. The French were on the Rhine, and fears were widely entertained lest incendiaries should set the whole country-side ablaze. George and Rose are a newly-married couple, happy and contented in their tranquil activity. Old Martin, Rose's father, has caught the Jacobin fever, pores over the papers and thrills to the news from France. His daughter and son-in-law care for nothing but their little holding, the landlord of which is a kindly nobleman. Schnaps, the clever villain of the piece, determines to play a trick on Martin, and brings him the uniform of a French prisoner, with a red cap and a tricolour cockade. He informs him that he has received a commission as Citizen-General for the French Republic. The Jacobin Club has heard of his liberal views and sent an envoy— witness the sword, cap, cockade, and moustaches which every such official must wear. The German Revolution, he adds, must begin at once and in that village. Schnaps then explains French principles, and proceeds to illustrate them by removing some eatables from the cupboard. He is soon discomfited and arrested, and the judge proceeds ponderously to unravel the threads of what he believes to be a formidable plot. At this moment the landlord appears, and is assailed with a volley of explanations and appeals from the judge and his incriminated tenants. He sees in a moment that the mischief has not gone far ; and the play concludes with a homily which voices the political philosophy of the author. ' My children,' he says to Rose and George, ' love each other and look after your land and household.' Old Martin is advised to allow foreign countries to settle their own affairs. ' Let every one begin with himself, and he will find plenty to do. Let him employ the peaceful time that is granted us ; let him honourably seek the advantage of himself and those dependent on him, and he will thus contribute to the general welfare.' The judge breaks in with a plea for punishment, only to receive an admonition in his turn. ' Not too fast ! Vindictive penalties only breed trouble. In a land where the prince is accessible to all, where all classes live in harmony, where no one is hindered in his activity, where useful knowledge is universal, there will be no parties. The drama of the world will attract attention, but seditious opinions will find no entry. Let us be thankful to have the blue sky over our heads at a time when too many fields are ravaged by hailstones. It means something that we can laugh at the cockade and the cap and the uniform which have brought so much evil on the world.'

The landlord's philosophy sounds a little naïve ; and it would ring hollow in the absence of those conditions of relative prosperity and kindly government which the author copies from the model Duchy of Weimar into his pages. But the merry little farce, beneath its light setting, contains the major part of his political creed. While not maintaining that revolutions are always avoidable, he suggests that wise rulers and tactful landlords can render them unnecessary, and that the most effective contribution to the common weal is the fulfilment of the duty that lies to hand. Of course Schnaps is nothing but a caricature of the missionaries, whether French or German, who spread the Gospel of the Rights of Man ; and in other works Goethe has shown that he realised at least something of the appeal of the principles of 1789. He set out to write a comedy, to catch a single aspect of the tempest which was shaking the earth to its foundations. Indeed, he confesses that its construction was largely determined by an accident.[1] 'A player named Beck had just entered our company at Weimar, and I wrote the part of Schnaps in reliance on his talent and humour.' The piece was played more than once ; but the news from France was becoming too grave for the appreciation of political comedy. ' The prototypes of the characters were too dreadful for their reflection not to excite anxiety.' The play was none the less the most successful of his efforts to portray the Revolution on the stage.

The comedy met with a varying response among its readers. ' Your praise,' wrote the author gratefully to Jacobi, ' is worth much to me. Though I am an old hand, I am not always aware

[1] In the *Annals* and in *The Campaign in France*.

what I am doing, and this time it was a particularly risky under-taking. It acts well.' Herder's judgment was also favourable. On the other hand, Prince August of Gotha, to whom the author had sent a copy, conveyed his displeasure in the form of rather ponderous banter. ' In the doubtful ending (for I do not gather whether Schnaps has acted simply from his own whim or at the instigation of the Jacobins), I seem to recognise the hand of Kant. I find much resemblance to the merry humour which runs through the " Critique of Pure Reason." It is not impossible, too, that Schnaps, seduced by the misconceived principles of liberty and equality, should become a thief ; for even among well-educated aristocrats, I find many who form ideas of the equality of rights like the fish-wives of Paris.' The author himself always retained his affection for the sparkling creation of his fancy. One day in 1828 Eckermann remarked that he had been reading the piece with an Englishman, and that both had felt the strongest desire to see it on the stage. ' It was a very good piece in its time,' replied Goethe, ' and gave us many a pleasant evening. It was excellently cast, and had been so admirably studied that the dialogue tripped along as glibly as possible. Martin was perfectly played.' ' The part of Schnaps,' continued Eckermann, ' seems to me no less felicitous. The scene where he enters with the knapsack and produces the things one after another, where he puts the moustache on Martin, and decks himself with the cap of liberty, uniform, and sword, is among the best.' ' That scene,' rejoined Goethe, ' used always to be very successful on our stage. The knapsack and the articles in it had an historical existence. I found it on my travels along the French border when the Émigrés had passed through, and one of them might have lost it or thrown it away. The articles it contained were just the same as in the piece. I composed the scene upon it, and the knapsack with all its appurtenances was always introduced, to the great delight of our actors.'

Shortly after completing his comedy, Goethe unwillingly emerged once more from his sheltered home at the bidding of the Duke to witness the wild surge of war. Custine had seized Mainz at the same moment that Brunswick's army was thrown back from France, and had held it throughout the winter. But his forces were small, and after six months the French garrison found itself besieged. The poet and his mother watched with delight the flowing tide of 1793 which followed the disaster of 1792. ' We cannot thank God enough that we have been delivered in good time from the Liberty fellows,' wrote Frau Rat. ' If only we never saw them again !'[1]

---

[1] Her letters to her son are published in vol. iv. of the *Schriften der Goethe-Gesellschaft.*

'How I congratulate you and all my friends and relatives on the removal of the crazy Franks,' wrote the poet to Jacobi, 'you can well guess.' The expulsion of the invader appealed to him far more than Brunswick's abortive crusade. Once again we can follow his adventures and reconstruct his ideas with the aid of letters and of the narrative which he compiled from his notes and recollections in later years.[1] 'The Theory of Colours again accompanied me to the Rhine,' he writes in the 'Annals.' 'I held fast to these studies as to a plank in a shipwreck, having for two years experienced the disruption of all ties.' 'Here I am again in camp,' he wrote on May 29 to Christiane, 'and it looks more hopeful this time.' Jupiter Pluvius was no longer a Jacobin, the operations were taking place on German soil, and the hardships were mainly on the side of the beleaguered garrison. But the horrors of war, though on a smaller scale, awoke the old compassion for the combatants on both sides and for the civilians whose sufferings were often scarcely less poignant. 'Every heart was burdened with sadness,' he wrote in 'The Siege of Mainz.' 'Every moment one was filled with anxiety for the Duke and one's dearest friends, and one forgot to think of one's own safety. As if enchanted by the threatened confusion, one rushed to the danger-points and let the cannon-balls fly over one's head and burst by one's side. For the gravely wounded one wished speedy release; and the dead one had no wish to recall to life.' 'My friends can be thankful,' he wrote to Voigt, 'not to witness the misery in this part of the world and in unhappy Mainz.' After the fall of the city, he reported that the sufferings of the citizens had been indescribable; but on the same day he informed Jacobi that the closing scenes of the siege and the capitulation were among the most interesting of his life.

Once again there is no trace of bitterness against the French, and his rebukes are reserved for the Clubists or German Republicans. 'The mischief they have done is great. That they are now deserted by the French serves them right, and may teach a lesson to unquiet folk.' He watched the French march out of the city, singing the Marseillaise. 'It was a poignant spectacle as the cavalry rode past—tall, thin men, no longer young. Individually they looked like Don Quixote, but in the mass they appeared extremely impressive.' When the crowd rushed at a Clubist, Merlin de Thionville, who was riding beside him, appealed to his dignity as one of the French political commissioners, threatened revenge for

[1] The Letters are in *Briefe*, x. 60–101. See Pollak, '*Zur Belagerung von Mainz*,' in *Goethe-Jahrbuch*, vol. xix., for a discussion of the published narrative.

any insult, and advised the mob to control itself, for it was not the last time they would see him there. ' The crowd stood silent, and not a man advanced.' The prophecy was correct, for next year the French were back again. Goethe explored the city, which he found in a terrible condition. ' What centuries had constructed was now in ruins and ashes.' He watched with shame and indignation the attacks on the Clubists, the sack of their houses, and the pillaging of shops. ' How hard it is,' he sighs, ' to recall an excited mob to tranquillity.' He carried away from his second and last campaign an intensified and life-long loathing of war, and an even stronger conviction that the hope of mankind lay in orderly development and the loyal performance of common duties. ' My vagrant life and the political atmosphere,' he wrote to Jacobi from Frankfurt, ' drive me home, where I can draw around me a cordon through which nothing can pass but love and friendship, art and science. But I will not complain, for I have learned much that is interesting and useful.' ' Aesthetic pleasures keep me going,' he announced in the autumn from the safe anchorage of Weimar, ' while almost every one else is suffering from the political disease.' [1]

On his return home from the capture of Mainz Goethe proceeded to sketch a new play on the Revolution, first named ' The Signs of the Times,' and finally ' Die Aufgeregten,' which may be rendered ' Agitators and Agitated.' [2] The subject was once again the effect of seditious propaganda on the ignorant masses ; but while the ' Civilian-General ' skated lightly over thin ice, and contrasted the coarse greed of the innovators with the idyllic content of the country-side, its successor dealt in a serious and comprehensive spirit with the causes as well as with the results of agitation. The play, though unfinished, embodies the most complete dramatic statement of the author's political creed. The scene is laid in a village, the inhabitants of which have been grievously wronged by a deceased lord and by the fraud of a steward. The grandfather of the youthful Count had generously remitted some feudal burdens ; but the emancipating document had disappeared. The existing copy possessed no legal force, and only reminded the villagers of the loss of their privileges. The son of the benefactor, a hard and selfish man, had exacted the old dues, and his widow, fearing to compromise the rights of her son, made no alteration, though her kindly heart prompted her to concessions. At this point the outbreak of the French Revolution brings the smouldering discontent of the villagers to a head. Breme, the village doctor, spends long evenings at the pastor's house reading the news from

[1] *Briefe*, x. 105, 128.   [2] Printed in vol. xviii. of the Weimar edition.

Paris, arguing the rights of man, and forming plans for asserting the claims of the peasantry. 'Whether the French Revolution bodes good or ill, I cannot say,' muses his niece, as she sits at home waiting up for him ; 'all I know is that it has helped me to make several extra pairs of stockings this winter.' The tutor of the young Count forms one of the reading circle, and the lad has to sit with him until he drops off to sleep with weariness. One night he falls and hurts himself, an accident which Breme regrets as threatening the success of his plot to demand by show of force the restoration of the village rights. 'If we are discovered,' he cries, 'the greatest and loftiest conception, which may influence the entire Fatherland, will be stifled at birth. For to-day things are possible which ten years ago were impossible.'

The second act opens with the return of the Countess from Paris, where she has watched the early scenes of the Revolution with discriminating sympathy. She renews her refrain that if it were her estate she would make generous concessions ; and indeed her experiences in France have made her more, not less, resolved to take action. She is equally aware of the strength of the new claims and of the human weaknesses of their champions. 'So many people side with liberty and equality,' remarks Luise, Breme's niece, who looks after the young Count, 'only because they want to make an exception for themselves.' 'True enough,' rejoins the Countess ; 'you could not have learned more had you been with me in Paris.' But when the Baron remarks that the country is disturbed, she quickly replies : 'That is nothing if we only treat the people wisely and show them their true interests.' Thus at the very moment when the villagers are preparing to obtain their rights by force the Countess is resolving to do justice by her own free will—a course of action which her large-hearted Councillor thoroughly approves. From this point we only possess the outlines of the play, with a few scenes worked out in detail. The revolt begins with the assembly of Breme's ragged regiment ; but tragedy is averted by the resolution of the Countess's daughter Friederike. The self-willed and masculine girl had always declared that discontented peasants must be shot down, and when the crisis arrives she is for resistance ; but her native goodness of heart quickly asserts itself, and at the point of the gun she compels the villain who possesses the secret to produce the missing document from its hiding-place. The play ends harmoniously, and the wilder passions of the time find no place in its scheme. The Countess and her Councillor are people of kindly and moderate temper, while Breme, the organiser of the revolt, is rather a talker than a man of action, and has no desire to proceed to extremities.

The rustics are as usual depicted with good hearts and no brains; but they are balanced by the Baron, an irresponsible pleasure-seeker. It is regrettable that the play was never completed; for even in its fragmentary state it is of considerable interest. Gervinus's complaint that all the prizes are awarded to the aristocrats is without justification. It breathes the spirit of balancing conservatism which separated Goethe as much from the Émigrés as from the Jacobins. A foul wrong has been committed against the village; and the peasants, for whom the poet always entertained the kindliest feelings, have abundant cause for discontent. The moral is drawn that abuses should be corrected without waiting for an explosion.

In conversation in 1824 the author explained the purpose of the play. ' Do you know my "Aufgeregten"? ' he asked. ' Yesterday, for the first time,' returned Eckermann, ' I read the piece in the new edition of your works, and I regret from my heart that it remains unfinished. Even as it is, every right-thinking person must agree with your sentiments.' ' I wrote it during the French Revolution,' continued Goethe, ' and it may be regarded in some measure as my political confession of faith at that time. I have taken the Countess as a type of the nobility, and with the words I have put into her mouth, I have expressed how the nobility ought to think. She has just returned from Paris. She has convinced herself that the people may be ruled, but not oppressed; and that the revolutionary outbreaks of the lower classes are the consequence of the injustice of the higher classes. " For the future," says she, " I will strenuously avoid every action that appears to me unjust, both in society and at Court, and I will loudly express my opinion concerning such actions in others. In no case of injustice will I be silent, even though I should be shouted down as a democrat." I should have thought this sentiment perfectly respectable. It was mine at that time, and it is so still; but, as a reward for it, I was endowed with all sorts of names which I do not care to repeat. What I have suffered on account of politics, I cannot tell you.' ' One need only read " Egmont," ' rejoined Eckermann, ' to discover what you think. I know no German piece in which the freedom of the people is advocated more strongly.'

Leaving his drama of peasant rights uncompleted, Goethe proceeded to another sketch of the revolutionary world; but of the ' Maiden of Oberkirch,' ' a tragedy in five acts,' only two scenes were composed.[1] Marie, the heroine, has long been in the service of a noble family in Strassburg, all the members of which, except

[1] It was discovered by Erich Schmidt among the papers of August Goethe. See his *Charakteristiken, Zweite Reihe*, pp. 167–76.

the Countess and her nephew, Baron Karl, have fled before the
driving storm. The Baron tells his aunt that he wishes to marry
her maid, adding that in existing circumstances he thinks such a
connection as desirable as was formerly an alliance with a great
and wealthy family. His plan is opposed by the parson, a friend
of the family, who warns him that the match will not free him from
suspicion and will render his wife suspect. ' The terrible Jacobins
are not to be deceived ; for they track down every honourable man
and thirst for his blood.' The Baron consents to postpone a final
decision ; but, meanwhile, Marie's beauty has attracted the Jacobin
rulers of the city, who command her to represent the Goddess of
Reason in the cathedral. To save her noble employers, she submits ;
but during the ceremony her self-control gives way, she protests
against the blasphemous ritual, and hurls herself and the
family into destruction. Though the Jacobins are painted in the
darkest colours, Goethe takes care, even in the few pages which he
completed, to remind his readers of the other side ; for the play
opens with the reading, by the Countess, of letters from her sons
and daughters who have fled from ' this land of horrors,' but who
bewail the insolence of the Émigrés on the Rhine.

' I presumed to hope,' we read in the ' Annals ' for 1794, ' that
this year, in compensation for the many privations I had recently
suffered, would divert my thoughts by manifold activity. For to
have been an eyewitness of revolutions threatening the peace of
the world, to have seen with my own eyes the greatest misfortunes
that can befall citizens, peasants, and soldiers, clouded my mind
with sadness. Yet how was relief possible when every day the
monstrous tumults in France alarmed and menaced us ? Robespierre's deeds had terrified the world, and all sense of happiness
had been so utterly extinguished that no one presumed to rejoice
over his destruction, least of all while the horrors of war were in
full blast. French revolutionary songs floated about in secret,
reaching us by the hand of persons one would not have suspected
of such conduct. News of fugitives from all quarters flowed in.
There was not a family, not a circle of friends, which had not suffered.
From the south and west money and valuables were sent to me
for safe custody. Several times I offered my mother a quiet
residence with me ; but she had no fear at Frankfurt, finding
comforting passages in the Psalms and Prophets.'

His disgust with the times led him to refashion the old beast-
epic, Reinecke Fuchs, which, though written as a satire on Courts
and courtiers centuries before, was as topical as ever. The fierce
onslaught against the perennial follies and baseness of mankind
was in keeping with the sombre feelings which oppressed him. ' I

sought hereby,' he wrote in ' The Campaign in France,' ' to escape
from the horrible panorama.   As I had hitherto occupied myself
ad nauseam with revolts of the mob, it was a real pleasure to hold
up the mirror to Courts and rulers.'   The fable was retold in spirited
hexameters, in which the cunning of the fox and the imbecility of
his dupes and victims lose nothing of their point.   It was a relief
to him to hold the mirror up to human animalism and to show what
thin partitions divided man from beast.   ' Here comes Reinecke
Fuchs, the rascal,' he wrote to Charlotte von Kalb, ' and expects
a warm welcome.   As the tribe is much admired in our time at
Courts, and even more in republics, and is indeed indispensable
there, nothing can be more suitable than to become familiar
with his ancestors.' [1]   The arresting modernity of the poem is
neatly expressed in one of the ' Xenien.'

Say you indeed that a poet sang thus in long distant ages ?
How can that be ?   For my tale deals with the themes of to-day.

The epic tells its tale and points its moral without ambiguity ; but
Goethe could not resist the temptation of interpolating a few lines
of his own in the middle of the story.

Yet I consider the worst is the arrogance of the delusion
That has seized hold of mankind, that the world can be ruled and
     adjusted
By every man who is drunk with the violence of his desires.
Would that every man kept his wife and children in order,
Knew how to manage refractory menials, sagely adopted
Frugal habits of living, whilst idiots squander their substance.
But in what way shall the world become better when every one follows
All his desires and strives to overcome others by violence ?
Thus we sink ever deeper and deeper into the mire.[2]

The Revolution obsessed Goethe to such an extent that he
seemed unable to write without direct or indirect reference to it.
In the winter of 1794 he amused himself with a new ' Heptameron,'
the French armies playing the part which in the days of Boccaccio
had been taken by the plague.   The stories are among the flimsiest
of his productions ; but the *mise-en-scène* is not without political
interest.   ' In those unhappy days fraught with the saddest consequences for Germany, for Europe, and indeed for the whole world,
when the army of the Franks broke through an ill-defended gap
into our Fatherland, a noble family left its possessions and fled
across the Rhine.'   Among the refugees and the friends by whom

they are welcomed are the contrasted types which the poet loves to
present to his readers.   The old world is represented by a Privy
Councillor of the principality in which they have sought shelter.
' His prince, the land, he himself, had all suffered greatly from the
invasion.   He had learned to know the licence of the nation which
spoke only of Law, and felt the tyranny of men who had always
the cry of Liberty on their lips.   He had seen that in this case also
the multitude remained true to itself, swallowing words for deeds
and the shadow for the substance.'   The new era is embodied in
Karl, a disinterested enthusiast, who looked to the innovations for
the healing and rejuvenescence of the old, sick world.   Though
his estates are in the hands of the enemy, he cannot hate the nation
whose principles he approves and whose generous assurances to
the nations he trusts.   The Privy Councillor scoffs at the credulity
of the young man, while Karl sharply censures the timidity of the
slave of precedent.   The siege of Mainz leads to a passionate altercation, and the merits and fate of the Clubists are sharply canvassed.
' How blind they must be,' exclaims the Privy Councillor, ' if they
imagine that a great nation, which at present is in convulsions and
at ordinary times reserves its admiration for itself, should feel real
sympathy with them ! '   They are regarded as tools, and will be
thrown away when they have served their purpose.   It is a delusion
to believe that they will ever be taken by France to her bosom.
' And do you really believe that the great nation, after all its
successes, will be less proud and insolent than a kingly conqueror ?
When the town surrenders, they will no doubt be left or handed over
to us ; and may they then receive the punishment they deserve ! '
At this point Karl breaks in with a chivalrous defence of the courage,
the insight, and the idealism of the Clubists.   ' Who can deny that
among their numbers are able and right-minded men, and who can
fail to pity them as the moment approaches which will shatter their
hopes perhaps for ever ? '   When the Privy Councillor taunts Karl
with the danger to children who play with fire, the young man loses
his self-control.   He cries out that he wishes success to the French
arms, and summons every German to make an end of the old slavery.
He is convinced that France will respect the noble Germans who
declare for her and treat them as her own children.   ' Nothing of
the sort,' rejoins the Privy Councillor ; ' they will fall into the
hands of the Allies, and I hope to see them all hanged.'   ' And I
hope,' bellows Karl, ' that the guillotine will reap a rich harvest in
Germany and that no guilty head will be spared.'   The Privy
Councillor hurries away in disgust, and the distressing scene leads
to the banishment of political topics from the circle of friends.   The
conversation was typical of many which were held at this time on

both banks of the Rhine, and Goethe was beyond doubt drawing on his own unwelcome experiences.[1]

Though tolerant and kindly by nature, the poet's nerves were set on edge by a good deal of the talk to which he was compelled to listen. ' It is very difficult,' he wrote in 1794, ' living with one's fellows just now, especially with some of one's friends. The Coadjutor (Dalberg) tells me that the Clubists become intolerably offensive directly the French armies score a success ; and I must confess that some of my own friends are now behaving in a way that borders on insanity.'[2]   Among the reasons for which at this moment he welcomed Schiller into his life was the loss of old acquaintances. ' I am forming pleasant relations with Schiller,' he reported in August, ' at a time when politics and party spirit threaten to dissolve all friendly fellowship.'[3]   Many years later, in the ' Annals,' he recorded his gratitude in the famous words : ' For me it was a new spring, in which everything secreted in my nature burst into joyous life.' In both men the old instinct of poetic composition revived, and the first-fruits of their co-operation was the series of ' Xenien,' compared by the authors to foxes sent into the land of the Philistines with burning tails to destroy the harvest of its inhabitants. It was their wish that the winged words should be regarded as their joint work, and it is seldom certain from which bow the arrow has sped. ' The Germans cannot cease to be Philistines,' complained Goethe to Eckermann in 1828. ' They are now squabbling about some verses which are printed both in Schiller's works and mine. Friends, such as Schiller and I, intimate for years, with the same interests, in habits of daily intercourse, lived so completely in one another that it is hardly possible to decide to whom the particular thoughts belong. We made many couplets together. Sometimes I gave the thought and Schiller made the verse, and sometimes the contrary was the case ; sometimes he made one line and I the other. What matters mine and thine ? ' The great Twin Brethren, secure in their friendship and their genius, and agreeing closely on most subjects of the day, declared war on their critics and enemies and denounced the purveyors of false doctrines. Only a selection was published in 1796, and it was not till 1893 that the complete harvest was garnered.[4]

The main themes of the ' Xenien,' the German Dunciad, are

---

[1] Closely allied to the *Conversations* is the symbolic story entitled *Mährchen* ; but its meaning is too obscure to attempt a definite political interpretation.

[2] *Briefe*, x. 174.   [3] *Ib.*, x. 186.

[4] The only complete edition is in vol. viii. of the *Schriften der Goethe-Gesellschaft.*

literary and political. If nothing is added to our knowledge of
the poets' political doctrines, we find at least new evidence of the
current of their feelings and the intensity of their dislikes.   Among
German democrats they single out for bitter attack Goethe's friend
Reichardt, the composer, and Cramer, the professor expelled from
Kiel.   When they have been pierced by a sheaf of arrows the storm
abates, and we are once more in the company of Olympian Jove,
and listen to the measured tones of the experienced observer of
life.   The masses, he teaches, possess many virtues, but not the
wisdom needed for rule.

Blind men can feel, as we know, and the sight of the deaf becomes
   keener.
Where is the organ by which crowds can philosophise too ?   (777)

Where is humanity's Majesty ?   Tell me, where shall I seek thee ?
Surely not in the mass ?   No, we must look to the few.   (91)

Wilt thou be free, my son ?   Live frugally, learn something honest,
And never raise thine eyes up to the topmost place.   (64)

Knowest thou how even small men gain worth ?   By doing the small
   things
Thoroughly.   Thus do the great ever accomplish great feats.   (67)

Freedom is truly a glorious ornament, fairest of jewels.
Nevertheless it is not suited to all, as we know.   (678)

Let constitutional rule be established.   How much to be wished for !
Only you babblers do not help us to gain such a prize.   (62)

   But Goethe is as ready as ever to trim the balance, and as little
tempted to burn incense before the throne.

Who is truly a Prince ?   The riddle is easy to answer.
He alone is a Prince who has the gifts for his task.   (69)

Who are the worthiest members of Government ?   Trustworthy
   citizens ;
And in an autocrat's land they are the pillars of State.   (68)

Thou art both King and Knight, and thou canst ordain and give
   battle ;
But if a contract be made, summon your Chancellor too.   (77)

Man of the world, you will err if you think that people are rascals.
Dreamer, you too are deceived if you consider them good.   (88)

Take it for granted that men in the mass desire the right things ;
But when you deal with each case, certain you never can be.   (87)

And here is a protest alike against paternal government and democratic zeal.

That constitution alone is good by which each is assisted
Rightly to think, yet is not ever compelled so to think.   (86)

He rebukes alike those who hope too much and too little.

Vain is your hope, ye Germans, of ever becoming a nation,
Seek ye a different task.   Learn to develop yourselves.   (787)

Yet this inner growth is hindered, not fostered, by the greatest event of the age.

That which the Lutherans did, to-day is done by the Frenchmen.
In such terrible times tranquil culture recedes.   (785)

It is the most celebrated couplet in the ' Xenien,' and embodies the poet's unchanging conviction.

The progress of French arms and the extension of the war to Italy filled Goethe with apprehension and sorrow. ' Into what misery has that beautiful land fallen,' he wrote to his Swiss friend Meyer in 1796. Once again he longs to wing his flight to the south. ' Anxiety and fear, partisanship and *Schadenfreude* are destroying almost the last trace of independence and sociability. I would give much at this moment to be with you.' [1] He was anxious about his mother at Frankfurt, and was thankful that Weimar at least was at a distance from the storm-centre. ' The French tempest,' he wrote to Schiller, ' is reaching the Thuringian forest. In future we will venerate the hills, which usually send us cold winds, as a goddess if they break the storm.' [2] Germany, he declared, was in for a strange Revolution ; and he gives vent to a characteristic aphorism. ' Let us stick to our own ways. The Universe does not trouble itself about us ; why should we trouble ourselves more than is fitting about the Universe ? ' No one in Germany more strongly approved the Peace of Basle, by which Prussia and the North retired from the war. ' We have all cause,' he wrote to Karl August, ' to be thankful to him (i.e. Karl August) who gave us neutrality at the right moment ; for there is no question that the French could and would ravage us as they ravaged the districts of the Rhine and the Main, or even worse.' [3]

[1] *Briefe*, xi. 87–9, 130.   [2] *Ib.*, xi. 144.   [3] *Ib.*, xii. 137.

Having recovered his poetic inspiration, the poet turned from the controversial fireworks of the ' Xenien ' to the production of the most exquisite of his works. ' Hermann and Dorothea,' he writes in the ' Annals,' ' kept pace step by step with the events of the day ; and the poem was written with a sense of ease and inward comfort. The subject possessed me to such a degree that I have never been able to read it without emotion.' While the framework was suggested by a narrative of the wholesale expulsion of Lutherans from the ecclesiastical principality of Salzburg in 1732, the background was altered from religion to politics ; and his own experiences of war gave point and poignancy to his picture of the sufferings of the refugees flying before the armies of Republican France. His most competent biographer has contended that ' Hermann and Dorothea ' is not to be classed as a political poem ; but we may confidently assert that it would not have been written without the stimulus of the Revolution, and it is against the dark background of war and confusion that the angels of Love and Hope stand out in sharp relief. Writing to Meyer in December 1796, the author dates the action in the preceding August, when fugitives came flying across the Rhine. ' I have tried,' he added, ' to smelt the life of a German village in the epic furnace and to reflect the great movements and changes of the world-arena in a modest mirror.' [1]

The host of the Golden Lion sits with his wife and friends enjoying the placid beauty of summer and the comforts of his home. Refugees, he hears, are streaming into the village, but he has no desire to witness their plight. His thoughts are of the peace for which all are longing and of the marriage of his only son. Hermann, who has been out to observe and assist, returns sickened by the suffering, but thrilled with the charm of a beautiful girl nobly engaged in aiding her fellow victims. ' Heartless is the man,' he bursts out to his mother, ' who does not feel for the lot of these poor driven folk, and mindless he who is not oppressed by the thought of his own and his country's welfare in these days. What I saw and heard to-day has stirred my heart. I looked round on the glorious landscape, the fertile hills, and the golden fruit. But alas ! how near is the enemy ! The Rhine is still between us ; yet what are floods and mountains to that terrible people which sweeps onward like a hurricane ? They summon old and young to their banners, and death has no terrors for them. And a German dares to stay in his house, and hopes to escape the threatening woe ! I am an only son, and our business is good ; but is it not better to resist at the frontier than to await sorrow and slavery here ? I feel within me the courage and desire to live and die for the Fatherland

[1] *Briefe*, xi. 272–3.

and to set a worthy example to others.   If the youth of Germany gathered on the frontier, they would never trample on our fair country, destroy the fruit of our fields, and ravish our women.   I will go, and shall not return home.'   But these brave words mean little ; for he confesses to his mother that it is not the conflict, but the love of woman, that beckons him.   ' The fearful fatality of the cruel war thąt has ravaged the world and overthrown the foundations of mąny a solid edifice has driven her forth.   Are not men of high rank now wandering in misery, princes fleeing in disguise, and kings living in exile ?   And so is she, unmindful of her own misfortunes, unhelped yet helping.   Great is the sorrow which springs from this catastrophe ; shall not one flower of happiness spring from the soil of pain ? '

The village parson now sallies forth to collect information, and learns their story from one of the fugitives.   ' Our sufferings make a long tale, for we have drunk the bitter draught of all the years ; all the worse that our fairest hopes were dashed.'

For who will dare to deny that his heart was exalted within him,
And that his spirit enfranchised had throbbed with a purer devotion,
When he beheld the first and most radiant glory of morning,
Heard of the rights of man, to be shared in common with all men,
Learned of fair liberty, learned of equality, greatest of prizes ?
Every man hoped to live as his nature prompted.   The fetters
Seemed to be loosened that, forged by the hands of the idle and
   selfish,
Hitherto had ensnared so many lands in their bondage.
During those strenuous days, were not the eyes of all nations
Turned to the spot that so long had been the world's capital city,
Now, more than ever before, deserving that glorious title ?
Did not mankind wax strong in courage, in spirit, in utterance ?
Were not the names of those men who first spread abroad the good
   tidings
Equal in fame to the loftiest heroes among the immortals ?

' But the sky soon darkened.   A corrupt generation strove for mastery ; men murdered each other and oppressed their neighbours, and we thought of revenge.   May I never again see man in this horrible mood !   A raging beast is less hideous.   Let him not speak of liberty till he can rule himself.   When the restraints are gone, all evil is unloosed which law had kept under guard.'

Before Dorothea becomes Hermann's wife, she tells the story of the ring on her finger and of her first love.   ' Grant me a moment for my memories of the good man who gave it to me on leaving his country for ever.   He foresaw everything when the love of liberty

and the desire for action in a new and transformed world drove him
to Paris, where he found dungeon and death. Farewell, said he,
I go forth, for the whole earth is in travail. Fundamental laws
collapse in the strongest States, the owner is parted from his property
and friend from friend. Man is a wanderer on the face of the earth,
now more than ever. The world seems determined to dissolve
itself in black chaos and to emerge in new form. Thou wilt keep
thy heart for me, and if we meet again among the ruins we shall
be new creatures, transfigured, free, independent of fate ; for what
could fetter the man who had lived through such days ? Thus did
he speak, and I never saw him more.' So the new ring is placed
beside the old, and the poem ends with the grave and manly words
of Hermann. ' The greater the universal upheaval, the stronger
be our bond ! We will hold fast to each other and our fair possessions. For the man who falters when the earth is rocking increases
the evil ; but he who stands fast shapes the world to his own pattern.
It is not for Germans to foster the terrible movement or to stagger
to and fro. Let us keep what is ours. For it is the resolute peoples
who receive the meed of praise—those who have striven for God
and the law, for parents, wives, and children, and those who stood
and fell together in face of the enemy.'

It is impossible not to feel that here is a poem saturated with
politics, its message proclaimed in trumpet tones. The text and
the moral are those of the dramas. ' The bonds of the world are
unloosed ; who will join them together ? ' States, like individuals,
fall to pieces when the restraints of law are removed. To build
and maintain one happy home serves mankind better than all the
talk about the rights of man. Yet once again Goethe parts company
with those who see in the French Revolution nothing but an
explosion of folly and wickedness. He is well aware of its alluring
appeal to the noblest hearts and minds in France and beyond her
frontiers. The hope of a brighter age inspires the judge to eloquence,
despite his sufferings and disappointments ; and Dorothea's
betrothed, in whom we may perhaps discern the lineaments of
Adam Lux, had counted the cost of his adhesion. ' For life is no
more than other earthly possessions.'

In a long and penetrating analysis of the poem, which gave
genuine pleasure to its author, Wilhelm von Humboldt aptly remarks
that the personal theme is transported into a higher sphere by the
Revolution.[1] It is neither an idyll nor an epic, but an idyll within
an epic. The foreground is filled with peaceful labour, love, and
hope ; the background with the wild surge of the revolutionary wars.

[1] *Ges. Schriften*, vol. ii. Cp. Chuquet's Essay in his *Études de Littérature
Allemande*, vol. i.

O

The stage is enlarged, the atmosphere is charged with electricity, the Old World is falling in ruins. Hermann and Dorothea find happiness in each other ; but though the foreground is bright, the heavy clouds are not dispersed. The danger is not over, and the story closes on a note of responsibility. Hermann is now a man with a wife to defend, and he is ready to fight for his country against all foes. The most perfect of the poet's creations is also among the most virile. The lines in which the hero laments the distress and disunion of his country were to be quoted by one of Lützow's Jäger as evidence that Goethe was also a poet of national liberty. But the poem also makes an universal appeal. ' He knows no fatherland or party,' wrote Böttiger in delight after hearing the author read the beginning of the work. ' It can be enjoyed beyond the Rhine no less than here. The scenes are human, not national. It can be read in every language.' [1]

In the summer of 1797 the poet paid one of his rare visits to his mother at Frankfurt. ' Staying here just now is very interesting,' he wrote to Böttiger, August 16 ; ' every one is full of recent events. Intercourse with the people who have known almost all the important actors in this war-drama is most instructive. One sees the French Revolution and its effects much more directly, because it has had such great consequences for this city, and because one is here in such manifold relations with that nation.' Next day he drew a picture of the French character. ' What a curious people they are ! The Frenchman is not still for a moment ; he walks, chats, jumps, whistles, sings, and makes such a noise, that one always expects to see in a town or village a larger number of them than there is. If one does not understand them they grow irritable. They seem to demand that the whole world should know French ; but if one can talk with them they show themselves at once *bons enfants*. In armies of this kind one sees a peculiar energy and power at work. Such a nation must be terrible in more than one sense.' [2] He had no more desire than other Germans to see the Fatherland under the yoke of the conquering Republic. ' May things turn out well for Germany on this side of the Rhine,' he wrote in 1798. ' May it receive a decent constitution without the complete overthrow of its political existence, and not, like so many lands, including Switzerland, fall a slave to the French.' [3]

Ten years after the meeting of the States-General, Goethe made a final attempt to embody the cataclysm in dramatic form. ' The memoirs of Stephanie Louise de Bourbon-Conti ' (published in 1798), he writes in the ' Annals,' ' suggested to me the plan of " The

---

[1] *Literarische Zustände u. Zeitgenossen*, i. 74.
[2] *Briefe*, xii. 240, 247–50.   [3] *Ib.*, xiii. 118.

Natural Daughter." [1] Into this work, as into a vessel, I desired, with an earnestness worthy of the theme, to pour the reflections of many years on the French Revolution and its consequences. In 1801 I called up before my mind the complete plan which had been lying for years among my papers. At the end of the year the first act was ready.' 'Amid all the tumults of this year,' he adds under 1802, 'I never ceased to nourish in secret my pet " Eugenie." The whole having become entirely familiar, I worked indifferently at any part of it.' 'The first part,' he records under 1803, 'was written, played, and printed. The plan lay clearly before me ; nor had the attraction this piece had exercised over me for years in any way abated. The second part was to be laid in the country-seat, the residence of the heroine ; the third in the capital. I rejoiced in the friendliest appreciation from many sides. The conclusion drawn from the piece was all that I could wish ; but I committed the great and unpardonable mistake of coming forth with the first part before I had concluded the whole.'

Of the trilogy which was to unfold the story, only the first part was completed, and its stately proportions increase the regret that the statue remains a torso. Eugenie is the natural daughter of the Duke, the uncle of the King of France. Her mother, now dead, having been a member of the royal house, she has lived in retirement ; but her father desires to introduce her to the world. He asks his nephew to recognise her as a princess of the blood, and the good King promises to do so on his birthday. The Duke's son, learning of the intention, grudges his half-sister the share of the family inheritance which will fall to her on recognition, and orders his secretary to remove her, if necessary by death. The secretary is engaged to Eugenie's lady-in-waiting, who, to save her mistress's life, agrees to take her across the sea. The princess is hurried away to the tropics, heart-broken at leaving her beloved Fatherland, and convinced that fever will carry her off. There is, however, her lady-in-waiting assures her, one way of saving her life, and regaining her country—namely, to marry beneath her, and to hide her rank and residence. Indeed, she may do so at once, for a magistrate of high character is a candidate for her hand. Eugenie refuses on the double ground that she cannot marry without love, and that she has no wish to step down into the drab monotony of bourgeois life. But this resolution is quickly overthrown by a conversation with a monk, from whom she learns that the French monarchy is nearing the abyss. She had heard hints of the coming crisis from her father and the King, and she

---

[1] Gee Bréal, *Deux Études sur Goethe* (*Les Personnages originaux de la Fille Naturelle*) ; and Kettner, *Goethe's Drama, Die Natürliche Tochter.*

now determines to pay the price of her return. She will marry and live in her husband's country home, ready to help in the hour of danger to throne and Fatherland. Her father is informed that she has been killed in the hunting-field, and so disfigured that he could not bear to see her face before burial. Her brother thus again becomes sole heir, while Eugenie, her character strengthened by suffering and sacrifice, prepares herself for the great part which she is convinced awaits her.

Eugenie ranks high among Goethe's heroines, none of whom are painted with greater power or more loving care. While the other characters of the drama are types rather than individuals, and are only known by their title or their office, she fills the stage with her robust womanliness. Mind and heart are fully developed, and she is born for great deeds and great sacrifices. The drama makes no claim to be more than an overture, suggesting the archi-tecture of the piece, and indicating some of its themes. We find ourselves in a spacious vestibule, and every act and scene, wrought with cunning skill, increases our impatience to pass beyond the threshold. We are acutely conscious of the approach of tragic issues, of throbbing unrest, and the ferment of revolutionary ideas. The background is the French monarchy, under a kindly King. slipping into anarchy. Through the later parts of the trilogy the high-souled heroine would have moved in stately progress, occupy-ing the centre of the stage, connected with the Court through her birth, and with the people by her marriage. The noble fragment received ungrudging praise from the poet's friends. 'The high symbolism,' wrote Schiller, 'neutralising all the crude material and making everything a portion of an ideal whole, is truly wonderful. It is pure art.' 'It is the master's supreme achievement,' wrote Fichte, 'clear and unfathomable as the light, and, like light, melting into the infinite.' Herder described it as beautiful fruit ripened under the influence of the greatest event of the times. Karl August wrote after the first performance to congratulate the poet on the strength of his loins. But, like the other political plays, it never won a foothold on the stage. 'By over-attention to motives,' frankly remarked the author to Eckermann many years later, 'I spoiled my pieces for the theatre. My "Eugenie" is nothing but a chain of motives, and that cannot succeed behind the footlights.' No doubt it struck its hearers, as it strikes many of its readers, as cold and frozen—as if the action were taking place at a great distance, and only muffled sounds reached the ears of the audience. And yet beneath the polished marble surface we can feel the throbbing of subterranean forces. The measured reserve of the overture would have melted away when the curtain drew up and revealed the lightning playing round the head of the doomed and helpless monarch.

No German man of letters made so many attempts to embody the French Revolution in literary form as Goethe. If the charge of political indifference may be plausibly urged against him in the years of Napoleonic domination, it is merely ridiculous if applied to the period which preceded it. With the exception of ' Hermann and Dorothea,' not one of these endeavours met with complete success ; and that refulgent gem is the least directly concerned with politics. That so many were unfinished, or indeed only outlined, proves at once the fascination of the theme and the master-builder's dissatisfaction with his efforts. The reason lay deep in his own nature, which yearned for harmony in life as well as in art, and was disquieted by the storm and the earthquake. He complained that since the Revolution ' a restlessness had seized the minds of men, so that they hankered after a change in their position, or desired to move from place to place.' Though the political plays, poems, and sketches do not occupy the highest place among his works, there is not one without interest as a revelation of his personality and of his judgment of the greatest event of his life. While the opinions of most of his contemporaries swung from enthusiasm to detestation, his attitude remained unchanged throughout. He disliked the Revolution from the first, and feared its impact ; but he was well aware of the causes which had produced it, and of the probability of similar catastrophes elsewhere in the absence of just and efficient government. His attitude towards France is that of pity rather than indignation. The Revolution, he reiterates, reads a lesson both to rulers and ruled—to the former that they have duties no less than rights, to the latter that violence is more calculated to increase than to diminish their sufferings.

In conversation with Eckermann the Nestor of German literature repeatedly discussed his attitude to the Revolution and to the problems of government. ' It is true that I could be no friend to the French Revolution,' he remarked in 1824 ; ' for its horrors were too near me, and its beneficent results were then not apparent. But I was as little a friend to arbitrary rule. Indeed, I was perfectly convinced that a great revolution is never the fault of the people. Revolutions are utterly impossible so long as governments are just and vigilant. Because I hated the Revolution, I was named a friend of the powers that be. I must decline that title, because it denotes little less than the friend of the evil and the obsolete. All premeditated revolutions are unsuccessful, for they are without God, who stands aloof from such bungling. If, however, there exists an actual necessity for a great reform amongst a people, God is with it, and it prospers. He was visibly with Christ and Luther.' A year later he renewed his complaint. ' I do not know that I ever joined in any way against the people ; but it is now settled, once for all, that I am not their friend any more than I am a friend of Louis XV. I hate every violent upheaval, because as much good is destroyed as is gained by it. I hate those who achieve it as well as those who give cause for it. All violent transitions are revolting to my mind, for they are not conformable to nature. But am I therefore no friend to the people ? ' Eckermann once defined his adored master as a mild aristocrat ; and the poet would not have seriously quarrelled with the label, though he preferred another. ' Dumont,' he once remarked, ' is a moderate Liberal, as all rational people are and ought to be, and as I myself am. It is in this spirit that I have endeavoured to act throughout a long life. The true Liberal endeavours to effect as much good as he can with the means at his disposal ; but he would not extirpate evils, which are often inevitable, with fire and sword. He endeavours by judicious advances gradually to remove glaring defects without at the same time destroying an equal amount of good by violent measures. He contents himself in this ever imperfect world with what is good, until time and circumstances enable him to attain something better.'

' In all grave political questions,' wrote Goethe in ' The Campaign in France,' ' those spectators who take sides are best off, for they joyfully seize what favours their opinion, and ignore the rest. The poet, however, must by his nature be impartial.' He endeavoured to carry out his own prescription ; for he stood not only above parties, but above nations. Discussing the political plans of Béranger, he remarked that Paris was France. ' But we have no city, nay, we have no country, of which we could deservedly say—There is Germany ! If we inquire in Vienna, the answer is— This is Austria ! And if in Berlin, the answer is—This is Prussia. Only sixteen years ago, when we tried to get rid of the French, was Germany everywhere.' ' You have been reproached,' interjected Eckermann, ' for not taking up arms at that great period.' ' How could I take up arms without hatred ? ' answered the old man. ' And how could I hate without youth ? I have never shammed. I have never given utterance to what I have not experienced. I have only composed love-songs when I have loved. How could I write songs of hate without hatred ? And, between ourselves, I did not hate the French, though I thanked God when we were free of them. How could I, to whom culture and barbarism are alone of importance, hate a nation which is among the most cultivated on earth, and to which I owe so great a part of my own possessions ? There is a stage where national hatred vanishes altogether, and where one stands to a certain extent above the nations and feels the weal or woe of a neighbouring people as if it were one's own.' It is the voice of Olympian Jove.

'In his fifty volumes,' cried Börne in anger, 'Goethe has not written a word for Germany's freedom.' Such petulant outbursts were rebuked by Börne's greater friend. In a striking image Heine compared the poet to a venerable oak. Some, he declared, were angry because they could not make it a 'tree of liberty,' or fashion a barricade out of its timber. 'The tree was too high. They v ere unable to plant on its summit the *bonnet rouge*, or to dance the Carmagnole at its feet.' There is, indeed, at all times an atmosphere of aloofness, of aristocratic reserve, about him. He belongs to the governing class, and he looks down on the struggling masses as from the housetops, though without contempt. French doctrines, he felt, were not for men who enjoyed a secured position in life. 'Sieveking may be rich or clever,' he wrote to a friend visiting Hamburg ; 'yet he does not see that the Marseillaise is not suited to well-to-do folk, but is written to comfort and encourage poor devils.' [1] The two ruling conceptions of the eighteenth century were those of benevolent autocracy and cultured individualism ; and in both Goethe remained to the end the child of his age. His lot was cast in pleasant places, and he failed to understand the type of mind which resolves to overthrow the citadel of wrong, even at the risk of being buried in the ruins. Political passion was as unintelligible to him as religious fanaticism, and democracy meant to him the enthronement of mediocrity. His comparison of the Revolution to the Lutheran rebellion is as much the expression of his temperament as of his opinions. As Erasmus had watched with dismay the Peasants' Revolt, the religious war, and the frenzy of the Anabaptists, so the Erasmus of a later age was confirmed by the Revolution in his conviction that short cuts to the millennium were the longest way round. The risks were so great, the prizes so problematical. He lacked the belief in the instinctive sanity and potential wisdom of the people, which is the foundation and inspiration of the democratic faith. His creed is embodied in two hoary maxims : *Festina lente*, and *Ne sutor ultra crepidam*. 'The weak often have revolutionary sentiments,' he remarked. 'They think they would be well off if they were not ruled, and fail to perceive that they can rule neither themselves nor others.' [2] He ardently desired a completer humanity ; but he believed that loyal fulfilment of duty, not politics, was the best and indeed the only road to the goal.

[1] *Briefe*, x. 123.
[2] *Sprüche in Prosa*, 301, ed. Loeper. No. 216, in Bailey Saunders, *Goethe's Maxims and Reflections*.

CHAPTER VIII

SCHILLER

IF the Revolution had burst upon the world a few years earlier, or Schiller had been born a few years later, he would have been one of its most whole-hearted partisans.[1] As the subject of a prince conspicuous for his grinding tyranny, he experienced in his own person the ills from which his country was suffering. At Ludwigsburg he saw with childish eyes the extravagant display of a German Versailles out of all proportion to the resources of the little duchy, and his experience in the Duke's school implanted in him the contemptuous loathing of despotic rule which breathes through one and all of his youthful dramas. Karl Eugen, the evil genius of his country, became for the young poet ' the old Herod,' the symbol of princely oppression, the indignities of which sent the hot blood coursing through his veins. His chief political teacher was not any French or German theorist, but his own patron and Sovereign.

Schiller's intellectual development was precocious; and in his schooldays at Stuttgart he drank thirstily at the two chief springs of revolutionary idealism. In Rousseau, to adopt his own words, the indignation of outraged human dignity found content and form, satisfaction and goal; and he sang his praises in a brief paean.

> Undying record of the infamy
> Of France—the outrage of the century—
> My lyre greets the grave where Rousseau lies !
> He sought in vain for peace and rest—he found
> A resting-place in this small plot of ground.
> Sweet peace, come down and close his weary eyes.

[1] The best biography is that of Berger, as Minor's great work is uncompleted. Caroline von Wolzogen's Life of her brother-in-law remains indispensable. The best appreciation of his mind is the study written by Wilhelm von Humboldt as a preface to his *Briefwechsel mit Schiller.*

Once it was dark, and wise men passed away.
Now the wise perish in the light of day.
How shall this ancient wound be cicatrised ?
While Socrates was slain by sophistry,
Rousseau is slain by Christianity :
He by whom Christian men were humanised.

The Genevese philosopher pointed the path back to happy innocence, to emancipation, to rejuvenescence. His darkly-shadowed picture of modern society, which exactly corresponded with the young student's own limited experience, made his dream of securing universal happiness by a return to nature the more alluring. Scarcely less explosive was the influence of Plutarch, the trumpeter of valorous deeds, the janitor of a vanished world in which men had grown to their full stature. 'He raises us above the dead level of our generation,' wrote Schiller, 'and makes us contemporaries of a better and stronger race.' While these leavens fermented in his brain and heart, the fate of the most famous and most courageous of Swabian poets stirred him to his depths. He listened to Schubart's battle-cries with ecstasy ; and it was to one of his stories that he owed the theme of his first drama.

'The Robbers,' as we know it, is strong meat ; but in its original form it boils with passion. Karl Moor declaims with even greater violence against the accursed inequality in the world and the superfluous existence of despots. Begun before the author was of age, the drama appeared in 1781. Despite his anonymity the dramatist awoke to find himself famous, as Goethe had leapt into celebrity with 'Götz' and 'Werther.' He was well aware what he was about. 'I will make a book,' he remarked to a friend, 'which will have to be burnt by the hangman.' It was a flaming declaration of war against the abuses of State and society, a trumpet-call to men of spirit to throw off the burden which was crushing out the manly virtues. It was no novelty among the German writers of the 'seventies and 'eighties to tilt against caste and tyranny ; but never had such a ringing challenge been thrown down to the pano-plied powers of evil. From the title-page of the second edition glared an angry lion with the menacing legend 'In Tyrannos.' Though autocracy, as such, is not set in the pillory, its tools and flatterers are castigated with unflagging energy. The flaming defiance awoke a joyful response in adolescent Germany, and the proclamation of human dignity kindled a new hope in the hearts of crowded audiences. Schubart was rotting on the Asperg ; but his followers had found a new leader. 'Give me an army of fellows like myself,' cries Karl Moor, ' and Germany shall be a Republic in comparison with which Rome and Sparta were convents.' ' All the young Swabians of intelligence,' wrote Reinhardt, ' are members of Schiller's sect.' His very crudities increased his popularity and his influence. ' The theatre,' reported an eyewitness of the first performance at Mannheim, ' was like a madhouse ; eyes rolling, fists clenched, husky cries. Women fainted, and strangers fell sobbing into each other's arms.' To the spectators it was no longer a drama, but life itself : a gospel of good tidings, a signal of deliverance, a warning to oppressors. Its danger to the existing order was quickly grasped ; but wherever it was not forbidden, it was received as a revelation. While ' Damocles,' and other youthful dramas of Klinger, lacked conviction and therefore awoke no response, ' The Robbers ' enshrined the burning message of Rousseau in all the compelling power of its revolutionary appeal. The drama forms a landmark not only in German literature, but in German history. In 1795 a Viennese paper branded Schiller as the father of the revolutionary spirit, and though this was the exaggeration of panic, his youthful manifesto had assuredly sown dragons' teeth.

If Schiller owed the suggestion of ' The Robbers ' to Schubart, he owed the theme of his second play to Rousseau, who declared that Fiesco was a man worthy to sit for his portrait to Plutarch. In ' The Conspiracy of Fiesco ' the young Swabian gave ardent expression to his glorification of republicanism. ' The Robbers ' preached the gospel of social revolt, ' Fiesco ' of political rebellion. Both alike were variations on the theme of liberty. It was his first historical drama, and the comparative scarcity of his sources encouraged him to independent treatment. Andreas Doria, the tyrant of Genoa, is not without nobility, while Fiesco, the ambitious liberator, has feet of clay. The hero of the play is Verrina, the grim and unbending Brutus, who in the moment of victory slays his leader and saves the city from a new tyrant, worse than the old. ' "The Robbers " may die, but " Fiesco " will live,' cried the author as he smelted his ore. But his prophetic instinct was at fault. The success of the first performance in Mannheim was limited. ' Republican liberty,' he complained, ' is here a mere name ; no Roman blood flows in the veins of the Palatinate.' In Frankfurt, Berlin, and other cities, it was warmly welcomed, and increased the number of Germans who looked to Schiller to express their inarticulate longing for a wider measure of political and social liberty, and a more ungrudging recognition of human worth. The personal intensity which made ' The Robbers ' so poignant was lacking ; but the republican zeal is far from being purely academic.

If Andreas Doria is a majestic shadow, his nephew, Gianettino, the villain of the piece, is real enough. The drama is a cry for the recognition of human right, and for government by honest men. Though the scene is laid in Italy in the year 1547, it continually suggests memories of the author's time and country. Like all his early plays, it is at once a clarion warning to rulers and a fulminating declaration of the Rights of Man.

In his third play Schiller returned to his own time and drew directly on his own experience. ' Love and Intrigue ' breathes in every line the fierce resentment of a man whose soul was seared by the cruelty of irresponsible despotism. Of the four anti-revolutionary dramas it is by far the boldest, for it was most intimately related to the life of the moment. It is inferior in workmanship to ' Emilia Galotti '; but, while Lessing's haunting tragedy is staged in Italy, the young Swabian boldly flagellates the vices and crimes of the petty tyrants of his own race. Never before or after did he unveil with such unflinching hand the festering sores of German politics, and no writer of his time lanced the abscess with such dauntless courage. It is the most resounding condemnation in German literature of the abuses of the *ancien régime*, which in its main features was soon to be swept away by the lava stream of the Revolution and the sword of Napoleon. It was more revolutionary than ' The Robbers,' for it was more concrete. The dramatist had merely to photograph the ruler of his own or some neighbouring State with his mistress and his favourites, the nobility with their privileges, and the bourgeoisie in their helplessness. The conflict of classes supplied many a theme to Lenz and Klinger and other leaders of the *Sturm und Drang* ; but never was it employed with such skill and power. Beside the president, an able scoundrel, stand the chamberlain and the secretary, the noxious weeds who flourish in the rank soil of a corrupt Court. The centre of extravagance is the *maîtresse en titre*, Lady Milford, whose favour is the only road to wealth and power. From the midst of this poisoned world emerges the figure of Ferdinand, son of the president, a high-souled idealist and a disciple of Rousseau. He loves the daughter of a poor musician, who represents the solid virtues of the bourgeoisie, and in whom the poet reproduces traits of his honoured father. The humble girl, however, lacks the courage to rise above the fetters of her class-consciousness, and plunges herself and her lover into destruction. The *dénouement* is weak and unconvincing ; but its success all over Germany recalled that of ' The Robbers.' Half a century later Zelter described to Goethe the electric shock which he and the youth of his day had received from the drama ; nor has it lost its place on the German stage. Its position is assured ; for, like 'Figaro,' it is not only literature, but history.[1]

The fourth and greatest of the political dramas was also the last. 'Don Carlos,' produced in 1787, had taken five years to mature. In its early form the young prince fills the stage, and the drama is a tale of love, not of politics. But as the author proceeded, Carlos lost favour, and his teacher, the Marquis Posa, took his place. The hero was no longer the unripe, passionate prince, but his radiant friend, the herald of a State based on ordered freedom and the recognition of human dignity. Posa towers above all Schiller's didactic figures in force and eloquence. Unlike earlier plays, ' Don Carlos ' was written in verse, and its ringing declamations became and have remained the current coin of reformers. The play also reveals an advance in intellectual maturity. The poet had begun his career with passionate denunciations of despots and crowned heads ; but he learned to admire the kingly virtues of Frederick and Joseph, and he had tasted the goodness of the Duke of Weimar. Princes must now, therefore, be included in his vision of a regenerated world, and Posa's dream includes a prince, who, as father of his people, will foster and defend the rights of man and freedom of thought. In the kindling scene with Philip, where he pours forth the flood of his eloquence, the great idealist utters the hopes and demands not only of his creator, but of the mass of his contemporaries in the years immediately preceding the convocation of the States-General. We might, indeed, be listening to the magic tones of Vergniaud. The play reveals Schiller's entrance into a wider as well as a more tranquil world of thought than its predecessors, and marks the transition from *Sturm und Drang* to the standpoint of broad humanity which Herder and other leaders of thought already occupied. There is not less emotion, but there is more reflection ; not less criticism, but more construction. With ' Don Carlos ' the period of dramatic composition is interrupted for nearly a decade ; for ' The Misanthrope ' was laid aside almost as soon as commenced. His occupation with Philip II led him to study the revolt of the Netherlands. His history of its outbreak, a fragment of what was destined to be a large and comprehensive work, is a paean to national and religious freedom only less eloquent than the declamations of Posa.

In the summer of the year in which ' Don Carlos ' appeared, Schiller was profoundly influenced by the study of Kant's essay

---

[1] The identification of Lady Milford with Lady Craven in the *Memoirs of Sir Robert Morier*, ii. 300, is untenable ; for she only reached Anspach some years later.

on ' Universal History.' He learnt, in his own words, to think of
every detail and every phenomenon in reference to the whole of
which it forms a part, or, in other words, to regard it in a philosophic
spirit. He begins to consider the abuses of State and Church more
coolly, and to expect the ennobling of man not from revolt or the
imitation of foreign models, but from virile and independent thought.
The way to reform lay through the self-education of society,
not through revolution. He begins to turn from the mass to the
individual. A striking letter·to Caroline, his future sister-in-law,
in November 1788, prepares for the future quietism of ' The Letters
on Aesthetic Education.' [1] ' Wolzogen's verdict on Paris is natural
enough. The object is too big for him. He has brought a yard-
measure for a Colossus. Whoever has an instinct for the great
world must rejoice. How small and petty are our civil and political
conditions in comparison ! But one must have eyes which are not
offended at the evils which are inseparable from large movements.
Man is always a great being when he works in mass, however small
the individuals and details appear. Paris may perhaps make an
unpleasing impression on the philosophic observer, but not a petty
one ; for even the errors of such a highly educated State are imposing.
To me, in my little nut-shell, the great political society appears like
a man to a caterpillar. I have infinite respect for this vast, heaving
human ocean—but I am quite happy in my nut-shell. I believe that
every single soul, developing its powers, is more than any society.
The largest State is a human product, while man is the work of
Nature. The State is a creature of accident, a product of human
power, while man is a necessary being, the source of the power and
the creator of the idea itself.'

The cult of the individual was encouraged and strengthened
by ardent study of the Greek world, the magic of which he expressed
in ' The Gods of Greece.' He contrasts the drab colours of his age
with the radiant beauty of the past, and in the yearning lament
over Paradise Lost there is still a touch of Rousseau ; but the place
of an imagined Arcadia is taken by the glorious reality of Greece.
The ancient world offers to the poet an ideal of humanity towards
which he is urged both by the demands of life and art—a balance
of mind and sense, of nature and spirit. As he plunged into Homer
and the tragedians, the angry surge around him began to echo more
faintly in his ears. He shared not only the individualism but the
cosmopolitanism of his age, and his study of history made him feel
more than ever a citizen of the world. ' We moderns,' he wrote
to Körner in October 1789, in discussing historical composition,
' have a field of interest unknown to the Greeks and Romans and

[1] *Lotte*, i. 100–1.

far wider than the patriotic, which is only important for immature peoples and remote ages. It is a petty ideal to write for a single nation, and for a philosopher such a barrier is intolerable. Who can be content with such a changing, empirical and capricious form of humanity ? What else is the greatest of nations but a fragment ? The historian can only kindle for a nation in so far as it is an essential element in the progress of civilisation.'[1] It was in this spirit that the new professor delivered his inaugural lecture in Jena, in May 1789, on the meaning and study of Universal History.

Schiller had only recently, but none the less completely, emancipated himself from the explosive radicalism of his youth when the Revolution broke out.[2] While his friends read the news of the fall of the Bastille and the overthrow of autocracy with hopeful enthusiasm, he was critical and apprehensive from the start. ' During the first winter,' writes Caroline von Wolzogen in her biography of her brother-in-law, ' events in Paris were often the theme of his conversation. I remember how when we (Caroline and Lotte) were praising the spirit and the fine speeches of the Assembly, he remarked that the French were incapable of pure republican sentiments, and that nothing sensible could be settled by six hundred people.' His fears were confirmed by accounts of the early excesses sent home by Wilhelm von Wolzogen and the poet Salis ; and the more favourable descriptions of Friedrich Schulz made no impression on him. ' Schulz was with me to-day,' he wrote to Lotte and Caroline on October 30, ' back a week ago from Paris.[3] Would to heaven that all he says were true ! ' He gave no public expression to his opinions, and was reserved in his letters to intimate friends. ' What say you to the latest occurrences in France ? ' wrote Körner from Dresden in the same month. ' Nothing is impossible, and I should not be surprised if France broke up into separate republics. Scarcely any other course is open to the Assembly if it is to be consistent.'[4] But the poet made no reply, and we find no judgment on the Revolution in the extant letters of 1789. He began to accept articles on the crisis for the ' Thalia ' in 1790, but only for the sake of circulation.

The first reference occurs on April 15, 1790, in a letter to Körner. ' The political world interests me just now. I tremble at the thought of war, for we shall feel it to the remotest ends of Germany.' ' You ask me about politics,' replied Körner ; ' that is a new departure

[1] *Briefwechsel mit Körner*, ii. 128.
[2] The best summary of his attitude to the Revolution is by Rieger, *Schiller's Verhältniss zur Französischen Revolution.*
[3] Jonas, *Schiller's Briefe*, ii. 352–3.
[4] *Briefwechsel mit Körner*, ii. 131.

for you. All I can say, offhand, is that I still bet on peace.'[1] Here
is merely an expression of personal apprehension, not a verdict.
He had not yet reached a stable position or formed a clear view of
events. All that can be said with certainty is that he was never
carried off his feet. He read the political writings of his friends
and was interested in their views. ' Reinhardt is in Bordeaux,'
he wrote to Wieland, ' and is busy penning his reflections on the
Revolution and collecting the most important pamphlets as a
foundation. An essay of his on the subject is decidedly clever and
reveals close acquaintance with his theme.'[2] At this moment
Burke's ' Reflections ' were becoming known on the Continent,
and Körner wrote to call his friend's attention to them. ' If you
can procure a copy, do not let the Gallomaniacs prevent you from
reading it. Of course there is plenty of partisanship, declamation,
and one-sided reasoning ; but there are also many admirable
observations clothed in noble and virile eloquence.'[3] Nothing
impressed him more than Mirabeau's tract on education, ' which
reveals a solid and philosophic mind directed to securing the permanence of the Constitution by a national system of instruction.'

It was not surprising that some of Schiller's early friends should
look to him for a trumpet-call. ' It is ten years ago,' wrote Reinhardt
from Paris in 1791, ' that I had the happiness of making your
acquaintance. " The Robbers " had already revealed the man you
had become. Though separated from German literature for six
years, I have not forgotten it. I have read " Don Carlos," " The
Revolt of the Netherlands," and " The Thirty Years' War." I need
not say what pleasure you have given me. I cannot decide whether
to give the prize to " The Revolt " or to " The Thirty Years' War."
In the latter I detect the more practised eye, which covers a wider
field with less exertion. But what attracted me most in the former
is the bold, free spirit which anticipated the epoch when the French
Revolution should unchain the European mind. May I speak
frankly ? In your later work you sometimes seem to neglect the
principles, and by too great striving after impartiality you seem
on occasion to have become partisan. In a period when the great
law-suit between rulers and subjects rose to such prominence, a
man whose voice carries so far as yours should not concede a jot
of the rights of man, not even from fear of seeming to approve their
misuse.'[4]

On August 26, 1792, when Paris had overthrown the monarchy
and was preparing for the September massacres, the Assembly
proposed to confer the title of *Citoyen français* on distinguished

[1] *Briefwechsel mit Körner*, ii. 186.   [2] *Briefe*, iii. 139.
[3] *Briefwechsel mit Körner*, ii. 238.   [4] Urlichs, *Briefe an Schiller*.

foreigners who by their writings and courage had served the cause of liberty. The list included Washington and Kosciusko, Paine and Hamilton, Bentham and Wilberforce, Klopstock and Cloots, Campe and Pestalozzi. Before the motion was put to the vote, Rühl, an Alsatian, rose and proposed the addition of ' le sieur Giller, publiciste allemand.' The amendment was accepted and the vote passed unanimously. Forthwith appeared in the ' Moniteur ' and other French papers the name of Giller, Gillers, Gisler, Gilleers, and Schyler. Not once was the name of the new French citizen correctly rendered ; for he was in truth but little known in France. ' The Robbers ' appeared in an abridged and undistinguished translation in 1785 ; but under the old régime its performance was impossible. With the Revolution theatres sprang up like mushrooms, and a new taste, to which ' The Robbers ' might be expected to appeal, came into existence. Adapted for the French stage by an Alsatian, the play was given on March 10, 1792, in the Théâtre du Marais, the same stage where ' Figaro ' had triumphed a few years earlier. The Robber chief, wearing the Jacobin cap and pouring forth the fashionable revolutionary rhetoric, won storms of applause, and prepared the way for the grant of French citizenship. The honour gave little pleasure to its recipient ; but it was ignorantly believed to carry with it a certain influence. ' We are living here in great anxiety,' wrote the poet's father from Württemberg early in 1793, ' as the war is not far away. It is possible that we may have a visit from the French. If anxiety passes into danger, it occurs to me that we should be safe if my dear son, as a French citizen, would procure from the Convention a safe-conduct for his father and household. Then his citizenship would be of some use to us.'[1] A year later, Eberlin, a theologian, wrote to ask the poet, as a French citizen, to petition the Convention for the release of a young officer.[2]

The dramatist heard of his distinction almost at the same moment as of the overthrow of the monarchy. He now became absorbed in the tragedy, and at last began to feel the need of giving public expression to his opinions. ' Göschen is going to ask you to write on Cromwell for his Calendar,' he wrote to Körner in November. ' It is very interesting, especially at this time, to give vent to a healthy confession of faith on the subject of revolutions ; and as it must be to the advantage of their enemies, the truths which must necessarily be told to governments will not sound disagreeable.'[3] If Körner would accept the task, he would aid him. Admirers of the Revolution took it for granted

---

[1] Wolzogen, *Schiller's Beziehungen zu Eltern, Geschwistern*, etc., p. 109.
[2] Urlichs, *Briefe an Schiller*, p. 193. [3] *Briefwechsel mit Körner*, ii. 346.

that Schiller shared their views. ' What do you say to France ? '
wrote Baggesen's German wife excitedly to Lotte. ' What a
triumph of liberty and dawning reason ! How the author of
" Don Carlos " will rejoice ! ' [1] He certainly did not rejoice ; but
for a brief period he was impressed, almost overawed, by the titanic
energy of the young Republic. ' Since I have read the " Moniteur," ' he wrote to Körner, 'I have entertained greater expectations
from the French. If you do not read it, I strongly advise you to
do so. You find there all the proceedings of the Assembly, and you
learn to know the French in their strength and weakness. If they
disappoint my hopes, perhaps I may derive better ones from
the same source.' [2] The next letter records the not unexpected
disappointment. ' I hoped much for the French,' he wrote on
December 14, ' from the happy issue of their war. The consciousness of their strength, I believed, would give them a new moral
impetus, and I expected the horrors would cease, as they are only
the fruit of weakness and desperation. But alas ! there now appear
new horrors of insolence, ingratitude, revenge, egotism. Some
great men are overborne by a thoughtless mob or by the degraded tools of ambitious scoundrels.' [3] His verdict on German
sympathisers with the Revolution was equally severe. ' I cannot
interest myself in the Mainz folk,' he wrote to Körner, ' for all their
actions display rather a foolish desire to advertise themselves than
sound principles. Forster's conduct will surely find no defenders,
and I foresee that he will look back upon it with shame and
regret.' [4]

The supreme tragedy was now approaching, and the spirit of
the *citoyen français* waxed hot within him. ' Do you know any
one,' he wrote to Körner in the same letter, ' who can translate
German into French, in case I need him ? I can hardly resist the
temptation to mix myself up in the trial of the King and write a
pamphlet on him. The enterprise seems to me important enough
to claim the pen of a reasonable being ; and a German writer,
expressing himself with freedom and eloquence, might very possibly
make some impression on those empty heads. If some individual
publicly expresses his judgment, people are inclined to regard him
as the spokesman of his class, if not of his nation ; and I believe
that the French, particularly in this affair, are not altogether un-
responsive to foreign opinion. Moreover, this subject is well suited
to admit a defence of the good cause which is not in danger of
misuse. The writer who breaks a lance for the King dares to give
utterance to more weighty truths than other men. Perhaps you

---

[1] *Charlotte von Schiller u. ihre Freunde*, ii. 449.
[2] *Briefwechsel mit Körner*, ii. 350.　　[3] *Ib.*, ii. 352.　　[4] *Ib.*, ii. 357–8.

P

will advise me to keep silence ; but I think one ought not to sit with folded hands in such circumstances. There are times when one must speak out.' Körner replied without giving much encouragement to the idea. ' It would interest me more if it were already accomplished before the King's fate is settled. I know a good translator, and if you stick to your plan, you can send me the manuscript. It is difficult to decide if one should speak or be silent. I do not deny that a celebrated foreigner might influence the French by an eloquent appeal ; but I doubt if the effect would be lasting. Political sophistry has never been carried to a higher pitch than in this people, and the oscillation of opinion from one extreme to another makes it easy for the latest speaker to cancel the impression of the last but one.' [1] The form of the publication was settled with Göschen ; but the work was delayed by ill-health, and Körner's fears that his friend might be too late were realised. ' What do you say to French affairs ? ' wrote the poet when the tragic news arrived. ' I really began writing for the King, but I did not get on well with it, and now there it lies before me. The last fortnight I have not read a French paper, so disgusted am I with these horrible knackers.' [2]

Schiller turned away from France in disgust. He wrote to a friend that he had abandoned the youthful dream of forcing improvement on men, since unprepared minds were unable to make use of the purest and the best. His return to the orthodox fold was hailed with satisfaction by his conservative friends. ' Is he now quite converted,' wrote Frau von Stein to the Duchess Luise, ' and may I now call the members of the Convention robbers without him flaring up as he once did ? I am glad that he is a German—otherwise he would have been guillotined long ago ; for wherever they find a drop of noble blood they destroy it.' [3] He continued to read the political writings of his friends and prominent contemporaries. He asked Göschen to send him Gentz's annotated translation of Burke's ' Reflections,' and urged him to publish Humboldt's ' Ideas on the State.' His opinions at this time are described by his old friend Hoven, after conversations with the poet during his visit to Württemberg.[4] ' He was no friend of the French system of liberty, in which I was so deeply interested, and he saw no fair prospects of a happier future. He regarded the Revolution as the natural result of bad government, of the extravagance of the Court and the grandees, of the demoralisation of the people, and of the work of discontented and ambitious men who exploited the situation for their selfish ends—not as a work

---

[1] *Briefwechsel mit Körner*, ii. 359–60.   [2] *Ib.*, iii. 23.
[3] Düntzer, *Charlotte von Stein*, i. 384.   [4] Hoven, *Autobiographie*, p. 133.

of wisdom. He admitted that many true and valuable ideas, which had hitherto existed only in books and in the minds of clear thinkers, had become common property; but that was not enough to fashion a really beneficial constitution. Firstly, the principles of such a constitution were not sufficiently developed. Secondly, the people must also be ripe for it ; of which at present there was no indication. He was therefore convinced that the Revolution would cease as quickly as it began, that the Republic would collapse into anarchy, and that salvation would be found in the appearance of a strong man to restore order.'

Schiller's chronic need of money was generously relieved by unsolicited assistance from the Duke of Augustenburg, a young prince of enlightened views who had welcomed the Revolution and had later turned from it in disgust. The poet repaid his Maecenas by addressing to him a series of letters of portentous length on the subject which filled his thoughts for the two years following the death of the King of France. These epistolary essays showed that he had at last reached a definite standpoint, from which he judged the Revolution and all other political phenomena. ' Is it not untimely,' he began on July 13, 1793,[1] ' to occupy oneself with the needs of the aesthetic world when the events of the political world offer so much more immediate interest ? On the other hand, may we not choose our occupation ? Events and the tendency of literature have given the time a false direction, and turned it more and more away from ennobling art. The occurrences of this last decade of the century are of no less challenging significance for the philosopher than for the man of action. So you can fairly expect me to discuss this remarkable matter in our written conversations. A law of the wise Solon condemns the citizen who does not take sides in a revolt. If ever this law is applicable it is now, when the fate of humanity is in question and when a man can hardly remain neutral without incurring a charge of indifference. An intelligent, courageous nation, long regarded as a model, has begun to desert its positive institutions and to return to the state of nature in which reason is the only legislator. If legislation were really entrusted to reason, man respected and treated as an end in himself, law enthroned and true liberty made the foundation of the State, I would bid eternal farewell to the Muses and dedicate myself wholly to the noblest of all tasks—the Monarchy of Reason. But it is precisely these suppositions that I venture to doubt. In fact I am so far from believing in an incipient regeneration in the field of politics that events rob me of all hope for centuries. Before recent events, we could flatter ourselves with the beautiful

[1] *Schiller's Briefe*, iii. 329–40.

dream that the steady and imperceptible influence of thinkers, the seeds of truth planted during centuries, the accumulated store of experience, must have attuned men to the reception of higher things and prepared an era when light would triumph over darkness. We had advanced so far in the theory of civilisation that the hoary pillars of superstition were beginning to shake. Nothing seemed lacking but a signal for the great transformation and unification of the human spirit. It has sounded—but with what result? The attempt of the French people to obtain possession of the holy rights of man and to win political freedom has only exhibited its incapacity and unworthiness, and has swept back along with it a considerable part of Europe into barbarism and serfdom. The moment was most favourable, but it found a corrupt generation. The use it has made and is making of this great gift of opportunity shows indubitably that the race is not yet of age, that the light yoke of reason has come too early, and that he is not fit for civic freedom who still falls far short of the full stature of man.'

As Schiller proceeds with his picture, keeping his eye on Paris, the tints become ever darker. ' Man mirrors himself in his acts; and what a scene lies before us! In the lower classes we see only lawless instincts which hasten to their bestial satisfaction now that the restraints of society are removed. So it was not moral control, but external coercion, which hitherto held them back! So they were not free men, as they declared, oppressed by the State! No, they were merely wild beasts. At the other end of the scale the more civilised classes reveal the even more repulsive qualities of lethargy and degeneracy. *Corruptio optimi pessima!* When civilisation degenerates, it falls lower than barbarism can ever reach; for the latter can only become a beast, while the former lapses into a devil. Any attempt to reform the State according to principles is in my eyes premature, and every hope based upon it illusion, till the character of man is again raised from the abyss— a task demanding a century and more. We shall, of course, hear of many an abuse swept away and of many a victory over prejudice; but what ten wise men build up, fifty fools will destroy.' In the closing paragraphs he points the moral of his pessimism. ' Shall we then cease to strive for political regeneration? Nothing of the sort. Political and civic freedom remains for ever the holiest of possessions, the noblest goal of every effort, the axis of civilisation; but this glorious edifice can only be built on the solid foundation of ennobled character. We must make citizens before we present them with a constitution. Character is moulded by the rectification of ideas and the purification of sentiment. The former is the work of philosophy, the latter of aesthetics. Philosophy alone is insufficient, for it is a long road from the head to the heart, and most actions are determined by feeling. The most urgent task of our time appears to me to be the elevation of our sentiments and the moralisation of the will ; for much has already been accomplished for the enlightenment of the mind. Aesthetic culture is the most potent instrument in the formation of character, and it can be applied without the help of the State.' In a further letter he adds religion to the influences needed to construct a higher humanity. ' For the mass of the people it is a counterweight to its passions. The educated classes, too, are civilised without being moralised. In both, the examples of true virtue are the exception, not the rule. In France a revolution has overthrown religion and destroyed good taste, and the character of the nation is not strong enough to dispense with these supports.' [1]

In the summer of 1794 Cotta pressed the poet to undertake the direction of a political newspaper, which he had resolved to found. Schiller fought against the proposal on the ground that he was convinced of the political immaturity of his contemporaries, that it would be a waste of his special powers, and that his health was unequal to the strain. He therefore urged his publisher to begin with a political quarterly, which he could edit with less difficulty. Even this he would only undertake for the sake of the salary, as he could not muster up any enthusiasm for political journalism. He finally persuaded Cotta to found a literary journal, into which he could honourably promise to put his whole strength. ' Die Horen ' was to seek for truth and beauty ; and the fleeting interests of the day and controversy on constitutions were to be rigorously excluded. The limited scheme provoked criticism in several quarters. Jacobi wrote to ask how far ' the Interdict ' on political subjects extended.[2] ' All reference to State religion and political constitutions is to be excluded. But this limitation, literally interpreted, would be unendurable for the philosopher ; for with what can he ultimately deal but politics and religion ? ' The Editor referred him to the first number, adding that he would find that the philosophic mind was in no way forbidden to deal with the subject. ' Only it must not take sides in present happenings and must abstain from direct references to any particular State or event. In body we shall remain citizens of our time, because we cannot help it ; but in mind it is the privilege and duty of the philosopher, like the poet, to belong to no people and to no age, but in the literal sense of the word to be the contemporary of all the ages.' When Reichardt asked him for a few words for his political journal, ' France,' Schiller replied that at first he was almost annoyed to see an artist (the only

---

[1] *Briefe*, iii. 411. [2] Urlichs, *Briefe an Schiller*, p. 192.

free creature in the world) travelling on the lumbering political diligence. 'From me,' he concludes ironically, 'you must ask neither judgment nor counsel in this province, for I know little of it, and it is literally true that I do not live in my century ; and though I have been told a revolution has occurred in France, that is about all I know.' His affectation of indifference broke down when the French entered Stuttgart in 1796. 'Political affairs,' he confessed to Goethe, 'which I always, wished to avoid, do touch one, after all, very closely.'

Schiller's change of attitude had remained unknown, and his admirers naturally continued to regard him as the author of the dramas of revolt. One of them wrote in 1794, imploring him to strive for the liberation of Lafayette, 'the living incarnation of Posa.'[1] 'Your portrait,' he adds, 'hangs before me. These eyes say, It was not the mere jingle of words when I sang in my " Ode to Joy "—

> Rescue from the tyrant's chains ;
> Succour where the innocent weep.'

A year later an old schoolfellow from Mömpelgard wrote in similar ignorance.[2] 'I have been cast into Paris a year ago by this world-revolution. I have rejoiced to hear of your interest in these movements of freedom, and to know that French citizenship has been granted to you and that you have kept it. The present moment is critical. Good men are seeking to end the Revolution, and it is high time. But just for that reason bad men are working to postpone tranquillity. You, great Schiller, are doubtless observing the events of our pregnant epoch, and will, I hope, enrich the world with their history. Perhaps I could be of service to such a plan by a regular correspondence. I am thinking of writing something for foreigners. I shall try to familiarise the new Republicans with German literature and philosophy ; one could hardly render them a greater service. I and some of my friends will translate your works, which are known here only by name.' But the poet's thoughts were elsewhere, and such letters were left doubtless without reply.

The line of thought sketched out in the correspondence with his patron was developed in the 'Letters on the Aesthetic Education of Man,' published in 'Die Horen' in 1795. Though the theoretical portion is based mainly on Kant's 'Critique of Judgment,' the political background and conclusions differ widely from those of the philosopher of Königsberg. While Kant to the end of his life

---

[1] Urlichs, *Briefe an Schiller*, pp. 205-6.   [2] *Ib.*, pp. 239-40.

continued to believe in the value of mass movements, Schiller fervently proclaims the cult of the individual, which was the hall-mark of the Weimar circle. ' I have never taken up my pen to discuss political troubles,' wrote Schiller to Goethe, ' and what I say here is said only that I may never have to speak again.' With Kant, aesthetics were related to morals ; with Schiller, they were related not less to politics and sociology. The failure of the French Revolution to improve humanity imposed on its critics the duty of discovering and announcing another path towards the desired goal.

' It would appear unseasonable,' we read in the Second Letter, ' to search for a code for the aesthetic world when the moral world offers matter of so much higher interest, and when the spirit of philosophic inquiry is challenged by the circumstances of to-day to occupy itself with the supreme work of art—the establishment and structure of true political freedom. The eyes of the philosopher as well as the man of the world are anxiously turned to the theatre of political events where it is presumed the destiny of man is at stake. It would almost seem to betray a culpable indifference to the welfare of society if we did not share this interest. It would have been most attractive to me to inquire into such an object. But I can justify my resistance and my preference of beauty to freedom by showing that to reach a solution even in the political sphere, the road of aesthetics must be pursued, since it is through beauty that we arrive at freedom.' The succeeding Letter explains the principles which guide reason in the task of legislation. ' As a moral being, man cannot possibly rest satisfied with a political condition imposed on him by necessity. Every one must adapt himself to the highest end which reason has set up in his personality. It is in this way that an adult people is justified in exchanging a condition of thraldom for one of moral freedom. The term natural condition can be applied to every political body which owes its establishment originally to force, not to law ; and such a state contradicts the moral nature of man. Yet this natural condition suffices for the physical man, who only gives himself laws to escape from brute force. Moreover, the physical man is a reality, while the moral man is problematical. The task therefore is to keep physical society from dissolution while moral society is being formed. The living organs of the State have to be repaired while they act. A prop must therefore be sought to underpin society while it is being rendered independent of natural conditions. This support cannot be found in the natural character of man, which is selfish and violent, nor in his moral character, which has to be formed and on which the lawgiver can never rely. It is therefore necessary

to produce a third character, differing from but related to both.
Only when such a character prevails can a revolution be free from
evil consequences, and nothing else can secure its permanence.   A
people is unworthy to exchange the state of necessity for that of
freedom unless it possesses totality of character.'

After this preliminary argument the author inquires whether
the era in which he is living possesses the requisite character.   ' Man
has woken up from his age-long lethargy and demands with impressive unanimity to be restored to his rights.   Indeed, he not
only demands them, but seizes by force that which he believes to
have been unjustly wrested from him.   The edifice of the natural
state is tottering, and a possibility occurs to place law on the throne,
to honour man as an end in himself, and to make true freedom the
basis of political union.   Vain hope !   The moral presupposition
is lacking.   In the present drama man is observed either running
wild or in a state of lethargy—exhibiting the two extremes of
degeneracy at the same time.   In the lower strata, coarse, lawless
impulses come to view, breaking loose when the bonds of civil order
are burst, hastening to satisfy their savage instincts.   Society
collapses into its elements, instead of hastening upwards towards
organic life.   At the other end of the scale the civilised classes
present the still more repulsive spectacle of lethargy and depravity
of character. *Corruptio optimi pessima.*'   In his wrath he repeats
the very words of the Letter to the Duke of Augustenburg.

In the Sixth Letter we discover that the author is all the time
contrasting the darkness of his own generation with the blinding
radiance of the classical world.   ' Have I gone too far in my portrai-
ture of our times ?   I do not expect any such reproof.   Who among
us can step forth, man to man, and wrestle with an Athenian for
the prize of the highest humanity ?   Our modern State is a leveller,
in whose eyes it is but seldom a recommendation to possess superior
capacity.   Thus the individual life is smothered and the governing
authorities lose sight of humanity, while the people offer but a tepid
welcome to laws which address themselves so little to their personality.   At length society, weary of carrying a burden that the State
takes such scanty trouble to lighten, crumbles to pieces—a destiny
that has befallen the majority of European States.'   The later Letters
develop the contention that it is useless to seek political improvement by political means.   Nothing but the aesthetic disposition
of the soul can raise mankind from savagery to civilisation and
can give birth to liberty, which only begins when man completes
himself.   Everyone carries in himself the germ of the ideal man.
When the individual rises to the ideal of the species by perfecting
himself, he is labouring not only for himself, but for the community.

The work ends with a paean to the goddess of whom Schiller had
become the most ardent of votaries. 'Beauty alone confers
happiness on all, and under its influence every one ceases to be
mindful of his limitations. Beauty alone can give man a social
character; for to create harmony in the individual is to bring
harmony into society.'

The Letters were hailed by Gentz as a welcome aid in his anti-
revolutionary campaign, and were criticised by Körner with his
usual discriminating sympathy. 'You have thought it necessary
to prove the need of aesthetic education, since public attention is
chiefly directed to political amelioration. The road you have chosen
is original, but not, to my thinking, the shortest. You are unjust
to our age. Pure republican spirit has always been rare, especially
in moments of passion. Aesthetic education is an end in itself and
needs no recommendation as a means. Yet even as a means it is
of service for those who have eyes only for political objects. All
political change is the work of barbarians if it has not a worthy
ideal. The State is purely means; humanity is the only goal.
The ideal of the State therefore presupposes the ideal of humanity,
and the latter bases itself on the laws of beauty. The State can
never compel the transformation of the individual; it can only
provide the opportunity and remove obstacles. This purpose
determines its general ideal. Whether this ideal should be realised
by gradual or sudden change depends on the health of the State.
If sick to death it can only be healed by revolutions. The realisation
of the ideal, whether sudden or gradual, is impossible without the
personal worth of the majority, or at any rate of a section which
atones for lack of numbers by its strength. Hence the necessity
of the highest development of individuals if one evil is not to be
substituted for another.'

The author soon realised that his attempt to train the character
of the nation by the gospel of beauty was doomed to failure. His
philosophic essays found little response and incurred the charge
that they were frigid and unintelligible. The public declined to
rally round the banner of aesthetic culture. 'Schiller,' remarked
Goethe to Eckermann in 1824, 'had the good fortune to be looked
upon as the particular friend of the people; but between ourselves
he was much more of an aristocrat than myself.' As a matter of
fact there was nothing to choose between the great twin brethren
in their middle years; for both looked down on the thronging
masses who worshipped the idols of the market-place. The mood
of disillusion is expressed in his poem 'The Promenade,' a
philosophic survey of human destiny. He shows that man is born
for society, and assisted by society to great achievements. But

he falls into excesses which breed anarchy and lead to a new and savage state of nature.   The poet depicts the horrors of revolution in dark colours.   He asks if the race must despair of salvation, and answers that it depends on institutions which secure true culture through moral simplicity.   If it was over-bold to hope that the community would win true dignity, the individual can and should strive for totality.   The poet was in no mood to confine himself to lamentations over the failure of his educational crusade, and he combined with Goethe to carry the war into the enemy's camp. The ' Xenien ' threw down a challenge to those who sought salvation for society in French doctrines and practices, and who, consciously or unconsciously, were endeavouring to introduce them into Germany. ' I spend several interesting hours every day with Schiller,' wrote Humboldt to Wolf in 1796.[1]   ' We have talked about the " Xenien " a good deal.   As to the separation of authors, he usually avoids the subject, and he has expressly asked me, for the fun of the thing, to keep to myself what I have learned from him.   But I can assure you that we have made big mistakes, even where we thought error impossible.'   The confusion is unimportant, as the political convictions of the two men were virtually identical.

In 1798 Schiller was greeted by a voice from the past.   The grant of French citizenship in 1792 had been followed by the preparation of the diploma which was to be delivered by Custine, with a covering letter by Roland, in the course of his campaign on the Rhine.   But as the name was written ' Gille,' and there was no address, the parchment travelled no farther than Strassburg. Nearly six years later it was sent by a Strassburg citizen, an ex-adjutant of Custine, to Campe, who forwarded it to Jena.   ' Honoured fellow citizen,' wrote the Brunswick pedagogue, ' I am most grateful to the French Government for the opportunity, in sending you the enclosed, of assuring you of the warm veneration to which I have given expression in more than one of my writings.'[2]   'On your diploma of citizenship sent you from the dead,' wrote Goethe, ' I can only congratulate you in so far as it finds you in the land of the living.   Wait a bit before you go and join your distinguished fellow citizens.   Campe seems to be afflicted with a most dangerous form of madness, like many another good German.   Unhappily it is as difficult to cope with this plague as with any other.'[3]   Schiller accepted the suggestion of Karl August that the document should be preserved at Weimar.   ' I will have it copied,' he wrote jestingly to Goethe, ' and get an attestation that the original is in the library, in case any of my children ever wish to settle in France and make

---

[1] Humboldt, *Ges. Werke*, v. 172, ed. of 1841.
[2] Urlichs, *Briefe an Schiller*, p. 292.   [3] *Briefe*, xiii. 84–5.

use of this citizenship of mine.' [1] 'I will forward you a copy,'
replied Goethe, 'recording that the original is preserved in the Duke's
library. It is very good of you to fall in with the Duke's wishes.
Something of the sort is there already—the proclamation, in many
languages, to all peoples of the earth, of the glorious French
Revolution.'

A year later the poet made detailed reference to the Revolution
in the greatest of his lyrics. ' The Song of the Bell ' teaches in
imaginative form the same lesson as ' The Letters on Aesthetic
Education.' The casting of the molten metal requires a master's
hand in the life of the State not less than in the forging of a bell.
' Woe if the seething mass liberates itself and spreads destruction
around ! ' he cries, as the scenes of terror once more pass before his
eyes. But there is hope, not less than warning, in these haunting
lines. The perfect bell is the symbol of an ideal society, a union
resting on love and brotherhood, which forms the eternal if
unattainable goal of human endeavour.

> The mould is broken by the craftsman
> In due time : but 'tis ruin dire
> When of its own accord the metal
> Bursts forth in streams of molten fire !
> Blindly it thunders in its madness,
> Shattering its bonds with savage force,
> And from the jaws of hell emitting
> Destruction in its fiery course.
> Nought that is noble can be fashioned
> Where brutal tyranny prevails.
> When nations take to revolution
> Prosperity declines and fails.
>
> Alas, when in the heart of cities,
> Where faggots lie in readiness,
> The people, casting off their fetters,
> Rise in their wrath to seek redress.
>
> Struck by the hand of insurrection,
> The bells resound with brazen din,
> And, once attuned to peaceful music,
> Now ring the reign of violence in.
>
> ' Freedom ! Equality ! ' they clamour ;
> The peaceful burgher flies to arms,
> Crowds fill the streets, and bands of murderers
> Roam round, increasing war's alarms.

[1] *Briefe*, xiii. 91.

Insensate madness fills the women,
Who, breaking into frightful jest,
As fiercely as with teeth of panthers
Pierce and devour the foeman's breast.

Reverence is flung aside—they sever
All sacred ties on every hand ;
The good man yields to evil-doers
And crime stalks boldly through the land.
'Tis perilous to wake the tiger,
To rouse the lion in his den :
But the most dreadful of all terrors
Is the unbridled rage of men.
Alas for those who deem such blind ones
Lighted by wisdom's heavenly rays !
This lightens not—it only kindles,
And sets both town and land ablaze.

The beautiful little poem on ' The Opening Century ' is no less
sombre.

Tell me, O friend, where shall a place of refuge
Be found where peace and freedom may abide ?
The century has closed in storm and tumult,
The new age dawns in war and homicide.

The bonds are loosed by which lands were united,
Old institutions perish and decline ;
The ocean cannot drown war's fearful tumult,
Nor ancient Nilus, nor old Father Rhine.

Vainly, alas ! thou seek'st in earth's dominions
The dwelling-place of liberty and truth,
The everlasting spring of freedom's garden,
Where blossoms the undying flower of youth.

Enter the holy temple of the spirit,
If thou would'st flee from life's discordant throng :
For freedom dwells but in the realm of visions,
And beauty lives but in the poet's song.

Here is the Weimar gospel in all its purity ; but as Schiller had
passed in a few years from insurgent radicalism to philosophic
quietism, so he now, like Fichte, emerged in middle life from cosmopolitan individualism and gave deathless expression to the sentiment
of nationality, which had been preached by the conquering armies
of the Revolution and appropriated by their suffering victims.

Though a poetic, not a political, mind, he was intensely sensitive to changes in the atmosphere, which he faithfully reflected in the shining mirror of his prose and verse. ' The German emerges unfortunate from the conflict,' he wrote after the Treaty of Luné-ville ; ' but he has not lost that which constitutes his worth. German Empire and German Nation are different things. The majesty of the German does not rest on the head of his princes. German worth is a moral greatness which, dwelling in the culture and charac-ter of the nation, is independent of its political vicissitudes. Every people has its day ; but the day of the German is the harvest of the whole span of time.' In these noble words the gospel of inward-ness is joined to a new pride in the land of which Schiller was one of the brightest ornaments. The worth of national life found its first classic embodiment in German literature in the trumpet tones of ' The Maid of Orleans ' and ' Wilhelm Tell.' Though cut off at the age of forty-seven, the poet lived long enough to enshrine at different periods in imperishable verse the conceptions of liberty and nationality which were destined to govern the nineteenth century.

CHAPTER IX

THE ROMANTIC SCHOOL

In Germany, as in France and England, the Romantic movement was the work of two generations, the pioneers emerging in the third quarter of the eighteenth century, to be followed by the main army during the Great War and the early years of the Restoration.[1] If the watchword of the classical age was order, that of its successor was revolt. Content was placed above form, emotion above reason ; while individuality, imagination, and wonder came to their own. Romanticism was the work of young men, intolerant of tradition, resolved to follow their fancy wherever it led them. Such was the mood of Goethe and Schiller, of Lenz and Klinger, of Heinse and Gerstenberg, in the years of spiritual ferment which divided the Seven Years' War from the meeting of the States-General. When the Revolution broke out the pioneers had passed from youth to middle age, leaving their romanticism behind them. Their places were soon to be filled by a younger generation endowed with less genius than Goethe and Schiller ; but fired by the same determination to be a law to themselves, the same unfaltering resolve to suck out all the beauty and joy that life had to offer. The leaders—August and Friedrich Schlegel, Novalis and Hölderlin, Tieck and Wackenroder, Schleiermacher and Schelling—were born between 1767 and 1775, and were just crossing, or just about to cross, the threshold of manhood when the tempest burst upon the world. To precocious youth, starting out on the great adventure of self-realisation, the spectacle of a whole nation engaged on the same task came like a draught of water to the thirsty throat. While Goethe and Schiller averted their faces from insurgence and disorder, the new standard-bearers of the army of romance greeted the dawn with cries of delight. But it soon became clear that the juniors were as unpolitical as the seniors, and that both alike were far more interested in the individual

---

[1] See Haym's classical work, *Die Romantische Schule* ; Brandes, *The Romantic School in Germany* ; Huch, *Die Romantik* ; Pötzsch, *Studien zur frühromantischen Politik u. Geschichtsauffassung*.

than in society or the State. Politics, complained Justinus Kerner, were the death of all true poetry. ' Your horrible cries, your vivats and drums and trumpets, drown the sweet music of thrush and nightingale.' Novalis alone worked out a political system, and Görres alone plunged into the dust of the political arena.

I

The most influential members of the circle were August and Friedrich Schlegel, whose father and uncle were among the minor poets of the Frederician era.[1] While the elder was the greater critic, the younger was the more daring and original mind. August was content with literature and art, while Friedrich pressed forward to the problems of social and political life. The precocious brothers troubled themselves but little with politics till the coming of the Revolution, and the colder temperament of the elder remained almost unaffected by the excitement ; but Friedrich's ardent soul responded eagerly to the stimulus. His enthusiasm for the civilisation of Greece and Rome extended to their short-lived liberty, and disposed him to sympathise with modern attempts to establish a republic, which he believed to offer the best soil for the growth of personality. He studied political theory not less carefully than the march of events. ' You advise me to read Burke on the French Revolution,' he wrote to his brother in 1791. ' I have already read Girtanner, who is most useful in giving laymen a tolerable idea of the situation, as he provides extracts from the principal writers and is very impartial.' Sometimes it was Friedrich's turn to offer counsel. ' You should read a very interesting essay by Wilhelm von Humboldt—" How far should the care of the State for the welfare of the citizen extend ? " He promises to be a very good writer.' [2]

When others were turning their back on the Revolution, Friedrich's sympathetic interest continued to grow, and for a year or two politics became his main preoccupation. He enrolled himself among the disciples of Fichte, who, he claimed, had overthrown Rehberg in single combat. ' History and political science bulk largely in my future scheme of life.[3] I have read the chief modern books, but Rousseau alone repays exhaustive study. For some months it has been my favourite relaxation to follow the mighty, mysterious unfolding of events. If you want to know my thoughts,

---

[1] See Meinecke, *Weltbürgertum u. Nationalstaat*, chs. iv. and v. ; Rougé, *Frédéric Schlegel et la genèse du romantisme allemand* ; and Friedrich Schlegel's *Briefe an seinen Bruder*.
[2] *Briefe*, pp. 17, 80.   [3] *Ib.*, pp. 127–8.

read Kant's "Theory and Practice." You should also read Klop-stock's Odes. It is a fine thing to carry the life of a noble people in one's heart ; but to dare such Odes at such a time is indeed exalted virtue.' A month later he replied to a letter in which August expressed his detestation of French excesses. ' I reverence your noble humanity, which abhors the smallest violence, whether committed in the name of order or of liberty, and I agree with you as to the affiliation of all peoples to the French Republic ; yet I desire the preservation of freedom in France. But enough! My heart is quickly enflamed. My political reading is not mere dilettantism, but a preparation for a work on our national history, which will form my chief task in Dresden.' [1] The tightening reaction, however, suggested greater caution in his utterances. He announces that he will not compromise himself and will not discuss politics freely in letters which may be opened.

Friedrich believed the historical treatment of the problems of the Revolution to be the safest ; and in 1795 he composed an essay on ' Ancient and Modern Republics,' in which he argued that a revolutionary genius was necessary to comprehend the political mind of the ancients. The dissertation was rejected by the review to which it was sent, and no trace of it has been found ; but portions were doubtless utilised in the essay on ' The Conception of Republicanism,' published a year later in Reichardt's new journal ' Deutschland.' [2] ' I am tired of criticism,' he wrote, ' and shall work at the revolutions with incredible enthusiasm. I shall also write something popular on Republicanism. I shall be happy when I can revel in politics. I will not conceal from you that Republicanism is nearer my heart than divine criticism and the still more divine poetry.' [3] The essay was suggested by Kant's ' Perpetual Peace,' in which he regretted to discover some distrust of democracy. He challenges the philosopher's veto on insurrection, and authorises it when the ruler overthrows the constitution or when an organised despotism, which he defines as the negation of a State, is established. A Republic, he contends, is necessarily democratic. The individual has the faculty of self-communication, and the ego ought to be communicated. Therefore, political liberty and equality for all are the two postulates of moral liberty. The ' will of all ' is most accurately expressed by the majority, and the only aristocracy is that of merit. But he is no blind doctrinaire. Representation he pronounces to be better than direct government.

[1] *Briefe*, pp. 145-6.
[2] His early essays and fragments are published in his *Jugendschriften*, two volumes, edited by Minor.
[3] *Briefe*, pp. 277-8.

Demagogy is despotism, and Nero and the *sansculottes* are equally scourges of mankind. Happily such afflictions do not last ; while oligarchies, feudalism, and caste are more or less permanent. Monarchy is often the best government for peoples not yet or no longer worthy of a republic, the value of which depends on the measure of liberty, equality, and fraternity that it embodies. The Greek spirit should be revived and applied to politics. ' The moral education of the people is impossible till the State is organised on republican principles ; but equally a widely diffused morality is the condition of perfection. Only universal and perfect Republicanism would constitute a sufficient foundation of perpetual peace.' Schlegel, unlike Kant, believes a world-republic to be no less practicable than desirable ; but his cautious liberalism safeguards the rights of the individual better than Kant, while avoiding the philosophic anarchy of Humboldt. It was no small feat for a young man of twenty-four to mate the aspirations of the Revolution with the lessons of history.

Schlegel's political philosophy was further explained in his essay on Diotima, in which he emphasises the beauty of Greek society and the connection of Greek art and literature with republican institutions. In ' The Limits of the Beautiful ' he defines the Republic as the ' true State,' and glorifies the patriotism which only grows in such a fertilising soil. His glowing tribute to Forster offers further evidence of his democratic sympathies. No German writer of the time applied a more independent mind to the problems of politics and society or reached more liberal conclusions ; but his liberalism ended with his youth, and he gradually approximated to the standpoint of his brother, who, in his Lectures in 1803, glorified the Middle Ages, attacked the Aufklärung, and poured contempt on the English Constitution. On his reception into the Roman Church in 1808, Friedrich definitely enlisted in the army of the counter-revolution. His elder brother had long affected the contempt for politics which was fashionable at Weimar. ' In my youth,' declared Tieck to Köpke, half a century later, ' cosmopolitan ideas were even commoner than to-day. How often have I wrestled with August Schlegel, who was devoted to them ! It was a matter of complete indifference to him by whom he was ruled and how.' [1]

Though Friedrich Schlegel composed no systematic work on politics, his mind continued for some years to play round its problems. Of the hundreds of ' fragments ' published in the ' Athenaeum,' in 1798, a considerable number deal with the Revolution or with political philosophy. ' One may regard the French Revolution

[1] Köpke, *Tieck*, ii. 247.

as the greatest phenomenon in the history of States ; as a world-wide earthquake or an immeasurable flood.   These are the ordinary views.   One can also regard it as the centre and summit of French national character, of which it combines all the paradoxes ; as the most fearful grotesque of the age, where the deepest prejudices and the most powerful emotions are mixed in dark chaos into a vast tragicomedy.'   A well-known but paradoxical fragment pronounces the 'French Revolution, Fichte's 'Science of Knowledge,' and 'Wilhelm Meister,' ' the dominant tendencies of the age.'   His more general reflections are not without shrewdness.   ' Perhaps no people is worthy of liberty ;   but that is a matter for the judgment-seat of God.'   ' The perfect Republic must be not only democratic, but also aristocratic and monarchic.   Within the circumference of liberty and equality, education must outweigh and direct ignorance.' ' Is not that an absolute monarchy where the essentials are secretly settled in the Cabinet, and where a Parliament is allowed pompously to discuss and disagree about the forms ?   An absolute monarchy might very well possess a sort of constitution which to dull minds would appear republican.'   ' The revolutionary desire to realise the Kingdom of God is the hinge of progressive culture and marks the beginning of modern history.'   In some further fragments of the following year, published as ' Ideas,' a growing alienation from politics becomes manifest.   ' The few revolutionaries there were in the Revolution were mystics, who made their doings a religion. In future history it will appear the highest of its achievements that it was the most powerful awakener of religion from her slumbers.' ' Do not waste your faith and love on politics ;   but in the divine world of science and art make a sacrifice of your innermost self in the holy lava stream of eternal culture.'   From such sentiments it was only a step to the complacent quietism of the Restoration era.

II

The life and thought of Novalis spans the gulf between revolutionary fervour and the mystical conservatism in which nearly all the leaders of the romantic movement ended their days.[1]   He greeted the dawn with the same intolerant ardour as his young friends, and warned his brother to eschew controversy with their father and uncle on the ground that they were two old fogeys.   ' My heart is heavy,' he wrote to Friedrich Schlegel, ' that the fetters do

---

[1] See Heilborn, *Novalis* ;   Dilthey's fine essay in *Das Erlebniss und die Dichtung* ;   Meinecke, *Weltbürgertum u. Nationalstaat*, ch. iv. ;   Novalis's *Schriften*, ed. Heilborn.

not already fall to pieces like the walls of Jericho.   But this feverish
mood melted away, and the conservative temperament of the poet
asserted itself.   Though he never wrote a treatise on the Revolution
there are many references to it in his 'Fragments,' and his anti-
revolutionary philosophy is fully stated in the pamphlets of the
later years of his short life.   ' All the leading ideas of the romantic
school of the Restoration,' declares Haym with truth, ' are in
his aphorisms, free from all hardness, all partisanship, and all
obscurantism.'

Novalis was the most national and the least cosmopolitan of the
circle, and he wrote proudly of his countrymen.   ' The instinctive
universalism of the Romans is also implanted in the German people.
The best that the French have won in their Revolution is a certain
portion of the German spirit.'   Though a student of Burke, he
held aloof from the reaction.   ' Most observers of the Revolution,
especially the wise and well-born, have pronounced it a dangerous
and contagious disease.   But they have not looked beyond the
symptoms, which they have confused and misinterpreted in mani
fold ways.   Some have taken it for a purely local ailment, others
have diagnosed it as nothing but the crisis of puberty.   One cannot
accuse the publicists of audacity.   Not one of them has thought
of inquiring whether monarchy and democracy must not, and
cannot, be combined as elements of a State.   The constitution of
monarchy is the character of the ruler, and its guarantee is his will.
True democracy is Protestantism.   The limited constitution is
half State, half nature—an artificial and brittle machine, and
therefore distasteful to genius ; but it is the hobby-horse of our
time.   If this machine could be quickened into a living organism,
the great problem would be solved.'

To this ambitious task Novalis addresses himself in ' Faith and
Love ; or, the King and Queen,' published in 1798.   Glowing with
mystical devotion, the poet finds the spirit of the people incarnate
in the young Prussian pair.   The idea of the State, he contends, is
purest in monarchy.   ' A true royal couple appeals to the whole
man, a constitution to reason alone.   A constitution only exerts
the same interest as a document.   What is a law if it is not the
expression of a beloved, revered person ?   Does not the mystical
Sovereign, like every idea, need a symbol ?   And what symbol is
worthier than a kindly and excellent man ?   Besides, a born King
is better than an elected ruler ; for he is not intoxicated by his
position.   And is not birth the primitive choice ?   It is a pity that
our age is so divorced from nature, so lacking in comprehension of
family life, so inimical to the most beautiful and poetical form of
society.   The King is the worthy life-principle of States, like the

sun among the planets. He is the creative artist who brings the idea of the people nearer perfection. It is an error to describe him as the first official of the State ; for he is neither an official nor a citizen. It is the essence of monarchy that it rests on the belief in a man of superior birth and on the hearty acceptance of such an ideal being. From among my equals I cannot choose a superior. The King is raised to be an earthly Providence. Such poetry alone satisfies the higher longings of our nature. The time will soon come when all will realise that no King can exist without a Republic, and no Republic without a King, and that they are as inseparable as body and soul.'

The poet now passes to an even more radiantly tinted picture of the Queen as a vivifying and spiritualising element in the life of the State. 'Those who nowadays declaim against princesses, as such, and find salvation only in the new French system, and only recognise the Republic if it is accompanied by Electoral Assemblies, Directories, and Trees of Liberty, are miserable Philistines—empty in mind, poor in heart, slaves of the letter. The Queen's sphere of operations is not political, but domestic. First there is the supervision of her children, the education of her sex, the care of the poor, the supervision of public morals. She must close all houses of ill-fame. Her example will be of infinite importance. Happy marriages will become more common. She will be the model of dress —that faithful barometer of habit. Every woman and mother should have a picture of the Queen in her room, or that of her daughters. The King and Queen jointly are a greater protection to the monarchy than two hundred thousand men. No State has been governed more like a factory than Prussia since the death of Frederick William I. However necessary is such a mechanical adminis- tration for its physical health, it will collapse if it is treated to this diet alone. The conduct of the State depends on public sentiment, and the ennobling of this sentiment is the only basis for reform. It is no true monarchy where the King and the intelligence of the State are no longer identical. The King of France was dethroned long before the Revolution, as indeed were most other European princes.' Thus ends this ecstatic homage to the young couple, the father and mother of their people. It is mystical royalism exalted into a political system. He found States ' scarcely any- thing but legal and defensive institutions,' and his dream is to transform them into living personalities.

Having rehabilitated the throne, Novalis proceeds to rehabili- tate the altar in his most important political work, ' Christendom or Europe.' For the first time a Protestant accepts the Catholic reading of the Ages of Faith, and we find ourselves on the road which leads to Chateaubriand, de Maistre, and de Bonald. From the era of rationalism and unrest in which he lives, he looks back with longing to the safe anchorage of the Middle Ages. 'They were glorious times when Europe was a Christian land, with one faith, one head, one common interest. It was an era of childlike trust in the clergy and in their message. With what a light heart every man went about his daily task, when a safe future was secured for him by these holy men and every error received their forgiveness! They were the experienced pilots on the vast, uncharted ocean of life, in whose keeping the storm was no longer a terror. They preached nothing but love to the Virgin, and recorded the lives of the saints. Rome was the New Jerusalem. Princes submitted their disputes to the father of Christendom. The unity of Europe was secured by Christianity—the peace of God, resting not on material interests, but on religion. How beneficent, how perfectly adapted to the deepest nature of man, was this régime is shown by the mighty development of human capacity under its auspices.' Novalis omits to date this idyllic picture, the German counterpart to the 'Génie du Christianisme'; but he confesses that it did not last long. These, he declares, were the beautiful, essential traits of the truly Catholic or truly Christian times. But the race was not ripe for this noble régime, and deterioration set in among the clergy and laity alike. What could be more natural than the Lutheran revolt? Yet though many good principles were introduced and many abuses were removed, the Protestants sundered the indivisible Church and tore themselves away from the unity in which alone true and lasting regeneration was possible. Thus religion lost at one stroke its pacifying and unifying influence. Protestantism dried up the fountains of the spirit, and the worldly element became supreme. Christendom ended with the Reformation. Study the new revolutionary centuries, and the soulless Aufklärung. Is not the revolutionist a Sisyphus? The stone will roll down again if there is no celestial magnet to keep it on the heights.

However apprehensive, Novalis is by no means without hope. Shall a Revolution, he asks, occur in France alone? With the coming of peace a new and higher life will begin. In Germany, which marches slowly but surely in advance of other countries, indications of the new world are already visible. While others busy themselves with war, party, and speculation, the German is educating himself to a higher standard of culture. All around us we see intellectual effort. The faults of the old institutions are manifest, and the line of advance is taught by the Middle Ages. 'What if a closer and more manifold connection of European States were to be the historical goal of the war ? If a new movement of hitherto slumbering Europe were to occur ? If a State of States were to confront our vision ? ' It sounds like an echo of Kant ; but there is a note in the melody which his lips never framed. Only religion, declares the author with deep conviction, can awaken Europe, reconcile the peoples, and restore Christendom. Once more there must be a visible Church, caring nothing for territorial landmarks, taking to her bosom every son athirst for the spiritual life. ' When ? Patience—it must and will come, the holy time of perpetual peace.'

Some of the fragmentary utterances jotted down in the closing months of his life show that Novalis was by no means blind to the results of republicanism. The peculiar charm of a Republic is that everything finds expression so much more freely. ' In our towns the objects of our conversation are local. General and important matters occupy no one. It is better in Republics, where the State is the main concern of everybody, and everybody feels his part of a mighty society—his life bound to a mightier life ; and thus mind and imagination are enlarged.' Yet republicanism, which appeals so forcibly to youth, is as insufficient as the mechanical rigidity of a bureaucratic monarchy ; for both lack consecration. The basis of authority is not force, but faith ; not law, but the compelling personality of a benign and beloved ruler. Such is the ringing challenge thrown down to the rationalisation of politics. It is the product of an unpolitical and unobservant mind ; for in truth the age of chivalry, as Burke bitterly lamented, had vanished for ever. Moreover, we detect the germs of the servility of the later romanticism, when the misty idealism of youth shall have melted into the harsh outlines of autocracy and obscurantism.

III

The German Keats, though less of a political thinker than Novalis, was more powerfully attracted to the ideals of 1789.[1] As a boy Hölderlin abhorred the restrictions of school, and spoke with indignation of the imprisonment of his fellow-Swabian, Schubart. A student at Tübingen when the Revolution broke out, he shared in the general rejoicing, and joined a club where the French papers could be seen. ' I have been instructing myself a little about the Rights of Man in the great Jean Jacques,' he wrote at the end of 1791, ' and I am nearly ready with my " Hymn to Humanity." ' [2]

---

[1] See Litzmann, *Hölderlin's Leben in Briefen*; Dilthey's fine essay in *Das Erlebniss u. die Dichtung* ; and the *Sämmtliche Werke*, ed. 1913.

[2] Litzmann, p. 139.

The Hymn was completed in 1792, and bears a characteristic motto from Rousseau. ' Les bornes du possible dans les choses morales sont moins étroites que nous ne pensons. Ce sont nos faiblesses, nos vices, nos préjugés qui les rétrécissent.' A couple of stanzas will give some idea of the fine poem with its boundless hopes.

> Youth, when arrayed beneath the flag of freedom
>   Already knows itself to be divine,
> And, bursting through all fetters, is determined
>   To vanquish the presumptuous libertine.
> Bold in his wrath, behold the unconquered spirit
>   Of truth and right on lofty pinions rise :
> The eagle brings the lightning of the avenger,
>   And thunders victory's paean to the skies.
>
> Ring forth, ring forth, glad messages of triumph,
>   Sung by no mortal voices hitherto !
> We have avenged our wrongs, and now have proudly
>   Wrought what the power of aeons could not do.
> The legions of our fathers have arisen,
>   Rejoicing o'er their children's kingly deeds :
> By heaven itself humanity is vaunted,
>   And mankind follows where the ideal lèads.

A ' Hymn of Liberty,' composed in the same year, breathes the spirit of Rousseau in all its rapturous purity.

> Free and great and glorious is thy message,
> Queen, to whom be praise in word and deed !
> Now behold the dawn of new creation ;
> See fruit springing from the fertile seed.
> Newly risen o'er the boundless ocean,
> Like the planets in their majesty,
> From the distance, lo ! thou smil'st upon us,
> Century of new-born liberty !
>
> When the final victory is accomplished
> At the dawning of the harvest day,
> When the seats of tyranny are scattered,
> And the tyrant's menials cast away,
> When the life, love, labour of my country
> To the world's great brotherhood belong,
> Once again, fair goddess, I will hymn thee :
> Thine shall be my muse's parting song.

It was natural that the sympathies of the young idealist should be with France when war broke out in 1792. ' Now it will soon

be settled between the French and the Austrians,' he wrote in June.[1]
' Believe me, dear sister, we shall have a bad time if the Austrians
win. The abuse of princely power will become terrible. Take my
word for it and pray for the French, the champions of human
rights.' After the republican triumphs in the autumn he wrote
to his mother in the same strain. ' Do not worry about the war.
Wherever it has penetrated in Germany, the good citizen has lost
little or nothing and gained a great deal. It is touching to think
that in the French army at Mainz there are a lot of boys of sixteen
and seventeen.' On leaving the University in 1793 he outlined to
his brother his political creed.[2] ' Individuals mean less to me than
of old. My love is the human race—not, of course, the corrupt,
servile, idle race that we too often meet. I love the great, fine
possibilities, even in corrupt people. I love the race of the centuries to come. This is my dearest hope—the faith that gives me
strength and determination—that our grandchildren will be better
than ourselves, that freedom must arrive some day, that virtue will
thrive better in the warming light of liberty than in the icy zone of
despotism. We live in a time when everything is working towards
amelioration. These seeds of enlightenment, these silent wishes
and strivings towards the education of the race, will broaden and
strengthen, and will yield glorious fruit. This is the sacred goal of
my wishes and my activity—to plant the seeds which will ripen
in another generation.' Passing from Tübingen to Jena, the young
poet sat at the feet of Fichte, whom he calls ' the Titan,' and who
nourished both his idealism and his will to action. ' Hölderlin's
interest in cosmopolitan ideas,' wrote his friend Hegel, ' is always
growing.' A no less potent formative influence was the oracle of
Königsberg. ' The beneficent effect of philosophical and political
study on our national culture is obvious,' he wrote to his brother.
' We needed it more than any other nation. The common virtues
and failings reduce themselves to a Philistine domesticity. Kant
is the Moses of our nation, who led us forth from Egyptian lethargy,
and brings the law of energy from the Holy Mountain. Our
horizon is expanding.'[3]

The hopes and ideals with which Hölderlin was filled found
repeated literary expression in the decade of creative activity
which the poet was to enjoy before madness descended on him
like a cloud and blinded the eyes of the soul. His prose poem,
' Hyperion,' perhaps the most perfect of his works, was planned
at Tübingen. Like Friedrich Schlegel, he steeped himself in the
prismatic beauties of ancient Greece, deriving from their contem-
plation an ardent determination to renew them. The scene of his

[1] Litzmann, pp. 149–50. [2] *Ib.*, p. 169. [3] *Ib.*, pp. 467–9.

story is laid in modern Greece during the revolt of 1770. Hyperion, who is the poet himself, throws himself into the struggle, filled with the loftiest thoughts of national liberty. His teacher, Alabanda, is Fichte or Posa, or both, in a composite photograph. Their unselfish idealism stands out in sharp relief against the brutality of the Greek rebels, which quickly manifests itself. The story ends with the flight of Hyperion from the land of disillusion to the country of the poet's birth. He thirsts to live in a world of freedom and beauty, and, when he fails to catch a vision of the Grail in Greece, he renews the quest elsewhere. Germany, too, falls short of the ideal ; but while he scolds, he pities and loves. ' Happy is the man who has a flourishing fatherland. When I am reminded of my own, I feel as if the coffin-lid is closing over me.' Nowhere in German literature do we hear higher or sweeter notes of hope and faith, of noble endeavour and selfless zeal. Nowhere is the great and ennobling vision of a better world, which thrilled the age of the Revolution, rendered with more intensity of conviction and more consummate art than in this exquisite casket, richly studded with precious gems.

Romanticism at its best embraced the world in its vision. ' I no longer hug the individual so closely,' he wrote. ' My love is the race. The time has come when mankind can deliberately embark on the perfecting of itself. The divine in us is liberated. The partition between classes is broken down. The highest pride of the new-born citizen, his warmest love, his death, his heaven, is the Fatherland.' Hölderlin is not content with setting forth his ideals, but calls on his countrymen to fulfil them. In a series of impassioned poems he asks when thought will give place to deeds, when the soul of his country will awake and become creative. ' Scoff not at the child when he sits proudly upon his hobby-horse,' he cries in his stanzas ' To the Germans ' ; ' for we, too, are rich in thought, but poor in deed. May not the deed emerge like a flash from the clouds ?   May not the golden fruit spring from the written page, as from the umbrageous grove ?   May not the silence of the people be the moment of consecration before the festival ?   O genius of our race !   When wilt thou appear in thy creative power ?   When in thy completeness, soul of our Fatherland ?   Willingly would I perish if our cities were touched with a purer flame and the hills of our land were hills of the Muses, and under the golden heaven of the Fatherland the free, clear joy of the spirit were to shine.' ' Death for the Fatherland ' strikes an even more exalted note of patriotic sacrifice. ' The battle is ranged, and the youths stream down from the hills. Make place for me in your ranks, that I die no common death. . . . I longed to die for the Fatherland,

and now 'tis done! To you, my friends, I come—to you who taught me how to live and die. How often, in the days of light, I thirsted to see you, heroes and poets of old ! And kindly will you greet the unknown stranger. Tidings of victory reach us ; the battle is ours. Long life to you, my Fatherland, and reckon not the dead. Not one too many has fallen in your sacred cause.' A poet who could strike such virile chords on his lyre would surely have been found at the side of his master, Fichte, had he been privileged to take a conscious share in the revival of the national spirit after passing through the valley of humiliation. But while embracing the national ideal with religious fervour, he retained the generous democratic faith, without which nationalism is a mere formula of power and aggrandisement. ' Thou art God's voice,' he wrote in a poem, ' The Voice of the People.' ' So I thought in my youth, and I say so still. The waters purl without troubling about my wisdom, and yet gladly do I listen to them and they strengthen my heart. They may not follow my guidance, but they find their own way down to the sea.'

IV

None of the Romanticists possessed a less political nature than Tieck ; but he shared the academic radicalism prevailing among young writers in the years immediately preceding the outbreak of the Revolution.[1] His introduction to politics occurred when he heard Mirabeau declaiming with fierce eloquence in a Berlin restaurant to members of the French colony. He was naturally carried away by the news of the fall of the Bastille, and, after studying Linguet's famous book, composed a dramatic poem glorifying the insurgents and shedding tears of joy over the breaking of the fetters. His father watched events with very different eyes, and ended the discussions with his ardent son by a grave warning. ' Only confusion and folly will come from it. The people is not fit for such things.' The young poet stuck to his guns, and at Göttingen called himself a democrat, prating of liberty and equality to whoever would listen to him. His play, ' Alla-Moddin,' written in 1790-1, breathes the pure gospel of Rousseau.[2] The native King of Sulu, an island in the Pacific, visits the Philippines, and is treacherously imprisoned with his wife and child at Manila by the Spanish Governor. He is offered liberty if he will become a Christian ; but he declines. The Governor has qualms, but is dominated by a fanatical Jesuit, the villain of the piece. After

[1] See Köpke, *Erinnerungen aus dem Leben Tiecks*, two volumes.
[2] *Schriften*, vol. ii.

two years of suffering, the noble Alla-Moddin is released on the arrival of a ship from Spain with orders for the recall of the Governor and with news of the dissolution of the Jesuit Order. He returns to his home accompanied by Valmont, who has secured his release and who voices the ideas of 1789. ' I have left Europe for ever,' he cries. ' My country is bound in fetters by a cruel tyranny. I cannot live among men who are ashamed to be men. These rulers and their slaves offend my eyes. If the Old World ever improves, I will return to it. Till then, I will make my home in Sulu.'

Tieck spent his happiest hours in Reichardt's house in Berlin, where he met not only artists and actors, but men of advanced political opinions. When war broke out he sympathised openly with the enemy. ' Oh! to be in France! ' he wrote. ' It must be a glorious experience to fight under Dumouriez, to send the slaves flying, and even to fall ; for what is life without liberty ? I salute the genius of Greece, which I see hovering over Gaul. France is now my thought day and night.' The overthrow of the monarchy, the September massacres, and even the impending fate of the King, left him undismayed. In 1795 he gave expression to his dislike for the Émigrés, in his ' Hanswurst as Émigré,' in which the adventurer, Hanswurst, masquerades as Artois, who, for lack of a horse, has to ride on the back of his servant. Though the bright little comedy, which ends with the exposure of the impostor, would hardly have caused a revolution, it was not printed till after his death.[1] When the jealous Kotzebue endeavoured, in 1802, to injure his rival by reading the parade scene at the Prussian Court, the King paid no attention to the reader's malicious comments and insinuations ; for Tieck had been cured not only of his radicalism, but of his interest in politics. ' Did I not tell you what would occur ? ' asked his father, as the news of tragedy after tragedy arrived. ' Was I not right ? ' And the son sat silent, shuddering at the horrors, and seeking refuge in the green pastures of literature.

Tieck's bosom friend, Wackenroder, the gentle idealist who was snatched away at the age of twenty-six, shared both the romantic enthusiasm for the dawn of liberty and the profoundly unpolitical nature of the members of the circle. A letter to Tieck, written a few days before the death of the King, reveals the mind not only of the writer, but of the school to which he belonged.[2] ' I have long wondered that you have not asked me what I think about the French. Well, I think just like you, and heartily share your enthusiasm. I never mention them here, because people speak of their mighty deeds with a smile which makes me wish to box their ears. Besides, I think very little about the whole business, and I

[1] *Nachgelassene Schriften*, vol. i. [2] *Briefe an Tieck*, iv. 239–40.

have no time to read the papers.   If I were a Frenchman, I should be proud of my country ; but I should not be a soldier, as I prize life and health too much and lack physical courage.   I know you will fail to comprehend how one can be zealous for a cause without possessing sufficient resolution to work for it, and for a few hours my confession will provoke your wrath.   I am far from despising these bodily virtues—but I do not possess them.   And I am so built that beauty is to me above everything.   I find it impossible to be very interested when I read in the papers that the Prussians have taken this place and the French that.   It is all too remote, too difficult to visualise, too repugnant to the idealistic flight of my imagination.'   But though his interest was weak, his sympathies remained unchanged.   'The execution of the King,' he wrote to Tieck, 'has sickened the whole of Berlin, except myself, of the French cause.   I have not changed my opinions.'

V

In addition to the members of the inner Romantic Circle, two famous names call for notice.   Though belonging to theology, not to literature, Schleiermacher was for some years the closest friend of Friedrich Schlegel, and for the purpose of this chapter he may be reckoned a temporary member of the group.[1]   His early training at Herrnhut taught him to think lightly of the need for State control and to number toleration among the sovereign principles of human society.   At the outbreak of the Revolution the young theologian, then tutor in the family of a count, expressed his satisfaction at events and welcomed above all the separation of Church and State.   The laws on divorce and other ecclesiastical innovations provoked an expression of satisfaction that 'superstition and prejudice do not lie nearly so deep in the soul of the people as was imagined.'   The death of the King called forth a revealing letter to his father.   'I know not how it was that till now I have never spoken to you of these events ; but the affair occupies me too closely to keep silence.   As I always tell you all my thoughts quite frankly, I am not afraid to own that, on the whole, I love the French Revolution very much—of course, without praising everything which human passions and extravagant principles have wrought, or things which, though perhaps inevitable, cannot be approved.   I have loved it honourably and without partisanship ; but this event has filled my soul with sadness, for I regard the good King as perfectly innocent, and I abhor this savagery from my heart.   But I have been almost as much angered

[1] See Dilthey, *Leben Schleiermachers*, vol. i.

by the manner in which many people speak of it as by the thing itself. Many condemn it only because it is the fall of an anointed head ; others excuse it as part of the fortunes of politics, and only regret the lack of decorum. I say that no policy justifies the murder of an innocent man ; but if the death-sentence is ever legitimate, and Louis had committed a crime for which death is the legal punishment, his consecration should not save him from his fate. People shriek at one for having no feelings. That has been my fate thousands of times all through this French affair. While I cannot help attacking the partisanship of those around me and try to make them hear the other side, I get into trouble in both camps, and I, poor fellow, who seldom have an opinion on things and belong to no party, am taken by the Democrats for a defender of despotism and by the Royalists for a Jacobin. It is just the same in theology, where I am charged indifferently with being an evangelical and a rationalist.' His father replied with words of sympathy and warning. ' I am sorry that in political matters you have such struggles. Are there so few philosophical heads in your part of the world ? Will they not see that, if the French Revolution is very instructive for rulers and people, it cannot take place according to the ideal which has been formed of it, if one takes human nature as it is ? Our moral and political perfecting is as impracticable as Plato's Republic or the peace dreams of St. Pierre and Henri IV, as impracticable as the French system of liberty and equality will prove to be. Ask your radical friends if they really believe that a democratic republic of the size of France will ever be able to exist. There is certainly no precedent for it.' [1]

The execution of the Girondins was an even greater shock to Schleiermacher than the death of the King, and his lively sympathy was excited by Lafayette's captivity ; but he abstained from all public utterance. In 1796 he worked at an essay on the contract theory, suggested by the controversies of the Revolution. Though the essay was never written, notes survive to show that he fully accepted the conception of natural law, the main foundation of democratic theory. But his heart was in theology, and, like Friedrich Schlegel, he turned his back on political speculation before he had crossed the threshold of middle age.

VI

Though Jean Paul Richter belonged to an older generation than the Romanticists and had no close personal connection with them, he was none the less a standard-bearer in the army of literary

[1] *Aus Schleiermacher's Leben, in Briefen,* i. 114, 118–119.

revolt.[1] The Aufklärung had no power over the satirist, who did
as much as any of the Romanticists to kill it. He was born a
democrat, as Goethe was born an aristocrat, and he was ever ready
to denounce political and social wrong. In his ' Greenland Trials '
he scoffed at the old nobility, which he compared to maggot-eaten
cheese, and bitterly denounced the petty oppressions of German
rule. The ' Selections from the Devil's Papers,' published in 1789,
renew the attack on the abuses of a petty German State as he knew
them in his own Ansbach and Bayreuth. An essay on ' How a
Prince may support his Subjects after the Hunt,' bitterly satirises
the ruinous policy of conscienceless princes. There is no harm in
letting soldiers starve ; for if they are too weak to stand, they can
always fire on one knee. The sale of subjects to foreign potentates
for war is praiseworthy, since nothing can so surely save them
from the horrors of starvation as the sword of the enemy. State
lotteries are the simplest method of filling the humblest subjects
with the greatest hopes. In these attacks on princes and nobles
we find the deep sympathy with the disinherited and the oppressed
which accompanied him throughout life and which honourably
distinguish him from all his literary contemporaries. He complained that his countrymen were too patient of oppression. In
an essay, written shortly after the ' Devil's Papers,' he laments that
the German has no national pride, and compares him to a servant
who wears the cast-off clothes of other nations. The tax-paying
and uncomplaining Teuton is like Milo, who by daily carrying a
calf found himself after a time with an ox upon his shoulders. ' The
Journey of Rector Florian and his Pupils to the Fichtelberg '—that
incomparable picture of a tasteless pedant—is directly suggested
by the events of 1789. The French Revolution, declares the head
master, would have been impossible if people, instead of studying
the French *philosophes*, had been content to edit the classics.
When his pupils read the Orations against Catiline, he explains
how all the French revolutionaries are Catilines. He bids his class
meditate on the tranquillity of the great philologists, who have
never revolted and have only taught. They have praised no
republics save those of Greece and Rome, and those only for the
sake of the Greek and Latin languages.

' The Invisible Lodge,' the first of Richter's longer novels,
finished in 1792, presents a picture of the life of princes modelled
on his own ruler, the Margrave of Bayreuth and Ansbach. With
bitter irony he describes the death and burial of the prince. ' His
stomach digested as much as his conscience, especially large blocks
of land, and better than his head, which found truths and

[1] See Nerrlich, *Jean Paul Richter*.

remonstrances difficult of assimilation.' On growing tired of signing decrees he used a stamp, which lightened the burden of rule. The prince can listen unmoved to the sighs of his people, but not to those of a beauty. He would rather owe money to his Estates than to his violinist, and is more ready to restore a torn wig than a town in ashes. These pungent thrusts recall the early dramas of Schiller and the dashing skirmishes of the *Sturm und Drang.*' Richter made no secret of his radical opinions. On his visit to Weimar in 1796 he found Herder and other members of the circle which gathered round his clever and emancipated friend, Charlotte von Kalb, ' the keenest republicans,' and in this congenial company he aimed arrow after arrow at the lords of creation.

In 1799 the novelist wrote his celebrated essay on Charlotte Corday, whom he hails in impassioned accents as a second Joan of Arc, whose dagger-stroke was an ' execution.'[1] His eloquent paean closed with a glorification of Adam Lux, which drove his daughter to suicide, and was in after years to inspire Sand to the murder of Kotzebue. No German work on the Revolution breathes a more ardent love of liberty or hotter indignation against its French murderers. This glorious essay, remarks Hettner, stamps him as one of the few who held to the ideal origin and goal of the French Revolution. The conversation takes place at the residence of a petty ruler, whose hobby is the collection of portraits and books relating to heroes. ' I went to him on the anniversary of the death of Charlotte Corday,' relates the author, ' and found him with his President of the Council. The President quoted the verdict of Girtanner that Charlotte was worse than Marat, who only arranged murders, while she committed one.' ' Oh, God ! ' I replied, ' just the reverse. That is more cowardly.' ' Is murder ever lawful ? ' queries the President. ' Yes. While Ravaillac is blamed, Brutus is praised. And Charlotte fought and stabbed, as a warrior slays an enemy in civil war, or as a healthy member destroys a cancerous germ. We wish not only to inhabit the city of God, but to enlarge its area.' At this point the Count breaks in. ' Our morality is too homely—too much convention, and too little action. A literary genius or a superman will hardly appear once in a century. All the mountains and elevations in history were raised by the volcanic fires of such supermen as Bonaparte, who destroy and construct at the same time. What great men accomplish in enthusiasm, in which their whole being and the higher humanity in them raises and glorifies and reflects itself—that is right for them and their fellows, but for them alone.' ' Yes,' I added, ' there must be something loftier than mere law, or the

[1] *Werke*, vol. xxiv., ed. 1842.

avoidance of wrong ; but it is as little subject to measurement by the thumb-rule of custom as the figures of Raphael by mathematical symbols.' ' Want of courage, not want of goodwill,' resumes the Count, ' makes men cold and flabby. Such courage is divine— its arms are wings. With these wings, the eagle moulds the soft world more than with claws and beak. I should not like to live where no great spirit touched and penetrated and moulded—on a stage where there was only the chorus of the crowd, with old men, slaves, women, soldiers, and shepherds. What a difference there is between dying of something and dying for something!'

' I told the Count that I had prepared a sketch of Charlotte Corday for the anniversary. He thereupon chose for our reading the open expanse of heaven, an altar beneath two lime-trees. My host produced a portrait, and after gazing fixedly at this second Joan of Arc, I began reading. The Terror slew the life of the Revolution. Not they suffered most bitterly who lost property or life, but they for whom each day murdered a hope of liberty. When the Girondins, the last of the Republicans, died and left the field to the plebeians, their death touched the great heart of a woman.' After a full account of her journey to Paris, the assassination, and the execution, the author concludes : ' Let us not weep, but let each of us, like her, sacrifice what God desires of him, even if it be his life.' ' When the story was completed, I seized the hand of the Count, who tearfully kissed the portrait ; and we meditated in silence on the heroes and heroines of liberty.' In these burning pages the democracy of France is wedded to the sentimentalism of the German Romantic movement.

Richter's educational treatise, ' Levana,' afforded him an opportunity of renewing the expression of his democratic faith. The section on the education of a prince launches a vigorous attack on war, which the tutor must render ' hateful to his pupil ' by explaining its horrors. ' The poisonous air of Courts makes princes thirst for excitement ; but the people alone should decide on war, as they alone cull its bitter fruits.' The right kind of war is the struggle for reform. ' A truly brave people carries on its war of freedom at home against every hand which would stay its flight or blind its eye. This is the longest and bravest conflict, and the only one which admits of no truce.' The prince must be taught to know realities if he is to rule well. Let him visit every part of his country and obtain a thorough acquaintance with the life of the people. It is the ideal of ' the first servant of the State,' whose power, however, is shared with his subjects. The theory of enlightened autocracy is modified and supplemented by the principle of democratic control taught by the French Revolution.

The famous novelist shared the general sympathy for the early achievements of Napoleon, hailing him as the guardian angel of Germans and begging for a federation of princes under his protection; but he had no desire for universal monarchy. The humiliation of Jena made him a nationalist, and he confidently predicted a revival. But it was rather as a Mentor of princes than as a tribune of a nation that he spoke in the political pamphlets which preceded and followed the downfall of the Emperor. Political writers, he declared, were essential for national welfare; for they were ambassadors to a prince, who must tell him the truth about his own and other countries, disinterestedly and objectively, without interference from the censor. The Tree of Knowledge, he teaches, grows like the Tree of Liberty. The limitation of academic freedom is particularly foolish. When princes see everything, and see it in the right light, better times will come; for rulers, like other mortals, sin more in a search for good than for evil. After the wars of liberation he issued a noble appeal to princes to trust the people. A nation must obtain free government in order to become worthy of it. Thus to the end Richter's love of the people was the foundation of his political thought; and, though he taught mainly in parables, he holds an honourable place in the history of German democracy.

R

CHAPTER X

DURING the period of the French Revolution the most popular dramatists in Germany were not Goethe and Schiller, but Iffland and Kotzebue. Though the former is now remembered mainly as an actor, and the latter for his tragic end, for many years their plays drew crowded and enthusiastic houses in every part of the country. Gifted with immense inventive facility, and possessing a sure grasp of technique and telling situations, their dramas dealt with the experiences and emotions of ordinary sentimental men and women. Never soaring beyond the capacity of their audience, nor scaring them by moral and political paradox, they remained on the safe ground of bourgeois morality, and were rewarded by the unstinted homage of the bourgeoisie.

I

Consumed from boyhood with a passion for the stage, Iffland obtained employment at the theatre in Mannheim, then under the enlightened direction of Dalberg, the brother of the Coadjutor of Mainz. His opportunity arrived with the early plays of Schiller, and his fame is bound up with Karl Moor and Verrina, Wurm and Don Carlos. Called to the Prussian capital in 1796, as director of the national theatre, he raised the Berlin stage to the position of supremacy hitherto occupied by Hamburg and Mannheim. He was equally at home in comedy and tragedy, in Molière and Shakespeare. Though lacking the majesty and intensity of Talma, his fame is secure as the first of German actors in celebrity, if not in merit ; for he was not only a dramatist and an actor, but a conspicuous figure in the social and intellectual life of the time. He raised the prestige of his profession by his high character, his wide culture, and his friendship with the first writers of the day. ' You make the theatre a school of morals,' remarked his director, Dalberg ; and for Goethe he was ' the incomparable master.'

Iffland's Autobiography[1] presents a vivid picture of the early years of the Revolution as witnessed from Mannheim, where large numbers of Émigrés took refuge. The sensitive actor quickly marked the presence of a new element in his audience. They seized situations more rapidly and showed their appreciation of the play with less reserve. The temperature became warmer, to the great satisfaction of the actors. ' We watched the motley throng with their idiosyncrasies and their follies, and we enjoyed conversation with the more intellectual among them. After the first storms in Paris were over, the great events there gave promise of immense benefit to mankind without paying an exorbitant price. Everybody took interest in the event, rejoiced at the removal of oppression, and welcomed the assurance that the policy of France was to reform and defend the country, not to make conquests. We did not then foresee the conflict which was to destroy our peace and the peace of the world.' In the middle of 1791, and still more in the early part of 1792, the scene had changed, and opinion had changed with it. Persons and occurrences which had hitherto been the theme of witty sallies or grave conversation were now the cause of embittered controversy. The war of opinion began, and social intercourse was disturbed. The friction was felt in the theatre, one or other party advertising its view by calculated frigidity or boisterous enthusiasm. The Émigrés were the worst offenders, and their ebullitions annoyed quiet citizens. Some weeks after the Royal Family had been arrested at Varennes, Grétry's opera, ' Richard Cœur de Lion,' was being played. ' The performance was interrupted by sobs and ejaculations; and when the castle was stormed by Blondel, and the King released, the Émigrés stood up in their seats and embraced one another, uttering loud cries of " Louis Seize." ' At the end of the piece the actors were called to the stage, and Iffland cried in French, ' May the King find a Blondel to save his life.' The Émigrés were delighted, and at the time no voice was raised in criticism ; but the episode was to cause trouble to the great actor and stamp him as a partisan of the counter-revolution.

The impression was confirmed by a play which had been sketched in the spring of 1791 and was published at the end of the year. On a visit to Mannheim, his fellow actor, Schröder, read the outline of ' The Cockades,' and pronounced it excellent, though he believed that it would never be acted. The prophecy was not fulfilled. Of Goethe's plays on the Revolution, ' The Civilian-General ' alone caught the ear of the public ; and that was merely a *jeu d'esprit*. The most effective dramatic treatment of its problems was provided

[1] The best edition is that of 1898.

by Iffland in his five-act tragedy, the inception of which the author describes in his Autobiography. ' In 1791 I received an unexpected command from the Emperor Leopold to write a play on the Revolution of 1660, by which the Kings of Denmark regained their power. As I disliked the subject, I suggested that I should exhibit a prince and his people separated by misunderstanding, and draw the portrait of a true ruler. In that way, I could give utterance to the feeling of something like suffocation which began to oppress me. My proposal was accepted, and I wrote " The Cockades," which has been so harshly misjudged. Many took me for a furious aristocrat ; but the few who knew me were as surprised at the accusation as myself. I have never said that one class was first or another third.' As the play is almost unknown in England, it may be well to offer a fairly full summary.[1]

Privy Councillor Bangemann is the virtual ruler of a tiny principality in the absence of its prince. The French Revolution is in full swing, and its reverberations echo through Germany. Bangemann is a conscientious official, but inflexibly opposed to the doctrines around him. ' Every one now wishes to rule,' he complains to his wife, ' and every one bawls " Liberty " among the ruins. The rights of fathers and mothers have disappeared. Everybody goes his own way. I quite expect my children to betray me, and my nearest relative to put a halter round my neck.' At this moment of anxiety and stress, the Court Chamberlain arrives with a message of gratitude for his handling of the rebels. Though everything points to rigorous measures, declares the messenger, the Prince is inflexible in his policy. ' What I do not obtain from the love and conscience of my subjects, I will not possess.' Furthermore, he will not compel taxation, and will continue the pensions of widows and others in distress. ' The example of one people,' concludes the Chamberlain, ' is always dangerous to the rest. When newspapers and zealots by tongue and pen exalt such a revolution as the height of virtue, it is natural that the masses should revolt. At the word Revolution, they only think of cutting down silk curtains, taking four horses out of the shafts, and tapping a cask of old wine. That is their idea of equality ; and the carnival is kept going by men of education.'

Before the last words are out of his mouth, Hahn, the schoolmaster, enters the room with his hat on his head and his hands in his pockets. ' Here is the third number of my Journal of the Rights of Man,' he cries. ' When it reaches the people, the bomb will burst, and a heap of rubbish will fly into the air. It is our turn now. Our tongues are swords, our newspapers are armies.' As the Chamberlain leaves the room, Hahn adds ' In my next issue

---

[1] It is printed in Iffland, *Theater*, vol. xvii.

I shall deal with Chamberlains.' Bangemann turns angrily on him
and charges him with tempting peaceful citizens to disloyalty,
banishing peace from earth, and preaching a happiness that cannot
be realised.   Hahn's reply is effusively to embrace Jürge, an honest
old peasant, who enters unexpectedly, and to tell him to be seated
and keep his hat on.   When Hahn has gone Jürge gets up, but
is persuaded to resume his seat and to tell the story of the revolt.
' How did it all happen so quickly ? ' asks Bangemann.   ' When we
first heard the news from France,' is the reply, ' we did not think
much of it.   But later, as we read in the paper that all men are
equal and that the peasants in France can say what they think and
that we now count for a little more than we did, then we grew to
like it.   And in the evening as we sat under the lime-trees, Brother
Hahn joined us and explained things.   And now we have all made
up our minds not to pay anybody any more.   There will be no
more rent, for everything will be divided up.   You see, if I were
to pay you, I should be a slave.'   The old man, though not
disrespectful, has been converted by the specious tongue of the
schoolmaster, and talks like a parrot.   News now arrives that
the town has risen in revolt, and the Privy Councillor hurries away
to confront the danger.

Bangemann's colleague and friend, the Burgomaster Rechfeld,
is the bogey of the revolutionaries ; and Rechfeld's son loves his
daughter.   The second act opens with the arrival of the brewer,
who demands to see Frau Bangemann and tells her that he is sent
by her son Franz, whom all the citizens respect.   ' Pity that his
father and younger brother are on the enemy's side.'   Pressed
by the anxious mother to tell what is going on, the brewer replies
that her son is the leader of the revolt and a wonderful orator.
He adds that the people are searching for the Burgomaster.
Albertine, the daughter, enters and asks her mother how she is.
' Very sad ; your brother is crazed with folly.' ' He goes too
far,' rejoins Albertine ; ' but folly is a hard word for a noble
endeavour.'   Her sympathies are with the rebels ; for are not
her brother and her fiancé among the leaders ?   The mother breaks
into tears on discovering that her daughter is also perverted.   Her
younger son, Bernard, who remains unshaken, enters with the
news that young Rechfeld has appealed to the mob to pardon
his father as an old man in his dotage, and that the crowd has
allowed him eight hours in which to lay down his offices.

Albertine : Then see that he does so.

Bernard : Listen to her ; nature made her gentle and good, but
she too——

Albertine : Is a citizen, and thanks God that at last the rights of
man are restored to her sex.

Bangemann returns in time to hear his daughter's declaration of independence, and cries angrily : ' You're ill ; be off with you ! ' He tells Bernard that Rechfeld is hidden in the house.   When Franz returns his father begins a lecture, but breaks down in an appeal to filial piety.

Franz : My convictions cannot change ; why do you tug at my heart-strings ? One is driven forward. Our duties often involve terrible sacrifices.   Think, for instance, of that scandalous serfdom.

Bangemann : I would shed my blood for the Constitution under which till now we have lived in peace and happiness.

Franz : Slept, you mean.   I am fired with the conviction that I am doing good.   [*Hearing the beating of drums, he hurries off to the meeting of gilds summoned to depose the Burgomaster.*]

Bangemann : He who has sown the seed of revolt in the boy's heart cannot have been a father himself.'

The third act opens with a message from the Prince, urging the Privy Councillor to restrain his son. ' They are all wearing the white and yellow cockades as the symbol of liberty,' adds the Chamberlain, ' and they have marked some of the houses.   The Prince refuses to allow the palace to be closed.'   On his departure, Jürge and a mob of peasants, armed with rustic weapons, swarm into the room. ' We mean no harm,' cries the old man, ' but everything has got to be shared.'   ' If not, we'll burn the house,' shout the rest.   Bangemann asks them whether they also want to rule.   The conversation proceeds peacefully till Hahn enters with an armful of cockades. ' Dear brothers,' he cries, ' force alone breaks your fetters.'   He distributes the cockades, explaining to Bangemann that they are made by his daughter, ' my pupil.'   Franz now enters with his mother, who has found him and persuaded him to return.   He starts on seeing the room crowded with the rebels, and falters : ' Father, this is not my doing.' Bangemann replies by giving Franz the Prince's message—that he does not wish to use force, but has sent a warning.   When Franz remains deaf to all appeals, Bangemann utters the solemn words : ' He will never have a father's blessing.'   Turning to the peasants, who are resolved to burn the palace, he adjures them to spare it, and adds that the Burgomaster is not there.   Some of them try to seize him ; but he is defended by Franz, and they rush out. The son then falls at his father's feet.

The fourth act begins with a family altercation. ' Our sex has lived all this time in subordination,' says Albertine ; ' now for the first time we possess the rights of citizens. It is an inspiration to co-operate in the transformation of a world.'   ' You

are on the road to becoming one of the Furies who murder and
burn,' cries her father angrily. Franz declares that he is torn
between nature and his oath, and adds ' My will is no longer my
own.' ' Such is your freedom,' retorts his father bitterly. The
tragedy now approaches. Hahn enters and tells Bangemann that
if he will not reveal the hiding-place of Rechfeld he must suffer.
The Privy Councillor embraces his family and forgives his daughter,
but utters a curse on her marriage. Armed peasants surge into
the house and demand the surrender of the Burgomaster. A
struggle ensues, in which Franz defends his father. In the confusion Rechfeld appears. He is offered his life if he will resign
his office and wear the cockade ; but he refuses the terms, and spurns
the hated emblem. The mob seizes him and Bernard, and carries
them out, while the house bursts into flames.

In the fifth act the curtain rises on the throne-room of the
castle, decorated with busts and pictures of the Prince's ancestors.
The townsfolk and peasants stream into the hall, crying ' Liberty !
Liberty ! ' while many sit for a moment on the throne. ' The great
task is accomplished,' cries Hahn ; ' humanity is delivered.'
' Hurrah for equality ! ' answers the crowd. ' Old Bangemann
is in chains,' continues Hahn. ' Thousands are waiting to see what
we now resolve.' He adds that taxes and dues must be paid ; but
there is a chorus of protest, and some one suggests appropriating
the treasures of the hall. When a rope is thrown round one of
the statues, a voice is raised : ' He founded the hospital,' and
the statue is spared. As the next is threatened, some one recalls
the fact that he had suppressed extravagance at Court. Old
Jürge remarks reflectively, ' We have had a lot of good rulers.'
Opinion is beginning to swing round, and it is suggested that the
advice of Bangemann be sought ; but it is too late. He is brought
in chains, with torn clothes and mortally wounded in the attack
on his house, in which his son Bernard and the Burgomaster had
perished. He is at the point of death, and in a few minutes he
expires. As they are about to carry him away the Prince himself
enters, unattended, and kisses and weeps over the body, while
all but Hahn and the brewer look on with respectful sympathy.
After a brief silence old Jürge speaks for the rest. ' We work hard
for a pittance. Then we were told we could be free. So we were
carried away.' The Prince addresses the crowd, and asks what
injury he has done to any of them. While he speaks, one after
another silently throws away his cockade, till only Hahn and the
brewer are left. The Prince forgives his subjects, saying, ' I see
you were misled.' He denounces Hahn as a murderer, orders
him to remove his cockade, and commits him for trial. The crowd

gather round the Prince, kiss his hand, and lay their cockades at his feet. The wheel has come full circle.

The Prince : My children !
All : God preserve our good lord !

It is a political sermon on the same text as Goethe's ' Civilian-General.' The ruler is a true father of his people. The masses being poor and ignorant, the new doctrines work like a poison in their blood. The ringleaders are men of some education, who use their authority to mislead the crowd. The gospel of liberty and equality brings discord in the family, confusion and bloodshed in the State. Finally the misguided multitude awake as from an evil dream. Iffland makes himself the champion of the patriarchal State ; and, though he puts the ideas of '89 into the mouth of Franz and Albertine, he has obviously no sympathy with them. The teaching of the play was sharply criticised, among others by Schlözer, who censured it for confounding the noble striving for liberty with the intrigues of impostors, and for scoffing at the enthusiasm for equality of classes, instead of teaching rulers to respect the rights of their injured subjects. The author at once wrote to defend himself. ' I wish you had lived in certain parts of Germany and seen the fury with which most travellers on their return from France—and, above all, many of the Intellectuals— praise the Revolution, influence man, woman, and child, and drive them towards rebellion with lips of foam. I resolved to break a lance for the side which is everywhere scoffed at and ill-treated.' Such a play, he argued, was not an attack on liberty, but the fulfilment of a citizen's duty.

II

Though a native of Weimar, Kotzebue[1] possesses few points of contact with the Immortals ; for, like Klinger, he left Germany as a young man to enter the Russian service, and his appearances in his native town were fleeting and unhappy. His first impressions of the Revolution were not wholly unfavourable, and Metternich speaks of him in his Autobiography as at that time an ardent follower of the school which was one day to murder him ; but the author of ' Menschenhass und Reue ' had little interest in politics and no sympathy with democratic ideas. His scurrilous attack on Bahrdt, published in 1790, inveighs not only against the ribald adventurer, but against Mauvillon, Campe, and other German Francophils ; and the little Diary, in which he described his three weeks' visit to

---

[1] See Rabany, *Kotzebue*.

Paris at the close of the same year,[1] testifies both to his dislike of the Revolution and to his incapacity of judging it. The journey was undertaken as a distraction from grief on the death of his wife, and he records that though he stayed some time in the capital he knew little of it. He came prepared to grumble, and he naturally found plenty to criticise. Of liberty he hears talk *ad nauseam*, and he finds daily proofs of the impertinence of the people. A coachman addressed his fare as ' Mon ami,' and in reply to the question whether he really thought he was a friend, rejoined ' We are all equal.' On another occasion an incident occurred which the dramatist was to introduce into his literary skit on the Revolution. ' Our lackey, who fetched us a carriage to-day for the opera, asked us to let him come inside, as the weather was bad.' A wig-maker referred to the Queen as ' la coquine,' or ' la femme du pouvoir exécutif,' and many expressed regret that she had not been killed on October 6. He found no relief in the theatre. ' In the present fever of liberty, people only wish to see the tragedies of tyranny.' Violent declamation was in fashion, and topical lines were frantically applauded. A play on the last days of Rousseau was received with wild enthusiasm. On the eve of his departure he paid a visit to the Assembly. ' Before we entered we heard the voice of Liberty in the distance—the laughter of the mob. I came with great expectations and left with an unsatisfied soul.' On the last day he wrote : ' I will stay no longer. I should never feel at home. A crowd of trivialities make life intolerable : the habits, the meals, the beds, the noises, the air. The intolerable egotism of the people oppresses me.'

From such a man the ideas of '89 were likely to receive short shrift. On receiving a title he proceeded to defend nobility, ' at a time when the equality of all classes is the hobby-horse on which young poets ride.' In his philosophic picture of Louis XIV he had criticised despotism ; and his comedy ' Wampam,' written in 1794, a satire on rulers, was one of the grounds for his arrest and brief banishment to Siberia by the Emperor Paul. Appointed Court dramatist at Vienna, in 1798, he was denounced as a Jacobin. But the authorities were on a false track. His early sarcasms against hereditary nobles were never repeated. A generation after the outbreak of the Revolution he returned to Germany as a spy in the Russian service, denounced the students' movement, and was murdered by the half-crazy Sand in 1819.

Among Kotzebue's two hundred plays, one little skit alone is devoted to the French Revolution.[2] ' The Ladies' Jacobin

---

[1] *Meine Flucht nach Paris*, 1791.
[2] ' Der Weibliche Jakobiner-Klubb ' is printed in Kotzebue, *Theater*, vol. ii.

Club,' a political comedy in one act, published in 1791, is as merry as Goethe's ' Civilian-General,' and even lighter in texture.   Duport, an old officer, is sitting in his house in Paris when his little son enters in national uniform, carrying a cardboard gallows on which a cardboard man is hanging.

Louis :   Look, father, here's a lamp-post, and there hangs an aristocrat !
Duport :   Stupid boy !   Who told you that ?
Louis :   Mother cut out the lamp-post, and I made the man.   And mother let me have this lovely uniform so that people can see I am not an aristocrat.
Duport :   Do you know what an aristocrat is ?
Louis :   There hangs one.
Duport :   I would give you a drubbing, boy, if grown-up children did not think and behave just like you.   Go and read your catechism, and don't trouble your head about aristocrats.
[*As the boy goes away in tears his mother bounces in to know what he has done.*]
Duport :   He talks nonsense about aristocrats without knowing what he means.
Mme. Duport :   He must be told.   One must begin to instil correct principles in good time.
Duport :   That means that he must learn to respect virtue wherever he finds it, whether in a democracy or aristocracy.
Mme. Duport :   He'll never find it in the latter.
Duport :   Henriette, you are forgetting your own husband.
Mme. Duport :   You are led astray by thinking of your own interest, while I only think of the public welfare.
Duport :   Tell me, have you gained anything from this Liberty ?
Mme. Duport: No; but the community has, and that's enough for me.
Duport :   Society is composed of individuals.   Everybody praises Liberty, and yet nobody is satisfied.   The tree has grown apace, but its fruit is bitter.   What do you say to our garden being turned into a wilderness and our beautiful statues and vases lying broken on the grass ?
Mme. Duport :   Mere trifles !
Duport :   What do you say to the peasants on our farms playing the master and paying us no rent ?
Mme. Duport :   Trifles !
Duport :   And what of giving up your darling scheme of a visit to Switzerland ?
Mme. Duport :   Oh, we've money enough for that.
Duport :   Paper enough, you mean.   But that is not money.   Why, I am short of a dowry for our daughter.
Mme. Duport :   Time to think of that when she marries.
Duport :   She is going to marry the Marquis de Rozière in a few days.
Mme. Duport :   That aristocrat ?   Never !
Duport :   He is of good birth.
Mme. Duport :   Men are all equal.

Duport : He loves Julie, and she him.

Mme. Duport : She is a child. [*Rings the bell for the butler.*] You are not to admit the Marquis.

Duport : Admit him whenever he comes.

Butler : Thank heaven ! I am a free Frenchman, or I should not know what to do.

Both : Whom will you obey ?

Butler : Neither. [*Goes.*]

Duport : Here's another sweet fruit of Liberty. If I go out, the fellow walks at my side. If I drive, and it begins to rain, he asks to come inside. Very soon he will sit by my side at table.

Mme. Duport : All men are equal.

[*At this point Julie enters, and her father declares that she shall decide the quarrel.*]

Duport : Does your heart choose democracy or the monarchy of a husband ?

Julie : I am for a monarchy in which the monarch is bound to his subjects by the bond of love.

Mme. Duport : We'll convert her. To-day is the first meeting of a woman's Jacobin Club which I have founded, and our dining-room is tastefully decorated for the occasion. You, Julie, shall become a member ; and we'll soon teach you different principles.

The Marquis de Rozière appears, denounces the Revolution, and declares his intention of living with Julie in Switzerland ; but Madame Duport argues that the consent of the mother is required. Julie turns for help to her maid, who suggests that the Marquis should represent the wax figure of a chained aristocrat in the *salon*, where the club is to meet. The room is embellished with portraits of Mirabeau, Lafayette, and other heroes. Madame Duport and six ladies enter, and take an oath never to marry an aristocrat, or, if already married to one, to plague him. When Julie is brought in, she refuses to bind herself not to marry an aristocrat, remarking that she does not understand political quarrels.

Mme. Duport : If she wishes for an aristocrat, there sits one. Let her go and make love to him.

Julie : Do you really mean I am to regard this aristocrat as my husband ?

Mme. Duport : Yes, and we will all be your witnesses.

Julie : [*To the wax figure.*] I swear to you eternal fidelity.

The Marquis : And I to you.

While the ladies are speechless with astonishment, the husbands enter the room. ' Come along, gentlemen ! ' cries Duport, ' we'll storm the Jacobin Club.' Each falls at the feet of his wife, and the **couples embrace.**

CHAPTER XI

KANT

' THE life-history of Kant,' writes Heine in a brilliant passage, ' is not easy to describe ; for he had neither life nor history. He lived a mechanical, almost impersonal, bachelor existence in a quiet corner of Königsberg. The cathedral clock did not perform its daily task with less passion or greater regularity. Everything had its appointed time. The neighbours knew it was half-past three when Immanuel Kant, in his grey coat and cane in hand, left his house and moved towards the little row of lime-trees, which is still called the Philosopher's Walk. Eight times up and down he strolled, whatever the weather. What a contrast between the outer life of the man and his world-convulsing thoughts ! If the burghers of Königsberg had known their full significance, they would have shrunk from him more than from the executioner. The great destroyer resembled Robespierre in many ways. Both had the same inexorable, prosaic honesty. Both possessed the same talent of suspicion : the one directing it against ideas and calling it criticism, the other against human beings and calling it republican virtue. Above all, they were both petty bourgeois, whom Nature designed to measure out coffee and sugar ; but destiny ruled that they should weigh far different articles, and placed a King in the scales of one and a God in the scales of the other. We had our revolts in the world of mind, and the French in the world of matter ; and we were as excited over the destruction of the old dogmatism as they over the storming of the Bastille.'[1]

Kant was an old man when the Revolution broke out ; but he was young in spirit, and he greeted it with a cheer. The greatest rationalist of his age saw, or thought he saw, the enthronement of

---

[1] *Religion and Philosophy in Germany*, Book iii. See Stuckenberg, *Life of Kant* ; *Kant's Principles of Politics*, edited and translated by W. Hastie ; Kuno Fischer, *Kant*; Vorländer, ' *Kant's Stellung zur fr. Rev.*,' in *Philosophische Abhandlungen Hermann Cohen gewidmet*, 1912 ; and Schubert, *Kant u. seine Stellung zur Politik, Hist. Taschenbuch*, vol. ix.

reason in public affairs ; and even when France plunged headlong
into anarchy, he refused to burn what he had adored.   While most
of his compatriots had never given serious attention to politics, the
oracle of Königsberg had meditated deeply on the conditions of
human progress, and had given expression to a reasoned optimism
in more than one of his writings.   No German was so well prepared
by age and temperament, by study and reflection, to pronounce on
the portent flaming in the western sky and to forecast its effect on
the thought and practice of the world.   His interest in political
theory was aroused in middle life by the writings of Rousseau
Borowski relates that the only known occasion on which he missed
his afternoon walk was after the arrival of ' Émile.'   The master—
or the slave—of the worst style in Germany was overpowered by
the magic of the limpid French prose, and he confessed that he had
to read and re-read till the beauty no longer disturbed him.   His
knowledge of the history of mankind was as extensive as that of
Rousseau was meagre, and he rejected the paradox that civilisation
was a fall from a higher state ; but he embraced the central doctrine
of his faith.   To Rousseau he owed his conversion to democracy,
and he nobly acknowledged the debt.   ' There was a time when
I believed that knowledge constituted the worth of man, and I
despised the ignorant masses ; but Rousseau set me right.   I
learned to honour men ; and I should feel myself of far less use
than the artisan if I did not believe that my reflections would aid in
restoring the rights of humanity.'

While Rousseau turned the Professor into a political thinker,
the quarrel of England with her American colonies transformed him
into a watchful student of current events.   On one occasion his
strictures on the policy of George III led an English merchant,
resident in Königsberg, to challenge him to a duel.   The Philosopher,
however, continued the discussion with such convincing eloquence
that Green asked pardon for his anger, acknowledged the strength
of his arguments, and became his inseparable friend.

Shortly after the close of the American War. Kant published
two brief but pregnant dissertations on the nature and conditions
of progress, the first of which, ' What is Enlightenment ? ' appeared
in the ' Berliner Monatschrift ' in 1784.[1]   Enlightenment, he argues,
is the emergence of man from his voluntary minority—that is, the
incapacity to use one's understanding without guidance.   It may be
described as voluntary when the cause lies in the lack not of understanding but of courage.   ' Dare to make use of your intelligence,'
is the watchword of the Aufklärung ; but the trumpeter's call falls,

[1] The best edition of his works and correspondence is that published by
the Berlin Academy.

as a rule, on unheeding ears. Laziness and cowardice explain the
fact that so great a part of mankind contentedly pass the whole
of their life as minors. It is so comfortable to remain in tutelage ;
and the guardians, who have so kindly assumed their ' direction,'
succeed in convincing most of their wards—' including the whole
of the fair sex '—that coming of age is a difficult and dangerous
proceeding. ' They have made their cattle stupid,' he adds bitterly,
' and carefully prevent the tame creatures from going one step
beyond their pens ; and then they impress upon them the danger
of the path if they try to walk alone.' It is therefore difficult for
the individual to emancipate himself from the wardship which has
become a second nature. Indeed, he is at the moment incapable
of using his understanding because he has never been allowed to
try. It is much easier for a whole community to enlighten itself ;
for there will always be some independent thinker—even among
the guardians of the herd—who, having himself thrown off the yoke,
will spread the conception of human worth. But though collective
action is possible, it is not easy, and the community can only march
slowly towards the light. A revolution may perhaps bring a
diminution of despotism and repression, but it will not produce
a true reform of thought ; for new prejudices will serve as well
as old to keep the thoughtless mass in leading-strings. For true
enlightenment nothing is required but liberty in its most innocent
shape—namely, liberty to make public use of our understanding.
But from every side we hear the words, Do not use your reason !
The officer says, Do not reason, but drill ! The Minister of Finance
says, Do not reason, but pay ! The parson says, Do not reason,
but believe ! Our ruler (Frederick the Great) says, Reason as much
as you like, but obey ! Everywhere we find the limitation of liberty ;
and yet the unfettered use of our understanding is the only path
to enlightenment. Of course, exceptions must be made. An army
without implicit obedience is unthinkable ; but in the other provinces of citizenship the rein should be kept as light as possible.
For instance, a man must pay his taxes ; but, as an economist, he
may contend that they are bad ones. If a parson cannot teach as
he has promised, he must resign ; but as a student he has a right
to reason and discuss, for there are no unchangeable formulas of
belief.

The essayist now turns to the situation and prospects of his own
country. If it is asked, Are we living in an enlightened age ? the
answer is No, but in an age of enlightenment. Men are still far
from being in a position safely to use their own understanding in
religion without guidance ; but the field is now opened to them to
work freely, and the obstacles to general enlightenment are gradually

diminishing. The King of Prussia allows religious freedom to all laymen, and even the clergy possess a certain measure of liberty ' as scholars.' Every one is now aware that this freedom does not constitute the slightest danger to public order or unity. Men gradually extricate themselves from barbarism if not artificially restrained. What is applicable to religion applies *a fortiori* to the arts and sciences ; for a ruler who allows religious liberty is aware that there is no danger in any sort of public discussion. In his closing sentences, the champion of liberty of thought raises his eyes to more distant horizons and contends that freedom spreads in a widening circle, each advance facilitating and indeed necessitating a farther step. ' A larger measure of civic freedom appears favourable to liberty of thought. The instinct of free thought gradually works on the mind of the people and finally on the principles of the government, which finds it possible to trust man, who, after all, is more than a machine, according to his worth.' Thus the essay ends with a plea for political advance as involved in the conception and ideal of the Aufklärung.

Kant's virile belief in the rationality of mankind and in the prospects of the race found renewed expression in the same year in his pregnant little treatise, ' Universal History from a Cosmopolitan Point of View,' a survey of the whole movement of humanity in order to determine its goal. He lays down a number of propositions or principles as a guide to the interpretation of the process.

1. All capacities implanted by nature are intended to unfold themselves fully in accordance with their object.

2. The capacities which are directed towards the use of human reason find their complete development in the race, not in the individual.

3. Nature demands that man must obtain everything beyond his animal needs by employment of his reason ; for in giving him reason and free will she clearly indicated her intentions.

4. Nature's instrument for developing the capacities of men is the friction of society, which becomes the cause of a social order regulated by law. After establishing these preliminary propositions, he proceeds to sketch a bold programme of political construction. The supreme problem for the race, to which Nature urges us forward, is the establishment of a civil society administering right according to law. It is the highest and the most arduous of human tasks, and it can never be completely fulfilled. ' Of such crooked wood are we that nothing quite straight can ever be made of us ; it is only the approximation to this ideal that Nature enjoins.' The establishment of such a perfect civil constitution depends on the creation of a legal relation between States ; for Nature urges them

towards federation as the only chance of security from perpetual war. History is the realisation of a hidden plan of nature to create a perfect constitution as the only medium in which all our aptitudes can be fully developed. War will become so expensive and so uncertain that States will prefer arbitration. A philosophic attempt to write a history of mankind on these lines would popularise the conception and offer a justification of nature or rather of Providence.

The message of these pregnant essays was that man is formed to climb the ladder of perfection, that the chief instrument of ascent is the unfettered use of his reasoning faculties, and that his greatest task is to create a federation of States by which the desolating waste of war can be prevented. With such belief in the might and majesty of reason, the blessings of liberty, and the lofty destinies of the race, the sage of Königsberg could not fail to welcome the overthrow of autocracy and obscurantism in France.[1] ' It was his firm conviction,' wrote his friend Jachmann after the Philosopher's death, ' that all men have by nature the same rights. With these ideas you can guess how his attention was strained when a great civilised Power set about their realisation. With his knowledge of the world and of men, he anticipated the progress of this momentous event ; and every occurrence which appeared to foster or hinder it he followed with the liveliest interest. It was remarkable how often his predictions revealed truly prophetic insight. He was so anxious for the papers at critical moments that he would have gone miles to meet the post, and we could give him no greater pleasure than by bringing early and authentic news from France. We saw with what impatience he awaited the solution of the problem. Despite the zeal he showed for the realisation of this ideal, his interest was in nowise selfish. It was the impersonal sympathy of a citizen of the world and of an independent philosopher observing the construction of a constitution on the basis of reason, just as a scientist watches an experiment designed to confirm a weighty hypothesis. His conversation lost something of its manifold character. The stupendous event occupied him to such a degree that in society he almost always reverted to it ; and there was no lack of instructive observations on the progress of the movement and the character of the actors.' [2] Like Klopstock he had hitherto depreciated the French character ; and like Klopstock he now

---

[1] In a review of Schubert's *Life of Kant*, Varnhagen (*Denkwürdigkeiten*, viii. 427) quotes notes made in 1817 of a conversation with Stägemann, who knew Kant well. ' Kant said to some friends, on hearing of the French Republic, with tears in his eyes, " Now I can say, like Simeon, Lord, now let Thy servant depart in peace, for I have seen this day of salvation." ' But the authenticity of this remark is not universally accepted.

[2] *Kant geschildert in Briefen an einen Freund*, pp. 125–32, and 141.

became aware of the nobler qualities half hidden beneath its glittering surface.

When all eyes were turned to Paris, some of the Professor's friends and pupils desired him to discuss the broad issues raised by the Revolution. 'In your next work on practical philosophy,' wrote Klein, the Berlin jurist, on the eve of the fall of the Bastille, 'will you consider what limits are set to the caprice of the legislator? It is a theme to which I have devoted much attention; but before I publish anything, I should wish to see it handled by you.'[1] The reply is lost; but its liberal tenure may be gathered from a further letter from his correspondent.[2] 'I have written in the " Berliner Monatschrift " a dialogue entitled " Is a Prince bound to rule his people well? " In several writings I have protested against princes being styled fathers of the Fatherland. I am glad that this assertion, which struck so many people as a paradox, finds support in your theory.' Kant expressed equal satisfaction with a pamphlet by Count Windischgrätz, sent him by Jacobi, 'On voluntary modifications of monarchical constitutions.' 'In the present European crisis,' he wrote to Jacobi, 'it must be of great influence: partly as a wonderfully realised prophecy, partly as wise counsel for despots. No statesman has yet sought in such lofty regions the principles of the art of government.' Even more welcome than dissertations on political theory were first-hand accounts of the titanic drama. A letter from a pupil, Jachmann, a brother of his biographer, written on October 14, 1790, describes his prolonged stay in Paris.[3] Its enormous length, filling twelve large pages of print, shows that the writer was aware of his master's voracious appetite for news; and its outspoken political judgments would never have been uttered to unsympathetic ears. ' At first I believed myself in the land of happiness; for every one, even the humblest, seemed to show by his bearing how deeply he felt that he lived in a country where the yoke had been shaken off, and where liberty and the rights of man were honoured and observed. For several days before and after the Fête of the Federation we witnessed examples of patriotism and equality in all classes, of which one could never have dreamed. But this spirit of edification only lasted as long as the fêtes, and then we heard grumbling that the Assembly was going too far, and that the mob observed no limits. Instead of enjoying the moderate liberty it now possesses, it strives for licence. France is ruled to-day by the crowd and by a few restless heads.'

From the outbreak of the Revolution Kant devoted his main activity to political science, and scarcely allowed one of his writings to appear without some reference to the crowning event of his life.

---

[1] Kant, *Briefwechsel*, ii. 61.   [2] *Ib.*, ii. 115.   [3] *Ib.*, ii. 201–13.

S

Even in the unlikely quarter of the ' Critique of Judgment,' published in 1790, we stumble on evidence of his preoccupation. In discussing the conception of an organism, he mentions as an analogy the new idea of political organisation.[1] ' By the recent wholesale reconstitution of a great people, the word organisation has been used to describe the arrangements of the whole body politic. For in such a whole every member must be not only means, but end ; and in assisting the purposes of the whole, he receives determination of his own place and function from the conception of the whole.' The philosopher had never expected the Revolution to run smoothly, and he was therefore less stunned than most of his contemporaries by its shattering discords. Jachmann speaks of his ' ardent and oft expressed desire that his country should not interfere in the affairs of a foreign nation ' ; and when war broke out he abated nothing of his sympathy for its aims. He expressed his views with perfect frankness ; but he had no passion for martyrdom. He was already a theological suspect, and he resolved to afford the Government no excuse for political heresy-hunting. In discussing the vagaries of the censorship in a letter to Biester, editor of the ' Berliner Monatshcrift,' in March 1792, he wrote : ' You do our political arrangements too much honour in asking for consistency. So far as it concerns me, my strict rule is to keep within the limits of the law.'[2] In the agony of the war, friends and pupils continued to demand light and guidance from the oracle. Spener, the publisher, implored him to reprint the tract on Universal History.[3] ' I am grieved to find that this admirable essay has not reached the princes and their counsellors, except the noble Crown Prince of Denmark. Is it not a duty to reduce by a drop of oil the terrible friction which threatens to crush hundreds of thousands ? Dare a man refuse the call ? Have not nine more years of observation and thought struck some new spark ? ' Kant at once replied, explaining and defending his silence. ' If the mighty ones of the earth are in a frenzy, a pigmy who is afraid of his skin will do well not to mingle in their conflict, even with the most gentle and respectful exhortations : above all, because they do not listen, and those who do are likely to misinterpret him. I am now seventy. How can a man at this time of life hope to exert an influence ? It would be a mere waste of effort.' A somewhat similar demand came from Kiesewetter, a teacher of philosophy at Berlin.[4] ' Your Ethics are eagerly awaited —all the more because just now the French Revolution has brought many of these questions of duties and rights into the foreground of discussion. I feel that there is much of interest to be said about

---

[1] Section 65. [2] Kant, *Briefwechsel*, ii. 315.
[3] *Ib.*, ii. 400–3. [4] *Ib.*, ii. 421.

its first principles and its rationality, if it were wise to write about it. Here, too, the subject is the only topic of conversation and controversy, which, unfortunately, ends in confounding the cause itself with its present representatives, or proving and disproving the correctness of its ideas by empirical tests.'

The great treatise on morals was not to appear for some years ; but in 1793 the old Professor reiterated his belief in liberty and his general sympathy with the moral affirmations of the Revolution. In his work on ' Religion within the Limits of Pure Reason,' he challenges the objection of ' some clever men ' that a certain people, engaged in working out a freedom based on law, is not ripe for liberty. ' Only they become ripe who are first set at liberty. We must be free in order to be able wisely to employ our powers in freedom. The first attempts will inevitably be imperfect, and experience alone will ripen the seed.' With the backwardness of his country in his mind, and the ever-present fear of the censor, he declares that he would postpone the act of emancipation in that particular case ; but to reject it would be ' an interference with the prerogatives of the Deity, who created man for freedom.'

In the autumn of the same year Kant dealt more directly and in greater detail with some of the controversial issues of the time. The second part of the treatise, ' Theory and Practice,' [1] deals with public law, and the sub-title, ' Against Hobbes,' suggests its character. He sets forth the axioms of a rational political organisation. Liberty means that nobody can compel us to be happy in his particular way, and that each of us may seek happiness in our own, so long as we do not interfere with the liberty of others to do the same. A paternal government, which treats its subjects as minors and children unable to distinguish what is good and bad for them, is the worst conceivable despotism. Not less necessary than liberty is equality, which means not equality of possessions, but equal opportunity for each to climb as high as his talent, industry, and fortune can carry him ; no hereditary prerogatives being allowed to stand in his way. As Figaro said that the nobles simply give themselves the trouble to be born, so Kant points out that as birth is not the act of him that is born, there can be no innate rights. The third axiom is not fraternity, but personal independence, which alone carries with it the right to the franchise. Wage-earning servants, and other dependents, are excluded, because they are not their own masters. Such hesitations support Kant's own testimony that he was never a democrat, however inconsistent they are with his doctrine of

[1] Wittichen argues that the treatise was suggested by and directed against the writings of Burke. See ' *Kant und Burke,' Hist. Zeitschrift*, xciii. 253–5.

natural rights. The social contract is rejected as a historical fact, and interpreted as a regulative idea of reason. It is the touch-stone of the legitimacy of every law and every constitution ; for all laws must be conceived as springing from the public will. But then he executes a *volte-face*, and pronounces all resistance to the supreme legislature the greatest crime, and rebellion inadmissible even if the government breaks the contract. For who can determine which is right ? Such conduct would destroy the foundations of the commonwealth and involve a return to anarchy. The people possess certain inalienable rights, but not the right of rebellion. As it is ridiculous to assert that the government cannot err, it is the right and duty of the people to tell the ruler when they think him wrong. The freedom of the press is the only palladium of popular liberties. In every community there must be both obedience and a spirit of freedom ; for every one demands to be convinced by reason that the obligations imposed upon him are legitimate. Kant's sketch is thus a pretty close anticipation of the theory and practice of a modern constitutional State.

The third part of the treatise deals with ' Theory and Practice in International Law,' and bears the sub-title, ' Against Moses Mendelssohn.' The philosophic Jew had maintained that the race does not really progress, but only moves forward and backward, like the stone of Sisyphus. Kant, on the other hand, assumes steady advance in culture and morality, often interrupted, but never brought to a halt. ' I need not prove it,' he adds ; ' it is for my opponents to prove the opposite. All round us is evidence that we have recently made moral progress, and the cry of degeneration arises from our standing on a higher platform, whence we can look farther ahead and realise more fully the difference between what we are and what we should be.' He then reiterates the fortifying conviction expressed in his early essays that Nature is shepherding the race towards the goal of perpetual peace. ' As universal violence compels a community to submit to law, so continual wars at last bring peoples, even against their will, into a cosmopolitan constitution, or at any rate into a federation according to an agreed international law. Human nature nowhere appears less attractive than in the relations of nations, and safety will only be found in laws to which every State must submit. If it be objected that this is only a theory of the Schools, I for my part place confidence therein. Since respect for right and duty is ever strong in human nature, I cannot and will not regard it as so sunk in evil that the practical reason will not one day, after many failures, prove victorious.' Thus the great rationalist reaches the comforting conclusion that what is true in theory is ultimately true in practice.

The treatise gave lively satisfaction to the Philosopher's friends. 'It is excellent,' wrote Biester, 'especially the second part, which gave me all the more pleasure as it appears to dispose of the rumour (which I always thought improbable) that you had spoken favourably of the French Revolution, which to my mind becomes ever more repulsive and in which reason and morality and all wise statesmanship and legislation are scandalously trampled underfoot.' A few months later the same friend wrote that the essay 'still keeps many pens and minds busy.'[1] Gentz paid less attention than Biester to the denunciations of revolt and more to the underlying principles of the argument, which, he declared, contained the whole theory of the 'Rights of Man.' Rehberg criticised it in the 'Berliner Monatschrift'; but Kant made no reply, explaining to the editor that his own rationalism was too far removed from his critic's empiricism to render discussion profitable. His own judgment on the performance is preserved on the back of a letter received from a friend. 'I do not think I shall be accused of having flattered rulers with the indefeasibility of their rights; but, equally, I cannot be accused of flattering the people, though I vindicate its right to express its opinion on faults of the government. Hobbes asserted that after the conclusion of the contract the people possessed no more rights. He should have said that though they do not possess the right of resistance, they have the right of making known their ideas of improvement. The people has no right to undertake hostilities against its overlord, since he represents the people. Reform must proceed from the will of the Sovereign; but the pen must enable the ruler and the people alike to perceive what is unjust. What a people cannot ordain for itself—for instance, a new creed—the Sovereign also cannot impose.'

Kant shared the feelings of horror with which his countrymen heard of the death of the King, which he was to denounce in his 'Philosophy of Law' as a crime beyond forgiveness. But he refused to despair of the future or to lose faith in the ideas of 1789, and he sometimes astonished his friends by his unconsidered utterances. 'He is still a thorough democrat,' wrote the pious Nicolovius in 1794.[2] 'He said all the horrors in France were unimportant compared with the chronic evil of despotism from which France had suffered, and the Jacobins were probably right in all they were doing.' His medical colleague, Metzger, describes 'the boldness and fearlessness with which for years—if to the end, I know not—he championed the principles of the French Revolution against all comers, even against men of the highest

---

[1] Kant, *Briefwechsel*, ii. 440, 471–2.
[2] Quoted by Hettner, *Gesch. der deutschen Lit.*, iv. 39.

position in the State. There was a time in Königsberg when everybody who had a word to say for the Revolution was entered on the black books of the authorities as a Jacobin. Kant, however, did not let himself be frightened, and he was so respected that he was left in peace.'[1] A little further information is supplied by Jachmann.[2] ' In no direction, perhaps, did he make so many friends and enemies as by his political ideas. You knew that he pronounced every revolution to be wrong, even under the oppression of cruel despots, and wished reform to take place by the slower but safer road of moral advance. Our task is to strive for a new organisation in which, and not in the caprice of the ruler, the guarantee of equal rights and freedom is entrenched. The main point is to separate the legislative from the executive power. In such a constitution, perfect freedom and the maintenance of equal rights are attainable ; in such, the general will of the people expresses itself ; in such, there is true republicanism ; and it is of no great importance whether the representative of the people is one or many. He saw no harm as a true patriot in letting his thoughts dwell on the Revolution. He held with conscientious strictness to the laws of his country, entertained a hearty devotion to his princes, and was proud to be a citizen of a State in which inflexible justice obtains and whose rulers strive for the ideal of a perfect polity. He was not in the slightest degree a revolutionary, and he would have been the first and strongest opponent of every attempt at a *coup d'état*. In his own person he showed how to combine free citizenship of the world with unbending patriotism.' His friend and constant companion in later years, Wasianski, describes his insight into politics as ' so profound that we often thought we were listening to a man who was acquainted with the secrets of Cabinets. At the time of the Revolution he made many forecasts, especially in regard to military operations, which were accurately realised.'[3]

A man so outspoken and so eminent could hardly hope to escape molestation in the Prussia of Frederick William II ; for the omnipotent Wöllner distrusted even his metaphysics. The lectures on the ' Kritik,' delivered by his pupil Kiesewetter in Berlin during the first winter of the Revolution, were watched by agents of the obscurantist Minister. In 1790 the King was urged to forbid the Philosopher to write ; and in the same year his pupil Reuss, professor in Würzburg, issued a pamphlet to rebut the charge that the French Revolution sprang from the

[1] In his anonymous *Ausserungen über Kant.*
[2] *Kant geschildert in Briefen*, pp. 32–125.
[3] *Kant in seinen letzten Jahren*, pp. 25–7.

master's teaching. The work on Religion, published in 1793,
provoked the appearance of a pamphlet ' On a great but invisible
union against the Christian Religion and Monarchies,' designed to
show the danger of Kant's activity to the Church.   In the following
year Wöllner struck his blow, denouncing Kant as disloyal to the
youth of Prussia and to the King in his attacks on religion, and
threatening punishment if they continued.   The professor replied
that he would discontinue his lectures and writings on religion
as ' His Majesty's most faithful subject.'   When the King died
three years later, he declared that he had chosen the phrase in
order not to bind himself beyond the lifetime of the ruler to whom
his promise was made.   Such sophistry was unworthy of the
illustrious moralist ;   but a portion of the blame must be borne by
the reactionary Minister.

Kant had opposed the entry of Prussia into the war against
France and rejoiced at her withdrawal, only regretting that England
and Austria were resolved to continue the conflict.   His dislike
of war had been clearly expressed in his essay on ' Universal
History';   but a curious passage in the ' Critique of Judgment '
showed that certain prejudices still lodged in his mind.[1]   ' War,
if conducted in accordance with rules and with respect for the rights
of civilians, has something sublime about it.   A prolonged peace
favours a commercial spirit and a debasing self-interest, cowardice,
and effeminacy, and tends to degrade the character of the nation.'
But the horrors of the first three years of the European struggle
had revived and intensified his destination.   The idea of a
federation had been adumbrated by Sully and Penn ;   but it owed
its effective introduction to European thought to the Abbé Saint-
Pierre.   Kant's treatise on ' Perpetual Peace,' published in 1795,
repeats and elaborates the propositions of his earlier dissertations,
and endeavours to establish the connection between democracy
and peace.[2]   It is this latter contention which forms the chief
novelty of the treatise, and it is to the Revolution that we owe
its elaboration.   He seizes on self-government, the central idea
of the Revolution, and rears upon it the still loftier ideal of a
supernational organisation.   If law, based on reason and morality,
is the foundation of the life of the State, it should equally regulate
the relations of States to one another.   The family of nations
needed a constitution not less than France and Prussia ;   for so
long as each State recognises no authority above itself, and no
duty except to itself, wars will continue.   As individuals have been

---

[1] English translation (1911), pp. 112–13.
[2] See the translation (with Introduction) by Miss C. Smith, 1903.   Cp.
Jacob ter Meulen, *Der Gedanke der internationalen Organisation, 1300–1800.*

forced to sacrifice their lawless freedom for their own good, so States must submit to some limitation of sovereignty in their own interest. Kant calls his work a philosophical sketch, and in a letter it is described as a dream. It is rather his political testament, which expresses his inmost convictions better than the formal ' Philosophy of Law.' It is the most arresting of his political works, and in its pages we catch the highest notes ever struck by a German publicist.

' Perpetual Peace,' he begins, was the legend on a Dutch inn-keeper's signboard above the picture of a churchyard. But this little witticism forms the prelude to a treatise as arid and repellent in form as it is practical and human in substance. He takes for granted the evil of war, and plunges at once into a discussion of how it may be avoided. The first section enumerates the ' preliminary articles of peace.'

(i.) No treaty is valid if it contains the secret reservation of material for a future war.

(ii.) No State shall be acquired through inheritance, exchange, purchase, or donation. For a State is not a property, but a society of human beings, of which no one but itself has the right to dispose. For the same reason, no State is entitled to hire the soldiers of another country.

(iii.) Standing armies shall one day be abolished. For they are always threatening other States with war and lead to a competition in numbers, till at last armed peace becomes more oppressive than a brief war. The practice of hiring men to kill or be killed implies that they are mere machines. Very different are the voluntary, periodical military exercises of citizens who thereby seek to secure themselves against attack.

(iv.) No national debts shall be contracted for external purposes —that is, for war. For such loans render war easy and encourage the inclination of rulers towards it ; an inclination apparently planted in human nature.

(v.) No State shall forcibly interfere with the constitution and administration of another. What could justify such an act ? It would be a violation of the rights of an independent nation struggling with internal disorders and would make the autonomy of States a mere name. (Though France is not mentioned, no reader could fail to catch this pointed allusion.)

(vi.) No State shall treat its prisoners, employ treachery, or conduct itself in such a manner as to make the restoration of confidence impossible.

These articles are, of course, mere counsels of perfection, so long as the destinies of nations are in the hands of irresponsible autocrats ; and the author therefore proceeds in his second section to establish the fundamental conditions, or, as he phrases it, the definitive articles of a permanent peace. The need for them arises from the unhappy circumstance that war, not peace, is the natural condition of mankind.

The first article is that the constitution of each State shall be ' republican,' the only form which has its origin in the idea of the original contract, on which the lawful legislation of every nation must be based. It recognises the supremacy of law and the equality of its members, and it is also the only constitution which ensures peace. For if the consent of subjects is needed for the making of war, they will think twice before they undertake such a bad business. But where the State is non-republican— that is, where the subject is not a citizen with a vote—plunging into war is the easiest thing in the world, and requires no greater effort on the part of the ruler than to issue orders for a hunt ; for he suffers no personal loss, and continues to enjoy the pleasures of sport and the table. When selfish and capricious autocracies are replaced by representative institutions, a new system of relations between States becomes possible. ' Republican' constitutions are not necessarily non-monarchical, but include every kind of genuinely constitutional government, the criterion of which is the separation of the executive from the legislature. No worthy constitution is possible without representation. Every nation must become master of its own fate. The second article affirms that the Law of Nations shall be founded on a federation of free States. Peace cannot be preserved when some are bond and some are free, but only when the voice of the people is clearly heard in a representative assembly in every country. For war and victory can never decide the question of right. Such a transformation of Europe must not be expected, and cannot occur all at once. ' If destiny ordains that a powerful and enlightened people should form a republic— which by its very nature is inclined to peace—this would serve as a nucleus of federal union.' Through different unions of this kind the federation would gradually increase in size and authority. A world-republic—not, of course, a world-empire—would be the only real solution ; but the nations will not have it. ' Hence, if all is not to be lost, we must have its negative substitute—a federation for averting war. And even then there will be continual danger.' The third article claims what is described as universal hospitality for individuals in whatever State they may find them-selves. Now that the intercourse of nations has so greatly increased, the old explicit or instinctive hostility must be laid aside. The idea of world-citizenship is the complement of the unwritten code of the public rights of mankind.

What ground have we to anticipate such a beneficent change in the relations of States as will lead to the cessation of war ? In one of the brief supplements to the treatise the philosopher offers some reasons for his great hope. Nature, he declares, points us towards peace ; for she makes harmony spring from discord—even against the will of man—and fills the earth with contiguous peoples who gradually learn their interdependence by being driven to supply each other's needs. The commercial spirit cannot co-exist with war, and, sooner or later, it takes possession of every nation. An appendix, dealing with the antagonism of morals and politics, returns to the Revolution and gives renewed expression to the author's demand that the French Republic should be allowed to work out its own salvation. 'If through the violence of the Revolution—the product of a bad government—a constitution more in accord with the spirit of law were attained, even by unlawful means, it should not be considered right to force the people back into the old paths. Moreover, a nation cannot be asked to surrender its constitution, even though it be a despotism (which is the strongest where foreign enemies are concerned), while it runs the risk of being swallowed up by other States.' Thus the work, which sets forth an ideal even loftier than the ideas of 1789, ends on a note of sympathy with the struggles of France towards the light.

In a curious passage sandwiched in between the discussion of weightier issues, the author pleads for the class of which he was the most eminent living representative. The opinions of philosophers, he declares, should be considered in regard to the conditions of a peace. That kings should turn philosophers, or philosophers become kings, is not to be expected or desired ; for power is fatal to the exercise of reason. Kings and nations should therefore not allow the class of philosophers to disappear nor forbid the expression of their opinions. In the present instance he had no reason to complain that the expression of his opinions was hindered or that they were met by disdainful indifference. The little treatise was diligently studied in every part of the country, and, despite its scholastic form, the first edition of fifteen hundred copies was exhausted in a few weeks. 'I wish I could describe with what delight the best minds have read it,' wrote Kiesewetter from Berlin.[1] 'Posterity will learn to thank you when it tastes the fruit of your labours. That it does not find the same welcome everywhere is inevitable. Gentz has spoken out against it, and will perhaps take up his pen. I regret that it will only be read by Germans, for it certainly would do much good in the great nation which has already made such gigantic strides along the

[1] Kant, *Briefwechsel*, iii. 47–9.

road of political enlightenment. I am going to send it to a friend
who has gone to Paris, and shall ask him to translate it.' After
a long delay the translation was made, and in 1798 Kiesewetter
informed the author that he heard from France that it had been
welcomed with enthusiasm, and that extracts had appeared in
the 'Moniteur.'[1]

In the Weimar circle 'Perpetual Peace' found a respectful
welcome. 'A little work of Kant has surprised me,' wrote Goethe
to Schiller. 'It is a very valuable product of his well-known
method of thought, and, like all coin from his mint, contains the
most glorious passages ; but in composition and style he out-Kants
himself.'[2] The view of the two poets was shortly after expressed
in the 'Xenien' (72 and 73).

PERPETUAL PEACE

Let each but grasp his truest advantage and grant to his neighbour
Equal advantages, then permanent peace is secured.

PERPETUAL WAR

No man living is pleased with the share that Fortune assigns him ;
Thus the causes of war ever and ever recur.

A third couplet (775) enshrines in a picturesque image the almost
boundless admiration of the poets for the greatest of German
thinkers.

KANT AND HIS COMMENTATORS

As a rich man provides for the needs of numberless beggars ;
So, when monarchs construct, carters have plenty of work.

Humboldt's opinion of the book was rather more critical.[3]
'On the whole,' he wrote to Schiller, 'it is not very important. It
contains no idea that is not already to be found in his books, and
a great deal of it comes from the Abbé Saint-Pierre. But I welcome
the little work for its faithful and interesting picture of the
individuality of the author. In parts, too, it shows genius, and
it is written with much warmth and fancy. A democratic vein,
which often peeps out, is not altogether to my taste, nor, I expect,
to yours.' Körner was openly hostile. 'It has not satisfied
me,' he confides to Schiller.[4] 'He does not seem to me to be

---

[1] Kant, *Briefwechsel*, iv. 264. [2] *Briefe*, xii. 301-2.
[3] *Briefwechsel mit Schiller*, p. 189.
[4] Schiller, *Briefwechsel mit Körner*, iii. 310.

quite in his province. From one-sided observations he deduces propositions which will not hold water.' Greater sympathy was expressed by a pupil writing from Würzburg on the French invasion, who informed his master that he had visited a battlefield on the day after the struggle.[1] ' It is not to be described,' he added, ' and here one learns to wish for perpetual peace with all one's heart.' In spite of the critics and the sceptics, Kant's prophecy will never be forgotten by those who are in earnest in having it fulfilled. Whoever desires to become ' a good European ' need only resort to the oracle at Königsberg.

A few months after the Treaty of Basle and the publication of ' Perpetual Peace,' an attempt was made to bring two of the most remarkable men of the age into personal relations. Early in January 1796, Karl Theremin, an East Prussian, who had taken a post under the Republican Government, wrote the following letter from Paris to his brother, a pastor in Memel.[2] ' Yesterday I visited Sieyès, who has occupied himself a good deal with metaphysics. He explained some of his principles, and when I told him they agreed with those of Kant, he seemed highly flattered. As I know that Kant respects Sieyès, and has spoken of his worth in some of his essays, I wished that a correspondence could be established which would be of use both to philosophy and to the French nation. Since peace now reigns between the two peoples, such communication is lawful, as indeed it ought to be even in war.' On receipt of this letter the pastor wrote to Königsberg : ' My brother in Paris often tells me that he is urged to make your philosophy known in France.[3] The chief mover appears to be Sieyès. If you would enter into an academic correspondence with him, which he greatly desires, you would see how far he and his countrymen are capable of assimilating your ideas. As a true philosopher, you are of course a citizen of the world, and would doubtless gladly assist to enlighten a great nation. If you will write a few words to Sieyès, I will forward them in a letter to my brother.' An inaccurate report of the project quickly found its way into print. ' What I have long yearned for, I now see in the papers is accomplished,' wrote an old pupil living in Elberfeld, ' namely, that the French nation, through Sieyès, has invited you to examine their intended constitutional laws, with a view to removing what is superfluous and suggesting improvements.' Another pupil wrote in similar terms from Würzburg. ' I cannot tell you how enthusiastic people are here about the news in the papers that you are summoned to France as legislator and restorer of tranquillity, and that you have obtained the permission of your

[1] Kant, *Briefwechsel*, iii. 101–2. [2] *Ib.*, iii. 59. [3] *Ib.*, iii. 58.

King.'[1] Thus the legend grew. But to the letters of congratulation, as to the original invitation, Kant made no reply. His attitude is explained by Jachmann. ' That he was a true patriot is proved not only by his affection for his fatherland, but by his oft expressed wish that our State should not interfere in the affairs of a foreign nation. For this reason he declined the correspondence which Abbé Sieyès suggested to him. He knew how far a citizen, even a citizen of the world, could go.'[2]

In the ' Philosophy of Law,' published in 1796, Kant reiterated and expanded the ideas already expressed in his ' Theory and Practice.' The preface informs the reader that parts of the book are only a sketch, since questions of public law are now so much discussed and so important that a final judgment may well be deferred. The duty of the State, he argues, is narrowly limited ; it has to secure justice, not happiness.[3] Once again the disciple of Rousseau maintains that the highest criterion of legislation is the will of the united people ; that liberty, equality, and independence are inalienable attributes of the citizen ; that the contract is the foundation of political rights, and that perpetual peace is the goal of society and law. Once more does he condemn all attempts at forcible change. ' The alteration of the constitution can only be effected by the Sovereign by way of reform, not by the people by way of revolution.' Rebellion is like the sin against the Holy Ghost, for which there can be no pardon in this world or the next. The execution of Charles I and Louis XVI was worse than dethroning them, which might be right ; and worse than murder, which might be an act of defence. It was an error of judgment on the part of the French King to have conceded the legislative power, and, above all, the control of taxation ; but, once granted, the Assembly was not bound—indeed, as the representative of the popular will, was not at liberty—to surrender it. When a revolution has succeeded, the illegality of its origin and its execution is no sufficient reason for good citizens to withhold their obedience. Thus the moral claim of the Revolution is once more recognised.

In his last important work, written in 1797 at the age of seventy-five, and published in 1798, Kant returns to the problem of progress, which had formed the theme of his first political essays and to which the chequered course of the Revolution had given poignant actuality.

---

[1] *Briefwechsel*, iii. 62, 69.

[2] *Kant geschildert in Briefen*, pp. 125–32.

[3] His theory of the State is well discussed by Caird, *The Critical Philosophy of Kant*, vol. ii. book ii. chs. 6–8 ; and Wilbrandt, *Kant und der Zweck des Staats ; Schmoller's Jahrbuch*, vol. xxviii.

The second part of ' The Conflict of the Faculties ' deals with the relations of philosophy and law, and discusses ' whether the human species is advancing towards improvement.' The three possible answers are : that it is going back, going forward, or standing still. The most arresting phenomenon of the age, he declares, is the drama in France, to which he once more offers a striking testimonial. ' The Revolution of a gifted people which we have witnessed may succeed or fail, and it may be so filled with misery and cruelties that a right-thinking man would not care to repeat it. It finds, however, in all onlookers a sympathy which borders on enthusiasm, and is therefore moral in its nature. This moral cause is twofold. First there is the right of a people not to be hindered by other Powers in giving itself such a constitution as it thinks best. Secondly, there is the object (which is also the duty) that this constitution should be in accordance with law and morally right, and so constructed as to avoid aggressive war (which only a republican constitution can do), and thus prevent war, the source of all evils and the destruction of morals, and thereby provide a negative guarantee of progress to humanity, despite all its fragility, by avoiding interruptions in its advance. At this point the author interpolates a protest against the political heresy-hunting prevalent in Prussia. He does not advocate that a people with a monarchical constitution should claim the right or even harbour the design to alter it ; for perhaps the geographical situation of the State renders monarchy the safest defence against powerful neighbours. Again, the grumbling of subjects at the hindrances placed in the way of other States in their efforts to republicanise themselves is no proof of dissatisfaction with their own constitution, but rather of love for it ; since the more other peoples republicanise themselves, the more security against danger does the State obtain. And yet slanderous sycophants, to invite attention to themselves, have tried to represent this innocent talk as Jacobinism, which threatens danger to the State ; though there was not the least cause for such apprehensions—above all, in a land so distant from the theatre of the Revolution. Enthusiasm is only inspired by moral ideals, and cannot be based on selfishness. The opponents of revolutions could not be bribed to the zeal and exaltation produced by the mere conception of right ; and even the feeling of honour of the old fighting nobility vanished for those who had grasped the right of the people to which they belonged.

Kant now boldly proceeds to claim the right of self-realisation for adult nations. Why, he asks, has no ruler ever dared to say that he recognises no rights in the people, that they owe their happiness exclusively to the government, and that any claim of the subject to rights against him is a punishable offence ? Because such a declaration would band all citizens together in protest, even if, like obedient sheep led by a wise and good shepherd well fed and protected from danger, they had nothing to complain of in respect of material well-being. Beings endowed with freedom are not satisfied with the amenities of life ; the principle by which they secure them is the deciding factor. A being endowed with reason, conscious of this his privilege over the unreasoning animal, must demand for the community, of which he forms part, a government in which he shares. Men must thus work far beyond the thought of well-being ; for this right is a holy thing that is above all price, and which no government dare touch. The execution of this right, however, is subject to the rules of morality, which the people must not transgress ; for instance, revolution is always unjust. The philosopher next attempts to forecast the effects of the Revolution on the future of the race. Such general and disinterested sympathy, he repeats, can only be evoked by a moral appeal. France exhibits the evolution of a constitution based on natural law. Despite convulsive struggles it is not yet achieved ; but the striving is towards a republican and unaggressive system. Such a phenomenon in human history is never forgotten ; for it has revealed such a capacity for improvement in human nature as no politician ever dared to conjure up, and which only nature and freedom in combination can produce. Even if the goal were not to be reached, if the revolution or the reform of the constitution ultimately failed, the prophecy loses nothing of its force. For the event is too great, too intermingled with the interest of humanity, and too widely spread in its influence not to be recalled when favouring circumstances recur and provoke fresh attempts. It is therefore not only a fair-weather maxim, but one which carries the strictest proof and defies all sceptics, that the human race has always been advancing and will continue to advance. This conclusion opens up a boundless vista, if one looks not only to what ·may happen in a single people, but conceives all nations of the world taking their share in the procession of the ages. Confronted with the omnipotence of nature, or rather with her unfathomable First Cause, man is only a trifle. Yet it is not a trifle, but the negation of the purpose of creation, that his rulers treat him as such, heaping burdens on him as if he were an animal, making him a mere tool of their plans, and driving him forth to be butchered in their quarrels.

The idea of a constitution in conformity with the natural right of mankind—that is, that those who obey the law should help to make it—lies at the foundation of every variety of State. An absolute king is one who can make war by himself ; a limited monarch is one who must consult the people.   It is not the theory, but the practice, that matters.   For instance, the English consti- tution is nominally a limited monarchy ; but the King, by bribery and other methods, contrives to make himself absolute.   With advancing progress the violence of the mighty will gradually diminish, and obedience to law will increase.   There will be more well-doing, less litigation, fewer broken covenants ; and this spirit will gradually spread till it embraces the relations of people to one another.   A cosmopolitan society can be formed without any increase in the moral capital of the race, for which a new creation or supernatural influence would be necessary.   We must never expect too much from man in his march towards improve- ment, lest we provoke the scoffs of the politician who would gladly dismiss the hope as the illusion of a brain on fire.   It is a delight to plan out constitutions based on the postulates of reason ; but it is an offence to urge the people to overthrow the existing system. Plato's ' Atlantis,' More's ' Utopia,' and Harington's ' Oceana ' have never been tried.   It is only a sweet dream to hope to see such a State ; but it is the duty of rulers to set their course in that direction.

Kant's last published work, the ' Anthropology,' appeared in the same year, 1798.   He had often lectured on the subject, and his notes kept pace with his studies and the progress of events. In its final form he essays a brief characterisation of the leading nations.   The portrait of France is painted in the conventional colours employed by most German and English artists of the revolutionary age.   ' The French nation is polite and pleasant, and supreme in the art of conversation.   The reverse of the medal is excessive liveliness, an over-readiness to abolish certain forms simply because they are old, and a contagious spirit of liberty which drags reason into the arena, produces a subversive enthusiasm, and goes beyond all bounds.'   As usual, a few references to the Revo- lution creep into the text.   He describes the era of the Committee of Public Safety as that of ' public and nominally legal injustice,' and remarks that he can understand how honourable men preferred suicide.   On the other hand, ' though the equality of the Con- vention only consisted in formalities, it is better to have even the appearance of this ennobling blessing than to be robbed of it.' The portrait is severe ; but the picture of his own nation is scarcely more flattering.   ' The German, of all civilised peoples, submits most easily and most continuously to the government under which he lives, and is farthest removed from the spirit of innovation and opposition to the established order.   His less admirable side is his tendency to imitation, his slender opinion of his own originality, and, above all, a certain cult of method, a readiness to allow himself to be classified with other citizens, following the principle not of equality, but of privilege and rank. All this, of course, may be attributed to the form of the German constitution, though its pedantic structure issued from the spirit of the nation and from the natural tendency of Germans to erect a ladder from top to bottom, on which each rung is marked with the prestige attaching to it ; and he who has neither profession nor title is of no account.' But the veteran thinker is less interested in the fortunes of any single nation than in the destiny of the race. It is characteristic of his consistent optimism that the last sentence of his last work looks forward to his favourite ideal of gathering the human family into a cosmopolitan system.

By his individualism and his cosmopolitanism Kant belongs to the eighteenth century ; but the greatest of philosophers was also one of the boldest and most suggestive of political thinkers. He lived and died an impenitent Liberal. He was a child of the Aufklärung in his belief in the majesty of reason and in his rationalistic treatment of politics ; but in his demand for the co-operation of the people in the work of government he stretches out his hand to the democratic forces which the Aufklärung despised. His philosophy was grounded on his conviction that man was a rational being and that Nature or Providence was irresistibly urging him onwards and upwards. Every human being was born with inalienable rights, which he could neither voluntarily nor involuntarily surrender. Long afterwards Schön recalled his master's saying : ' My whole being shudders when I think of serfdom.' The authority of the State and the rights of the people rested equally on the social contract, and each party was bound to respect the domain of the other. The best security for ordered liberty he found in the separation of powers ; for he was not less a disciple of Montesquieu than of Rousseau, taking his theory from the latter and his machinery from the former. He never asked that the people should possess executive power, with the significant exception that no war could be declared without the approval of their representatives. Though holding no reform to be impossible, he fully realised that time was necessary for even a partial fulfilment. The best hope of progress lay in freedom of discussion and in giving ear to the counsels of thinkers. It was for the subject to say what was wrong, and for the ruler, aided by representatives of the people, to set it right. He was not a blind optimist ; but he felt that politics were ultimately dependent on morals, and would therefore improve with the advance of reason and virtue. No German of

T

his time surpassed Kant in his robust belief in the essential sanity of human nature and the sterling worth of the individual. In noble words, which embody his political as well as his moral philosophy, he declares that man cannot get away from the idea of right. ' In every man we must honour the dignity of the whole race, and no human being must be used as a mere instrument of the ends of other men.'

CHAPTER XII

FICHTE AND HEGEL

I

THOUGH generally known to the modern world as the first great literary champion of German nationalism, Fichte began life as a cosmopolitan radical.[1] Born of humble Saxon parentage, he sat at the feet of Kant, and made his début by an anonymous treatise on religion, which was widely ascribed to the master. Like most of his youthful contemporaries, he hailed the Revolution with delight ; but while others turned away from its excesses in disgust, he continued to hope throughout the dark days of the Terror. So convinced was he of the necessity of sweeping away the old order in France and Germany that he was prepared to pay a high price. His writings are trumpet-calls to action, and his pages glow with passionate zeal for humanity.

When the King of France was dead and Germany and Austria were at war with the Republic, it required no little courage to publish even an anonymous tribute to ' French ideas '; for the risk of discovery was considerable. Undeterred by danger, Fichte launched his first political pamphlet in the summer of 1793, ' A Demand for the restitution of freedom of thought from the Princes of Europe who have hitherto suppressed it.' His scathing attack on the rulers of his country is described as an Address, and the title-page bore the legend ' Heliopolis, in the last year of the old darkness.' It is one of the characteristics of the age, he begins, to blame princes and the great ones of the earth, though most German princes show good will and encourage learning. He

[1] See J. H. Fichte, *Fichte's Leben u. Litterarischer Briefwechsel*; Kuno Fischer, *Fichte*; Adamson, *Fichte*; Lasson, *Fichte im Verhältniss zu Kirche u. Staat*; Windelband, *Fichte's Idee vom deutschen Staate*; Zeller, ' *Fichte als Politiker,*' in his *Vorträge u. Abhandlungen*; Meinecke, *Weltbürgertum u. Nationalstaat*, ch. vi.; Treitschke, ' *Fichte u. die Nationale Idee,*' in his *Aufsätze*, vol. i.

therefore trusts that they will not feel themselves insulted by his tone or matter. He is aware that the conduct of a neighbouring Protestant State is contrary to his principles (the reference is, of course, to Prussia under the Wöllner régime), and in some other Protestant States conditions are even worse. Every government will now have an opportunity of proving the sincerity of its liberal professions by permitting the sale of his book. Reform, he continues, may be achieved either by a sudden leap or by gradual advance. By revolutions, or lightning strokes, a people may advance more in half a century than in a thousand years; but in like manner it can be thrown back into the barbarism of the remote past. Forcible revolutions are always a risk. If they succeed, they are worth the effort; if they fail, they increase the prevalent misery. The safer course is gradual progress towards enlightenment and improvement of the constitution. At this moment the prospects are darkened by a sinister attack on freedom of thought. If an attempt is made to stop the progress of the human mind, either we cease growing and give up the struggle, or, more probably, the dammed up flood breaks through and carries away landmarks in its course. Thus mankind revenges itself in the most cruel manner on its oppressors, and revolutions become necessary. It is now high time—if indeed there is still time—to open the dams.

Fichte now turns to address the people, coupling them in his condemnation with the rulers whom they slavishly obey. ' You peoples,' he cries, ' surrender everything but freedom of thought, that heaven-born palladium, that pledge of a destiny higher than suffering and degradation. Your fathers won in bloody strife what you can maintain by merely displaying a little firmness. Hate not your princes, but yourselves. One of the sources of your misery is your exaggerated estimate of these personages, whose minds are warped by an enervating education, indulgence, and superstition. It seems almost a miracle that one finds in history far more weak than bad princes. I reckon as virtues all the vices they do not possess, and thank them for all the evil acts which they do not commit. These are the men who are exhorted to suppress freedom of thought. Raise your voice as loud as you will, the satellites of despotism will not hearken. They will coerce you by hunger, prison, or death. Cry aloud to your princes that you will never permit your freedom of thought to be filched from you. We must combat the notion that it is the task of a prince to secure our happiness. No, Prince, you are not our God! From Him we await our happiness; from you the defence of our rights. We ask of you not favour, but justice.'

The Introduction is sufficiently rhetorical; but the Oration itself, in its volcanic eloquence, anticipates the fervent appeal of the ' Addresses to the German Nation.' Such fiery denunciations of despotism and oppression had never been heard in Germany. It was the voice of Fichte ; but it was the message and the authentic accent of the French Revolution. ' The dark ages are over, you peoples, when you were told in God's name that you were herds of cattle set on earth to fetch and carry, to serve a dozen mortals in high place, and to be their possessions. You are not their property, nor even God's property, but your own. You are stronger than they, for their strength is in your arms, as recent events have proved. Their knowledge is no greater than yours. You will now dare to ask the prince who wishes to rule you, By what right ? If they reply, By inheritance, you will ask, How did the first of your line obtain the right ? Moreover, can we be inherited like flocks and herds ? Man cannot be inherited, nor sold, nor given away. He is subject to conscience alone. If he admits any other principle, he sinks to the level of the beasts. He has a right to everything which conscience does not forbid ; and liberty and personality are not only not forbidden, but inalienable. Some rights can be bartered for others, hence the institution of contract ; but such transactions can only relate to externals, not to our innermost convictions. It is contrary to right to accept laws from any one but oneself. Only when I freely accept it, does legislation become binding on me. The prince derives his whole power from the people, and he can only possess the rights which society itself possessed. But is the State or society entitled to limit our freedom of thought ? Certainly not ; and freedom of thought involves free expression of thought. You allow us to think, because you cannot prevent it, but not to express our opinions. It is indecent for thinking-men to grovel at the foot of the throne and crave permission to be the doormats of kings. Free discussion is the noblest link between men. If you reply, You may speak truth but not error, I rejoin, What is truth ? Where is your infallible criterion ? Under the early Christian Emperors truth changed at every coronation. The community has no more right to demand the surrender of freedom of thought than has the individual the right to comply. You foretell infinite misery from such freedom. You remind us in the papers of a gentle people sunk to the level of cannibals, thirsting for blood and exhibiting bleeding fragments of its citizens. We will not remind you of the bloodier fêtes which despotism and fanaticism in their traditional alliance provided for the same nation. Such things are not the fruit of free thought, but of ages of intellectual slavery.' The Oration closes on a note of tense republican passion, in which the ruler is once again roughly reminded that he is made of common clay. 'Every man of sense honours society in you, not yourself. A straw figure, bearing your robes and sceptre, would be your equivalent. The true worth of kings is only estimated when they are dead. Search for your enemies, and you will find them among those who counsel you to leave your peoples in ignorance and to make your kingdom a dominion of darkness.'

No such slashing attack on kings and princes issued from a German printing-press during the era of the Revolution; and young and eager hearts thrilled in grateful response. 'Blessings on the great man,' wrote Schelling to Hegel. 'Have you read the "Demand for Freedom of Thought"? If not, get it. Who could mistake its author?'[1] Fichte remained proud of his performance, though it is obviously the work of a young man, full of sweeping generalisations and massed superlatives. 'In his violent outbreaks against the nobility,' remarks Treitschke, 'speaks the wrath of the Saxon peasant's son'; and Zeller discovers in its flaming pages the spirit of the 'Robbers' and the Convention. The argument rests on the social contract, so interpreted that the individual retains in perpetuity certain fundamental rights against society and the State. The full-blooded doctrine of the sovereignty of the people, imported from France, is blended with the passion for the spiritual liberty of the individual, which forms the most precious legacy of the Aufklärung. The author avoids the mistake of expecting constitutional changes alone to produce a better world. Improvement is, above all, a spiritual process to be attained not only by the conversion of princes, but by the efforts of individuals. He summons his fellow citizens to throw off their creeping servility and to raise themselves to their full stature, while the government is commanded to withdraw its clumsy fingers from the delicate machinery of life and growth. As man is born with inalienable rights, he is under no obligation to a government or a social system which fails to respect them. If the individual is thus captain of his soul, how much more is it the right and duty of a whole people to remove all obstacles to the pursuit of a free and elevated existence. A nation can never abdicate its right to liberty and self-realisation.

A longer and less rhetorical treatise appeared in the same year, entitled 'A contribution to the formation of a correct judgment on the French Revolution.'[2] Though it was published anonymously, like its predecessor, the tone was far less aggressive and the treatment more philosophical. There is more argument and less tropical

[1] *Aus Schelling's Leben*, i. 74.
[2] Both works are published in his *Sämmtliche Werke*, vol. vi.

declamation. 'The French Revolution seems to me of importance for the whole of mankind. I am not speaking of its political consequences to France and to her neighbours—the latter only produced by their uninvited interference. Every event is an object-lesson set up by the Great Educator of the race for us to learn what it behoves us to know. The Revolution, for instance, is a sermon on the theme of Human Right and Human Worth. The only way to prevent such eruptions is to instruct the people in their rights and duties. Things have become the subjects of conversation to which nobody had given a thought. Talk of the rights of man, of liberty and equality, of the sacredness of contracts, of the limits of royal power, replaces gossip about fashions and adventures. We are beginning to learn.' The reader, however, is cautioned not to direct these principles against governments. Most constitutions are very bad, and the inalienable rights of man are generally abused; but emancipation can only come peacefully from above. 'It may be argued that if we make ourselves worthy of liberty, the monarchs will not grant it. Do not believe it. We are living in the dawn, and the full light of day is not far off. Be just, ye peoples, and your princes will not be able alone to remain unjust.'

After this conciliatory Preface we reach the Introduction, which inquires by what criterion political transformations should be judged. No constitution, it is clear, can be unchangeable, for the simple reason that none is perfect. Secondly, all parties to a contract equally possess the right to amend it. Thirdly, only he whose heart feels a warm reverence for human right and human worth can be a judge in the case. The author is convinced of the capacity of mankind both to know and to do what is right. 'Man can do what he ought; if he says he cannot, he merely means that the will is lacking.' Two distinct questions must be asked about the French or any other Revolution. The first refers to its justification, the second to its wisdom. The first book of the treatise deals with the former. In arguing for justification the author repeats the assumptions of his earlier treatise in almost identical words. Man as a reasonable being is subject to the moral law alone, and no one has a right to place him under another jurisdiction. If he allows a law to be imposed on him by an alien will he makes himself a beast. The moral law is the state of nature, and the moral will is the only legislator. He recognises no binding authority in existing States, for their morality is inferior to that of their subjects. The tendency of all monarchies is to unfettered autocracy within and to universal domination without. They do at once too much and too little; for abroad they make wars, and at home they resist change. ' Jesus and Luther, holy guardian angels of liberty,' he cries, ' look down on your successors and rejoice at the ripening harvest. A third deliverer will soon appear, who will complete your work and break the last fetters which hold man in bondage.'

After this ecstatic appeal to the two greatest revolutionists in history, Fichte reiterates the atomistic theory of the State which he had expounded in his earlier treatise. ' Every one has a perfect right to leave the State when he will.' We can only surrender alienable rights ; and the right to terminate every contract at will is not among their number. What has been freely made can be freely unmade. No one is the property of another. The dead cannot bind the living. Thus privileges, which imply a limitation of the liberty of others, cannot be handed down, for they exist only on sufferance. A long historical discussion of hereditary nobility leads to the conclusion that the State can terminate it if it is found inconvenient. It is not a question of right, but of expediency, whether a State retains one or more privileged classes. In like manner, no Church is justified in imposing its belief ; for both Church and State live beneath the august sceptre of the Law of Nature. Property can be withdrawn from the Church as the nobility can be deprived of their privileges ; for both are usurpations. Strictly speaking, the Church has no rights in the visible world. The author was particularly proud of his treatment of the latter theme. ' I should write the chapter on the nobility quite differently now,' he wrote to Reinhold a year later ; ' but I have said much that is new on the Church.' [1]

The first book thus decides affirmatively the question whether the French Revolution was justified. But at this point the treatise is interrupted ; for the second question, dealing with its wisdom, was never answered. The work is thus a fragment, confining itself to theoretical prolegomena, and containing scarcely any direct reference to the cataclysm which inspired it. Fichte leaves his readers in no doubt as to his opinion not only of revolutions in general, but of the French Revolution in particular. Tradition, authority, vested interests, prerogative, and privilege melt away before the breath of his displeasure. Armed with the sword and spear of reason and conscience, it is the duty as well as the right of citizens to alter their constitution at need, to banish the foul shadows of the past, and to carve their way towards the liberty which is the hope of the world.

In a brief postscript, added to the unchanged second edition of 1795, he records that the book had been published as a specu-

---

[1] J. H. Fichte, *Fichte's Leben*, i. 223.

lation ; and for a time it seemed still-born. It was rescued by
a laudatory notice in a monthly journal, and thereafter attracted
considerable attention. His friend Reinhold not only praised it in
the press, but identified the author. ' I see that you have given
a favourable notice of my book,' wrote Fichte, 'and you believe me
to be the author. Well, I am. I have told nobody here, but
a friend in Switzerland has let it out.' [1] Shortly after he wrote
to Stephani : ' My book has made a good deal of stir, and I hear
that it is unfortunately generally attributed to me. Reinhold
revealed the secret.' [2] In a letter to Kant he explains his
anonymity. ' I must confess that something of mine is already
in print of which I do not at present wish to admit the paternity,
as I have attacked many injustices with great freedom and zeal
without at present suggesting peaceful ways of removing them.
If you will allow me, I will send it to you, for you are the only
man in whose judgment and secrecy I place full confidence. On
political topics, alas ! almost everybody is a partisan, being either a
servile adherent or a furious enemy of tradition.' [3] The reception
in Königsberg, however, was not encouraging. ' That Kant is not
pleased with it, I can well believe,' wrote the author to Schön ;
' but his reason—that I withhold my name—is not the right one.
I am no longer satisfied with most of it : not because I went too
far, but because I did not go far enough. The science of politics,
like all philosophy, must be profoundly modified. I conceal my
name, because my present situation demands circumspection.
It is universally known that I am the author ; but a public recognition might bring difficulties to my government, or, at any rate,
prevent a number of its subjects from studying at Jena. I have no
need to defend the work, because nothing worth answering has
appeared.' [4] Among its readers was Körner, who complained to
Schiller of a lack of urbanity in many of the best German writers.[5]
' Fichte, for instance, sometimes offends against good taste. Indeed,
I am not at all satisfied with the book. Much of it is admirable
and gives one a lofty notion of the author ; but much is very acrid
and not even correct. My fingers have often itched to reply. If
I did not think it dangerous to write on politics, I would break a
lance with him.' Still more hostile was the verdict of young
Niebuhr, who exclaimed : ' What remains for us but death, if such
principles should become dominant ? ' [6]

Both the ' Freedom of Thought ' and the ' Revolution,' we

[1] *Reinhold's Leben*, pp. 160–1.   [2] J. H. Fichte, *Fichte's Leben*, ii. 394.
[3] *Ib.*, ii. 170–1.   [4] *Aus den Papieren Schöns*, i. 39.
[5] Schiller, *Briefwechsel mit Körner*, iii. 180.
[6] *Niebuhr's Life and Letters*, i. 35–6.

learn from the author without surprise, were forbidden in Berlin. It was, indeed, fortunate for him that he was safely anchored at Jena in the service of one of the most enlightened of German princes. When his appointment was under discussion, his democratic ideas had been mentioned as an obstacle ; but Hufeland, his backer, explained that there was a gulf between theory and practice. Fichte, he declared, only defended democratic principles in the abstract, and would not seduce the youth of the little duchy. ' Goethe,' wrote Voigt, after a conversation, ' greatly wishes that Fichte would not give his name or his anonymity to a new edition of "The French Revolution." He thinks Fichte promised him this.'[1] Whether or not such a promise was given, the edition of 1795 was the last. Both publications were none the less high explosives ; and it is not surprising that they won him the names of democrat and Jacobin, and dogged his footsteps for many years.

In 1794 Fichte delivered five lectures on ' The Vocation of a Scholar,' prompted by the excesses of the Jena students. Though mainly devoted to academical morality, they throw light on the author's political ideas, which were always in process of development. He is still a staunch individualist of the school of Humboldt. ' Political society is no part of the absolute purpose of human life, but only a possible means towards the formation of a perfect society. The State constantly tends towards its own annihilation, since the final aim of all government is to render itself superfluous. We may have to wait for aeons ; but one day all political combinations will become unnecessary.' For this advance the lecturer looks not to the statesman, but to the scholar—the teacher and pilot of the race. ' I know that an effeminate and nerveless generation will dislike these ideas ; but I speak to young men, and I would gladly contribute to spread a more self-reliant tone of thought, a more ardent zeal to fulfil our destiny.' He condemns Rousseau's glorification of the state of Nature and his repudiation of art and science as factors in individual and social well-being. ' He took account of the sorrows of the race, but overlooked the power which it possesses to help itself. The ultimate aim of society is the perfect equality of all its members. What the individual cannot accomplish, the community can.' But though Fichte's advice is to march forward instead of backward, he pays a generous tribute to one of his favourite teachers. ' Peace be with Rousseau's ashes, and blessings on his memory ; for he has kindled fire in many souls.' The young author was rapidly growing in reputation and authority. ' The greatest metaphysician now alive,' wrote Friedrich Schlegel

[1] *Goethe's Gespräche*, i. 214.

to his brother, ' is a popular writer. You can see it in his famous book on the Revolution. Contrast the contagious eloquence of the " Lectures on the Scholar " with Schiller's declamations. Every trait in his public life seems to cry, This is a man ! ' [1]

While the ' Vocation of the Scholar ' reiterates the unbridled individualism of his earliest utterances, the treatise on the ' Foundations of Natural Law,' published in 1796, records a distinct advance. Fichte's mind never stood still, and to the end of his life he continued to work at the problems of society and the State. He now begins to construct breakwaters against the surge of popular passion. The State, he admits, is necessary because men are still very imperfect. His system still rests on a philosophy of free will, and civil society reposes on the recognition of individuality. He declines to discuss in detail the best form of government for a particular State, on the ground that it is a question not for the science of right, but for the art of politics ; but he offers a few guiding directions. He clings to the sovereignty of the people and the social contract, and his fundamental axiom is that the people must decisively outweigh the government in the scales of power. Representation is not only wise and useful, but is involved in the conception of rights. The government should be neither despotic nor democratic—that is, not wholly in the hands of ruler or people. States unaccustomed to strict obedience to law need a monarchy, while for those who have long enjoyed orderly rule a republic is most suitable. Rulers should have few friends, so that they may escape partiality. If law and justice cease to be effectively secured, action must be taken by the Ephorate—a small body which, while possessing no executive power, is entrusted with the task of watching the government, and, in case of need, of summoning a national convention to pass judgment on the offenders.

This curious work, though free from the hyperbole and credulous idealism of his earlier utterances, constitutes no great advance towards a workable theory of the State. The main novelty of the treatise, the Ephorate, shows that he is feeling his way towards the necessity of stable government ; but every one, except the author, at once realised that the Ephors were anaemic phantoms. If the executive were wicked enough and strong enough to trample on the rights of the people, would it not *a fortiori* possess the will and the power to bend or break a handful of decorative supermen ? But the critic is absolved from his task by the author's ultimate recantation of his errors. When Reinhold sharply criticised the Ephorate on its first appearance, the author replied that it presented no difficulties ; but in the last year of his life he dismissed it as

[1] F. Schlegel, *Briefe*, pp. 235–6.

impracticable. For who, he asks, could prevent it attacking the government unfairly, and who could prevent the government suppressing the Ephorate ? But this is not the only flaw in Fichte's structure. In his eyes the community is only an aggregate of individuals, and the State, being purely mechanical, possesses no more strength than a heap of sand. He reiterates the contention of his earlier works that the contract between the State and the individual possesses no binding character, and he refuses to recognise any essential connection between the citizen and the society into which he is born. ' Every man must be a member of some State ; but he is entitled to a free choice.' The constitution of every State must be the creation of its citizens, and the vote, as in Poland, must be unanimous. Those who are dissatisfied can join a group more to their liking. While insisting on the representative principle, he refuses to admit its implications. He sees nothing but the State and the individual in actual or potential antagonism, lacking all organic unity. The State is a purely external mechanism, a provisional and unwelcome necessity, to be vigilantly watched lest it oppress the people.

In 1799 Fichte was deprived of his chair at Jena on a charge of atheism ; but he contended that the real ground of his dismissal was political. ' I have never imagined that they are persecuting me as an atheist,' he wrote to Reinhold. ' They are attacking a freethinker who is beginning to make himself intelligible, and a democrat.'[1] It was now universally known that he was the author of the two pamphlets of 1793, and the subsequent qualifications of his system had not sufficed to retrieve his reputation. ' I am supposed to be a Jacobin,' he wrote indignantly in his ' Answer concerning Atheism,' ' and it is notorious that I am in consequence unspeakably hated. But in my " Natural Law " will be found a stronger opposition to a democratic constitution than in any other writer. You will notice that I demand a subjection to the law and its control over the doings of citizens, which is to be met in none of your political thinkers or constitutions. The common criticism, indeed, is that I am unfair to liberty. So far am I from preaching anarchy. If a young man who had given up his fatherland and was connected with no State, and was angered by the glorifications of the limitless power of the mighty—if he, too, exaggerated a little in order to restore the balance ; if it was but a fragment ; if he has in the interval become a mature man and written on the same theme in a riper work ;—is it fair to make this juvenile and unfinished essay the measure of the political principles of his manhood ? '

[1] *Reinhold's Leben*, p. 205.

The eloquent Professor spoke the truth when he declared that he was moving steadily away from the uncompromising individualism of his early years. In ' The Foundations of Natural Law ' he had imposed on the State the duty of attending to the material welfare of the individual. He was now to go much farther. Individualism blends with socialism in the contention that every one has a right to the physical necessities of life. In the following year his remarkable economic treatise, ' The Exclusive Commercial State,' described by its author as an appendix to the ' Natural Law,' saddles the State with new and onerous responsibilities. In the social contract, he declares, each surrenders his natural claim to property in order to obtain a definite and equal share. The State is now a socialistic insurance society for material subsistence. To achieve this object it must determine how many shall work in each branch of industry, and fix prices on the principle that equal labour must command an equal share of the good things of life. To avoid the overthrow of the equilibrium, the State alone must undertake foreign trade. The idea is fanciful enough, and it is curious that the fiery champion of liberty should now entrust his old enemy with such extended powers. He was the first German seriously to study the social question, and he had also come to realise that liberty needs to be secured. But in his efforts to secure it he had overshot the mark. In his system of despotic radicalism, to borrow a phrase of Treitschke, the man is lost in the citizen.

In the first stage of his thought Fichte's State is merely a policeman. In the second, the demand for material welfare leads to a socialist organisation of work. In his ' Lectures on the Characteristics of the Age ' he repudiates the philosophic anarchy of his early writings. ' The political character of our age is the interpenetration of the citizen by the State ; and this is a necessary purpose of the State and nature, not a subject of censure, as it has been made by a certain visionary scheme of unrestricted freedom. True freedom can only be attained by means of the highest obedience to law.' This is a notable advance ; but he is still a resolute cosmopolitan. ' Where is the fatherland of the truly cultured European ? It is Europe, and more particularly that State which at any given time occupies the highest point of culture. From this cosmopolitan standpoint, we need not trouble ourselves as to the doings and fortunes of particular units.' But this was the last utterance of the eighteenth century. Modern nationalism is the child of the French Revolution, and Prussia learned at Jena what France had learned at Versailles. But even before the thunder of the guns awoke North Germany from her slumbers, he showed signs of the coming change in his ' Dialogues on Patriotism.' While remaining a cosmopolitan, he emphasises the value of the nation and the State as a limited field of action, which enables the individual to carry on his work for his own culture and for that of the race. The recognition of the State' as a political entity is carried a stage farther in a striking essay on Macchiavelli, written in 1807.[1]

In the ' Addresses to the German Nation,' delivered in Berlin in the winter of 1807–8 within earshot of the French garrison and at the peril of his life, Fichte emerges as the loud-tongued herald of a powerful national State. His evolution is now complete, and the patriotic note is sounded in the opening discourse. ' I speak for Germans, brushing aside all the differences which unhappy events have created during centuries in the single nation. These Lectures, delivered first to you, are meant for the whole nation. They are intended to kindle a patriotic flame.' He no longer paints his princes black and their subjects white. All, he cries, are responsible for the great collapse, and all must co-operate in the work of reconstruction. The most crying need is education. The eloquent voice of the Professor echoed through the country. The nation had become self-conscious, and nationality involved the recognition of the necessity, the utility, and the majesty of the State. While Humboldt and Kant express the loftiest ideals of the age which was passing away, Fichte embodies the transition to the dominating principle of German thought in the nineteenth and twentieth centuries. But in becoming a convert to the national idea he never completely outgrew the cosmopolitanism and radicalism of his early manhood. In the political writings and fragments of the last year of his life he pleads for a temporary Prussian leadership, to be followed by the supreme ideal of a republic without princes or hereditary aristocracy. The generous ideas of 1789 revive as he wraps himself in the prophet's mantle. ' For the first time, a true kingdom of right will be created by the Germans, such as the world has never seen, in all the enthusiasm for the liberty of the citizen which we find in the classical world and without the slavery of the majority.'

In early life Fichte wrote to his wife : ' I intend not only to think, but to act.' His aim was realised. All his writings, remarks Treitschke, are orations ; and they are also calls to action. His books and lectures are addressed not only to the mind, but to the will of his readers and hearers. Half in jest and half in earnest, Heine compared him to Napoleon. Both, he declares, represented the great, implacable Ego to which thought and action are one. Fichte was the most impressive lay preacher of his time, and no

[1] *Nachgelassene Werke*, vol. iii.

writer strove so hard and so successfully to transform Germany
into a political nation ; and this great elemental force was set in
motion by the French Revolution.

II

Hegel, complained Börne, wrote against revolutionary ideas on
the parchment of a Prussian drum.[1] But the position of rigid
conservatism, reached in later life, was far removed from the ideas
of his youth. Born in the household of a conservative official,
the young Württemberger entered Tübingen in 1788 as a student
of theology and philosophy. Among his fellow students were
Schelling and Hölderlin ; and the young men read Rousseau,
worshipped at the shrine of classical Greece, and welcomed the
French Revolution, in which they saw the triumph of Reason. A
political club was founded, and French newspapers were provided.
'Hegel,' records his pupil and biographer, Rosenkranz, 'was one
of the most enthusiastic orators of liberty and equality, and, like
all other young heads, he was devoted to French ideas.' One
Sunday, in the spring of 1791, he joined Schelling and other friends
in planting a Tree of Liberty in a meadow near the town. A member
of the club betrayed its existence, and Duke Karl hurried from
Stuttgart to make inquiries ; but the displeasure of the Government
merely increased the enthusiasm of the recalcitrants. Excitement
was increased by the presence of a corps of Émigrés in the vicinity ;
and if any of them appeared in the town the students openly
displayed their enmity. Hegel's birthday album is embellished with
entries which leave no doubt as to its owner's sentiments—' In
tyrannos !' 'Vive la liberté !' 'Vive Jean Jacques !' 'Fatherland
and freedom !' 'Perish the detestable policy which claims absolute
power over the human heart !' 'For what was true and great
in the Revolution,' records Rosenkranz, 'he always retained an
almost tender reverence, though the hollowness of mere declamation
on liberty and equality soon dawned on him.' With the Terror
his sympathy changed to disgust, though he continued to follow
events with eager interest. 'I have met Oelsner, the author of
the "Letters from Paris" in Archenholtz's "Minerva," he writes to
Schelling.[2] 'He told me of some of our Württembergers in Paris,
and of Reinhard, who has an important post in the French Foreign
Office. You know that Carrier has been guillotined ? Do you read

---

[1] See Rosenkranz, *Hegel's Leben* ; Kuno Fischer, *Hegel*; Caird, *Hegel*;
Dilthey, *Die Jugendgeschichte Hegels*; Adolf Stahr, ' *Hegel als Politiker*,' in
his *Kleine Schriften*, vol. i. ; Meinecke, *Weltbürgertum u. Nationalstaat*, ch. ii.
[2] *Briefe von u. an Hegel*, i. 7–9.

the French papers ? I think I have heard they are forbidden in Württemberg. This trial is very important, and has unveiled the whole scandal of the Robespierrists.'

Hegel left the University in 1793 and became tutor in the house of a Bern patrician family, the grandfather of his pupil being one of the leading men in the State. Though his first writings were on theology, his main study was Thucydides, Montesquieu, and Gibbon. He parts company with Fichte and Schelling by this historical grounding, and with the historical school by his retention of the critical and liberating spirit of the Aufklärung. He studied the English Constitution, followed the English debates on the Poor Law, excerpted English papers, and wrote a lengthy commentary on Stewait's 'Political Economy.' Though the atmosphere was intensely conservative and he detested his three years' residence in Switzerland, the young tutor watched the last days of the proud oligarchy with interest. In writing to Schelling in 1795, in reference to the choice of the Sovereign Council, he remarks with severity : ' To know an aristocratic constitution one must have spent such a winter here before the election.' His abiding interest in Swiss politics has been revealed by the discovery of his translation of ' Cart's Letters on the relation of the Pays de Vaud to Bern.' [1] The book was published in 1793, the German version, with preface and notes, in 1798. Vaud had been ceded by Savoy to Bern in 1564, but was never reconciled to its lot. Excited by the French Revolution, it revolted in 1791 ; but the rising was bloodily suppressed. Its cause was pleaded by Laharpe and Cart, a lawyer, who wrote the ' Letters on the historic rights of Vaud and their violation by Bern.' As a convinced champion of the Vaudois, Hegel associates himself with Cart, and sharply castigates the clique of ancient families which monopolised the administration. He rebukes those who say ' There is such low taxation'—' as if it were better to pay a few thalers less than to possess civic rights.' In free England, he adds, taxation is highest, though he blames Pitt for his encroachments on political liberty. He quotes with approval the revolt of the American colonists against a small tax. He appeals throughout to historic rights, not to abstract theory ; to Montesquieu, not to Rousseau. His literary début aroused no interest and was at once forgotten ; but it is worth notice as a milestone on his course.

A more striking expression of his liberal ideas was given in the same year in a pamphlet ' On the latest events in Württemberg,' suggested by the struggle of the new Duke Frederick with the old

[1] See Falkenheim, *Eine unbekannte Politische Denkschrift Hegels, Preussische Jahrbücher*, November 1909.

oligarchy. He intended to dedicate his pamphlet ' To the People of Württemberg'; but as he learned from friends that it would please neither side, it was never published. Its demands are, indeed, bold and far-reaching. He pleads for representative government, the limitation of the ducal power, and the removal of abuses. He complains of the Constitution that ' everything turns on a single man, who concentrates all power in his hands and gives no guarantee of recognition or respect for the rights of man.' But the conflict was not directly between the ruler and his people. Frederick was fighting for autocracy, his opponents for the privileges of the old oligarchy ; and Hegel attacks them both, convinced that both alike are out of date, and that ' institutions, constitutions, and laws, which no longer harmonise with the opinions of mankind and from which the spirit has departed, cannot be artificially kept alive.' ' It is time,' he writes in the Introduction, ' that the people of Württemberg should cease to oscillate between fear and hope, between expectation and disappointment.' He summons all hands to aid in the reform of the Constitution. ' The picture of better, juster times has flashed on the souls of men, and a longing for a purer, freer condition has set all minds in motion.' But the realisation of new political ideals must be gradual, and the franchise must at first be confined to ' enlightened and honourable men.' Concrete measures, moreover, are not enough. Justice, courage, self-sacrifice for the redemption of the Fatherland are also needed. There is a breath of the hopeful idealism of 1789 about this eloquent and earnest plea for reform.

The advocacy of reform in his own State was followed by a more ambitious work on the constitution of the Fatherland, sketched in the Imperial city of Frankfurt, where he lived as tutor from 1797 to 1801, and written directly after his appointment to the Chair of Philosophy at Jena. The publication of this unfinished treatise in 1893 from the MSS. in the Berlin Library, of which Rosenkranz and Haym had only given fragments, reveals Hegel once again as a bold and convinced reformer.[1] The most important question for every German, he declares, is the future of his country. His aim is to quicken the national consciousness. He sees Germany as Macchiavelli saw Italy—a prey to petty despots and foreign enemies ; and cries aloud that she must become a State. Where the old generation thought in terms of individuals, the new thought in terms of nations. ' The last generation,' he declares, ' stood for orderly dominion over one's property, and the enjoyment of one's little world. Now a better life has breathed on our time, an instinct for new conditions ; and the new inner world must have a new legal

---

[1] *Kritik der Verfassung Deutschlands*, edited by G. Mollat.

U

expression.' He recalls the collapse of 1792, Marengo and Hohenlinden, which heralded the approaching dissolution of the Empire.
How can Germany emerge from anarchy and become a State again ?
For she cannot properly be called any longer a State—that is to say,
a body able to provide for defence of its possessions. But to urge
reform is not to plead for a centralised despotism. ' What a dry
and mindless life develops in a modern State, where everything is
ordered from above, is shown by the French Republic. The framework of German institutions is founded deep in that which has
made us famous—our instinct for freedom. This it is which, after
all other European peoples have surrendered themselves to a single
authority, has prevented us doing the same.'

He proceeds to survey the history and condition of the Imperial
army, finances, legislation, and justice, and laments the loss of
territory up to the Treaty of Lunéville. Religious differences had
broken up unity, and Germany was like a heap of round stones, from
which no pyramid could be built. The fault was not in the people,
but in the Constitution, which condemned them to impotence
and anarchy. In one respect alone—its system of representation
—the Empire was abreast, or even ahead, of other States. France's
misfortunes must be traced to the utter decay of feudalism ; for,
through the cessation of the States-General, the nobility no longer
met in its representative capacity, and the Third Estate possessed
no representation. Yet he speaks enviously of France, England,
Spain, and other countries which have made a State, ' and thenceforward enjoyed a period of power, wealth, and ordered prosperity.'
The supreme lesson of the French Revolution is that order and
liberty must be combined. ' For ten years Europe has fastened its
eyes on the terrible wrestling of a people for liberty, and in consequence conceptions have changed and have shed their vagueness.
Europe is less sensitive now to the blind cry of freedom. In this
bloody drama the cloud of liberty has melted, in embracing which
the peoples have fallen into the abyss of misery. The conviction
has been deeply implanted that a settled government is necessary
for freedom, and that the people must co-operate in laws and the
most important concerns. Without a representative body freedom
is unthinkable.' The work concludes with proposals for the reform
of the Constitution, and utters a solemn warning that if the country
is not to share the fate of Italy and be divided up among foreigners,
it must reorganise itself.

The treatise was never published, and in any case the warning
would have been too late. This powerful, practical, and deeply
patriotic book shows Hegel at his best. He has recovered from
the intoxication of Tübingen, and has not yet ossified into the

champion of Prussian autocracy. In his conviction that the State must, before everything, possess a power of self-defence, he is a thorough realist. But his urgent demand that the people should share in the task of government shows that French ideas had not lost their hold ; and his assumption that the ordering of every department of life from above paralyses the development of the individual suggests that, like Stein and Niebuhr, he had learned one of the most fruitful lessons that England had to teach.

As the years advanced, Hegel's tone towards the ideas of 1789 steadily hardened. ' Universal freedom,' he writes in the ' Phenomenology of Mind,' with reference to France in the years of revolution, ' can produce no positive achievement.[1] There is left for it only negative action. It is merely the rage and fury of destruction. The sole work accomplished by universal freedom is death.' He will hear nothing of the equality of man. On the other hand, he has not enlisted in the army of reaction ; for at Heidelberg, where he held a chair for two years after the restoration of peace, he helped and advised the young Burschenschaft movement, and in 1817 he issued the most vigorous and effective of his political manifestoes.[2] In accordance with Article 13 of the Treaty of Vienna, the King of Württemberg, like other South German potentates, granted a Constitution, which, instead of evoking gratitude, aroused a fierce outcry at the abolition of ancient liberties and privileges. Hegel intervened in the conflict, and once again traditional rights and privileges make no greater appeal to him than to the thinkers and actors of the French Revolution. His main concern is to sweep away antiquated rubbish, to build up a strong and enlightened State, and to combine order with liberty. Denouncing the ' French abstractions ' and ' atomistic principles,' he takes his stand boldly on the side of the King, and emphasises the infinite importance of the rights he had granted. ' We see in the action of the Württemberg Estates exactly the opposite of that of France, twenty-five years ago, when everybody contended that nothing should be accepted in a constitution but reason. One might have feared that the leaven of the revolutionary principles of that time, the abstract principles of freedom, was not yet digested, and that assemblies would seize the opportunity to make similar attempts and thereby introduce danger and confusion. But Württemberg has given consoling proof that this evil spirit no longer stalks abroad ; and that the colossal experience of France and Europe was not forgotten—namely, that the rigid maintenance of vanished conditions and the rival extreme of abstract theory are alike the sources of misfortune in every land. The beginning

[1] Baillie's translation, 1910, p. 598.   [2] *Werke*, vol. xvi.

of the French Revolution was the conflict of reason with positive law and privilege ; but now it is the exact reverse. And this is done in the name of the people ! One might say of the Württemberg Estates as of the Émigrés—they have learned nothing, and forgotten nothing. They seem to have slept through the last twenty-five years—the richest in history and for us the most instructive.' This eloquent work breathes a virile conviction that men are living in a new world. He sees in the controversy nothing but a conflict between pedantic traditionalism and rational reform, between antiquated particularism and efficient organisation. It is the spirit of the Emperor Joseph, and the philosopher forgets that there is no security in a constitution that is granted by an autocrat.

Hegel's faith in its final form was enshrined in ' The Philosophy of Right,' published in 1820 ; but only the references to France concern us.[1] In speaking of the will, he holds up the Revolution as a terrifying object-lesson. In war, he declares, the will has no limits. ' A manifestation of this freedom is the fanaticism of political and religious life. Of this nature was the terrible epoch of the French Revolution, by which all distinction in talent and authority was to have been superseded. In this time of upheaval and commotion, any specific thing was intolerable. Fanaticism wills an abstraction. It finds all distinctions antagonistic to its indefiniteness, and supersedes them. The people abolished the institutions which they themselves had set up, since every institution is inimical to the abstract self-consciousness of equality.' In discussing rival theories of the State he pronounces an even sharper verdict. ' When Rousseau's abstractions attained to power, there was enacted the most tremendous spectacle which the human race has ever witnessed. All the usages and institutions of a great State were swept away. It was then proposed to begin all over again ; but as the undertaking commenced with abstractions, it ended in scenes of tragic cruelty and horror.' Among the factors that drove Hegel to his glorification of the State, the memory of the blood-stained anarchy of the Revolution occupies a foremost place. Power has become far more important than liberty, and a strong executive needs the firm hand of a monarch. The people should be consulted, but the decision lies with the ruler.

' The Philosophy of Right ' disappointed most of the author's friends, and the attack on Fries was particularly resented ; but it has often been contended that he did not really change when he went to Berlin. His provocative challenge, ' the real is the rational,' lent itself to an ultra-conservative interpretation ; but it was flung

[1] Translated by Dyde as *Hegel's Philosophy of Right.*

at those who denied all right to the *status quo*. That he was as far
as ever from the grovelling obscurantism of the *ancien régime* or
the Restoration, is indicated by an entry in his diary relating to
Scott's onslaught on the Revolution in his life of Napoleon. ' Scott
says that Heaven, to punish the sins of France and Europe, gave
power to men who were only the tools of its vengeance. If so, the
Revolution was necessary—not a new crime, but a punishment for
old ones. Even an ignorant Capucin would barely be forgiven
such nonsense.' [1] And when he was addressing his students,
memories of his youth would sometimes urge him to more
generous sentiments than found a place in the bleak world of the
' Philosophy of Right.'

Hegel's latest judgment of the Revolution was presented in the
lectures on the ' Philosophy of History.' [2] The course was delivered
five times between 1822 and 1831 ; but it was not till 1830 and 1831
that he treated at length the problems of the Middle Ages and
modern times. Though the text was prepared after his death from
the notes of the lecturer and some of his hearers, its rendering of
his thought, if not his actual phraseology, may be accepted as
accurate. His picture of the *ancien régime* and of the effects of
the Revolution might have been signed by any German Liberal.
' The political condition of France presented nothing but a confused
mass of privileges altogether contravening Thought and Reason,
with the greatest corruption of morals and spirit. The change was
of necessity violent, because the work of transformation was not
undertaken by the Government.' The Court, clergy, and nobility
were unwilling to surrender their privileges. ' The idea of Right
asserted its authority, and the old framework of injustice could offer
no resistance to its onslaught. It was a glorious mental dawn.
All thinking beings shared in the jubilation. A spiritual enthusiasm
thrilled the world, as if the reconciliation between the divine and
the secular was now first accomplished.' To the French Revolution
Germany owed not only great suffering, but emancipation. The
country was traversed by the hosts of France, but was saved by
nationality. ' One of the leading features in the political condition
of our country is that code of rights which was certainly occasioned
by French oppression, since this brought to light the deficiencies of
the old system. The fiction of an empire has vanished. Feudal
obligations are abolished, for freedom of property and person has
been recognised as a fundamental principle. The offices of State
are now open to every citizen.'

The veteran Professor was not always in this mood of cheerful
gratitude ; for he lamented the French Revolution of 1830, and

---

[1] Rosenkranz, *Hegel's Leben*, p. 559.   [2] See part iv., section 3.

dreaded drastic change everywhere. His last utterance was an essay on the English Reform Bill, written in 1831.[1] ' Even if opinion was universal in favour of such reform as the Bill proposes, we must be allowed to examine its contents ; all the more, since we have not seldom experienced in recent times that the demands of public opinion are impracticable or undesirable, and that the general voice often violently attacks what it has recently with equal violence demanded. The Ancients, who themselves lived in democracies, thought very differently of the popular voice than is now the fashion.' His dislike of the Bill was due to his conviction of the need of a strong executive. ' Hostility to the power of the throne is the most inveterate of English prejudices.' The essay is the work of a tired and timid mind. He had ceased to care for constitutionalism, and he was content with the fact of representation without troubling himself as to its quality. Hegel is the founder of systematic political thinking in Germany ; but his contemptuous repudiation of cosmopolitanism and his marked preference of order to liberty led him to an exaggeration of the power and position of the State, which has moulded and injured large sections of German thought for a century.

[1] *Werke*, vol. xvii.

CHAPTER XIII

GEORG FORSTER

No German scholar identified himself more fully with the French Revolution, or laid a more precious sacrifice on its altar, than Georg Forster.[1] Taken to England at the age of twelve, he accompanied his father and Captain Cook, six years later, on a voyage round the world as the botanist of the expedition. He was deeply interested in every branch of natural science, and his first book was a detailed narrative of his adventures. In the year of its publication he was appointed Professor of Natural History at Cassel, and, in order to take up his post, trod German soil for the first time at the age of twenty-four. 'He is a splendid young fellow, and has won all hearts,' reported Jacobi, his first German host. He possessed a genius for friendship, and within a few years he was on intimate terms with the intellectual *élite* of Germany. His attraction was felt no less at the Courts of Cassel and Mainz, Vienna and Warsaw, than in literary and scientific circles. At Cassel his colleague, Sömmerring, the celebrated anatomist, became his bosom friend. The two professors joined the Masons and the Rosicrucians, and dabbled in alchemy ; but the craze soon passed away. Six years later he accepted a call to distant Vilna, whence he joyfully returned in 1788 to Mainz, where, through the agency of Johannes Müller, he was appointed Librarian of the University. Like Müller, he was nowhere wholly a stranger and nowhere altogether at home. Born in Poland, of German parents of Scotch descent, he had almost become an Englishman when he found himself a German professor. His roving life had made him restless and unsettled, and his constitutional inability to live within his income preyed on his spirits. His clever wife, a daughter of Heyne, brought him intellectual

[1] See Chuquet, ' Georges Forster,' in his *Études d'histoire*, vol. i. ; *Forster's Briefwechsel*, with biography by his wife ; Gervinus' study in *Forster's Sämmtliche Schriften*, vii. 1–78 ; Zincke, *Forster nach seinen Original Briefen* ; Hashagen, *Das Rheinland* ; Perthes, *Politische Zustände* ; Geiger, *Therese Huber* ; Jaurès, *La Convention*, i. 571–609.

companionship without love. Though one of the most brilliant and admired men of his time, he was not one of the happiest.

Before 1789 politics claimed little share of Forster's attention ; but he had learned to admire the English Constitution, and before the explosion in France he had broken a lance for Mirabeau, contending that gold was no less gold because it was seldom if ever found unmixed with dross. He had lost his religious belief, and he was thus prepared to witness far-reaching changes in Church and State without the tremors that beset more conventional minds. ' What think you of the French Revolution ? ' he wrote to his father-in-law.[1] ' That England has allowed it is a tribute to her heart, but not to her head. The republic of twenty-four millions will give her more to do than the autocracy. Yet it is fine to see what philosophy has ripened in the brain and then realised in the State. Such a comprehensive transformation at the cost of so little bloodshed is unique. It is the safest course to instruct men about their true interest and their rights ; then the rest follows of itself.' His satisfaction increased with the news of the fourth of August. ' What a sitting ! ' he wrote to Heyne. ' I believe it to be without parallel. I no longer anticipate perfection in human affairs ; but if a better state is obtained, that is all that mankind can achieve. We set up our ideal ; and though we do not reach it, we advance farther than we should without it. It is a mercy that no evil spirit prompts the English Ministry to hinder France in her great experiment, though politically England loses thereby.' On August 28 we catch the first note of apprehension. ' If only they do not drive too fast ! Of course, the suppression of the privileges of the nobles is bound to cause acute disturbance, as many of them live exclusively on their seigneurial rights.' ' There are disturbances everywhere,' he records mournfully on October 3. ' It is sad how rarely a revolution aids true liberty. Yet, is it not enough that it develops the latent powers of mankind and keeps the world from slumber and stagnation ? ' He regretted the absence of any leader worthy of the gigantic task which confronted France. ' I regard Mirabeau only as the leaven—a repulsive but indispensable element. Of Necker I can form no clear idea.' ' Since the last risings,' he wrote to Jacobi after the march to Versailles, ' I am fearful for liberty.' In December he pronounces a harsher verdict on the two leaders. Mirabeau is Catiline, Necker a mediocrity. ' It is clear that the Assembly, while following clever men, keeps an eye on their ambitions.'

In the spring of 1790 Forster paid a visit to Belgium, Holland, and England, with Alexander von Humboldt, returning via Paris,

[1] *Briefwechsel*, i. 819–56.

where he spent three days. His descriptive volume, 'Views of the Lower Rhine, Holland, England, and France,' the most popular of his writings, paints the decadence of Cologne and Aachen, and the spiritual darkness of Belgium, in sombre colours.[1] 'One hears *ad nauseam* from so many champions of despotism,' he writes from Brussels, 'that the Aufklärung is responsible for revolutions. They should try to apply that principle here.' He rejoices to revisit England after an absence of many years. The narrative unfortunately breaks off when he sets foot on French soil; but we can fill the gap from his letters. 'My rapid journey through France,' he wrote to Heyne, 'convinced me that there will be no counter-revolution. Everything is tranquil and promises well for the new arrangements. The enthusiasm of the people, especially in the Champs de Mars, where preparations are being made for a great fête, is uplifting in its universality and its disinterestedness. "We and our property are suffering," remarked several people to me; "but our children will thank us, for they will benefit."[2] On his return he told Johannes Müller that the Revolution would last, and that the nation would make good use of liberty. The news of the Fête of the Federation confirmed his optimistic mood. Mirabeau has now become 'the leaven which makes France ferment, the beneficent genius of French liberty, a nobler, greater, more patriotic Alcibiades. The history of Constantine and others teaches us not to reject a good thing because bad men share in it; and liberty is worth a certain number of atrocities.'[3]

Like other German Intellectuals Forster read Burke's 'Reflections' on their appearance, and he recorded his impressions in his survey, 'English Literature in 1790.'[4] He accepts the eulogy of the English Constitution, 'which, despite all its faults, secures the happiness and independence of the individual more fully than any other'; but he scornfully rejects Burke's analysis of the situation in France. 'The Revolution must be regarded as a work of natural justice. The clergy and nobility have been overthrown not by the wisdom or folly of the Assembly, but by their own incapacity.' 'It is very thin gruel,' he wrote to Heyne, 'and possesses no interest for Germany.' 'Burke,' replied the Professor, 'does not appeal to German heads, and he is certainly a bit theatrical; but he is not so worthless as you contend. I am not learned in the writings of the Revolution, and in him I discovered its key—namely, that things have been brought to this *impasse* by the capitalists, the lawyers, and the philosophers.' 'The work of such a man is of course not utterly worthless,' rejoined Forster;

---

[1] *Schriften*, vol. iii.
[2] *Briefwechsel*, ii. 12.
[3] *Erinnerungen an 1790*, *Schriften*, vol. vi.
[4] *Schriften*, vol. vi.

' but I think that on this occasion he falls below his standard.'
' He is not really so bad,' he adds a week later ; ' I was irritable
at first because I was so disappointed.'

Forster watched the progress of events with foreboding, appalled
at the lack of wisdom with which the world in general, and his own
country in particular, was governed. He pointed out that the
revolutionaries were not the first or the greatest of sinners. ' For
a king to shoot at his subjects is nothing,' he remarked ironically
' but the head of a guard, carried on a pike before the King—this
justifies a counter-revolution.' ' The King's flight has strengthened
the Assembly,' he wrote to Heyne after Varennes. ' The only
thing now lacking is war, and the Princes of Europe seem fools
enough to wish to start it. We could have got along for a century
without a revolution ; but war hastens it by more than fifty years.
The German nobility is blind with rage, and, instead of smoothing
things down by reasonable sacrifices, they urge the princes to war
against France and to tyrannise over their own subjects. They
are doing here what the French nobility has done, and it will be
their own fault if they share their fate.' Three days later he
returned to the theme in a long and interesting letter.[1] ' Politics
are as I anticipated. The people have been so scandalously mis-
handled, and rendered so stupid and blind, that it is no wonder that
the outbreaks cannot show an unsullied record. I never cease to
wonder that so much pure virtue, especially political virtue, exists
in a people which has groaned under the most hideous oppression
for centuries. There is not a blunder committed by the Assembly
of which the curse does not fall back on the old despotism. Who
denies that some members of the party of the autocracy deserve
pity, or that some rogues sit in the Assembly and that many belong
to the party of the people ? The French peasant has been freed
from half his burdens, and the people are happy. For the vast
class which lives from hand to mouth, two years are enough to
prove the excellence of the Constitution. Here in Germany abuses
are pretty bad ; but they are not intolerable, and things are still
quiet. So my advice to the princes is to look to the usurpations
of the nobility—for there lies the seed of revolution. A prince
who protects the Tiers État, and sees that the laws are observed,
need have no fears.'

' Things seem to be going well with the French,' wrote Forster
to Sömmerring in the last week of 1791 ; ' if only they were united ! '[2]
But it was not only the danger of disunion by which the country
was confronted. At the opening of 1792 it was pretty clear that

[1] *Briefwechsel*, ii. 76–80.
[2] *Forster's Briefwechsel mit Sömmerring*, p. 560.

war was at hand. 'The end of the troubles,' he prophesied to Heyne, 'cannot be expected for twenty years'; yet he continued to believe that the Revolution had been a blessing for the French people. 'You speak comfortingly,' replied the old scholar. 'I am not ashamed to say that the situation of the poor people in France often saddens me. I stick to my old principle—to confine myself within my little world, of which my study is the centre, and to peep out at the great Fools' Comedy without astonishment and without anxiety.' In his next letter the timid Professor advised his impulsive son-in-law to moderate his ardour, lest he suffered for it. 'In my house,' came the reply, 'there is more talk on the aristocratic side than on the other. I do not belong to the wild men in either camp. Far from wishing for an upheaval, I do my utmost to prevent it.' Heyne continued to pour out his laments. 'In France things are going from bad to worse; I dare say there will be a collapse. It is such a fanatical mob. If the Jacobin pack only had a Cromwell! I am grieved above all by the injury to the true principles of liberty. The men who are conducting affairs so badly deserve the malediction of present and future generations. The Jacobins are the most contemptible folk on God's earth; they play into the hands of Austria and Prussia.'

Forster, on his side, complained bitterly of the Émigrés, with whom the Rhine cities were swarming. 'They have doubled prices,' he wrote, 'and the young vegetables, to which we have been looking forward all the winter, are not procurable, as they go straight to the kitchens of the rich French families. Would that some decisive event might rid us of this army of locusts!' When war began he remarked prophetically that he would not give a farthing for the life of the Royal Family. 'The fury of the Jacobins will stick at nothing. When the crisis is at its height they will come forward. Everything will have to yield to the armed democracy of the clubs; and who knows how mad it will be?' None the less, he rendered justice to their services. 'No party is free from fault; but I am rather for than against the Jacobins. Without them the counter-revolution in Paris would already have triumphed. If all the ground gained since 1789 is not to be lost, they had to act as they did. The guilt of all the horrors lies on the Court, the nobility, the priests, and the foreigners. The abolition of monarchy is in sight.' When he expressed his sympathy with the *enragés*, his father-in-law invariably responded with a warning. 'Do not play us the trick,' he wrote, 'of running off to Strassburg or Paris and turning Jacobin. Lafayette is the only Frenchman whose virtue I envy, and whom I hope to be able to admire to the end.'

Forster had no belief either in the military talent or political wisdom of the Allies in peace or war. 'Archenholtz is here after a visit to Paris,' he wrote in June. 'He says the Allies may defeat the French, but will not penetrate far into France nor even be able to hold their ground.' But military defeat was not the only danger ahead. 'I fear that the abolition of abuses, which would have been so easy if taken in hand, will lead, even in Germany, to a ferment which will degenerate into anarchy—all the more that we have no commanding figure to lead us. Equally little real greatness is to be found among the rulers.' Meanwhile the news from Paris grew worse. 'Poor France is nearing her total dissolution. She has no head. If either side had one, there would be no civil war ; but now it is inevitable.' The criminal blunder of the Brunswick Manifesto was promptly denounced. 'If it was desired to goad the French to resistance, nothing better could have been done. Now they must in self-respect fight with desperation, and they will. Paris will not be reached so speedily as is expected, and France will certainly not be conquered.' Forster, however, still kept his opinions for his correspondents and his intimate friends. 'I take no part in what goes on here,' he assures Jacobi, 'and I set a watch on my lips. If I offend, it is because I refuse to advertise my devotion to what I cannot respect.'

As the tide of invasion rolled towards Mainz, Forster's letters are full of the panic flight of the nobles and clergy. Heyne approved the decision of his son-in-law to remain in the city ; but a crisis in his fate was at hand. 'My position has never been so insecure,' he wrote to Voss, a publisher in Berlin ; 'the Elector can no longer pay me my salary. Till now I have kept aloof from affairs; but the hour of decision is approaching, and I shall have to take sides. The Rhine must be the frontier of the Republic. It would be madness to dream of maintaining the integrity of the Empire. Hesse and Swabia await their deliverers. Everything demands peace with France and the sacrifice of the bishoprics of Trier and Mainz. The nobility, the Elector, and the clergy have fled in shameful terror at the first breath of danger.' The irrevocable decision to throw in his lot with France as the best course, both for himself and the country, was soon taken. 'With my rather philosophic temperament I am not cut out for a demagogue,' he wrote to Voss ; 'but I heartily wish the Mainzers freedom. I am convinced that if the city returns to Germany at the peace, France will secure us a relatively free constitution. If the Elector returns, I can always earn my bread in France. I wished the present Constitution to last, as I was not convinced that Germany was ripe for a change ; and a premature revolution is not a pleasant experience. But

people must take note of the feeling which makes it impossible
for the rotten barriers to hold when they are buffeted by freedom's
flood. It is one of the decisive epochs in history ; since the birth
of Christianity there has been nothing like it. The enthusiasm,
the zeal for liberty, is irresistible. That is as clear as the sun at
noonday, and only madness or blindness could doubt it. I waited
two weeks, and then took the plunge.'

There was at last good reason for one of Heyne's pastoral
epistles. ' The violence of your last letters frightens me. One
would think you were already heart and soul a Jacobin. Surely
you do not imagine that things will stay as they are ? I implore
you to control yourself. Do not plunge so passionately that you
lose the faculty of calm judgment. The aristocrats are hated
here and elsewhere, and the French people is not grudged its
liberty ; but we are not blind to the other elements in the situation.
I am older than you, and so I think ahead.' Forster at once replied,
stoutly defending his action. The whole town and district had
accepted the French constitution, tranquillity prevailed, and the
invaders set a good example. Officers and privates were like
brothers, eating at the same table. ' The most curious feature is
that it is all happening without either excitement or enthusiasm,
as it were automatically. I can only swim with the stream. To
be neutral is impossible. One can only do good if one takes sides
and proceeds on firm and moderate lines. I could not emigrate
without losing everything, and my friends here approve my conduct.'
This cool and half apologetic letter went far to assuage the old
Professor's feverish anxiety. ' I feel sure you will do neither
too much nor too little, nor be too prominent; so that you are
prepared for any possible change.' But the counsels of Polonius
were to fall on deaf ears.

As the French troops entered the city Forster cried ' Vive la
République ! ' but he was not the first of the Intellectuals to join
the new régime. Wedekind, the Elector's doctor, asked for the
title of French citizen; Metternich donned the tricolour, and
Hofmann rendered active assistance to the invaders. A political
club was founded by Stamm and Georg Böhmer, who became
respectively the secretary and aide-de-camp of Custine. The
Elector's librarian waited several days before burning his boats ;
but the support of the most distinguished man in the city was
ardently desired not only by the French, but by the Germans
who had already embraced their cause. He joined the club on
November 5, and at once became in the eyes of Germany the
personification of the Mainz Revolution. Wilhelm von Humboldt
explained his friend's conduct in a letter to Schiller by the disorder

of his finances[1]; but though he was as usual in debt, that consideration can only have played a subordinate part in his resolve. The desire for a leading rôle, the example of his friends, his contempt for the old régime, and his belief in French principles, were the deciding factors.

On November 15 he delivered his maiden speech in the club.[2] ' In three weeks,' he began, ' we have changed from oppressed, maltreated, and silent serfs of a priest into erect, articulate, free citizens, bold friends of liberty and equality.' The difference of language, he argued, need not divide the races. ' Let the victorious chant of liberty peal out ominously in the German dialect. Now is the time when every good citizen must take sides and express his opinions. Here are mine. (i.) The freest constitution is the best. (ii.) We could not face God or the world if we let slip the opportunity of securing a constitution. (iii.) We must not sacrifice the liberty and happiness of a town or State to consideration for a few individuals. (iv.) We must defend to the death the liberty and equality offered us by our Frank brothers.' When Custine demanded a large sum from Frankfurt, a neutral town, he defended the levy in a pamphlet, which ended with a paean. ' Oh, eternal honour and imperishable glory of my France! Oh, divine majesty of liberty! Long live the French Republic!' On the reconquest of the Imperial city by the Prussians, he adjured the French Government to regain it. In spite, however, of his apostolic zeal, he at this moment accepted money from Hertzberg, who had offered help before the entry of Custine, in the hope that his old friend would remain ' a good Prussian.' The assistance had at first been refused; but he was now driven to accept it. ' Necessity commands,' was his terse comment, ' and my scruples vanish.'

His headlong plunge created surprise and indignation among his friends. Heyne emphasised the ingratitude to the Elector; Wilhelm von Humboldt bluntly declared that it revealed him as lacking nobility of character. His father renounced him, and publicly expressed a desire to see him hung. ' There is only one opinion about Forster,' wrote his bosom friend, Sömmerring, to Heyne; ' he is lost to Germany.'[3] Heinse scoffed at his old colleague for allowing himself to play a part in the ' farce of liberty,' and to be devoured by the Revolution. ' Forster's behaviour will surely be blamed by everybody,' wrote Schiller to Körner, ' and

---

[1] This explanation has been adopted by Perthes and Hashagen. His champion, Zincke, on the other hand, argues that his wife's infidelity drove him into politics.

[2] *Schriften*, vi. 413–31.

[3] *Briefwechsel mit Sömmerring*, p. 608.

I foresee that he will emerge with shame and regret.'[1] 'I hope God will soon restore you to the sciences and your friends, and bring tranquillity to your soul,' wrote Schlosser, after reading some of his speeches and declarations ; 'only your name on them could make me believe that you could speak and write in such a way.'

To most of these critics Forster made no reply ; but Sömmerring's rebukes could not be left without an answer. 'I have chosen a cause to which I must sacrifice my tranquillity, my studies, the happiness of my home, perhaps my health and my life. But I take things calmly, because they are the consequences of accepted principles. My conscience is clear.'[2] An exhortation from his publisher, Voss, to be 'a good Prussian,' provoked a spirited rejoinder.[3] 'I was born near Danzig before it became Prussian, and therefore I am not a Prussian subject. I have lived in England as a savant, circumnavigated the globe, and taught in Cassel, Vilna, and Mainz. Wherever I was I tried to be a good citizen. *Ubi bene, ibi patria* must remain the motto not only of the scholar, but also of the free man condemned to live in countries which possess no constitution.' In letters to his wife, who had left Mainz for Strassburg, he refers quite calmly to the storm that was beating about his head. 'I hear from Voss that all Germany is angry with me, that I pass for the chief author of all the mischief in this city, and that the savants of Berlin are making free with my name. It is, however, better to be free, or, let us say, to strive for freedom, than to beg one's bread from a despot.' Having taken the plunge, he was swept away into the maelstrom, and persuaded himself that the execution of the King of France was just and necessary. 'To contend that the Convention could not try him is mere sophistry. His death was a measure of safety ; it had to be, not by the decree of codes but by the law of nature. Moreover, he had made a will, describing himself as King of France, expressing the hope that his son would rule, and recommending the Émigrés to him ; and this he did after the nation had unanimously constituted itself a republic and forbidden talk of the restoration of monarchy on pain of death.' His next letter blamed his wife for allowing herself to be influenced by friends of moderate views. 'One is either for absolute freedom or absolute tyranny. A half-way house does not exist, for limited freedom always relapses into despotism.' Once again he justifies the death of the King. 'All your doubts about the legality of his conviction are only juridical sophistries.'

[1] Schiller, *Briefwechsel mit Körner*, ii. 357.
[2] *Briefwechsel mit Sömmerring*, pp. 570-1.
[3] *Forster's Briefe an C. F. Voss.*

Forster devoted his whole strength to his new task. He was disgusted by the wastefulness and rapacity of the French, and he carried his complaints to Custine ; but he continued to praise the Republic, and scolded his fellow countrymen for rejecting the offer of liberty. ' The German indolence and indifference of these people excite my indignation. They wish nothing, and do nothing.' He proposed to create a new department of the French Republic, which would, of course, send deputies to Paris. ' I know who will be one,' he told his wife. On December 15 a decree of the Convention ordered the formation of primary assemblies to organise an administration. Only those were to vote or serve who took the oath to liberty and equality, and the Convention sent its agents to supervise. On January 13, in the presence of Custine, he planted a Tree of Liberty in the Elector's capital, and delivered an oration. In addition to his labours in the club, he edited a paper, the ' New Mainz Gazette, or Friend of the People,' and translated the proclamations of the Government. He also took part in the preparations for the Rhine Convention, which was intended to demand annexation. He was ready for harsh measures against those who refused to take the oath. When the Convention met, he became its vice-president and its leading spirit. Every evening the leading clubists met members of the Government at his house to prepare the decrees which were to be voted on the morrow. The opening of the Convention was hailed in his journal as ' the most holy of days, which generations have impatiently awaited and which will be the salvation of future generations—the great day of deliverance.' This was mere rhetoric ; for he well knew that the mass of the people hated the foreign yoke, and that the Convention had been called into being with the sole object of facilitating annexation. The creation of a new State, independent alike of France and the Empire, was rejected in favour of annexation to France, proposed by Forster, who argued that a small independent State could not defend itself. ' The free Germans and the free French henceforth form one indivisible people.' Three deputies were chosen by the Convention to inform Paris of the vote ; and Forster, accompanied by Lux and Potocki, at once set out for the Mecca of Liberty.

On March 30 the head of the mission addressed the Convention in Paris in a flamboyant oration. ' The free Germans who are asking for union are eager for a share in the glory which surrounds the French name.' He then read the address of the Rhine Convention, drawn up by himself. ' We offer ourselves in gratitude to those who have broken our chains.' Next day he spoke at the Jacobin Club. His life in the French capital is mirrored in the letters to his wife, which followed one another in rapid succession. The first, written on the day after his address to the Convention, briefly announces that he is still satisfied with the Revolution. A week later he writes more critically. 'One should not judge this movement in terms of happiness or unhappiness, but as one of the great instruments of fate to produce transformations in the destiny of the race. I am as little edified by the French as their enemies; but I also recognise their virtues, and I regard no nation as ideal. The French are selected—perhaps as a punishment—as martyrs for the good which the Revolution will produce in the future, just as the Germans were martyrs for the common good in the Reformation.' Three days later we hear a new and bitter note. 'I stick fast to my principles, but I find very few who are true to them. Everything is blind, passionate fury, angry partisanship, explosive temper. The cool heads are either very few, or else they are hiding. The nation is superficial and uncertain—as it always has been—without firmness or warmth, love or truth. It possesses brains and imagination, but neither heart nor feeling.'

Forster turned with relief from the mob of French politicians to the society of Mary Wollstonecraft, Helen Williams, Christie, and other Francophils, who formed the British colony in Paris. 'It does one good to be with English people, and their tranquil sense of liberty is better than the over-wrought fanaticism one finds here.' But nothing could comfort him now that the mirage of liberty has faded away. 'You ask me to write a history of this terrible time. I cannot do so. Now that I know there is no virtue in the Revolution it fills me with disgust. They are devils—heartless devils. It is just self and passion. Who can stand it? Every day and hour strengthen my conviction that my political career is ended. As I was right—according to my then knowledge—to enter the political arena, so it would now be wrong to remain, unless the whole tendency changes, which appears impossible. Had I known, eight months ago, what I know now, I should have gone to Hamburg and not into the club.' The Revolution, he moaned, was a foul labyrinth; the Jacobin Club was occupied by the excrement of humanity. 'History will only think of the beneficent results of this great movement; but its immediate outcome is horrible.' He admired Charlotte Corday scarcely less than his fellow envoy, and witnessed her execution. Though his sympathies had been Girondin, he undertook missions to the provinces from the Jacobins, feeling bound to support the new system in spite of its vices. The Revolution was necessary, and the storms would pass. He came to feel himself purely French, and called his countrymen 'our enemies.'

W

During the closing months of 1793 Forster sat down to compose an ' Account of the Mainz Revolution ' and ' Paris Sketches.' [1] The former opens with a vivid and contemptuous picture of the panic in the city on the approach of Custine. ' The idea of resistance never occurred to any noble Mainzer. Each thought only of his own possessions.' The interesting narrative breaks off with the entrance of the French troops. The ' Paris Sketches,' written for his countrymen, passed lightly over the horrors, poured contempt on the conventional critics of the Revolution, denounced the Émigrés and the Cabinets of the Allies, foretold their defeat, and praised the Revolution for its attack on the egotism of Courts and the narrow materialism of man. As Germany had borne the burden of the Reformation, and England and Holland had bled for political liberty, so France was now undergoing a martyrdom from which Europe would derive benefit. But the work was not destined to be completed, and he died too soon to witness the benefits which he foretold. He was aware, too, that these benefits were not likely to be realised without fresh sufferings. ' As a man, a citizen of the world, a European, a German, a Frank,' he wrote in his last letter to Voss, ' my most earnest wish is that it may be the design of Providence to remove the blindness which, if it lasts another year, must infallibly drag all Europe into dissolution.' [2] Lonely and broken-hearted, his strength was insufficient to carry him through an illness, and his troubles ended early in 1794. No man ever less regretted leaving life. The Revolution had deceived him, and his wife was only awaiting his death to marry the man she loved. The pathos of his end was deeply felt by his friends, though not one of them wished him back. ' I loved him beyond words,' wrote Heyne to his daughter. ' What knowledge was accumulated in that head ! He was the noblest character, the best heart, and he was always the object of my sorrow and sympathy. He deserved happiness more than most men, but never found it.' [3] ' It was good fortune for him not to live longer,' remarked Wilhelm von Humboldt ; ' his destiny would not have been happy.' ' His death affects me like that of a hopeless invalid,' observed Zimmermann. ' Forster, the navigator,' wrote Heinse to Gleim, ' longed for rough seas again, and has been engulfed. His ship of State was no English man-of-war, but a crazy bark ; and Custine was no Cook.' [4] Alexander von Humboldt referred to him long after in ' Cosmos ' as ' my distinguished teacher and friend, whose name I can never mention without heartfelt gratitude.' Goethe had never ceased to think kindly of him. ' Is anything known

[1] *Schriften*, vol. vi. [2] *Briefe an C. F. Voss*, p. 216.
[3] *Forster's Briefwechsel*, ii. 662–3. [4] Heinse, *Werke*, ix. 251.

of our Forster ? ' he inquired of Sömmerring in December 1793. When he heard the news of his death, soon after, he wrote : ' Poor Forster has expiated his errors. I regret him heartily.' None the less, when he came to compose the ' Xenien,' Forster was too tempting an object to spare.

> ' Freedom, equality ! ' shrill is the cry. I hear and will follow ;
> And since the stairs are too long, let us jump down from the roof.

That is harmless enough ; but the second arrow is sharper.

> Fool that I am ! a raving fool, and all men are madmen
> Who plant Liberty's tree, acting on woman's advice.

' You are not the first to ask me for some memorial to our good friend,' wrote Lichtenberg from Göttingen to Archenholtz ; ' but in recent times I quite lost sight of him. I could not approve his political activities. He was a great but a very young man, as he showed, alas ! at the end.' [1]

The most whole-hearted tribute came from Friedrich Schlegel, who discussed his achievements and ideas at considerable length in an essay of 1797.[2] ' One rarely lays down anything of his without feeling oneself stimulated, enriched, and enlarged. No German prose-writer breathes such a spirit of advance ; for in even the best of German writers one is conscious of the air of an enclosed room. Every pulse-beat of his ever active spirit struggles forwards. He never tried to argue away the crimes and follies of men ; but the idea of perfection was the foundation of all his works.' Half a century later Schlegel's glowing testimonial was countersigned by Gervinus in the eloquent study written for the ' Collected Works.' Forster, he maintained, far from being a doctrinaire, was born for action. He admired England and the United States for the opportunities of self-realisation they afforded ; and it was the same principle which attracted him to the Revolution. His decision to embrace the French cause was both inevitable and consistent, since he was a German neither by birth nor training. Even more remarkable is the verdict of Jaurès, who pronounced him ' the boldest revolutionary fighter of Germany, the only man of action thrown up by the German democracy.' [3] But these resounding eulogies overshot the mark. He was not a political nature,[4] and his skin was too sensitive for the perilous encounters

---

[1] *Lichtenberg's Briefe*, iii. 117.   [2] *Jugendschriften*, ii. 119–40.
[3] Jaurès, *La Convention*, i. 568–609.
[4] This view is strongly supported by Hashagen, *Das Rheinland*.

of public life in the hurricane season. ' Bold revolutionary fighters '
and ' men of action ' do not die of a broken heart a few months
after they discover that their ideals are not in process of realisation.
He was the weakest of men, testifies Caroline. He lacked the
qualities of virility, judgment, and decision that are needed by those
who would guide and govern their fellow men. ' As long as he
regarded the evils of the Revolution as the price of the good, he
bore them,' writes his wife, who knew him best ; ' but when he
saw all the selfishness and the treachery, his heart broke.' His
death was a loss not to democracy, but to scholarship and society ;
and Perthes is guilty of no exaggeration in describing him as the
greatest sacrifice offered by intellectual Germany to the French
Revolution.

CHAPTER XIV

THE GERMANS IN FRANCE

I

AT the outbreak of the Revolution by far the most distinguished German resident in France was Baron Melchior Grimm, who had settled in Paris as far back as 1748, and had earned his living by supplying German princes with tit-bits from the Mecca of culture.[1] The 'Correspondance Littéraire' was carried on by its founder till 1773, when it was entrusted to his Swiss colleague, Meister. The editor quickly won his place among the brilliant spirits who taught France to ask questions about politics and religion ; but the witty freethinker had no sympathy with political radicalism. 'Man is made neither for liberty nor for truth,' he wrote in the 'seventies. 'They are senseless dreamers who long for great revolutions in State and society. The gain would not be worth the sacrifice.' He lamented the progress of democratic ideas, and in the opening days of 1789 sorrowfully confessed that the evil spirit could no longer be held in check. Such a man naturally detested the Revolution from the outset. 'I observe that you want to surpass the English and the Americans,' he remarked to a friend on the eve of the States-General ; 'take care not to fall short of the Poles.' The demolition of the Bastille filled him with dark forebodings, which were quickly realised. 'I can prove geometrically that France is ruined beyond recall,' he wrote in August 1790, 'and that unless a god descends to save it, there will only remain on the map the black spot which Burke and I and others have foreseen from the beginning.' He described Necker and Lafayette as the innocent cause of the trouble. 'There is nothing more reprehensible than innocents who mix themselves up in great affairs ; and for the

---

[1] See Scherer, *Melchior Grimm*. His voluminous letters to Catherine the Great, and her letters to him, have been published by the Russian Historical Society, vols. xliv. and xxiii. For the subject of the whole chapter, see A. Mathiez, *La Révolution et les Étrangers*, 1918.

first time, perhaps, necessity has not created the leader or leaders required to save the country. I see only men who have set in motion a machine which they cannot guide, and by which they are swept away. It was an unpardonable blunder on Necker's part to convoke the States-General without troubling to secure a majority. To double the representation of the Tiers État was right enough ; but the King should have insisted on every deputy being forty years old and a landed proprietor, which would have saved the Monarchy from falling into the hands of the lawyers. Yet when I recall the previous efforts of France to govern herself, I am tempted to think that her fate was sealed when the States-General were summoned.'

On his way to Germany at the end of 1790 Grimm visited Bouillé at Metz, and reported his impressions to Catherine. ' He is a man after my own heart ; but he can no more restore order than anybody else. Your Majesty is quite right. A man at the head of eighteen thousand soldiers on whom he could rely might be the tyrant or saviour of the country. The French army is now on the level of the Turks. To save France a foreign force is requisite as a nucleus round which the national forces could rally ; and such a body does not exist. Only one Frenchman could have achieved this miracle—the King ; and he refuses.' On reaching Frankfurt at Christmas he had remarkable conversations with the Emperor and the Nuncio. ' I told the former that I feared the return of barbarism and the destruction of arts and letters. He replied that the return of superstition and the empire of the priests seemed to him near and inevitable. I added that the French had proved themselves unfit for liberty by the use they had made of it, and that their extravagances could only lead to a rigid despotism. Caprara remarked to me : " I have no fear for the authority of the Church. You and I are perhaps too old to see it reborn from its ashes ; but reborn it will be. Your Jacobins have rendered that inevitable." '

Before leaving Paris Grimm had adjured Catherine to order the Revolution back into its cave by a blast of her trumpet, and he now pictured Russia as the only bulwark against the flood. ' If the French delirium is not promptly repressed, it may be more or less fatal to the heart of Europe ; for the pestilential air must inevitably ravage and destroy everything it approaches. The overthrow of military discipline will be one of the immediate effects of this systematic insubordination. Russia alone is beyond the orbit of this Gallic madness, and Russia will prevent the Turks from overrunning Europe. Then two Empires, Russia and America, will monopolise the prizes of civilisation—letters, arts, arms, industry—and the rest of us will be too degraded to know, except as a vague memory, what we have once been.' To keep Russia free from the contagion he forwarded a copy of a report on ' some apostles of French regeneration,' so that if any of them found their way to the banks of the Neva they might receive the ' promotion' they deserved. Grimm watched the decline and disappearance of the moderates with regret, but without surprise. ' I should not be astonished if Lafayette were to end his days in America, like Necker in Switzerland,' he wrote in 1791. ' He has combined disinterestedness and many romantic qualities with abstract and metaphysical ideas. Mirabeau's death is generally considered a misfortune, as he might have saved the Monarchy in spite of all the harm he had done to the country. Nothing proves the madness of the nation more than the incredible honours paid to a man generally despised in his lifetime.'

These anti-revolutionary sentiments were generally known in Paris, and his friendship with Catherine increased the suspicion with which he was regarded. His movements were, however, for the present untrammelled. Having left Paris in 1790, he spent the summer of 1791 in Frankfurt and Aachen. At this moment Catherine begged him to burn her letters, and he returned home in the autumn not to destroy but to remove them from the danger zone. He left France in haste on the eve of war in 1792, but was unable to take his papers and property with him. Three years later he sent a vivid description of the circumstances to the Empress. ' I was reproached for having only aristocrats for my friends and for being in relations with several of the tyrants of Europe. A number of Sansculottes among my neighbours warmly defended me, testifying that, before the Revolution, I had always been a friend to good patriots, and maintaining that, as a foreigner, I was under no obligation to hold the republican faith. My enemies were thus compelled to make more definite charges, and therefore spread the report that fifty thousand Russians were about to join the Coalition, and that, if I had not persuaded your Majesty to this step, I was at any rate in your secrets. Before long, fifty thousand Russians were believed to be hidden in my house, ready to fall on the people.' He proceeds to relate that his maid valiantly remained on watch in the house after her master's precipitate flight and during the examination of his papers. Though the search lasted for fifteen days, nothing of a compromising character was found ; for Catherine's letters had been removed. A further incident of these critical days is preserved by Eckermann.[1] ' We were one day dining at Grimm's,' said Goethe, ' and the host

[1] *Goethe's Conversations with Eckermann*, February 14, 1830.

remarked, " I wager that no monarch in Europe possesses so costly a pair of ruffles, and that no one has paid so high a price as I have." You may imagine that we were incredulous, particularly the ladies, and that we were all very curious to see so wonderful a pair of ruffles.   When he produced them we all burst into loud admiration. We endeavoured to set a price on them, but we could not value them above a hundred or two hundred louis d'or.   Grimm laughed, and exclaimed : " You are very far below the mark.   I paid 300,000 francs, and was lucky in laying out my assignats so well. Next day they were not worth a groschen." '

Grimm found refuge at Gotha, of which Court he had long been the diplomatic representative at Paris.   The Duke was friendly and the Empress continued his pension ; but he pined for the scintillating talk of the best society in Europe. He acted as Catherine's agent in assisting the Émigrés, and poured out his soul in interminable letters to St. Petersburg. He had never grasped the necessity of fundamental changes, nor realised the explosive power of the revolutionary gospel. He agreed with Catherine's verdict that France had been delivered of a rotten and stinking monster.   Knowing nothing of the strength of New France or of the weakness of Old Europe, he anticipated the speedy triumph of the Coalition armies, and the collapse of the campaign filled him with sorrow and anger.   The death of the King affected him less than the danger of the Queen, which moved him to an outburst faintly recalling the glorious declamation of Burke.   ' The rigour of her lot has nearly destroyed the little wits that I still possess. When I think of the moment I saw her for the first time in Vienna, the year before her marriage, when she spoke to me with childlike curiosity of the royal palace which was to be so fatal to her ; when I think of the young Archduchess, envied perhaps by all her sisters, starting for France, and now delivered to the executioners without a shadow of offence against the nation ; when I think of the intoxication of this frivolous and ferocious people for her and its love of the King in the early years of his reign, I almost go mad.' Her execution drove him to fury.   ' One would die of grief at belonging to the race of man if one could not turn one's eyes to an empire governed for thirty-two years by wisdom and virtue. The alternatives are to exterminate the impious race which has seized the helm in France, or to submit to the ruin of all ordered government and the sacrifice of centuries of civilisation. And yet Europe deliberates, and there are sovereigns and governments who are indifferent.   If at the end of next year this hydra still exists, it may be all up with the Continent.   I have never feared the contagion of their principles.   Though lawyers and men hungry for power are to be found everywhere, her neighbours have too much good sense to let themselves be led away by the sophisms which have transformed the French into a horde of brigands. The danger is that these brigands, when there is nothing more to pillage at home, will hurl themselves on their neighbours, and famine and perhaps pestilence will make Europe one vast cemetery. In that case Russia would bear away culture into Asia.'

France's shame and Europe's extremity were Catherine's opportunity. 'My creed is brevity itself,' he wrote in a strain of fulsome eulogy. 'I believe in Catherine II, the only hope of humanity in these times of darkness, the only support in these days of desolation. I believe that her genius watches over Europe to save it from the terrible effects of the barbarism and ferocity of this impious and sacrilegious race which hell has vomited on to the earth for the terror of all decent folk. I believe that hell will not prevail against the imperturbable constancy of her magnanimous heart.' When voices were raised for peace with the Republic, he wrapped himself in the mantle of Burke. 'No peace or security in Europe is possible,' he wrote in January 1794, 'so long as this horde of savages exists in France.' He even denounced his old friend and patron, Prince Henry, as a Jacobin for his share in the Treaty of Basle. The death of the Empress a year later was a crushing blow; but her son and grandson continued the pension, and the old Baron lingered on till 1812, when he had reached the age of eighty-four. No German had loved the old France or hated the new more heartily than the Bavarian pastor's son, who had risen to rank and celebrity beyond the Rhine and closed his life in exile in his own land.

II

While Grimm shook the dust of the revolutionary capital off his feet, a considerable number of Germans turned their footsteps towards the Mecca of Liberty, where not a few of them were to find glory or death. Among the latter was Anacharsis Cloots, known to all the world as the Orator of the Human Race.[1] Yet he was something more than a hero of melodrama. Sprung from a family of Dutch descent, he was taught French at home, and received his education at Brussels and Paris. At the age of fifteen he entered the Berlin Academy for young nobles, founded by Frederick the Great; but his heart was in France, and when he came of age and found himself his own master, with an income of 100,000 francs, he

[1] See Kayser, *Anacharsis Cloots, Preussische Jahrbücher*, March 1895; and Selina Stern's excellent monograph, 1914.

settled in the French capital. It was not long before the young Prussian nobleman had made the acquaintance of all the leaders of thought and society. He visited Franklin at Passy and Rousseau at Ermenonville; but his god was Voltaire, whose anti-clericalism was surpassed by the vitriolic zeal of the disciple. In these early years he was far less interested in political reform than in combating intolerance and fanaticism. He wrote on the history of religion, and desired to present an address to the King urging him to ordain the cult of Natural Religion, and thereby emancipate his twenty million subjects from superstition. His rabid talk brought him into conflict with the police, and in 1785 he left Paris, declaring that he would not return till the Bastille had been overthrown.

The next four years were spent in travel. On a visit to England he met the Whig leaders and stayed with Burke at Beaconsfield, carrying away with him the Whig doctrine that the English Constitution left too much power to the King. The outbreak of the Revolution found him far away in southern Europe, and he hurried back to Paris in high glee. 'As I look at the map of the world,' he wrote to Burke, 'it seems to me as if all other countries had vanished and only France exists, with her rays filling the universe.' Till now he had only desired a religious revolution. He had admired the enlightened autocracy of Frederick the Great, and had shared the Aufklärung's contempt for the masses. By a sudden *volte-face* he now convinced himself that behind the aristocratic veneer was concealed an evil heart, while behind the rude simplicity of the *plebs* lay noble qualities. He sought the society of the Fourth Estate in the Halles and the Cabarets, and rejoiced to find his own detestation of priests so widely shared. ' The noblest revolution in history ' was far more than a mere revolt against oppression. It was the beginning of a new era of political liberty and philosophic enlightenment. Realising to the full the importance of the press, he became a zealous and effective journalist, contributing articles to most of the journals, above all to that of Camille Desmoulins 'Writers are the pillars of the Constitution,' he cried, ' the immovable generals of the citizen army. If we desire to keep our newly-won liberties, let us retain unfettered liberty of the press.' When hereditary nobility was abolished in 1790 he called himself Anacharsis Cloots, thereby surrendering his ' Gothic title ' and also his Christian name : the latter in order to ' debaptise ' himself. He now signed himself ' Cloots, Baron in Germany, citizen in France.' He was among the earliest members of the Jacobin Club, where he preached distrust of the King at a time when nearly every Frenchman still believed in his good will. He was by this time a familiar figure in the revolutionary world ; but it was not till the Fête of the Federation that he won national and international fame. He collected a number of foreigners resident in Paris, some of them fugitives from despotic lands, and propounded his plan of appearing at the bar of the Assembly as delegates of the human race. The idea was applauded by his listeners, who hailed him as the Orator of the Human Race.

On June 19, 1790, thirty-six of ' the Committee of Foreigners in Paris,' clothed in their national costumes, entered the Assembly. Cloots, standing between an ' Arab ' on his right hand and a ' Chaldean ' on his left, read an address from ' the holiest embassy ever known ' to the body whom he greeted as the ' Oecumenical Council of Reason.' ' The trumpets which proclaimed the resurrection of a great people echoed to the four corners of the world. The Fête of the Federation will be the fête of the human race. The joyful songs of a choir of twenty-five million free men have awakened the peoples of the south, buried under age-long slavery. And so foreigners from every clime beg leave to present themselves in the Champ de Mars as a pledge of the speedy emancipation of their unhappy fellow citizens. Rome bound the chiefs of conquered peoples to her chariots. It is your privilege to see free men assisting at your triumphal progress. We are the true ambassadors of the one sovereign, Mankind.' The Assembly granted leave to the deputation to express its sentiments and to take part in the fête, ' on condition that you tell your fellow countrymen what you have seen.' The ' Turk ' stammered a few words of gratitude in broken French, and the unique ceremony was at an end. Sceptics declared that the Baron had picked up his deputies in the gutter, and that the ' Turk,' the ' Arab, ' and the ' Chaldean ' were fetched from the Opera ; but the impresario paid no attention to the cackle of unfriendly tongues. He presented certificates of presence to the members of the deputation, dated from ' the capital of the globe,' and was henceforth regarded as the patron and spokesman of Francophil foreigners in Paris. Half a million copies of his speech to the Assembly were printed, and addresses flowed in from every part of France. He now dubbed himself with unction the Orator of the Human Race, ' a man penetrated with the conviction of human worth ; a tribune burning with the love of liberty and the detestation of tyrants ; a man who has received the sanction of his world-apostolate in the bosom of the legislature of the world, and then dedicates himself exclusively to the voluntary defence of the millions of slaves who from Pole to Pole sigh under the rod of aristocrats ; a man whose menacing voice reaches every throne, whose comforting accents penetrate every workshop ; a man who banishes himself from the scenes of his childhood and travel and sweet memories in order to reside in the capital of independence,

declining all posts of honour and emolument to which his zeal and
his talents entitle him.   The mission of the Orator of the Human
Race will only end with the overthrow of the oppressors of mankind.'

The idea of propaganda was implicit in the principles of 1789,
and it was the commonplace of orators in the Assembly and the
Jacobin Club ; but with Cloots it assumed practical form.   ' I leave
father and mother, brother and sister, Lares and Penates,' he
exclaimed, ' for the regeneration of France and the Universe.'   He
was convinced that liberty would moralise the world.   An enslaved
nation, he contended in a book published early in 1791, committed
more crimes in a day than a free nation in a century.   As individuals
have improved their lot by forming communities, so peoples will
benefit by combining into a single nation.   When national sentiment is abolished, the whole world will be the fatherland of every
individual.   There will be no more Émigrés and no more war.   They
will be free citizens of the world, who now drag the chains of princes
and kiss the slippers of priests.   The French Assembly will then be
the representative body of the thousand departments of the world,
each returning ten members, and Paris will be the capital of the
globe, the Vatican of Rèason.   ' All the land will be a Garden of
Eden ; East and West will embrace.   Rome became the metropolis
of the world through war, and Paris will become its successor through
peace.'   Other countries would not belong to France : they would
be subject to law alone.   ' The world will enjoy perpetual peace ;
but to reach it there must be one more war against tyrants.'   In
his cosmopolitan zeal, the author never forgets his hatred of
Christianity and clerical rule—the pillars of tyranny.   Religion,
he cries, is too useful to tyrants to be necessary for the people.   Its
very name, ' twice bound,' betrays the snare of the fowler.   Belief
in the sovereignty of the race is religion enough for a free man.   His
creed should be ' One interest, one law, one reason, one nation.'

Cloots rejoiced at the opening of hostilities, and gave twelve
thousand francs to equip forty or fifty soldiers for ' the holy war of
men against crowns,' which would inaugurate perpetual peace.
He was certain of victory, and convinced that the peasantry would
everywhere support the French arms.   When Prussia joined Austria
he was instrumental in forming a Prussian Legion, and marched
with some of his countrymen to the bar of the Assembly.   ' These
petitioners,' he announced, ' have sworn to deliver their country.
We offer you a Prussian Legion.'   The offer was accepted, and his
services were recognised by the grant of French citizenship.   He
became the only German member of the Convention, and rose to
be chairman of the Diplomatic Committee.   He had refused to join
a society for tyrannicide, ' for iron only kills tyrants, not tyranny ' ;

but he had no objection to the systematic extermination of un-
desirables. He approved the September massacres, and expressed
his regret that any priests had escaped. He voted for the death
of the King, and desired a similar fate for Frederick William II,
' and all other tyrants.' ' I have seen the head of a monarch jump,'
he wrote after the final scene in the Place de la Révolution. ' I
will wash my hands in the blood of the last tyrants of Europe, hands
which are already red with the blood of Louis XVI.' He supported
the Jacobins as the advocates of centralised power against the
Girondins, whose detestation of him is reflected in the caustic
pages of Madame Roland.

The famous decree of the Convention, offering liberty to all
peoples, war on the châteaux, peace to the cottages, breathes the
cosmopolitan radicalism of the Prussian Baron. He spoke frequently in the Convention and the Jacobin Club, and wrote in the
press on the annihilation of kings and the establishment of a world-
republic. Such was the orthodoxy of the moment ; but he was
playing with fire in advocating his other pet project—the abolition
of Christianity. For a time he rode on the crest of the wave, and
was elected Chairman of the Jacobin Club. When the first Fête of
Reason was held in Notre Dame, he thought the long battle was
won, and saw in imagination the worship of Reason subduing the
world. But he had reckoned without Robespierre, who ingeniously
argued that atheism was aristocratic. The eloquent Deist carried
the club with him, and Hébert and Chaumette drew in their horns.
Cloots was denounced as a rich Prussian nobleman, and Robespierre
adroitly interpreted his notorious cosmopolitanism as a lack of
patriotic zeal. ' He wishes to be called a citizen of the world. He
was never the defender of the French people, but of the human race.'
His attack on religion, continued the indictment, gave pleasure to
the enemies of liberty. ' And he, a foreigner and a noble, was
chairman of the club. Aliens rule there, aliens spy upon us.' The
arrow sped to its mark. Foreign members were expelled : Cloots
vainly contending that his fault was to love the race too much and
parties too little, and claiming Robespierre as his pupil in political
philosophy. ' I believe in the infallibility of the people—there
is my creed.' On Christmas Day Robespierre carried the war into
the Convention, which in turn expelled him as an alien. Two days
later he was arrested with the Hébertists, who were accused of
plotting a civil war. ' Time will revenge us,' he cried on hearing
his sentence ; ' the people will judge its judges. I appeal to the
human race ; but, like Socrates, I am ready for the hemlock.' When
Hébert feebly bleated that liberty was lost, his stout-hearted comrade
rebuked him. ' You know not what you are saying. Liberty cannot

die.' He perished with a smile on his lips, bravely claiming the hideous privilege of being the last of the batch to mount the scaffold.

Cloots was a man of extreme views ; but he was as ready to die for them as he was to consign to the scaffold those who refused to share them, and his personal character was unblemished. He resisted Robespierre in the plenitude of his power, and denounced his old friends, the Girondins, when he believed that the Jacobins could more effectively defend the Fatherland. It was in vain that his mother had warned him of danger in 1792, and had urged him to seek safety in the United States. He detested compromise, and marched clear-eyed towards his doom. Though a French citizen, he could never think like a Frenchman. ' I demand the subordination of the French name to that of humanity,' he cried ; and his strident cosmopolitanism grated on the ears of the Jacobins when France was fighting for her life. Though neither a fool nor a madman, he was vain, eccentric, and ruthless. His ideals were undesirable as well as impossible ; and, despite his acknowledged bravery, not a soul in France or Germany mourned his inevitable fate.

III

Of the Germans who threw in their lot with the Revolution Reinhard alone rose to high office and played an important part in affairs.[1] But though he became a French citizen, and remained in the service of France till his death, he never lost his affection for the land of his birth. In an age of unexampled passion and excitement he never made an enemy ; and though denounced by the fiery Arndt as an apostate, he enjoyed the respect and friendship of most of the leading men in the two countries which were continually warring against one another. At Tübingen he drank in the French influences brought to the University by the French students from Mömpelgard ; and his poetic effusions were a mere versification of Rousseau. These juvenile outpourings are now forgotten ; but they were praised by Schiller who, next to Rousseau, was the hero of his early manhood. He left the University with relief. ' I owe nothing to those five years but a heightened desire for liberty, the fruit of painful abstinence. I know not if it was owing to the elasticity of my character or to Providence that my mind was not weighed down to the breaking-point.' In 1787 he became tutor in a Protestant family in Bordeaux, unwittingly taking the decisive step which was to determine his career. In the eager commercial and intellectual life of the great port he found the bracing atmosphere he had craved ; and his liberal views secured him a welcome at a

---

[1] See Wilhelm Lang's masterly work, *Graf Reinhard*.

time when France was girding herself for her great adventure. He wrote poems in French—an epistle on Religious Liberty, dedicated to Raynal, and an ode to Liberty, suggested by the meeting of the Estates of Béarn at Pau, of which he was an interested spectator.

Reinhard's delight on receiving news of the fall of the Bastille was described in a letter to a Württemberg paper. ' If the world used to scoff at the French claim to be the first nation in the world, a universal chorus will now award the palm to this noble people. England will regard without jealousy her rival following and surpassing her example. Of course we cannot anticipate the future. An unexpected catastrophe might restore despotism ; but it is improbable. The triumph is too complete, the nation too unanimous. Wise men are apprehensive as to the unsteadiness of the national character ; but, in any case, no people and no epoch has witnessed such a venerable Assembly or such a momentous revolution.' A second letter, written in September, describes the effects of the events in Paris on the provinces, and reviews the debates on the Constitution. The constitutional effort may fail ; but success is more probable, as the King is behind it. ' Besides, the universally accepted principles of the Assembly are a seed which, sooner or later, is bound to bear fruit throughout Europe.' Yet he has no wish to see Germany imitate France. With a country split into innumerable fragments, any revolution would be local and ineffective. Moreover, it is unnecessary. ' As good and enlightened princes greatly outnumber the bad ones, most German States, even where no Estates exist to limit the princely power, are happier and have less burdens and purer morals than France will ever possess. Besides, public opinion and a virtually free press hold despotism and vice in check.' On the other hand, he regretted that enthusiasm for the Revolution was not universal in his own country. ' Not all my countrymen love your Revolution,' he wrote in a Bordeaux journal, ' and it is the scholars who bark the loudest. To these folk fraternity appears a chimaera, like all the lofty reforms which have been accomplished under their eyes. They remind me of the German professor who was proving the impossibility of the balloon at the very moment that two rose majestically into the air.' As the Revolution progressed, Reinhard felt himself increasingly drawn to the country which was striving for liberty, and ever less inclined to return to the land of petty tyrannies in which he was born. He began his political career in the local branch of the Society of Friends of the Constitution, and for a month took his turn as president. When the flight to Varennes became known in Bordeaux, 2400 citizens promptly enrolled themselves for the defence of the country ; and in these hours of exaltation the young tutor crossed the Rubicon.

' I saw the Revolution begin, I embraced it with enthusiasm, and on the day when the news of the flight reached the city, I recorded my resolve to live and die a Frenchman.'

When the Legislative succeeded the Constituent Assembly, Reinhard accompanied his friends Vergniaud and Ducos to Paris, where he quickly found his feet. ' When I saw you in the Assembly,' he wrote to Lafayette, ' my heart beat. I blessed you when you were traversing the wilds of America.' He joined the Jacobin Club, and wrote in the early numbers of Archenholtz's ' Minerva.' Shortly after his arrival he dispatched a long letter to Schiller.[1] ' For two months I have been here with a pupil and in the company of two deputies of the Gironde, who have already distinguished themselves in the new Legislature and whom I am allowed to call my friends. You can well believe that I have taken sides wholeheartedly in the events of which I have been a witness for three years. I saw in the French Revolution not the affair of a nation with which I shall perhaps never wholly sympathise, but a gigantic step forwards in the progress of the human mind, and a fair prospect of ennobling the whole destiny of the race. Even if all the terrible pictures drawn abroad of the excesses of liberty were true, I should still have forgiven the goddess her bloody revenge. The plan of the new Constitution seemed to me a new experiment which France was trying at her own risk for the good of the race ; and I have never forgiven my compatriots for blaming such a magnanimous undertaking. Of course, the corruption of morals and the incredible egotism seemed at the beginning an insurmountable obstacle ; but observation and reflection soon brought me to a more hopeful attitude. Unlike the friends of the English Constitution, I maintain that the building must rest not on experience, but on principles. If these are correct, the results will soon obtain the necessary modifications from circumstances. The success has till now fully justified this expectation. The nation as a whole has gained enormously in enlightenment. Even its moral character, except in the case of the upper classes, has become ennobled to an incredible degree. Nearly all prevailing prejudices have been smashed to pieces by principles. The opposition of the nobility led to the abolition of titles. The opposition of the clergy led to the untying of the knot which bound the Catholic religion to the State, and perhaps the stroke is not far distant which will cut it through. You saw how in Varennes the last sacred shimmer disappeared in which political superstition veiled the Crown. With a second Varennes, the throne itself would perhaps disappear for ever. The irresistible power of principle makes St. Domingo the theatre of a fearful negro rebellion ;

[1] Printed in full by Urlichs, *Briefe an Schiller.*

and if the League of Princes matures, will it not make all Europe a St. Domingo ?

'I have watched this marvellous revolution in large perspective. When I say that the French nation has raised itself, that is merely relative to the abyss in which the Revolution found it. I do not mean that it has reached a high standard of moral and intellectual worth. I will give you an indication of our atmosphere here. You know the Society of the Friends of the Constitution, and the mother-lodge, the Jacobins in Paris ; but perhaps you do not know that there are now thousands of these societies in France, all more or less connected. They have rendered infinite service to the Revolution, and without them there might have been no constitution. I can assure you that the reputation of the mother-lodge rests far more on a sort of voluntary, childlike respect than on the efforts of its leaders. We have had no one during the Revolution with the strength of a Cromwell, able to stop or even to direct the machine. Even Mirabeau, in order to influence it, had almost always to follow its momentum. The secret conspiracy of the enemies of the Revolution could nowhere gain ground in face of these vigilance committees. The meeting-places were opened to the public, and the leading men thus became known to the people. The ruling passion of the new legislature is patriotism ; but there are so many secondary traits in its physiognomy that it becomes repulsive. Every member thinks that the Chamber is still the arena of the society in which he began, and thus every one wishes to play a leading rôle. Thus arises a conflict of vanities, an intolerance, a tumult which would disgrace a beer-house. Even wise resolutions are carried in such a curious way that their wisdom appears doubtful. In short we see everywhere mediocrity, lack of dignity and education ; and perhaps nothing but a new crisis can give this Assembly the tone which corresponds to its true character and put the shouters in their place. Nothing is more certain than that such a crisis must soon occur. I see a fivefold danger—the financial chaos, the convulsions of fanaticism, the storm in the colonies, the plans of the Émigrés, the lack of specie combined with the high price of food. The sixth and most threatening is that the control over such a new and complicated machine is in the hands of an untrustworthy government. Meanwhile if, as I hope, some happy result issues from this long and terrible uncertainty, mankind will find its path to perfection made smoother. Perhaps France will be the victim of her own enterprise ; but may not the principles of equality be transplanted into more receptive soil ? In the temples of Jerusalem only the Koran is heard ; but all Europe turns to the Cross. I do not know if I have the right to deal so fully with a subject which

X

must of course be of infinite significance in your eyes, but which you will perhaps regard from a totally different standpoint. I am only worrying you because I hear that you have accepted an old article of mine for the " Thalia." In payment I venture not only to ask for a reply to my letter, but to dictate its contents. I should like to know your confession of faith in the French Revolution and the Constitution. If it is not asking too much, would you give me some account of how the leading German publicists and authors look at these matters ? If you honour me with a correspondence, I would give you information, not lacking in interest, which my position enables me to collect.' No reply from Schiller has been preserved, and the young enthusiast does not appear to have sent his friend a further bulletin.

With such influential friends as the Girondin leaders, Reinhard soon found responsible employment. Having procured formal permission from the Duke of Württemberg to enter the French service, he made his début in diplomacy as First Secretary to the French Embassy in London, under Chauvelin. On the outbreak of war with England, in the following year, he was transferred to Naples. When Naples in turn declared war against France, he returned to Paris. The Girondins had fallen, and he was for a time in danger ; but he was given a post in the Foreign Office. To the end of his life he shuddered at the name of Robespierre, and spoke with emotion of those gruesome months when death was never far away. When the Terror was over, he was appointed Minister to the three Hansa cities. The post was thoroughly congenial ; for he had never lost his love for his fatherland. He rejoiced to find himself in the liberal and cultivated atmosphere of Hamburg, where he married a daughter of Reimarus. Three years later he was removed to Florence, and in 1799 became Foreign Minister of the French Republic till Talleyrand displaced him after Brumaire. He returned to Hamburg, and later became Minister to King Jerome at Cassel ; for, though he disliked Napoleon, he kept his thoughts to himself. After Waterloo he represented the Bourbons at Frankfurt, and died a Peer of France in the same year as Goethe, his revered friend and correspondent. His belief in the value of the Revolution never faltered, and his faith in the future never waned.

IV

Among the Generals to whom France looked with confidence at the crisis of her fate was a German veteran.[1] Born in 1722 in

---

[1] See *Le Maréchal de Luckner, Revue des Questions Historiques*, April 1898 The article is based on MSS. in the French War Office.

Bavaria, in humble circumstances, Luckner entered the Bavarian army at the age of fifteen, fought against the Turks, and subsequently took part in the War of the Austrian Succession and the Seven Years' War. In the latter struggle he had fought for Hanover; but when peace was restored, he was no longer needed by George III. Feeling himself slighted he offered his sword to Louis XV and was appointed Lieutenant-General at a high salary. The post was a sinecure, for he lived in Holstein, and paid only three short visits to France before the outbreak of the Revolution a generation later. In 1790 he once more visited Paris: drawn not by devotion to the principles of 1789, or a feeling of duty towards his employers, but solely by fear of losing his pay. A mercenary adventurer throughout life, he was guided solely by considerations of personal interest. He had turned Protestant to win a rich wife, and he now turned Republican because Louis XVI had refused him a Marshal's bâton. He joined the Jacobin Society in Strassburg, and delivered patriotic speeches; but he had no political convictions. He would assure the King of his devotion, while informing the Jacobins in his hideous jargon, 'Moi aussi ché suis Chacopin.' For a few months his name was on every lip, Mirabeau and Dumouriez joining in his praise. His age and long experience, it was believed, would make him a skilful and intrepid defender of the soil of France. Even before fate exposed his nakedness, Madame Roland's sharp vision took his measure at a dinner party to which she invited him. 'I never saw such mediocrity. He is half stupid, and possesses neither mind nor character. O my poor country, you are doomed if you have to entrust your destinies to an alien of that stamp!' On the eve of war he was created a Marshal, 'for consecrating his talents to France and her struggle for liberty. The guarantee of your devotion is your choice of France in preference to any other country.'

On the outbreak of war Luckner led the French army against the Austrian troops in Belgium; but his military inefficiency at once became manifest. Though neither a coward nor a traitor, he was irresolute and incapable, and let opportunity slip through his fingers. With such a sham leader, defeat was inevitable. He was moved to Metz, where he proved himself equally incompetent. Deprived of command he lived in disgrace but unmolested, till, at the end of 1793, he foolishly ventured to Paris to demand arrears of pay. He was promptly denounced by his fellow countryman, Charles of Hesse, condemned as a traitor, and executed. He had inflicted more damage on his adopted country as a French Marshal than when he had fought against her as a German officer.

V

Equally incompetent as a soldier, and far more repulsive in character, Prince Charles of Hesse-Rheinfels had entered the French army as a young man and obtained a good position through the favour of Louis XVI.[1]   He had nothing but his title to recommend him ; for he was of almost bestial appearance, his teeth clattered when he talked, and he was at once a coward and a braggart.   He welcomed the Revolution not from conviction, but in a spirit of revenge.   Incensed against the Court for refusing him an independent command—though he was destitute of military talent—and against the nobles for treating him with disdain, he watched with malicious glee the humiliation of his foes.   'The courtiers of the *ancien régime*,' he had complained, ' look down on me as a German prince, very patient and very stupid.'   He was now to have his revenge. He joined the Jacobin Club and became a satellite of Orleans.   ' We call him Monsieur Hesse,' reports Anacharsis Cloots.   In 1791 he asked for employment, and was made commandant of Verdun. He at once began to denounce real or imaginary plotters, in order to attract the attention of the Jacobins, whose rise to power he foresaw.   At the Jacobin Club, in April 1792, he made a fulsome speech.   ' I loved the Revolution before it broke out.   I love it now, and I always shall, though I had the misfortune to be born a prince.'   He was successively commander at Strassburg and Lyons, where he denounced suspects—including General Montesquiou, the conqueror of Savoy—and organised atrocities.   ' I have won in the south the honourable title of General Marat,' he wrote proudly from Lyons to the Committee of Public Safety.   He received the news of the overthrow of the Monarchy at Besançon.   ' Thank God,' he cried, ' that we have no longer a King and that we are now all brothers.'

The unchanging policy of Charles of Hesse was to sow tares and to shout with the largest crowd.   ' This worthless creature, whose mind is as degraded as his body,' wrote d'Espinchal in his Journal, ' threw himself heart and soul into the Revolution, being influenced quite as much by love of money as by his opinions.   He is a rabid Jacobin, and one of the most unprincipled of all.' [2]   But no zeal, real or affected, could wipe out the original sin of his birth.   In October 1793 he was dismissed from the post of Commander of Orleans, since Jacobin feeling in Paris demanded the eviction of all nobles.   At last the sinister personage who had sent so many

---

[1] See Chuquet, *Un Prince Jacobin, Charles de Hesse.*
[2] *Journal*, p. 223.

innocent men to prison was himself arrested and imprisoned for
a year without charge. His worthless life was saved by Thermidor ;
but he was never employed again. He was the butt of verses and
squibs, and angrily resented being called prince—'that ridiculous
title which I so heartily despise.' Expelled the country by Napoleon,
he returned to Hesse, where he lived at the expense of his cousin.
He stands in history as the blasphemer who said ' I would denounce
God the Father, if He was not a Jacobin.' While other German
Jacobins marshalled in this chapter were for the most part men
of character or ability, the name and fame of Charles of Hesse are
beyond redemption.

Another German princelet, Frederick of Salm-Kyrburg, lord of
a tiny territory on the left bank of the Rhine, met a harder fate.
He had raised troops for the ' Patriots ' of Holland in their struggle
against the Statthalter in 1787 ; but his courage had failed when
the Prussians had appeared on the scene, and he was deserted by
his men as a traitor. A quarrel with the Empire drove him abroad,
and after the fall of the Monarchy he settled in Paris, surrendering
his princely title for that of a French citizen. His bloodthirsty
flatteries of Robespierre revealed once again the baseness of his
nature, and no tears were shed over his death in the feverish days
of Thermidor. ' He was doubtless guillotined unjustly,' wrote
Grimm to Catherine, 'like so many others under the reign of
Robespierre ; but he was a *mauvais sujet* who, crippled with debts,
had at the beginning of the Revolution entered the National Guards
to save himself from his creditors, against whom Robespierre, in
one of his moments of clemency, wished to guarantee him for
ever.' [1]

VI

When France declared war in 1792, a proposal to organise ' foreign
legions ' was simultaneously made from many quarters ; and the
Legislative Assembly offered rewards to deserters from the enemy.
The decree was sent over the frontier in parcels, was affixed to trees,
and otherwise brought to the notice of likely recruits. ' Legions '
were organised from Holland, Belgium, and Savoy ; and the formation of a German Legion was undertaken by Cloots and Saiffert—the
latter a native of Leipsic, who called himself the Saxon Doctor.[2]
He had settled in Paris as a young man, and numbered among
his patients Égalité and Princess Lamballe. Known before the
Revolution as a democrat, he was among the first to join the Jacobin
Club. He translated the ' Declaration of the Rights of Man ' into

[1] *Lettres de Grimm*, p. 664.   [2] See Chuquet, *La Légion Germanique*.

German, and dispatched copies to the principal cities of the Father-land. The two organisers proposed the appointment of a Prussian, ɩ Dutchman, an Austrian, and an Alsatian as chiefs of the Legion ; and these six men formed the committee, which Saiffert grandilo-quently pronounced the foundation-stone of the future liberty of Germany. He composed a marching song for his motley band of warriors. ' Arise, oppressed people ! Be free like the French. Nature made us equal. My brothers, renounce your slavery ! ' Two thousand six hundred men were to be enrolled, and the command was entrusted to Dambach. On August 12 the histrionic Cloots presented some Prussian volunteers to the Assembly. ' Legislators ! ' he cried, ' we offer you a Prussian Legion.' First among them was Dambach, a veteran of the Seven Years' War, who was introduced as ' covered with fifteen honourable wounds,' Saiffert adding that he had lived for several years in France and married a French wife. The real leader of the Legion was Heyden, a member of a Dutch family settled in Prussia, who had taken part in the American War and made his home in France. There were a dozen other German officers, nearly as many Dutch, and a sprinkling of Belgians and Poles, Italians, and Swiss. In spite of its name, most of the officers and men were French, among them Marceau and Augereau.

Recruiting continued through the autumn of 1792 ; but the Legion never reached the number expected, as there were few deserters from the invading hosts. The corps rendered useful service, and sections of it were sent about the country to restore order and quell riots. But its harmony was destroyed by the friction between the German and French elements, and its career was short. The French officers determined to secure the first places for themselves, preached insubordination, and denounced the foreign commanders. Its enemies contended that it was far below strength, extravagantly expensive, disloyal, and badly equipped. As the war grew fiercer, foreigners became increasingly suspect. In 1793 the Bavarian and Belgian Legions were dissolved, and Marat's attack on the German body was equivalent to a sentence of death. By the summer the foreign officers were in prison; but, though deprived of its leaders, part of the Legion aided in the suppression of the Vendée revolt. When Saumur was taken by the royalists, it alone fought bravely for the Republic. Several of its members, however, joined the royalists after the fight, and the corps was dissolved. Saiffert and Heyden published answers to the attacks upon its record and protested against its dissolution. The subsequent history of the leaders of an enterprise which began with such high hopes is one of death, suspicion, and neglect. Cloots perished on the scaffold.

Dambach's end is lost in obscurity. Heyden lived to receive a few crumbs from Napoleon's table. In 1794 Saiffert dispatched his poems to a friend,' from an imprisoned singer of liberty and equality.' Liberty and equality were out of fashion, and France was ruled by ruthless and suspicious despots.

VII

The most original and attractive personality in the German colony was Count Schlabrendorf, the son of a high official in Silesia, who, after leaving the University, like many a young noble-man set forth on his travels.[1] He accompanied Stein to England, where he spent six years, and made a minute study of English institutions. He returned to Paris on the eve of the Revolution, and found it so enthralling that he never left it. He welcomed the events of 1789, and remained steadily attached to 'French prin-ciples' when others threw them over. To his house every German resident and visitor turned his steps. 'Schlabrendorf is a very clever democrat and a man of ripe experience,' wrote Forster, on his arrival in the city ; 'he knows Europe very well and England best of all.'[2] Though the Count abstained from overt action, his friendship with Brissot, Condorcet, and other Girondins made him a suspect. He spent eighteen months in the Conciergerie and the Luxemburg, in daily expectation of death, but untroubled in spirit and unchanged in conviction. Obtaining money from home through Switzerland, he distributed it among his fellow prisoners, who rewarded him with the name of The Benefactor. When death appeared inevitable, he transferred his whole fortune to Oelsner, who, though also suspect, was still at large and allowed to visit him The Count urged him to instant flight. 'If we meet again, give me what is left ; if I am guillotined, it is yours.' Oelsner escaped to Italy and, despite his poverty, never touched the money, which in happier days he was to restore to its owner.[3]

Among all the hairbreadth escapes from the guillotine none was more remarkable than that of the Prussian nobleman. When his name appeared on the list, he answered the call without flurry or protest. After dressing himself, he sought for his boots, the gaoler assisting in the search. As they were not to be found, he remarked to the gaoler : 'I cannot go without boots, as you will admit. Take me to-morrow ; one day makes no difference.' The

---

[1] See Fähler, *Schlabrendorf*; Varnhagen, *Vermischte Schriften*, i. 422–71 ; and *Denkwürdigkeiten*, iii. 167–228.

[2] *Forster's Briefwechsel*, ii. 460–1.   [3] See Richter, *Oelsner*.

boots were found, and next morning he stood ready for the tumbril ; but the summons did not come. The gaoler took no steps to repair the oversight, and he remained forgotten till the prison doors were opened by the death of Robespierre. On regaining his liberty, he quietly resumed his former life. Every German in Paris sought and found assistance or advice from the man who kept no servant and dressed like a beggar. Zschokke was amazed to find him 'intellectual, noble, rich, yet with dirty, torn clothes, in a dark room littered with books.'[1] In 1811 Dorow brought an introduction from the Count's old travelling companion, Reichardt, and was fascinated by the talk of the old man with long hair and a torn grey coat.[2] ' I learned more about Paris and France in a few hours' conversation than from any book.' He also sent large sums to the Prussian prisoners in France, never ceasing to feel himself a German ; and the Iron Cross, sent him by Frederick William III as a reward for his work for Prussia, was richly deserved. Next to philanthropy, his chief hobby was conversation. He called himself the Diogenes of Paris, receiving innumerable visitors in his tub. He would talk for hours, and his friends never wearied of his eloquence and learning. He was a born student, and followed literature and philosophy as carefully as politics. He detested Napoleon as the enemy of liberty ; but as he never intrigued, and rarely left his house, he was regarded as a harmless eccentric, and escaped the attentions of Fouché's police.[3]

We owe a lifelike portrait of this delightful figure to Varnhagen, who, having made his acquaintance on a visit to Paris in 1810, passed much of his time with his fellow countryman when the Allied armies occupied the capital in 1814. ' He was as bright and sprightly as ever, and looked out at the world with proud confidence. He rejoiced at the fall of Napoleon, which he had always expected. He cared for nothing but liberty, and never changed his principles, which he had convinced himself were essential to the welfare of the State ; but he was forbearing in his judgments of men and things, and always looked for the best. He was the first, and perhaps the only man, who on the day of the Emperor's fall thought of a Republic. A firm friend of the French, he wished to secure the results of the Revolution, so that none of its dearly

---

[1] Zschokke's *Autobiography*, in his *Historische Schriften*, i. 18–21.

[2] Dorow, *Erlebtes*, iii. 69–72. Cp. Helmina von Chezy, *Unvergessenes*, i. 242.

[3] Fähler and Holzhausen (*Die Deutschen in Paris*, ch. i.) attribute to him the pamphlet *Napoleon Bonaparte and the French people under his Consulate*. The author, describing himself as ' a free citizen of the world,' declared that the First Consul despised the French nation as much as it hated him. To free Europe from the mortal enemy of princes and free peoples, the only way was a new Fürstenbund.

bought advantages should be lost. He had much to say against
kings, and spoke of them with a freedom which astonished one :
especially as he talked thus frankly to the Frenchmen of all parties
and the Germans of all ranks who crowded his room. He was at
home to visitors day and night. He would describe the Revolution
in broad, living strokes. He stopped talking for nobody, and
contributed most of the conversation himself. There one heard
the latest news and the most secret intrigues. To what debates and
arguments I have listened ! When alone with a friend he would
leave solid earth and rise into the ideal world of politics, philosophy,
and ethics. Though refusing to write, he would give us outlines of
his ideal republic. All limited monarchy, he would say, is only a
stepping-stone to republicanism. Freedom is indivisible ; if you
admit a part, the rest will follow. The French Revolution could
not succeed straight off ; for no people, unaided, can accomplish
such a task. But now, since all Europe willingly or unwillingly
has taken a share, it may succeed as a co-operative achievement.
The peoples are closer to each other than is generally thought, and
they are moving in the same direction. Man misses the highest
prize of life if he does not belong to a free community.'

Hardenberg, Humboldt, and Gneisenau repaired to the oracle ;
but Stein, who expressed a wish to see him, would not risk meeting
Jacobins and Bonapartists. The Count therefore visited his old
friend on the eve of his departure. There was only time for a
few words. As Stein drove away, he called out ' Auf wiedersehen
in Deutschland! If Prussia gets a Parliament, you must come
and be Speaker of the Upper or Lower House, whichever you like.'
But Prussia had to wait for her Parliament, and Schlabrendorf
remained in the city of his choice. The firstfruits of Bourbon
rule were little to his taste, and he told Varnhagen that now for
the first time he had thoughts of returning to his native land. He
had always loved Paris till the Government issued regulations on
Sunday observance, which foretold a régime of clericalism and
cant. But habit and inertia prevailed, and he spent the remainder
of his life in the house which he had occupied since his arrival
in 1789. He had intended to write his memoirs, and collected
thousands of books and pamphlets relating to the revolutionary
era as raw material. But he lacked concentration, and when
he died in 1824 he left nothing but the memory of a man who,
in spite of birth, wealth, and ability, never found worthy employment for his powers. Yet his life had not been in vain ; and on
his death, Oelsner once again paid a tribute of gratitude to one
who had comforted the afflicted in prison and had sent no man
empty away.

VIII

The name of Oelsner, though familiar enough in France and Germany at the time of the Revolution, fell into oblivion for nearly a century ; and it is only in our own generation that his anonymous writings have been identified and the thoughtful publicist has come to his own.[1] Starting on his travels in 1787 the young Prussian was in Switzerland when the States-General met at Versailles. He felt the call of the Revolution, and arrived in Paris in time for the fall of the Bastille. Lasting friendships were contracted with Schlabrendorf and Reinhard, Georg Kerner and Archenholtz. When the Editor of ' Minerva ' was forced by the outbreak of war to return to Hamburg, Oelsner became his principal correspondent. On reaching Paris, Forster wrote to his wife : ' Oelsner has made many friends and picked up a good knowledge of the place. He knows how to call everything by its right name, understands the art of conversation, makes himself agreeable to the ladies, and fires off polite observations like a Frenchman.' ' He is a very good fellow,' he added a few months later, ' but young and partisan. He cannot find the ideal in the world, and so he becomes angry.' [2] Varnhagen and Zschokke also noticed and praised the combination of French and German virtues. His society was, indeed, widely sought and appreciated--not least by Helen Maria Williams and other democrats of the British colony. He joined the Jacobin Club, of which he was a regular attendant ; but in May 1792 he withdrew, unable to bear the ' hypocrisy and bloodthirstiness ' of Robespierre and ' the convulsions of fanaticism.' He fearlessly mingled in every throng, picking up information and observing opinion in the making. He extended his knowledge by journeys through the provinces, and was a constant attendant at the debates of the Assembly. In private he met the leaders of the different parties—Égalité, Sieyès, Barnave, Danton, and Robespierre ; but it was among the Girondins that he found his closest friends, and he was a welcome guest in the *salon* of Madame Roland. No member of the German colony approached him in first-hand knowledge of the men and events of the Revolution, or brought to bear a more critical judgment on the changing scenes of the drama.

Having no desire to play an active part, Oelsner confined himself to the rôle of spectator and recorder. He was profoundly

---

[1] See Stern, *Oelsner's Briefe u. Tagebücher, Deutsche Zeitschrift für Geschichtswissenschaft*, iii. 100–27 ; and Richter, *Oelsner und die französische Revolution*.

[2] *Forster's Briefwechsel*, ii. 460–1 and 594.

convinced of the significance of the cataclysm and of the corresponding responsibilities of a philosophical publicist. His aim
was to describe events ' as history will see them, with sympathy
and truth, but without partisanship.' His principle was to separate
the ideas of the Revolution from the outward husk. ' For mankind
must not use against liberty arguments which are only applicable
to revolutions.' His devotion to freedom never changed. He
avowed himself a disciple of Sieyès, who, he declared, impressed
a holy character on the movement. ' Liberty! Equality! The
right to burn incense on your altars is confined to men of
virtue. The aristocrats who do not believe in your existence
are atheists ; and the rabble who persecute those who worship
you in their own way are fanatics.' After the flight to Varennes,
when the Jacobins hardly dared to speak against the Monarchy,
he urged banishment on the ground that the King would never
be loyal to the Constitution ; but he denounced the doctrinaires
who condemned monarchy unconditionally, pointing out that
free constitutions could be of various kinds. When, however,
war and invasion brought new dangers, he declared boldly for
a Republic as the sole alternative to anarchy. He looked to
Girondin friends to reconcile order with liberty, and the old millennial
hopes surged up once more. The Revolution was the darling of
Providence. Princes who opposed it were like children building
a wall against the tide. If only, instead of resisting liberty, they
would grant it to their countries !

The execution of the King filled the horizon with dark clouds.
' I am not concerned about the foreign Powers or the dangers of
insurrections, but about the foolish carelessness which, like Pali-
nurus sleeping at the rudder, steers the noble cause of liberty
to destruction.' The fall of the Girondins turned apprehension
for the Republic into despair ; but he never lost faith in the
Revolution itself. ' The French Revolution deserves to be known
with all its savage elements. How can the work of man be perfect
when even God's handiwork is faulty ? Its aim was noble and
necessary. If it were to fail, war against Providence would be
justified.' His outspoken radicalism caused his editors, Wieland and
Archenholtz, to mix water with his wine ; but the value of his work
was generally recognised. The best articles in ' Minerva,' pronounced
Forster, were all from his pen. Like Schlabrendorf he collected
material for a history ; but as the danger in Paris waxed he burned
his treasures. At the end of 1792 he wrote : ' Paris is now thoroughly
unpleasant. Suspicion peers from every eye. Nobody dares to
express his opinion.' The danger grew, and in May 1794, on
a warning from Meister, he escaped from the city of blood.

Oelsner was welcomed in Switzerland by liberal friends ; but he craved for Paris, and in 1795, when the Terror was over', he was back again, accompanied by Zschokke, who desired to study the working of the Republic. He wrote for the papers of Huber and Usteri, and defended his ' darling ' Sieyès, whom, he records, ' I honoured and loved.' When the Abbé regained influence in 1795, he sent Reinhard to Hamburg and offered Oelsner a post in Switzerland ; but he refused to enter the service of a foreign country. When, however, Frankfurt appointed him its representative in Paris in 1796, he accepted the task of securing neutrality for the city and recognition of its independence in any changes in the Empire. He was often asked for advice by the Directory, which he adjured to make friends with the little States beyond the Rhine, where he had visions of a league under French auspices. In 1798 he visited Germany after an absence of ten years ; but he was arrested and kept under watch in his native village as a suspicious character. These experiences chilled such shadowy patriotism as he still possessed, and he returned to the city of his choice. He abhorred the rule of Napoleon, and his contributions to the ' Allgemeine Zeitung ' had to be dispatched in secret. On the fall of the Empire he accepted a post in the Prussian Embassy in Paris, where he died in 1828. The keenest pleasures of his later years were his intercourse with Schlabrendorf and his correspondence with Varnhagen and Rahel.

IX

Georg Kerner was the elder brother of the poet Justinus Kerner, whose autobiography remains among the principal authorities for his short and ardent life.[1] While sharing the Swabian love of poetry and the past, he was also fired with the passion for self-realisation which stamped the romanticist era. In the educational system of Württemberg, he records, subordination was the chief principle, and the creation of obedient subjects the supreme goal ; but the designs of autocrats are not always realised. At the outbreak of the Revolution he was in the Karlsschule at Stuttgart, where he joined a students' club which celebrated the first anniversary of the fall of the Bastille with fervid declamation. His contribution to the Fête was the burning of the patent of nobility of his family. In the Easter and summer holidays the more adventurous boys would pay a flying visit to Alsace and catch a brief glimpse of the Promised Land. Their escapades reached the

---

[1] See Wohlwill, *Georg Kerner* ; and Justinus Kerner, *Das Bilderbuch aus meiner Knabenzeit.*

ears of the Duke, who at the end of the summer term of 1790 warned them to behave themselves, as they would be jealously watched. Such admonitions had no terror for Kerner, who in the summer holidays trudged with his friend, Marschall von Bieberstein, to Strassburg, where he donned a French cap and displayed open sympathy with the 'Patriots.' With people of conservative leanings he would enter into eager arguments, and prove from Greek and Roman precedents that the new Constitution would be a blessing. After visiting the altar of Liberty he wrote to Reinhold: 'When shall we see such altars in Germany? A happy vision shines before me of a land where everyone will determine his own worth in society, a land of liberty whither people will flock from Germany and other States to pay homage to this goddess, safe from the power of despots, and will find peace and a new fatherland.' In these prophetic words the young man had sketched his own future career.

Declaring that he must study medicine at a foreign University, Kerner settled in Strassburg in 1791 ; but his goal was not medicine but politics. A few weeks after his arrival he joined the Society of Friends of the Constitution, of which he was elected German secretary, and before which he was soon delivering eloquent orations in French. The indignant Duke deprived him of his scholarship, and his father angrily ordered him to pursue his studies in Vienna. 'To leave France,' replied the impenitent rebel, 'would kill me. The thought that I am freer here than in any other land binds me to this country. Vienna is to Paris as hell is to heaven.' He was given his head, but supplies were cut off. He reached Paris on foot in the autumn, and earned his living by giving German lessons and, later, as a correspondent of the 'Minerva.' He was quickly in touch with Reinhard and Schlabrendorf, and with Kosciuzko and other knights of liberty. But the Promised Land proved disappointing on closer acquaintance. As a liberal royalist he welcomed the Constitution of 1791, and was indignant at the attacks upon it. On August 10, 1792, he hurried to the Tuileries to fight for the King, and had a narrow escape. He detested the Jacobins, who, 'blinded by their passions, instead of treading in the footsteps of the great Romans, are following the example of bandits.' At the end of the year he wrote to a friend lamenting the murders, deceit, corruption, and ignorance. 'Imagine the despair which the scenes of August and September caused me!' Robespierre was a fool, Condorcet a knave, and the whole Convention only contained a few honest men. England alone presented an attractive vision. But his faith in the cause, of which the Jacobins were the unworthy trustees, remained unchanged. Still convinced that France was destined to bring liberty to the world, he welcomed the defeats of his countrymen ; but the King's death was too much for him. He expressed a desire to return home ; but his father replied that the journey was unsafe. In April he wrote : ' The present position of affairs no longer corresponds to my principles. I love freedom, which is no longer recognised here.' But he was in no mood to join the enemies of the Republic. Though represented by bloodthirsty degenerates, the cause of France was better than that of the league of tyrants. Better anarchy than to be under the heel of despots. ' The little Swabian,' wrote Forster to his wife, ' belches forth liberty like a volcano. He is original and good-natured, and combines brains with energy.' [1]

Such sentiments were not enough to save him from danger. He championed the Girondins before and after their fall, and denounced the Revolutionary Tribunal as a Spanish Inquisition. He detested Marat, and on the news of his assassination he hurried to Schlabrendorf, exclaiming ' She has anticipated us.' His name was on the list of the proscribed in 1794, and he owed his life to Reinhard, who procured him a pass to Switzerland. ' Dr. Kerner, who has distinguished himself by devotion to the cause of liberty, reported the secretary to the French Embassy in Switzerland, ' though proscribed by the Duke of Württemberg, has been carried away by his zeal to return to his country to instruct and unite the Patriots, and even to revisit Stuttgart, where he is not afraid of facing the Duke if he asks to see him. While admiring his courage, I am alarmed by the step, and I shall only regain my tranquillity when I know he is safely at Schaffhausen, where he will reside in order to carry on his correspondence with Germany.' [2] His apprehensions were justified, for Kerner was quickly expelled from Württemberg. He returned to Paris at the end of 1794, and enrolled himself in the newly constituted National Guard, in order to combat the counter-revolution. He accompanied his fellow Swabian, Reinhard, as secretary, to Hamburg, and spent three happy years in the stimulating atmosphere of the Hanse towns. His zeal for the Republic remained unabated ; but on the rise of Napoleon he withdrew from political life and settled in Hamburg. Like Reinhard, whom he in so many respects resembled, he never lost faith in the ultimate triumph of the principles of 1789.

X

The most romantic of the foreign victims of the guillotine was Adam Lux, whose association with Charlotte Corday has thrown

[1] *Forster's Briefwechsel*, ii. 460-1.　　[2] *Papiers de Barthélemy*, iv. 351-4.

the aureole of immortality round his head.[1] No more devoted or disinterested champion of liberty made the supreme sacrifice than the young martyr of Mainz. His Doctor's thesis on Enthusiasm specified among its varieties ' the enthusiasm of the heart transported by a great and sublime action '—a prophetic vision of his doom. He studied the ' Contrat social ' with passion, and expressed a wish to be buried opposite the tomb of his master. When Custine entered Mainz, he was among the first to join the club. Once described as ' a philosophic peasant,' he was now a man of culture and attainments, an orator, and a master of French. He took an active part in working up the vote for annexation, and persuaded his own village to plant a Tree of Liberty. Two hundred and thirteen out of 223 in his village signed the Red Book at the town hall ; of the remainder, eight were absent and only two refused. Such a magician naturally exerted an influence in the club ; and he was elected to the Rhine Convention, in which he proposed the incorporation of the Electorate in France. He compared the State of his birth to ' a weak orphan girl, whom a strong and tender mother offers to adopt. She assures you that she will fulfil all her maternal duties. Do not delay to fly into her arms. Brothers, Vive la République française ! '

Who could better represent the Mainz Republic in Paris than this eloquent and blameless idealist ? On reaching the capital with Forster, he received the fraternal kiss of the President of the Convention, swore in the Jacobin Club to live as a republican or perish, and was allotted a subsistence grant. But the process of disillusion was unequally rapid. Like most foreigners he admired the Girondins ; but the humane enthusiast was horrified by the savage cruelty of the Jacobins and the Assembly. He resolved to recall the Convention to its right mind and to reunite its parties by the heroic remedy of committing suicide at the bar as the climax of an impassioned appeal. Farewell letters were dispatched to his wife and friends ; and the speech to the Assembly, and Reflections to be read to it the following day, were duly composed. When everything was ready his friends dissuaded him from throwing away his life ; and he contented himself with publishing his ' Avis aux Citoyens français.' ' I would be silent,' he begins, ' if the Jacobins were capable of saving the Republic.' But they were the chief offenders. They had commenced with the September massacres, and proceeded to the overthrow of the Girondins. They were mere anarchists and murderers, whose tyranny was worse than that of Versailles. In calling down punishment on the Jacobins

[1] See Börckel, *Adam Lux* ; Chuquet, *Études d'histoire*, vol. ii. ; and Bamberger, *Charakteristiken*.

and the Commune, he adds that he knows himself to be in their power, but is not afraid of the guillotine.

At the very moment that he thus hurled defiance at the ruling powers Marat was murdered. Though he disapproved of assassinations he was filled with exaltation at the courage of the deed. At white heat, and in a moment of mystical exaltation, he threw off his manifesto, ' Charlotte Corday.' Her pure blood had transformed the scaffold into an altar, and he begged for the guillotine. He asked that his head might receive as many blows from the executioner as hers. In vain did Forster, who read the manuscript, implore his friend to keep it in his desk. The old passion for self-immolation flamed up with tenfold fury. Why should he live any longer in a world of darkness ? He was arrested, and his papers were seized. ' The good fellow has quite lost his head over the girl,' wrote Forster to his wife, ' and thinks nothing more blessed than to die for her.[1] For eight days he has scarcely eaten anything—perhaps nothing all day but a quarter of a pound of bread. I have always urged him not to give rein to his imagination ; but it was like talking to the wind. Even the fear of compromising me—the only argument which had any weight with him—did not hold him back. It will be impossible to do anything for him, and he does not wish it.' For three months he lingered in prison, where he was visited by Kerner and other friends, who marvelled at his longing for death. When one of them tried to save him by asserting his madness, the prisoner retaliated by calling the attention of Fouquier-Tinville to his case. He went to his death with rapture, and Forster records that he sprang upon the scaffold.

Lux was an *intransigeant*, to whom compromise was anathema. He loved liberty so much that death for the cause was ecstasy. More than any other foreigner he was consumed with the revolutionary flame—the sublime folly which immolates itself for an ideal. His blood wrought no redemption for France, for even precious blood had become too cheap to ransom a nation's soul ; but the sacrifice impressed his countrymen. Georg Kerner sung his praises in verse, and Richter coupled him with Charlotte Corday in his memorable prose poem. ' This superb Lux, of celestial heart, this Roman Cato—let no German forget him ! ' Above all, he stands—though without name—in ' Hermann and Dorothea ' as the embodiment of the high and splendid ideals with which the best minds of the Revolution era marched to assault the citadel of injustice and wrong.

[1] *Forster's Briefwechsel*, ii. 520–1.

XI

No figure of the eighteenth century had a more romantically tragic career than Freiherr von Trenck, who, after fighting in the War of the Austrian Succession, lost the favour of Frederick the Great, was arrested, escaped, was re-arrested, and spent many years of his life not only in prison but in chains. The story of his hardships and adventures, related in his Autobiography, made his name familiar throughout Europe on the eve of the Revolution ; but, though now an old man, his spirit was unbroken. After a long visit to Paris, shortly before the meeting of the States-General, he had returned to Austria ; but though his property was restored to him by Frederick William II, he revisited the French capital in 1791 and was caught in the trap. His ability was undoubted but his character was unattractive. ' I have seen Trenck,' wrote Forster to his wife.[1] ' As I expected, he displeased me as he displeases all men of judgment. He displays vanity, repulsive harshness, selfishness, and a mixture of arrogance and servility ; but he also possesses a rare energy of mind and temperament which renders work easy to him.'[1] Being a practised writer he resolved to start a paper, and dunned his German friends in Paris for help. In June 1793 he urged Wolzogen to collect subscriptions for the forthcoming Journal, and begged him for a loan to pay in advance for the first number, ' as I am a German Émigré.' [2] ' Do you know any friends of the naked truth ? If so, make them support my paper. Directly my work sees the light it will find a welcome.' If the paper ever appeared, which is uncertain, its life was short. His attempt to save Custine from death increased the suspicion which necessarily attached to an alien nobleman at the height of the Terror. He was arrested as a foreign agent and a conspirator to restore the Monarchy, and was guillotined a few days before Thermidor, at the age of sixty-eight.

XII

In German University circles no one greeted the Revolution with more immoderate delight than Cramer, Professor of Rhetoric at Kiel, an eccentric and unbalanced but wholly disinterested scholar.[3] He had formed one of the circle of students at Göttingen who were sealed of the tribe of Klopstock, and had rejoiced at the American revolt and the symptoms of approaching reform in France.

[1] *Forster's Briefwechsel*, ii. 514–15.
[2] Caroline Wolzogen, *Lit. Nachlass*, ii. 404–7.
[3] See Krähe, *Cramer bis zu seiner Amtsenthebung*, pp. 226-46.

Y

Klopstock dedicated to him his ode, ' The States-General,' and in 1790 wrote a hymn to the Revolution entitled ' To Cramer the Frank.' He set no guard on his lips, storming against monarchs and trouncing the nobility as ' the worm that gnaws at the root of mankind.' He gave a banquet to celebrate the Revolution, and exhibited a stone from the ruins of the Bastille. In 1791 he began to publish a chaotic rhapsody in eight volumes, entitled ' Human Life,' stuffed with paradox and eccentricity. ' Cramer,' wrote Boie, an old Göttingen friend, ' has written a book of Liberty in eight parts. It is bizarre and foolish, but it will certainly not make a revolution.' [1] He refused to take the ' arch-democrat ' very seriously, and, instead of arguing with him, made fun of his opinions. Knebel, on the other hand, discovered in it a better political judgment than could be expected in a German.[2] But, as the reaction increased, the Professor's position became more difficult. In 1793 he commenced, in a Hamburg paper, a translation of essays by Pétion, whom he heralded as a lover of humanity and a martyr of righteousness. ' All great men,' he added significantly, ' are persecuted—from Socrates to Jesus Christ, from Jesus Christ to Brissot.'

The eulogy of Pétion, whom he mistakenly believed to have voted against the death of the King, was harmless enough ; but it provided the authorities with an excuse for action. ' I am on the road to martyrdom,' he confided to a friend, ' for I am ordered to offer an explanation.' His answer, entitled ' My Destiny,' was anything but conciliatory, and in 1794 the Danish Government ordered his expulsion not only from his Chair but from the city. He had always praised the liberality of Danish rule, and his bark was well known to be worse than his bite. The Kiel professors protested, lauding the character of their colleague, though admitting that his judgment was erratic. ' Are you dismissing without trial the harmless Cramer,' wrote Voss to a Danish friend, ' a man who never hurt anybody but himself ? He has plenty of enemies ; but few of them will think the verdict just. Everybody is enraged at such a thing happening under such a prince and such a minister.' [3] The friend replied that he had seen Bernstorff about the case. Cramer has been dismissed not for what he has published but for what he has written. In any other country he would have been more harshly treated. Another protest came from Baggesen. He is only punishable on aesthetic grounds,' wrote the Danish poet ' his errors only deserve to be tried by the tribunal of the

[1] Weinhold, *Boie*, June 11, 1792.
[2] *Von und an Herder*, p. 385.
[3] Herbst, *Voss*, ii. 291–3.

Graces.' Bernstorff was inexorable, and the Professor left Kiel for ever.

Cramer naturally gravitated to Paris, though the overthrow of the Girondins had damped his ardour. 'France is no longer the Promised Land. The Republic has become an oligarchy.' But there was useful work to be done, and he became the mediator between French and German literature. He translated some of the writings of Klopstock and Schiller's 'Maid of Orleans' into French, and rendered the famous pamphlet of his new friend Sieyès on the *Tiers État* into German. With the help of Sieveking he started a bookseller's business, and sent full reports on current events to his friends in Hamburg.[1] Like other foreign enthusiasts he was shocked to discover how far the reality fell short of the ideal. 'If one does not hold fast to the principles which founded the Republic, and which will one day be restored,' he wrote to Klopstock in 1796, 'if one does not shut one's eyes to the colossal suffering of mankind, if one seeks in the Republic only virtue or even the absence of vice, one is oppressed by the spectacle of waste, deceit, and injustice.' The worst, however, was now over. 'The sudden change since Thermidor, from the height of cruelty to the extreme of mildness, is astonishing, and it proves that neither quality resides in the character of mankind or of a particular class, but that everything depends on the accident which makes criminals or men of character the shepherds of the flock. I consider the return of the Terror as impossible as the restoration of the autocracy.'[2] A year or two later Brinckmann, the Swedish poet and diplomatist, reported to Klopstock that he had met Cramer in Paris, and found him 'the happiest and most immovable admirer of all that happens, so long as the order is printed on republican paper.'[3] His most congenial task was to act as the steward of Sieveking's generosity. When the kindly merchant heard of the need of Bailly's widow, he promptly sent help; and he assisted Condorcet's widow by purchasing his papers. 'Believe me,' wrote the bookseller in 1797, 'there are an infinity of foreign republicans, Germans included, who are angry at the national ingratitude which neglects the dependents of the illustrious martyrs, and who ask nothing better than to repair these revolting wrongs.' He was among the principal victims of the 'Xenien,' and was the hero of the bitter couplet 'Germany's Revenge on France.'

Many a lackey you sold us as being a man of distinction.
Cramer we forward to you, warranted man of deserts.

[1] See H. Sieveking, *G. H. Sieveking*, ch. v
[2] *Von und an Klopstock*, pp. 371-3.   [3] *Ib.*, p. 395.

He was indeed conspicuous neither for ability nor judgment ; but his zeal for liberty was never quenched by the sufferings in which it involved him, and his store of good-will towards his fellow men was inexhaustible.

XIII

In the ranks of German Jacobinism the greatest scoundrel, with the possible exception of Charles of Hesse, was Eulogius Schneider.[1] The peasant's son was educated in a Jesuit school at Würzburg, but was expelled from the University for his evil life. Despairing of his future, he entered the Franciscan Order, combining the study of theology with the composition of frivolous verse. After serving as Court Chaplain to the Catholic Duke Karl of Württemberg, he was summoned to the University of Bonn by the Elector of Trier, who was waging war against the Pope and the clericalism of Cologne. The new Professor entered zealously on his task, sharply attacking the Jesuits and the system of Catholic education in Germany. In addition to his University lectures on rhetoric, he taught religion in the Gymnasium ; and his instruction was negative enough to suit the taste of the most exacting rationalist. In his Apologia he denies the charge of heresy, maintaining that he had only assumed a critical attitude towards relics. There is no doubt, however, that he launched his arrows against many of the dogmas and practices of the Church. The Elector soon regretted the appointment of the eloquent scamp, and ordered him to refrain from discussing the celibacy of the clergy in school. His politics, no less than his theology, aroused alarm ; for he expressed agreement with the most advanced opinions of the Revolution. On the news of the destruction of the Bastille he composed a poem and read it to his class.

> No royal edict, no ' Such is our will,'
> Shall henceforth shape the burgher's destiny.
> Behold ! in ruins lies the proud Bastille ;
> The sons of France have won their liberty.

In 1790 he published ' A Catechism on the Principles of Practical Christianity,' which emphasised the ethical side of religion and made no secret of his democratic convictions. The Elector's patience was now exhausted, and the Professor was dismissed with

---

[1] See Mühlenbeck, *Euloge Schneider* ;   Wegele, *Preussische Jahrbücher*, vol. xxviii. ; Lady Blennerhassett, *Deutsche Rundschau*, July 1889 ; Venedey, *Die deutschen Republikaner*.

a year's salary. As employment in his own country was out of the question, he gladly accepted an invitation to occupy the Chair of Canon Law at Strassburg.

Alsace was the main channel of communication between democratic France and the democrats of Germany ; and Strassburg, which experienced a miniature revolution in the summer of 1789, was the goal of eager young Germans who wished to catch a glimpse of the Promised Land.[1] Though the *ancien régime* was less oppressive in the Rhine provinces than in old France, the peasants had to pay taxes to the French Crown and feudal dues to the petty German lords. Pfeffel, the blind poet and pedagogue of Colmar, drew a picture in his ' Three Estates ' of Liberty visiting France and finding a man in rags and chains on his knees, with an archbishop and a noble standing over him. The goddess observes his sweat and tears, and asks : ' How long have you lain thus prostrate as a slave at the feet of your brothers ? Arise, and break your chains ! ' He did ; and he was as tall as they, indeed taller. ' Here is a fine spectacle, friend—provided that the holy laws of reason and justice govern the giant.' Not less zealous was Oberlin, the saintly reformer of the Steinthal. A vivid sketch of the capital in 1790 was drawn by Varnhagen in his Autobiography. ' My father was not the last to embrace and proclaim the beautiful hopes of a new world. In Strassburg it was hardly possible to move a step without meeting the new ideas in fact or symbol—Trees of Liberty, inscriptions, the tricolour on every hat, the songs of street urchins. My father joined the National Guard, and when I first saw him in uniform my heart beat for joy. Now I felt that we really belonged to the new Fatherland. There was no dislike of kings, but only of aristocrats ; yet there was even then a small party which aimed at violence.'[2]

The virtual unanimity with which the Revolution had been welcomed was destroyed by the Civil Constitution of the clergy, and still more by the crazy demand that Catholic priests should swear to it. The oath was refused by the great majority of the Alsatian clergy, including Cardinal de Rohan. His successor, the constitutional Bishop of Strassburg, appointed Schneider his Vicar, and the fortune of the ex-Franciscan was made. He was enrolled as a citizen and shortly elected to the Town Council. An address in the cathedral, ' On the harmony of the Gospel and the French Constitution,' warmly defended that instrument as embodying the spirit of Christianity. He soon ceased, however, to appear in

[1] See Reuss, *L'Alsace pendant la Révolution* ; Seinguerlet, *Strasbourg pendant la Révolution* ; Heitz, *Les Sociétés Politiques de Strasbourg, 1790-1795*.
[2] *Denkwürdigkeiten*, i. 38-40 and 60-75.

the pulpit, and devoted his energies to the Society of the Friends of the Constitution. Like its parent, the Jacobin Club in Paris, the Strassburg Club was at first the stronghold of constitutional royalism, of which Dietrich, the first mayor, was one of the leading supporters.[1] But from the beginning there was a disturbing element which kept pace with the eddying currents in Paris and ended by dominating the club. With this section of opinion the time-server Schneider naturally identified himself. When Reichardt, the composer, visited the city on his way to Paris in the spring of 1792, he found the citizens separating into two camps. ' On entering the gates I at once donned a tricolour cockade. Thus constitutionally attired I hurried to the club, of which two meetings were held every week, French and German being used alternately.' He recognised the chairman, Laveaux, a renegade French monk, who had for some years taught French at Berlin and was now engaged in editing a French paper. The club split into two parties : the constitutional royalists, led by Dietrich and Turkheim, the representatives of the old families, while the worthless Laveaux belonged to the republican group, which events in Paris were soon to raise to undisputed power. On another occasion Schneider was presiding. ' At the very first glance his vanity disgusted me, and his conduct in the chair confirmed my low opinion.' [2]

When the Monarchy fell Dietrich and the constitutional royalists fell with it ; but they refused to desert their principles, and bravely pleaded for the life of the King in a courageous address to the National Assembly. His friend Schweighäuser, the celebrated editor of ' Polybius,' joined in the protest and was rewarded by exile and imprisonment.[3] The city was now at the mercy of the newly elected Jacobin Council, of which Schneider was the leading figure. In February he had answered the question ' Are we Republicans ? ' by an emphatic negative ; but he was merely waiting for the Republican tide. Rouget de Lisle, the author of the Marseillaise, had denounced him as *le scélérat* ; and after August 10 he swung over in a moment and hailed Robespierre as the ideal citizen. When the French Republicans began to quarrel, opinion in Strassburg favoured the Girondins ; and when the latter fell, the suspect city felt the wrath of the Jacobins, who declared a state of siege and appointed a Committee of Public Safety in Alsace. Of this body Schneider was a member, and he quickly added to his duties that of Public Accuser to the Revolutionary Tribunal at Strassburg. The ex-monk now revealed his true character. Always a trifle

[1] See Spach, *Frédéric de Dietrich.*
[2] Reichardt, *Lettres.*
[3] See Rabany, *Les Schweighäuser.*

suspect as a foreigner, he determined to prove the purity of his
Jacobin faith by zealous imitation of the methods of the Terror.
' People bleat of consideration and humanity,' he cried. ' Death
to evil-doers is a service rendered to men of sound principles.' With
equal zeal he adopted the Cult of Reason, and insulted believers in
a series of parodies and satires. His paper, the ' Argus,' lived up
to its name, and its denunciation of suspects added a new terror to
life. The first head fell under the guillotine in Strassburg on
November 5, 1793, and Schneider greeted the newcomer in savage
verse.

> O dear Guillotine, how welcome you are !

A few days later St. Just and Lebas, the Representatives on Mission
of the Convention, arrived and conducted themselves as if in
conquered territory. A huge forced loan was levied, and Schneider
was ordered to proceed on circuit through Alsace.

Accompanied by a guillotine the ex-monk started forth on his
Bloody Assize. In five weeks twenty-nine heads had fallen, mostly
of insignificant peasants and artisans, charged with maligning the
Revolution. He won the name of the Marat of Strassburg ; but
on returning to the city he was promptly arrested by order of St.
Just and Lebas. His offence was that in his paper he had attacked
the tyranny of the Commissioners ; and St. Just was resolved to
destroy all critics of the Terror. He was placed on his own guillotine
and exposed to the angry crowd for some hours, after which he was
hurried to Paris and thrown into prison. His first task was to
compose and to forward an apologia to the Jacobin Club. ' I am
called the Marat of Strassburg, and I am proud of the name. When
I was appointed Public Prosecutor of the Department, a second
Vendée was in preparation. I hurried to the danger zone and by
executing the three leaders prevented the revolt. I was also the
first journalist in France to reveal the deceit of the Gironde, and I
was almost alone in Strassburg in fighting the friends of the rebels
of Bordeaux. Then I was made Civil Commissioner to the Revolutionary army ; and though it never existed, its name struck terror
into the aristocrats. I had the guillotine paraded through the
streets of Strassburg ; and when the city was cleansed I went on
tour to ferret out the correspondents of the Émigrés. Eleven heads
fell in ten days. On my return St. Just arrested me. In my
judgment every aristocrat deserves death ; and those against whom
facts can be established must be exterminated. I believed that the
Commission had entrusted me with this terrible but necessary
operation, and I performed the task.' When Robespierre heard
of the appeal he broke up the plates ; but the compositor rescued

the manuscript from destruction. The Dictator then launched terrible charges of immorality and savagery against the man ' whose crazy tyranny renders credible all that is recorded of Caligula or Heliogabalus.' The prisoner had once expressed a wish to live long enough to bring Dietrich to his doom ; and his sinister ambition was fulfilled. After a long incarceration the ex-mayor perished in the last week of 1793 ; and after a brief interval his deadly enemy followed him to the scaffold. The ex-monk left a blood-stained memory, at which Alsace has never ceased to shudder ; but voices were not lacking to defend his character and actions Venedey believed in him, and among his papers was found a letter of Schneider's sister to a friend, written from Strassburg in 1798. ' Have the calumnious echoes of his " Heliogabalism " turned you against him ? I do not believe it. You know him too well for that. Posterity will crown him for his pecuniary disinterestedness, his zeal and courage in defending liberty against all opponents, and his sacrifice of life in the cause.' His sister's view of his innocence was shared by his pupil, Geich, who defended him in his Bonn paper ; but the verdict of history is inexorable.

CHAPTER XV

WOMAN'S RIGHTS

In an era of revolt and excitement, when tradition was sharply challenged and new ideas sprouted with the rank luxuriance of tropical vegetation, it was inevitable that the relation of the sexes should come up for review ; and the tendency to revaluation was strengthened by the fact that at that moment Germany could boast of a larger number of clever women than ever before or after. Henriette Herz, Rahel, Caroline, Therese Huber, Charlotte von Kalb, Frau von Stein, Princess Gallitzin, the Duchess Luise of Weimar, Johanna Schopenhauer, Caroline von Wolzogen, Goethe's mother, Schiller's wife—such are the figures which greet us in the portrait gallery of the revolutionary epoch ; and all of them, except the Princess Gallitzin, who was too busy with her soul to trouble about politics, followed the crowding events with lively interest.

The first *salons* on the French model—those of the Jewesses, Henriette Herz and Rahel Levin—gave women a share in the making of opinion which they have never again enjoyed in Germany. Henriette, the wife of a Berlin doctor in large practice and an old pupil of Kant, possessed rare social gifts and an inexhaustible fund of sympathy ; and all the Intellectuals in the Prussian capital gathered around her.[1] In her ' Reminiscences ' she frankly confesses that in comparison with the eager interest of many other women in politics she had little taste for them, and indeed was often bored by the stream of political talk. Her sympathies, however, were liberal, and she shared the enthusiasm for the revolting American colonists. A year or two after their victory the circle was fluttered by the appearance of Mirabeau. ' He was hideous,' she writes, ' but one forgot everything directly he began to talk. When he became one of the first heroes of France, I was not surprised at anything I heard of the electric effect of his speeches.' In this cultivated

[1] See Fürst, *Henriette Herz, Ihr Leben u. ihre Erinnerungen* ; Hargrave, *Some German Women and their Salons.*

atmosphere the Revolution was assured of a warm welcome. 'The Revolution was not at first called by that name ; and even when we began to recognise it as such, few anticipated what was before us. How many tears of sympathy were shed by us women as we read of the victims who looked back with sorrow to their prison, so strange had light, air, and freedom become to them ! And then the beautiful and romantic Fête of the Federation ! The joyful, elevating impression still remains with me.' Before long the interest of the hostess and her friends became centred in the King ; and with the flight to Varennes the veil was torn from their eyes. 'From ardent supporters of the Revolution, we became its bitter enemies—and this was a pretty general change. We were far from seeing in the bloody horrors the baptism of a new era, and we would never, have purchased it at such a cost. Nor, though our wishes for our fatherland were ardent, would we have desired their fulfilment at the price paid by the French.' The whole drama, she adds, gave rise to endless chatter. 'I say chatter advisedly, for with most people, even in the educated classes, hardly a trace of deeper political thought existed. It was chiefly speculation on coming events, for which the long intervals in the arrival of news provided the opportunity. For the Berlin papers then appeared only twice a week, and their contents were meagre and stale, being often anticipated by the courier. As papers began to appear oftener, and fuller information was available, idle conjectures gave way to reasoning, and people began to have views and principles.' But though· the charming Jewess detested the excesses committed in the name of liberty, her *salon* never became a temple of the counter-revolution. However much the sad fate of the King was lamented, she records, the war against France found little approval, and the Peace of Basle was generally welcomed.

A far more striking and original figure was her younger friend, Rahel Levin, whose acute mind and magnetic charm won the life-long homage of the cleverest men of her time.[1] Even more than Henriette, the girl of sixteen was impressed by the personality and eloquence of Mirabeau ; and her friendship with Moses Mendelssohn and his enlightened friends strengthened her innate tendencies to a liberal outlook on life. Since few of her early letters survive, and she never wrote her reminiscences, we cannot recover her opinion of the Revolution ; but it doubtless passed through the usual stages from sympathy to detestation. Her time and thought were given to her friends, not to events on the Seine. For brilliant young writers like Humboldt and Gentz, on the threshold of their career;

[1] See Mrs. Vaughan Jennings, *Rahel : Her Life and Letters* ; and Varnhagen, *Denkwürdigkeiten*, viii. 563–820.

it was a liberal education to enter the charmed circle, and to share in the discussions for which her *salon* was celebrated. But though no province of life or thought was ruled out, it was no more political than that of Henriette Herz ; for Rahel's main interests lay in the domain of personality and in the problems of the human heart. The sympathies of an original mind, on whom tradition laid the lightest of yokes, were naturally liberal, and her marriage with Varnhagen strengthened and established her in the faith ; but the Revolution in its political aspects meant less to her than to most of her clever contemporaries.

Among her friends was Dorothea Veit, the accomplished daughter of Moses Mendelssohn. A letter to Rahel, written after a visit to Prince Henry's private opera at Rheinsberg, reveals the extent to which French ideas appealed to her sympathies and convictions.[1] Her anger was stirred by the luxurious palace surrounded by tumble-down cottages and ragged children. ' Accursed Aristocrat ! I could not help crying. I saw how a whole people could in a moment rise against the self-indulgent tyrants who drown the cry of misery in the music of their orchestras. I imagined France to be like that, and now I understood the French. Forgive my zeal, my dear Aristocrat !—Only, you should see Rheinsberg.'

The name of Therese Forster is closely associated with that of Caroline, for they grew up in the same Göttingen atmosphere ; but Heyne's daughter was less gifted and far less wayward.[2] The two girls, however, were equally attracted to advanced opinions in politics and religion. At nineteen she visited a friend at Gotha, where the old Duke showed marked kindness to her ; but she was not thereby reconciled to the life of Courts and the principle of hereditary rule. ' As a republican,' she wrote long after, ' I wished to sweep all that sort of thing away.' Her marriage to Georg Forster linked her to one of the most eminent men of the time ; but they were unsuited to one another, and Therese, like Caroline, was destined in later years to follow the promptings of her heart. ' I was very unhappy,' she confessed, ' in loving Huber and not my husband. If the Revolution had occurred at that time, I should have hurried to the scenes of blood, and should have taken part in them in order to experience a feeling which reflected the desperation of my breast.'

Therese, like Forster, welcomed the Revolution. ' Our mood,' she wrote many years later in her ' Life of Huber,' ' was a childlike but noble passion for what appeared to us the best happiness of

---

[1] See Dorothea von Schlegel, *Briefwechsel*, i. 3–7.

[2] See Geiger, *Therese Huber*; and Zincke, *Georg Forster nach seinen Originalbriefen*, vol. ii. ch. ix.

mankind, though we recognised the mixture of human folly and deeply deplored the excesses.'[1] Filled with scorn for the flying Elector, she lived through the excitements of the French occupation of Mainz, sharing her husband's views but not his zeal. Her father and Sömmerring were, however, not alone in thinking that she influenced Forster's opinions, for anonymous plays and pamphlets published in Mainz spoke of her political rôle and pointed to her as his seducer; and the well-known 'Xenion,' already quoted, enshrines a similar conviction on the part of the great Twin Brethren of Weimar, who make him lament his weakness in yielding to feminine guidance. It is impossible to be certain how much ground existed for such charges, for the evidence is conflicting. 'She was heart and soul for the cause,' wrote her rival Caroline, when Therese left Mainz[2]; and the latest writer on Forster and his circle pronounces her a passionate republican.[3] Geiger, on the other hand, her indulgent biographer, accepts the portrait of herself drawn by his heroine in her biographies of her two husbands and in her letters. 'I am not fanatical,' she wrote to her father, when Forster had thrown in his lot with the French invaders; 'but I saw that his path led this way! I will never put myself or the children in danger. If necessary I would go to France where I should find help, and where the humanity of the inhabitants is itself a support. Liberty develops the intelligence of our degenerate Mainzers, who are thinking aloud about their rights, and for the first time feel the divine rays of their own worth and will. Little has happened so far, for the people are paralysed and possess slender capacity; but if their halting gait is little calculated to arouse one's enthusiasm, it is at any rate an antidote to fanaticism.'

When Forster was planning his mission to Paris his wife and children left the city of danger and migrated to Strassburg. She lodged with a shopkeeper whose daughter represented the goddesses of Liberty and Reason in the city fêtes, and her husband alarmed himself without need when he exhorted her to stand fast in the republican faith. After the recapture of Mainz she wrote to General Kalckreuth, begging for the return of her property and contradicting the rumours as to her opinions. 'My father tells me that all efforts on my behalf at the Court of Mainz failed because I was accused of being a clubist. Neither I nor any other woman could be, as the Jacobins once formally resolved to admit no woman and to permit no woman's assemblies.

Therese had never loved her husband, and as early as 1790 she transferred her affections to Huber, a young protégé of Schiller and

---

[1] *Huber's Werke*, i. 63.   [2] Caroline, *Briefe*, i. 278.   [3] Zinckc

Körner, who was appointed secretary of the Saxon Legation in Mainz.[1] On parting from Forster she entrusted herself and her family to his hands, and, on finding herself a widow, married her lover. In editing Forster's Letters she speaks frankly of the matter. ' As the French Revolution suspended the usual bourgeois considerations for us *exaltées*, I followed the major morality at the cost of the minor; and terminated a dishonouring relationship.' Huber shared Forster's enthusiasm for the Revolution. ' It is good that at last a passionate emotion, as in the Crusades, begins to unify the peoples and interrupts the monotonous villainy of the Chancelleries. To accept the Revolution as one of the greatest epochs in history, one need not know its issue.' When Körner reproached him for being a democrat, he replied that the democratic passion was more noble, more just, and more necessary than the aristocratic passion. He approved Tom Paine's ' Rights of Man,' and ' cried with joy ' at Mackintosh's reply to Burke. He justified the rising of August 10 as a reply to the treason of the Court, but was shocked by the September massacres ' Is it not terrible to fall from the enthusiasm of preceding years into the fanatical horrors of the Ligue ? And most unhappy are those who believed in the century of reason and have now lost their belief.' Yet he greeted Custine's victories as ' the first appearance of liberty in Germany.'

A man of such opinions was not welcomed by the authorities in Neuchâtel, where Therese joined him from Strassburg, and he had to prove that he had never been a Jacobin ; but husband and wife quietly maintained their general sympathy with progress. ' My only violent emotion,' she wrote to Caroline after Forster's death, ' is the freedom of France ; people mean little to me now.' But even this ' violent emotion ' was not very intense. ' She never reads a paper,' wrote Huber to his father-in-law a year later, ' as she has no time. When I read to her she enjoys it—if it is not a newspaper. And so it is with her political enthusiasm. Of course she will only lose her lively sympathy with the liberty of our times at death ; but this interest is as far removed from political activity as from Hebrew. Our attitude is harmlessly democratic. We are far too little on the side of the aristocracy or the counter-revolution not to be reckoned as democrats ; but we can appeal to the good opinion of our neighbours, which would be impossible if there were any taint of political fanaticism or of unwomanly pretence to erudition in our household.' In spite of her political reserve she regarded herself as half French through Huber, and she felt quite

---

[1] See the biography by his wife, prefixed to his *Werke*, vol. i.

at home in French Switzerland. 'His enthusiasm for the French Revolution has greatly cooled,' wrote Madame de Charrière in regretting his departure from Neuchâtel in 1798. 'He has always feared change in a country which is, on the whole, happy and flourishing.'[1]

In 1796, when the Terror was at an end, Therese wrote a political novel which for a time enjoyed as great a popularity as those of Klinger and Lafontaine and moved many readers to tears. As she had never been an uncritical enthusiast, she had escaped the violent reaction which overtook most of the early idealists; and 'The Seldorf Family' presents a quiet, objective view of the great drama. Sarah Seldorf is the daughter of a French officer who, on returning from a long journey, finds that his wife is unfaithful. Sarah lives in retirement with her father and brother (after the death of her mother and the illegitimate child) near Berthier and his son. The latter loves Sarah, who fails to return his devotion. The Revolution now throws its tremendous shadow across the scene. The elder Berthier is a Republican, while his son joins the Royalists. Meanwhile a Count settles near the Seldorfs, falsely pretending to be a Republican, and seduces Sarah, who gives birth to a child. The Count refuses to marry her, but brings her to Paris, where she learns that he is married, and meets his wife. In desperation she joins the Revolutionists, fights heroically as a man in several battles, and secures the death of the Count who has so foully wronged her. On suddenly meeting her brother, she faints and betrays her sex. She now again refuses Roger Berthier, who, in spite of all that has happened, renews his request for her hand. There is no political message in the book, but it skilfully portrays the atmosphere of terror and excitement in Paris and in the army, in which love and death, bravery and cruelty, crimes and virtues, are inextricably intermingled. In her long years of widowhood Therese maintained herself and her family by her pen, but politics faded out of her life. Her qualities of head and heart secured her affection and admiration wherever she went. The friend of her youth, Wilhelm von Humboldt, never lost sight of her, and on her death in 1829 he paid her a worthy tribute. 'In intellectual power she was one of the most remarkable women of her time. She knew a great deal and possessed a high degree of cultivation. But that was quite overshadowed by her innate intellectual power and by her rich and creative imagination.'[2]

A fourth clever Jewess, the most brilliant and seductive figure in our gallery, was the daughter of Professor Michaelis, the Göttingen

---

[1] Godet, *Mme. de Charrière*, ii. 280.
[2] *Briefe an eine Freundin*, vol. ii. Letter 5.

orientalist.[1] Caroline met men of distinction from her earliest
years, and won a reputation for precocious originality no less
than for beauty and social gifts. The publication of her correspondence, two generations after her death, has enabled us
to compare her portrait, as painted by herself, with the pictures drawn by her friends and enemies. The emancipated
girl, who, like Madame Roland, possessed 'a cosmopolitan soul,'
welcomed the Revolution with greater zeal than any other German
woman of distinction, and stoutly championed it against doubters
and enemies. ' It is not at all nice of you,' she wrote to her intimate
friend Meyer in October 1789, ' always to be running down the
exalted French nation.'[2] A long visit to the Forsters at Mainz,
beginning in February 1792, brought her nearer the scene of action
and intensified her interest. 'We may have lively scenes if war
breaks out; but nothing would induce me to leave. Fancy if I
can tell my grandchildren how I lived through a siege, and how
the long nose of an old priest was pulled and his effigy burned by
democrats in the market-place ! We are living at a very interesting
moment.'[3] The Émigrés, she added, made things very expensive.
In August she defended herself against the attacks of Meyer. ' The
red Jacobin cap which you place on my head I toss back to you.
We know the heroes of the Brissot stamp only too well ;—invective
is his element. We make you a present of the Assembly, the
Jacobins, Lafayette—everything but the Cause. No one here
prays for the success of the Imperial and Royal arms. Despotism
is abhorred, but not every individual aristocrat ; for there is a
noble impartiality abroad. A curious trait is the bitterness of the
Émigrés against their helpers ; and of the Prussians they speak
like disgruntled democrats. The Duke of Brunswick alone
commands their respect.'[4]

When Custine's troops entered the city, her brother-in-law,
Böhmer, became secretary and interpreter to the General. She
wrote to tell Meyer of the flight of the Court and the nobility, and
of her refusal to follow them. 'We are staying on partly from
curiosity, and partly because we have a good conscience. We are
in the hands of the enemy, if you can call our brave and courteous
guests by such a name. What a change in a single week ! If they
were beggars and rabble, or if the pride in their cause did not possess
them and teach them magnanimity, it would be impossible thus

[1] See Mrs. Alfred Sidgwick, *Caroline Schlegel and her Friends* ; Janssen,
Zeit- und Lebensbilder, vol. i.; Haym, *Die Romantische Schule* ; Scherer,
Vorträge u. Aufsätze ; M. Bernays, *Schriften*, vol. ii. Erich Schmidt's edition
of her Letters supersedes that of Waitz.
[2] *Briefe*, i. 186.   [3] *Ib.*, i. 250.   [4] *Ib.*, i. 264-5.

to avoid all disturbances. The middle classes, however, have no wish to shake off the yoke ; for the bourgeois never feels comfortable if it is not resting on his neck. How far is he below the most insignificant Sansculotte out there in the camp ! Business is at a standstill, and that is all that he thinks about. As for the Elector, there is only one opinion, and that is that he will never see his beautiful city again. And only four months ago the Concert of the Powers met here to plan the overthrow of France ! ' [1]

To a fascinating young widow, without moral ballast, the French occupation was a danger as well as a stimulus ; and she yielded to the seductions of an officer after dancing the Carmagnole at a ball. When the invaders were expelled in the summer, Caroline, who was expecting her confinement, found herself in disgrace without a friend at hand. Her association with Böhmer and Forster gave her a Jacobin reputation, which she did not deserve. ' Since January,' she wrote after the siege, ' I lost all interest in politics.[2] At first I was a real enthusiast, and Forster's opinions naturally carried me away. But I have never been an open or secret proselytiser, and never have I been more discreet than in this democratic time.' She was, however, imprisoned in a fortress near Mainz, whence she was extricated by the efforts of friends. After a temporary refuge afforded her by the kindness of Göschen,[3] the publisher, she accepted the helping hand held out by the elder Schlegel. The loveless marriage gave her a home, restored her to respectability, and introduced her to the Romantic circle of which she became the queen. She retained her sympathy with France, and converted her husband to kindlier views. ' He thinks now rather differently of my friends the Republicans,' she wrote to Friedrich Schlegel in 1795, ' and is no longer in any way an aristocrat. His impartiality on this subject gives additional charm to his conversation. I will learn from him to be passionless, and then my education will be complete ! Does not the main difference between your ancient Greeks and my new Franks lie in the different degrees of passion ? Had they rather cooler blood, all nations of the earth would be compelled to envy and to love them. But how is the heat to be eradicated ? ' [4] Caroline never discovered the answer, and in a few years she left the chilly Schlegel for the young and ardent Schelling. She lives in the vivid pages of Friedrich Schlegel's ' Lucinde,' and in Schiller's revealing nickname, Frau Lucifer— a typical child of an age when the foundations of the earth were rocking.

It is the highest praise of Schiller's wife to say that she was

[1] *Briefe*, i. 273–6.
[2] *Ib.*, i. 297.
[3] Göschen, *Life of Göschen*, ii. 173–81.
[4] *Briefe*, i. 366–7.

worthy of her husband.   Without possessing the brains of Caroline
Michaelis or Rahel Levin, Lotte von Lengefeld was a thoughtful
and well-read woman, fully competent to hold her own in the
intellectual circles of Weimar and Jena.[1]   Though less gifted than
her sister, the poet by a sure instinct chose the younger to be his
partner for life.   Schiller's correspondence shows how closely the
pair followed events in the world both of thought and of action.   On
the eve of the Revolution Caroline's friend Wolzogen, afterwards
her second husband, was residing in Paris, whither he had been
sent by the Duke of Württemberg to complete his training as an
architect ; and his reports were eagerly studied by the trio.   ' He
is quite at home there,' she writes to Schiller at the end of 1788,
' though he still sees it too much through German eyes.   He will
discover many people there to be better and truer than he thinks.
My own impression of France was just the same.   A journey to
Paris would give you much material, though indeed you do not
need to look outside yourself for that.'   But nobody judged the
most prominent of Frenchmen more severely than the sisters, who
read his ' Secret History of the Prussian Court ' with disgust.   ' One
must be very mistrustful of travelling Frenchmen,' wrote Lotte ;
' if I were a prince, I would admit none to my Court.'   ' I am
thankful in reading Mirabeau,' added Caroline, ' that those I love
have nothing to do with politics.   The author is the worst character
in his book.   It is to the credit of the Duke of Weimar that he has
fallen foul of him.'

' I cannot write fully,' reported Wolzogen to Caroline on July 23,
1789, ' for caution is necessary.   I can only say that for the honour
of mankind the Bastille is no more.' [2]   His enthusiasm was shared
by the sisters.   ' In after days,' records Caroline in her ' Life of
Schiller,' ' we often remembered how the destruction of the
Bastille, a monument of dark despotism, seemed to our youthful
minds the herald of the victory of liberty over tyranny, and how
delighted we were that it occurred at the beginning of our happiness.
Throughout the summer the Revolution formed the chief topic of
conversation.   ' I am enjoying the happenings in France,' wrote
Lotte in September, ' and now the connection has become clear to
us.   I shall make everybody talk about it, instead of talking about
themselves, which does not interest me.' [3]   After the October attack
on Versailles, however, doubts begin to gather.   ' Beulwitz has
written from Paris telling me stories of women, which I hope are

---

[1] See Berger, *Schiller* ; Bär, *C. v. Lengefeld* ; *Schiller u. Lotte, ein Briefwechsel* ; *C. v. Schiller u. ihre Freunde* ; Caroline von Wolzogen, *Lit. Nachlass* ;
and *Schiller's Leben.*

[2] Caroline, *Nachlass*, i. 71.   [3] *Schiller u. Lotte, ein Briefwechsel.*

Z

untrue. Some of them are said to have gathered round a dead soldier, torn out his heart, and drunk his blood in cups. Things must have come to a pass if they have so utterly forgotten their sex.' By the following spring France had grown to be a name of ill omen. 'You have not learned any French habits, have you ? ' wrote Lotte to Wolzogen.[1] ' I cannot imagine you so changed.' She had read Plutarch as diligently as Madame Roland, and she now turned to the other oracle of revolutionary France. ' I have been reading Rousseau's "Confessions,"' she wrote to Schiller early in 1790. ' His character is not attractive, and it does not really interest me. The everlasting distrust and vanity repel me. It is a sad fate not to believe in virtue, and to see an enemy in everyone.' ' I am reading diligently in Rousseau,' she added a week later, ' and it has interested me greatly to learn the origin of his Julie. As he has lived long in the country near Paris, he feels an emptiness in his heart which he could never wholly fill, and the need to love, till he at last begins to live in the world of his own making and to cherish the creations of his fancy.' Wolzogen wrote from Paris that he had visited the Hermitage, and expressed a wish that Lotte could share in the pilgrimage.

The sisters had greater hopes of the Revolution than Schiller permitted himself to entertain ; but they soon joined the ever-growing army of critics. Caroline was a guest in Dalberg's residence at Erfurt when the news of Varennes arrived, and heard the host's cold-blooded observation: ' What are the events of our little earth to the boundless heaven ? ' Such detachment from the interests and sorrows of humanity was impossible to his friends. ' I would gladly go to France as Schiller proposes,' wrote Caroline to Lotte in November 1792, ' but I have no belief in the permanence of anything with that superficial people.' She was equally little disposed to idealise her own countrymen. ' The liberty of Mainz will come to nothing. The Germans are too uncultivated to base it on principles, and far too phlegmatic to lose themselves in a beautiful dream.' Custine's privates, she added, were said to discuss the French Constitution with wonderful sense and point.[2] The sisters shared the poet's indignation at the imprisonment and death of the royal victims. ' I am delighted at the Austrian victories,' wrote Lotte in April 1793.[3] ' Since the cruel death of the King the Franks have lost all credit with me. The way they try to convert people to liberty in the Rhineland is really too much. If that is not despotism, then still less is the conduct of kings, past and present. One is so drawn into politics that one can

[1] Caroline, *Nachlass*, ii. 195.
[2] *C. v. Schiller u. ihre Freunde*, ii. 57-8.   [3] *Ib.*, i. 340.

hardly stop talking. I never imagined they would interest me so
much.' The subsequent victories of the French armies on the
Rhine filled her with gloomy forebodings. ' Your feelings about
the war are quite right,' wrote Frau von Stein in August 1794 ;
' I fear we shall all be gobbled up.' [1] The prophecy was to be
fulfilled twelve years later ; but by that time Schiller was in his
grave.

In Germany, as in England, the closing years of the eighteenth
century witnessed the first serious literary attempt to do justice
to the claims of woman. Kant was singularly narrow in his views
of the fair sex, opposing projects for their higher education and
discouraging their interest in things of the mind ; and it was left
to lesser men to raise the standard of revolt against tradition and
convention.[2] The most eloquent and enthusiastic champion of
feminism was Hippel—the German equivalent of Mary Wollstonecraft—a man of sentiment and gentle humour, a romanticist of the
tribe of Richter and Rousseau, whose names were often on his lips.[3]
But the Prussian official was more a man of the world than Jean
Paul, and he was a welcome guest in University circles in Königsberg. Published in 1774, his little book ' On Marriage ' breathes
the spirit of liberty and equality which was beginning to find its
way into German literature.[4] ' Why does the male sex, the
Adam,' he begins, ' forget that it has a helper in the female sex,
Eve ? What right have men to regard women as little more than
a vacuum ? ' Like a modern suffragist, he protests against the
bride's vow of obedience. Men, he chivalrously contends, are
responsible for most unhappy marriages. He is so indignant at
the civic inferiority of women that he credits them with all the
capacities of the stronger sex for public life. ' When and where
has woman renounced the business of State ? The longer we
neglect to give her the vote and a place in all that concerns the
welfare of State and the Fatherland, the more violently will she
break out directly the barriers of coercion and slavery are torn
down. She has little if any belief in laws, since she has had no
voice in making them. If you wish to hear sharp judgments on
rulers, their souls and bodies, go to a clever woman. Over her sex
broods the spirit of revolution. Many gallantries arise not from
passion but from desire for power. History shows that if women
have not exercised direct rule, everything has been settled by their

---

[1] Düntzer, *Frau von Stein.*
[2] Stuckenberg, *Life of Kant*, pp. 183–7. Cf. Hanstein, *Die Frauen in der
Geschichte des deutschen Geisteslebens.*
[3] See Gervinus, *G. d. Deutschen Dichtung*, v. 211–21.
[4] *Werke*, vol. v. It is republished in Reclam's *Universalbibliothek.*

influence.' In a revised edition of 1792 the gospel of equality is preached with even greater fervour, and the French Revolution is naturally pressed into the service of the cause. ' It is difficult to understand the absence of plans for the civic amelioration of the fair sex, since everybody now talks of the rights of man and of civic liberty. For this amelioration requires no *lanterne*, and would notably foster the welfare of the State, both in culture and in morality. By the Rights of Man is really meant the Rights of Men.' Such a distinction, he declares categorically, has no foundation in reason or justice.

A later work, ' The Civic Advancement of Women,'[1] published in 1792, repeats and develops the argument of the earlier. Only a German, he begins, would think of writing such a book. France, where everything is unequal, has left the sex as it was. Unpardonable! How can a people which exists for the fair sex neglect it in this era of universal equality? Quite recently the emancipation of the Jews has been demanded. If they are to be freed, why not the women? Is it not beyond forgiveness to permit half of the human resources of the world to slumber unknown and unused? Women raise the tone in every society; and will this not also occur in the State when their light illumines it?[2] Are there any fundamental differences between the sexes? Certainly not, answer Catherine the Great, Christina of Sweden, Joan of Arc, and other mighty souls. Woman will not fulfil the full intention of nature till she also is a citizen, and no longer merely a ward of the State. She asks for rights, not privileges. If it is objected that only a few have proved themselves great, the reply is that in face of so many obstacles it is wonderful that the number is so large. And men themselves suffer by the subordination of women. A glance at primitive society explains the origin of male predominance. How did it arise? By strength alone. Where liberty is suppressed nothing human can grow to its full stature. In the East woman is a toy; and even the Prussian code, ' the New Testament of Carmer,' is lamentably out of date.

The closing chapter deals with projects of reform. ' France now frightens with liberty those Powers which threaten to oppose the bold decrees of the Assembly. Good God! to think that at the end of the eighteenth century one can terrify people with liberty! Even for the man who is brought up in chains the name of liberty is an illumination, for it is the divine spark which makes us what we are. Woman has never tried to obtain civic rights by negotiation

[1] *Werke*, vol. vi.
[2] The same argument that they would raise the tone of political assemblies was simultaneously employed by Gorani. See Marc Monnier, *Gorani*, p. 281.

or force, and she unselfishly awaits them from our generosity.
Shall we let her wait, and shall we reject with an emphatic negative
the petition of nature at a time when the Rights of Man are
proclaimed on the housetops? All persons have equal rights. All
the French, men and women alike, ought to be free and citizens.
Yet the new constitution, to its shame, overlooks half the nation.
We deceive ourselves if we think that women have no feeling for the
honour of mankind or for the struggle of liberty against autocracy.
They have proved, and not by their applause alone, that they
recognise its worth. Would all the lynching have happened if
they had been on the voters' list? Where God has granted strength,
has He not also given the right to use it? Shall women wrap up
their talent in a napkin and not lay it out at interest, which would
bear fruit for the State a thousandfold? The monopoly of man
must be broken down. Women must be jurors, judges, doctors.
What they can do they have a right to do.' In demanding equality
of opportunity between the sexes, Hippel was as far in advance of
the teaching of the French Revolution as Kant in pleading for the
federation of the world; and a large part of his emancipating
programme remains unfulfilled a century after his death.

Hippel was but the most eager and unflagging champion
of woman's rights. Salzmann translated Mary Wollstonecraft's
'Rights of Woman.' Bahrdt appealed to women to interest themselves in public affairs and to become citizens of the world. In
his 'Lectures on Political Science' Spittler warmly defended the
claim to vote.[1] Democracy, he argued, existed nowhere; for even
in republican France and Switzerland women were excluded from
a share in legislation. 'This exclusion has no rational ground.
The whole series of arguments by which male despots defend it is
untenable. People talk of the difference of spiritual capacities—
as if women had not sufficient nerve and knowledge to cast a vote.
What inconsistency! People allow themselves to be ruled by a
woman but will not admit her to the franchise. If she possesses
less knowledge and experience, it arises from lack of opportunity.
Man has tried to exclude woman as the noble has tried to exclude
the burgher. Let her have a better education and a more careful
training, and then we shall see how far it is a question of incapacity.'
The feminism of Friedrich Schlegel, on the other hand, was rather
philosophical than political.[2] In his 'Essay on Diotima,' published
in 1795, he praises Plato's ideal woman, 'combining the grace of
an Aspasia and the soul of a Sappho with a lofty independence
—a picture of complete humanity.' His scheme of womanhood

[1] *Werke*, xv. 52–5.
[2] See his *Jugendschriften*; and Rougé, *La Jeunesse de F. Schlegel*.

embraces mind and culture no less than innocence and charm. He desired the complete development of individuality, not the accentuation of differences. While Humboldt and Schiller considered that neither man nor woman alone could realise the full human ideal, which was only to be reached through love, Schlegel taught that each individual could embody the integral humanity which stands above the differences and limitations of sex. In his essays on Condorcet and on the ' Conception of Republicanism ' he pursues the theme, demanding not only the equality of the sexes but its symbol in the vote. Despite such powerful backing, the idea of the civic equality of women never took root in Germany, and the conventional view was expressed in the question put to Schlegel by his bosom friend Schleiermacher : ' If women become engaged in politics, would it not involve the loss of love and of the impalpable influence with which nature endows them ? ' As far as Germany is concerned the question remains unanswered ; for the experiment is only now beginning to be tried.

CHAPTER XVI

PRUSSIA AND THE REVOLUTION

I

THE death of Frederick the Great, like the death of Richelieu, was hailed by his subjects with mixed feelings of relief and apprehension. ' I remember the expression of dull amazement created by the news in all classes,' wrote General Boyen in his ' Memoirs.'[1] ' Men of iron wept like children. Even those who had opposed him asked anxiously, What will happen now ? ' When, however, the first shock was over, warmer airs began to blow. It was felt that the period of strain was at an end and that a milder rule was dawning, since it was beyond the power of the new King to stretch the bow of Ulysses. The reign began well with the abolition of the hated monopoly of tobacco and coffee, and it was widely believed that further beneficent changes would follow. The most bold and comprehensive programme of reform came not from a Prussian but from a Frenchman. In his ' Open Letter to Frederick William ' Mirabeau grappled with fundamental issues. Though generous in praise of the dead monarch, he declared frankly that his rigid system was out of date. A national militia should be substituted for the expensive army, the peasantry emancipated, class-barriers thrown down, the censorship abolished, education improved. He implored the new King ' not to govern too much.' The concluding sentences of his vast descriptive treatise, ' The Prussian Monarchy,' compiled with the aid of Mauvillon, reiterated the advice to seize the golden opportunity afforded by the death of Frederick. The noble edifice, he declared, rested on comparatively fragile foundations. His prescription was Peace and Liberty. ' Civil, industrial, commercial, religious liberty, liberty of thought and of the press—there is the whole art of government ; therein, as in a fruitful germ, resides the prosperity of empires. The Prussian monarchy is more ready than any

[1] Boyen, *Erinnerungen*, i. 13.

to gather in the bounteous harvest. Everything is ripe for the great transformation, and no overwhelming obstacle blocks the path.'[1] Mirabeau was right in maintaining that to avoid a great revolution far-reaching reforms were essential—the abandonment of a stifling mercantilism, the abolition of the exclusive privileges of the nobility, the overthrow of feudalism, the reform of taxation. But no attention was paid to his demands. In the remorseful words of Queen Luise, ' We went to sleep on the laurels of Frederick the Great.' It required the double shock of the French Revolution and the catastrophe of Jena to convince the rulers of Prussia that they must set their house in order.

The hopes excited by the accession of Frederick William II were soon disappointed.[2] The new King was keenly interested in foreign affairs, and the Dutch campaign of 1787 revealed a flickering energy ; but his dissolute life sapped his energies and unfitted him for the routine labour without which autocracy is nothing but a name. Alexander was gone and the Epigoni ruled in his place. Government by Cabinet councillors replaced government by the King. The mainspring of the machine was broken. In the words of Massenbach, Prussia had changed from a monarchy into an aristocracy. It was in the early days of disenchantment that Mirabeau's ' Secret Letters from the Court of Berlin ' appeared.[3] He had arrived in the capital shortly before the death of Frederick, and in an incredibly short time had acquainted himself with the conditions and leading personalities of the Hohenzollern realm. The descriptive sketches were written to Talleyrand and Lauzun ; and, being intended for the eyes of the French Court, were rendered designedly piquant. We are offered a picture of a State in decadence, languishing under an idle King. ' Frederick William's character is compounded of falseness, egoism, and greed. No State has ever experienced a quicker collapse. It is being undermined from every side. It is rotten before it is ripe.' The letters, slightly toned down before publication, appeared in the summer of 1787, were at once translated into German, and sold by thousands. When the Prussian Government complained to the Court of Versailles, the offending volume was solemnly burned by the

---

[1] *De la Monarchie Prussienne*, iii. 703, ed. 1788.

[2] See Philippson, *Geschichte des Preussischen Staatswesens*, vol. i.; Heigel, *Deutsche Geschichte*, vol. i.; Cassel, *Friedrich Wilhelm II* ; Gilbert Stanhope, *Frederick William II*.

[3] The best edition, though far from good, is in Welschinger, *La Mission Secrète de Mirabeau à Berlin* ; cp. Stern, *Das Leben Mirabeaus*, vol. i., chaps. xi. and xii. ; and *Forschungen zur Brand. und Preus. Geschichte*, xiii. 214–23.

executioner; but its author escaped punishment. Its exaggerations were as patent as those in Wilhelmina's acid sketches of Potsdam and Wusterhausen. Hertzberg compared the author to Procopius and Aretino; while Trenck, Zimmermann, and Posselt issued replies. But the damaging impression remained, and the King's reputation never recovered from the indictment. The Austrian Minister contemptuously described the monarch to Kaunitz as ' an enormous machine of flesh,' and the scandals of his domestic life were the talk of Europe.[1] When the French thunderstorm broke in fury, Prussia was totally unfitted to confront its challenge. The State was in the grip of the landed aristocracy, a brave but ignorant class; the bourgeoisie were powerless, and the peasants were serfs.[2]

Though Frederick William at first made no spectacular changes among the Ministers of the Great King, the helm was immediately seized by a little circle of men who had won his favour before his accession. At their head stood the unworthy Wöllner, who had begun his career as a rationalistic pastor and a Mason.[3] A request for nobility had been refused by Frederick, who curtly dismissed him as a deceitful and intriguing parson. He was then persuaded by Bischoffswerder to enter the Rosicrucian Order, and the two men commenced a systematic campaign to secure the favour of the heir to the throne. Frederick William was received into the Order, whose claims and antiquity were set forth by Wöllner; and the circle was enlarged by Haugwitz and Goldbeck. The Prince grew to regard Wöllner as his oracle, and studied the memoranda in which he set forth his ideas. Though a scheming egotist, the future Minister was not lacking in statesmanlike notions. He had already written with authority on agriculture, and he now urged the abolition of serfdom and the lightening of the burden of taxation on the peasant. His attacks on the godless régime of Zedlitz and his sceptical master also found a responsive echo in the heart of the orthodox Prince. The abolition of the Regie formed an obvious plank in the platform of an heir to the throne in search of popularity. The early months of the new reign were a honeymoon, and a rash panegyrist claimed that Augustus had followed Caesar. The zealous educationist, Zedlitz, obtained the promise of more generous support for the elementary schools; and in the sphere

---

[1] Vivenot, *Quellen*, i. 230. His kindness and charm are recognised by his cousin, Princess Luise of Prussia, *Forty-Five Years of My Life*; and Countess Voss, *Sixty-nine Years at the Prussian Court*.

[2] See Lehmann, *Das alte Preussen, Hist. Zeitschrift*, vol. xc.

[3] The fairest account is that of Bailleu, in the *Allgemeine deutsche Biographie*.

of justice a good impression was created by the restitution of the magistrates unjustly punished for their conduct in the Müller case. The rapid and victorious campaign in Holland added to the prestige of the new reign. But the halcyon days were of short duration, and the new ruler soon declared his hand. Wöllner, Bischoffswerder, and the Rosicrucians became supreme, supported as they were by Madame Rietz, the Prussian Pompadour, who retained her influence after the King had transferred his affections and had contracted successive morganatic marriages.[1] The open breach with the Frederician tradition came with the Religious Edict in 1788. Semler's life-long protest against the rigidity of dogma, in the name both of piety and scholarship, was in harmony with the best thought of his age ; but open attacks on religion from the pulpit, and capricious alterations of the formularies, had become fashionable, and among highly paid ecclesiastical dignitaries were men without dogmatic belief. Edicts had been issued in Württemberg and Saxony against similar anomalies, and an injunction to the clergy to preach the faith of the Church or resign their posts would have met with general approval ; but the substitution of Wöllner for Zedlitz as Minister of Worship and Education denoted a more ambitious policy.

The edict, drawn up by Wöllner's own hand, declared war on the Aufklärung, and muzzled philosophical as well as theological discussion. It provoked a crop of spirited and abusive replies : among them that of Bahrdt, the *enfant terrible* of the Aufklärung, who was promptly arrested. The blow was followed up by the Censure Edict at the end of the same year. Though the document was drawn up by Suarez, and did little but repeat the Frederician regulations, it was disliked as the twin of the Religious Edict, and resented because the press had enjoyed almost complete liberty since the death of Frederick. In his crusade for orthodoxy Wöllner found zealous lieutenants in Hermes, a pietist pastor of Breslau, and Hillmer, a creature of Hermes, both fanatical enemies of the Aufklärung. The latter informed the King that ' the monthly and other papers are most read by all classes, and do more harm to tranquillity and good order than larger theological and ethical works ' ; and he therefore asked to have all papers and pamphlets sent to him for censure. The request was granted, and his activity soon bore fruit in the removal of Nicolai's journal to Kiel and of the ' Berliner Monatschrift ' to Jena. ' God wills that I should obey my superiors,' declared Pastor Ewald in Berlin in 1790. ' I sin against Him if I do not. If I believe myself unjustly treated, I

[1] See Dampmartin, *Quelques traits de la vie privée de Frédéric-Guillaume II*, 1811 ; Gräfin von Lichtenau, *Memoiren* ; Cölln, *Vertraute Briefe*, vol. 1.

may beg them for grace, but I must submit. That is the teaching of Christianity, and the only enlightenment the people needs on its rights.'[1] Such were the craven accents that Hermes and Hillmer desired to hear.

The reaction was in full swing before the Revolution; but it was naturally strengthened by events in France. Wöllner quickly dropped his enlightened views on privileges and peasant disabilities; for the King saw in a strong nobility a breakwater against the onrush of the revolutionary tide. The signal of repression given by the Emperor's circular of December 3, 1791, ordering the princes to prevent and punish the authors and circulators of seditious writings, was warmly welcomed in Berlin.[2] The King, in a Cabinet Order, expressed entire agreement with the circular ; adding that ' a more watchful eye than hitherto was necessary to suppress revolutionary writings.' On the following day he ordered Finckenstein, as *doyen* of the Ministers, to call a Council, and advised the supervision of booksellers as well as of newspapers. The Council, however, pointed out that it was impossible to censure all books, and equally impossible to compel foreign editors to supply specimen copies for inspection. Carmer argued that the Censure Edict of 1788 rendered a new law unnecessary, and the members reported that there was not the slightest tendency to disloyalty. The censorship was none the less tightened. The ' Moniteur ' was forbidden, except for ambassadors and high officials several German papers were refused permission to circulate in Prussia and the Berlin Censor vetoed political comment and allusions. In February 1793 Finckenstein warned Spener, the owner of one of the two chief papers of the capital, to amend his Gallophil tone, ' so different from that of the " Vossische Zeitung." ' The Prussian Minister in Hamburg cautioned editors to omit certain French news, if they did not wish their papers to be excluded. Hermes and Hillmer actually vetoed the second part of Kant's treatise on religion ; but the King, broken in spirit and body, gradually lost his anti-revolutionary fervour. With the disappointment on the Rhine he lost confidence in the Rosicrucian circle, and the end of the reign was milder than the years of war.

The state of political feeling in Prussia at the outbreak of the Revolution is fairly described by Boyen, afterwards Minister of War.[3] ' The opening scenes made no great impression among a

---

[1] Biedermann, *Deutschland im 18ten Jahrhundert*, i. 162.

[2] Consentius, *Die Berliner Zeitungen während der Franz. Revolution, Preussische Jahrbücher*, September 1904.

[3] *Erinnerungen*, i. 24-5.

people which had given little thought to France, except in respect of fashion. The Prussians despised the evil government of France and the immorality of the *noblesse* and higher clergy, and opinion did not blame the French for seeking to remove all these abuses, as we felt we were much better off. On the whole the inhabitants were comfortable, and nearly all regarded the happenings merely as objects of curiosity. But the success of the American Revolution and the failure of the Dutch revolt against the Statthalter laid the foundation of other views. In general the bourgeoisie and many of the scholars were favourable. They looked forward to the abolition of burdensome feudal privileges, class distinctions, and waste. There were plenty of landowners, especially in East Prussia, who approved the abolition of serfdom and feudal services. The nobility and the officers, on the other hand, especially the older members, were utterly opposed to any action which threatened their position. On myself the abolition of many foolish privileges of the nobility and the emancipation of the peasant from his crushing burdens made a favourable impression. In the Declaration of the Rights of Man I saw an ideal of legislation never before reached ; and my inexperience caused me to overlook the imperfections and unpractical character of this famous manifesto, which should have mentioned duties as well as rights.'

II

The most distinguished and experienced of Prussian statesmen was Hertzberg, who had aided Frederick the Great in the conduct of foreign affairs for a generation.[1] No German of his time possessed such a profound acquaintance with the history of diplomacy or the secrets of the Prussian archives as the Foreign Minister ; but his interests were wide, and he admired the literature of his country as heartily as Frederick despised it. His tenure of office became precarious with the death of his old master ; and with the rise of Bischoffswerder he was ousted first from the control and then from the knowledge of foreign affairs. He welcomed the Revolution not only because he believed that it would weaken France, but because he approved its principles ; and he told Posselt that the suspicion of democracy was one of the causes of his fall in 1791. He retained his position as Curator of the Academy, which he desired to transform from a predominantly French corporation into a body representing German scholarship. A second innovation, the reading of political and economic discourses, had begun in 1781.

[1] See Preuss, *Hertzberg*, and Harnack, *Geschichte der Akademie der Wissenschaften zu Berlin*, pp. 262–377.

An address delivered in 1784 urged the emancipation and representation of the peasants.   After the death of Frederick the Curator
delivered an annual survey of the preceding year, accompanied by
the discussion of some problem of political science.   In 1789 he set
out to prove that the Prussian monarchy was not despotic, and in
1790 he discussed hereditary nobility.

In 1791 Hertzberg enlarged on Revolutions, and gave free rein
to his views on current events.   ' It is much to be desired that the
Revolution, the most extraordinary in history, had been carried out
with less violence; that the dignity of the Sovereign had suffered
less, that the differences of class and birth had been less drastically
diminished, and the Rights of Man not been pushed too far
and subjected to the whim of democratic despotism.   But France,
enlightened and stimulated by the newer philosophers, desires to
create the best possible constitution and to surpass the English,
inasmuch as it combines monarchy and the republic, giving the
legislative power to the nation and the executive to the King, yet in
such a way that he remains subject to the representatives of the
people.'   Republicanism, he added, stood for peace, and the French
had surrendered the ambitious designs which menaced their neighbours.   This address, which spoke with approval of the revolutions
of 1688 and 1789, was delivered in the presence of the King and the
Crown Prince, and confirmed the rumour, spread by his enemies,
that he was a Jacobin in disguise.   His ideal was an enlightened
monarchy, in which reason should be the real ruler.   If reason ruled,
it was a trifle whether the constitution was monarchical or republican.
His views were not changed by the events of 1789 ; but what was
theory before now appeared a danger in the eyes of the King and his
counsellors.   Alois Hofmann denounced the old Minister as the
worst patron of revolutionary propaganda, and maliciously suggested
that the Convention had begged the King to send them his writings
and portrait.   In 1793 he read a discourse on the reign of Frederick
the Great, proving that monarchy could be good and even preferable
to a republic.   He lent the MSS. to the King ; but a few days earlier
Frederick William had removed Condorcet from the list of Foreign
Associates, and in his anti-revolutionary zeal he would hear no
more of ' the democrat.'   Though not deprived of his post, he was
known to have lost the last traces of royal favour, and the political
sessions of the Academy came to an end.   Two years later the last
political representative of the age of Frederick the Great was dead.

Unlike Hertzberg, the governing caste was naturally alarmed by
the Revolution and by its implicit challenge to the autocracy and
feudalism of Prussia.   Their opinions were voiced by Marwitz, the
frankest spokesman of the Junkers, to whom any change was rank

Jacobinism. 'All was well at that time,' he writes with naïve complacency in his ' Memoirs ' ; ' aristocracy was perfectly regulated and authority was undisputed.' When he met a man who talked democracy, he scarcely believed his ears. ' I had read of such notions, but never imagined that they could take root in our country. I silenced him by a threat to throw him out of the window.' He soon found that there were other offenders. A *savant* who was not a liberal, he complains bitterly, was as rare as a white raven. Liberty, he contends, already existed in France—' the true liberty, individual, corporative, and local '—though it had been somewhat circumscribed by recent monarchs. It was not till the rebels were in control that real oppression and despotism were experienced.[1] Marwitz naturally applauded Burke, and expresses his gratitude to Frederick William II for his efforts to preserve Prussia from the plague. The Religious Edict, he declares in an essay written in 1834, was admirable, and might have been an effective weapon against the French poison; but it was never carried out. ' If all conscienceless preachers, professors, and teachers had been sternly dismissed, and the French Revolution had been at the very beginning combated with the same earnestness by other rulers as by Frederick William II, arrogance, godlessness, and demagogy would never have been able to scourge Germany. It is impossible to admire as it deserves the profound wisdom with which the King perceived the root cause of all the evils which flooded Europe, and his courage in defending his country against it in time. But here, as in foreign affairs, he failed to reach his goal through lack of men to carry out his policy.'[2] Moreover, while the King of Prussia was purely disinterested in entering on the war, the Emperor Leopold was himself a liberal. Even among Prussian officials the doctrines denounced by Marwitz found an occasional champion. In a remarkable address on ' The Spirit of Revolutions,' delivered in 1790, Professor Mangelsdorff of Königsberg declared Prussia a model State, ' whose subjects were happy beyond conception. But if it is a pleasant duty to obey a good monarch, it is equally the right of unhappy peoples to refuse obedience to despots. If the yoke becomes intolerable, and the sceptre turns into the iron staff of the Pharaohs or the knout of the Tartar Khans, the people is entitled to stand up to the oppressor and throw off the horrors of despotism.'[3] Scarcely less advanced opinions were entertained, if not expressed, by Suarez, Klein, and other members of the ' Wednesday Society,' which met weekly for political discussion.

[1] Meusel, *Von der Marwitz*, i. 58–9.
[2] *Ib.*, ii. 107–22.
[3] Prutz, *Preussische Geschichte*, iii. 291.

III

There was one important class which expected to gain by the Revolution, and whose sympathies, like those of Marwitz, were dictated by their interests. There was no ferment in the, towns ; but the peasantry was thoroughly discontented. News of the Revolution penetrated to the remotest parts through French agents, Émigrés, or newspapers, and encouraged ideas of personal liberty by showing that they were capable of being carried out. The scene of the chief revolts was Silesia, whence endless petitions for relief had reached the Government, and where in the first winter of the war several villages refused to pay their dues to the lords.[1] Far graver incidents occurred among the Silesian weavers on the Bohemian frontier, where wages had fallen owing to the war. Hunger and discontent led to revolts in the spring of 1793, and Hoym, the Governor of the province, reported to the King the existence of a widespread conspiracy and of ' evil ideas arising from French propaganda. This spirit of unrest,' he added, ' must be stifled at birth.' In spite of warnings the revolt spread, and the cry was occasionally heard, ' We only wish the French would come.' Hoym, now thoroughly scared, demanded heavy punishments ; but the good-natured monarch prescribed mild measures and full investigation. The trouble spread to Breslau, where the apprentices and the mob came into collision with the police. The soldiers fired, and several lives were lost ; but Hoym was uncertain of the temper of the troops. A paper with the words ' We soldiers wish to help you, so that we may obtain a free Republic,' frightened the Governor into conciliation, since the greater part of the army was on the Rhine or in Poland. It was lucky for the State, he reported, that the lower classes possessed no organisation ; for the spirit of lawless dissatisfaction was more general than was realised. Many communes refused their dues or demanded redress of grievances before paying them. At the end of the year a revolt broke out among the Silesian Poles. The officials were expelled, and cries were heard that the French Revolution must be reproduced. As a result Breslau was allowed to choose twelve representatives to be consulted on important occasions; but no remedial measures were taken. In April 1794 the Breslau Chamber launched a threatening decree against all who, in private houses, ' praised the unhappy French Revolution.' In 1795 the custom of beating the peasants with sticks was abolished ; but a year later the Silesian authorities complained

[1] Most fully described by Philippson.

once more of ' the spirit of revolt ' among the peasants, which they attributed mainly to the influence of the soldiers from the Rhine campaigns, ' who talk to the peasants of the French Revolution, liberty, and equality.'

Hoym's troubles were not over ; for he was soon confronted with the so-called conspiracy of Held and Zerboni.[1] Hans von Held, a young Silesian, was a loyal Prussian official ; but as a Mason and an ardent disciple of Rousseau he welcomed the Revolution with rapture. On becoming Finance Minister in 1791 Struensee was the recipient of some joyful verses from his young protégé. ' A brighter day begins to shine on the lower ranks of society. Hoary folly falls in ruins. The gloomy walls of slavery collapse. The joyful songs of the peoples ring from both hemispheres. The world will never retrace its steps.' In 1793 Held moved to Posen, and discussed the problems of the time with his friend Zerboni—an able and patriotic man destined to high rank in the official hierarchy of Prussia. Zerboni was a friend of Fessler, an Austrian refugee, who suggested the creation of a secret society—a favourite pastime in that era—to further the reforming aims which were common to them all. The ex-Capucin has described the escapades of his youth in his Autobiography. He had known Martinovich, the ex-Franciscan, ' a convinced atheist and political fanatic, a Catiline,' who, on the death of Leopold II, planned a conspiracy against the State, and paid the penalty with his life. He himself was never inclined to violence, and asserts that his new friends were ' far removed from all political tendency,' and only strove for moral and educational reform.[2] The triumvirate formed a society called the Euergetes, which was conceived as a branch of the Masons, among whom they expected to enrol members. The Order was joined by Zerboni's younger brother, just back from Paris, by Captain von Leipziger, a writer on war, and by Contessa, who was engaged in business. ' I believe I am worthy to be a republican, and I desire to live in a republic,' wrote the younger Zerboni. ' I hate everything that will allow one man to tyrannise over others. I abhor kings and their slaves, and I will only pardon them when their crowns are broken for ever.' Contessa was also a republican ; but the other members were content with constitutional monarchy. A further element of discord emerged in Fessler's zeal for the use of ceremonies. Thus the tiny group broke up as quickly as it formed, and the friends of its founders rightly regarded the episode as a

---

[1] See Grünhagen, *Zerboni u. Held* ; Varnhagen, *Hans von Held*, in his *Biographische Denkmale*, vol. vii.; Hüffer, *Zerboni u. Held, Preussische Jahrbücher*, July 1898.

[2] See Fessler, *Rückblicke*, pp. 115–16, 173.

harmless extravagance of youth. Held proceeded to translate Chénier's poem on the removal of Rousseau's ashes to the Pantheon, and other French and Latin verses in praise of Liberty ; and, like all Francophils, he rejoiced at the Peace of Basle, believing the two peoples to be destined by nature to co-operate. ' Call back your brave army,' he adjured the King, ' and let us be brothers of the Franks.'

In 1795 Zerboni, Leipziger, and Contessa formed the idea of a new secret society with political aims, since the perfecting of man was impossible without political liberty. The little group of reformers found a task ready to its hand in counter-working Hoym. The Governor's long tenure of office, and the confidence of the Court, had made him virtually independent of Berlin ; and throughout the province his word was law, while his protégés occupied every post. The French Revolution rendered the people more critical and Hoym more reactionary. When New South Prussia, the fruit of the second partition of Poland, was entrusted to his hands in 1794, the friends determined to ferret out abuses and to reveal them to the public or sue the offenders in court. Contessa spoke of ' the moral Vehmgericht,' which was to be the terror of evil officials. A seal and cipher were made, and in 1796 the attack was opened by Zerboni. Hoym forwarded the letter to the King, and denounced the writer as a republican. Zerboni was imprisoned, and among his papers were found particulars of the two secret societies. The clue was followed up by the seizure of the papers of Leipziger and Contessa, and the Vehmgericht stood revealed. Hoym was delighted at the turn of fortune, and urged his master to treat the society, which he described as ' a revolutionary club,' as treasonable. Its members were imprisoned in different places without trial ; but they were released by the new monarch in 1798, though the court decided that the imprisonment was just. ' That Leipziger has tried to disturb public order is most improbable,' wrote Knesebeck. ' So far as I know him, he is a warm Prussian patriot. Mere opinions, I hope, will not be crimes ; else it would be as easy to find or make 80,000 Jacobins in Prussia as Burke discovered in England.' [1] Zerboni, feeling himself both innocent and injured, published a documented apologia in 1800. The book aroused considerable attention, and the author underwent a further short term of imprisonment. The conflict was carried on by Held, who, though not a member of the second society, hated Hoym. His indictment, ' The True Jacobins in Prussia,' bitterly attacking Hoym and the Chancellor, Goldbeck, was called ' the Black Book,'

[1] See Lehmann, *Aus dem Leben Knesebecks, Preussische Jahrbücher* vol. xxxiv.

from its binding, and was succeeded by ' the Black Register ' on the squandering of State lands. Many of his accusations, however, have been proved groundless ; for most of the lands were given or sold at the command of Frederick William II to his Generals or other servants. After a year in prison Held was ultimately restored to the service of the State, but passed the rest of his life in obscurity.

IV

Apart from some insignificant disturbances among the artisans and apprentices, the peace of the Prussian capital was unbroken. A few unguarded utterances were heard, such as the war-cry of the popular preacher, Jenisch—

> Flee all ye tyrants for your thrones are rocking,
> Now right and liberty, your foes, appear.

But such explosions were purely academic, neither exciting their readers nor alarming the Government. A few superficia changes were noted in Caroline de la Motte Fouqué's sketches of social life in Berlin. 'For a time the upper classes discarded French for English as the language of polite society, in order to exhibit their contempt for France. In less exalted circles, on the other hand, French fashions and symbols were never more popular. The *modistes* made bonnets *à la Carmagnole*, and babies were thus decked out for christening. Even when our troops marched against the enemy, fashion clung to the tricolour stuff and ribbons which Paris sent us. As the first French prisoners passed through the city, many pressed forward to greet them. Despite their squalid and unkempt appearance, the people watched with curiosity the dances of the republicans, one of which represented the washing of hands in the blood of aristocrats. With the usual German admiration for everything foreign, people made presents to the barbarians, and bought toy guillotines made by the prisoners as a pastime on the march.' [1]

The French colony, which numbered about five thousand souls, caused no anxiety to the Government. In Prussia, as elsewhere, the descendants of the Huguenot refugees had proved themselves loyal and industrious citizens.[2] They welcomed the fall of the intolerant Bourbons ; but there was little ferment in their ranks.

---

[1] *Der Schreibtisch*, pp. 52–9.
[2] See Muret, *Geschichte der Französischen Kolonie in Brandenburg-Preussen*.

The venerable Erman, the historian of the refugees, was a member of the Prussian Academy and Historiographer of Brandenburg.[1] Of a younger generation the most influential were Ancillon and Lombard, both of whom rose high in the service of the State. The former was pastor of the French colony ; and his political orthodoxy was as unimpeachable as his piety. Lombard had recently entered the State secretariat, where his services were found extremely useful.[2] He frankly praised the ideas of 1789, which he believed could be applied to Prussia in diluted form ; and he shared the prevailing view in Berlin that the war was a mistake. Accompanying the King on the campaign as his private secretary, he was disgusted by the conduct of the Émigrés and by the pillaging habits of the Prussian troops after crossing the frontier. ' That is the way to make all France one party,' he exclaimed, ' and to raise up twenty-four million enemies.' He quickly perceived that the old régime possessed no friends among the privileged classes. But, though a critical observer of Prussian policy, he never gave offence ; and he approved the expulsion of Borelly, a professor at the Military School, and Chanvier, the Royal Librarian, at the end of 1792, ' on account of their scandalous language and the Jacobin sentiments they proclaim.' Bitaubé, the translator of Homer, had left Prussia for Paris some years before the Revolution, and narrowly escaped the guillotine during the dictatorship o. Robespierre.

The even tenor of life in the capital was disturbed for a moment by rumours of a plot, in which, however, the offender was not a Prussian. The Alsatian, Leuchsenring, had led a wandering life.[3] He had accompanied the eldest son of the Duke of Hesse-Darmstadt on a visit to Paris, and lived for a time with the Landgrave of Hesse-Homburg, one of the best of the German princelets.[4] In 1784 he was appointed by Frederick the Great tutor to the future Frederick William III, then a lad of fourteen ; but he quarrelled with the other tutors, was accused of dangerous teaching, and withdrew after two months. His wide information and clever talk made him a welcome addition to literary circles. Goethe had long known and liked him, though he made fun of him in ' Pater Brey.' But he was eccentric and suspicious, and the ardent Illuminé saw everywhere ' crypto-Jesuits,' and other masked assassins of truth. ' What a strange being he is,' wrote Johannes Müller to

[1] See W. Erman, *J. P. Erman.*
[2] See Hüffer's excellent biography.
[3] See Varnhagen's biographical sketch in his *Vermischte Schriften*, i. 494–532.
[4] See Schwartz, *Friedrich V, von Hessen-Homburg,* i. 130–9.

Jacobi; 'for him everything is done by secret societies.' He threw down the gauntlet in 1786 in an article in the 'Berliner Monatschrift,' which inaugurated the long conflict of the Berlin rationalists against crypto-Jesuits and crypto-Catholics. He was aided by Nicolai and Biester; while the cause of religion was defended by Jacobi, Lavater, and Schlosser. The crusade was ineffective, for the conspiracy was a mare's nest.

Like most of his friends, Leuchsenring was a cosmopolitan. When he visited Lavater in 1786 a violent disagreement took place, as the Swiss stood up stoutly for patriotism in general and Switzerland in particular. The outbreak of the French Revolution filled him with delight as the realisation of his dreams of liberty, equality, and universal peace. He returned to Berlin after further wanderings, became an *habitué* of the French Embassy, and gathered round him the Francophils of the capital. He openly praised the speeches of Vergniaud and Isnard, and spoke against the coming war. He delivered lectures on philosophy, which were attended by ladies of the Court; and his eulogies of the new France reached the ears of the King, who gave him money to travel in order to be rid of him. While he lingered on in the capital, further evidence reached the Government which led to his expulsion and the seizure of his papers. The air was thick with rumours of plots, and well-known names were mentioned as his dupes or accomplices, including that of the reigning favourite.

'A very curious affair has occurred at Berlin,' wrote Count Bray, the French Minister to the Diet at Regensburg.[1] 'A club of pretended Jacobins has been discovered. Madame Dönhoff is supposed to be at the head, with one Leuchsenring, and two other women. This discovery has made a prodigious noise, and her credit has been undermined. The King has treated her with much mildness and generosity; but she has left Berlin, and is said to be in Switzerland. Leuchsenring has been dismissed. I am told on good authority that she has produced a correspondence which goes far to justify her and to compromise Bischoffswerder. It is said that the Princess of Orange and the Duke of Brunswick had determined to overthrow Bischoffswerder by showing the King what sort of people surrounded him.' Eden's dispatches from Berlin to Lord Grenville were filled with the affair. 'The expulsion of Leuchsenring without any form of trial has given rise to many reflections. From his aged figure he could not inspire any tender passion; but he had made many fair proselytes to his exalted notions, among others Mlle. de Bielefeld, a young lady who was governess to the King's youngest daughter. She has of course been

---

[1] Bray, *Mémoires*, pp. 289–90.

turned out of her place. By her extravagant eulogy of Mirabeau and the principal demagogues, she had given offence to Baron Rolle and others of the French agents here, who have long been seeking to effect her disgrace.' Two days later he added that the Dönhoff had been disgraced, as Leuchsenring's papers proved a connection with the Jacobin party. In a third dispatch he explains Frederick William's mild treatment of his favourite. ' Certain it is that she was in correspondence with Leuchsenring ; but the King rather attributes her wishes to prevent his interposing in the affairs of France to tenderness for his person than to a desire to thwart the schemes of Bischoffswerder or to promote the destructive doctrines of French demagogues.' [1]

The chief offender found but little sympathy. ' I saw him in Erfurt,' wrote Schiller to Körner. [2] ' I wonder if extremity will make anything of him. He has been collecting materials for twenty years and written little or nothing. Now writing will be his only resource, and we shall see what he will produce.' ' Leuchsenring may not be so innocent as he pretends,' replied Körner. ' I know he has been suspected of a plot against the Royal Family, and things have been found in his papers which rendered his dismissal inevitable. I do not know him.' Suspicion fell on some of his friends. Mencken lost favour though not office, since nothing was proved against him ; and Zelter, the composer, was in danger of being expelled at the same time. But the whole incident was a storm in a teacup, and the arch-conspirator was a very harmless individual—a dilettante in politics not less than in literature. Fräulein von Bielefeld, who was arrested with him, accompanied him to Paris, where they were married and made their home. He lived by teaching languages, and, despite his poverty, refused offers from the Directory and the Empire ; but he accepted help from the ever generous Schlabrendorf, from Oelsner, and from Humboldt. He was called ' Le vieux de la mare ' by the children who played in the Bois at the side of a pond, to which he paid a daily visit ; and he died in Paris in 1827, poor and forgotten.

A second victim of French sympathies was the composer Reichardt, who had been appointed Kapellmeister to Frederick the Great at the early age of twenty-three, and had become the centre of musical circles in Berlin. [3] In 1785 he paid a long visit to Paris, where his music was much appreciated ; but his enemies intrigued against him during his absence, and on his return he lost interest in his work. His hospitable house and clever talk, however,

---

[1] *Fortescue MSS.*, ii. 276–7.
[2] *Schiller's Briefwechsel mit Körner*, ii. 316, 318.
[3] See Schletterer, *Reichardt's Leben* ; and Pauli, *Reichardt*.

continued to attract men of advanced opinions. 'In 1791 he resigned his post ; but the resignation was declined, and he was given leave of absence for three years. The composer utilised his leisure for a visit to France, in order to study the Revolution at close quarters. Fragments of his letters home appeared in his own Musical Journal in Berlin, and the complete series was published anonymously on his return.[1] The preface to the first volume was dated August 15, 1792, and the title-page was adorned with a vignette of the red cap of liberty and two tricolour cockades. The journey began in the early weeks of 1792, and led him through the Rhineland to Strassburg. The traveller reports that nearly all the people he met at Lyons desired war. ' If they are attacked,' he added, ' the advantage will be theirs.' Arriving in Paris, he revisited the site of the Bastille. ' Do you remember that moving evening, years ago, when we walked round the formidable fortress ? Filled with horror at tyranny, touched by a profound pity for both innocent and guilty who were suffering behind those walls, we forgot the sum of good which even in Paris reconciled man with his lot.' He found the city in trouble, but entertained hopes of her recovery. The Revolution, he wrote, had made so many mistakes, owing to the inexperience of its leaders. Mirabeau alone foresaw the difficulties, and his death was as great a misfortune as the loss of a pilot at sea. ' Before France can enjoy the tranquillity and order which all elevated minds desire for her, at least twenty years must elapse. And what are twenty years for a great revolution ? If in that period she can secure a constitution assuring her centuries of repose and prosperity, history will only see in it a time of difficult but fruitful harvest. This is doubtless cold comfort for the victims of a great cause ; but I feel that foreigners who watch and criticise the Revolution should employ more calmness and perspective in their judgments.'

On his return to Berlin Reichardt found his position impossible. The authorship of the Letters leaked out, snatches of his talk were reported to the authorities, and his adopted son left the University to fight as a volunteer in the French army. He was dismissed from his post as Kapellmeister, and bitterly attacked both by Gallo-phobes and rival musicians. His friend and patron, the Princess of Dessau, appealed on his behalf to Bischoffswerder, who replied that he dared not mention his name to the King ; but the kindly Frederick William, himself a musician, appointed him director of salt-mines at Halle, a lucrative sinecure. He had, however, no intention of hiding himself or his views, and he founded two journals,

[1] Reprinted in 1892 as *Un Prussien en France en* 1792. *Lettres intimes de J. F. Reichardt.*

called 'France' and 'Germany,' the former appearing in Altona, the latter in Berlin. 'Germany' was a feeble performance, filled with excerpts from other papers and abstract declamations on freedom ; but 'France' was a more ambitious journal, in which the editor struck out at the enemies of liberty. A criticism of Goethe's 'Conversations of the Refugees' led to a terrific retaliation. He had composed music for Goethe's poems, and had been a welcome guest in Weimar ; but politics had sundered the friendship. 'Reichardt threw himself with furious fanaticism on the side of the Revolution,' we read in the 'Annals' for 1795. 'I, on the other hand, who with my own eyes observed the ghastly, ungovernable consequences of the violent dissolution of all bonds, and clearly perceived a similar secret agitation in my own country, held fast to the established order. In the sphere of music he remained a friend, but in politics he was an antagonist.' Schiller, on the other hand, had always detested him. 'The conductor, Reichardt, of Berlin,' he wrote to Lotte in April 1789, 'is staying with Goethe. It would be hard to find a more impertinent fellow. Fate has thrown me across his path, and I have had to put up with his acquaintance. No scrap of paper in the room is safe from him. He puts a finger into every pie, and I hear that one must be very careful what one says to him.'[1] The angry poets launched their sharpest 'Xenien' against the Jacobin composer ; and the most cutting phrases were contributed by Schiller.[2]

Two newspapers he issues, or even three ; I advise you,
Keep your writings locked up, hunger may drive him to theft.

One hand seizes on France, while the other boldly embraces
Poor old Germany : yet both, being paper, are light.

Aristocratic dogs are always snarling at beggars,
And silken hose provoke yelps from the democrat cur.

Do you consider the Germans so dense, Apostles of Freedom ?
Every one sees through your game. All that you want is to rule.

Holiest freedom ! noblest instinct of man for improvement !
Truly, though look where you will, worse priests you never shall find.

Shape the State how you like. You never will be of importance.
Light on the surface floats always and ever the cork.

[1] *Schiller u. Lotte, Ein Briefwechsel*, i. 228.
[2] See the notes to the *Xenien*, edited by E. Schmidt and Suphan.

Truly the health of the State is not in such imminent danger
That it should risk a cure, life or death at your hands.

Priests of liberty ! You have never looked on the goddess ;
Never with gnashing of teeth is the Divine shadowed forth.

Despite this bombardment Goethe and Reichardt resumed friendly
relations within a few years.

On the death of Frederick William II Reichardt reappeared in
Berlin, where his compositions were played with success. For his
journalistic work he secured the services of Friedrich Schlegel, who
contributed some of the best of his early essays ; but the young
critic soon cut himself adrift. 'Reichardt is here,' he wrote to
his brother from Berlin in 1797. 'Outwardly we get on well
together. The man has much that is good in him ; but, as he is
not generous, it would be folly to remain in literary partnership
with him. His so-called republicanism, political and literary, is
only the Berlin Aufklärung—an opposition to obscurantism, and a
leaning to the French, whom he, as a German, hates and despises,
just as he also despises the Germans as a Frenchman.' [1] The
composer paid another visit to Paris in 1802, and in 1807 accepted
the post of Kapellmeister to King Jerome at Cassel.

V

While in France the Revolution provoked not a little socialistic
speculation, in Germany only one anonymous pamphlet exists to
show that the deeper implications of the new doctrine of equality
were recognised. In one of his letters Forster mentions a brochure
published in Berlin in 1792, 'On Man and his Condition.' More
than a century later Jaurès, stumbling on the reference in Forster's
correspondence, asked that search should be made. The pamphlet
was found, and extracts have been published by Bernstein.[2] The
unknown author described himself in the preface as a pupil of
Wieland. 'My guides were Wieland's works. But my views
diverged more and more every day from the prevailing opinions, so
that I could no longer repress the wish to publish them. Can it
be a dishonour to Wieland to have opened my eyes, which, after
all, remain my own ? '

The writer's opinions are voiced by Philemon, while the conventional view of education, society, and the State is presented by
Erast. The opening phrases of the dialogue reveal the influence

[1] F. Schlegel, *Briefe an seinen Bruder*, p. 299.
[2] In his *Dokumente des Sozialismus*, i. 114–31.

of Rousseau and the Philosophes, strengthened by the teaching of the Revolution. Current ideas are mercilessly criticised, and traditional arrangements are haled before the judgment-seat of Reason. The first topic is education.

Erast: Am I not to train my children for the State ? Is there a nobler goal for the educator ?

Philemon: It may be noble, but not right. Do you think man is in the world to be a member of this orthodox State ? He must recognise the obligations of membership ; but they are not the goal of his being. The man is prior to the citizen.

On reading further we discover that the author is a communist, and that it was to expound his views on property that he rushed into print.

Philemon: If private property ceased and the citizens, like children in their father's house, satisfied themselves at the common table, what a vast mass of crime would vanish with the disappearance of greed, envy, and vanity !

Erast: Equality is a dream. For whom shall I work if my children do not reap the benefit ? Will not the thought that strangers gather the fruits of my labour make me idle ?

Philemon: Why is your neighbour a stranger ? Owing to our imperfect organisation, the love of man has concentrated itself too much. So long as each one plants his goal to the right or left, near or distant, so long will there be painful collisions. We have common destinies, common rights, a common goal. The existence of each must no longer be entrusted to his own weak hands. The whole of society must be responsible. Good and bad fortune will lose its power ; for the community will bid it defiance.

Erast: I confess that I can only think of my own household.

Philemon: Don't you want your poor neighbour to be happy also ?

Erast: Of course I do ; but who can help him ?

Philemon: There are several people in the village who have more than they need. And which of us is sure that he may not himself be in need ? One ought to weep at the idea of being happy alone.

Erast: You say that strong passions—for instance, those of possession and power—are incompatible with human welfare ; but do not great deeds spring from them alone ? Great achievements demand great motives.

Philemon: The thirst for greatness has made man very small. The truest greatness is to do right. Heroic deeds are a very poor compensation for the misery they have caused. Corpses are the steps to the temple of fame. Men either overestimate or underestimate themselves.

The treatise ends on the note of lofty individualism with which it began. The form of the Constitution, argues Philemon, is of secondary importance. ' The freedom of a State resides not in its outward forms, but in independence of the caprice of others, and in the impossibility of some imposing their will on others, either legally or illegally.' Thus communism is to be the instrument by which for the first time the individual is to discover and to emancipate himself.

VI

The atmospheric currents prevailing in Prussia during the era of revolution may be profitably studied in the story of the ' Allgemeines Landrecht.' [1]   Among the many beneficent projects of the Aufklärung was the reform of the law, based on the substitution of reason for tradition ; and some of the most eminent of European jurists laboured at the production of codes.   When Frederick the Great drew breath after the Silesian War, he commissioned Cocceji to prepare a code in German, ' based wholly on reason and the constitutions of the country ' ; but the workman was not equal to his task, and the project was shelved five years after its inception. Nearly thirty years later the King's interest revived ; and in 1780 the new Grand Chancellor, Carmer, was commanded to frame a new code, based on existing law and practice, but corresponding to the spirit of the time.   Carmer had won fame as Minister of Justice in Silesia, and he brought with him from Breslau his colleague, Suarez, to be his chief of the staff.   Suarez drew up a sketch which, after modification by Carmer and other judges, was printed in 1784. The draft was canvassed in numerous memorials from those affected, ranging from provincial governments to private citizens. Prizes were offered for the best essays on the project, and the whole educated class took its share of responsibility.

The first part, dealing with the law of persons, appeared in the lifetime of Frederick the Great, who, while approving its provisions, ordered the Estates of the different provinces to formulate their views.   A *précis* of the memorials and criticisms was ordered by Suarez, who wrote a report on it, to which Carmer added his reflections.   The change of ruler made no difference to the project, and at the end of 1789 the King was informed that the first and most important part of the Code would be ready for publication in the following summer.   At this point, however, obstacles began to

---

[1] See Stölzel, *Suarez* ;   Philippson, i. 297–320, and ii. 46–60 ;   Meier, *Preussen u. die Fr. Rev.* ii. 142–9 ;   Hinschius, ' Suarez der Schöpfer des Preussischen Landrechts,' *Preussische Jahrbücher*, March 1890.

appear. Wöllner was now in the saddle, and the King accepted his guidance, despite the fact that he had been trained as a theologian. It was accordingly decreed that the Code should come into operation in 1792, but that provincial privileges should remain in force, and that it should only operate in their absence. The provincial laws, however, were to be revised within three years and arranged on the plan of the Code by a meeting of the provincial judges and the Estates, in order that local differences might be abolished. In the spring of 1791 the Chancellor forwarded the first three volumes to the King, and announced that the fourth would soon follow. ' Then a work will be completed which will not only contribute to the strength and progress of the State, but immortalise your name among the benefactors of humanity.' On the title-page stands the bust of Frederick William II, ' the legislator.' Little did the authors dream that their proud edifice was to be overthrown before their eyes.

There was little enough of ' liberalism ' in the Code as it issued from the hands of Carmer and Suarez ; for the Chancellor was broadly content with the Frederician system, in which the burgher was sharply divided from the noble above and the peasant below. But while a benevolent autocrat is presupposed, the Code defines, and in effect limits, his power by safeguarding the individual against the caprice of the government. For instance, the inter-ference of the ruler in judicial cases is categorically condemned as of no effect ; and legal disputes between ruler and subject are to be tried in the ordinary courts by the ordinary law. The indepen-dence of the bench is buttressed against further attacks by the provision that judges can only be removed by the courts, not by the executive. Some paragraphs in the Introduction also point to an atmospheric change since the heyday of the enlightened despots. ' The laws and ordinances of the State must not limit the natural liberty and the rights of citizens more than the general interest requires. The universal rights of man are based on the natural liberty to seek his own welfare without injuring the rights of others.' Title 13 of Part ii denies by implication the unlimited power of the prince by drawing up a list of his rights, and the authors make a practice of employing the word ' citizens,' or ' inhabitants,' in place of ' subjects.' Prussia would thus become a limited, though not a constitutional, monarchy : a State founded on law, not on undefined prerogative.

Though we catch an echo of 1776 and 1789,[1] the main structure belongs to the Frederician era. The privileged position of the

[1] One of its authors, Klein, had defended the decrees of the Fourth of August.

nobility in the army and the State, which was the corner-stone
of that system, is retained. 'The noble,' declares the Code
categorically, 'has a special claim to positions of honour. As the
strength and security of the State rest mainly on noble landowners,
the class must be kept free from contamination by lower elements.'
If a noble elects to take up some form of industry, or 'to choose
a career which degrades him to the level of the common people,' he
must lose the privileges of his class. He cannot legally marry
a peasant or 'lower' burgher; but he may contract a morganatic
marriage—a curious revival of the Roman *concubinatus*. The
peasant, in turn, though contributing two-thirds of the population,
remains a serf. Suarez, who was far more liberal than his chief,
disliked serfdom, and, though willing to allow the continuance of
the services which were the equivalent of his holding and cottage,
he desired the peasant to be no longer *glebae adscriptus*. This
extension of civil liberty was vetoed by Carmer, and peasant rights
were narrowed instead of enlarged. He remains a hewer of wood
and a drawer of water. He and his children are forbidden to follow
a burgher's trade. He must obtain his lord's permission to marry.
The lord and his tenants may chastise him and send him to prison
for a week. In one respect alone—namely, the clauses dealing with
seduction—were more humane provisions introduced. While the
position of the upper and lower class was thus elaborately defined,
the burghers are clumsily described as consisting of 'those who
do not belong to the noble or peasant class.' In the sphere of
religion the Code is conservative: only the three recognised Christian
Churches—Catholics, Lutherans, Calvinists—being credited with
rights, though freedom of conscience is assured to all. The stout
Erastianism of Suarez is visible throughout.

The Code of Carmer and Suarez, though in many respects
behind the best Prussian opinion, was, broadly speaking, in advance
of Prussian practice. It went far beyond a mere codification of
existing law; and for this reason it aroused the fierce hostility of
the feudal, pietistic, and absolutist clique which was now in control
of the country and the King. A paper compared passage after
passage with the 'Declaration of the Rights of Man,' in order to
prove that the famous seventeen articles were reproduced either
in phraseology or in spirit. The Estates of Minden-Ravensberg
presented a bitter protest, claiming that nothing should be altered
without the consent of all the provincial bodies. These spokesmen
of Junker particularism disliked the permission of marriage between
nobles and higher burghers—such as officials, substantial business
men, or scholars—though it had long existed in practice. They also
complained that 'the laws relating to equality and promises of

marriage bear the unmistakable stamp of the now too fashionable philosophy, of which one of the chief principles is equality of classes. How detrimental is the application of this principle in human society we observe in the hideous anarchy which is devastating France ; and who can be sure that the same consequences will not occur in the rest of Europe if the law accredits such principles ? France would never have lost the form of limited monarchy if more pains had been taken to retain the privileges of the nobles and the consequent devotion to the King.' The obligations imposed on the seducers of peasant girls also aroused their anger. The Estates of another province asked for four years' delay in which to compile their provincial code.

The most dangerous enemies of the Code were not the Estates. In April 1792 the Silesian Minister of Justice, Dankelmann—a tool of Wöllner and Bischoffswerder—urged the King to postpone recognition, ' as the many innovations of a dangerous and anti-monarchical character would produce unsuitable political results and require further consideration.' It was in vain that Carmer pointed out that every part had been approved by the Commissioners and passed by the King, and that ten thousand copies had been piinted. In April its inauguration was indefinitely postponed, ' because the public has not had time to familiarise itself with its provisions.' Dankelmann renewed the attack, complaining of the name ' General Code,' and attacking the limitation of the prerogative and the use of such phrases as ' free citizens.' Goldbeck, already marked out as Carmer's successor, pronounced it ' quite wrong to mention the relation of the ruler to his subjects, as this is not the concern of judges. It is also wrong to make new law, as the plan was merely to codify existing law, under which the land was happy and prosperous.' He was on firmer ground in attacking the morganatic marriages, and he sketched an order to Carmer to remove certain features of his work. The document was approved by the King, who instructed the author to suggest omissions. Among his excisions were the limitation of the royal power in legal cases. When the emasculated Landrecht finally became operative in 1794, it had lost its quasi-constitutional character. In the last year of his life Frederick the Great had declared against the incorporation of the principles of public law ; and in this respect, at any rate, Wöllner and his friends could quote the authority of their great enemy. ' The standpoint of the Landrecht,' declares Meier, ' was not that of retrogression, but of opposition to an advance.' All references to natural rights and citizens disappeared, and the attempt to limit autocracy was repudiated. Even now it was only to occupy a subsidiary position ; for it was at first only to apply where the laws of the province were not in conflict with it. Provincial laws were to be harmonised, as far as possible, by 1796, after which unwritten customs were to have force no longer. A year after its publication Carmer fell.

In its original form the Code was a perfect reflection of an age of transition, providing weapons alike for the champions of the Old World and the New ; and even when some of its teeth were drawn, the monster aroused consternation in the ranks of the Junkers, who saw in it an insidious threat to their privileges and to the historical foundations of the Prussian State. The Code, declared Marwitz in an essay written in 1834, was revolutionary, and the King was talked over and misinformed by its designing authors.[1] 'These jurists and theorists were by their nature and the trend of the spirit of the age ideologues, trained and initiated into the philosophy and the fashionable ideas of their century. These ideas were transferred bodily into our Code from the " Rights of Man " of Tom Paine and the utilitarian notions of the Constituent Assembly. It is penetrated by the idea that the monarch is only an official, whom the people have commissioned to rule over them. He is always called the head of the State, so that all his attributes are applicable to any one at any moment who is strong, clever, or evil enough to seize the helm. Though the King commanded the omission of all that concerned public law and the Constitution, and all that did not flow from the existing laws, the ideologues led him by the nose. Apart from the morganatic marriages and such trifles, I find no difference between the Gesetzbuch and the Landrecht ; indeed, the Jacobin principles are clearly retained. This plight of our jurisprudence was very favourable to the revolution in our country.' But the dreaded ' revolution ' was only to take shape after the material and spiritual debility of Prussia had been twice exposed to the world by the rough challenge of arms.

[1] Meusel, *Marwitz*, ii. 123–31.

CHAPTER XVII

PRUSSIA AND THE WAR

I

THE King of Prussia, like most other rulers who had come into diplomatic or military conflict with the French monarchy, welcomed the Revolution in the belief that it would cripple a formidable rival ; and Goltz, the Prussian Minister in Paris, who was in friendly touch with many of the leaders, was instructed to tell them that their new-found liberty was in no wise distasteful to his master. In September 1790 the Jewish banker Ephraim, the Bleichröder of his day, was dispatched on a secret mission to Paris to arrange for an alliance with, or at least the benevolent neutrality of, France in the event of war between Prussia and Austria.[1] He met Mirabeau, Lafayette, Barnave, the Lameths, and Montmorin, the Foreign Minister ; but he aroused the suspicion of the Austrian Minister, who secured his arrest and recall. The Émigrés for a time regarded Frederick William rather as a foe than a friend. ' What strikes me most,' wrote Vaudreuil to Artois from Venice in October 1790, ' is that the sect of the Illuminés is the cause and instigator of all our troubles ; that one finds these sectaries everywhere ; that even the King of Prussia is imbued with this pernicious system ; that the man who possesses his chief confidence (Bischoffswerder) is one of its chief heads.' [2]

There was nothing in the principles of 1789 incompatible with the peace of the world ; but two concrete causes of friction between the new France and the old Europe arose in the abolition of the feudal rights of German princes on the left bank of the Rhine and the harbouring of the Émigrés on German soil. By the Treaty of Westphalia the House of Hapsburg had ceded Alsace on the conditions of its own tenure, the King of France succeeding the Emperor

[1] J. Kühn, *Ephraim's Pariser Geheimsendung von* 1790–91, disproves the legend that his instructions were to cause a rupture with Austria by urging Égalité and others to kill the Queen.

[2] *Corresp. de Vaudreuil et du Comte d'Artois*, i. 342.

as political sovereign, while the princes and other petty potentates retained their possessions and their jurisdiction and continued to levy feudal dues. Further treaties concluded by Louis XV with a number of secular and ecclesiastical rulers guaranteed their ancient rights in return for the recognition of French sovereignty. The position was in any case one of considerable difficulty; for many princes of South Germany and the Rhineland possessed fiefs in Alsace, including the Ecclesiastical Electors, the Bishops of Strassburg, Speier, and Worms, the rulers of Württemberg, Baden, the Palatinate, Zweibrücken, Hesse-Darmstadt, and Nassau. When the Constituent Assembly abolished feudal rights, Alsace was naturally included in the edict of emancipation; and when the Departments replaced the old provinces, the lands held by members of the Empire were treated as French soil. Treaty rights were plainly infringed, and the princes vigorously protested. The grievance was frankly admitted by the King of France and his Ministers; and in April 1790 the Constituent Assembly, at the suggestion of Mirabeau, reluctantly sanctioned the payment of an indemnity. A few of the rulers, recognising that protest was useless and fearing the anger of France, were ready to compromise; but the majority flatly declined to bargain away their rights, and demanded that the Emperor should secure the abrogation of the obnoxious decrees. The intransigeant princes found a leader in Schlözer's old antagonist, the Bishop of Speier, an industrious but quarrelsome despot, who abhorred not only the Revolution but the liberal principles of the Aufklärung. In December the Emperor formally complained on behalf of the Empire. In March 1791 France replied that the matter only concerned the individual princes; to which the Diet rejoined that it was the affair of the Empire, and declared the action of France null and void. The Emperor supported the claim of the Diet, and renewed his contention that the territory of German princes could not be taken, even in return for compensation. Juridically the princes occupied an impregnable position; but in setting her house in order France could not reasonably be expected to treat Alsace as a foreign enclave. The difficulty was by no means insoluble, and generous compensation would have ensured a fair settlement of undoubted hardships; but the controversy had become embittered by new and wider differences, and the question was left to the arbitrament of arms.[1]

The problem of feudal rights in Alsace, thorny though it was,

---

[1] The best survey of this difficult problem is by Theodor Ludwig, *Die deutschen Reichsstände in Elsass und der Ausbruch der Revolutionskriege*, 1898. Cp. Wille, *August Graf von Limburg-Stirum, Fürstbischof von Speier*.

would never have caused war ; and the fuse which provoked the explosion was the *Émigration*. France entertained no objection to the representatives of the old régime seeking shelter in the pleasant cities of the Rhineland ; but she could not be expected to watch with unconcern the feverish efforts of Artois and Calonne to mobilise the armies of Europe against the Revolution. Louis XVI, who never thought of foreign intervention till he had been compelled to accept the Civil Constitution of the Church, warned Leopold not to aid and abet their violent plans. The advice agreed with the temperament and opinions of the Emperor, who desired a limited monarchy for France on the lines of Mirabeau. Frederick William, on the other hand, prompted by Bischoffswerder, lent a ready ear to the pleadings of Artois, who assured him that all good Frenchmen were sighing for the arrival of foreign bayonets. An attempt to reconcile the Prussian and Austrian standpoints was made in the Declaration of Pillnitz, which, though described by Mallet du Pan as an ' august comedy,' and falling far short of the Émigré demand for immediate hostilities, embodied a conditional threat, and placed a weapon in the hands of the revolutionary leaders whose minds were beginning to turn in the direction of war.

The policy of Austria under Leopold and Kaunitz was steadily directed towards neutrality. ' From several parts of the Empire,' wrote the old Chancellor early in 1791, ' the Court has been warned of the presence of French emissaries who try to stir the subjects of the governments to revolt ' ; [1] but in spite of provocation, he held on his way. The Pillnitz Manifesto breathed an Austrian rather than a Prussian spirit ; and the Austrian Minister told Kaunitz that it was ' only the incredible violence and importunity of Artois ' that caused the issue of a Declaration at all. The acceptance of the Constitution of 1791 by Louis XVI was hailed with lively satisfaction in Vienna, where Kaunitz expressed his belief that the King was a free agent. In November the Chancellor jotted down some reassuring reflections on the situation. ' The new Constitution renders France far less dangerous than she was under the old régime. If it is a bad one, she will be the only sufferer. The pretended danger of the possible effects of the evil example of the French on other peoples is nothing but a nightmare. Nothing is more unsubstantial than the pretended interest of all the Powers in co-operating for the more or less wholesale destruction of the new French Constitution. The enterprise would be unjust, the success doubtful, the risks and costs incalculable. The King and

[1] Vivenot, *Quellen zur Geschichte der deutschen Kaiserpolitik Oesterreichs*, i. 104, 236, 284–6, 290–303.

BB

his advisers are the best judges of the situation. The restoration of the *ancien régime* is an illusion.' Not that Kaunitz had any belief in the principles of 1789 ; for undated fragments dictated in 1791-2 contain hostile comments on each separate article of the ' Declarations of the Rights of Man.' He was equally convinced that the existing Constitution could not endure; and that the restoration of the old régime was impossible.

Despite the moderation of the Emperor and his experienced adviser, Europe drifted steadily towards war during the autumn and winter of 1791. After Varennes Frederick William's zeal to rescue the Royal Family from danger, and to slay the hydra of revolution, grew to fever-heat. Count Ségur was sent to Berlin to avert war ; but the mission was condemned in advance.[1] ' Bischoffswerder read me a dispatch from Strassburg,' reported the Austrian Ambassador to Kaunitz on January 14, 1792, 'to the effect that Ségur had met several Jacobins there and arranged to apply all methods of propaganda to seduce people here. So he will be watched.'[2] Meanwhile the numbers of armed Émigrés on the Rhine continued to grow. The first signal of the approaching conflict was trumpeted forth when in the last days of the year France threatened the Elector of Trier with war, unless he dispersed the Émigrés ; and the Emperor rejoined that he would defend the Elector if he was attacked, adding some peremptory words on French propaganda. France had expected to be attacked long before Europe determined to attack her, and she became in consequence irritable and suspicious.

To many of the ardent idealists who made and led the Revolution it was not merely a social and political reform, but a universal religion which it was the mission of France to impose on the world. Armed propaganda, however, formed no part of her intellectual outfit in the first two years of the crisis. The decree of the Constituent Assembly dealing with the power over war and peace, passed on May 22, 1790, solemnly declared that ' the French nation renounces wars of conquest and will never employ its forces against the liberty of any people.' The article was inserted in the Constitution of 1791 ; but as the prospect of a war about concrete issues took shape, the orators and journalists began to speculate on the chance of other peoples rising against their rulers. ' It is a crusade of universal liberty,' cried Brissot in the Jacobin Club at the end of the year. ' Every soldier will say to his enemy : Brother, I do not come to cut your throat, but to release you from the yoke under which you groan. Like you, I was a slave. I have armed myself, the tyrant has disappeared, and now I am free,

---

[1] See Ségur, *Esquisses*, pp. 246-51.   [2] Vivenot, *Quellen*, i. 323.

and you can be, too.' In vain did Robespierre object that nobody loved armed missionaries. 'The first counsel of nature and prudence is to repel them as enemies. The invasion of Germany would revive the memory of the devastation of the Palatinate and subsequent struggles rather than sow constitutional ideas.' But these wise counsels fell on unheeding ears. The Girondins assumed power in the spring of 1792, and promptly declared war against Austria.[1]

II

When war was declared by France, Kaunitz remained as critical as ever. In a dispatch to Reuss he denounced the French princes and the Émigrés as the foes both of Louis XVI and the Powers.[2] 'They claim that the princes and their counsellors should be the directors of the whole operation, putting the Émigrés at the head of every enterprise, and informing the French nation in advance that the Emperor and the King of Prussia intend the annihilation of the new Constitution and an integral restoration of the ancient forms of monarchy. As it is an axiom that of a hundred thousand people in France perhaps not one would tolerate such a programme, and equally notorious that the princes—above all, Calonne and many of the Émigrés—are the object of universal detestation, such a policy would unify virtually the whole nation.' But the cautious old Chancellor's day was over, and in the summer the young Emperor Francis parted with the trusted adviser of his father and his grandmother.

The outbreak of hostilities aroused equally little enthusiasm in

---

[1] The responsibility for the Great War has been passionately debated for a century. While the older French writers attributed the outbreak to the threats of the Powers, historians of other lands, following Sybel, have usually traced it to the chauvinism of the Girondins. Their responsibility is admitted by Sorel, who delivers judgment in a single pregnant sentence. 'It was a war of France to extend her frontiers, and of Europe to prevent her.' Ranke discovered the cause rather in circumstances than individuals. Politicians, he declares in his dispassionate work, *Ursprung u. Beginn der Revolutionskriege*, sought peace ; the universal antagonism pointed to war. Recent writers differ no less than those of an earlier generation. Ranke's view has been supported by Glagau and combated by Wahl, who repeats Sybel's contention—that it was not an inevitable war of principles, but an enterprise started by certain individuals for definite and practical ends. Heidrich, on the other hand (*Preussen im Kampfe gegen die F. R.*), contends that France merely anticipated the coming attack, like Frederick the Great in 1756, and that she was justified by Austria's refusal to discontinue military preparations and by Prussia's obvious wish for war. The evidence is carefully sifted by Clapham, *The Causes of the War of 1792*.

[2] Vivenot, *Quellen*, vol. ii. May 22.

Prussia. 'Though I cannot blame the princes for fearing the French propaganda,' writes Boyen in his 'Memoirs,' 'it was a great pity that Austria, by the selfish cries of the Émigrés, which found a ready response among the Viennese nobility, succeeded in dragging Prussia into a war of principles against France. To restore all the evil customs which the Revolution had abolished, as they declared their intention of doing, was an outrage on reason and morality: indeed, indirectly a reproach to Prussia, whose great kings had gradually abolished many of the abuses from which the French desired to free themselves. The nation thought the war unnecessary, and only some of the officers were glad for professional reasons.'[1] 'The event was expected,' wrote Morton Eden to Lord Grenville from Berlin.[2] 'Certain it is that the enterprise is very unpopular and even reprobated. The operations of the campaign are talked of by those in place as likely to be very trifling and of short duration; but the undertaking continues to be very unpopular, and it is even maintained that it would be wiser to draw a cordon, as in the time of the plague, to prevent the spirit of innovation from entering the country, than to send so many men out to imbibe its pernicious principles.' Alois Hofmann bitterly complained of the indifference shown in Germany; and Bailleu decided that the only man in all Prussia whose heart was in the struggle was the King.

A different picture is drawn of political opinion by Massenbach but not of the military anticipations. 'One can imagine the uncontrolled joy of many, almost all, at the prospect of war. To Paris! one heard people cry. It was to be like a hunting-party— Rossbach over again.' Bischoffswerder remarked to Massenbach in May: 'Do not buy too many horses. The farce will not last long. The liberty imposture is burning itself out in Paris. We shall be back in the autumn.' Brunswick, who was better informed, remarked to Massenbach that it would not be so easy as it had been in Holland;[3] and other warning voices were not lacking. 'The French soldiers of liberty will perhaps be not less formidable than those of America,' wrote Archenholtz. 'They may win victories, and even conquer German provinces. The Prussians will not reach Paris.' Even the admonitions of the Minister of Finance were contemptuously brushed aside. 'It is incredible how the check of the French patriots has excited the military spirit here,' wrote the French envoy, Vicomte de Caraman, from Berlin on May 8. 'The tone of the Court has changed amazingly, and to-day it speaks in tones of the most ardent determination. Struensee, an old friend

[1] *Erinnerungen*, i. 112–13.
[2] Clapham, *The Causes of the War of* 1792, Appendix iii.
[3] Massenbach, *Memoiren*, i. 22, 25–6.

of Mirabeau, is displeased at all that is going on. He wished to raise objections and present calculations, but was told to make provision and supply money and to keep his scruples to himself.' [1] His employers, who regarded the French Revolution as merely the latest of the periodical spasms with which the history of modern Europe was filled, failed to realise that in fighting against the restoration of the hated feudal régime, and the subjection of their country to foreign arms, France was likely to prove unconquerable.

The defeat and retreat of the Allied troops in the Valmy campaign, following on the French *débâcle* in Belgium, created surprise and excitement in Germany. The troops were impressed by their experiences, and Prussian officers learned to admire the energy of the Republic which they had despised. 'The rage of liberty,' prophesied Dumouriez, 'will seize all the mercenaries who attack us'; and it was widely feared that the forecast would be fulfilled. Prince Reuss reported to Vienna that the Prussian army was growing democratic. The Prince of Nassau-Siegen remarked to the King of Prussia: 'Your Majesty does not know what your officers say in favour of the rebels, whom they call their friends. The number of democrats is great.' The King, however, was well aware of it; for he confessed to Breteuil, 'I know all the democrats talk against me.' The whole army talked politics, and the campaign of 1792 strengthened the Republic and brought Louis XVI to the scaffold.[2] 'The increased boldness of our Republicans since the Duke of Brunswick's retreat is very striking,' wrote Grenville to Auckland in November.[3] 'The same spirit is attempting to be raised in Berlin. I know this train is directed from Hamburg by the French agent there. I wish to put the Prussian Government on their guard and to tell them that if they could get at his papers they would probably get possession of the whole conspiracy, with the names of those concerned at Berlin, some of whom are stated to be in the palaces.' But there seemed little hope of energy or wisdom from the Court. 'Bischoffswerder, Haugwitz, and Lucchesini, with their female appendices,' wrote Eden to Auckland, 'have the whole sway, and to a dismal state they have reduced the country.'[4]

The contrast between the victorious energy of the young Republic and the fumbling of the old dynasties was not lost on observant minds in Germany. 'They behave in such a way,' wrote Vincke, then a student at Marburg, in reference to Custine's march to the Rhine, 'that they leave only friends, not enemies, of

[1] *Corresp. de Fersen*, ii. 269–71.
[2] See Chuquet, *Guerres de la Révolution*, iii. 218–21.
[3] *Fortescue MSS.*, ii. 332.   [4] *Ib.*, ii. 347.

their cause wherever they pass. That will not produce the best effect in Germany. In Hildesheim a peasant recently calculated how much they would save by exchanging princes and chapters for a simpler government. The Hessian in Cassel sings *Ça ira*. The Hanoverian wears a red cap, and cries, Long live the Jacobins and the French nation! The worst of it is that people no longer distinguish between good and bad princes. And now our brave countrymen return vanquished from the land of liberty! Oh, the unhappy war, and the crazy people who egged on our good, weak King to shoulder the burden! How much better it would be to unite with the children of Liberty than this unhappy bond with Austria!'[1]

The failure of the campaign of 1792 made Austria eager to secure the assistance of the Empire; but it was no easy task. 'The Austrians hate everybody devoted to the French Republic,' wrote a French agent in November. 'The partisans of the Court of Vienna have taken care to represent to the Diet everything that has happened in France in a false light. They have even forbidden it the French papers, so that none of the Ministers can obtain them by the ordinary post. The Austrians fear that if I pitch my tent at Regensburg, I should easily open the eyes of most of the Ministers, and even encourage the opposition, which cannot fail to take umbrage at the monstrous coalition of the two Courts. The discontent is very great in Regensburg, and opinion is embittered against them and their despotism. This unpopularity of the Allied Courts seems to me pretty general throughout the Empire, especially in the Free Cities, where the democratic party is everywhere preponderant.'[2]

A further difficulty with which the Allies had to cope was the seductive influence of French propaganda. On November 19, 1792, the celebrated decree was issued which reverberated throughout Europe. 'The Convention declares in the name of the French nation that it will accord fraternity and help to all peoples who wish to recover their liberty, and charges the executive power to order the Generals to carry succour to those peoples and to defend citizens who have been or may be persecuted for the cause of Liberty.' The commanders were ordered to print and proclaim the decree in the languages of all the countries entered by the Republican armies. The provocative manifesto was cancelled in the following spring, when Danton assumed control of foreign affairs; but it had already exerted a considerable influence on the Rhineland. To counteract foreign propaganda and sectional jealousies, the Ministers of Austria and Prussia issued an appeal to German patriotism in

[1] Bodelschwingh, *Vincke's Leben*, i. 44–50.
[2] *Papiers de Barthélemy*, i. 40.

February 1793. ' The Fatherland is in danger. The Constitution, religion, property, tranquillity—all are menaced by near ruin. The bloody projects of the French are unveiled. The sweet names of Liberty and Equality cannot hide the abyss which opens under our feet ; and this year, unless we rally all our forces, will be the last in which we shall be able to embrace our children, dwell in our houses, or enjoy the consolations of religion. True enough, the first operations of the French Revolution naturally exerted general approbation. Every friend of humanity watched with interest the efforts of a people bent under the weight of old abuses, groaning under enormous taxes. What a touching spectacle to see a good King, surrounded by the wisest men, redressing every abuse ! But what grief when this happy expectation was disappointed ! When the Emperor raised his voice against the violation of the rights of German princes, the French declared war.' The appeal concludes with an exhortation to all who care for the Fatherland in danger to make every sacrifice to save it. The Diet declared war, and issued a decree against clubs, papers, and preachers of French ideas. The Emperor confirmed the decree, and launched a condemnation of ' the dangerous principles of the Revolution, spread by conscienceless philosophers.' [1]

The outbreak of war failed to produce unity or resolution in the Empire. ' I am told,' wrote a French agent, ' that the King of Prussia, while announcing the necessity of his presence to settle affairs in Poland, went direct to Berlin on hearing that a conspiracy was on foot, of which the centre was the French colony, stirred up by the Jacobins of Paris and their emissaries. The King was convinced of its reality, and seized Hertzberg and Bischoffswerder as suspects. This requires confirmation ; but everything suggests that if there are plans of insurrection their explosion should come soon in Prussia, where minds are more disposed to it and philosophy has made more progress than in Austria.' [2] ' We must make the light penetrate into Germany in all possible ways,' wrote Bacher, the secretary of the Embassy in Switzerland, ' and especially among the military.[3] The French Government would have vastly increased the number of its adherents beyond the Rhine if it had adopted my proposal to print in small *format*, and in Gothic characters, a translation of the best books on the Revolution. This well-chosen collection would above all have exerted a powerful influence on the minds of the German women, who are naturally indolent, and on the young officers who, like youth everywhere, ardently seize on

---

[1] See Aulard, *La Diplomatie du Premier Comité de Salut Public*, in his *Études et Leçons*, vol. iii.

[2] *Papiers de Barthélemy*, iii. 216.   [3] *Ib.*, iv. 351-4.

democracy.   The war against France has no longer any charm for
the German soldier.   The partisans of the French Revolution
increase daily, and one can reckon two-thirds of the population as
patriots.   The watchword of the French, Perish the tyrants ! makes
the Courts tremble.   No prince can now count on the attachment
of his people.'   Though these reports were over-sanguine, they were
not wholly without foundation.   It was a sign of the times that at
this moment the clergy and nobility of Paderborn surrendered their
immunity from taxation.

A far more important factor than French propaganda in the
weakening of the Allies was the friction between Berlin and Vienna.
The old rivalry, concealed for a time between common professions
of anti-revolutionary fervour, burst out afresh when the failure
of the campaign of 1792, and rival ambitions in Poland, led to mutual
recriminations.   Moreover, the Prussian Court was a poor advertisement of the cause of monarchy and religion.   Successive British
Ministers to Berlin spoke with something like loathing of their task.
' From the wretched and dirty intrigues that pervade this Court,'
wrote Sir Morton Eden to Grenville, ' the transaction of all business
becomes every day more difficult.[1]   The most able of the Ministers
have no weight but through the favourite (Bischoffswerder), the
sect of Illuminés, or the tribe of mistresses, past and present.   There
are not fewer intrigues going on in this Court than in those of the
East.   Your Lordship will see the difficulties and disgust that must
often attend a foreign Minister's situation.   The Sovereign is
immersed in pleasure, and becomes every day more adverse to
business.'   Equally lurid descriptions were sent home by the
experienced Malmesbury.[2]   ' The inside of this Court is really a
fit subject only for a private letter.'   It was distrust of the King,
of whom George III spoke uneasily as an Illuminé, and his advisers
that made the British Government less willing to supply funds for
the prosecution of the war.   On April 5, 1794, Malmesbury reported
to Grenville a conversation with Haugwitz.   ' His professions of
faith are as right as possible, particularly in his abhorrence of the
principles and conduct of the French.   He tells me General Kalkreuth
is an unprincipled character and a rank Jacobin.'   But Malmesbury
saw ' Jacobins ' everywhere.   ' Many Prussian officers have decided
Jacobin leanings,' he added.   ' There is a strong taint of democracy
among officers and men, and a dislike to the cause for which they
ought to be fighting.'   He discovered that French opinions had
made considerable progress in Germany—' not those of to-day but
of 1789'—and attributed it largely to the professors.   Grimm, on

[1] *Fortescue MSS.*, ii. 273.
[2] Malmesbury, *Diaries and Correspondence*, iii. 42–5, 123, 137–9.

the other hand, professed to find an increase of zeal in the army.[1]
' At the end of 1792 and 1793,' he wrote to Catherine, ' the majority
of officers were democrats, and almost the whole of the army openly
attacked the war ; but at the beginning of 1794, when the Prussian
Ministers spoke of the necessity of peace, the whole army declares
for a continuation of the war against a fierce and powerful enemy.'
But Grimm, buried alive in quiet Gotha, was not in close touch with
the body he described, and his opinion was not shared by those who
were.

The war had never been popular, and its lack of success rendered
opinion ever more critical.[2] ' Egoism and avarice,' declares Sorel
with just severity, ' dominated all the designs of Europe. In default
of ideas and principles, it could only reduce the Revolution by
force ; and force was lacking.' ' Without the systematic procrastination of the Austrians,' confessed General Thiébault, ' we should have
been ruined a hundred times. They alone saved us in giving us
time to make soldiers, officers, and generals.' Among continental
statesmen and soldiers Catherine and Suvorof alone possessed the
ability and determination needed for a successful war ; but it was
the policy of Russia to involve her rivals in a costly struggle in the
west of Europe and thereby secure herself elbow room in the East.
' It is hardly to be imagined,' wrote Walpole, the British Minister
at Munich, in 1794, ' that the complex and languid body of the
Empire, which could not be brought into action last year by the
joint efforts of the two preponderant Powers of Austria and Prussia,
should be capable of exertion now when the Powers have different
views and drag different ways.' The fall of Robespierre strengthened
the peace party in Prussia, where Hardenberg had already drawn
up a memorandum advising his master to recognise the Republic
and prepare for peace, since the restoration of the Monarchy was
impossible. As France could not be compelled to pay indemnities,
Prussia might recoup herself by the secularisation of ecclesiastical
principalities. When the King, whose health was broken and whose
treasury was empty, reluctantly consented to treat with the regicides,
negotiations had already begun without his knowledge. The
French negotiator was Barthélemy, a man of high character and
moderate views, who detested the Terror and the Terrorists ; and
he was assisted by Bacher, an Alsatian, who numbered Prince Henry
and other prominent Germans among his friends. Wöllner, who
had never approved the war, now brought his influence to bear, and

---

[1] *Lettres*, p. 553.
[2] Even the pious Heynitz, who hated the French even more fiercely than
his friend Stein, urged the King and the Government to make peace in 1794.
See Steinecke, *Heynitz*, in *Forsch. zur Brand. u. Preuss. Geschichte*, vol. xv.

in October besought the King ' to follow the wish of the whole nation
and give up the unhappy French business.' The only influential
voice raised against peace was that of Prince Louis Ferdinand, who
expressed his readiness to lead the army if it refused to sheathe the
sword. The last to be converted was the King himself. As he
lay dying, two years after the peace, he whispered to Haugwitz, ' I
ought never to have made war against France.' [1] Beyond the
boundaries of Prussia the withdrawal naturally aroused a good
deal of angry criticism. ' The sheep are told to leave the shepherds,'
cried Johannes Müller, ' and the dogs are ordered to live at peace
with the wolves.'

III

The principal Prussian author of the Peace of Basle and the leader
of the Francophil party before, during, and after the Revolution,
was Prince Henry, the eldest surviving brother of Frederick the
Great.[2] The Prince won fame in the Seven Years' War only second
to the King, who generously declared that he alone of his generals
had never made a mistake. A true son of the Aufklärung, Henry
was a lover of literature no less than an ardent politician. The
first partition of Poland was discussed on his visit to Catherine the
Great, with whom he maintained a lively correspondence till the
Revolution drove them into opposite camps. His palace at Rheinsberg, the scene of the happiest years of Frederick, was visited by
all travellers of distinction ; and French guests were particularly
welcome. He paid his first visit to Paris in 1782, and in 1787
informed his French friends that he would probably settle in France.
Louis XVI sent him word that he would be welcome ; but he
contented himself with a long visit during the winter preceding the
outbreak of the Revolution. He foresaw the crisis, which, he
believed, would produce a good constitution and render France
the greatest of monarchies. He was royally fêted, and told Ségur
that he was struck by the knowledge, the sense, and the goodness
of the King.[3] The diplomatist in return described the distinguished
visitor as ' a valiant warrior, a clever general, a profound politician,
a friend of justice, of science and art, a protector of the weak, and

---

[1] See Ranke, *Hardenberg*, i. 399. The controversy has raged ever since.
Häusser and Sybel discovered the villain of the piece in Thugut, who was
stoutly defended by Vivenot, Hüffer, and Zeissberg. Ranke and Sorel,
Bailleu and Heigel, working in a calmer atmosphere, have analysed the
complex factors which rendered the partnership a failure.

[2] See Krauel, *Prinz Heinrich als Politiker* ; and Krauel, ' *Prinz Heinrich in
Rheinsberg*,' *Hohenzollern-Jahrbuch*, vi. 12–37.

[3] Ségur, *Mémoires*, ii. 140–8.

a friend of the unfortunate.' Mirabeau, on the other hand, who had met him in Berlin, drew a very different picture. ' His Gallomania served us badly. He is false. Everything is small in his soul, though his mind is gigantic.' But the author of the ' Secret Letters ' dipped his pen in gall, and no malefactor could be hung on his unsupported testimony.

The Prince welcomed the upheaval, and exerted himself to keep his country from spoiling the game. The King visited his uncle at Rheinsberg, and received the advice to follow the example of the Great Elector by welcoming the Émigrés and making use of their talents. ' I only wish,' wrote the host, ' that this King, who has such a splendid heart, was always surrounded by honourable people, for then our country would be the paradise of the world.' Frederick William, however, soon developed violent hostility to the Revolution ; and the Prince, who once more found himself wholly without influence, poured out his angry disappointment in letters to Grimm. He spoke bitterly of the chauvinism of ' King ' Bischoffswerder and the obscurantism of ' King ' Wöllner. Every French emissary, official or unofficial, found a welcome at Rheinsberg, which became the focus of opposition to the idea of war. Not that the Prince watched events in Paris with uncritical eyes. ' I confess that I abhor the Jacobin party,' he wrote in April 1792 to his brother Ferdinand, ' and I would give the world to see them annihilated. France is in a horrible condition. If I thought force would be useful, I would support it ; but I am convinced that those who, under those circumstances, would steer the ship, would do more harm than good.' Brissot he denounced as a ' terrible, turbulent, violent man.' Nor was he a blind admirer of England. ' I have never suffered from Anglomania. I esteem their Constitution, and the philosophers, historians, and *beaux-esprits* which they have given to Europe ; but it is the most boastful and perfidious of nations.' In spite of these views he was generally regarded as a democrat and a Jacobin, and the King suspected everybody who did not echo his crusading fervour. Among his critics was Catherine the Great, who gave vent to her angry contempt for her old friend in her letters to Grimm.[1] ' As you are going to Karlsbad,' she wrote in June 1792, ' you will doubtless see Prince Henry, and you must tell me if it is true that he has become a fiery democrat.' Two months later she thanked her ' fag ' for his report, adding that she knew the Prince had been threatened during the past winter with imprisonment at Spandau for his seditious language. This was, of course, mere gossip ; but his movements were closely observed. When war was decided, he went to Karlsbad to escape shadowing ;

[1] *Lettres à Grimm*, p. 569.

but Bischoffswerder warned the Austrian Government to keep a sharp lookout on him.

The Prince foretold that the invasion would fail, and that the French people would never welcome the troops. ' I have a very bad opinion of the prospects of the campaign,' he wrote in the autumn. ' The Manifestoes have spoilt everything.' [1] After the disastrous retreat he sent a memorandum to the King, recalling his warning and urging him to retrace his steps. ' These people,' he declared bitterly at a later stage, ' can neither conduct war nor make peace.' While the fall of Robespierre seemed to some observers the signal for a monarchical restoration, the Prince saw in it rather the hatred of rule by a single person. He had at first looked for a constitutional monarchy, but he now felt the Republic to be safe for the present. He remarked how the republican spirit gives the mind a certain power of soaring, whereas in autocracy the vanity of one individual hinders the development of the powers of the masses. Such democratic talk increased his unpopularity in Court circles, and even Brunswick was horrified to hear such doctrines from the lips of a prince. The Duchess of York, a daughter of the King of Prussia, complained that Rheinsberg, from the guests to the lowest menial, was nothing but a Jacobin club, and she wondered how the King could tolerate such a coterie in his dominions. The charge was unfounded, for the kind-hearted and hospitable Prince welcomed Émigrés no less than Republicans to his beautiful home ; and none of his visitors gave him more pleasure than Madame de Sabran, accompanied as usual by the witty Boufflers.

The Prince boldly endeavoured to extricate his country from the war, and in 1794 co-operated with Struensee and the peace party. ' It was begun in folly and has been conducted in folly,' he remarked to Massenbach early in 1795. ' It is contrary to the interest of our country, and must be stopped. We have other enemies than the French. Peace is assured. I have initiated it.' [2] He corresponded with Bacher, secretary of the French Legation in Basle, who described him as the born defender of all Frenchmen. The war had never been popular, and no single Prussian did so much to end it. He had an exalted opinion of his abilities, military and diplomatic, and he boasted that in Brunswick's place he could have settled things by negotiations with France and have saved the King. Though his desire to act as Prussian plenipotentiary was not fulfilled, the year of the Treaty of Basle registered the high-water mark of his influence and activity.

Catherine's letters to Grimm keep up a lively artillery fire against

[1] H. v. Donnersmarck, *Briefe der Brüder Friedrich des Grössen*, p. 58.
[2] Massenbach, *Memoiren*, ii. 92.

her old friend.[1] She thanks her correspondent for the fragments of talk at Rheinsberg. 'Where does he want to go ? To America ? I maintain, in opposition to the Prince, that nothing but unlimited power will please the French people. And, besides, a republic always ends in monarchy. He says he has serious tasks. I don't believe it. He is like the *petit-maître* who, to make people think he has a rendezvous, leaves the company and shuts himself up at home.' A few days later, on the arrival of the news of the Peace of Basle, the Empress takes a graver view of the errant Prince's power and achievements. 'The great Henri has pushed the King into breaking his treaties with the Emperor, England, and myself. He hates his nephew cordially. If he had cared a little bit for him, he would never have driven him into courses so disastrous and dishonourable.' She lent credence to the ridiculous rumour that he was about to ascend the French throne. 'If he becomes King of France in reward for the disgraceful peace, one must hope that if he is not guillotined he will execute justice on the enemies of his cause.' 'Some people say the regicides are planning to make Prince Henry regent to Louis XVII, when they restore him,' she wrote two months later. 'If so, I wager he will be guillotined in less than six months.' In September she is equally spiteful and still more mendacious. 'As for the great little Henri, he got the peace signed with the sole object of becoming tutor to Louis XVII, and, after his death, King of France. That is what Madame de Sabran and the Chevalier de Boufflers nursed him for in the name of the constitutionalists. What a joke ! the great peacemaker believes that I forbade you to go to Rheinsberg, and that I treat him as a monster. Well, this great little man is mistaken. I leave him his glory, and I laugh at his insults. I suppose he ranks me with Robespierre. Everybody, including the Prussian Minister, says that he has integrally adopted the system and conduct of Philippe Égalité, of infamous memory.' Henceforth she speaks of the 'Court of Citoyen Henri.' Shortly before her death she wrote, 'This Citoyen is always mounted on stilts.' It was a sad ending to an old and once valued friendship.

Shortly after the Treaty of Basle restored diplomatic relations, Caillard, the Ambassador of the Republic, paid one of his first visits to Prince Henry.[2] 'I found him in Berlin as we saw him in Paris—gentle, affable, witty, always displaying the most marked leaning towards France and the French, in fact, just what we should

---

[1] *Lettres à Grimm*, pp. 623–4, 626, 635, 637, 640, 646, 652, 660, 674.

[2] Bailleu, *Preussen u. Frankreich*, i. 430, 454–6. Cp. Sir George Jackson, *Diaries and Letters*, i. 279 (1805) : ' Prince Ferdinand has been throughout a warm admirer of the French Revolution.'

wish ; for the Revolution has in no way altered his sentiments in regard to us. He told me how distressed he had been at this unfortunate war, and how glad he was to have contributed to the restoration of peace. He appears to be as keen on our successes as we are. To-day I was presented to Prince Ferdinand. He has not the same vivacity or enthusiasm for the French nation, but at bottom his sentiments seemed to me identical.' After helping to make peace, however, Prince Henry never again enjoyed political influence. ' The vanity of the uncle and the vanity of the nephew,' reported Caillard in 1797, ' are in conflict. The Prince is rightly indignant at not being consulted, and the King would be in despair if people were to think he needed the Prince. The Crown Prince esteems him, but he has no power.' Three days later he describes a further visit. ' He is a real friend, and I did not fail to stimulate his sentiments by everything flattering to his self-esteem—a chord which vibrates powerfully in his ear and heart. He had told the King that the France he loved was the France of old : that of to-day being only a foreign Power. It was, therefore, no longer by a personal sentiment that he favoured it, but in the interests of Prussia.' A less flattering picture was naturally drawn by Prince Reuss, the Austrian Ambassador.[1] ' Prince Henry is always active, and never doing anything ; always occupied in trying to obtain recognition, and always condemned to the same nullity by the Sovereign and his Ministers, whom he overwhelms with memoranda which nobody reads.' The verdict of a later and more distinguished emissary of the Republic was the same as that of Caillard. ' I admired the clarity of his thought and the purity of his conversation,' reported Sieyès after his first interviews with the old man. ' As for his opinions, I felt that I was talking to a Frenchman. But, as you are aware, he has no influence.'

Soon after the termination of the war Lord Elgin informed Grenville of a conversation in which Struensee, the Minister of Finance, declared that peace had been inevitable, being founded on the necessities of the Treasury, and that the general temper of the army was against the war. Inevitable or not, the peace was certainly popular. An interesting, if somewhat caustic, picture of opinion is drawn in the dispatches of Caillard.[2] ' When I arrived, I received an extraordinarily warm welcome. I have not found a man who did not pretend that he had disapproved the war from the first ! Here, as elsewhere, nobody will confess his faults ; but the fact is that, with the exception of Prince Henry and perhaps General Möllendorf, everybody in Berlin shared more or less in the frenzy of the Coalition. Above all, the King was the determined

---

[1] Bailleu, *Preussen u. Frankreich*, i. 535.   [2] *Ib.*, i. 430–1.

enemy of the French Revolution. Peace was not made for love of France ; but, in my judgment, the nation, the Ministry, and all the princes, except the King, are now entirely for us. They pardon us our revolution, for it is over. They wish us well—success abroad and tranquillity at home.'

Liberal views were not unknown in the army. In December 1794 there appeared at Frankfurt a brochure, ' Europe and Peace,' with the name of Sieyès on the title-page, but of which Knesebeck confessed the authorship in response to an inquiring friend.[1] ' In the summer of 1793 I was employed to sound imprisoned officers on French views of peace. I heard from Hardenberg that Prussia desired it, and I wrote a memorandum in its favour, which was the foundation of my pamphlet. It was wrong to use the name of Sieyès, but I sought to enter into his mind. I also wrote two essays, " How to avoid violent Revolutions," and " Is Perpetual Peace compatible with human failings ?" These show that, even if I think republicanism the best form of government, I condemn violence and wish the goal to be reached by gradual enlightenment. The first essay maintained that revolutions were not necessarily evil, since those of Jesus Christ and Luther were confessedly beneficial. It is only violence that is bad ; and violence must be obviated by timely reforms. The nobles must share the burdens of the State, and the King be the first citizen under the laws. The only two classes are the educated and the uneducated. If equality is a chimaera, so is pride of birth. In most States the government is a century behind its citizens. Institutions must change as the youth becomes a man. Happy is the State where the ring is enlarged in time before it is burst by the tree.'

The attitude of France was now at least outwardly correct. ' There is no intention of stirring up the peoples of Germany,' reported Sandoz-Rollin from Paris, January 1797.[2] ' Here is a proof. An emissary from the districts on the right bank of the Rhine has presented a memorial with fifteen hundred signatures, asking the Directory, despite the treaties with Württemberg and Baden, to protect and guarantee the insurrection and independence of those peoples. The emissary was dismissed and told that the Republic, faithful to its treaties, would never listen to such proposals.' The death of Frederick William II in 1797 improved relations by removing the main author of the war. Prince Reuss at once reported to Vienna the new King's ' aversion to the French of all shades and his cordial hatred of the democrats '[3] ; but this

---

[1] See Lehmann, *Aus dem Leben Knesebecks, Preussiche Jahrbücher*, vol. xxxiv.

[2] Bailleu, *Preussen u. Frankreich*, i. 108.   [3] *Ib.*, i. 536.

view was not shared by the men who knew him best. His abilities were mediocre ; but he was no implacable opponent of the spirit of the age. He had imbibed a slight tincture of liberalism from Suarez's private lectures ; and he recorded his ideas in some notes written shortly before his accession, which reveal a certain hospitality towards reforming ideas.[1] ' Whole sections,' comments Lehmann, ' read like the well-meaning wishes of a capable petty bourgeois who has become rich, who will know nothing of the privilege of birth, and will guard himself against the temptations of wealth and power.' ' The Thoughts on the Art of Government ' begin with a eulogy of peace. ' The greatest happiness of a land consists in a prolonged peace ; and therefore our policy is to observe this principle so long as our neighbours do not attack us.' Non-intervention in French affairs is not enough ; and the section on ' The Chief Qualities of a Ruler ' shows that the writer was alive to the lessons of recent history. ' A sound understanding, correct judgment, and the strictest love of justice are essential. No good government can exist when the ruler does not possess them, or makes himself contemptible by laziness, vice, or failings. Such a one does not deserve to rule, and it is therefore no wonder when at last his oppressed subjects, tired of such a government, combine to procure themselves a better. The French Revolution affords a terrible object-lesson to all bad rulers who are not there, like good princes, for the good of their land, but suck its blood like leeches and waste the money of their subjects in sensual pleasures.'

The young King inherited Haugwitz and the policy of neutrality from his father, and nothing could turn him from his convictions. The Directory, anxious for an alliance with Prussia as a means to enforce peace with Germany and Austria, dispatched Sieyès on a special mission to Berlin in 1798.[2] His ability made him a worthy representative of the Republic ; but the Prussian Court had not forgotten his regicide vote. The day after his audience he attended the coronation of the new sovereigns ; and his austere profile, his unpowdered hair, and the large tricolour scarf folded over his breast sent a shudder through the brilliant throng. ' A terrible omen,' wrote Marwitz bitterly in his Autobiography. ' Except the Ministers, who had no choice, nobody in the higher circles spoke to him. Yet some of the Berlin savants visited him to learn political wisdom.'[3] Haugwitz and his master proved immovable, and Sieyès reported that Prussia would do absolutely nothing for

---

[1] See Lehmann, ' *Ein Regierungsprogramm Fr. Wilhelm's* III.,' *Historische Zeitschrift*, lxi. 441–60.

[2] See Sorel, v. 328–38 ; and Clapham, *The Abbé Sieyès*, pp. 203–12.

[3] Meusel, *Marwitz*, i. 134–7.

peace. ' When one sees this country, so little known to Frenchmen in spite of the big and the little books of Mirabeau, one is astonished that it can have a following in France.'

Though Prussia resolutely declined an alliance with the Republic, the French leaven continued to ferment and political discussion never ceased. An Edict issued in 1798 prohibited all societies which involved obedience to unknown superiors, all secret societies—such as Freemasons—and finally all associations the object of which was to discuss changes in the Constitution or administration of the State. ' Civilised society,' wrote Hugh Elliot to Grenville from Dresden, ' has been exposed perhaps to greater danger from the extension of the tenets of impiety and anarchy through the medium of the press than even from the success of the French arms. The partisans of revolution and innovation have not been more active in any country than in Germany ; and, unfortunately, the German Universities have been the centre of a spirit of democracy, which has thence been diffused into the learned professions.' Gross attacks on England and her policy were in circulation. ' Anarchists, Deists, and Republicans vent their malice in German publications without encountering an opponent.'[1] To meet these attacks Marsh published his well-known defence of British policy, both in English and German dress.

The King's progressive attitude was shared by some of his advisers, whose mild liberalism aroused apprehension in circles which were not wholly reactionary. ' The Cabinet Councillors,' complained Gentz, ' approve everything which makes for innovation, and assure the King of the urgent need of robbing the nobility and clergy of their privileges and influence. Their continual talk of educational reform is only one of their methods of inaugurating their revolutionary system.' ' Liberty and enlightenment,' echoed Clausewitz, ' appeared to them their principal task, and they looked on themselves as tribunes of the people who had to hold in check the aristocratic leanings of the Ministers of noble birth.' These arrows were aimed at Mencken,[2] the grandfather of Bismarck, an experienced and enlightened official of the age of Frederick the Great, and still more at Beyme, for some years the most influential adviser of the King in home affairs. The latter, who had worked on the Code under Carmer and Suarez and was later to claim an honourable share in the foundation of the University of Berlin, was pronounced by Gentz an avowed friend and protector of all who strove for enlightenment and the reform of States ; and the middle-class Cabinetsrath was well aware of his unpopularity with the conservative nobles. Nor were Mencken and Beyme alone in the

[1] *Fortescue MSS.*, iv. 281–2.　　　[2] See Hüffer, *Mencken.*

royal counsels. In 1799 Otto, the French Minister, reported to Talleyrand a remarkable conversation with Struensee.[1] ' You have only the aristocrats against you,' remarked the Minister ; ' King and people are decidedly for France. The very useful revolution you have made from below upwards will be made slowly in Prussia from above. The King is democratic in his own way. He works unceasingly to reduce the privileges of the nobility. In a few years there will be no privileged class in Prussia.' A similar report was sent soon after by Duroc to the First Consul. ' People are very pleased about Brumaire. We have no one against us but the higher nobility. The King, his army, and the people love and esteem the French.' [2]

If there was but little ' love and esteem ' for the French, there was at any rate a certain leaven of liberalism among the younger generation of officials—especially those of East Prussia, who had sat at the feet of Kant and Kraus at Königsberg. ' The Wealth of Nations ' was hailed as a new gospel. ' I consecrated this morning to the reading of the divine Smith,' wrote the Westphalian Vincke in his diary in 1796, ' and I am resolved to begin the work of each day with a chapter.' Next to Zerboni and Held the most radical figure was that of Morgenbesser, who, like Schön, had been a pupil of Kant. His anonymous ' Contributions to a Republican Code,' published in 1798 at Königsberg, praised republicanism as the only constitution suited to human nature, the only guarantee against despotism and war, and the only means to unite the race in a single society. A republic cannot be created by revolution, but is best reached through a well-organised monarchy. Despite his anti-obscurantism and his extreme views on marriage and divorce, which procured the prohibition of the book by the censor at Vienna, the author was to render assistance to Stein and to rise to the position of President of the Judiciary at Königsberg. Prussia, in fact, was well supplied with capable and enlightened officials, and the mass of the people was not discontented. No nation, declared Vincke, was freer or better governed, and Clausewitz declared that the people were satisfied with their ' mild liberal government.' From such facts Meier has drawn the conclusion that the French Revolution passed over Prussia without leaving a trace, and that the débâcle was unconnected with internal conditions. The assertion is as one-sided as the rival contention that Prussia before Jena was rotten to the core. The reform movement, declares Hintze, was not a break with the past or a sudden importation of foreign models. But if the ideas were there, there was no power to translate them into action. Despite the friendliness to reform

[1] Bailleu, *Preussen u. Frankreich*, i. 505.   [2] *Ib.*, p. 514.

in the highest quarters, the only real advance achieved in the early years of the reign was the emancipation of the serfs on the royal domain. The kindly monarch desired to extend the measure to private estates ; but he lacked the resolution to sweep away vested interests and carry out far-reaching changes. A few minor administrative reforms were made ; but Prussia remained bound in her feudal fetters till the guns of Jena finally convinced her ruler that the world had changed since the death of Frederick, and that he must change with it.

CHAPTER XVIII

SAXONY, BRUNSWICK, AND HANOVER

I

THAT none of the larger German States was less affected by the Revolution than Saxony was mainly due to the personality of its beloved and respected ruler.[1] Frederick Augustus, named by his subjects ' the Just' and by Napoleon ' the truest of the true,' though not a statesman, was a man of unblemished character and excellent intentions. Destitute of ambition and conscious of his intellectual limitations, he desired to stand aloof from the maelstrom of politics and to rule over a peaceful and secluded Arcadia. His merits were widely recognised beyond the limits of the Electorate. Findlater, a Scotch peer, who travelled all over Europe and was acquainted with Catherine the Great, drew up a long memorandum on the civil condition of different States, which has been preserved in Grimm's correspondence with his Imperial patron. ' My journey to Dresden has confirmed my idea of its good government. The Prince occupies one of the first places among the sovereigns of his country by the wisdom of his administration. From the bankruptcy and devastation of 1763 it has risen once more to prosperity ; and the improvement has been achieved without fuss or fine phrases. His constant preoccupation with his subjects' welfare redeems his two faults (in his subjects' eyes)—his religion and his hunting. If he were. a Protestant, altars would be raised to him.'[2]

Though the surface of the waters was unruffled, there was ground enough for discontent in the villages, and the news of the Revolution brought a message of hope. A newspaper read by the peasants narrated the dramatic story of the sitting of August 4 and the

[1] See Böttiger, *Geschichte Sachsens*, vol. ii. ; Bonnefons, *Un Allié de Napoléon, Frédéric Auguste* ; Treitschke, *History of Germany*, iv. 289–329 ; Rühlmann, *Die Öffentliche Meinung in Sachsen*, 1806–1812.

[2] *Lettres de Grimm*, pp. 598-603.

abolition of feudal privileges, and produced the inevitable ferment.
' Apprehensions have been entertained here for some time,' reported
Morton Eden, the British Minister at Dresden,[1] on October 4,
' that the spirit of insurrection, which has appeared in different parts
of Germany since the late Revolution in France, should be communicated to the Electorate. Various reports have been propagated
of riots in different parts of the country ; but they have been found
to be without truth or greatly exaggerated. Though the great
burden of taxes falls upon the lower classes, and their services with
respect to game are rather hard, the mildness and moderation of
the Government in other respects make it unlikely that any serious
disturbances will happen.' The Minister was unduly sanguine ;
for in the following summer he filled several dispatches with details
of an alarming revolt. ' The peasantry have at different times
expressed much discontent at the quantity of game which infest
their fields,' he wrote in June. ' Formal representations were
made to the Elector, who ordered their number to be diminished,
but the evil is as great as ever. The high price of grain and a
severe drought have roused the people from ineffectual complaints
to active exertions in their own behalf. Last week two or three
villages near Dresden began to drive the deer and the wild boars
from their neighbourhood. Their example was immediately
followed by adjoining villages, and is extending itself throughout
the Electorate. However much their conduct is contrary to the
laws, in other respects the peasants behave themselves with great
prudence and moderation. A Commission of Inquiry has been
ordered. Orders have again been given to diminish the numbers
of the game, and the Elector has been advised to put a stop by
gentle means to complaints so very general, and in the present
time so peculiarly dangerous.'

A fortnight later his tone becomes graver. ' The spirit of
revolt that pervades so considerable a part of Europe seems to be
gaining further ground, and requires the most serious attention
of the Government in their country. Such appears to be the
spirit of the people that nothing but the total extermination of
these destructive animals, or shutting them up in parks, will satisfy
them. A deputation of twenty peasants arrived last week at
Pillnitz, the Elector's summer residence, to complain of some
grievances respecting the services, or _corvées_, required of them.
The Elector received their petition, and promised that their complaints should be inquired into.' It was soon obvious that a mere
promise of inquiry would not avert the gathering tempest. ' It is
probable that the peasants do not mean to stop till they have

[1] Dispatches in the Record Office, Saxony.

nearly extirpated that race of animals. The Government, thinking it dangerous to oppose, or even to check, a spirit so determined and so universal, has thought proper to pass unnoticed what has happened, and, by sending out the Elector's huntsmen to accompany the peasants in pursuit of the game, has given a countenance of legal authority to excesses which could not be prevented. Some of the *chasseurs* have been ill-treated by the peasants, who allege that they did not sufficiently exert themselves in killing the game ; and the Government has ordered parties of dragoons to be stationed in some of the villages for the purpose of preventing either party from hurting one another. A Commission is expected for inquiring into the losses from the game and to allow compensation for damages.'

For a moment the harvest claimed the attention of the incensed peasantry ; but the Government, blind to the signs of the times, let the situation drift. The peasants had struck first at the game ; but their other burdens were almost equally distasteful. ' The spirit of innovation continues,' reported the Minister on August 22. ' A general association is formed among the peasants to refuse the usual *corvées* and feudal services, since they allege that, the Electoral domains and the estates of the nobility being exempted from the greater part of the taxes, it is absolutely impossible for them, in the present time of scarcity, to afford the usual services and to maintain their family. In general their language is not that of common peasants, but appears to be dictated by persons of superior education. The Government seems to be more and more embarrassed and uncertain what steps to pursue. In Lusatia, and among the miners at Freiberg, alarming symptoms have appeared ; but it is principally in the circle of the mountains and in the neighbourhood of Meissen where the conduct of the people has been uncommonly riotous. Some of the most active and clamorous were seized at Meissen ; but their companions compelled the commanding officer to deliver them, and then proceeded to beat and abuse several gentlemen whose severity was well known ; and they obliged others to make a formal resignation in writing of all their rights and feudal services. Some regiments and cannon have been sent to check this daring insurrection.' The next letter reported that the leaders of the peasantry were not always peasants. ' A very considerable number have been committed to jail. A clergyman has been apprehended for preaching seditious doctrines, and a lawyer has been seized who is suspected of having had a considerable share in raising the disturbances. It is thought that some obscure plot had been formed for seizing the Elector, had he gone to hunt, and extorting his consent to all their demands.' A

week later the worst was over. ' Some little remains of the tumults
among the peasantry still continue ; but they are gradually
appeasing, and Government resumes its former confidence. The
consternation was for a time very great. Without a full and
satisfactory redress the discontents are only appeased for the
moment.'

The Elector and his advisers had no intention of making any
real change in the system of government ; and, like many other
rulers, Frederick Augustus believed that the root of the trouble
lay less in concrete grievances than in the teaching of ' sedition.'
It seemed easier to suppress the expressions of discontent than to
eradicate its causes. ' Though the most perfect tranquillity now
prevails,' wrote Morton Eden in February 1792, ' Government
has published an edict, and ordered it to be read from all pulpits—
that no person ought to presume to redress his own grievances,
and forbidding all meetings, clubs, or assemblies whose object is to
animadvert on, or oppose in a body, any of the public ordinances,
and strictly prohibiting the publication of all libels, satires, pas-
quinades, or any books of an inflammatory tendency respecting the
Government.' A Commission of Inquiry reported that the peasants'
knowledge of the French Revolution was one of the principal causes
of the revolt, though no trace of foreign emissaries had been found.
The Elector's policy was now to draw a cordon round his dominions
and to supply antidotes to the poison that had already found
entrance. Mauvillon, though a Brunswick official, was forbidden to
enter Saxony on the ground of his friendship with Mirabeau ; and
help was refused to the son of a French employé, desiring to study
medicine in Paris, ' because he would only imbibe evil principles.'
Six thousand copies of a Gotha pamphlet, entitled ' Rebellion Fever,'
were ordered for distribution. Measures of literary coercion were
apprehended. ' A heavy blow is threatening our liberty of the
press,' complained Körner to Schiller early in 1792. ' The talk is
of severe regulations for the censorship. The Diet is said to have
set the Elector in motion as the prince responsible for the districts
of Upper Saxony. I hold that the necessary limits to literary
freedom should be drawn not by legal compulsion, but by elevation
of taste.' ' Surely,' replied the poet, ' the Elector will not be such
an enemy to Leipsic as to attack the liberty of books ! ' He was
right ; for the fear of damaging the trade of the great city kept the
Government within bounds.

The counter-revolution appealed to the Elector as little as the
Revolution itself ; and, though sympathising with the sufferings
of the Royal Family and the Émigrés, he had no wish to join in
the crusade against the new France. Though the Declaration of

Pillnitz was issued from his own castle, the most pacific prince in Germany took no part in the conference and made no secret of his own dislike of the policy of intervention. ' I have been very positively assured that no actual interference will take place in the affairs of France,' wrote the British Minister. ' The reception of the Count d'Artois by all these illustrious personages was evidently very cold, and perhaps humiliating. Many here think that the assurances were extracted by dint of importunity, and that they will not be of any real effect.' Frederick Augustus continued to be more interested in his favourite pastime than in high politics. ' The Elector and the Electress have returned from hunting the wild boar,' wrote Eden in November, ' and are by no means satisfied with the behaviour of the peasants. Accounts from different parts of the country agree that the same spirit of discontent with respect to game and feudal services which broke out last year is far from being extinguished.'

When France declared war in April 1792, the Elector was urged by Austria and Prussia to join in the crusade ; but he refused to take part except at the bidding of the Empire. He disapproved the Brunswick Manifesto ; but on the deposition of the King he broke off diplomatic relations with France. The September massacres, following on the Tenth of August, awoke horror even in distant Saxony. ' A sense of the danger to which the lives of their Majesties is hourly exposed prevails among all ranks of the people,' reported Hugh Elliot, who had succeeded Morton Eden at the Saxon Court. ' The Elector paid many compliments to that spirit of liberality which had imbued so many individuals in England to subscribe towards the relief of the unfortunate priests who had fled from France.' The death of his cousin Louis XVI was the greatest shock of the Revolution. ' As soon as the Elector received the intelligence of the atrocious crime,' wrote the Minister, ' he ordered the suspension of all the amusements of the Carnival, and the remainder of the sum destined for balls and entertainments to be distributed among the poor. The public theatres have been closed for the week. It has excited the horror and resentment in the superior ranks of society which it was natural to expect ; but it is with pain I confess that, to the best of my observation, the inferior classes of men in Germany have not manifested those just feelings which we learn to have been so loudly proclaimed by the unanimous voice of the humane, generous, and loyal people of England.'

Despite his grief at the tragic fate of his relative, the pacific Elector was as unwilling as ever to draw the sword. ' He appears to have formed a fixed resolution of taking no further share in the

war than what is prescribed to him as a co-estate of the Empire or
than what the immediate defence of his own frontiers may require.'
He conceived his main task to be that of keeping his dominions free
from infection. ' In closing the Diet the Minister read a speech
in the Elector's name, which contained several allusions to the
pernicious principles inculcated by the French or their emissaries,
and ended with a warm exhortation to the members of the Diet to
second his efforts for the maintenance of good order and tranquillity.' Though the British Minister would have preferred more
zeal for the anti-revolutionary crusade, he could not deny that the
Elector's policy secured the well-being of his subjects. ' The able
and steady system of the Government secures interior tranquillity.
His subjects enjoy a degree of liberty which they have the good
sense to consider sufficient for their happiness, the liberty of
attending to their individual interests, unmolested by the tyranny
of revolutionary clubs or ambitious demagogues. Agriculture,
manufactures, and commerce have spread a glow of prosperity over
this beautiful country which I have never seen equalled beyond
the precincts of our fortunate isle.   The just value the Elector sets
on peace gives little room to foresee that he will endanger its
stability.'

When, however, the Empire's declaration of war against the
Republic compelled him to enter the fray, an apologetic message
was informally conveyed to Le Brun, the French Minister of
Foreign Affairs, a copy of which was sent home by Hugh Elliot.
' The Elector took no share whatever in the Convention signed at
Pillnitz, and never gave his approbation or encouragement to the
intended attack on France or to the cause of the French princes.
He waited for the decree of the Diet before he furnished a single
man towards carrying on the war against France, and kept strictly
to the number of troops prescribed by his place in the Empire. He
gave no asylum to emigrants, but constantly refused them leave
to reside within his dominions. He also refused to provide soldiers
to be paid by the Empire.' Such a half-hearted combatant was
not likely to prove a very formidable enemy.

A year after Saxony's entry into the war domestic disturbances
broke out once more, though on a smaller scale than in 1790. ' The
tranquillity of the city,' wrote Hugh Elliot in the summer of 1794,
' has been interrupted by a combination of apprentices and journey-
men who committed various acts of riot on pretence of obtaining
satisfaction from the magistrates for an imaginary offence of the
most trivial nature ; but they have been quelled without bloodshed.'
When the troubles were repressed in the capital the flames broke
out in the country. ' The utmost tranquillity prevails among all

classes,' reported the Minister a fortnight later ; ' but I am sorry to learn that there have been various symptoms of a rebellious spirit among the peasants in certain districts of Lusatia, which could not be subdued without the aid of military force.   Though there is no reason to believe that any French agents have been able to extend their intrigues to this country, yet it is a melancholy truth that the success of the French arms is productive of bad effects on the minds of the multitude, even in this central part of the Empire.'   ' I do not mean that the body of the people are actuated by any particular spirit of hostility against the French,' he added on November 16. ' The inclinations of perhaps the majority have manifestly a contrary tendency, but, fortunately, not so decidedly as to prevent them from concurring in all the constitutional measures of their government.'   When Prussia and the north withdrew from the war in 1795, Saxony soon followed their example, and the Elector returned to the policy of placid neutrality from which he had never desired to depart.

During the revolutionary era the Electorate was distinguished neither for the quality nor the quantity of its intellectual life ; and there was but little speculation and discussion even in its two leading cities.   The most distinguished subject of Frederick Augustus was the celebrated geologist who presided over the School of Mines at Freiberg.   ' Werner was a thoroughly patriotic Saxon,' wrote Steffens, his admiring pupil, ' devoted to his prince and country.   His fame in France was great, and the Republican leaders, anxious to pay him homage, sent him a diploma of citizenship, which plunged the timid legitimist into embarrassment.   He at once took the diploma to Court ; but I do not remember if he was allowed to accept it.' [1]   The most cultivated circle was that which gathered round Körner in Dresden.   Schiller's closest friend lives in history rather for what he was than for what he did.   After accompanying Stolberg on a long journey through England and France, he announced a course of lectures on law at Leipsic ; but as the response was disappointing, he accepted a minor post in the State service, and devoted his leisure to study and reflection.   Like nearly all the highly educated bourgeoisie he was devoted heart and soul to the Aufklärung ; but he was never carried away by the Revolution, being convinced that liberty of thought was more vital than political change.   The internal troubles in Saxony aroused in him contempt rather than apprehension.   ' The latest revolutionary tricks seem to me more childish every day.   Low antics no one side, a fire of straw on the other—a disgusting spectacle. Never has the lack of great men in our time showed itself more

[1] Steffens, *Was ich erlebte*, iv. 213.

conspicuously.'[1] The events of the autumn of 1792 filled him with
sadness. ' I hoped much for the French from the happy result
of their war. The feeling of their strength might have given them
a new moral impetus, and the horrors, which were merely a consequence of their weakness and despair, ought to have ceased. But
alas ! now there arise new horrors of arrogance, ingratitude, ignoble
revenge upon the vanquished and self-seeking. Great men are
overborne by a thoughtless mob or by the infamous tools of
ambitious rascals.'[2] He was smitten with a passing desire to write
on politics ; ' but on reflection I feel that the fire now raging is the
work of a higher hand, and that one should add neither oil nor water
to the flames.' He adhered to his resolution, but did not wholly
escape molestation. ' I suppose I owe it to Huber's connection
with Mainz,' he wrote to Schiller early in 1793, ' that I have become
an object of suspicion to the Government and have already received
serious warnings.'[3] But with Körner, as with most other moderate
liberals, the Terror marked the end of even Platonic sympathy
with the Republic.

If Körner's moderate views disquieted the Government, the
conservative opinions of the pious Göschen could give no cause for
alarm. The friend and publisher of Wieland, Goethe, and Schiller
naturally advocated liberty of the press ; but he was not a political
head, and he deemed moral reform the supreme need of the age.
' People speak much in our days of civic freedom,' he wrote.
' Would that the people might begin to be morally free ! But
they are becoming day by day more miserable slaves of their
passions, of luxury, and selfishness. Their own egotism is their real
tyrant. I sometimes meditate on politics, and it appears to me
as if the genius of the eighteenth century had become an old man
who plays with liberty and equality. Is the spirit of strength, of
moderation, of simplicity in life, of virtue, no longer in us—that
spirit which alone can expect, preserve, and endure liberty ? Those
below desire to pull down those above, but none wish to raise others
up to their own level. That is the spirit of our age, and I do expect
little from it.'[4] Despite his religious and political orthodoxy, the
publisher for a time employed and gave his friendship to the
romantic and adventurous Seume, who had been compelled to fight
for George III against his revolting colonists, and who ever after
contended that all the misery of nations arose from privilege.[5]

From time to time a young Saxon felt and answered the call of
liberty. At the age of twenty-three Von Miltitz fled to Paris to

[1] Schiller, *Briefwechsel mit Körner*, ii. 325.   [2] *Ib.*, ii. 352.
[3] *Ib.*, iii. 74.   [4] Goschen, *G. J. Göschen*, i. 440, 458–9.
[5] See Goschen, ch. xxiv. ; and Planer und Reissmann, *J. G. Seume.*

offer his services to the Minister of War. His mother, aware of his opinions but not of his flight, wrote him a final appeal. ' Only one thing has really upset me—that you should join the side of France. I should survive your death but not the loss of your reputation. I have only one request—do not make me ashamed of you.' Such cases, however, were rare. More overtly Gallophil than any native publicist was Rebmann, a clever young jurist from Erlangen, who settled in Dresden in 1792 and edited a paper in which he defended the principles of 1789.[1] ' The greatest event of all the centuries,' he wrote, ' gave to many a young man a powerful impetus that set all his capacities in motion. Nobler and grander than it can ever be realised in practice arose the ideal of universal brotherhood.' The first task of his journalistic career was to attack the war, which he attributed to the Émigrés. He proclaimed the prowess of the French armies, but denounced the September massacres, admired the Girondins, and detested their Jacobin conquerors. He warned Germany against revolt, and expressed a hope that the press would persuade the princes to initiate reforms. Early in 1794, at the height of the Terror, he issued a pamphlet entitled ' Naked Truths.' The Constitution, he argued, had been ruined by the intrigues of the King and by the war, while the Terrorists had been brought to power by the fear of invasion. If the Revolution were to fail, it would be no proof of the error of its principles ; for the Rights of Man were based on a sure foundation. Such doctrine was not very revolutionary ; but Rebmann was kept under observation, and now found it wise to flee from the Electorate.

The tranquillity of the people forcibly struck Morritt of Rokeby, the friend of Scott, when he visited Dresden in 1794.[2] ' Like true Englishmen we have been employed all the morning in quizzing the natives. However, it is hardly worth while, for it quite fails of its effect with a German ; if you were to spit in a man's face here, he would only wipe it off. I always thought what I heard of the phlegm and sleepy temperament of these people exaggerated ; but you would swear the whole nation was asleep. The composure with which they let you scold them is inconceivable ; and when we have done, we might have held our tongues, as a German is never in a hurry. Voltaire, somewhere, calls them the old men of Europe. Burke would delight in a German ; for he never makes innovations.' This sprightly sally, despite its humorous exaggeration, was less inapplicable to Saxony than to almost any part of the country. The extremes of revolutionary and anti-revolutionary passion were unknown, and the distance from the danger zone

---

[1] See Wrasky, *Rebmann*.   [2] *Letters of Morritt of Rokeby*, p. 11.

facilitated the formation of moderate judgments. ' I could forgive you everything,' remarked a Saxon pastor in 1807 to a French visitor, ' if it were not for the death of your good King.' Saxony emerged from a generation of turmoil and ferment shorn of nearly half her territory, but the same loyal, stagnant, and caste-ridden community that she had been in the tranquil years preceding the cataclysm of 1789.

Equally unaffected by the storms and stimulus of the Revolution were the Mecklenburg duchies, the Sleepy Hollow of Germany, where the Junkers were so firmly entrenched that the personality of the ruler mattered as little as in Poland.[1] At the very moment when in most other parts of Germany the power of the Crown was increasing, the settlement of 1755 recognised and enlarged the rights of the Estates. Despite the popularity of the well-meaning Frederick Francis of Schwerin, who began his long reign in 1785, and of Karl, the father of Queen Luise of Prussia, in Strelitz, the ruler remained a mere shadow, and was regarded by the arrogant nobles as merely *primus inter pares*. During the years of the Revolution the surface of the stagnant waters was ruffled by a few half-hearted peasant tumults ; but the old order lingered on, and the abolition of serfdom had to wait till 1820.

II

The high reputation earned by the Duke of Brunswick before the Revolution was confirmed by his conduct during its early stages ; for he never allowed events in France to interrupt the patient reorganisation of his little State.[2] In 1790 he abolished every extraordinary tax ; and in 1794 an edict gave the Estates a measure of control over the revenues of the principality and even of the Domain. In order that his economies should not be in vain, he decreed that the property of the State should not be pawned or sold without the consent of the Estates. It was the high-water mark of princely concession registered in Germany during the era of upheaval. In this enlightened Court it was natural that the Revolution should receive a friendly welcome ; and it was said in Berlin that Brunswick had become the *foyer* of the Revolution in Germany. The charge was in so far true that unfettered liberty was allowed to journalists and scholars. Campe's ecstatic letters

---

[1] See Treitschke, *History of Germany*, iv. 393–405.

[2] See Fitzmaurice, *Charles William Ferdinand, Duke of Brunswick* ; Heinemann, *Geschichte von Braunschweig u. Hannover*, vol. iii. ; Treitschke, iv. 381–93.

from Paris appeared in the 'Brunswick Journal,' to which his radical friends, Trapp and Mauvillon, also contributed ; and Friedrich Schulz dated his 'Genealogical Almanach' from Brunswick in 'The Year of Liberty,' 1789.

The Duke's sympathy with the Revolution was so confidently assumed in Paris that in 1792, when a conflict was in sight, Narbonne, the Minister of War, sent François de Custine, the son of the General, to offer him the command of the French armies.[1] The French Ministry expected war with Austria alone, and looked round for another Marshal Saxe. The Duke's devotion to France and the Philosophes, his own reforms and his liking for foreign reformers, were well known. His praises had been sung by Mirabeau and many other French visitors, and he was admired by the Girondins and by Dumouriez. There was even some talk, which found its way later into the Memoirs of the period, of deposing the King of France in his favour—a project attributed to Sieyès, Brissot, Condorcet, and some of the Jacobins.

Custine had married Delphine, the daughter of Madame de Sabran, and, though only twenty-three, he was well equipped for his difficult mission. Starting in January 1792 he stopped at Frankfurt to inquire whether a loan could be raised. ' I find here plenty of good wishes, but little optimism,' he wrote. ' Those who believe in the stability of the Constitution do not believe in our finances. Bankruptcy is thought to be almost inevitable.' On reaching Brunswick he had several tentative conversations before he launched his thunderbolt. The Duke gradually thawed. ' He told me that he would talk to me unofficially, and would consider himself as a cosmopolitan withdrawn from the affairs of Europe. He appeared to identify himself with the new order of things and in general with our principles, some of which he has always approved. His truly philosophic mind sometimes clashes with his feelings. For instance, in discussing the *noblesse*, he said : " I admit it is prejudice ; but, as it exists throughout Europe, Europe could not watch with indifference your efforts to destroy it." ' He impressed the envoy as a philosophic Grand Seigneur, a friend of liberty of thought, but with no taste for democracy. Like Frederick the Great and Voltaire, his zeal for reforms was joined to a profound contempt for the ignorant crowd. ' Every conversation showed me, beneath the mask of an impenetrable circumspection, a superior mind, free from prejudices, raised above all ideas of absolute power. He often reproached us with our disorders, but he renders homage

[1] The curious story was told in detail for the first time by Sorel from the reports of the envoy, ' *La Mission de Custine à Brunswick*,' *Revue Historique*, vol. i.

to the majority of our principles.   He dislikes our Single Chamber, and is interested in the fate of our princes and Émigrés ; but he repudiates all interference in our affairs.'

One day Brunswick spoke of the war in Holland in 1787, remarking that some Frenchmen had blamed him for it. ' It was only aristocracy against aristocracy.   The interests of the people were so little the object that there was never any question of forming a good national representation, the only true foundation of all free government.'   These observations encouraged the envoy to broach his proposal, begging him to accept the proffered honour on the ground that he was the only man who could maintain order in France and who enjoyed consideration abroad.   ' I recognise the grandeur of the idea,' replied the Duke, ' and am profoundly touched by the offer.'   Custine then handed him Narbonne's letter, and the Duke made inquiries about the army.   He spoke of the difficulties of success, and ended by saying that he must think it over.   Next day brought the refusal.   ' I am perhaps capable of sharing your sentiments, but I have no acquaintance with your methods, and I am too old to change my own.   I foresee too many difficulties.   I know your country well enough to feel how hard it is for a man to maintain his credit and reputation there.   You have too many clever heads.   Opinion is too changeable.   Perhaps if you were threatened at this very moment by an invasion, say from Spain or Italy, I might undertake the task.   But your neighbours will leave you in peace, and the Courts of Germany have no intention of arming against your liberty.   I am not unconscious of the attraction of a leading rôle on the first stage of the world ; but I should be presumptuous did I not recognise the impossibility of success.   I have too much pride to wish to risk my reputation. My business is to command the Prussian army in war and to rule my duchy in peace.'   He repeated his reasoned refusal in a letter to Narbonne.   Custine believed that there was still a faint hope, and urged that the King of France should write to him ; for he only needed to be assured of success.

The young envoy was ordered to Berlin as *chargé d'affaires* ; for Ségur, who had been sent on a special mission to detach Prussia from Austria and to express the desire of France for peace, had been so coldly received that he asked for his recall.   Before leaving Brunswick he had a final conversation with the Duke, who confidently expected to be in command if there was war.   He hated the Émigrés and Austria, but he was in the service of Prussia.   He reiterated his refusal of the French offer with such emphasis that even Custine realised that the game was up.   Brunswick confessed that he might have to fight France, and added that he knew French valour would be as great as ever. 'The equality of rights on which our Constitution rests,' reported the envoy, 'appeals to his reason, but not to his feelings. He approves it, perhaps, but he certainly does not love it. I must add that the debates in the Assembly on foreign Powers, which have echoed through Europe, have contributed not a little to bring him to this position.' Shortly after this conversation the Duke followed Custine to Berlin in order to discuss the plan of the coming campaign. Nothing was known in Paris of the mission and its failure, and the Duke continued to be popular. Even when the armies were gathering for the invasion Carra wrote of him as the greatest warrior and statesman of his century. 'Perhaps he only lacks a throne to be—I will not say the greatest of kings, but the restorer of liberty in Europe. If he reaches Paris, I wager that his first expedition will be to the Jacobin Club to don a red cap.' But in the twinkling of an eye he was hurled from the pedestal to the abyss. He had unwillingly consented to lead an enterprise which he disapproved, and he was well aware of the moral and material strength of France. He disliked the leaders as well as the policy of the Émigrés, and his closer acquaintance with them at Coblenz deepened his dislike into detestation. 'He paid them compliments and made them a thousand bows,' records his friend Massenbach ; 'but his cheeks glowed and his eyes glittered like those of a tiger.' His heart was not in the war ; and in an evil moment he set his hand to the infamous manifesto which enshrined the blind fury of the Émigrés, provoked the September massacres, and turned the war into a struggle for liberty and independence. 'Ah! that unlucky manifesto,' he remarked some years later, 'I shall repent it to the last day of my life. What would I not give never to have signed it ! '[1]

The Duke's reputation for statesmanship vanished in a moment, and his fame as a soldier quickly followed it. 'The Duke started out holding in his hands the destiny not only of France but of all Europe,' wrote Grimm to Catherine. 'All eyes were fixed on him. All hearts rendered in advance to the hero of the century a tribute of respect and admiration.'[2] The disappointment was in proportion to the expectation. The disasters of the Valmy campaign were due in part to the jealousy between Austria and Prussia, partly to the interference of Frederick William II, partly to the unceasing downpour ; but when full allowance has been made for these and other contributory causes, the irresolution of the Commander-in-Chief must carry its share of responsibility. 'He will always remain a timid General,' reported Reuss to the Emperor after the terrible retreat, 'and nothing virile is to be expected

[1] Massenbach, *Memoiren*, i. 236.   [2] *Lettres de Grimm*, p. 556.

from him.'[1]   'For a long time,' writes Massenbach, 'I was deeply
impressed by his personality ; but I gradually came to recognise
that he lacked greatness of character.   He had the power to save
Germany ; that he would not use it the world can never forgive.'
Brunswick resigned the command in the opening days of 1794, and
returned, soured as well as saddened, to the less exacting task of
ruling his little duchy.   He watched the progress of French arms
with sombre apprehension, and remarked : 'I am convinced that
the flames of the volcano will destroy us all.'[2]   He spoke of France
with mingled bitterness and envy; and after the Peace of Basle
French animosity against the nominal author of the Manifesto
waned.   Indeed, when Sieyès was looking round for a soldier to
overthrow the Directory, his mind turned to Brunswick before
Bonaparte ; but the Duke was too old for adventures and had no
desire to befriend the Republic.   With the rest of his countrymen
he grew less cosmopolitan and exerted himself to counterwork
French designs.   'The Duke,' reported De Luc to George III,
'explains that he selected as his representative at Rastadt a
professor of law at Helmstädt, named Häberlin, a declared Jacobin,
in order to discover the views of the French deputies.'[3]

In 1799 the veteran soldier-statesman drew up a remarkable
memorandum for the King of Prussia and the Duke of Weimar,
which emphasises his unchanging conviction that the Great War
was a conflict of spiritual no less than of material forces, and that
in both spheres the enemy possessed the advantage.[4]   'The present
war against the French Revolution is a proof how far a nation can
be misled by the distortion of the recognised principles of religion
and morality.   The seducers of France did not confine themselves
to upsetting the pillars of religion and government on the pretext
of liberty in France, but made it a principle to spread their
revolutionary maxims everywhere by force of arms.   The picture of
an ideal liberty, which taught the rights of man without the corresponding duties, worked on the short-sighted, uneducated, passionate
masses—especially the youth—and on a class which sought the
satisfaction of their egoism in turning the heads of the growing
generation by sophisms.   The unobservant part of mankind, unaware of the results of such ideas, called the war of defence against
France a war against ideas.   This false phrase had more effect
on the armies ranged against France than was imagined.   They
believed they were being led against ideas of liberty which promised
general happiness ; and the luck of war, which was on the side of
the French usurpers, owing to the lethargy and want of resolution

[1] Vivenot, *Quellen*, ii. 322.   [2] Massenbach, i. 228.
[3] *Fortescue MSS.*, iv. 53.   [4] Bailleu, *Preussen u. Frankreich*, i. 322–4.

DD

on the part of Germany, was regarded by too many as the result of the struggle of liberty against tyranny, so that few of the armies can flatter themselves not to have secret adherents of the French Revolution in their ranks.   This mood relaxed discipline and military spirit.   The results of this growing attitude, the germinating idea of the fragility of existing governments based on birth or descent, the secret wish to see a change in the existing political constitution of Europe by the success of French arms—all this exerted such an astonishing influence on the destiny of Europe that it is remarkable they have been overlooked.   Seduction and timidity together rose to such a height that people openly declared that nothing could withstand the French armies ; and instead of uniting for Germany's independence, security was sought in piecemeal treaties.'

While the Duke watched the early stages of the Revolution with mingled feelings, one of the most distinguished of his subjects felt a personal interest in its course.   Mauvillon, the son of a Huguenot father, had devoted his life to military science and economics, and had served in the Seven Years' War as an engineer.[1] When Mirabeau visited Germany and resolved to compile a detailed survey of the Prussian Monarchy, he found in him the assistant he required.   While the Frenchman supplied the scheme of the book and paid its expenses, Mauvillon collected and arranged the material. ' I did the work,' wrote the latter, ' and he gave the child a suitable dress for its appearance in the world.' [2]   Mirabeau, in turn, publicly expressed his obligations to ' my German collaborator ' in his preface, and privately pronounced the work ' truly excellent in every respect.'   The two men took to each other at once, and the Brunswicker described himself as the only man in Germany who agreed wholly with his views on economics and administration.   As a democratic liberal Mauvillon welcomed the Revolution, and followed the activity of his friend with sympathetic admiration. After Mirabeau's death, when the reactionary tide began to flow, his association with the orator was cast in his teeth.   He replied by publishing his letters, which deal largely with their collaboration in ' The Prussian Monarchy,' and reflect honour on both.   He remained none the less a marked man, and his letters were opened in the post.   One of them, written to a friend in Hesse-Cassel, expressed his joy that the Constitution was taking root, and expressed the hope that in a year or two he would see the flame of revolution shooting up in Germany.   The Landgrave sent a copy to the

---

[1] A biography of Mauvillon is needed.   He was one of the Abbé Barruel's bogeys ; *Memoirs of Jacobinism*, vol. iv.

[2] See his Preface to *Mirabeau's Lettres à un de ses amis en Allemagne*.

Duke, asking him to dismiss the writer from his post; but the Duke declined to take action.

Mauvillon was no more of a Jacobin than Mirabeau. He abhorred the horrors, wrote his friend Dohm, as much as he abhorred the old despotism; but he refused to abate a jot of his democratic faith when the skies darkened.[1] A pamphlet entitled 'Dr. Martin Luther,' published in 1793 and universally attributed to him owing to the numerous references to Mirabeau, sharply castigated the reaction. Wieland was denounced for comparing the Jacobins to cannibals, and the princes were flagellated for their suppression of free speech and their intervention in France. 'What a tragedy it was,' he cries, 'that Charles V and Francis I prevented the Reformation reaching its goal of purifying the teaching and practice of the Church! Let not the Revolution now be hindered in purifying the teaching and practice of the State. The French will never again allow themselves to be ruled by mistresses and favourites. Let them work out their own salvation. Neither the Jacobins nor the King and the armed States of Europe will save the threatened State. The peasant, the merchant, the official, the soldier—they are the regenerators. There is a little animal which wakes the sleeper when scorpions and other poisonous creatures approach; and the friends of truth and enlightenment play the same rôle. It is a patriotic duty, not treason, to raise a warning voice against knavery and folly.' Mauvillon denounced German reactionaries and French doctrinaires with equal vigour. In 1793 the preface to the second edition of 'The Prussian Monarchy' repeated the attacks on the autocracy and obscurantism of the rule of many German princes. In an introduction to a translation of Malouet's 'Letters on the Revolution,' written in the same year, he censures the teaching of Brissot, Tom Paine, and Forster, and gravely declares that 'certain limits must remain in human society.'

Among Mauvillon's friends was Benjamin Constant,[2] who spent most of his time between 1789 and 1794 at the Court of Brunswick; and though his resolve to write a biography was never fulfilled, he retained a grateful memory of Mauvillon's personality. 'I have had a loss,' he wrote, 'which absolutely changes the character of my sojourn. He consoled, supported, and encouraged me. Without him I should have become as dull as my surroundings. He was the friend of Liberty and Light, whose lofty opinions on morals, politics, and religion agreed in every particular with my own. I am stunned by the loss. I always left his presence better informed

---

[1] See Dohm, *Denkwürdigkeiten*, v. 396–423.
[2] See Rudler, *La Jeunesse de Constant*, pp. 413–16, 473–88.

and more active and alert.' Constant had been turned to liberalism by his experience of the Bern aristocracy, and heartily despised the philosophy of the counter-revolution. ' There are as many absurdities as lines in Burke's " Reflections," ' he wrote ; ' hence its complete success in all English and German circles.' His liberal faith was strengthened during his residence at Brunswick, both by the influence of Mauvillon and by the suspicions of the Court. ' I do not go to Court,' he wrote to Madame de Charrière in 1792 ; ' I only leave the house to walk or to see Madame Mauvillon. I am never invited, and prudent democrats avoid seeing me for fear of being stamped as Jacobins.' The picture was somewhat over-charged ; for though ' French ideas ' fell into disfavour, there was no persecution of men of liberal opinions. But the brilliant and irritable Swiss publicist belonged to the class of men who are never satisfied either with their own surroundings or with themselves.

Campe[1] never lost the vivid interest in the Revolution which his visit to Paris had inspired ; and he greeted the Constitution of 1791 with a poetical *Nunc Dimittis*. His utterances aroused the wrath of Alois Hofmann, who angrily inquired how long cosmopolitan and philanthropic writers were to be allowed to pay homage to the wildest intoxication of liberty. ' Campe's Letters must have been written in an asylum. No other excuse for them is possible.' When the impenitent Brunswicker proceeded to attack the Powers for their crusade against France, Wöllner complained to his employer, who ordered him to abstain from political criticism, while privately assuring him of his continued favour. Campe was, however, more affected by the September massacres than by the admonitions of governments, and explained his position in an address ' To my Fellow Citizens ' at the end of the year. ' At first I sympathised ; but now I shed bitter tears over the handful of murderers who are a curse to the world.' His services to liberty had been recognised by the grant of French citizenship in company with Klopstock and Schiller ; but as the diploma had not reached him, he could not return it. This manly apologia stopped the outcry against him, and Campe felt no further call to intervene in politics.

III

The second Guelf principality enjoyed a mild if lethargic government.[2] ' Hanover,' wrote Wraxall on his visit in 1777,

---

[1] See Leyser, *Campe*, vol. i. ch. i.
[2] See Heinemann, *Geschichte von Braunschweig u. Hannover*, vol. iii. ; Treitschke, iv. 351–81 ; Ford, *Hanover and Prussia*, 1795–1803 ; Thimme, *Die inneren Zustände Hannovers unter der Französischen Herrschaft*, vol. i.

'presents the image of departed greatness—palaces without inhabitants, a capital without trade, and an Electorate without a sovereign.'[1] Though George III instituted a 'German Chancery' in London, internal questions were usually settled by the Privy Councillors on the spot. Any proposals for important changes or for an increase of taxation, on the other hand, required the assent of the provincial Estates, which under an absentee ruler increased their power at a time when in most parts of Germany it had passed to the prince. But though each province possessed its Diet, there was no central representation, and customs were levied on goods passing from one district to another. The reforming age of Münchhausen was over, and the King, the bureaucracy, and the Estates were agreed in desiring the minimum of change. Though Spittler was justified in describing the Government as the mildest in Germany, only the nobility and the higher bourgeoisie had reason to be satisfied. The peasantry wore their feudal fetters, and the neglect of trade and industry kept the towns small and poor. Political criticism was as yet unborn, for Schlözer had learned by experience not to aim his shafts at the bosom of his masters. Well might Scharnhorst lament 'the intellectual No thoroughfare! exhibited by our land.'[2]

In such a soil the French appeal to abstract ideas naturally found little favour, and the Hanoverian nobility and officials watched the struggle with pitying contempt. 'You know that if anybody hates despotism and a corrupt aristocracy it is I,' wrote Ompteda on hearing the false news of the escape of the King ; ' but I dread ochlocracy still more ; and that, with its sister anarchy, was all that confronted the people—a people seemingly incapable of rational liberty.'[3] It was not till the summer of 1792 that the sleepy country was visited by the troubles to which, in different degrees, the ideas and influences of the Revolution gave rise in nearly every State. Opposition to oppressive taxes in the bishopric of Hildesheim spread to Hanover. At the end of the year a memorial from a number of the citizens of Celle was presented to the Luneburg Estates. ' In our land, as well as in others, we feel humanity has reached a stage where much that is old is out of date. For instance, the position of the privileged class must be modified, since the old arrangements out of which it grew have long passed away. The love of justice which has already changed certain features in our taxation is most praiseworthy. Put the finishing touches to this great work, exalted representatives of the people! Abolish all distinctions and privileges ! In future, let the only difference be that the wealthy citizen contributes in proportion to the protection afforded to his property by the State.' The memorial added a request for publicity in the accounts of the province, and for a juster representation of the taxpayers. The Estates stiffly rejoined that they could not forward to the King demands for the annihilation of legal or traditional rights, since their oath bound them to maintain the privileges of all classes.

The authorities were further alarmed by rumours that the loyalty of the troops was being undermined, and General von Freytag, a veteran of the Seven Years' War, founded a military union, which he desired to extend throughout Germany and Austria, to defend the armies against revolutionary propaganda. For this purpose a general order was issued to the army in December 1792. ' Remarks have been made in conversation on French principles and questions of government which are incompatible with the duty of an officer. Such talk is forbidden.' The old warrior was firmly persuaded that emissaries of the Illuminati were plotting to destroy the morale of the army, and he therefore dismissed or degraded the suspects. The Electorate sent no troops when the Empire declared war against France in 1793, compounding for its duty by cash ; but as 16,000 troops fought in English pay, the wrath of the conquering Republic was not averted. When the French armies reached and crossed the Rhine the ferment increased. ' Then appeared in Calenberg,' wrote Berlepsch, ' not only audacious pamphlets and seditious pasquils— especially against certain of the nobility who were threatened with lynching—but meetings and conventions were held with a view to overthrow the existing representation and land system.' The poll-tax was withdrawn, and the storm abated ; but in Osnabrück military measures were required, and some blood was shed. It was also in the old ecclesiastical principality, soon destined to be incorporated in the Electorate, that the precocious young poet, Broxtermann, embraced the cause of the French Revolution with passionate zeal, even to the extent of defending the death of the King.[1]

When Prussia's expected withdrawal from the war threatened to leave the Electorate in a position of dangerous isolation, a bold step was taken by Baron von Berlepsch, once a friend of Hardenberg and now a judge and high official. In the Diet of the province of Calenberg, which included the capital, he proposed that the Elector should send a declaration of neutrality to France on behalf of ' the Calenberg nation ' ; failing which, direct negotiations should be commenced. No vote was taken ; but when Berlepsch published

[1] See the biography prefixed to *Broxtermann's Werke.*

the resolution in the papers he was deprived of his offices. He appealed to the Imperial Court at Wetzlar, which ordered his reinstatement ; whereupon the Hanoverian Government brought the case before the Diet at Regensburg, and banished the agitator. He had held radical views since his student days at Göttingen, and possessed a political imagination rare among the stolid Hanoverian officials ; but he was a general without an army, and ' the Calenberg Mirabeau ' was regarded rather as an eccentric than as a conspirator. It would have been well for Hanover if his advice had been taken, and the Government had followed the example of Hesse-Cassel and negotiated a formal peace, instead of merely acquiescing in the neutrality created by the Treaty of Basle.

Such slight ferment as existed was to be found in Göttingen, to which many anxious eyes were directed. ' I see you have had liberty influenza in your town,' wrote Lichtenberg to Forster in September 1790 ; ' so have we, but not so badly.' [1] The University was thoroughly cosmopolitan, and the most troublesome students came from beyond the borders of the Electorate. A lively picture of town and gown is painted by the Ritter von Lang in his vivacious Autobiography.[2] ' In Göttingen—where a king of England ruled, where it was the policy of the professors never openly to take sides, and where many of the students were sons of the wealthiest nobility of Hanover, Mecklenburg, and other States—a favourable view of the principles of reform, though not of bloody executions, was found rather among the lower bourgeoisie than in the University, where the mannikin Girtanner shouted his opposition. My brother at Frankfurt, who was heart and soul for the French, sent me all sorts of bulletins, papers, and pamphlets, with the music of *Ça ira* and the Marseillaise, to which I put words to be sung by the choir-boys in the streets. These songs, which one continually heard, were soon forbidden, and my brother's parcels were first opened in the post and then prohibited. One night, excited by punch, I called out Down with the Duke of Brunswick ! and was warned against further offences.'

The views of Schlözer and Spittler have been examined in another chapter ; and none of their colleagues followed events so closely or expressed themselves so frequently. Heyne, the brightest star in the Göttingen firmament, is described by his conservative biographer and son-in-law, Heeren, as having regarded the Revolution ' in the right light ' ; but though on the whole hostile to the great experiment, he was wholly free from intolerance.[3] His only political utterances were in Latin, and therefore passed unnoticed.[4]

[1] Lichtenberg, *Briefe*, iii. 13.   [2] *Memoiren*, i. 245–7.
[3] Heeren, *Heyne*.   [4] *Opuscula*.

He sought warnings and parallels in the classical world, which he knew far better than his own.   One of his themes was that the recovery of liberty rarely brings its expected fruits ; another, the vain attempt of the Roman Senate to restore the liberty of the State ; a third, the picture of liberty and equality in Athens drawn by Aristophanes.   In these and other dissertations he writes quietly, as a student of history rather than of politics.   His opinions on current events are more clearly expressed in his voluminous corre-spondence with Georg Forster.   His chief convictions were that all violence was detestable and that scholars should never embark on the stormy sea of affairs.   He noted with wondering pity the ravages of the malady of the age.   ' I can well imagine the situation you describe,' he wrote to Sömmerring in 1792.[1]   ' People who are bubbling over with enthusiasm cannot bear those who are not. Intolerance is as closely connected with the so-called Liberty instinct as persecution with religious zeal.   People see everything through coloured glass.'   ' I have read with pleasure of the retreat of the French,' he wrote to another friend about the same time.   ' If only they would take their principles back with them !   But I hear they have taken deep root in Brunswick.   Thank God ! that is not the case here.   We were not afraid of Custine.   We see the storm in the distance, but have no fear that the waves will reach us.' Despite Forster's championship of the French régime in Mainz, Heyne rejoiced at the refusal of the citizens to swallow the bait. ' People are now everywhere pretty unanimous that they will not have French democracy.'   But his detestation of French principles never soured him, and he recognised the better motives of his erring son-in-law.

The least academic of the professors was Lichtenberg, who was as eminent in literature as in science, and whose cool and sceptical mind poured equal scorn on the zeal of the revolutionists and their enemies.   ' That France has gone mad,' he wrote in 1793, ' arises partly from her evil draughts and partly (as usually happens) from the remedies applied.   When people explain everything by deep-laid plans that are gradually being unmasked, I can hardly repress a smile.   Nothing of the sort !   It is merely passion and fury.   The professors make the authors of the evils into malicious pedagogues, and the philosophers discover philosophic systems everywhere.' ' I have the good fortune, doubtless rare in Germany, of living under a Government which I greatly respect,' he wrote to Archenholtz. ' I ask nothing better than to live as I am living now.   I care little how much of my happiness is owing to the Government and how much to myself.   One should never make great demands on the

---

[1] Forster's *Briefwechsel mit Sömmerring*, p. 597.

Government till one has done everything for oneself.' On the eve of Thermidor he confessed that he could hardly look at the papers. ' Who would have thought that in the middle of Europe a robber-nation would arise, and that it is to this nation that we used to send our rulers to learn manners and culture ? No one has yet proposed in the Convention to eat the bodies of the guillotined ; but that, too, will come.' Thermidor brought a certain *détente*. ' The fall of Robespierre improves the credit of the Convention. Perhaps we could take soundings for peace. The Allies and the Convention, at any rate, are brought nearer by their common conviction that Robespierre was the most infamous scoundrel the world has ever seen.' Despite his horror of Jacobinism Lichtenberg laughed at the notion that it had infected the steady, easy-going population of the Electorate. ' Have you read an article in the " Journal de Paris," he wrote in February 1795, ' stating that if a revolution broke out it would begin in Hanover, and that Göttingen had expressed astonishing sentiments of liberty ? Is it not monstrous ? I wish, my dear friend, that you knew the Göttingen of to-day. Among the professors there is not one who holds or has held revolu-tionary principles. Of course they weigh and compare ; but there is not one who would not give his life for the Government. I hear that talk is much bolder in Hanover, but equally friendly. It grieves me to think that our excellent King must believe part of what he is always being told by the infamous libellers of Göttingen.' [1] Similar regrets were expressed by the veteran Pütter, who declared in his Autobiography that the reproaches were wholly undeserved.[2] The best tribute to the University is to be found in Heeren's testimony that it was denounced alike by aristocrats and democrats.

The only professor who was really suspect was Feder, whose Autobiography presents a vivid picture of the difficulties of an academic Liberal. ' My text-books,' wrote the Professor of Philosophy long after, ' show that I had held some of the principles of the French Revolution ; but in my lectures I always opposed the anti-monarchic and anti-aristocratic principles of Rousseau—such as the sovereignty of the people and the dependence of all authority on the whim of the majority. Young democrats found much in my lectures that was by no means to their taste. My only complaint was that no commoner could be a high officer.' When the Revolution broke out he found himself between two fires—suspected by the authorities and denounced as a coward by the left wing. ' And thou, Feder,' wrote one of his critics, ' who first taught me the rights of man ; thou seest how they are trampled underfoot,

---

[1] Lichtenberg, *Briefe*, iii. 98–9, 117, 121, 134, 146.
[2] *Selbstbiographie*, pp. 834, 838–9.

yet keepest silence.' ' It is true,' replied the Professor, ' that much that one could say or write before the Revolution must now arouse suspicion.   It is also true that the friends of Liberty and of the Rights of Man do not always express their hopes and joy with the requisite moderation.   I said openly that I deemed myself happy to live through such momentous and hopeful changes, and I said so to the Minister who had appointed me.   Some of us, though with no evil intentions, spoke with great levity about politics.' [1]

Hanover, like Saxony, emerged almost unchanged from the storm and stress of the revolutionary era and from the ten years of French domination.   The old-world institutions and practices which had been swept away by the Kingdom of Westphalia were restored.   The country was governed from London by Count Münster, who was profoundly convinced of the excellence of Hanoverian institutions.   His chief agent, Brandes, had not grown less conservative ; but his desire to remove a few of the more glaring abuses aroused the resentment of the nobles and led to his fall.   In Hanover, as in Saxony, Mecklenburg, and Brunswick, it seemed for the time as if the French Revolution had, after all, left few if any traces of its stormy passage across the scene.

[1] *Feder's Leben*, pp. 131–54.

CHAPTER XIX

HAMBURG, WEIMAR, AND GOTHA

I

COSMOPOLITAN by tradition and liberal by conviction, with one foot in the Empire and the other on the threshold of a wider world, Hamburg welcomed the French Revolution with disinterested sympathy; for her citizens desired that other countries should share the blessings of liberty which they themselves enjoyed.[1] The applause was led by Klopstock, whose poetical ecstasies embodied the sentimental optimism of most of his friends. The first anniversary of the fall of the Bastille was celebrated at a private party attended by eighty guests, including English and French, Americans and Swiss.[2] 'Young girls in white, wearing scarves in the French colours,' records Sieveking, one of the hosts, 'added to the romantic character of the scene. Songs were sung and toasts were drunk to Liberty and its heroes.' Sieveking himself contributed a poem. 'Free Germans,' it began, 'sing the hour which broke the fetters of serfdom! Let your hearts be altars of liberty!' The poem with its chorus found approval far beyond the walls of Hamburg. 'Dear Sieveking,' wrote Frederica Brun from Copenhagen, 'we often sing the Song of Liberty.' Though the fête took place in a private house the whole city was soon talking of it, and the fame of Klopstock spread the news all over Europe. 'I cannot tell you,' wrote Frau Voght to the Chevalier de Bourgoin, 'how I share the enthusiasm of the Fête of the Federation. We also have celebrated the great day. We were eighty. The ladies wore white, with tricolour sashes. Klopstock read two odes, crying with joy, and Dr. Reimarus gave an address. Then we danced, dined, sang, and danced again. We have formed a club to meet on the 14th of every month. Perhaps it will be for some years a *vox clamantis*; but Germany's time will come. Perhaps it is

---

[1] See Wohlwill, *Neuere Geschichte Hamburgs, insbesondere von 1789 bis 1815.*
[2] See H. Sieveking, *G. H. Sieveking,* pp. 48–53.

best that it should not come till we are sufficiently enlightened; for we are still rather backward, except, of course, the Hamburgers.'[1] The Imperial Minister reported to Vienna, however, that such pronounced sympathy existed only in a few merchants and writers, some of whom he had warned to be careful.

An interesting picture of opinion among the younger generation is drawn in the Autobiography of Rist, the Danish diplomat, son of a clergyman, living just outside the territory of the city.[2] ' My father was rather critical of the Revolution, and pointed out to me its dangers. I hated it from the first—hated even the word Liberty. I longed to serve in the war, and in imagination I joined the army of the Princes at Coblenz. I got a medallion of the Duke of Brunswick and hung it over my desk. But I was converted (at the age of seventeen) by a pamphlet of Hennings, denouncing absolutism and vindicating the rights of the people. I was now on the side of the majority. Not only young men were filled with zeal for the new dispensation, but the merchants felt themselves carried away. Everybody of note in the intellectual world made vows for the welfare of the people and declared war against tyrants. A fête, at which the Marseillaise was sung, completed my conversion; but I never approved the cruelties, and I saw my mother weep bitterly at the death of Louis XVI.' Hamburg, in fact, was liberal, not revolutionary, and the stormy years passed over it almost without a ripple. ' The city has been for some days past in a state of confusion,' wrote the British Minister in August 1791, ' owing to the conduct of the different gilds of handicraftsmen. The Senate has been under the necessity of using force.' But the trouble was soon over. ' The city is at present in a state of perfect tranquillity,' he reported a week later. ' The Senate applied to me to use my authority with the masters of the British vessels here, in order that they might prevent their crews from interfering.'[3] The dispute turned on concrete issues, and was not complicated by theoretical appeals to the rights of man.

Hamburg was a city of newspapers, and both the liberal and conservative schools of thought were ably represented. ' The best poems remain unread,' complained an author. ' People will look at nothing but papers and pamphlets which satisfy their craving for politics.' The most eminent and influential of the Hamburg publicists was Archenholtz, a Hanoverian noble who had fought in the Seven Years' War and had written its history.[4] In the

---

[1] Grimm, *Correspondance Littéraire*, xv. 140–1.
[2] Rist, *Lebenserinnerungen*, vol. i. ch. i.
[3] Record Office, Hamburg.
[4] See Ruof, *J. W. von Archenholtz*.

succeeding years of peace he travelled and resided in many parts of western and southern Europe. He spent six years in England, where he attended the debates and the law-courts and became an ardent admirer of the Constitution ; and prolonged sojourns in France and Italy made him familiar with their literature, institutions, and ideas. His travels and studies convinced him of the necessity of free institutions ; and though he retained his admiration of the genius and achievements of Frederick the Great, his teacher was Montesquieu and his model was at Westminster. To the Mason, the freethinker, and the liberal cosmopolitan, the Revolution was naturally welcome, and he rejoiced that ' the divine word of Liberty penetrated the cells of the Bastille.' He congratulated the French, 'long accustomed to kiss their chains,' on having broken them and attained a larger measure of liberty than the Greeks or Romans, the Americans or the British. Burke's ' Reflections ' struck him as a senseless production, provoking the pity both of friends and enemies. He paid the new France the supreme compliment of settling in Paris with his family, intending to pass the remainder of his life in the land of Liberty. With his practised glance he studied the new conditions and tendencies of the city he had known so well under other circumstances, and he was a constant listener to the debates of the Assembly and the clubs. He quickly discovered that the real centre of power was the Jacobin Club. ' I was an enemy of this detestable society,' he wrote in 1799, ' from the moment I entered the den in October 1791.' He refused to become a member, and made no secret of his contempt for the ability of the chief stars of its dusky firmament.

Archenholtz was a practised and popular writer, and early in 1792 he founded the journal ' Minerva,' which appeared at Berlin but was quickly moved to Hamburg. There was room for such a political organ, as Schlözer's course was nearly run, and most other political journals were violent or ill-informed. While the editor resided in Paris the new paper was almost wholly devoted to French affairs. His principal contributors were Reinhard and Oelsner ; but his own contributions formed the chief attraction. As a liberal royalist he defended the Constitution of 1791, though he expected it to fail. When war loomed in sight he foretold the defeat of the interventionists, realising, as no German outside the French capital could realise, the immense strength of France. His frank criticisms of the Jacobin leaders rendered his position increasingly precarious, and in June 1792 he fled. His standpoint was clearly defined in an article entitled ' The Political Confession of the Editor.' ' I love the French Revolution as the abolition of countless abuses and unspeakable cruelties. I revere the French Constitution with

all its obvious defects.   I regarded the Constituent Assembly as a
respectable Senate : the majority as highly deserving, and a few of
its members as really great men.   On the other hand, I regard the
Legislative with quite different eyes, for its good members are weak
and possess no influence.   I despise the Jacobin leaders, on whom
alone, as seducers of the masses, the curse of the nation and all
impartial people abroad must rest.   I pity the King.   I abhor the
aristocratic Émigrés who thirst for the old despotism and are
ready to wade through streams of blood of their fellow citizens to
restore it.'   His faith was now placed in Lafayette, ' the first of
French citizens and the best hope of France ' ; and he laboured
for his milder treatment in his Austrian captivity.

On returning to Hamburg Archenholtz published a brochure
entitled ' The Jacobins, a historical narrative from   personal
knowledge.' [1]   ' The patriotic societies in France,' he begins, ' are
the most remarkable of all the effects of the Revolution.   They
found their model in England, but they abused it.   At first they
were innocent and praiseworthy ; but certain individuals soon
determined to bend these powerful machines to their personal
use.'   The oratory in the Jacobin Club, he declares, was poor,
though Robespierre's was the best.   The club had 3500 members,
and 760 societies in France were in connection or correspondence
with it.   The pamphlet is vivid, but severe ; for at the time it was
written the author's gloomy forecast had been fully realised.   Like
every other journal, the ' Minerva ' denounced the Terror ; but the
editor never entered the reactionary camp, and his paper was much
appreciated by moderate men.   ' Every new number is a festival
for me,' wrote Lichtenberg in 1794.   ' In my judgment you
leave all similar journals far behind you.' [2]   And nowhere were
its well-informed columns more eagerly studied than in Hamburg
itself.

The opposition was led by Schirach, whose monthly ' Politisches
Journal' enjoyed a large circulation ; for, like Schlözer, the editor
possessed correspondents in the chief cities of Europe.[3]   At first
the clever Jew shared the almost universal expectation among
German writers of a happier age ; but he lost his faith as early as
August 1789, and became ever more critical and apprehensive.
' Never was the personal attention of princes more necessary than
now,' he wrote in 1790, ' if the shock is not to run like electricity
through Europe.'   As the circulation increased a Russian edition

---

[1] The British Museum possesses a copy.
[2] Lichtenberg, *Briefe*, iii. 118.
[3] For the Hamburg press, see Salomon, *Geschichte des deutschen Zeitungs-
wesens*, vol. i. ; and Wenck, vol. ii.

appeared in Moscow, and several governments made use of the paper. The French *chargé d'affaires* in St. Petersburg complained that the Hamburg papers, ' which everybody here reads,' show a very hostile tone. The editor's hostility soon passed into hatred, and his paper denounced not only the Revolution, but the Aufklärung and its principle of free speech. He clasped the Émigrés to his bosom, and filled his pages with stories of revolutionary plots and propaganda. The Swiss, Girtanner, rendered a less effective support to conservative ideas in his review of events in France, which was only read for its news.

The great city was famous for its tolerance ; but the ' Mercury,' founded by Schütz, the secretary of the French Minister, Lehoc, overpassed the limits by lauding the Revolution to the skies. Never, he declared, was so great a transformation so rapid and so relatively bloodless. Every contribution to the extirpation of despotism and fanaticism, he added, was welcome. But though he described Hamburg as the place where the unbiassed observer could watch events and criticise the follies and injustices of the day, his paper was forbidden after two numbers. He proceeded to publish it under a new title, close by, at Danish Altona, and glorified the events of August 10. ' Arise, ye peoples, still under the slave-yoke of despotism, and be free ! Now is the time.' When he proceeded to denounce the German princes who took up arms against the Revolution, the paper was once again forbidden. It changed its title for a second time, and finally circulated in manuscript ; but in April 1793 the incorrigible editor was turned out of Hamburg. These and other papers used hand-presses, which were not easy to track ; and, if they appeared in Altona, the Holstein officials had to refer to Copenhagen for instructions. As the Hamburg Senate was no heresy-hunter, the city witnessed the publication of more writings for and against the Revolution than any other part of the Empire. Though loyal to the Empire it was disinclined to join in the war, less out of active sympathy with France than from a desire to avoid a breach with a good customer. After the fall of the Monarchy it forbade the exhibition of pictures of Louis wearing a red cap. The Prussian Minister, however, was suspicious, and reported that the Senate was in the pocket of the Convention. ' The Marats and Robespierres here are in the ascendant,' he complained ; but he also reported that the mass of the population was anti-revolutionary. A tiny group of extreme men gathered round the rich merchant, Schuhmacher, and drank to the Terrorists, while two of their number, Albert and Leonard Wächter, edited a short-lived review ; but the horrors excited as much indignation in Hamburg as elsewhere. Lehoc was a zealous but not a violent champion of his country. When slight labour troubles occurred in 1791 in Hamburg and Bremen, arising from questions of wages, he frankly reported that enthusiasm for political freedom played no part in them, though there were traces of the spirit of the time in the cry of a procession, ' Long live the Convolution ' (a blend of Constitution and Revolution). In the words of Bourgoing, ' the people of Hamburg are happy in laws of their own making, secure alike from despotism or oligarchy.'

The leaders of opinion were men of solid character and moderate views, fully competent to separate the gold from the dross of the Revolution. Next to the editors, the most influential arbiters of opinion were substantial business or professional men of the type of Reimarus and Sieveking, Voght and Büsch. Reimarus, son of the author of the heresies unearthed by Lessing, was a doctor whom Varnhagen declared to possess something of Benjamin Franklin and Justus Möser.[1] His ' Dialogue on Liberty ' contrasted the happy institutions of the city with the abuses prevailing elsewhere, and preached the folly of violence. He also wrote pamphlets combating privileges and demanding liberty of the press. ' Of course the French are frivolous and prone to excess,' he wrote to Erhard in October 1791 ; ' but a gentle, phlegmatic people would never have thought of making such a revolution, which, if by no means perfect, possesses the outstanding merit of waking up other peoples, as we already observe in several praiseworthy examples, with more to come. The Revolution has produced many good things which despotism cannot efface. Let us spread sound principles more and more. Rulers are for the benefit of the ruled. Conquerors are like robbers. No war should be begun except on the advice of the representatives of the nation. Peoples should not be transferred or sold like cattle.' [2]

Though French principles were excellent, French politicians aroused the growing distrust of the Doctor and his household. ' Alas ! that the French alienate the good will of all other nations,' he wrote to Knigge at the end of 1791. ' The French are not a nation with which one can unite in brotherly relations,' lamented his wife, the clever sister of Hennings, in December 1792.[3] ' Who does not shudder when Roland is accused ? O Liberty ! why have you not fallen into better hands ? ' The death of the King aroused no less horror in liberal than in conservative circles. ' The spectacle is so hideous,' she exclaims, ' that I do not understand how we could have been so blind. What would I not give to be

[1] *Denkwürdigkeiten*, i. 167–75; cp. Böttiger, *Lit. Zustände*, ii. 15–32.
[2] Varnhagen, *Biographische Denkmale*, x. 24.
[3] *Sieveking's Leben*, pp. 156–69.

able to recall the sentiments which animated us three years ago, when we celebrated the fall of the Bastille, and when everything was so pure ? Would that I could go to sleep till the Revolution is over ! ' Yet even in the Terror she returned to her earlier belief. ' To judge calmly one must project oneself forward thirty years. At that period of time, one will look back and see only slavery at the beginning and happiness and liberty at the end.' The *élite* of Hamburg did not allow itself to be permanently soured, and visitors to the city continued to find faith and hope as well as delightful conversation. ' The hours I have passed with Reimarus and Sieveking are among the happiest in my pilgrimage,' wrote Böttiger after a visit in 1795. ' Reimarus is cosmopolitan in the noblest and widest sense.' [1] Detestation of the Terrorists did not extend to innocent Frenchmen or to foreigners who had entered the service of France, and when Reinhard arrived he found a warm welcome from the Doctor and his wife, and won their consent to the marriage of their daughter.

The history of Hamburg presents no more attractive figure than that of Sieveking, a merchant prince who was also a lover and patron of literature, an enlightened citizen of the world, and a generous benefactor.[2] His wife, to whom Rouget de Lisle presented his poems, was a granddaughter of the theologian Reimarus. His hospitality was boundless, and sometimes seventy guests would meet at his house on the Elbe outside the city. His sympathies were strongly attracted to the Revolution, and the festival of July 14, 1790, was held at his house. He refused to allow the inevitable excesses to cloud his judgment. ' The liberty of France will cost blood,' he wrote in the spring of 1792, ' but it will become the liberty of the world. That some Frenchmen and many Jacobins are not ripe for nor worthy of liberty does not make me doubt my principles.' [3] Though he considered Louis XVI a traitor to his country, he condemned his execution. A citizen of such prominence and of such liberal opinions naturally became an object of suspicion. The firm of Voght and Sieveking, which sent many consignments to France, was accused of forwarding munitions of war. On the expulsion of Lehoc he was forced to swear that he was not a Jacobin, and his house was searched for arms. These attacks on his honour he rebutted in a pamphlet, ' To my Fellow Citizens.' He was called a Jacobin, he complained, and President of a Jacobin Club ; but he owed no one an explanation of his views on the French Revolution. ' The welfare of France is of great

---

[1] Böttiger, *Lit. Zustände*, ii. 15–32.
[2] See the admirable biography by H. Sieveking.
[3] *Sieveking's Leben*, pp. 156–69.

importance to me as a man, a merchant, and a Hamburg citizen. What I praised in the Revolution, every impartial man must also praise. What I hoped, every friend of humanity desired. I thought well of men, I loved them, I wished their happiness. That I never defended anarchy, disobedience, irreligion, cruelty, murder, I need not inform those who know me. I despise many of the leading actors in the Revolution. Perhaps, when I have heard the French denounced as robbers and murderers, a violent expression of protest may have escaped me. It is a lie that I rejoiced at the death of the King ; indeed, I forwarded a defence to a friend in Paris. Lehoc is a friend, and I am proud of his friendship. Is it a crime to love a Frenchman ? The so-called Jacobin Club in this city began as a harmless reading-circle. The "Jacobin" with whom I corresponded in Paris is my agent and my old friend, Schlüter, who takes no active-interest in the Revolution.' It is the dignified and manly apologia of an enlightened liberal.

For a time it seemed as if Sieveking must leave Hamburg ; but the storm blew over. His sympathy with France brought a great volume of trade to the city ; but he was no uncritical admirer, and he expressed his joy to Schlüter at the arrest of 'the infamous Carrier.' His views at this time are expressed in a letter to his partner, Voght, whose zeal for the Revolution had faded away.[1] ' We, for our part, have not yet given up the beautiful hope which inspired us at the beginning of the great struggle for liberty. And even if we are dreaming, leave us our dream. We know as well as you that in France selfish robbers and murderers rule, and we are not blind to the misery the Revolution has brought on a large part of France and the world. Yet we hope that the salvation of mankind will be the end of the bloody struggle of good and evil, and that the race will be wiser, better, and happier than it would have been without this moral earthquake. And we observe the great and overwhelming benefit which already manifests itself, this astonishing unfolding of forces which would have waited long or would never have come to the birth, this spread of enlightenment and humanity.' It is the letter of a generous and far-seeing mind, of whom any city and any country might be proud.

Closely connected with the circle of Reimarus and Sieveking was Hennings, a Holstein official, who had applauded the revolt of the American colonists and approved still more strongly the overthrow of the old régime in France.[2] Yielding to the new-born desire to influence opinion, he turned to journalism. Though Denmark took no part in the war, its Government was compelled by Prussia to

[1] *Sieveking's Leben*, pp. 165–7.
[2] See Böttiger, *Lit. Zustände*, ii. 68–86 ; and *Sieveking's Leben*, pp. 156–69.

punish his ' Schleswig Journal ' for publishing Voss's translation of the Marseillaise. He passionately opposed the war against the Republic. ' I no longer worry about the fury of the French. My heart has become quite Jacobin against the Prussians and Austrians.' He was equally enraged by the death of the King; but he subsequently founded the ' Genius der Zeit,' which during its nine years of existence (1794–1803) was widely read by men of advanced views in North Germany. No less of a celebrity was Büsch, the veteran Director of the Trade Academy and the author of numerous treatises on economic theory and practice.[1] Though an economist rather than a politician, he welcomed the Revolution, and advanced a certain distance under its guidance. A passage in one of his early books, approving the privileged position of nobles in the State service, was modified in an edition published after the cataclysm. As the Revolution advanced he was filled with almost equal contempt for the excesses of the French and for the anti-revolutionary fervour of the Powers. Though less liberal than Sieveking and Reimarus, and though, according to Varnhagen, somewhat conceited, he was none the less an ornament to the city.

When war broke out Lehoc remained in neutral Hamburg as an unofficial representative of his country, and the city continued to trade with France. ' M. Lehoc remains here,' reported the British Minister, September 25, 1792, ' but he carefully avoids making any formal application to the Senate of this Republic, being aware, I suppose, that it could not have any weight. He continues, however, to enjoy all the honours and privileges due to a foreign Minister.' His position was rendered impossible by the execution of the King, which ' filled the minds of everybody here with the justest and liveliest sentiments of horror and indignation. It seems pretty certain that the remonstrances made here against him were chiefly personal, as he is suspected of having employed emissaries in Prussia and other States for the purpose of propagating the very destructive principles of the present French Government. Several merchants here are likewise accused of having assisted him in these views. His departure has occasioned a very great sensation, as the Hamburgers are very fearful lest it should prove detrimental to their trade; and it is believed that a present was made to him to induce him to represent the circumstance in as favourable a light as possible.' Lehoc took his departure without waiting to be expelled, receiving presents and expressions of good-will from the city in which he had made many friendships. Even then a certain amount of trade continued. ' The Senate is resolved to humour the French nation so far as is compatible with our duty to the Empire,' wrote

[1] See Roscher, *Geschichte der Nationalökonomie in Deutschland*, pp. 559–76.

Syndicus Matsen to Haugwitz, ' for France could do us infinite harm. The French nation will still exist when the rule of cannibals ends. If there is a collision of duties, we shall hold to the Empire.'

When the Empire declared war the old Hanse city was of course involved in hostilities, but it endeavoured to conduct them on the principle of limited liability. The Senate forbade the sale of grain, cattle, and munitions, but a good deal of contraband trade was carried on. In 1794 the Chamber of Commerce asked Schlözer to write on behalf of neutrality—a request which was angrily declined. ' While the French torment the Franconians and the Rhineland,' he cried, ' the Hamburger trades with the inhuman enemy. Fie on these petty mercantile gains ! ' The rebuke brought no blush to the cheeks of the Senate, and Büsch calmly replied that their prosperity was of benefit to the whole country. When Prussia withdrew from the struggle in 1795, many Hamburgers expressed their wish for neutrality, and Reinhard was sent by the Directory to renew diplomatic relations ; but the city hesitated to recognise him, as the Empire was still at war, and it was important not to alienate England.[1] In this moment of difficulty Sieveking, now re-established in the confidence of his fellow citizens, was sent to Paris, where he negotiated a commercial treaty and persuaded the Government to allow Reinhard to reside in Altona and to enter into unofficial relations. Thus nobly did he requite the unworthy suspicions of which he had been the object.

As the century drew to its close the stock of the French Republic began to fall. Reichardt's monthly journal, ' Frankreich,' in which he received assistance from Poel, preached liberal doctrine from the safe anchorage of Altona. Reinhard, Villers, and Matthieu Dumas formed a Republican coterie, and Varnhagen has described the welcome of Lafayette after his release from an Austrian dungeon ; but the tide was no longer flowing towards Paris. Enemies of the Revolution—such as Jacobi from Düsseldorf, and Schlosser from Baden—made their home in the old city. A number of Émigrés, driven from Belgium and the Rhine, found a temporary haven, among them Rivarol, the wittiest Frenchman of his age ; and a French bookshop was started as a centre of counter-revolutionary propaganda.[2] The French Minister was recognised after the Treaty of Leoben ; but the popularity of his country was diminished by its demands for money. Gallomania was succeeded by Anglomania, and for a time the English language and fashions, newspapers and books were in the ascendant. A few years later Anglomania was in turn replaced by a vibrant patriotism in the days of disaster, and nowhere was Napoleon more detested. It was in Hamburg that

[1] Lang, *Graf Reinhard*, ch. viii.   [2] See Lescure, *Rivarol*.

Perthes founded his publisher's business for the revival of national feeling. With Crabb Robinson's picture of the city in 1807 we may bid farewell to the Hamburg liberals. ' Of all my acquaintances the most interesting is Mr. Poel. He is the brother of my landlady, proprietor of the " Altona Mercury," a man of letters, affluent and hospitable. He keeps a good table and gives dinners and suppers several times a week. He was an ardent friend of the French Revolution, but is now in all things an anti-Gallican. But he is one of the few who, like Mrs. Barbauld's lover, will still " hope though hope were lost." He is persuaded that, in the end, the good cause will conquer. His wife was also a woman of great personal worth, a daughter of the celebrated Professor Büsch. His sister was a very sensible and interesting woman. These ladies had a friend, Madame Sieveking, who formed with them a society which in few places is equalled. She was a widow, and the daughter of the well-known Reimarus. On the borders of the Elbe Poel had a country house, where, especially on Sundays, there used to be delightful dinner-parties. In this house my happiest hours were spent.'[1]

II

Among the petty States of central Germany, Weimar, Gotha, and Anhalt-Dessau were honourably distinguished by the excellence of their rulers and the relative prosperity of their inhabitants. The two Courts at Weimar agreed in dislike of the Revolution. The Dowager Duchess, who was in Italy when the drama commenced, explained her attitude in a letter to Knebel. ' I will not pronounce on it ; but I think one may say with the Greeks, " with you the wise men discuss and the madmen decide." So far it is utter anarchy, and only time will show if any good will come of it.'[2] While retaining her love of French literature Anna Amalia had no sympathy with ' French ideas,' and her good wishes accompanied the invading armies, which were led by her brother, the Duke of Brunswick, and accompanied by her son. Karl August, though no reactionary, was equally deaf to the appeal of the Revolution, and he soon began to hate it. He had carried out reforms in his own little State and saw no need for a violent upheaval in France or anywhere else. ' He who observes the French nation at close quarters,' he wrote to Knebel on his return from the Valmy campaign, ' must feel a perfect detestation for them.[3] They are all very well informed, but every

---

[1] *Diary*, i. 122–5.
[2] See Bode, *Amalie Herzogin von Weimar*, iii. 184 ; and Gerard, *Life of Anna Amalia*.   [3] Knebel, *Nachlass*, ii. 177.

trace of moral feeling is extinguished. I hope these times will implant such disgust in my children's minds that they will cultivate the utmost simplicity, which alone brings lasting happiness. What is the good of the so-called and highly praised Atticism to the French, when they have lost all honesty?' Despite this philippic, the Duke placed one of his country residences at the disposal of Mounier, the distinguished constitutional royalist, who opened a school to prepare young men for the public service, and for six years occupied an honoured place in the life of the little capital.[1] Neither revolutions nor political theories, believed Karl August, were needed if rulers and ruled alike performed their allotted duties. His view of the princely office was shared by the most distinguished of his subjects, who repeatedly acknowledged his debt to his ' Augustus and Maecenas.'

Modest and small is my master among Germania's princes ;
　　Circumscribed is his land, limited what he can do.
But if we only made use of our powers after his model,
　　Then what honour and pride were it a German to be.
For he has given me that which is seldom vouchsafed by the mighty,
　　Friendship and leisure and trust, meadow and garden and house.[2]

' I have been intimately connected with the Grand Duke for half a century,' remarked the poet to Eckermann a century later, ' and I have not known a single day in which he has not thought of doing something for the benefit of the land. It is said that I am a slave to princes. If that is so, it is my consolation that I am the slave of one who is himself a slave to the common weal.'

The Duchess Luise, though of a thoughtful and independent mind, shared her husband's opinions, and had no leanings to democracy or cosmopolitanism. It was friendship, not the ideas of 1789, which made her implore her friend Frau von Stein to drop ' Madame ' and ' Yours obediently ' in her letters. On the death of the Emperor Joseph she wrote a gloomy letter to her brother.[3] ' What do you say to the commotion in France ? Do you think all will go well, or will the country become bankrupt ? Are you an enthusiast for the so-called liberty, for tyrannical democracy, for the confiscation of property ? For my part I am satiated with all these grand sentiments, which are, as a rule, nothing more than words and fine phrases. People are always the same, possessing the same passions, and allowing themselves to be ridden by them ; and in spite of all

[1] See Lanzac de Laborie, *Mounier*, ch. xiii.
[2] *Venetian Epigrams*, No. 34.
[3] Bojanowski, *Luise, Grossherzogin von Sachsen-Weimar*, p. 223.

our philosophers and all our culture they will remain the same.'
' Anacharsis Cloots,' she wrote to Frau von Stein in 1792, ' has
suggested in the Assembly the murder of the King of Prussia and
of " cannibal " Brunswick, with great applause.   Really this nation
has neither shame nor decency.   Just think that all foreign writers
who have spoken favourably of the Revolution must receive French
citizenship.   Schiller is among them, but I hope he will refuse.'   A
week later she wrote to the same friend on the September massacres.
' I have never observed that mankind grows better ;   and these
horrors prove clearly that human nature remains the same.   Virtue
is the private property of certain individuals and will never be
universal.' [1]   The death of the King and Queen roused her flaming
indignation.   ' If God would only overthrow the *Sansculottes*,' she
wrote to her brother, ' and take pity on honest folk !   How sad
that one can no longer count on miracles ! '   She rejoiced in the
recapture of Mainz.   ' Our *beaux esprits* complain that the clubists
are to be punished.   As if these rascals had the right to commit
crimes with impunity ! '   She felt pity and sympathy for the
Émigrés.   ' Eisenach is full of them,' she wrote to her brother, ' and
their society is very agreeable.   Poor things ! I fear they will never
see their country again.' [2]

To Frau von Stein, as to her mistress, the Revolution—even in
its most hopeful days—made no appeal ;   and she marvelled that all
Weimar did not share her views.   ' Knebel,' she wrote in 1790, ' is
quite mad.   We have had such a quarrel about the French Revolution that he will not come near me for a week.' [3]   Her old friendship
with the Duchess grew more intimate in their common opposition
to the new doctrines.   She wrote angrily to Lotte on hearing that
Schiller had been made a French citizen.   ' Tell me what he has
written in praise or defence of the Revolution.'   She described how
Blumenbach, the Göttingen professor, on a visit to Weimar, no
longer took off his hat or said ' Your obedient servant.'   ' Would to
God the French had kept to these foolish trifles ! '   Hearing of Herder's
explanation that he loved not the French, but the triumph of reason,
she exclaims excitedly : ' Is it possible to call the triumph of robbers
the triumph of reason ? '   The news of Thermidor comes as balm
to wounded spirits.   ' Robespierre's fate did not surprise me,' she
writes to Lotte ;   ' I regard it as preordained that these monsters
should gobble each other up.' [4]   On the other hand she notes with
dismay the gradual weakening of the anti-revolutionary fervour.
' The warring Powers in Germany seem tired of bloodshed, and are
ready to give up everything for the sake of peace.   To imagine the

[1] Düntzer, *C. v. Stein*, i. 363–9.   [2] Bojanowski, pp. 231, 235, 238.
[3] Düntzer, *Charlotte von Stein*, i. 350–1.   [4] Düntzer, ii. 11–14.

beautiful Rhine as a French possession gives me a stab.   One thinks
with terror of the moment when the King of Prussia will perhaps
withdraw his troops.   The Empire does not give him sufficient help.
Who knows if it will be the last time that we shall pass together in
peace ?   For the French, or French principles, will one day make the
world a great wilderness.'   Her dark forebodings proved only too well
founded ; for she lived to hear the thunder of the guns at Jena, and
to see Weimar a prey to the drunken soldiery of an omnipotent
Emperor.

'These fatal politics,' wrote Privy Councillor Voigt to Schiller
in 1793, 'exhaust and divide us.'   Goethe was hostile from the
beginning, while Schiller's indifference passed into detestation, and
Wieland's support was never more than lukewarm.   On the other
hand Herder remained Gallophil, and was stoutly supported by
Knebel, the most radical member of the Weimar circle, despite his
military training and his long association with the Court.[1]   'My
heart expands in view of the many new prospects for our life and the
life of mankind,' he wrote joyfully to his sister in January 1790.[2]   'I
live exclusively in the latest news from France, which uplifts my
mind and heart.   We in Germany are wrapped in fog and night and
Gothic darkness ; but surely before long a ray of daylight will break
for us, and man will become aware what he can achieve if he only
dares.'   'It is good when people grumble,' he added a few weeks
later, 'for even widespread suffering is preferable to bovine satisfaction.'   Like other observers he was disappointed at the development of events ; but his change of attitude was not so great as was
reported to the Duchess.   'I am glad to find that your views are
altered,' she wrote in October 1790 ; 'for now you will have to leave
that country and its democrats to its fate and its Utopian dreams.'
His views were expressed in frequent letters to Herder.   'I try to
make a little France within myself.   The world always pursues an
oblique course, and we must train individuals before we can create
regiments.   I cannot blame the Duchess for being so anti-Gallican.'
He lamented the indifference of Germany, adding that the spirit of
the nation could never soar so long as the happiness of the individual
depended entirely on princes.   He abhorred the plan of armed
intervention in French politics, and in the summer of 1792 described
the situation in Weimar to Herder, who was taking the waters in
Aachen.   'Everything here speaks of war ; everywhere one sees
cannons and standards.   The general effect is childish and repulsive.
In these marching regiments one sees humanity in chains, dull and

[1] See Düntzer, *Freundesbilder aus Goethe's Kreise*.   A full biography is
needed.

[2] *Aus Knebel's Briefwechsel mit seiner Schwester*, p. 107.

sad, set in motion and kept in order by force alone. The two stimuli without which the sight of soldiers is offensive—namely, defence of the Fatherland and desire for conquest—are lacking in these mechanical figures. The whole war seems to me like a debauch.'[1]

Though he detested the war, and foretold its failure, Knebel found little to cheer his spirits in the conduct of France. 'Since the Fête of the Federation the spirit of faction has displaced the love of liberty. Self-indulgence and passion appeal to man more than reason. There are, however, many signs that the spirit of liberty is growing in Germany.' Like all humane men he was appalled by the events of August and September. 'The French have saved us the trouble of taking an intelligent interest in their affairs. Yet we must not pass a final judgment. Perhaps some good will emerge from all this folly. At any rate the campaign will not develop as the German heroes anticipate.'[2] Like Herder he denounced the Terror, and expressed the universal admiration for Charlotte Corday in halting verse. 'The Judge of Life stood before Marat and said, Die! thou hast shed blood. And the Angel of Liberty came to him, and he died by the hand of the noblest of women.'[3] He continued to lament the absence of divine discontent among his countrymen. On a visit to Bayreuth in 1797 he found the people comfortable, but unimaginative. 'They are so used to subjection that there is no fear of a revolution. Nobody reads any paper but the local journal.'[4] He was profoundly convinced that the Revolution was needed, and that its influence would continue to operate. 'It was a revolution of Humanity,' he remarked to Luden in 1813, 'which only broke out in the sorest point, and to which none of the plasters, hitherto applied, brought healing. Even Napoleon only restored the surface of the body.'[5]

The University of Jena naturally felt the breath of the new spirit. 'When the paper arrives,' wrote Reinhold, the popular Professor of Philosophy, to Jacobi in 1790, 'I am forced to put aside my work, however urgent it be. I expect as little as you from " government by reason " ; but I cannot help rejoicing at the intellectual forces which I note beneath the extravagances. I believe that spirit has never had a greater share in a revolution, though even in the present instance it is not the first nor the chief of its motive powers.'[6] An attempt was made by some of the more enlightened students to employ ' French ideas ' as a weapon for the

[1] *Von und an Herder*, iii. 72, 74, 81–2.
[2] *Ib.*, iii. 85, 91.   [3] *Nachlass*, i. 79.
[4] *Briefwechsel mit seiner Schwester*, p. 127.
[5] *Nachlass*, iii. 108.   [6] *Aus Jacobi's Nachlass*, i. 127.

suppression of the duel.[1] A flaming manifesto of 1792 to their 'German brothers' dreams of a union of students for the purification and elevation of University life. 'Everywhere the spirit of nations raises itself to secure the recognition of their divine rights, and even princes step down from the throne of caprice to make place for it, and feel themselves ennobled by their act. Shall we not, German brothers, share in this great enterprise ? Shall not we youths, nourished on the sciences, seek a place among the heroes of our time who strive to make the rights of reason prevail over hoary prejudices ? We lucky contemporaries of a philosophy which sets up the purest principles for legislation and thereby lays the foundation of the highest morality, shall we alone, amid the universal striving around us towards the ennobling of mankind, feel no vocation to make reason our lawgiver ? '

Though the movement was frowned on by the Government and came to nothing, the University was regarded by French agents as generally sympathetic. 'A young French citizen returning from Jena,' reported Bacher, secretary to the French Embassy in Switzerland, 'relates that the professors celebrate the great events of the Revolution and develop its principles, while the liberty of the press is unlimited.' Further details are provided in a report by the same diplomatist, written a few months later. 'The University is now the home of reason. The French Government would do well to send thither some students, ardent patriots, who would inflame their German comrades, who, in turn, would propagate French principles in their homes and render priceless service in the formation of opinion. Some old professors, stuffed with ancient prejudices, seeing that their pupils, electrified by some young Frenchmen, deserted their lectures and let them die of hunger, have joined the revolutionary dance, so that the whole University is now up to the standard of events. These details should be brought to the knowledge of the Committee of Public Safety, which will be glad to hear that the Duke of Weimar, from the beginning of the Revolution, has deserved well of the friends of liberty.'[2] This was an over-sanguine view, and the little principality did not wholly escape the deadening influence of the counter-revolution. 'French affairs,' wrote Privy Councillor Voigt, 'are throwing back our liberty of thought and utterance many years. No prince will permit anything which seems to diminish servile obedience.'

[1] See *Die Jenaer Duellgegner des Jahres* 1792, in *Quellen u. Darstellungen z. Geschichte der Burschenschaft*, vol. iv. ; and Keil, *Geschichte des Jenaischen Studentenlebens*, ch. vi.

[2] *Papiers de Barthélemy*, iv. 77, 351–4.

III

Next to Weimar, the most enlightened Court of the five Ernestine houses was Gotha.[1]   In his youth Ernest II had travelled widely, learning in Holland and Switzerland to admire liberty, and in Paris making acquaintance with the Philosophes.   ' Young man,' said Diderot in kindly warning, ' you are not made for this world, and your ways are not those of Paris.   Do not linger too long among us ; we might corrupt you.'   Succeeding his blameless but common-place father in 1772, he governed his little duchy with conscience and skill ; counted Voltaire and Grimm, Goethe and Herder among his friends, and joined the ranks of the Illuminati.   He was born for study rather than for rule.   He had something more than an amateur's knowledge of physics and astronomy, was a member of the Royal Society, collected books and coins, encouraged education, and reformed the Poor Law.   To a ruler who approved the English Constitution and sympathised with the American Colonies, the summoning of the States-General brought unfeigned satisfaction ; but the development of events distressed him, and for a time he feared the spread of violence over Europe.   But he desired to spare his subjects the horrors of war, commuting the obligation to supply troops in 1793, and only dispatching them in 1795, when he was compelled.   ' His thoughts,' records Friedrich Jacobs, ' turned to the United States as a haven where he might live as a free citizen for himself and for culture.   This idea he nursed for years, and he selected strongly bound books to accompany him, which he called the American library.   Among them were French works, including Raynal's " History of the Indies." '   Throughout the years of excitement and conflict the kindly Duke kept his balance, tolerating the expression of every variety of opinion.

' On a visit to Gotha,' reported Grimm to Catherine in November 1790, ' I found an excellent atmosphere, and discovered that our writers had not succumbed to the *mal français*, like so many other German *beaux-esprits*.'   Three months later he combats the report of French agents as to sedition in Weimar and Gotha.   ' The poison-sellers are not so stupid as to pitch their tents in little towns where they would be unmasked in a moment.   They need large theatres for their operations.   I do not know enough of Weimar to speak with authority ; but an excellent spirit prevails in Gotha among those who write for public instruction.   It was to writings published there that the prompt restoration of tranquillity among the peasants

---

[1] See Beck, *Ernst der Zweite* ;   Jacobs, *Vermischte Schriften*, i. 1–86 ; and Reichard, *Selbstbiographie*.

in Saxony was due.'[1] But while the conservative Grimm approved the steadiness of the Duke, men of more advanced views were delighted to find him such a staunch liberal. ' Meister, an excellent Zurich patriot, favourably known in Paris by his sentiments and high literary merits, has been to see me,' reported the diplomat Barthélemy from Switzerland in 1793.[2] ' In speaking to me of the Duke, whom he knows well, he said : " His ideas are as revolutionary as my own." We ought to have cultivated the smaller princes of Germany, who are afraid of Prussia and Austria ; for we could have made them valuable agents of division.' The Duke was a moderate liberal, not a revolutionary ; but his wife, a princess of Saxe-Meiningen, made no secret of her radical opinions, and when excesses became frequent she accepted them as a fitting punishment of the great. ' She took the side of the Revolution very strongly,' records Reichard.[3] ' In her rooms were the busts of the leaders, from Bailly and Lafayette to the Directory, one following the other into the rubbish-room to make place for the new-comers, like the originals in Paris.' When Reichard published his ' Revolutionsalmanach ' in 1792, she ordered a dozen copies ; but finding it hostile to the Revolution, she returned them in anger to the bookseller.

Her views were shared by Prince August, brother of the Duke, who was known throughout Germany as a friend of the Revolution.[4] His wide culture and expansive disposition made him a popular figure, and he counted Goethe and Herder among his friends. Responsive to all the new ideas of the time, he zealously embraced the ideals of the Illuminati. A political and religious freethinker, he saluted the dawn of liberty in France, and regretted that his country lagged so far behind. ' In France,' he wrote to Herder, ' the collision of old and new ideas produces a ferment before which our inveterate short-sightedness shrinks back with derision ; but it will undoubtedly exert as mighty an influence on the destiny of all peoples in the centuries to come as the invention of the magnetic needle, paper, printing, and gunpowder has had on the last three or four centuries.' He was passionately opposed to the war. ' As the King of Prussia has graciously resolved to turn France into a heap of ashes, his way lies over Erfurt and Gotha.' The conservative Reichard bluntly declares that ' the Prince stood on the side of the Jacobins ' ; and the Abbé Barruel, who naïvely traced the

---

[1] *Lettres de Grimm*, pp. 382, 407.
[2] *Papiers de Barthélemy*, iii. 248–50.
[3] *Selbstbiographie*, p. 287.
[4] See Suphan, *Goethe u. Prinz August von Gotha, Goethe-Jahrbuch,* vi. 27–58.

Revolution to the secret societies, refers to him as Walther Fürst, his name among the Illuminati. He expressed his wishes for a French victory, and remained friends with the enemy. When the first skirmishes ended in retreat and disgrace for the French levies, he wrote regretfully to Herder : ' I wish the vanquished a victory at some future opportunity, even if I have no great hopes of it. The fury and folly of a few thousands cannot quite outweigh my sympathy with the twenty-five million. It will be harder to overwhelm them on their own soil ; and if our beloved Duke is to flesh his sword on them, I hope it may be outside the frontiers of France.' After Valmy he saw that the invasion had failed. ' I do not in the least believe that Paris will be reached after a promenade. *Ces messieurs ont compté sans leur hôte.* The bill will be all the heavier and the retreat the harder. But I will not be a Cassandra for our good friends (Goethe and Karl August). I hope they will get safely out of the trap ; but I wish they had not stuck their heads into it.'

Prince August was naturally shocked by the September massacres ; but he declined to believe in the immaculate innocence of the King. ' If he has only supplied the funds for a few hundred men in the service of his brothers, that is guilt enough ; for it is the people's money, and it is used against them. Let us draw a veil over so many horrors on both sides. And now I will tell you something for your ears alone. When two Cardinals meet they drink the health of Christ in *Lagrima Christi.* So I do with my friends in my letters, and I drink *La Salute della libertà* with them in secret.' He longed for the conclusion of the hated conflict. ' Perhaps Belgium will be lost to Austria this winter for ever, or perhaps there will be peace, if there is still any wisdom in the hearts and heads of rulers. That is my most urgent counsel and my dearest wish.' When Goethe visited the Prince in May 1793, he had convinced himself that the invasion had been a wholesale folly, and he agreed pretty closely with his host as to the responsibility of ' aristocratic sinners.' He warmly approved the Peace of Basle, and died before Prussia again plunged into the furnace of war. A singularly modern man, emancipated from tradition and scorning etiquette, he gave himself no airs, enjoyed the best society of his time as an equal among equals, and entrusted his bark without selfish fears to the democratic current which was hurrying the world towards uncharted seas.

In addition to the Duchess and Prince August, a third representative of advanced ideas lived in Gotha, to the dismay of all good conservatives. When the storm broke over the heads of the Illuminati in Bavaria in 1784, Weishaupt, the founder of the Order, found shelter and a pension in Gotha, where he lived in peaceful obscurity till his death in 1830. 'According to letters which I receive from Germany,' wrote the Abbé Barruel in his voluminous attack on Jacobinism in 1797, 'the Duke now recognises his mistake, and no longer allows Weishaupt to appear in his presence. But he is still admitted to the Duchess, and it is to her influence that his continued residence is attributed. I do not know if Prince August shares his brother's disgust for the Order.' [1]

The most active literary opponent of French principles was Ottokar Reichard, the son of a Gotha official, whose early years were devoted to travel, poetry, and the stage, and who at the outbreak of the Revolution occupied the post of librarian to the Duke. [2] On a visit to France in 1786 he had seen signs of the gathering storm ; but when it broke he at first felt ' not the slightest desire to declare himself for or against it.' Indifference soon deepened into hostility, and he exchanged literature for politics. Though a Mason and an Illuminé like his master, he was angered by the attitude of the Orders as defined in a Masonic address delivered in 1790 on the Duke's birthday. In face of the signs and wonders in France, declared the speaker, every Mason must cast off indifference and take sides ; and the soldiers present were adjured to observe a judicious neutrality, if their help was demanded for the suppression of popular revolts. This provocative address was followed by the withdrawal from the Orders of Reichard and other men of conservative leanings. 'Every moderate mind,' he writes in his Autobiography, 'must be embittered by the madness of certain unquiet heads in my Fatherland, who appear in writings and conduct as the heralds of the new rights of man, and against whose influence I exerted myself to the full, as my knowledge of many of these world-benefactors showed me their true motives.' With this object he issued a series of warnings addressed to public opinion in Germany and elsewhere. 'An appeal of a German to patriotic Swiss' exhorted them to watch French propaganda. 'A Dialogue between two Peasants on Rebellion and Government' was suggested by the peasant risings in Saxony, and was rewarded by a present from Dresden. 'An Appeal of a German to his fellow countrymen on the Rhine' brought distinctions and remuneration from Vienna and the Rhineland, while 'The Rights of Man on both sides of the Rhine' was published in the same year at the expense of the Emperor. 'A nice fellow,' wrote Sömmerring at this time to Forster ; ' but what an aristocrat ! ' [3]

[1] *Memoirs of Jacobinism*, iv. 262–3.
[2] See his *Selbstbiographie*.
[3] *Forster's Briefwechsel mit Sömmerring*, pp. 564–5.

In 1792 the eager propagandist established the 'Revolutions-almanach,' which lived for six years. The journal was warmly approved in conservative circles, and was brought to the notice of Catherine by the zealous Grimm. In sending a copy, ' the homage of the author, the wise Reichard,' he described its character and fortunes. ' This almanach, composed in an excellent spirit, is now in its second year. It is obtaining a wide vogue, though the German Jacobins have done their utmost to stifle it at birth, so that on its appearance the author could not secure its advertisement even for money. None the less, it will be the almanach of all wise folk, in spite of the contagion of the French leprosy, which has been arrested but not extirpated in Germany. Reichard has just brought me a further offering for your Majesty, called "The Guide of Travellers in Europe," dedicated to you. I note that for years past he has paid homage to you in all his productions, and that his name sometimes figures in the letters of the *Immortal* fills him with pride. If, in consideration of all this, you would allow me to make him a gift of forty or thirty louis, it would be money well spent. Not only would it add to his happiness but it would cause the German Jacobins to gnash their teeth.'

IV

Of the four petty principalities into which the Duchy of Anhalt had been divided in the seventeenth century—Zerbst, Köthen, Bernburg, and Dessau—the latter was the best governed. The exemplary Leopold Friedrich Franz, grandson of the Old Dessauer, was intelligently interested in art, literature, and education ; and it was in his capital and under his patronage that Basedow set up his famous secondary school, the Philanthropinum. During his long reign many material improvements were introduced into the little State ; and though he left the Estates unsummoned he proved as enlightened an autocrat as the Dukes of Gotha and Weimar. Georg Forster, who was not easy to please, confessed that Dessau reconciled him to the government of princes. ' I was glad to find how satisfied are the Dessauers with their prince,' echoed Novalis after a visit in 1794.[1] ' This little land is one of the happiest in Germany. He seeks in every way to augment the well-being of his subjects. His Court is not large, and there are few fêtes. His only extravagance is hunting.' ' I wish you could have the happiness of meeting this noble pair,' wrote Eliza von der Recke to Bürger. ' You would thank God that such princes live. Luise of Dessau is a rare and splendid soul.' [2]

[1] Novalis, *Schriften*, i. 421-2. [2] *Briefe von und an Bürger*, iii. 315.

The Landgrave Wilhelm of Hesse-Cassel had supported his father's sale of mercenaries to England and inherited a fortune without parallel in Germany; but whereas Frederick had spent the blood-money on buildings and in riotous living, his repulsive son was a miser, who increased his treasure by lending money to his subjects at high interest.[1] But though parsimony ruled at Court, debauchery continued, and no one was sure of the exact number of his bastards. Though an alumnus of Göttingen and a dabbler in literature and art, he dismissed the distinguished professors whom his father had summoned to Cassel. Detesting the Revolution, he took every means to keep his subjects in ignorance of its doctrines and progress. He forbade round hats as Jacobin symbols, while compelling the prisoners who cleaned the streets to wear them. He prohibited foreign travel and applause at the theatre to avoid encouraging the spirit of criticism; but his police were scared when they discovered that the lions which supported the Hessian coat of arms in the market-place of Hanau had been decorated with red caps of liberty. He kept a strict watch on opinion and opened letters in the post. His librarian, Kuhn, was punished for praising the French Constitution and describing Mirabeau as the first head in Europe. He was believed to sell his gaol-birds to the army of the Émigrés at thirty gulden apiece, and when they deserted he arrested them and sold them again. On the other hand he refused a petition from the brother of the King of France for the shelter of twelve thousand Émigrés, alleging that they would involve the country in danger; and, though the greedy ruler joined in the war of 1792 for a price, he was the first after Frederick William of Prussia to make peace with the Republic. Though he obtained the Electoral title in 1803, he lost his dominions for a time after Jena, hesitating through avarice to take sides till it was too late. No German prince of his generation was less accessible to generous ideas or was governed by more sordid considerations. On his return from a seven years' exile after the collapse of King Jerome, richer, greedier, and more autocratic than ever, he decreed the integral restoration of the *status quo* of 1806. The Code Napoléon and the beneficent legislation of the Kingdom of Westphalia were swept away, and the old burdens and abuses were restored.

Hesse-Darmstadt, on the other hand, the younger line of the Hessian house,[2] was blessed with a relatively enlightened ruler, Ludwig X, who succeeded his father, Ludwig IX, in 1790, and later received from Napoleon the title of Grand Duke. As Crown Prince he had consorted with Masons, and was believed to be a member of the Illuminati; and on his accession he did what could be done

---

[1] See Treitschke, iv. 329–51.   [2] Treitschke, ii. 691–6.

to compensate Karl Friedrich Moser for the ill-treatment he had suffered. He loved literature and the arts, and it was during his reign of forty years that Darmstadt awoke to a more vigorous intellectual life. Though determined to retain his authority, he moved with the time—abolishing the exemption of the nobility from taxation, and allowing considerable liberty to the press. He was, nevertheless, alarmed by the unrest caused by the Revolution, and in 1791 proposed joint action to his neighbour of Hesse-Cassel.[1] ' Events in Saxony last summer,' he wrote, ' show how quickly the spirit of revolt spreads. That it was soon extinguished there does not prove that it could so easily be tamed elsewhere. In the Rhineland there is special danger, as the people hate the nobility.' He therefore proposed a union of German princes for the maintenance of the German Constitution, headed by the two Hesses and Mainz, and the drawing of a line of defence. The Landgrave of Hesse-Cassel declined the proposal on the ground that there was no peril. Ludwig replied that the danger from discontent was very real, and that he expected a revolt in the Palatinate before long. After his rebuff in Cassel, Ludwig concluded a defensive alliance with Mainz, and took his full share in the wars of the Revolution.

Far more enviable was the lot of Hesse-Homburg under its Landgrave Frederick V, the friend of Klopstock, Goethe, and Lavater, who governed his tiny principality for over half a century with a father's loving care.[2] He sharply denounced ' the open or secret friends of France, the German-French '—above all, the Mainz clubists—as a disgrace to their country and as the main cause of the failure of the war ; but his rule was mild, and his reforms in trade and industry, education and the Poor Law, showed that it was possible to be a patriot without being a reactionary. The same lesson was taught in Catholic Münster, where the enlightened rule of Fürstenberg established a network of educational facilities to be found nowhere else in Germany.

[1] See Strippelmann, *Beiträge zur Geschichte Hessen-Cassels*, i. 1–13.
[2] See Karl Schwartz, *Friedrich V von Hessen-Homburg*. His thoughts on the French Revolution are printed in vol. ii. pp. 174–6.

CHAPTER XX

THE RHINELAND

WHILE the French Revolution reached North and East Germany through newspapers, pamphlets, and the reports of travellers, the associations of the Rhineland with its western neighbour were of necessity far more intimate.[1]   The fringe of the Empire was linked to France by the common possession of Roman traditions; while for generations German princes had been in French pay, and the younger sons of noble families had sought a career in French regiments. French was the language of polite society, and the detachment from intellectual currents in Germany was almost complete. Linked to French civilisation by so many ties, nothing but the vaguest sentiment of nationality existed in the Rhineland ; and the bewildering territorial mosaic of which it was composed offered an insurmountable obstacle to healthy political life and economic prosperity.   No portion of the Empire, except Thuringia, was broken up into so many fragments as the long strip of territory collectively described as the Left Bank.   The Duchy of Cleves and Guelders in the extreme north belonged to Prussia, whose southern frontiers marched with those of the Elector of Cologne.   To the west of the Electorate lay the Duchy of Jülich, the property of the Elector Palatine.   Journeying southward the traveller passed in succession through the Electorates of Trier, Mainz, and the Palatinate.   The southern portion of the Rhineland was divided among a crowd of petty potentates and principalities, including the Bishoprics of Speier and Worms, the Duchies of Zweibrücken and Nassau-Saarbrück, the domains of Imperial Knights, abbeys and religious Orders ; while the Free Cities were represented by Cologne and Aachen in the north, by Worms and Speier in the south.   The whole country was almost equally shared between ecclesiastical and

---

[1] See Perthes, *Politische Zustände* ; Hashagen, *Das Rheinland und die Französische Herrschaft* ; Sagnac, *Le Rhin Français pendant La Révolution et l'Empire* ; Rambaud, *Les Français sur le Rhin.*

secular masters, the standard of government varying with the character of the ruler and the tradition of the State. The administration of Prussia's provinces was eulogised by Mirabeau, while that of Jülich received a testimonial from Forster. Nassau-Saarbrück enjoyed a tranquil prosperity denied to its neighbour Zweibrücken, the luckless victim of its half-crazed Duke. The left bank portions of the Palatinate suffered no less than those of the right from its bigoted and extravagant ruler in distant Munich. The four Free Cities were stagnant survivals of the Middle Ages, misgoverned by their burgomasters and exploited by senatorial oligarchies.

I

The Left Bank followed the earliest scenes of the Revolution with less sustained interest than was felt in many other parts of the Empire, where feudal burdens were more onerous ; but within a few weeks of the fall of the Bastille, the political and social problems raised by the great upheaval were presented to the apathetic Rhinelanders in tangible form. ' One must distinguish between the voluntary and compulsory emigrations,' wrote Madame de Staël. ' After the fall of the Monarchy we all emigrated.' This distinction between ' the emigration of pride ' and ' the emigration of necessity ' was fully appreciated in the territories in which the newcomers sought refuge.[1] On the fall of the Bastille Condé rode post-haste from Chantilly to Versailles to urge the suppression of the Revolution by force ; and when the King rejected his advice, he shook the dust of France off his feet. By desire of his royal brother the Comte d'Artois left at the same time, accompanied by a suite of eighty-two, expecting to return in a few months and find the revolt at an end. To the advance guard of the Émigrés the ' principles of 1789 ' were a deadly heresy, to be extirpated by fire and sword. The sovereigns of Europe were expected to rally to their aid ; but the King of Sweden was the only monarch who really troubled himself about their misfortunes. Whatever the merits of their cause, its advocates were singularly ill-fitted to secure it support. Artois was vain, ignorant, and excitable, and his adviser, the frivolous Calonne, was worthy of his master. Condé was made of sterner stuff ; but his abilities were mediocre, and he had no head for politics. Moreover, from the outset the Émigrés constituted themselves an Opposition not only to the Revolution but to the King, who was prepared for reform and had no stomach for civil war. They

---

[1] See Daudet, *Histoire de l'Émigration* ; and Forneron, *Histoire des Émigrés*.

grumbled because they were forbidden to organise an army, and the King frowned on the endeavours of his witless partisans to force his hand. ' Till his death,' writes Ernest Daudet, the classical historian of the Émigration, with just severity, ' Louis XVI had no worse enemies than the Émigrés, who were the principal authors of his troubles. The princes were disobedient to their brother and disloyal to their country.' Artois was received by his brother-in-law at Turin ; but throughout the dominions of the House of Savoy he had few friends, and when the King of Sardinia declined to enter a coalition, Calonne urged his master to strike his tent. To all who had eyes to see, the first Émigration was a convincing pictorial condemnation of the *ancien régime*. ' By threatening us with the return of despotism,' complained Mirabeau bitterly in 1790, ' they will drag us willy-nilly to a republic.'

In 1791 the Émigration entered on a new stage. As the breach of the French Court with the Revolution became wider, the Émigrés grew more numerous and more audacious. Artois took up his residence in Coblenz at the moment of the flight to Varennes, the failure of which caused no sorrow to the more selfish of his followers, who feared that the King, if free, might compromise with the Revolution. It was now obvious to all the world, they argued, that he was no longer his own master, and that the direction of the royalist cause could only be undertaken by his brothers. The Count of Provence, who escaped with the King and reached Coblenz by way of Belgium, at first showed himself as intransigeant as Artois, and acted as if Louis was already dethroned. It was in vain that the French Court vetoed armed demonstrations, in which it read a sentence of death. From the arrival of the royal princes Coblenz was the headquarters of the Émigration, which swelled the population by twenty thousand. The newcomers were assured of a warm welcome from their uncle, a son of Augustus II of Saxony. The Elector possessed a kind heart and slender abilities ; and his power was limited both by the rich Chapter, to which he owed his election, and by the Estates whose consent to taxation was constitutionally required. His natural policy was to increase his control over the clergy and nobility by making common cause with the bourgeoisie ; but he had not the wit to profit by the reforming currents set in motion by the Revolution. He ostentatiously identified himself with his guests, and was swept away by the hurricane which they so rashly provoked. The official journal vigorously denounced the first excesses in Paris. Teaching was brought under strict supervision ; and he promptly receded from the militant Gallicanism of Ems, convinced that all Catholics should stand together in defence of the coming danger. But, in spite of his efforts to establish quarantine, the epidemic of liberty reached the Electorate. The citizens demanded the restoration of the Gild constitution and other old customs, and street notices called the people to revolt against the tyrant; but trouble was averted by a joint meeting of the Chapter and leading citizens, with power to remove all proved abuses. The Émigrés were horrified to find the monster, which they had left home to avoid, confronting them in a foreign country. 'The spirit of democracy is as rife here as everywhere else,' wrote Espinchal bitterly in his Diary, in recording a meeting of the Estates of Trier. 'The tone in which the Sovereign is addressed is quite new. They have been worked upon by the democrats, and have made some very insolent suggestions to the Elector, insisting that he should banish us in order to avoid the threatened invasion.'[1]

Despite popular grumbling the Elector was heart and soul with his nephews, and his resources were placed unreservedly at their disposal. The brothers set up separate Courts, in each case presided over by the *maîtresse en titre*.[2] The *salon* of Madame de Balbi, the real Queen of the Émigration, attracted those who loved political conversation, witty repartee, and high stakes at the gaming-table. But if Monsieur had more brains Artois possessed more heart. The Comtesse de Polastron was entirely free from Madame de Balbi's ambition to play a political rôle, and kept no poisoned arrows of malice and scandal in her armoury. She loved Artois for himself, not for his rank or prospects, and succeeded in chaining his wayward affections till her death. To this bicephalous Court every refugee from Paris turned his steps, bringing flattering tales and offers of service. The princes lived in a world of illusion, and believed that France was ready to rise in defence of the *ancien régime* at the word of command. Disinterested royalists like Fersen, who really cared for the King and Queen, looked with angry contempt on the selfish schemers at Coblenz, where the natural moderation of Monsieur was overborne by the fiery spirit of his brother and the hypnotic influence of Calonne. To men who thus mistook a mirage of their own creation for the map of France, the guarded Declaration of Pillnitz came as a bitter disappointment. The Émigrés declined to recognise the new Constitution or to believe that it had been freely accepted. The brothers continued to flout their lawful Sovereign, and planted their Ministers in the capitals of Europe. All pretence of harmony between the Tuileries and Coblenz had vanished. 'Le grand malheur,' remarked Condé to the secretary of Marie Antoinette, 'c'est que votre Maîtresse est

---

[1] *Journal of Comte d'Espinchal*, p. 227.
[2] See Vicomte de Reiset, *Les Reines de l'Émigration*, 2 vols.

un peu démocrate ' ; [1] and the Queen in her bitterness denounced the Comte de Provence as ' Cain.'

The autumn of 1791 witnessed the nadir of the fortunes of the Émigrés, repudiated alike by the French Court and by the Emperor and detested by the population among whom they dwelt. In November the King was compelled to complain of their assembling at Coblenz as a menace to France, and invited the Elector to disperse them. Their host replied that they were not an armed assembly but simple refugees. Similar notes were sent to the other Princes who harboured them, and the Rhineland now knew that war was inevitable unless they were dismissed. ' The whole Electorate has been trembling with panic,' wrote the harassed Elector to the Emperor on New Year's Day. ' Threatening letters arrive in great numbers. I am faced by the alternatives of revolt or invasion.' [2] A second summons broke his resolution, and he ordered the dispersion of the troops. But the stream of fugitives was again flowing rapidly. The clergy fled mainly to England, the *beau monde* to Brussels, Spa, and London, the poor to Lausanne, while the military still steered for Coblenz, Mainz, and Worms. The Emperor now announced that he would intervene if the princes of the Empire were assailed ; but he was still anxious to avoid any provocation from the German side, for he was well aware of the unpopularity of a crusade.

The German rulers differed in their treatment of the fugitives : Prussia showing herself particularly inhospitable, while Brunswick and Münster exhibited marked kindness. Individual sufferers received sympathy and assistance ; but the Émigration, as a whole, proved a more effective argument for ' French ideas ' than all the speeches in the Assembly. ' The scum of France gathered in Coblenz,' confessed Niebuhr. ' One of the keenest of French royalists said to me, " Whoever saw our Émigrés on the Rhine must have felt disgust and loathing for us." ' [3] ' I confess,' wrote Esterhazy in his ' Memoirs,' ' that the great number of women and young people at Coblenz recalled too much the life of Versailles and gave rise to intrigue and discontent. The Courts of the princes were too costly, and secrets leaked out.' [4] The Comte d'Espinchal, who had won the reputation of knowing everybody in Parisian society, describes the influx of sixty to eighty a day, and soon begins to enter in his Journal complaints of ' the immense establishment ' of the princes.[5] ' So much display is rather premature, and distresses sensible people. All these expenses are alarming to everybody

---

[1] See Augeard, *Mémoires*.   [2] Vivenot, *Quellen*, i. 308.
[3] Niebuhr, *Das Zeitalter der Revolution*, i. 243–4.
[4] Esterhazy, *Mémoires*, pp. 238–9.   [5] Espinchal, *Journal*, pp. 227, 244, 259.

except the incorrigible Calonne. Nothing is lacking to remind one
of the abuses of the Court. Coblenz is a hotbed of intrigue. The
princes, relying on promises which have not been fulfilled, have
been absurdly extravagant. It is undeniable, too, that among the
hordes that the Émigration has assembled, there is an incredible
number of scoundrels. In the Three Crowns a café has been started,
the most infernal gambling-hell ever known. The princes have in
vain demanded the suppression of this infamous establishment.
What a contrast between the *émigré* soldiers and the crowd of
swaggering triflers in this town of Coblenz! These men can do
nothing but dress up in fine clothes, like the women they take out
in their carriages.'

The heartlessness of many of the refugees aroused widespread
indignation. 'The death of the King has not affected them very
much,' wrote Fersen in his Diary. 'They console themselves with
the regency of Monsieur. Some of them have even been to the
play.' [1] Varnhagen was at Düsseldorf when the terrible news
arrived. 'Some tore their hair, while others said he deserved his
fate, as he had given way to the Revolution and betrayed the cause
of the Crown and the *noblesse*. Some kissed his picture, others
trampled on it.' The tragedy, indeed, appeared to affect the
Germans more than the French. 'My father deeply lamented him,'
writes the same observer, 'being convinced of his good-will. The
cause of the Émigrés was completely separated from that of the
King.' [2] When Augeard, the secretary of Marie Antoinette, paid
a flying visit to Coblenz, he was appalled by his experiences.[3]
'People talked of the King and Queen openly in the cafés and other
public places with the greatest licence. As a good Frenchman and
one who loved our real masters I was deeply afflicted. The town
was a sink of intrigue, cabals, follies, depredations, and apings of
the old Court. The Archduchess Christina asked me " What has
my unhappy sister done that she is torn in pieces by everybody ? " '

The *intransigeance* of the *noblesse* filled with disgust men of
different nationalities who had no sympathy with the Revolution.
'We passed through the main body of exiles,' wrote Lord
Mornington to Lord Grenville, while resting at Spa on his journey
home from Italy in the summer of 1791.[4] 'It is a curious circumstance that even the servants and suite of the princes are democrats.
They made no scruple of declaring that they would desert their
masters the instant they attempted to attack any part of French
territory. Nothing would content the principal persons who have

---

[1] *Le Comte de Fersen et la Cour de France*, ii. 63.

[2] Varnhagen, *Denkwürdigkeiten*, i. 117–18.

[3] Augeard, *Mémoires*, pp. 280–2.   [4] *Fortescue MSS.*, ii. 118.

left France but a complete restoration of the ancient despotism in all its parts. Those whom I met spoke of nothing but revenge and retaliation.' ' The number of French Emigrants resorting to Coblenz and other places along the upper Rhine is increasing daily,' reported Ralph Heathcote, the British Minister to the Ecclesiastical Electors, in October 1791.[1] ' Whilst their present abode at Coblenz becomes more burdensome to the Elector of Treves, the great circulation of money turns to the advantage of his subjects ; though, to say the truth, their morals are far from being improved, and the bad effect of the looseness now prevalent there—particularly among the lower classes—will be felt for many years to come.' Their arrogance and immorality were castigated by Pacca, the Papal Nuncio ; and an envoy from the Elector of Bavaria reported that he was tempted to imagine that Coblenz had become a French town, with the Elector as guest instead of host. ' The Émigrés only think of themselves,' wrote the Emperor Leopold bitterly to his sister Christina. ' They only covet money and distinctions, and care nothing for the King. They do nothing but talk and write scandal about you, me, and all who do not blindly follow their lead.'

If French and other foreign observers were shocked at the conduct of the leading Émigrés, it was not to be expected that they should be loved by the Rhinelanders. They had at first been welcomed not only as the victims of misfortune but as good customers with well-filled purses. This phase was soon over and the complaints became ever louder of their debts, their gambling, their duelling, their arrogance, and their immorality. The price of living rose by leaps and bounds, and the guests displayed little if any gratitude for the hospitality they received. The most terrible picture was drawn by Laukhard, who, after lecturing at Halle, enlisted as a private in the Prussian army, and spent some weeks in Coblenz on his way to the campaign of 1792. ' That the French nobles had long been leaders who sucked the blood of their fellow countrymen and drove a loyal nation to revolt is clear.' The girls and presentable women, he adds, flocked in from the villages, boasting openly of their lovers and their earnings. ' The whole river, from Basle to Cologne, was poisoned by this scum of humanity.'[2] Though Laukhard's loose character makes him a poor witness, his position and tastes enabled him to see much that was hidden from more respectable observers.

Almost every German memoir-writer has something to relate of the unwelcome guests. When Veit Weber was humming a French song on a Rhine boat with the refrain, ' Vive la Liberté ! '

[1] Record Office, Cologne and Cassel.
[2] Laukhard, *Leben*, ii. 10–22, edition of 1908.

some Émigrés attacked him and his unarmed companions, struck them with the flat of their swords, put ropes round their necks, robbed them of their money and passes, and brought them to Coblenz, where they were locked up till liberated by the arrival of the Prussians. In like manner, when young Varnhagen was sailing down the Rhine with his father, the Émigrés noticed a lad with the tricolour, and behaved so roughly that the other passengers threatened to throw them overboard.[1] 'Nearly everywhere, and especially at Coblenz,' wrote Reichard during his tour in 1792, 'they have to pay double or treble, and always in advance; else they are refused food and lodging.'[2] On reaching Cassel, on his way home from the campaign of 1792, Goethe was at first mistaken for an Émigré and informed that the hotel was full. The proprietor had resolved to refuse all further Émigrés on the ground of their arrogance and stinginess; 'for, despite their plight, they behaved as if they were taking possession of a conquered country.' When Lombard, the secretary of the King of Prussia, was in Coblenz on the way to the Valmy campaign, some nobles, flushed with insolence and wine, passed him in the street and called out 'I bet he is a democrat'; to which Lombard replied 'I soon shall be, if all the Émigrés are like you.'[3] Young and old alike, he adds, seemed to be the scum of the nation. 'Their conversation is atrocious,' wrote the young Archduke Charles to his brother the Emperor; 'if their fellow citizens were to be left to their vengeance, France would soon be nothing but a vast cemetery.' Of course there were numberless instances of quiet heroism and self-sacrificing fidelity to principle; but they were never popular, and the differences of race, language, and temperament were acutely felt. Schiller's friend, Hoven, the Ludwigsburg doctor, liked most of his patients; but he records that he never observed the phenomena of hysteria in such a degree and in such variety of form as in some of the French women.[4] An *émigré* family at Coblenz forms the subject of 'Klara du Plessis,' one of the most popular novels of August Lafontaine, who made acquaintance with the world he describes while acting as military chaplain during the campaign of 1792. The story tells of Klara's love of a commoner bringing her into conflict with her father, the Viscount, who stands for the unbending prejudices of caste which helped to plunge France into the abyss.[5] The Émigrés looked with pitying contempt on the *bons Allemands*, and the Rhineland returned their scorn with interest.

A very different kind of Émigré was Charles de Villers, a

---

[1] *Denkwürdigkeiten*, i. 82–91. [2] *Lettres*, p. 31.
[3] Hüffer, *Lombard*, p. 19. [4] Hoven, *Autobiographie*, pp. 134–7.
[5] Gruber, *Lafontaine's Leben*, pp. 224–38.

Lorrainer, who had defended the Revolution by tongue and pen.[1]
' I am not surprised,' he exclaimed, ' that the groans of the suffering
people suddenly turn into shouts of sedition.   How could it be
otherwise with such a contrast of opulence and poverty ? '   He
pleaded for constitutional monarchy ; but his open condemnation
of violence made him suspect, and after the tenth of August he fled
across the frontier.   While most Émigrés learned nothing of the
countries in which they found a haven, Villers resolved to study
Germany and to teach his countrymen.   At the age of thirty-one
he entered Göttingen as a student, and was delighted by its tranquil
atmosphere.   ' The professors are certainly the most learned and
enlightened men in Europe.'   His closest friend was Schlözer, whose
clever daughter initiated him into German literature.   A year later
he published ' Lettres Westphaliennes,' in which he discussed Kant
and defended philosophy from the charge of causing the French
Revolution.   There was, he argued, too little of it ; for it would have
rendered the Revolution needless by instituting timely changes.
The spirit of philosophy no more directed the Revolution than the
Gospel dictated the massacre of St. Bartholomew.   On leaving
Göttingen he visited Lübeck, where he made the acquaintance of
Stolberg, Voss, Jacobi, and their friends, and settled in Hamburg,
where he wrote for the ' Spectateur du Nord,' a political and literary
monthly.   Among his first tasks was a translation of Kant's tract
on Universal History.   ' These noble ideas of peace and perfection
have enlarged my own.   They seem as solid as they are luminous.'
He was happy in his task of interpreter.   ' The secret Providence
which watches over the perfecting of our race has allowed us to serve
as a means of communication between two great peoples,' he wrote
in an article ' On the destiny of literary Émigrés in Germany.'   He
refused to hate his country or his countrymen.   He compares
France to a volcano, the Émigrés to the rocks and débris cast
afar.   His own chief task was to study and interpret Kant ; and
his book on the philosopher, published at Metz, introduced him
to France.   Among its readers was Madame de Staël, who had
begun to interest herself in Germany in 1798, and had learned
the language.   Villers planned her tour and told her whom to
meet, and without him ' L'Allemagne ' might never have been
written.   He rejoiced at the success of a book which performed
a task beyond his own powers.   But while Madame de Staël
remained wholly French, Villers became thoroughly German.   He
maintained that his country must be regenerated by Luther and
Kant, and that France must have a more serious and profound
moral and intellectual life like Germany, in which he found

[1] See the excellent biography by Witmer.

his spiritual home. Though occasionally visiting Paris, Janus Bifrons—as Goethe called him—preferred to live in the land of his adoption, an apostle of peaceful intercourse between warring nations.

II

Of the States of the Rhineland the Ecclesiastical Electorates were the richest and most powerful; and at the outbreak of the Revolution the Elector of Cologne was the most prominent personage in Western Germany.[1] Brother of the Emperor and the Queen of France, lord of the rich abbey of Münster and the Duchy of Westphalia, in addition to his main territories on the Left Bank, the Archduke Max lived the life of a great secular prince at Bonn, endeavouring to realise the ideal of enlightened autocracy which he shared with Joseph and Leopold. But despite the educational and administrative reforms of its ruler, the Electorate of Cologne was the most backward of the three, and was to prove least hospitable to French ideas. Throughout the Rhineland the non-privileged classes —the burghers, the peasants, and the artisans—hoped with greater or less confidence for a mitigation of their burdens, and in every town a few Intellectuals greeted the principles of '89 with the assent of conviction; but the general desire, common to the Prince and his subjects, was for cautious reform, not revolution. The official journal expressed approval of the opening scenes, blamed the cabals of the Court, lauded the King for fulfilling the wishes of his people, and praised the zeal of the nation in abolishing feudalism. The public reading-room, often frequented by its founder the Elector himself, admitted French papers and pamphlets favourable to the popular cause; but the October raid on Versailles deepened the apprehensions which the governing classes had already begun to entertain. The veneer of liberalism fell away; for the nobles, clergy, and higher officials had merely coquetted with French culture, and were opposed to serious changes. Ecclesiastical policy was sharply altered early in 1790 when, at the wish of the Chapter, inquiries were ordered to be made into the opinions of the professors, and it was decreed that nothing should be taught in the University that contradicted the principles of the Catholic Church. While the Revolution strengthened the existing discontent, it also enabled the

---

[1] See Perthes; Hashagen; Biermanns, *Die Politik des Kurfürsten Maximilian Franz, 1789–1792*; Venedey, *Die deutschen Republikaner*; Essers, *Zur Geschichte der Kurkölnischen Landtage, 1790–1797*; Hesse, *Geschichte der Stadt Bonn, 1792–1815.*

privileged classes to discount the cry for reform as the voice of
sedition.

The march of events and opinion may be illustrated from the
dispatches of Ralph Heathcote, the British Minister at Bonn.[1]
'The Directorial Princes of the Circles of Westphalia and of the
Lower Rhine,' he wrote in September 1789, 'have lately taken a
resolution which no doubt will have the effect of maintaining the
public tranquillity and good order within the limits of both Circles,
in several parts whereof a spirit of revolt had some time ago begun
to prevail in a manner truly alarming.   A decree was published last
week that for the purpose of preventing all further troubles, such as
had first manifested themselves in France, they were firmly resolved
to employ every means in their power towards maintaining throughout the said Circle the Constitution of the Empire, prohibiting all
unlawful meetings or bearing of arms ; in short, everything which
might tend to excite any fermentation among the people.'   The
ferment, however, could not be allayed by proclamations ; and the
troubles of Liège filled the Elector with apprehension.   'In taking
such an active part in their business,' wrote Heathcote in May 1790,
'he has been actuated by no other political motive than that of
preventing the spirit of rebellion from spreading further, which
would undoubtedly happen should the people of Liège not be
compelled to submit.   His Highness's situation requires his utmost
endeavours for carrying this point as soon as possible ; for the Diet
of this country, whose sessions are usually over in the space of six
weeks, has now been assembled near three months on account of a
new mode of collecting taxes, the deputies of the burghers having
proposed a general and equal taxation throughout the whole
country ; whilst the clergy and nobility, who have been hitherto
exempted from it, will by no means give up their ancient privileges.
The Elector himself, persuaded of the necessity of yielding, has
declared that he would consent to his own private domains being
brought on the list of taxation ; but this offer, though it has
endeared him to the people, has not yet made so much impression
on the other two Orders of the Diet as to dispose them to follow so
laudable an example.'   Though thus willing to compromise with
the new spirit of equality, the Elector stiffly refused the French
offer of indemnification for the loss of rights in Alsace, and sharply
told the agent that he had nothing more to say to him.   'This
gentleman, I hear,' reported Heathcote, 'has received everywhere
answers of the like nature, and has been treated at some Courts in
a manner much more discouraging, particularly at Coblenz, where
the Elector of Treves, whose character is naturally very mild, was so

[1] Record. Office, Cologne and Cassel.

much exasperated by others obstinately insisting on and repeating his offers that he could not forbear menacing to send him to Ehrenbreitstein.' At the same time stricter measures were taken to defend the Electorate from evil communications. ' As it is now apprehended,' added the Minister, ' that a number of French emissaries are rambling over those parts of Germany which are situated on the Rhine, with a view of instilling into the minds of the people the principles now prevalent in France, a general rule seems to be established at many Courts that every Frenchman, if he be not particularly recommended by persons of undoubted credit, is watched with the most jealous eye and is not allowed to stay if the slightest suspicion rises against him.'

Though stray spies and travellers could be controlled or expelled, Custine's army seemed likely to plant seeds which it would not be easy to eradicate. ' It is strongly apprehended,' wrote Heathcote, ' that in case the French should maintain themselves long in their present possessions on the Rhine, their strange principles of liberty and equality will soon take strong roots among the middle and inferior orders of the inhabitants, and will be spread even further, as the people at large, however quiet, will in the end be allured to adopt them, if only for the sake of novelty.' No French coaching in any case was required to convince the Third Estate of the injustice of a system of taxation which imposed the whole burden on those least able to bear it. A pamphlet published in January 1790 by ' A Friend of Man ' had attacked the exemption of the privileged Estates on the ground of natural law, and urged the towns to abolish it, hinting that the time was now specially favourable. The question which had been raised in the session of 1790 continued to be discussed, and the cleavage of classes rapidly widened. ' The States are to assemble here on the first of next month,' reported Heathcote in February 1791. ' It is probable that during the course of the Diet the object of establishing an equal contribution to the taxes—which was already discussed last year with great warmth, but could not then be determined—will again be brought up and give rise to new disputes, as the Orders of the clergy and nobility will insist on their ancient privilege of immunity, and those of the people will found their pretensions on the necessity of being alleviated from burdensome contributions which but too long had fallen to their share alone.'

His forecast was correct. ' Last week,' he reported on April 25, ' the States closed their sessions. The Elector's Ministers, in consequence of His Highness's express commands, have supported by every means in their power the pretensions of the inferior Order, but without the desired effect. It was at last agreed that the whole affair should be decided by the ordinary Court of Justice, which is in the first instance the Electoral Aulic Council. The clergy and nobility hope, by protracting the lawsuit, to gain time before they are brought to submit to the proposed taxation, while the inferior Order trusts entirely to the equity of their cause, which they believe cannot fail to be decided in their favour.' In the following year the Estates again sat for two months, and again failed to settle the question. Another year passed by, and the Minister believed the end of the dragging controversy to be in sight. ' In two or three days,' he wrote in August 1793, ' it will be decided whether and in what manner the nobility and clergy are to contribute to the payment of taxes.' But he was too sanguine. ' The Elector left no means untried,' he reported a few days later ; ' but the clergy and nobility persisted absolutely in the maintenance of their ancient privileges. All that could be obtained was a declaration to pay equal taxes under the title of a free gift, and only for this year.' A year later the same grudging concession was made. ' The Estates have closed their sessions,' wrote the Minister in May 1794. ' The superior Orders consented at last to contribute equally with the burghers and peasants during this year only, with the reservation of being exempted for the future.' A few months later the Elector fled for the second time from his dominions, never to return ; and the privileged obstructionists, who had so stubbornly refused to bear their share of the burdens of State, were swept away by the broom of the Republican war-god.

Unlike his ecclesiastical colleagues Max had never allowed the Émigrés to settle in his capital or his territory ; and though he was the brother of Marie Antoinette he did not take the troubles of the royal pair very much to heart. ' Go and see the Elector of Cologne,' remarked the Elector of Trier to Augeard, the secretary of the Queen. ' He is very cool about affairs in France. His heart is good, but he does not know the Revolution. You must explain it to him and to his sister Christina.' The description proved correct. ' I found him very cold,' writes Augeard. ' He blamed us for taking as Minister that madman, Calonne, and also Necker, a foreigner, a Protestant, and a Republican. He ascribes our troubles to our own faults—such as rendering help to America and Holland against their lawful rulers.' [1] No German ruler was more unwilling to enter into a crusade against the French Republic. ' The Elector's political conduct from the beginning of the French Revolution,' wrote Heathcote in October 1792, ' has been quite different to that of the Electors of Mayence and Treves, and in every respect one of strict neutrality.' He later confided to the British Minister that

[1] Augeard, *Mémoires*.

he blamed both the Émigré princes and the rulers of Germany for dragging his State into war, adding bitterly ' We must suffer for the faults committed by others.'

When the French armies approached the Rhine in the autumn of 1792 the Elector fled ; but as the friendly Austrians alone entered his dominions, he returned in the spring, and ruled quietly for eighteen months till he fled for ever in 1794. For a time good order was maintained by Marceau ; but the arrival of the French was soon followed by the usual requisitions and by compulsion to accept the virtually worthless assignats at their face value. Like most other dispossessed princes, the Elector regarded the interruption of his rule as temporary. In September 1797 the British Minister, who had accompanied him in his flight, forwarded a translation of a Declaration to his subjects, issued in view of the anticipated creation of a Rhenish Republic. ' The good inhabitants—not the majority alone, but almost the unanimity—even in the midst of the calamities of the war, and in spite of every attempt to seduce them, have faithfully adhered to their true sentiments, and manifested that we and the Constitution of their ancestors are still dear to them. There have been, indeed, some little time ago, persons, part of whom unknown as yet, sneaking in the dark, who attempt to destroy the fortunate harmony subsisting between us and our subjects. Though we have no reason to be uneasy about the success of such contrivances, yet there is a possibility that our subjects may be overawed by force ; but never will they forget us, and never will they forget they are Germans. There exists only a small number of Germans who are forgetful of their country, and endeavour to influence others in such a manner as to become traitors to themselves.' But Max was well aware that the situation was graver than he admitted. ' The Elector of Cologne,' wrote Walpole, the British Minister to Bavaria, from Ratisbon, ' urges the Diet to entreat the Emperor to accelerate the peace of the Empire with France, as the spirit of revolution gains ground daily on both sides of the Rhine.' He had lost his hold on the country ; and if the French had few friends on the Lower Rhine, those who desired the restoration of the old régime were scarcely more numerous.

When the Elector and his Court fled across the Rhine, republican sentiment began to emerge. ' The revolutionary spirit now got into the head of my elder brothers,' wrote Sulpiz Boisserée in 1794. ' They frequented the revolutionary meetings, and one evening at my request they took me with them. When the French entered the city our manager, a great Francophil, demanded that the soldiers should be invited to supper, and set one at his side ; but he was much surprised when the soldier laid his head on his shoulder and with complete *sangfroid* extracted one of his watches out of his pocket and put it in his own.'[1] There were, however, a number of men who combined Francophil opinions with high character. Geich, an ex-Franciscan, preached a vigorous but by no means fanatical radicalism in his journals, which extended a discriminating support to the Republic. Venedey, a young Cologne lawyer, joined the club at Bonn, and delivered French and German addresses at the fêtes. He accepted the post of secretary of the cantonal government in Andernach ; but he quickly discovered and combated the shameless robberies of the French officials. His correspondence reveals the difficulties of honest and disinterested German republicans. He planted a Tree of Liberty at Andernach ; but few were present on such occasions.[2] The friends of the invaders had never been numerous ; and their numbers declined as experience of their methods began to spread.

The Free City of Cologne had even less right to prolong its existence than the Electorate which encircled it. The stronghold of bigotry and reaction on the Lower Rhine could not be expected to welcome the Rights of Man ; but the searching breeze from Paris caused a slight stirring of the dead leaves. ' The spirit of revolt,' wrote Heathcote from Bonn in September 1789, 'which some time ago reigned with almost unrelenting fury all over France, after having spread to the Bishopric of Liège, has, during the course of last week, begun to influence the inhabitants of the city of Cologne. Happily no excess has been committed, they having contented themselves to lay before their magistrates some grievances by a very numerous deputation of burghers, whilst the rest of them kept themselves in their houses, ready, however, to break out in case immediate redress should be refused. Their chief demand was that an ancient law of the city—according to which the burghers should have the right of electing and appointing the persons that constitute the magistrature, and of which, as they pretended, they had been unjustly deprived by degrees—should be restored to its former validity. This demand having been accompanied with some threatening expressions, the demand in question was, after some feeble discussions, illimitably granted and ordered to be published. After these transactions everything has remained in a sort of tranquillity, which, it is hoped, will be permanent, in spite of several other pretensions made by a very small minority of dissatisfied burghers. Upon the whole, my Lord, it is not improbable that this affray would have been productive of some serious consequences and would at least not have ended in so speedy and quiet a manner had the present disposition

---

[1] *Boisserée's Leben*, i. 10.   [2] Venedey, *Die deutschen Republikaner.*

of the people in general to acts of violence and revolt (after the example thereof in other countries) not intimidated, as it were, many of the ruling persons. It is certain that, some months sooner, the people of Cologne would not have dared to act as they have done at present ; for the authority of their magistrates would have been directly supported by some of the neighbouring princes.'

The protest was a mere flash in the pan, and the life of the corrupt oligarchy flowed on in its accustomed channels. ' We were glad to leave the dreary place,' wrote Forster after his visit in 1790.[1] ' How little does this extensive but half-deserted town correspond to the seductive picture it offers from the river ! No city possesses so many churches ; but there is not one for Protestants. There are said to be a number of rich families ; but that is no comfort to me, so long as I see nothing but crowds of ragged beggars who trade in idleness, bequeathing their post at a church door or employing it as a dowry. The clergy of all Orders, who swarm in every street, and make an unpleasant impression on every traveller, could achieve a great deal if they would encourage them to industry ; but they make no effort, since the beggars are their militia, whom they lead on the chain of the blackest superstition. A visitor from our enlightened Mainz is shocked by the mechanical piety of the place and the cult of relics. What a difference between Cologne and clean, prosperous Düsseldorf ! '

The authorities were stirred to repression, not reform. Political songs were forbidden in the cafés, and houses were searched. The city was naturally involved in hostilities when war was declared by the Empire ; but it was too weak to render effective aid. When the French entered in October 1794, an occasional Jacobin cap was seen in the streets or a Tree of Liberty was planted. Some revolutionary speeches were delivered, and a certain frothy enthusiasm was displayed by sections of the lower classes ; but the fleeting popularity of the invaders was soon terminated by their plundering and oppression. Early in 1795 the town council dispatched the burgomaster, Dumont, to Paris to protest against the financial exploitation ; but the deputation produced no improvement, and in 1796 the Council was supplanted by a Francophil municipality. The city was now under the French heel, and the wilder spirits had full scope for their propaganda. Biergans, an ex-monk, founded a journal, ' Brutus '—the German equivalent of the ' Père Duchêne '—the coarse and blasphemous violence of which disgusted the ' Patriots ' or moderate liberals. In 1798 the ' Constitutional Circle ' was founded in the ancient city. The Marseillaise was sung, and at the opening ceremony Venedey congratulated the

[1] ' Ansichten vom Niederrhein,' etc., Letter 5.

citizens ' on their admission into the great family of free men.'
He went on to eulogise Robespierre for his simple life and incor-
ruptibility, and attributed the Terror to lesser men who sheltered
behind his name. He exerted himself to reconcile French rule
with German interests, adjuring Rudler to appoint honest officials,
adding, ' The fate of the Left Bank is in your hands.' The Circle
justified its existence by fearlessly defending the people against
French exploiters, and by helping the peasants against those who
continued to demand the performance of feudal duties already
abolished by French law. On receiving news of the entry of the
French into Rome Venedey exclaimed : ' You see that the peoples,
under the aegis of the French Republic, are one by one regaining
their rights.' Despite their republican zeal the criticism of the
' Patriots ' was resented by the French administration, and the
Circles were crushed between the upper and nether mill-stones of
official disapprobation and popular dislike. In 1799, heartily
disgusted with his deliverers, Venedey resigned his post. ' As far
as my experience goes,' he cried bitterly, ' there is scarcely an
honest man among the French officials.' In 1799 the fall of the
Bastille was celebrated for the last time on the banks of the Rhine.
The chapter was closed by Brumaire. ' I have served the Republic,'
cried Venedey in anger ; ' I will serve no despot.' His disenchantment was shared by most of the ' Patriots ' on the Lower Rhine.
' Liberté, égalité, ou la mort ! ' wrote Boosfeld, a fellow ' Patriot '
of Bonn ; ' the only change needed in this formula is the
substitution of *et* for *ou*. Oh, this beautiful land of ours !
Such a paradise, and yet rendered so utterly miserable by its
thousand-headed rulers ! ' If such were the sentiments of the
Gallophil, what must men and women of conservative instincts
have whispered to one another in the evil days of the Directory ?

III

The lord of Mainz, like his brother Electors, detested the
Revolution, and was angered by the abolition of his feudal rights
in Alsace ; and when the Prince Bishop of Liège quarrelled with
his subjects, he sent fifteen hundred men to his support.[1] He
welcomed the Émigrés in his capital and lent Condé his palace at
Worms, partly from sympathy with their sufferings and principles,
partly from a desire to strengthen the prestige of his Court. Every

---

[1] See Perthes ; Hashagen; Bockenheimer, *Die Mainzer Klubisten*; K. Klein,
Geschichte von Mainz, 1792–1793 ; Chuquet, *Guerres de la Révolution,* vols. vi.
and vii. ; Remling, *Die Rheinpfalz.*

day hundreds of meals and the costliest wines were dispatched from his kitchens, and his table was crowded with the more distinguished of his guests. In public the Émigrés flattered their ' Père Protecteur ' ; but behind his back they laughed at *l'abbé de Mayence* or *le gentilhomme parvenu*. The easy tolerance of the days before 1789 was succeeded by a policy of repression. Liberals were watched, letters were opened, the press and the stage were censored, teachers were warned, reading circles were condemned. Eickemeyer described Mainz as a city of servility, ignorance, and superstition.[1] A Danish traveller found in his inn a warning against ' conversation hostile to religion, morals, and government.' The Elector persuaded the Prince of Thurn and Taxis, who controlled the Imperial post, to refuse the transmission of certain French papers ; and the Émigrés were allowed the censorship of the reading-room. To combat the growing reaction the future clubists met to discuss plans, and discontent grew rapidly. ' The French Revolution was beginning,' wrote Prince Metternich long after in his Autobiography, ' and from that moment I was its close observer.[2] As in all German Universities, the spirit of innovation appeared in Mainz. I was surrounded by students who employed the Republican Calendar ; and certain professors, among them Hofmann, interlarded their lectures with allusions to the emancipation of the human race. Georg Forster gathered round him numerous acolytes of the Revolution. I visited at his house, and saw the effect of the seductive principles to which so many youthful minds fell victim.' In May 1792 Villars, the new French Minister, arrived, and became the secret patron of the discontented. After his official reception he was excluded from Court ; but the Elector was too timid to check the intrigues of the man whose enmity he had provoked.

For the last time the sun shone on ecclesiastical Mainz at the reception of the last of the Holy Roman Emperors after the Coronation in Frankfurt in July 1792, when for two days the *élite* of Germany and Austria gathered within its walls. The Brunswick Manifesto was printed by the Court press, and the King of Prussia started from Mainz for the Valmy campaign. For a moment Mainz was the centre of the Empire ; but the city of Boniface was soon to pay dearly for her ruler's zeal in the cause of the counter-revolution. The Elector sent two thousand men to join in the attack on France ; but there was no enthusiasm behind the venture. The French Revolution was unpopular, and there was no disposition to imitate it ; but the Mainzers considered it unnecessary to support a war in which the Empire remained neutral, and which exposed the

---

[1] Eickemeyer, *Denkwürdigkeiten*, p. 40.　　　[2] *Memoirs*, vol. i.

Electorate to invasion.   The forebodings of the citizens were quickly
realised.   The country was totally unprepared for hostilities, and,
after the cannonade of Valmy had sealed the fate of the Austro-
Prussian invasion, Custine hurried from the south and seized in rapid
succession Speier, Worms, and Mainz.   The Elector and his Court
fled helter-skelter across the Rhine, carrying their gold and jewels
with them.   'The towns have fallen without striking a blow,'
noted the American Minister in Paris, Gouverneur Morris, in his
diary.   'The Declaration of the Rights of Man produces the
effect of Joshua's trumpets.'   Custine's first proclamation ' To the
oppressed people of Germany ' was cleverly conceived.   ' Your own
unforced will shall determine your fate.   If you prefer slavery
to liberty, you may choose which despot shall restore your fetters.
Let eternal infamy fall on those who prefer the rattle of their chains
to the sweet voice of liberty.'   He was pretending to act on the
principle of the Constitution of 1791, which renounced conquests ;
and it was therefore necessary to make the çonquered districts
declare their wish that the French should remain.   The General
reported to Paris that he was trying to spread the teachings of the
Revolution in the places occupied by the armies of the Republic ;
but he was not the most fitting apostle of the new faith.   Himself an
aristocrat—ambitious, garrulous and vain—he scorned republican
simplicity, living in the Elector's palace and driving out in his
gorgeous carriages.

Even before the craven flight of their ruler, some Mainz radicals
had established contact with Custine.   Böhmer, son of the famous
canonist, joined him after the capture of Speier, and became his
secretary—drafting his proclamations and editing the official
journal ; but his head was turned by authority, and he was least
esteemed by those who knew him best.   ' Those who push themselves on such occasions are never the best,' wrote his sister-in-law,
Caroline, with severity.   The ' Moniteur ' on the other hand gratefully pronounced him ' a useful and virtuous man, uniquely fitted
to spread the principles of liberty in Germany.'   Custine was
also encouraged to march on the city by Wedekind, the Elector's
doctor and Professor of Medicine at the University.   Five days
after his entry the General summoned the gilds, and asked them
if they desired to retain their Constitution or whether they wished
for a new one.   They replied that they desired neither the one nor
the other, but asked for certain specific reforms.   Only natives
should be officially employed, taxation should be equal, the unjust privileges of nobles and clergy should be abolished, and
the new Constitution, whatever it might be, should be included
in the articles of peace, so as to secure recognition by Europe

and the Empire. The gilds spoke only for themselves, but in demanding reform and declining French tutelage they were voicing the aspirations of the whole Rhineland. This, however, was by no means Custine's programme, and he accordingly founded the club as an instrument of propaganda. A few enthusiasts met in the palace, listened to a speech from Böhmer, and swore ' to live free or die.' The General appeared at the second meeting and delivered an address. The war, he declared, was being waged to punish the injustices committed against the Republic and to inform the peoples of the Rights of Man. Four hundred members were quickly enrolled, most of them officials, professors, and their pupils. Among the leaders were Wedekind, who on the entry of the French wrote to the Convention : ' I demand of the French nation the title of French citizen and its adoption of me among its children.' His brother professor, Hofmann, a man of superior ability and deeper convictions, had long instructed his students in French political theory, and wished Mainz to be annexed to France. Among other leading members were Mathias Metternich, Professor of Mathematics, and Blau, a teacher of Theology in the Mainz seminary.

The object of the club was not only to focus Francophil opinion but to persuade the inhabitants of the Electorate to ask for a new constitution, on the ground that the flight of the Elector had broken the contract between ruler and people. The Strassburg Club was commissioned to petition the Convention for measures of defence. ' Our brothers in Mainz,' wrote the Alsatian democrats, ' beg that the whole family of the French Republics, with whom they desire ever to remain linked in brotherhood, should defend them with all their power against the tyranny from which Custine has delivered them.' When this address was read in the Paris Convention the Alsatian member, Rühl, rose and declared that the Mainzers were, of all Germans, the most worthy of liberty, and harboured in their hearts an unquenchable hatred of tyrants. This fancy picture was traversed by Custine's petition for some good speakers who knew German. ' We need some political apostles,' he wrote confidentially. ' Our club is doing famously ; but we require men for Frankfurt, Worms, and Speier. The Mainzers also require waking up.' In response to his appeal three expert propagandists were dispatched to the city. The most competent of the political revivalists, Dorsch, had been sent to Paris to complete his education as a young priest, and had held the Chair of Philosophy at Mainz before the Revolution. In 1791, with some other rationalist theologians, he resigned his post and went to Strassburg, where he threw off his Orders and married, taking an active part in the club of the Friends of the Constitution. The vain and ambitious new-comer attached himself closely to Custine, whose favour he shared with Böhmer. The second propagandist, Cotta, a brother of the Tübingen publisher, had in like manner left his post as teacher in the Karlsschule at Stuttgart in 1791, to seek his fortune in Strassburg. The third, Pape, a Westphalian priest, also came from Alsace, where he had been employed as a teacher at Colmar. On arriving in Mainz he discarded his Orders and violently attacked the clergy. His Open Letter to Friedrich Wilhelm Hohenzollern informed him of the club's determination to expel all tyrants, and to hold a meeting of the friends of liberty and equality in the Castle of Berlin in the following summer, under the protection of a great Frank army. The Letter was signed 'Thine and all kings' enemy, the Republican Pape.' But the combined exertions of the trio availed as little as the proclamations of the General and the rhetoric of the clubists to wean the Mainzers from their allegiance to their country.

At Böhmer's suggestion two books were opened for signatures — the Red Book of life, and the Black Book of slavery. 'Hasten to inscribe your name,' cried Forster to his fellow citizens, 'and let the Franks see that liberty appeals to Germans too.' In spite of official pressure, however, not more than a thousand names were inscribed, and the contumacy of the citizens encouraged the French to act as conquerors, not as brothers. A tame administration was formed under the direction of Dorsch, who installed himself in the palace. 'We expect from you the most detailed information from the interior of Germany,' wrote the Jacobin Club in Paris to the Mainz Club; and Forster and Wedekind obediently replied that they would do their utmost to supply it. Forster had already expressed his view that the natural frontier was the Rhine; but the majority of the clubists desired to see the Electorate in unforced union with France. Even this, however, went far beyond the wishes of the bulk of the inhabitants. Throughout the Rhineland the aristocracy, the clergy, the officials, the gilds, and the Fourth Estate were almost unanimously opposed to French radicalism; and the fear of vengeance in the not improbable event of the return of the old régime counselled caution. 'The Frenchman is not beloved here, as we flattered ourselves,' runs a candid report to the Foreign Minister. 'Individual persons and individual towns may wish for liberty; but the mass of the nation, ever slow and superstitious, sees in its rulers privileged beings, and appears to love the yoke. Perhaps, however, the levity and mercurial temperament of the new apostles of liberty also contribute to make it appear less desirable.' 'When the Convention is assured that the Mainzers love the French and wish to be

free,' testified a second agent, 'they are being told lies. The
people do not ask for liberty. The holy word reaches their ear
but not their heart.' A third reported that all the efforts of France
on the Rhine were fruitless. ' Why should we continue to sacrifice
money and lives for ungrateful people who do not deserve them ?
The Germans will always remain Germans, and they will trick us
sooner or later.'

The French Government were under no illusions as to the
unwillingness of Mainz to don the livery of France ; but their
determination to annex the country was irrevocable. On New
Year's Day, 1793, three representatives of the Convention reached
the city. Their impressions confirmed previous reports. ' There
are few patriots in Germany,' wrote Merlin de Thionville, the leading spirit. ' The inhabitants, fashioned to the yoke, prefer apathetic
calm to the tempests of liberty.' Enthusiasm was confined to a
handful of Intellectuals, and the Trees of Liberty struck no roots.
' At last we enjoyed the longed-for happiness to be deemed worthy
of the same fatherly care as Savoy, Brabant, and Liège,' exclaimed
Forster ecstatically. ' Now we may hope that our indissoluble
union with the Republic may not be far distant.' Very different
was the verdict of Forster's friend, Sömmerring. ' I cannot imagine
that the French Constitution will make progress in Germany,'
he wrote to Heyne, ' so long as it is sponsored by such worthless
apostles as Wedekind and Böhmer.' With the arrival of the
politicians from Paris Custine was speedily eclipsed, and Böhmer
and Dorsch fell with him. Hofmann became the chief of the local
administration and of the club, and sharply attacked not only
Dorsch and Forster, but the General himself.

Preparations were now made for a Convention, chosen by the
newly created municipal bodies, and designed to vote annexation
to the French Republic. Nobles, clergy, and officials were ordered
to swear fidelity to the principles of liberty and equality, and to
renounce their privileges and the authority of the Elector ; but,
despite the efforts of the clubists, the oath was generally refused.
The Emperor had recently issued a decree, warning subjects of the
States composing the Empire against entering the service of France ;
and many argued that it was not in their power to separate themselves from the Reich. Only three to four hundred took the oath
in Mainz, and in Worms and Speier the refusal was equally general.
The attempt aroused widespread indignation. ' The barbarism
and severity with which the French treat the unfortunate Mainzers
is indescribable,' wrote Sömmerring to Heyne. ' It is intolerable,'
complained Fischenich, a Bonn professor, ' how the French impose their principles by force and are false to their own precepts.

They thunder against religious compulsion ; yet they compel citizens to break their oath with cannon, and promulgate liberty with fire and sword.' When the elections were over the club had done its work and was dissolved by Merlin, who had discovered that not all the members even of that select society were trustworthy.

' For centuries,' exclaimed the ' Moniteur ' after the first sitting of the Rhine Convention, ' Germany has not witnessed this imposing spectacle of an assembly of free men.' But they were not free. It was a picked body, summoned for a predetermined purpose. When Hofmann had been elected president and Forster vice-president, the latter moved and carried a resolution decreeing that ' the district between Landau, Bingen, and Mainz be freed from its lords, and that all its tyrants be for ever deprived of all their rights.' A second decree declared a free, indivisible State, and threatened any rulers who attempted to return with death. Independence was then publicly proclaimed to the sound of cannon, and Custine and Hofmann engaged in a theatrical embrace. Adam Lux desired real independence, while a few deputies advocated an ' alliance ' with France ; but it was too late for compromise. After a three days' debate annexation was voted unanimously, and three members of the Convention were appointed to communicate the decision to the Assembly in Paris. The Rhine Convention ended with the completion of its task, but on March 30, the day when the Convention in Paris accepted its petition, the city was surrounded by German troops and the siege began. On its fall, four months later, some of the clubists marched out with the French, though the terms of capitulation only allowed the invading force to go free. The German Jacobins had treated their fellow citizens roughly enough in the brief hour of their triumph, and it was now their turn to be assaulted and imprisoned. Some of them remained in durance till the doors were opened by the Peace of Basle. Those who reached Paris formed a society of Mainz Patriots under the presidency of Hofmann, whose evidence helped to bring Custine to the scaffold. His opinions never changed, and in begging Merlin for help in 1795 he could affirm with truth that he had sacrificed his property, his post, and his health to the Revolution. Wedekind, on the other hand, in a pamphlet on Jacobinism published in Strassburg in 1795, denounced his old associates as murderers of liberty.

If Frankfurt suffered somewhat less than its neighbour, the old Imperial city also shared the tribulations which the ebb and flow of battle brought on the Rhineland.[1] In his rapid advance, in the

---

[1] See Kracauer, *Frankfurt u. die Französische Republik*, 1795–1803, in *Archiv für Frankfurt's Geschichte u. Kunst, Dritte Folge*, vols. iii., v., vi.

autumn of 1792, Custine entered the city without striking a blow, and imposed an indemnity on the citizens which effectually discouraged Francophil sentiment. ' You saw the Emperor crowned here this year,' he cried prophetically to the hostile crowd in front of the Römer, ' but you will never see another.' Though Prussian and Hessian troops recaptured the city a few weeks later, the inhabitants were still unable to breathe freely. A Mainz journal spread the lying report that the Frankfurters had sworn to murder the French garrison, and had manufactured thousands of knives for the purpose, one of which Custine dispatched to the Convention. The City Council denounced the mendacious rumour ; but they could scarcely hope to remove the sinister impression it had created. Though compelled to send a contingent when the Empire declared war in 1793, the Council endeavoured to avoid giving an excuse for retaliation should the republican armies appear on the scene. Having entered the conflict with reluctance, the wealthy and aristocratic Frankfurters desired to withdraw as soon as possible. The negotiations for the Treaty of Basle seemed to offer a means of escape ; but the permission of the Empire was refused. The luckless city was bombarded and captured in 1796, and once more compelled to pay a crushing ransom. The alternations of hope and fear through which the residents passed during these stormy years are mirrored in the correspondence of Goethe's witty and stout-hearted mother.[1]

Though Frankfurt had no cause to love her French neighbours, her citizens were considered by some observers peculiarly liable to infection. In a city completely dominated by a ring of ruling families some friends of innovation were naturally to be found ; and a few voices had celebrated French victories and even defended the execution of the King and Queen. ' I send you the result of my inquiries and observations on the moral influence of the French revolutionary system on this part of Germany,' reported a Prussian agent in 1798, ' and on the way democratic agents try to agitate the Right Bank of the Rhine and to sow the germ of insurrection.[2] The preparations seem to me very dangerous. It is no longer the French agents, but the German clubists, whose efforts are directed to a rising. The effects become more marked every day, especially since the surrender of Mainz. This town contains a revolutionary Committee, presided over by the too famous Professor Hofmann —a dangerous man who, in the excess of his fatal ambition, would overthrow all governments. He has put himself at the head of

---

[1] See *Schriften der Goethe-Gesellschaft*, vol. viii. ; Reeks, *The Mother of Goethe* ; and Heinemann, *Goethe's Mother*.

[2] *Fortescue MSS.*, iv. 107–8.

this democratic assembly, and works at a large plan to seduce the mind of the peoples. He is not lacking in motives and means. If for the moment the French have renounced the invasion of North Germany, the prolongation of the residence of their troops on the Right Bank announces not less dangerous enterprises.' Frankfurt's worst troubles, however, were over, and under the rule of Dalberg it was soon to experience a tranquil prosperity not less than that enjoyed by the most favoured portions of the Left Bank.

IV

Next to Forster, the most prominent figure in the politics of the Rhineland during the revolutionary era was Görres.[1] Born at Coblenz in 1776, the precocious lad, who inherited the vivacious temperament of his Italian mother, followed events in France with passionate interest. ' In my earliest youth,' he wrote in 1800, ' ideas of republicanism and the improvement of political conditions thrilled me. I clung to them with warmth, devoted to them my best strength, and lived in them alone.' At the age of twenty he composed a little work entitled ' Universal Peace,' suggested by the treatise of Kant. Monarchy, he argued, was despotism, and democracy alone was compatible with personal liberty. He found his masters in Kant and Fichte, Rousseau and Condorcet. The French Revolution had created the model State, and France must now realise the idea of a great republic of peoples. ' The general will of all nations will then have a government which introduces an everlasting peace of God under the compulsion of the laws, and would thus open to humanity golden days.' To these alluring visions he appends an impassioned eulogy of revolutionary France. ' It was reserved for our generation to see a great nation appear which tore from its usurper the rights of men, which had become rusted with neglect. The dazzling light frightened the despots, who resolved to unite for its destruction. Nearly all the dynasties fell upon the young State, but were hurled back. For a time they stood in impotent wrath ; then they crept back, and one after another begged for peace from the foe they had despised.' No publisher dared to sponsor the outburst ; and the author therefore embodied his essay in seventeen articles, setting forth a plan for a general and lasting peace, and sent it to the Directory, which returned a polite acknowledgment. ' If in a despotic State,' ran Article X, ' public opinion, by a revolt or otherwise, expresses its wish to alter the Constitution, the rulers of other despotic States

---

[1] See Sepp, *Görres* ; Perthes ; Hashagen ; and Görres, *Politische Schriften.*

undertake not to intervene. Nor may the despot attempt to coerce his subjects back into prison.' This article attracted the attention of the Rhine ' Patriots ' ; and Görres quickly followed up his literary *début* by plunging into the politics of the Rhineland. The world, he cried, was covered with ' Egyptian darkness ' ; the Rhine was the new Jordan, France the Promised Land, Paris the new Jerusalem.

In the early summer of 1797 the rumour was circulated that France would not retain the Left Bank ; and those who desired to prevent the return of the rule of the crozier determined to create an independent ' Cisrhenan Republic ' before peace was signed, and thereby secure French protection in the hour of need. Görres desired to see France surrounded by a ring of republics in federal connection with her, while others hoped that in quieter times the Rhine Republic might join the German Fatherland.[1] A Cisrhenan Confederation was therefore organised from Coblenz. On September 14, 1797, the ' Confederates,' accompanied by French troops, planted a Tree of Liberty in Coblenz, adorned with flowers and ribbons, to the cry of ' Vive La République ' ; and Görres delivered his first public address. The Republic was voted by acclamation ; but the gilds and the town council denounced the scheme. The council was promptly dissolved by the French, and a new body was chosen from the Confederates. At this momon Hoche died, and Görres attended his funeral in the green uniform of the ' Patriots.' With his death the only disinterested friend of German liberty among French generals or politicians of the era of the Directory passed away. ' We said to one another,' wrote a Rhinelander in after days, ' if the French trail the principles of liberty in the mud, the Germans will prove that these principles can be applied without executions or bloodshed. We therefore desired independence, not annexation.' But victorious France cared nothing for such aspirations ; and in October 1797 the Treaty of Campo Formio surrendered the Left Bank, which was ruled by a Commissioner from Mainz.

Görres had supported the project of a Cisrhenan Republic ; but he was now ready with arguments that union with France was an even better policy for the Rhineland. No peace treaty could bind the princes, he contended. ' If we are united with France, with a

---

[1] While Perthes saw in the Cisrhenan movement an attempt to facilitate the transfer to France, Heigel accepts the assurances that it was designed to rescue Germanism on the Left Bank. ' It was the only path of salvation in their trouble and isolation,' declares Zschokke. ' The Republic speaks for, not against, the German spirit of the Rhinelanders.' The truth is that both views found champions.

colossus which by its weight can suppress the cabals of a party which has sworn enmity to the cause of humanity, she will defend us against all attacks. Nature made the Rhine the frontier of France.' He now printed his essay on Peace with slight alterations, with a dedication from ' A German Republican to the Frankish Nation.' ' The flag of liberty,' he cried, ' waves in the towns of our fatherland. Popular societies are beginning to disseminate liberal principles among the masses, and to sow the seed of future harvests.' He rejoiced at the recapture of Mainz by the French in the last days of the war. ' Mainz is ours,' he cried in a New Year's address in the club at Coblenz. ' This bulwark of despotism is lost, the integrity of the Empire at an end, the hope of despots destroyed, the bridge to the Left Bank broken down. They stand on the mountains beyond and gaze with impotent fury into the Promised Land of Liberty, which for ever forbids their return. The surrender of Mainz has given the *coup de grâce*. Rejoice, nations, your cause has triumphed!' The event moved him to the composition of his celebrated epitaph on the Holy Roman Empire and to the only verses he ever wrote. ' Mown by death's scythe, pale and without breathing, there lies here the Holy Roman Empire. Stranger, tread gently, or you may wake it, and it will once more rain decrees upon our heads. But for the French, we should not read upon this stone *Requiescat in Pace*.' With biting satire he announced the forthcoming sale of croziers, episcopal caps, and other symbols of defunct theocracy. So entirely did he identify himself with the French that he greeted the occupation of the Eternal City with the words ' Rome is free.' In his own city the petition for annexation received so few signatures that school-children were forced to swell the total ; and he reproached the Rhinelanders with their indifference to the proffered gifts.

Like all disinterested ' Patriots,' Görres was speedily disgusted by the difference between the principles and the practice of the French invaders, who settled on the land like vultures on their prey. His nature was too noble not to denounce the exploitation practised by officials, small and great—' the heartless and mindless men who are sent to govern us, adventurers, the scum of France. Many of us believed that the French had been transformed by the Revolution into angels ; but the arrogance of the proud conquerors waxed day by day, and there was no end to their extortions and exactions. Officials and priests, who lamented the loss of their power, stirred up the people ; and the affection of the German for his traditional forms and maxims rendered every novelty abhorrent to him. Everything combined to create a universal hatred of the French, and the cause was soon identified with its representatives. Hatred was felt not only for republicans, but for republicanism and liberty. I believe that the century for the introduction of democracy has not yet dawned, and will not dawn in a hurry. People have discarded their old principles and not yet had the time or the desire to procure new ones. We say with Vergniaud, We have deceived ourselves not in liberty but in the hour. We believed we were in Rome, but we found ourselves in Paris.' Such was the message of the ' Rothes Blatt,' founded in February 1798, which reveals the Rhine ' Patriots ' at their best. ' We work for the happiness of the people,' he announced in the opening number, ' and we have sworn eternal hatred of clericalism and monkery. We also labour in the interest of the princes by showing that they are not indispensable, and thus help to relieve them of the burden of rule. Let every citizen watch the conduct of the officials and denounce their failings to the people. What their own principles do not forbid, the fear of the pillory may perhaps avert. Our weapon is publicity.' The editor, in a word, loved the Revolution but not its representatives.

Görres carried out his programme of denouncing corruption and oppression with unflinching courage, and boldly compared the four Rhine Departments to Turkish Pashaliks at the mercy of the Janissaries. His complaints were echoed on every side. ' The Franks had issued proclamations promising respect of persons and property,' wrote the Gallophil Posselt in 1795. ' We expected defenders of the rights of man—indeed, a sort of philosophers— and we found soldiers, in whose dictionary the word Discipline was lacking.' Another writer compared them to a man with a dagger in his hand, swearing eternal friendship. After a few months the ' Rothes Blatt ' was transformed into the ' Rübezahl ' ; but nothing was altered except the name. ' France has behaved disgracefully to the champions of her principles and has degraded them to helots. She has vomited on to us the dregs of the age, and has trampled on right and justice with iron foot. She has sent us proconsuls without head or heart—mere toadies of those who appointed them.' On June 28 he summoned his friend to listen to an address to the Directory in complaint of the conduct of its representatives. ' The robbers grow ever bolder,' he concluded. ' Death to them all ! Let the union of brave republicans be our watchword. Our life for fatherland or liberty ! ' He carried his complaints to Paris, asking on behalf of the ' Patriots ' for annexation rather than such exploitation. ' To-morrow,' he wrote to his *fiancée*, ' I enter the land of heroes and weaklings, of the proudest republicans and the most contemptible slaves, of the great Republic and the little people.' [1]

[1] *Briefe*, i. 3.

To his dismay he found that the French on the Rhine were no worse than the French at home. The people had ceased to care for liberty; and several weeks before Brumaire he reported that in Napoleon 'the new Emperor' was at hand. 'There was a time when I regarded men as more or less ideal,' he wrote a week after his arrival, 'but these happy days of illusion are past.' His little book, 'Results of my Mission to Paris,' forms the political testament of his stormy youth. 'I saw the actors behind the scenes, without their costume. The passions were off the chain and careered about the stage. I must tell my fellow citizens what I witnessed, as my mission was official; but I cannot tell all I saw.' He denounced Paris as a prostitute, wearied by her excesses, dancing like a comedy actress on the world's stage. In rapid outline he recalls the early scenes of hope, and declares the failure due to lack of character. The Revolution was like a balloon which soared into the air, exploded and sunk to the earth in flames. Brumaire was the end of the chapter; and towards Brumaire 'a terrible convergence' was traceable throughout the years of ferment. 'On the pillar on which world-history carves its annals will stand these words: At the end of the eighteenth century the French people rose into the region of a loftier destiny; but, dragged down by time and by their own nature, they did not attain the goal for which they strove. Citizens of the future! study their errors, and complete what they first dared to think.' He withdrew from association with the 'Patriots,' discontinued his paper, and retired to his tent.

Many years later, when Görres re-emerged as a publicist, he defended himself vigorously against an attack on his early indiscretions. 'The movement only began,' he wrote to Stein in 1814, 'when the Left Bank was lost to Germany. The idea now occurred to me of preventing union with France by declaring these lands independent. My plan was to link Holland with Switzerland by a buffer State, including Belgium and Alsace. General Hoche was won for the scheme, and an assembly was about to meet in Aachen when he died. The Directory disliked the scheme, and Augereau, after an offer to assist it in return for a huge bribe, put the extinguisher on it. Now began my war against the French, which I waged so vigorously that for over a year I went about armed, was often attacked, and more than once found myself in prison. That is the history of my Jacobinism. I have nothing of which to be ashamed. I never used my power against my fellow citizens, and never attacked anything worthy of respect.' Four years later, in writing on 'The Relations of the Rhineland to Prussia,' he repeated his defence. 'These movements may be denounced as un-German and ill-advised; but the purity of motive, the power, the brains, and the insight of their best supporters must be honoured as they deserve. My chief fault was to attribute to my contemporaries more virtue than they possessed.' Görres may have had, as Treitschke maintains, an unpolitical mind ; but he was perhaps the most brilliant and effective journalist that Germany has ever produced, and in later days the ' Rheinischer Merkur ' was to earn the name of the fifth among the Powers allied against Napoleon.[1]

V

From 1794 to 1797, except for the too brief interlude of Hoche's sympathetic administration, the Left Bank was misruled and exploited by the military authorities ; but in the latter year the administration was entrusted to a civil commissioner, and sweeping changes were inaugurated.[2] Before the arrival of the French the territory had been ruled by nine archbishops and bishops, two religious orders, seventy-six princes and counts, four free cities, and a host of imperial knights. Every one of these rulers and systems of government had now passed away, and the nobility, with few exceptions, had fled across the Rhine. The country was divided into four departments. Feudal dues and tithes, privileges and exemption from taxation were abolished. The sequestration of the lands of the dispossessed pointed to their sale in the near future. The liberty of industry was secured by the suppression of

[1] A somewhat similar course was run by Rebmann, whom we have met in Saxony and who pitched his tent in Paris in 1796, whence he carried on his self-imposed task of converting his countrymen to democratic ideas by newspapers and pamphlets. Like most visitors, he found the real Paris very different from the city of his dreams ; and when, in 1796, he accepted office as a magistrate on the Left Bank, he soon accused France of regarding the Rhineland as a new Indies, in which every moral bankrupt could find office and spoils. He had now reached the relative impartiality which came to disillusioned enthusiasts of the type of Görres. ' Political salvation for humanity comes from France,' he wrote, ' but the light of the Aufklärung burns far more brightly in Germany. In Paris every one has read Voltaire ; but how many Departments there are into which no book has penetrated ? Our colleges, our academies, our towns have their literary needs, and there is a table spread for everybody.' Political conditions, on the other hand, were deplorable. No one urged the secularisation of the ecclesiastical States with more vigour and conviction. ' Away with the black squadrons ! Only so will the frontier incidents cease.' The rights of man, he was convinced, would one day be universally recognised. ' What we have sown in tears the generations to come will reap in joy.' See Wrasky, *Rebmann*.

[2] The story is told from the German side by Perthes and Hashagen, from the French by Rambaud and Sagnac. The most impartial picture is painted by Herbert Fisher, *Studies in Napoleonic Statesmanship, Germany*.

the trade corporations with their harassing rules and limitations ; and French weights and measures and the decimal system gave a further impetus to trade. An efficient police guaranteed public security, a uniform legal procedure took the place of the innumerable tribunals of spiritual and temporal lords, and the mild Criminal Code of 1795 was applied. The gates of the Ghetto at Bonn were opened, and the Protestants of Aachen and Cologne built their first churches.

On the debit side of the account stood a number of less welcome innovations and the imposition of heavy burdens. The first Commissioner, the Alsatian Rudler, was honest and relatively moderate ; but his rule was brief, and his successors—who spoke nothing but French—were either shadows or tyrants, the obedient tools of their masters at Paris. Conscription was the first and most detested of the penalties of conquest. The army of occupation lived on the country, and the burden of taxes and requisitions was increased by the dishonesty of alien and unpaid officials. The shock to religious sentiment was particularly resented. The clergy lost their endowments and received no salary from the State. Pilgrimages and religious processions were forbidden, and the Republican Calendar, with its three decades a month, virtually suppressed Sunday. While the parents went to church the children were in school ; and shops were closed not on Sundays, but on Decadi. There was no longer the idle pretence of consulting the people. Nobody wished for the return of tithes and feudal dues, but there was no enthusiasm for France. Public opinion expressed itself in apathy and passive resistance, not in open antagonism. The burghers refused to celebrate republican fêtes, to wear cockades, to attend the planting of Trees of Liberty, or to accept posts in the administration. Under the fanatical Lakanal the yoke became almost intolerable. Churches were closed, houses were searched, and incautious critics found themselves in prison.

With the incorporation of the four Rhine Departments in 1802, following the definitive cession of the Left Bank by the Treaty of Lunéville, the office of Commissioner was abolished and the Rhineland was thenceforward governed as an integral part of France. Though the higher administration was purely French, the subordinate posts were in the main filled by natives. The local assemblies and municipal councils were mere shadows, and there was as little liberty in the Rhineland as in the rest of Napoleon's dominions ; but the reconciliation with the Church was welcomed, order was introduced, and striking material progress was achieved. The property of the secular and ecclesiastical princes, the Émigrés, the corporations, and the communes was now thrown open to purchase by the peasants and burghers, who in working for their own profit rendered the soil more productive. The last traces of serfdom disappeared, education was extended and systematised, and the navigation of the Rhine facilitated. The Code substituted uniform procedure and modern ideas for a chaos of outworn practices. Roads were constructed, fruit-trees planted, agriculture and stock-breeding improved. Under model prefects—such as Jeanbon Saint-André and Lezay-Marnésia—the Left Bank experienced a period of tranquil advance after a decade of war, billetings, exploitations, and assignats.

' In the relatively short period of twenty years,' writes the latest French historian of the Rhineland in a passage of eloquent pride, ' the French accomplished an immense work, of which the Germans would never have dared to dream.[1] The country was divided up into ninety-seven little States, jealous of one another, and incapable of self-defence. It had remained feudal, and, being occupied by the petty interests of caste, was incapable of any comprehensive activity. It was called not immediately, but little by little, and at the request of a large part of its inhabitants, to enter into a modern and centralised State, rich and powerful, and vivified by economic liberty. To these weak and disunited peoples France gave what they needed most—protection and security. Having gone to war to liberate the peoples, not to enslave them, she brought all the free institutions which she had won in ten years of terrible strife. She abolished feudalism, liberated the soil, and transformed peasant serfs into free proprietors. She sold to the burghers and the peasants the possessions of the late rulers and the lands of the Church, and even a portion of the communal property, in order to multiply small freeholders and insure them a competence. She established civil liberty and equality. In these German lands, so unfamiliar with the equality of rights and with liberty, so respectful of ecclesiastical and noble castes, it was a profound revolution. No more distinction between citizens. Protestants and Jews found themselves on the same footing as the Catholics, who for centuries had governed the country in their own interest. The unity of laws was established. The Civil Code facilitated transactions from end to end of the Rhineland, and gave to the Rhinelanders the profound sentiment of the unity of their country and of their intimate union with France, who carried law and liberty in the folds of the tricolour.'

This is history seen through the invaders' spectacles, and overlooks not only the burdens imposed by an Emperor perpetually at war, but the ineradicable dislike of civilised Europeans for

---

[1] Sagnac, pp. 351–6.

alien rule. The dominant feeling of the Rhineland was in favour of a return in due course to German rule, combined with the retention of the reforms introduced by the conquerors. No one ever dreamed of the restoration of the sway of the crozier and of the feudal order, which had been swept into the dustbin by the revolutionary blast ; but absolutism had been unknown in the Ecclesiastical Electorates, and the *ancien régime* had left no such bitter memories of oppression and humiliation as in France. Moreover, attachment to the Church had continued unbroken, and had been strengthened by the attacks upon its practices and ordinances. In a word, the Rhineland, as a whole, was neither Jacobin nor reactionary, neither nationalist nor anti-national ; and for this reason, though not immune from the fell visitation of war, it was spared the horrors of revolution and counter-revolution. When peace returned to the world in 1815, the Left Bank reverted to German allegiance without regret and without enthusiasm. The reforms which had been introduced into the mushroom principalities of Westphalia, Berg, and Frankfurt were for the most part swept away on the fall of their creator ; but in the Rhineland, divided though it was between Prussia, Hesse-Darmstadt, and Bavaria, twenty years of French occupation and assimilation left abiding traces. Friendly memories of the tricolour, and legends of the Petit Caporal, lingered on till they were swallowed up in the pride and glory of the German Empire ; and the Civil Code remained as a link with the past till it was superseded by the Imperial Code in the closing year of the nineteenth century.[1]

---

[1] See Rovère, *Les Survivances françaises dans l'Allemagne Napoléonienne depuis 1815.*

CHAPTER XXI

THE SOUTH

I

THE Revolution found but little welcome in backward Bavaria ; but from the outset the ruling powers were alarmed, for they knew that the State was rotten to the core.[1] As early as 1789 the Government felt anxiety in regard to French emissaries in Munich ; and at the opening of 1790 a declaration warned the people against the evil spirit of the new ' destroyers of the State.' Before long the circulation of French newspapers was forbidden, and all writings on the Revolution, except refutations of its principles, were prohibited. The censorship was tightened, education was brought under stricter control, letters were opened, arrests and banishments became frequent, and all candidates for office had to swear that they belonged to no secret association. Reaction reigned supreme, and the last years of Karl Theodor, surrounded by his bastards, are among the darkest periods of Bavarian history.

In this atmosphere of decadence and obscurantism it was inevitable that active minds should look with sympathy on the ideas, if not on the actions, of the French reformers ; but the country was too lethargic to breed disturbances. The utmost efforts of an inquisitorial government only succeeded in unearthing a few harmless trifles. A club founded in Munich in 1791, with nightly meetings, proved to be a joke. On another occasion the authorities heard of a number of people who wore ' secret signs ' ; but further inquiry proved that the emblems were silk ribbons, distributed to the guests at a wedding party, and that the mysterious letters were the initials of the happy couple. In the little town of Neuötting, Lippert—commonly called the Grand Inquisitor of

[1] See Döberl, *Entwickelungsgeschichte Bayerns*, vol. ii. ; Perthes, *Politische Zustände*, 373-433 ; Schrepfer, *Pfalzbayerns Politik*, 1789-1793 ; and Treitschke, ii. 623-61.

Bavaria—discovered ' all sorts of French seditious pieces' : among them a copy of the Constitution, a parable of a grain of mustard growing into a Tree of Liberty, and a speech of Eulogius Schneider. In Ingolstadt a ' society of friendship' met to hear addresses on the latest news from Paris. Minor disturbances were reported from Augsburg and Passau ; but, in the main, Bavaria was as little affected by the revolutionary earthquake as Saxony.

A vivid picture of the state of opinion in the Wittelsbach dominions is drawn in the dispatches of Thomas Walpole, the British Minister, who moved from Munich to Mannheim and from Mannheim to Munich, as his diplomatic duties or his thirst for information dictated.[1]   While Bavaria was separated from French territory by a considerable tract of country, the Palatinate was exposed to the full force of the revolutionary gale. ' We receive daily accounts of new insurrections and troubles from the neighbouring frontiers of France,' he wrote from Mannheim in August 1789. ' At Landau, where a regiment had gone out to exercise, people assembled and shut the gates upon them, and then attacked the magistracy ; but a few light horse who had remained in the town forced the gates open. When the infantry re-entered, all the battalion joined the people. An engagement took place, and a great many lives were lost. At Strassburg Prince Maximilian of Deux-Ponts (the future Elector and King of Bavaria), in anger at seeing his regiment begin to mutiny, made use of the word *Canaille* in talking of the people, which so much irritated the soldiers of the regiment he commanded that they obliged him to accept the National Cockade and to drink a glass of beer to the success of the Tiers État, with other insulting circumstances too indecent to mention. He immediately after conveyed his wife and children to Heidelberg, and on his return to Strassburg found the gates of the town shut upon him. This seditious spirit has communicated itself to the neighbouring countries, and the Elector's Minister has been ordered to reside constantly in this town to watch more carefully the peace of the Palatinate. A cordon of troops is to be formed along the borders of Alsace. The Duke of Deux-Ponts has found it necessary to apply to the Elector for troops to suppress the riots in his dominions ; but no answer has yet been returned from Munich. One of the Duke's *baillis* has been carried off to Alsace and is there kept in prison by the people who are under arms.' ' The peasants in several districts of the Palatinate,' he added a fortnight later, ' have assembled, and deputations have been made to the regency to demand a redress of grievances, complaining particularly of the great mischiefs they suffer from

[1] Record Office, Bavaria.

the quantity of game. The insurrections have been hitherto easily quieted.'

From his watch-tower on the middle Rhine Walpole looked anxiously to the north, south, and west, fearing that the whole Rhineland would soon be aflame. ' The pillaging and universal uproar continue to range over the neighbouring parts of France,' he wrote in September, ' and this contagious disorder threatens to spread itself to all the bordering parts from the Low Countries as far as Basle.' Throughout the Rhineland the fires were smouldering, and there were not a few who believed that the rule of France could hardly be worse than their own. A pamphlet of 1792, ' By a Peasant to his Elector,' gave frank expression to the prevailing discontent. ' Shall we rejoice that we were allowed for fifty years to till our fields in the sweat of our brow in order to feed the boars and hares of his Excellency, or that he gave our hardly earned property to a band of noble and other robbers, chamberlains, mistresses, and adventurers ? ' On returning to Bavaria the British Minister found himself in a different world. ' This country continues in a state of perfect tranquillity,' he wrote from Munich in October ; ' but at Mannheim and in the Palatinate there have been tumultuous meetings, which have hitherto been easily kept under. The frontiers of Germany are always under a great alarm, and the Margrave of Baden has drawn a cordon of troops along the borders of his country, and will not permit above six people to pass at a time.' Throughout the first winter of the Revolution the dispatches tell the same story. ' Everything is very quiet here,' he reported in January 1790 ; ' but the last letters from the Palatinate have brought news of another insurrection in the *bailliage* of Simmern soon quelled ; and something of the sort has happened in the Duchy of Juliers.' ' The news from the Palatinate is very alarming,' he added a week later. ' There is much discontent, and every reason to apprehend an insurrection.'

In placid Bavaria the only danger that appeared to threaten came from the Illuminati, who were still widely believed to carry on their nefarious activities in many parts of Germany. ' Three years ago,' reported Walpole at the end of 1790, ' I often wrote about the Illuminati. The Elector has now appointed a secret Committee under the famous ex-Jesuit, Father Frank, to make search. It is supposed some discoveries of a dangerous nature must have been made, from the very violent rescript published yesterday, forbidding the meeting of the Illuminati and all other sects. The proclamation has created much uneasiness and surprise, because no ill-humour has appeared in the country or even of

late in this town, and I have no reason to believe the report of
there being French emissaries in this country.' Further measures
of repression followed at intervals. 'All private meetings under
the denomination of clubs or assemblies are forbidden,' wrote the
Minister in the summer of 1791, 'and the publication of books
which may serve to deprave the morals of the people. The post-
humous works of the late King of Prussia are prohibited under
the severest penalty. The Elector has struck out of the list several
favourite plays which alluded to the times. The principal towns
in the Palatinate are full of French emigrants; but very few
come this way and everything is perfectly quiet.'

The Elector detested the French Revolution; but he had no
desire to combat it by force of arms, and showed no zeal in vindicating his rights in Alsace. His ideal was to keep his dominions
free from French influences, and his method was as far as possible
to exclude Frenchmen of all parties. 'He has formed a cordon
of troops in the lower Palatinate on the frontier of France,'
reported Walpole in February 1792, 'to prevent the incursion of
vagabonds.' In his next dispatch he records the issue of an order
for the strict interrogation of French emigrants, 'when more than
two or three arrive together.' When war broke out the Elector
made no secret of his desire to preserve neutrality. 'The French
Minister is still here,' wrote Walpole in September, 'but he does
not appear in public. The Austrian Minister has again applied
very strongly for his removal.' The Elector, though not much of
a politician, refused to believe in the disinterested zeal of the
anti-revolutionary crusaders. 'The new alliance between Austria
and Prussia is very far from being popular,' commented Walpole on
the eve of the Valmy campaign, 'and almost all the German Courts
are apprehensive of the two preponderating Powers encroaching
upon the liberties of the Empire or the possessions of their neighbours.' The Minister's view was confirmed by a visit to Ratisbon.
'The close alliance between the most powerful sovereigns in the
Empire is cause of uneasiness and suspicion among the princes;
but the infamous doctrines of the French faction have given
such just alarm, and excited so much horror, that I have no
doubt the Emperor and the King of Prussia will be well
seconded in their efforts to destroy the present dangerous
anarchy in France.'

The Elector soon found that neutrality was unavailing to shield
an ill-governed State while other German princes were waging war
against the French Republic. 'Very alarming news comes from
the Palatinate,' reported Walpole in November. 'The peasants
refuse to pay their taxes, and are supported in their disobedience

by the French troops in the neighbourhood.' ' Our news from
the Palatinate continues very bad,' he repeated in December.
' The French troops overspread the country, seize upon the corn,
and poison the minds of the people with their abominable principles
of insurrection and hollow promises.' These trials, however, merely
strengthened the desire to avoid the greater evils of war. ' The
exposed situation of the Palatinate,' he reported early in 1793,
' prevents the Elector from renouncing a neutrality which has
hitherto been so beneficial to his subjects till the laws of the Empire
require it.' He was, indeed, utterly unprepared for hostilities.
He had entrusted the military administration to his favourite, Sir
Benjamin Thompson, who had seen service on the King's side in
the American War of Independence, but whose competence was
greater in natural science than in arms or statesmanship. For
years Walpole's dispatches were filled with references to the
unlimited favour enjoyed by the clever American, whose services
were rewarded in 1792 by the title of Count Rumford. ' The
great ascendency he has over the civil as well as the military power,'
he had written in 1791, ' and the steps he has taken to show his
authority, have made him great enemies among the first nobility
here ' ; but, while obviously disliking his character, the Minister
was not insensible to his energy and ability. When Bavaria was
compelled to enter the war in 1793, Rumford crossed the Alps ' for
his health,' and was not expected to return. ' He will not leave
the military on a better footing than he found it ; but I must do
him the justice to say his administration has been incorrupt, and
his establishments of the poor-house and military academy of real
benefit to the country.'

War involved increased expenditure, which in turn necessitated
the partial co-operation of the people. The Bavarian Diet had
never met since 1669, when the Estates and the Elector agreed to
empower twenty deputies to vote the annual supplies. As all
vacancies were filled by the Committee itself, the body quickly
lost touch with opinion. The summoning of the enlarged Estates
was as unwelcome to the Government as it was unavoidable, and
the first task of the new deputies was to purge themselves by oath
of ' Illuminatism.' But liberal ideas had filtered even into this
closely guarded preserve. ' Some maintain,' reported Walpole in
1794, ' that the Elector should be answerable to them for the
expenditure of public money, and show that it is employed in the
purposes for which it is voted. The Court maintains this to be
a new principle, and unknown to the constitution of the country.
He is only willing to give an account of all extraordinary sums
which they shall grant him.' The democrats failed to carry their

point ; but the dispute was of little practical importance, since the ruler, despite the loss of the Palatinate, confined his participation in the war within the narrowest possible limits. 'It is much to be feared,' wrote the Minister in cipher, in the spring of 1795, ' that he will soon relapse into his former system of neutrality.'

The dissolute old man hated business as much as he hated change, and after a period of eclipse the favourite reappeared at Court. ' Count Rumford has been appointed Minister of Police,' announced Walpole in February 1798. ' He appears to have regained all his influence with the Elector,' he added a fortnight later. ' His influence is unlimited.' His régime was mild enough —too mild, indeed, for the taste of the British Minister. ' His regulations concerning the police have been highly beneficial to the public,' he reported in the summer, ' however unwilling they may be to allow it ; for he has the misfortune to have many enemies among all ranks of people. He does not think it the business of the police to interfere with the people's private opinions as long as they keep them to themselves. I do not mean to accuse him of any predilection for republican tenets ; but we continue to see the dangerous effects of these principles.' The Elector's last mark of favour was to appoint the Count Bavarian Minister to the Court of St. James's ; but George III flatly declined to recognise the choice.

In the autumn of 1798 Arthur Paget succeeded Walpole at Munich, and sent home his alarming impressions of Bavaria in the closing months of the reign. ' I am ashamed to think,' he reported in October, ' there exist men in this country who little less than publicly espouse the French cause.' ' There exists a difference between the Elector and the Estates,' he added a week later, ' which is fomented by the secret machinations of a sect called the Illuminés, which, though not so openly employed, is as active as ever it was in the time of Weishaupt. Of those who compose the States there is one, Count Arco—in some respects a clever man, but a most violent Jacobin—who detests the Elector, and pays his court to the Duke of Deux-Ponts, whom he equally detests.' He felt it his duty to warn the Elector of the danger. ' In speaking with him of the internal enemies of the Government, particularly Count Arco, he not only agreed, but reprobated, if possible in stronger language, their conduct. He said he had a thorough proof of his guilt, but not a single legal proof. I insisted most strongly on the necessity of getting rid of him, and also of expelling once more from these dominions the Illuminés—a sect whose diabolical principles are almost universally spread, particularly throughout the higher classes.'

There was, indeed, a certain justification for these alarms. During the revolutionary era French agents circulated pamphlets and appeals in large numbers throughout the south. The propaganda was particularly active in Bavaria, and many reports of the year 1796 slumber in the archives of the Foreign Office. Those of ' Frey,' himself a Bavarian, expressed the hope that Germany would form one or more republics.[1] ' It would be difficult to make this country into a republic like Holland; but under a hundred despots it will never possess sufficient common sentiment to maintain its existence. It remains ever a passive Power, used by the stronger for their own ends.' In the closing years of the century the ferment increased, and a number of anonymous pamphlets appeared. 'On South Germany, by a South-German Citizen, presented to the French Government,' pronounced it riper for a republican government than any other country. ' Only the French bayonet,' argued the writer, ' is needed for the establishment of a South-German Republic.' Another pamphlet, entitled ' Outlines of a German Republic, by a Martyr of Truth,' argued that no sacrifice was too great for the goal. ' A survey of the History of the Bavarian Nation, and the Awakening of the Nations after a Thousand Years,' recalled the historic relations with France, and clamoured for the overthrow of clerical influences. Karl Theodor, however, lacked both the will and the capacity to save the State. His course was nearly run, and in the opening days of 1799 he died of a stroke.

The death of its degenerate ruler was the first step towards the revival of the country which lagged so far behind other German States ; and the accession of his successor was hailed as a deliverance by the small party of enlightenment. Max Joseph had been a Colonel in the French army and lived with his regiment in Strassburg till the outbreak of the Revolution, when he moved to Mannheim. The death of his half-crazy brother in 1796 made him Duke of Zweibrücken ; but as the tiny principality was already in French hands he remained in the capital of the Palatinate. Enjoying life, liking to see happy faces around him, tolerant and unassuming, he was universally beloved, and Bavarians waited eagerly for the day when he would enter Munich in state. To such an easy-going nature rancorous hate was impossible ; and he never lost his old affection for France. ' I was born there,' he remarked to the French chargé d'affaires on his accession to the Bavarian throne, ' and I beg you to regard me as a Frenchman. Please inform the

[1] His reports are summarised by Du Moulin Eckart, ' Bayerische Zustände und die Französische Propaganda im Jahre 1796,' Forschungen zur Kulturgeschichte Bayerns, ii. 168–211.

Directory that it has no truer friend than myself. Whenever I hear of the successes of the armies of the Republic, I rejoice to know that I am a Frenchman.'

The accession of the new ruler was particularly distasteful to the British Minister. 'The character of the present Elector,' he wrote in February, 'is such, I fear, as offers little prospect of happiness to his subjects : the more so, as he is surrounded by persons supposed to be devoted to the present French Government, and particularly a certain M. de Montgelas.' 'M. Montgelas,' he added in his next dispatch, 'was at the head of the sect of the Illuminés when they were driven out of Bavaria. He governs the Elector.' Paget's dispatches exhibit a crescendo of shrill invective. 'Jacobins and fomenters of revolution remain unmolested here at a moment when many respectable but unfortunate Émigrés are persecuted and ill-treated. I have lamented the influx of Illuminés into this country since the last Elector's reign. I have seen with pain the hordes of Jacobins with which this place swarms, and have in secret condemned the system by which they are tolerated.' These 'secret' conversations naturally reached the ears of the Elector, who showed himself very chilling in the only audience that he granted and proceeded to ask for another Minister. In the autumn Paget's successor, Walrond, reported an ordinance forbidding all secret societies for the discussion of politics, religion or science. 'It is considered a favourable prelude to further and more energetic measures for restraining the licentious principles that have hitherto been tolerated.' But Walrond, like his predecessor, was of opinion that the omnipotent Montgelas retained something of the Illuminati taint of his youth, and sent home a detailed biography of the Jacobin Count.

A year later, the Elector having joined the Second Coalition, French troops entered Munich, where their behaviour was exemplary. Moreau, their commander, was a student of German literature, and General Desolle loved German music. There was, however, some friction ; and after the battle of Hohenlinden it was widely believed that the dynasty was doomed. Republican brochures and songs abounded, an imitation Jacobin Club was formed, and plots were in the air. Mannlich, director of the Art Gallery at Munich, records in his 'Memoirs' that his nephew, a young soldier, was informed by two French officers of a plan for the establishment of a Republic under the protection of France.[1] The conspirators told Moreau of their plan, and gave him a list of their members, with the name of Utzschneider at the head. Our knowledge of the plot has been enlarged by the discovery of a report

---

[1] Mannlich, *Leben serinnerungen*, ch. viii.

by an Austrian agent.[1] The Illuminati, he declares, had the Elector and most members of the Government in their power ; and there was an independent and no less dangerous secret society called the ' Patriots.' The Illuminati were never really suppressed. The French Revolution suggested to the Order a new terminology, and it began to speak in the phrases of 1789. The ' Patriots ' were composed of men like Utzschneider, who split off from the Illuminati and formed a body of their own. Their pamphlets embodied far-reaching proposals, among them a Bavarian Landtag and the abolition of feudalism. When the French arrived they formed clubs, and tried to organise a revolt. Utzschneider suggested constitutional government, another member asked for a South-German Republic. Both Illuminati and ' Patriots' worked for a revolution in Church and State : the former by philosophy, literature, and politics, the latter by political action alone. The former were secret enemies, the latter open. The former found adherents in the higher classes, the latter in the lower. Only one party of the ' Patriots ' desired a Republic ; the others merely wanted to bind the ruler.

The French commander gave no encouragement to the conspirators, and the Elector was informed of the plot. ' A few excited, discontented, and partially ruined people,' writes Montgelas in his ' Memoirs,' ' vainly attempted to induce the enemy generals to revolutionise Bavaria, depose the officials, and establish a provisional government. This treason, in which some men whom one would never have suspected took part, failed on account of Moreau's refusal to co-operate. The Revolution had done enough harm in France, he argued, and there was no need to make other countries suffer in like manner.'[2] Max Joseph, though somewhat alarmed by the flood of pamphlets, displayed a healing moderation. He had no wish to see the blood of martyrs flow ; and Utzschneider himself, though deprived of his post, continued to receive his salary. After the conclusion of peace and the departure of the French, a voice was occasionally raised for a republic ; but the republican idea had struck no root, and a vigorous broom was to sweep away many of the causes which had fostered it.

Montgelas possessed the energy and ability which his weak and benevolent master lacked.[3] The creator of modern Bavaria

[1] See Fournier,' *Illuminaten u. Patrioten*,' in *Historische Studien u. Skizzen* ; and Du Moulin Eckart, ' *Eine Ehrenrettung*,' *Forschungen zur Kulturgeschichte Bayerns*, vol. v.

[2] *Denkwürdigkeiten*, pp. 48–9.

[3] See Du Moulin Eckart, *Bayern unter dem Ministerium Montgelas ;* Sicherer, *Staat u. Kirche in Bayern* ; O. Meier, *Zur Geschichte der römisch-deutschen Frage*, vol. i.

was the grandson of the President of the Senate of Chambéry, whose son migrated to Bavaria and married a German wife. The future statesman studied in Ingolstadt, Nancy, and Strassburg, and at the age of twenty entered the service of the State. His ideas were rather French than Bavarian, and he was drawn into the movement of the Illuminati. When the Order was attacked, his name was found among its papers. He lost the Elector's favour, and entered the service of Karl of Zweibrücken ; but the Duke was an impossible master, as short-sighted in his policy as he was ungovernable in his life.[1] ' At the very beginning of the crisis,' writes Montgelas in his ' Memoirs,' ' he spoke out boldly against the Revolution, and all his speeches and acts showed his conviction to be unchangeable. He seemed to forget that France was a neighbour, and that he was subject to invasion at any moment.' He gave splendid fêtes to the Émigrés, bitterly lamented his losses in Alsace, and persecuted his subjects. Such a policy led to its natural result in a French occupation. When Bergzabern revolted and asked for union with France, the Republic responded with the momentous Decree of November 19, 1791, offering help to peoples wishing to recover their liberty, or, as in the case of the Duke's subjects, threatened with punishment for their democratic zeal. But the young official had attracted the notice of the Duke's brother, Max Joseph, who, on succeeding to the title, made him his chief Minister ; and, when the Bavarian throne fell to his master, Montgelas became the real ruler of the country for eighteen years.

The Dictator looked like a French noble, and wrote and spoke French in preference to German. ' They were a singular pair of friends,' writes Treitschke ; ' the slovenly and homely King, side by side with the courtly figure of the adroit Minister. His appearance recalled the old French style, with his powdered hair, his embroidered red Court dress, and long silk stockings ; his keen yet shifty brown eyes, and great overhanging nose projecting over the large and satyr-like mouth—a countenance expressing in every lineament a penetrating understanding.' His aim was to reap the harvest of the Revolution, to accomplish for Bavaria what France had accomplished for herself. He approached his task with the critical detachment of a foreigner, and made no secret of his contempt for *cette nation bornée*. Like Frederick of Württemberg, he determined to remove all institutions which could thwart his will, beginning with the Estates and the Communes. Serfdom was abolished, the monasteries were reduced in number, prisons reformed, and torture abolished. An efficient bureaucracy and a

[1] See Mannlich, *Lebenserinnerungen*, ch. vi.

new provincial organisation were created, and the material regeneration of the country taken energetically in hand. Protestants
received equal rights from a prince who had married a Protestant.
The most successful of his reforms were in the sphere of education.
To root out Jesuit influence the University of Ingolstadt was
abolished, and a new seat of learning established at Landshut. The
Academy was revived, and scholars were imported from the
Protestant north. Elementary education was freed from clerical
control and rendered compulsory. In a few years the rubbish of
centuries was swept away, and Bavaria was transformed from the
most backward into one of the most advanced of German States.
' We are in the middle of a complete but bloodless revolution,'
wrote Anselm Feuerbach, the author of the new Criminal Code,
with delight in 1808. The Minister despised mankind and was as
little of a democrat as Frederick the Great ; but his lucid and logical
mind was offended by the absurdities of the old system, and he had
learned from France that revolutions could only be avoided by
drastic reform. He lacked, however, the statesmanship of the
Prussian reformers, for his policy of pitiless centralisation sapped
the vitality of provincial institutions. While Stein's Town
Ordinance created the conditions of a free and vigorous life, the
corresponding Bavarian law bound the municipalities hand and
foot to the bureaucracy. Hardenberg called him the first revolutionary Minister ; but, as he cared neither for liberty nor for
nationality, he is better described as the last survivor of the
Aufklärung.

II

It was not to be expected that Karl Eugen of Württemberg would
welcome the Revolution ; for he had only bowed to necessity in
accepting the partial limitation of his power by the Estates.[1] The
country occupied an exposed position ; and its Duke was also lord
of distant Mömpelgard, an enclave embedded in French territory.
Alone of German rulers, however, he visited Paris after the meeting
of the States-General, and was shown the sights by Wolzogen, a
diplomatic agent whom he had sent to France in 1788. The visit
angered the Émigrés, who misconceived its nature. ' The Duke
of Württemberg,' wrote Espinchal in his Journal, ' sold himself to
the Jacobins when last in Paris, where he habitually consorted
with those scoundrels, and frequently attended the sittings of the
National Assembly.' [2] It was true enough that he had used his eyes

[1] See Treitschke, ii. 588–623 ; Perthes, *Politische Zustände*, pp. 433–74.
[2] *Journal*, p. 252.

and kept his ears open ; but he never dreamed of renouncing the principles of a lifetime.   He was indeed no friend of the Émigrés ; and in 1791 he issued simultaneous orders against seditious writings and the fugitive *noblesse*. He complained to the Diet of French attacks on his rights ; but he took no part in the war of 1792, and only dispatched his troops when the Empire declared war.

When his long reign ended in 1793, Karl Eugen was succeeded by his two brothers, the elder of whom, Ludwig Eugen, was a keen opponent of the Revolution, and anxious to cast the full military strength of the duchy against the movement. But his zeal was not shared by his subjects. ' Just now there is a great disturbance in Stuttgart,' wrote Schiller's father to the poet in 1794. ' The cobbler apprentices have revolted, and the disturbance grew to such dimensions that yesterday all the troops from Ludwigsburg and some cannon were sent to the capital. The local Jacobins are probably mixed up in it, so there is ground for anxiety.' [1] His successor, Friedrich Eugen, was less zealous ; and when the French poured across the Rhine in 1796, his chief anxiety was to withdraw from the conflict—a desire intensified by continual friction with the Committee of the Landtag over the expenses of the war. His accession had been hailed with relief by young reformers. ' His activity and enlightenment give us hope of improvement,' wrote Schelling to Hegel, ' and the despotism of our philosophic mannikins will, I hope, get a good shock. It is incredible how much damage this moral tyranny has wrought. Had it lasted some years longer, it would have paralysed intellectual liberty more than any political despotism. They wanted no scholars, only orthodox theologians.' [2]

Unlike Bavaria, Württemberg could boast a considerable number of Intellectuals at the outbreak of the Revolution ; and with scarcely an exception they greeted the brightening dawn.[3] The veteran Friedrich Karl Moser, it is true, who returned to his native State in 1790, looked on with sombre forebodings. He felt no sympathy for France, and he believed that the Revolution would prove the scourge of Germany, for which he foretold the fate of Poland. His ' Political Truths,' published in 1796, showed how little he had changed, and he died in 1798 without having modified his belief in enlightened despotism. To the younger generation, on the other hand, the ideas of 1789 came as a gospel of hope and deliverance. ' Man is always trying to improve his

---

[1] *Schiller's Beziehungen zu Eltern, etc.*, p. 132.

[2] *Aus Schelling's Leben*, i. 78.

[3] See Wohlwill, *Weltbürgertum u. Vaterlandsliebe der Schwaben* ; and W. Lang, *Von und aus Schwaben*, iii. 57–130.

lot, and is accustomed to regard mere changes as improvements,'
wrote Schiller's schoolfellow, Hoven, in his 'Autobiography' ; ' and
this was the case with myself and most of my young friends. We
were powerfully stimulated by this great world-revolution, and,
like so many thousand Germans, we promised ourselves the most
blessed results for mankind. We talked about it every day. Of
course we had not seen it at close quarters : the war had not yet
broken out, and no French armies had come to plunder and to
burn. We regarded the drastic means adopted by the Assembly
as a necessary defence against the threat of foreign intervention,
and we placed the guilt not on French shoulders, but on those of
the Emperor and the King of Prussia, and, above all, on the
Brunswick Manifesto, which we at once predicted would provoke a
war to the death, the total dissolution of the Monarchy, and very
likely the execution of the King. In spite of the war and its horrors,
I and my friends in Ludwigsburg and Stuttgart never lost hope, and
we could not withhold our admiration for the energy of the nation
and the prowess of its armies.' [1]   The recollections of the Ludwigsburg doctor are confirmed by those of the ecclesiastic Pahl. ' There
was joy and hope in every hamlet. Despite the excesses and the
disappointments, the principles of the Declaration of the Rights
of Man were rooted in the heads and hearts of men, and strove
unceasingly for realisation. The French victories in Belgium and
Mainz convinced me that Providence had summoned France to
inaugurate the great task of world-reform.' [2]

Schubart had emerged from his dungeon in 1787 a broken
man ; but the news of the Revolution braced the old champion of
Washington and Paoli like a cordial.[3] ' Mankind is neither old nor
weak,' he cried, ' when a people whom we thought steeped in the
spirit of littleness gives such proofs of courage and greatness.' In
early manhood he had denounced French influences ; but he now
expressed shame that his countrymen were passed in the race, and
with bitter irony congratulated them on being ' the best of subjects.'
' There is nothing to compare with it in recent history,' he wrote
in his paper. ' The King is the first personage of a free people, the
rights of citizens are weighed in equal scales, and France is approaching the meridian of her greatness and strength. Brother Frank,
thy liberty will stand firm like God's mountain, if thou wilt only
preserve it by patriotism, virtue, and piety.' He rebuked the
forebodings of Schlözer and Schirach, and he was moved to rapture
by an invitation to a fête in Strassburg. ' One seemed to see the

[1] Hoven, *Autobiographie*, pp. 123-4, 145-6.
[2] Pahl, *Denkwürdigkeiten*, pp. 98-105.
[3] See Strauss, *Schubart's Leben in Briefen*, ii. 313-15, 423-4, 428-9.

heavenly Jerusalem and to hear the spirits of the blest shouting for joy in its crystal palaces.' In the winter of 1789 he prophesied that if the Powers intervened they would be repulsed with fury, and he was convinced that Europe would emerge in a new and better shape from the chaos of destruction. Ten years on the Asperg had, however, satisfied the poet's appetite for martyrdom, and in the last months of his life he was terrified by a rebuke for writing that Bischoffswerder had fallen and Wöllner was about to fall. He admitted that he might inadvertently have spoken without sufficient respect of the German Constitution ; ' for in dealing with the present Constitution in France I have been carried away by the popular rejoicing, and have often given utterance to democratic principles. I yield to none, however, in true, deep patriotism, and beg to be informed in future what I am to do or not to do.' But while his published utterances became more cautious, his letters were as outspoken as ever. ' You are royal birds, beating your wings in the empyrean of holy liberty,' he wrote to a friend in Strassburg ; ' and we are the ravens, the *servum pecus*. Germans are not destitute of the lofty sense of liberty ; but they can suffer more, and longer, than the Franks. When they awake, their uprising is all the more terrible. I believe that your free Constitution is firmly grounded. May you long enjoy the happiness of it—the foretaste of the Kingdom of God ! ' A few weeks later he was dead, and was spared the bitterness of seeing the collapse of his hopes.

Schubart's Journal was continued by his son, with the aid of Stäudlin, who sang the praises of the Revolution in mediocre verse. Like most foreign radicals, he lost his heart to the Girondins, whom he glorified as the guardian angels of liberty in a poetic sketch, ' The Genius of the Year 1793.' Vergniaud and his staff are likened to Solon, Demosthenes, and Pericles ; while Charlotte Corday is reverenced as a heroine and martyr. Though Robespierre and the Terrorists are flagellated, he retains his faith in the value of the Revolution. In spite of his outspoken Gallophilism, he tried to be fair to his own country, and during the war he praised the prowess of both sides. The Chronicle thus pleased nobody, lost readers, and was suppressed. He moved to the Breisgau, whence he could survey ' the fair land where the champions of liberty dwell.' He started another paper, but with no better success, and ended his troubles in 1796 by plunging into the Rhine.

Schubart was soon followed to the grave by his old colleague in critical journalism. Having spent his life in singing the praises of France Weckhrlin welcomed the Revolution, and congratulated himself on catching a Pisgah sight of the kingdom of philosophy and toleration. He refused to be perturbed by the excesses, coolly

observing that many of those who had been lynched would have
fared no better at the hands of justice. Comparing the fate of
Foulon with that of Damien, he asked : ' Are we used to greater
mildness from the laws ? Have their atrocities been any less ? '[1]
But the tightening grip of the censorship taught him caution, and
he finally took refuge behind a mask of indifference. ' Others may
preach revolt,' he remarks ; ' but we will preach peace. We gain
nothing by revolt, for new tyrants succeed to old. A philosopher
thinks too little of the mob to sacrifice his ease for it.' Despite
his assumption of detachment, Weckhrlin continued to be regarded
as a dangerous man ; and his death was hastened, if not actually
caused, by rough handling inflicted during an attack on his house
in 1792.

In no part of the duchy was enthusiasm for the Revolution
more whole-hearted than in its ancient and renowned University.
We have already seen something of the ferment in dealing with
Hegel, Hölderlin, and Reinhard ; but the life of Schelling supplies
further details.[2] ' As for the expressions of enthusiasm,' writes
the son of the philosopher, ' I could not learn of Trees of Liberty
in which Hegel and Schelling took part, though I inquired from
contemporaries ; but bold speeches were certainly made, songs of
freedom written, and renderings from the French declaimed. Above
all, the Marseillaise was honoured, and Schelling was said to have
translated it. Though this was not the case, the Duke believed
the report. Full of wrath he hurried to Tübingen, and ordered
the scholars to assemble in the dining-room, where Schelling and
other suspects had to stand forward. The Duke held out the
document towards Schelling with the words : ' Here is a song composed in France and sung by the bandits of Marseilles.' He looked
fixedly at Schelling, who returned his gaze without flinching. The
Duke was pleased by his courage and imposed no punishments.
After delivering a short exhortation, he again stepped up to him
and asked if he was sorry, to which the young man replied, ' We all
make mistakes in various ways.'

This was not the end of his troubles, as two letters to the Rector
from his father, a country clergyman, testify. ' Your magnificence
can well imagine the anxiety in which the news of our son plunged
his parents. Though he makes himself out quite innocent I
cannot believe his word without corroboration, and am full of
apprehension. Accept my thanks for your kindness to the short-
sighted youth, and let his sorrowing father and mother know what
we have to fear or hope, and whether I can do anything for him

[1] See Ebeling, *Weckhrlin*, pp. 190–8.
[2] *Aus Schelling's Leben*, i. 31–4.

II

at Court.' A month later he wrote to express his gratitude for letting his son come home. ' I confess, since the recent unhappy occurrence, I should have been glad to have him with me, and to lead him to a frank confession whether he knew of any forbidden associations. I have learned nothing from him, and he assures me he entered into nothing which the world might not know. But I am now much more tranquil. From his earliest years to the time he left home he has committed innumerable faults of youthful impulsiveness ; but I never knew him dishonourable or mendacious. So, even in this case, I must almost believe his consistent assertion of innocence. But I have given him the most emphatic warnings to be more careful in his conduct and in the choice of friends.' In these letters timidity almost passes into servility ; but the prodigal son continued to think for himself. When the French armies crossed the Rhine the impenitent young philosopher bitterly denounced the German princes, to whose obstinacy he attributed the sufferings of the Fatherland. A similar event was experienced in the Karlsschule in Stuttgart, where the students formed a political club and held debates. ' The object of the school,' wrote Georg Kerner, ' was to train Mamelukes, blindly devoted servants of the Government ; but the founder lived to see his students form an Opposition.' The Fête of the Federation was solemnly celebrated, the students entering the throne-room by night and delivering impassioned speeches before the busts of Brutus and Demosthenes and a clay statue of Liberty.

The outbreak of war brought Württemberg within the danger zone. ' The great revolution in France causes some apprehension in these districts,' wrote old Schiller to his son in August. ' It might easily occur to the great mob to pay a visit to Württemberg, which lies so close. Some preparations have been made on the frontier, but not enough if the internal chaos in France increases, and high prices and lack of money drive the people to robbery.' [1] Mömpelgard, or Montbéliard, was promptly occupied by the enemy, and permanently ceded at the peace. Many expressions were heard of the need of a *levée en masse* in Germany to resist the French.[2] In 1794 the Prince Bishop of Bamberg and Würzburg issued a fiery appeal to his subjects for military service—an example followed by other governments and by an Imperial decree recommending the arming of the frontier population. But there was little desire to fight for the existing régime. ' The *levée en masse* with which the Emperor wishes to frighten the Republic is a

[1] See *Schiller's Beziehungen zu Eltern, etc.*, pp. 99–100.
[2] See Wendland, *Versuche einer allgemeinen Volksbewaffnung in Süddeutschland.*

sham,' wrote Bacher, the French agent in Basle, to his Government. ' The people in Swabia and Baden would only rise to make a revolution. If the German princes were so foolish, it would be the end of their rule.' Over one hundred and fifty pamphlets appeared, demanding the abolition of abuses, extension of the suffrage, and the regular summoning of the Landtag.

Though sympathy with France was general in the opening months of the Revolution, it was never more than academic. 'In our day,' wrote old Moser in 1796, ' one can say much that our fathers hardly dared to think.' But the Terror taught even liberal-minded men to be suspicious of French theories. What Württemberg desired was not to transplant French institutions, but to restore and maintain its own constitutional rights—' the good old law ' granted by Duke Ulric in 1514. The accession of Frederick in 1797, the nephew of the three last Dukes, opens the most critical period of its history. Able, well-informed, and widely travelled, he had served as an officer in Russia and Prussia ; and he looked with contempt on the fossilised provincialism of the little country to which he returned in middle life. While impatiently waiting for the throne, he mapped out the scheme of policy which was to make him the absolute ruler of a centralised, homogeneous, and powerful State. The Landtag at once met in full session—for the first time since 1770—to discuss the war-debt. To the old opposition of the States was added a new and sharper criticism of abuses, which was attributed by observers to the influence of French democracy.[1] The quarrel now began which lasted throughout the reign. The Landtag was repeatedly dissolved and the leaders were banished. There was nothing revolutionary in the attitude of the Estates, whose foremost champion was Georgii, a constitutional monarchist, equally opposed to the unlimited claims of the Duke and the doctrinaire radicalism of France. ' You think there are still people who wish to revolutionise Swabia,' he wrote to Abel, the Minister of the Hanseatic Towns. ' So there are ; but they are rather foreigners than natives. I am certain that there will never be a revolution in Württemberg, unless the torch is applied from abroad.' Georgii fought for the Constitution as long as possible, and then, yielding to superior force, retired into private life.

In such an atmosphere of strife and suspicion rumours of plots were frequent. At the time of the Congress of Rastadt there was talk of an ' Allemannic Republic.' A Constitution was passed from hand to hand, and Georgii (without his knowledge) was designed as prospective President. Several arrests were made, but the conspiracy, if it existed, was insignificant. Pahl's name

[1] See Vreede, *La Souabe après la Paix de Basle,* Introduction.

was connected with it, but without reason. ' I was an opponent of every revolutionary or forcible movement,' he writes ; ' but I abhor the party of reaction still more.' His anonymous satires attacked the abuses of the State; but he was never a man of extreme opinions. None the less the brutal rule of the Duke prepared the soil for French propàganda. ' I have heard from Macintosh from Stuttgart,' wrote Thomas Grenville to Lord Grenville from Berlin, ' expressing the greatest apprehension at the progress of French principles in Württemberg under the active direction of Citoyen Mengaud and Citoyen Trouvé. The latter was once employed in England by Prussia ; but proving himself, as Haugwitz told me, a very mischievous democrat, they sent for him here to shut him up, which he avoided by escaping to France, and he has since become one of the most active agents for the revolutionising of Germany.'[1] When Moreau's armies swept over the Rhine Jacobin clubs were formed, and a pamphlet propounded the question ' What should we gain if Swabia became a Republic ? ' But the Duke proved himself capable of dealing with all opposition. Realising that he could not fulfil his ambitions without French support, he joined the side of Napoleon, trebled his territory, and acquired the royal title.

With the new Catholic territories which fell to his share in the liquidation of the Empire Frederick could do as he pleased ; but he refused to rule over a country in a portion of which his will was fettered by antiquated rights and claims. He therefore made a clean sweep of ' the good old law,' and introduced a uniform system throughout his dominions. ' The *coup d'état*,' writes Treitschke, ' was not the outcome simply of a tyrant's overweening love of power, but also of an undeniable political necessity. Over the united Old and New Württemberg all the terrors of despotism now raged ; but the autocracy endowed the country with the indispensable institutions of the modern State. The edict of religions, King Frederick's best work, overthrew the dominion of the Lutheran Church and gave equal rights to both creeds. By the secularisation of Church property, and the abolition of the treasury of the Estates, unity of the national economy was established and the duty of paying regular taxes was carried into effect. The defenceless country once more acquired a little army fit for war. With revolutionary impetuosity the enemy of the Revolution established modern legal equality in his own State.' The debauched and extravagant monarch was detested by his people ; but his work remained. Without the example of France to warn, to inspire, and to guide, neither Montgelas nor Frederick could have

[1] *Fortescue MSS.*, iv. 485–6.

overthrown the entrenched forces of tradition, nor carried out the revolution from above, of which South Germany stood in such desperate need.

III

As a life-long friend of France, Karl Friedrich of Baden [1] regarded her efforts for liberty with considerable sympathy; but the proximity of his State to the frontier rendered it peculiarly liable to the infiltration of disturbing influences, and concrete causes of friction soon appeared. The abolition of feudal rights in Alsace affected his finances, and though compensation was discussed, no settlement was reached. A second and even more thorny problem was that of the Émigrés, to whom the Margrave offered hospitality, while forbidding them to arm in his dominions. Determined to remain master in his own house and to resist pressure from whatever quarter it came, he drafted small garrisons into the towns, and guarded the crossings of the Rhine. Some villagers came to him, demanding immediate abolition of their grievances, and added: ' If you refuse, we shall compel you.' ' Come!' was the spirited reply, ' and I shall receive you as you deserve.' Trouble occurred in a few parishes; but the movement was not really revolutionary, and tranquillity was quickly restored by the combined energy and moderation of the ruler.

Karl Friedrich's initial friendliness to France turned into mistrust and hostility, much to the disappointment of his admirers among German Gallophils. ' I am surprised,' wrote Reichardt early in 1792, ' that the Margrave, who has always so prudently followed the *juste milieu*, now pronounces so openly in favour of the aristocracy. At the beginning his conduct was quite different, and he took no notice of Artois on his first appearance at Karlsruhe.' [2] But the ruler had no desire to do more than defend his little State from disturbance, and he had nothing in common with the Émigrés or the King of Prussia. He founded a secret society, called the Black Brothers, to counterwork the party of revolution, and to defend Christianity and patriotism. ' We have no right and no need to intervene in France,' wrote Privy Councillor Meier in his diary. ' Do not annoy her; do not support the Émigrés;

---

[1] See Kleinschmidt, *Karl Friedrich von Baden*; Treitschke, ii. 661–87; *Politische Correspondenz Karl Friedrichs von Baden*, vols. i.–ii.; Obser, *Baden u. die revolutionäre Bewegung im Jahre 1789,*' in *Zeitschrift f. d. Geschichte des Oberrheins, Neue Folge*, vol. iv.; Lenz, *Ein deutscher Kleinstaat in der fr. Rev., Preussische Jahrbücher*, December 1892.

[2] *Lettres*, p. 41.

accept the proffered compensation for our rights in Alsace.' And such was the policy of Karl Friedrich himself, in spite of the efforts of his chief adviser to frighten him into action. ' There will be a great stir,' declared Edelsheim on the meeting of the States-General. ' If the Court is firm, everything will be settled and the phœnix will rise from its ashes ; but for a long time the importance of France will be destroyed.' He soon realised, however, that France was by no means paralysed, and began to be heartily afraid of her. In June 1792 he officially complained to France that travellers from Alsace brought seditious writings into Germany ; ' and we have often been warned that there are emissaries in our dominions charged to seduce the inhabitants.'

Baden entered the war in 1793 with the rest of the Empire, but waged it without enthusiasm. After the Treaty of Basle the Republic redoubled its efforts to influence South Germany.[1] In 1796 a copy of a proclamation in German was discovered, promising French help to secure independence for Baden and other south-western States. ' The enemies of the French people are not the peoples, but the princes—your tyrants—who have robbed you of your rights. A French army is drawing near. We are all your brothers.' The document was forwarded to Karl Friedrich, who replied that it was known weeks before, and that there was no trace of its circulation in Baden. With the signing of peace in 1797 the danger from sedition passed away. The Dutch Minister reported on ' revolutionary movements ' in 1798 ; but they were unimportant and yielded to gentle handling. One evening in 1799 the Margrave heard the words ' Es lebe die Republik ' in a wood close to his residence ; but the three men arrested proved to be harmless enough. Baden, indeed, was less infected by the revolutionary leaven than Bavaria or Württemberg. ' It is an honourable trait that not a single German State joined in the mad orgy of which France had given an example,' writes the latest historian of the Rheinbund.[2] But in truth the Terror and the conduct of the French armies had cured Germany of illusions.

Opinion in Baden, as everywhere else, was divided. The most distinguished of the Margrave's advisers was Schlosser, the Frankfurt jurist, who had married Goethe's sister, and had entered the service of Karl Friedrich in middle life.[3] His sympathies, like

---

[1] See Obser, 'Der Marquis von Poterat u. die revolutionäre Propaganda am Oberrhein im Jahre 1798,' in Zeitschrift für die Geschichte des Oberrheins, Zweite Folge, vii. 385–413.

[2] Bitterauf, Geschichte des Rheinbundes, vol. i.

[3] See Nicolovius, J. G. Schlosser ; and Gothein, J. G. Schlosser als Badischer Beamter.

those of most of the highly educated bourgeoisie, were with the Aufklärung, and he enrolled himself among the Illuminati. Learned, upright, and independent, he was a model official, whose work was fully recognised by his master. His political ideal was a small State, with an enlightened ruler and representation by Estates ; and he assisted his master in the discussions preceding the formation of the Fürstenbund, in which, however, he lost interest when Prussia assumed the leadership. Having no belief in the wisdom or capacity of the people, he looked as coldly on the Revolution as on its adversaries. In the words of a biographer, he was a conservative from pessimism, not from conviction. ' We cannot prevent the people learning from the French example that things could be different,' he wrote in an essay on State Reform ; ' but it is possible to make the habit of obedience easier than the effort of resistance. A fair reduction of taxation, the limitation of game, the revision of dues, a helping hand to poverty, a wise assistance to industry, a firmer supervision and a more careful selection of the servants of the State, a more accessible system of justice—that is the only eloquence to restrain subjects from revolt, the only eloquence to convince.' This was courageous language ; but he never imagined that it was the rulers alone who needed good advice. In an essay on Machiavelli he gives the other side of the picture. ' Instead of, or parallel with, declamations on the abuse of princely power, the publicist must also take note of the faults of the people which caused them. When one observes how France is behaving, one cannot help seeing how much more the ass is to blame for carrying the sacks than is the miller for putting them on his back.'

Schlosser was often asked for his advice in writing ; and a series of memorials embodies his policy in the years of storm and stress. In 1790 he urges the surrender of Baden's trifling claims beyond the Rhine, and a compromise with France. The effect of the Revolution, he added, would long remain, though it would probably be succeeded by a despotism, after the English precedent. A war of the Empire, or the retention of rights in Alsace, was strongly deprecated. At the end of 1791 he discussed the Imperial decree on seditious writings. ' Such writings contain little danger for the present adult generation. But when they are gone, and the younger generation which is living through this epoch takes their place, I fear that, unless many things are improved, we shall have revolutions in Germany.' When Edelsheim attempted to push his master towards a policy of intervention, Schlosser, determined to keep out of war, intrigued with France behind his back, employing the Alsatian poet Pfeffel, whose brother resided in Paris, and whom we already know as a political correspondent of Schlözer. On May 8, 1792, Pfeffel forwarded to the French Foreign Minister a letter from ' one of the Margrave's chief Ministers,' stating that the action of Austria did not involve the Empire, and that the Swabian Circle desired to maintain neutrality.

Schlosser detested violent upheavals, even in the name of a good cause. ' Take my advice,' he wrote to Forster early in 1792, ' don't talk so loudly about liberty. I am very dissatisfied not only with the great ones of the earth, but with the common herd as well. Till I detect in the people the capacity to rule themselves, I would rather leave the old brew alone. I am a citizen of Frankfurt, and fifty-three years old ; in other words, I am not under a despot, and I have reached an age when one begins to long for rest. You are younger, and not a citizen of Frankfurt ; but even you can sacrifice a few traits in your ideal of liberty and a few paragraphs in your Code of Rights in order to live quietly under your own fig-tree.' A few weeks later, when the Great War had been unchained, he wrote again to Forster. ' I am not afraid of French threats, but I fear for the poor people ! For two years I have been warning, counselling, urging. If they had taken my advice, land and people would have been safe. But the aristocrats opposed me, and now we have the wolf by the ears.' His outlook grew ever darker. ' The sombre prospects of barbarism haunt my vision—I mean barbarism of the heart, not of the head. Instead of wisdom, justice, respect of property, we see cruelty, robbery, defiance. Do not tell me that great revolutions of necessity breed these excesses. France needs no great revolution, and cannot bear it. When the States-General met, the principal evils were easy to remove. The King was popular, and a few measures relating to finance, the army, the Church, and periodical meetings of the Estates would have been enough in the first years. Later on the people would unwittingly have obtained power, and the new order would have gradually been digested.' The death of the King was for Schlosser, as for most German liberals, the last straw. ' All the commonplaces about the rise and fall of mankind fail to comfort me,' he wrote to Dohm. ' I think of nothing but why I have to live to witness such a scene. The death of Charles I was contrary to law ; but he was taken with arms in his hands. If Louis sighed for foreign aid it was not in order to be a despot, but to frame a constitution dictated by patriotism, not by factions.'

The younger generation was naturally less conservative, and was represented by such historians and publicists as Rotteck and Posselt. ' The French Revolution and its wonderful events,' wrote a friend of the latter, ' were his idol. His mind, which at that time lived wholly in the great times of the Greeks and Romans, gave it a welcome of fiery enthusiasm, which inevitably passed into his writings. He who regarded republics as the synonym for all that was great and good, and as the element of great souls and heroes, naturally loved the French Republic, that beautiful meteor. When he described the deeds of the French with brilliant eloquence, the crowd called it partisanship.' Like all humane men, he was shocked by the death of the King ; and his ' History of the Trial ' sharply condemned ' the savages who have made one of the most significant of revolutions into the scorn of the world.' But he admired the Girondins, and translated Condorcet's sketch of the progress of the human mind. The Terror grieved him without destroying his faith in liberty, and he upheld the ideas of 1789 in the monthly ' European Annals,' which he began to edit for Cotta in 1795. His views cost him his Chair of History and Rhetoric in Karlsruhe, though the mild Karl Friedrich allowed him to draw half his salary as a pension.

When Schiller lost interest in politics, Cotta turned to Posselt, who became the first editor of the ' Allgemeine Zeitung.'[1] The most famous of South-German dailies began its career in 1798 with a sentence comparing the transformation achieved by the Revolution with some vast geological cataclysm. Goethe and Schiller exchanged notes on their friend's enthusiasm for the arrogant French conquerors. Even Archenholtz found the paper too radical for his taste, and his tenure of the editorial chair was brief. But his view of the Revolution was no longer so favourable. ' What at first nineteen out of twenty Frenchmen called holy is now held by Europe in horror,' he wrote in 1802. ' We have learned that there can be republics without liberty, and liberty without republics. Sieyès was right in saying that it was perhaps nowhere safer than in a limited monarchy.' If Baden was hardly a limited monarchy, it was, at any rate, not a despotism. During the Napoleonic era the Margrave bowed to the inevitable, and it was truly said that ' the guns of Strassburg commanded the policy of Baden.' But when Karl Friedrich died in 1811, after a reign of sixty-two years, he had increased his inherited territory tenfold, and had laid the foundations of one of the most prosperous and enlightened States of modern Germany.

The French Revolution left a deep and permanent mark on the rulers and subjects, the institutions and ideas of the west and south of Germany ; and men of a later generation looked back on it with gratitude as the inauguration of a better age. ' My birth

[1] See Heyck, *Die Allgemeine Zeitung*.

and childhood,' wrote Welcker, ' synchronised with the Revolution, before which nobody thought of a constitution.[1]   The proclamation of liberty and reform delighted Klopstock and Kant, and all men sound of mind and heart ; and the later excesses never, thank God, stole from my father the warm and abiding love of right and liberty.'   The fall of Napoleon restored German lands to German rulers, but the foreign leaven remained.   For a generation after Waterloo the liberals of the south and west looked to Paris for their inspiration, as the liberals of the north looked to England, and spoke more of the French occupation than of the Wars of Liberation.   The abstract and deductive method which had been the hall-mark of ' French ideas ' continued to prevail.   The two most popular historical works of the Restoration era in the south and west were the world-histories of Schlosser and Rotteck, both of which stretched kings and priests on the rack and shed tears over the sufferings of the oppressed masses.   While Prussia remained without a constitution till 1848, the South-German States were furnished with Parliaments within a few years of the conclusion of peace.   The French gospel of natural rights and the sovereignty of the people was proclaimed by Rotteck, the father of South-German liberalism, who asked for the republican spirit, if not for republican forms.   The central doctrine of the French Revolution— that the destinies of the country should be controlled by the people as a whole—found far fuller acceptance than in Prussia, and has coloured the political thought and practice of the south and west ever since.

[1] Wild, *K. T. Welcker*, pp. 324–6, 336.

CHAPTER XXII

CONCLUSION

' I OBSERVE that minds are fermenting in that Germany of yours,' wrote Mirabeau to Mauvillon at the end of 1789.[1] ' If the spark falls on combustible material it will be a fire of charcoal, not of straw. Though, perhaps, more advanced in education, you are not so mature as we, because your emotions are rooted in the head ; and since your brains are petrified with slavery, the explosion will come with you much later than with us.' The great tribune's prophecy proved correct ; for the main effects of the Revolution were manifested in Germany some years after the acute crisis in France was past. ' France did more than conquer Europe,' writes Sorel in an eloquent passage ; ' she converted her. Victorious even in their defeat, the French won over to their ideas the very nations which revolted against their domination. The princes most eagerly bent on penning in the Revolution saw it, on returning from their crusade, sprouting in the soil of their own estates, which had been fertilised by the blood of French soldiers. The French Revolution only ceased to be a source of strife between France and Europe to inaugurate a political and social revolution, which in less than half a century has changed the face of the European world.'[2]

I

The combined influence of the ideas of 1789 and of the Great War which followed their proclamation produced two concrete results in Germany of incalculable importance—the one of a negative, the other of a positive character. The first was the destruction of the political framework of the country. The proved weakness of the Empire in the war, the desertion of Prussia and the north at the height of the struggle, and the collapse of the Ecclesiastical Electorates, left no attentive observer in doubt that the old

---

[1] *Lettres à un de ses Amis en Allemagne*, p. 490. [2] Sorel, i. 548–9.

firm was in liquidation.   No ambitious and aggressive State could
have wished for a neighbour less fitted by its traditions and
institutions to parry the thrust of its conquering sword.   Well might
Napoleon write to the Directory from Rastadt : ' If the Germanic
Body did not exist, we should have to create it expressly for our
own convenience.'   When the left bank of the Rhine was annexed
to the French Republic, Görres wrote his celebrated Obituary.   ' On
December 30, 1797, at three in the afternoon, the Holy Roman
Empire, supported by the Sacraments, passed away peacefully at
Regensburg at the age of 955, in consequence of senile debility and
an apoplectic stroke.   The deceased was born at Verdun in the
year 842, and educated at the Court of Charles the Simple and his
successors.   The young prince was taught piety by the Popes, who
canonised him in his lifetime.   But his tendency to a sedentary
life, combined with zeal for religion, undermined his health.   His
head became visibly weaker, till at last he went mad in the Crusades.
Frequent bleedings and careful diet restored him ; but, reduced to
a shadow, the invalid tottered through the centuries till violent
hemorrhage occurred in the Thirty Years' War.   Hardly had he
recovered when the French arrived, and a stroke put an end to his
sufferings.   He kept himself unstained by the Aufklärung, and
bequeathed the left bank of the Rhine to the French Republic.'
Görres was right.   The Empire was not buried till 1806, but it
was slain by the Revolution.   It perished unwept, unhonoured,
and unsung, and its ghost had to be laid before Germany could be
reborn.

Secularisation was in the air before 1789 ; and when the Republican armies reached the Rhine, the princes whose interests were
affected sought compensation for their losses on the right bank.
When rude hands were laid on the ark of the covenant, they quickly
found imitators.   The doctrines of legitimism and conservatism
were conveniently forgotten.   By the Recess of 1803 the Ecclesiastical Electorates and principalities were swept away, the Free
Cities, with the exception of Hamburg, Bremen, Lubeck, Frankfurt,
Nuremberg, and Augsburg, disappeared, and the old organisation
of the Circles was broken in pieces.   In the College of Princes the
Protestants obtained a majority, and power passed from south to
north, from the Austrian to the Prussian camp.   The Hapsburg
ascendancy was overthrown by the eviction of the ecclesiastics
and by the aggrandisement of Bavaria, Baden, Württemberg, and
Hesse.   ' Few among the great transformations of modern history,'
declares Treitschke, ' seem so detestable, so base, and so mean as
this Princes' Revolution.   Not a glimmer of a bold idea, not a
spark of noble passion illuminated the colossal breach of public

law. And yet the overthrow was a great necessity. All that was buried was already dead. The ancient forms of the State vanished in an instant, as if they had been swallowed up in the earth.' [1] The judgment oi a recent English historian on what he describes as at once a salutary simplification and the most degrading page in the history of Germany is to the same effect.[2] 'The secular princes, eager for the spoils of the Church, sent their envoys to Paris to treat with Talleyrand, the Minister of Foreign Affairs. The base obsequiousness of the German envoys was only equalled by the timorous greed of their impatient masters; and the favours of the First Consul were supplicated in terms that would not have been exceeded for abjectness in Byzantium. The house of Talleyrand became the mart in which so many square miles, peopled by so many souls, could be acquired for so many snuff-boxes and so many francs and so many attentions to Madame Talleyrand's poodle. Princes and dukes, princesses and duchesses, paid huge sums to be comprehended in the indemnities. Some of the money was intercepted by swindling agents; but much found its way into the long purse of Talleyrand. The First Consul wisely kept himself aloof from the open traffic; but it was his policy which really guided events.'

The Princes' Revolution left the historic structure little more than a ruin; and it was clear that its respite would be brief. A year later, when the First Consul crowned himself in Notre Dame, the Hapsburg monarch assumed the title of Emperor of Austria. In 1805 the cannon of Austerlitz battered down what remained of the crumbling walls and towers of the Holy Roman Empire. By the Treaty of Pressburg, Württemberg and Baden divided Austrian possessions in the west, Bavaria and Württemberg became monarchies, and the rulers of the three great South-German States were recognised as fully sovereign within their own dominions. In the following summer the curtain was rung down on a thousand years of German history. After further bribery and haggling in the antechambers of Talleyrand, in the course of which the Imperial Knights and many petty principalities were engulfed, the Confederation of the Rhine emerged, with Napoleon instead of the Hapsburg as its titular head. A few days later Francis quietly discarded the title of Holy Roman Emperor. Thus the Emperor, the Electors, the Diet, the Court of Appeal, the Ecclesiastical Princes, the Imperial Knights, and the Free Cities collapsed like a house of cards at the touch of Napoleon's spear. For a few feverish years the Rheinbund, the creation and the obedient tool of Napoleon, provided

---

[1] *History of Germany*, i. 216.
[2] Herbert Fisher, *Studies in Napoleonic Statesmanship, Germany*, p. 41.

a partial and ineffective substitute; and when the German Bund emerged from the Congress of Vienna, there were only forty-one States in place of the myriad hosts who had composed the historic Empire. The outward transformation of Germany was as wholesale and almost as rapid as that of France; and it was accomplished without the savagery and sufferings which disgraced the noble experiment of 1789. On the other hand, the simplification of political geography brought gain rather to the princes than to the nation; for Germany as a whole secured neither unity, liberty, nor strength.

II

The second great concrete result of the Revolution, and one which requires a more detailed analysis, was the renaissance of Prussia; but it was not till the *débâcle* of 1806 that her rulers began to realise that they must learn lessons from their terrible neighbour. 'The Prussian monarchy,' declared Mirabeau, 'is so constituted that it could not cope with any calamity'; and the calamity had now arrived. The work of Stein and Hardenberg was rendered possible as well as urgent by Napoleon's thunderbolt; but the ideas· to which they gave practical shape were in large measure those of 1789. Among the counsellors of Frederick William II and his successor were men like Mencken and Lombard, who desired the application of French principles in diluted form; and young Custine pronounced Struensee as much a partisan of the French Revolution as a Prussian Minister could be. But they were not statesmen of the first rank, and they never seriously attempted to carry out the changes which they knew to be necessary. The hour of reform arrived when the logic of the stricken field had revealed the need of building from the depths, and when men of ability and resolution received the more or less reluctant permission of the monarch to carry out some of the most essential tasks. France had shown how to develop and apply the latent strength and capacity of a nation; and the grandeur of her achievement impressed even those who staggered under her blows. 'No man of insight,' declared the jurist Feuerbach in the Bavarian Privy Council in 1809, in an address on the Code Napoléon, 'can conceal from himself that Europe has changed and that the memorable words of a famous statesman, *La Révolution française fera la tour du monde*, are true. The principles of the Code are that every subject is a free man, and that all subjects are equal before the law. And to these fundamental ideas we must adhere.'[1]

[1] *Anselm Feuerbach's Leben*, i. 163–6.

In her desperate plight Prussia was fortunate in securing for a longer or shorter period the services of the best political brains and the highest organising capacity in Germany. In the memorable words of the King, it was necessary to seek compensation in spiritual forces for what had been lost on the material plane. The supreme task of the moment was to revive the courage and mobilise the resources of the nation by inviting it to share in the burdens, the privileges, and the responsibilities of government. ' In your ministries, your councils—if possible in your law-courts, and in your administration '—wrote Napoleon to the King of Westphalia, ' let the greater part of the persons employed be non-nobles. The declared principle is to choose talents wherever they can be found. That is the way to the heart of Germany.' [1] It was the lesson of the French Revolution taught by its testamentary executor, and it was now to be at any rate partially learned by his German victims. ' The military as well as the political chiefs,' writes Cavaignac, ' were penetrated by the examples of the Revolution, imbued by its spirit, convinced that Prussia and Germany would only find salvation by following the paths it had opened.' [2] And this was recognised as frankly by Stein and Niebuhr, by Scharnhorst and Gneisenau, who hated it, as by the eclectic Hardenberg, and by Schön, the radical doctrinaire.

Though Stein [3] was the son of an Imperial Knight, and was therefore subject to no superior but the Emperor, his youth was closely associated with Hanover and the English influences which it embodied. Like most young German nobles destined for a public career he studied at Göttingen, where his chief friends were Rehberg and Brandes, the disciples and interpreters of Burke. At the age of thirty he visited England for the technical study of mining, and took occasion to acquaint himself with the working of British institutions. In Cleves and Mark, where his administrative career began, his conviction of the value of local self-government was confirmed by harmonious co-operation with the Estates. He spoke of Rousseau as ' the man with a sick heart, and irritable and brooding imagination ; but for Montesquieu he entertained the reverence common to all admirers of constitutional government. Though a noble himself, he was wholly free from a belief in the monopoly of virtue and capacity by his class. He condemned serfdom in Poland, and had no use for unlimited monarchy.

Owing to the destruction of his early correspondence, including

---

[1] *Corresp. de Napoléon*, xvi. 174.
[2] *La Formation de la Prusse Contemporaine*, i. 406–7.
[3] Lehmann's great biography supersedes Seeley and Pertz.

that with his bosom friend Rehberg, we have no direct evidence of his attitude towards the opening scenes of the Revolution. 'Stein repudiated and raged against all ideas,' wrote Schön long after. ' His greatest word of blame in affairs of State was Metaphysicus.' [1] But his dislike of abstract ideas was no stronger than his hatred of abuses. He doubtless approved the policy of the Anglophils who occupied a commanding position in the first months of the Constituent, and he afterwards reckoned Mounier and Bailly among ' the best of men.' Moreover, as a keen Protestant, he was not opposed to the attacks on the Pope and monastic vows. In his manuscript history of the Revolution he pronounced Burke's ' Reflections ' ' the work of a great and experienced statesman who, with deep knowledge and splendid eloquence, defends the cause of civil order, religion, and morality against empty and criminal innovations.' But this verdict was delivered twenty years later ; and the first contemporary indication of his attitude occurs in a letter to Frau von Berg, written in the spring of 1792.[2] ' You ask me what I am reading. I am just finishing Brandes's new book on the influence of the French Revolution on Germany, which has given me great pleasure. You will find it in a spirit of moderation, observation, and precise acquaintance with the ruling ideas and tendency of the age. It correctly describes the whole chain of causes and circumstances which prepared the overthrow of a mass of old and useful conceptions and customs, and fostered the tendency to the spirit of innovation. I recommend you to read it.'

Stein had no qualms as to the justice of the war, and he felt confident of the rapid success of the Allies when he saw the Prussian troops at Coblenz on their way to the campaign.[3] ' The spirit of the army,' he wrote, ' the spirit of discipline, courage, and readiness to face danger, is very admirable. It is uplifting to recognise herein the work of the great monarch too early lost to us, in spite of his long reign.' The failure of the invasion saddened but did not alarm him. ' French anarchy and immorality will not infect the tranquil, moral German,' he observed.[4] ' He may not conquer this unhappy nation, but he will certainly not be beaten. The object-lesson of the excesses and sufferings of two illustrious Estates will perhaps remove many a prejudice and accelerate many an improvement. I anticipate a war of many years ; but its influence is of value, for it restores energy and courage, gives a new charm to activity, and will increase repugnance to the odious French nation.' His dislike of the French was confirmed when he watched the soldiers march out of Mainz on the recapture of the

[1] Schön, *Briefwechsel mit Pertz u. Droysen*, p. 173.
[2] Pertz, i. 108–9.   [3] *Ib.*, i. 114, 131.   [4] Lehmann, i. 154.

city. ' The expression of arrogance, foolish pride, and immorality
on the faces of the garrison was intolerable,' he wrote to Frau von
Berg ; ' there was not a countenance at which one could glance
with satisfaction.' After Thermidor he spoke with horror of ' the
monster, Robespierre, who revenged the King on his persecutors
and on the corrupt nation by streams of blood, till he himself, ripe
for hell, came to a horrible end.' He admired the heroism of the
Vendée rebellion, and praised ' the religious enthusiasm and true
devotion to the throne of the pious countrymen who fought against
the blind passion of bloodthirsty opponents and their great armies.'
He was at first inclined to sympathise with the Émigrés, finding
the Count of Provence good-natured and sensible, and Artois fiery
but clever ; but, like other Germans of all schools of thought, he
was soon disillusioned. ' On the whole they were burdensome in
their claims,' he wrote long after, ' and their frivolity and super-
ficiality prevented them from winning respect.' He agreed with
them, however, in denouncing the Peace of Basle as perfidy ; for
he regarded France as the representative of the principle of
despotism, which he hated beyond everything in the world. ' The
windy Frenchmen must be driven with the whip of a Louis XI, a
Richelieu, or a Louis XIV,' he wrote in 1802. ' The satisfaction of
his vanity compensates him for an evil administration—previously,
the honour of being a subject of the greatest of kings, now the airy
phantom of equality.'

Many years later Stein found himself an exile, without prospect
of employment so long as Napoleon bestrode the world like a
Colossus. He carried with him an undying hatred of the French
nation as well as of its ruler, which is reflected in the notes and
writings of this sad period of his life. ' In no history,' he wrote
at Brünn in 1810, ' does one find such immorality, such moral
uncleanness, as in that of France, and nowhere more so than in the
Revolution, the trend of which was vicious and criminal as soon as
the weakness of the government was recognised and the nation
was able to display its character without fear of retribution.' But
he was as far as ever from accepting the unhistoric explanation of
the Revolution common in reactionary circles. ' It arose from
the wish to improve the constitution of society. This wish was
universal, and was awakened by the reforms of two eminent rulers,
by the state of the sciences, and by the interest in political science
created by the American War. The deficit was a contributory
influence, but as little a real cause as were Indulgences that of the
Reformation.' [1]

The fallen statesman was not content to pronounce opinions.

[1] Pertz, iv. 443, 446.

KK

'To employ his leisure profitably,' wrote Varnhagen, 'he under-took a serious study of the Revolution.[1] He wished to get to the bottom of these events from which the fortunes of the world were directly derived, and to explore their strength and weakness. He read the writings of all parties as well as the "Moniteur." At every visit I found him further advanced, and I was able to note the impressions left by each of its epochs. His hatred of the Revolution was unmeasured, especially in its early stages, when on so many occasions everything could .have been altered by limited measures and a little courage. The French of 1789 were to him the same as those of 1811, and the republicans were already the serfs of Napoleon and the oppressors of Germany. The events in which the populace scored successes filled him with bitterness, and he would gladly have placed his abilities at the service of the Court, the Ministers, and the Generals. If Mirabeau and Lafayette found some grace in his eyes, it was because they were subsequently to oppose the popular tide ; but, with these exceptions, he included all the actors in the same condemnation. One day I found him unusually excited. He had reached the Convention ; and here, where his hatred must have reached its culmination, he found himself driven to admiration of the iron strength with which the Committee of Public Safety ruled France and presented a victorious front to the foe. He could not stop talking of all they had achieved, and blamed me for not recognising it ; for, though I had admired the Constituent and lamented the Girondins, the Jacobins and their atrocities had always filled me with horror. But at my next visit his admiration had turned to disgust.'

The fruits of his studies were a 'History of the Era 1789–1799 '—in reality the narrative covers the years 1786–1794—and a 'French History from the Earliest Times till 1799.' The manuscript is in the main a summary of his authorities, and has therefore never been published ; but the passages which record his opinions are of considerable interest.[2] 'The Revolution,' he declares, 'broke out without any cause being given by the King, who, indeed, willingly surrendered his privileges, and was fully prepared for the co-operation of the Estates. The French nation was superficial, immoral, irreligious. Party leaders endeavoured to turn the Monarchy into an empty shadow, and pursued a crazy goal by even crazier means—revolt, plunder, and murder—without consideration of the rights and feelings of their fellow citizens. And they in turn were overthrown by even more violent and ambitious men, who founded their rule on corpses, robbery, and atheism ; and

---

[1] Varnhagen, *Denkwürdigkeiten*, ii. 285–9.
[2] Lehmann, iii. 98–100, 102, 103, 116.

these, too, fell under the knife of their fellows.' He condemns the weakness of the King, the doubling of the representation of the *Tiers État*, the low franchise, the 'usurpation' of power by the Assembly, the decrees of the Fourth of August and the Constitution of 1791. In other words he condemns not merely the excesses and the later developments of the Revolution but its opening scenes. His condemnation, however, is not unqualified. Patriotism, he declares, made France accept even the rule of the Convention rather than allow the Coalition to tear the country to pieces. ' Detestable as was the Committee of Public Safety, it deserves imitation and admiration for its services in releasing and organising the fighting forces of the nation.' He has, moreover, no words of approval for the old régime. He still praises Montesquieu and his idea of ' a monarchy limited by national representation.' He firmly maintains the right of a State to abolish serfdom, which he describes as ' in contradiction to the original and inalienable rights of mankind.' He still retains his admiration for English models. And finally his hatred of the Revolution does not involve an indulgent verdict on its enemies. ' No leaders were to be found,' he writes of the First Coalition, ' capable of moulding public spirit, supporting the sinking burden of the European system, satisfying the reasonable wishes of the nations, or mending the faults of constitutions. One found everywhere mediocrity, weakness, and egotism, which only aimed at its own advantage and gave way to despair in times of anger.'

When Stein accompanied the victorious Allies to Paris in 1814, he refused to separate the French people from Napoleon. ' This impure, shameless and undisciplined race abuses the Tsar's magnanimity and must be ruled with a rod of iron. The levity and demoralisation of the nation make me apprehend new dangers to the peace of Europe and, above all, of our poor country.' He was among the strongest champions of the restoration of the Bourbons. ' What had Louis XVI done that he deserved to be executed ? Did he, like James II, conspire against the liberty and religion of the people ? Did he not rather display a confidence and consideration which made him the unhappiest of kings and his nation the most criminal in history ? The House of Bourbon has done nothing to forfeit its right to the throne.' In like manner he pronounced the expulsion of Charles X in 1830 tragic and unmerited. ' I hate the French as cordially as a Christian may hate anyone,' he remarked in the last year of his life. ' I wish they would all go to the devil.' [1]

The Revolution had been saddled and bridled by Napoleon

[1] Lehmann, iii. 359–60, 373–4.

before Stein was called in middle life to play a commanding part
in the affairs of Prussia ; but its influence on his reforming ideas
and achievements is indubitable.   After his appointment as
Minister shortly before the battle of Jena, he drew up a memorandum sharply criticising the organisation of the Cabinet.[1]   He
compares the Prussian State to a machine which only functions
properly when controlled by a superman, and therefore demands a
limited monarchy. .The memorandum was seen by the Queen,
but was considered too outspoken for the eyes of the King.   His
biographer, Lehmann, finds traces of ' the ideas of '89 ' ; but there
is nothing in it which would not occur to a student of the British
Constitution.   Of far greater importance was the so-called Nassau
Programme, written in his ancestral home on the eve of his appointment as First Minister.   ' If the nation is to be uplifted,' he
declared, ' the submerged part must be given liberty, independence,
property, and the protection of the laws.'   He agrees with the
French reformers with regard to the emancipation of the peasants,
the liberation of industry, the equalisation of taxes, and the abolition
of patrimonial jurisdiction.   ' There is no catalogue of the Rights
of Man,' comments Lehmann ; ' but the emphatic demand for the
right of the nation to administer itself rules out the patriarchal
system of old Prussia and implicitly contains the whole charter of
citizenship.' [2]

Stein's historic ministry was cut short before he had time to
carry out more than a fraction of the Nassau Programme ; but the
emancipation of the peasants and the grant of municipal self-
government stand as everlasting monuments of his brief rule.   In
the former case Prussia was a laggard rather than a pioneer, though
something had been done on the royal domain.   Joseph II had
abolished serfdom in his dominions in 1781, Baden in 1783, Denmark
in 1788, Schleswig-Holstein in 1797.   The idea was the common
property of the Aufklärung ; but the French Revolution provided
a new and powerful impetus by exhibiting the marvellous results
secured by every approximation towards equality and by every
release of individual aptitudes.   An advance was so generally
expected by the peasants that unimaginative officials attributed
the ferment to seditious agitators ; [3] but Stein knew better.   As
the emancipation of the peasants owed much to Schön, who had
drunk deeply at French springs—and, indeed, the abolition of
serfdom in East and West Prussia had been proposed before Stein
reached Memel—so the Town Ordinance, which revived communal
life after a progressive decline of two centuries, owed much to the

[1] Lehmann, i. 401–14.   [2] Ib., ii. 86–8.
[3] See Knapp, Die Bauern-Befreiung, i. 98.

radical Frey, another friend and pupil of Kant and an honoured Königsberg official.[1] In his preliminary sketch of the measure he studied the French decree of 1789 on municipalities, and envisaged the representatives of the local bourgeoisie as a kind of miniature Parliament. Reform in the direction of equality was in the air, and Stein was merely the principal agent of a change rendered ultimately inevitable by the ferment of the Revolution.

' What was it,' asks Lehmann, ' that attracted these thoroughly German minds in Königsberg to the revolutionary legislation of France, which they only approved with large reservations ? The answer is that they desired to attain for their country the position of power which those laws had secured for France.'[2] As it was the abstract ideas of 1789 which had appealed to the writers and thinkers of Germany, so it was their concrete results which many years later converted conservative statesmen to a policy of sweeping reform. Stein and his comrades were, accordingly, denounced to the King by Marwitz as democrats and Jacobins, who were out for a constitutional monarchy and accepted the ideas of the Constituent Assembly. ' French corruption,' wrote the indignant Junker in his Memoirs, ' hardly touched the nobility and the peasantry ; but the educated bourgeoisie was terribly affected.[3] The women in particular were unable to resist French politeness and flattery, and Masonry was another connecting link.' Moreover the keys of the fortress were handed over by the very man whose supreme duty was to defend it to the last. ' Stein brought the Revolution into our country, and it cost the land so much that Napoleon's exploitations were a trifle in comparison. He collected a gang of ideologues, drones, and chatterers round him in the Tugend-bund, and began revolutionising the Fatherland, inaugurating the war of the propertyless against property, of industry against agriculture, of crass materialism against the divine order. He began the co-called regeneration of the Prussian State with laws based on the principles of Rousseau and Montesquieu. The ideologues from the Garonne to the Niemen hailed the Emancipation Edict with a hymn of praise.' An essay on Stein's ' Political Testament '[4] argued that the Minister, ' despite great intellectual power, had the fault of being deceived by appearances ' ; and in a later essay on ' The Causes of the Increase of Crime ' he argues that the root cause was ' THE REVOLUTION '—that is, the breaking down of barriers and the abolition of old regulations. Gentz was alarmed at the revolutionary spirit in the Königsberg bureaux in 1808, and scented democracy in the proposal for universal service.

[1] Lehmann, ii. 447–91.   [2] Ib., ii. 548.
[3] See Meusel, *Marwitz*, i. 324–7.   [4] Ib., ii., part ii. pp. 446–75.

A Memorial of the Pomeranian Estates, presented to the King in 1809, denounced the abolition of serfdom as an attack on private property, demanded the retention of judicial power as one of the inalienable rights of the nobility which only disciples of Rousseau could attack, and protested against conscription as a fruit of the French imposture of liberty and equality. Even Ancillon called Stein ' a republican and revolutionary ' for his conduct in 1812–13.[1]

[1] The publication of Lehmann's biography led to a lively discussion of Stein's debt to the French Revolution. The Göttingen Professor occasionally made the mistake of attributing to the Revolution ideas which Stein had derived from the English Constitution and from the Aufklärung ; but he never suggests that France was more than one source of his inspiration, or that he made uncritical use of French models. ' Stein did not, indeed, surrender himself to the ideas of '89. He desired to modify them and to combine them with the inherited conditions of Prussia and Protestant ideals.' His estimate, however, was sharply attacked by the Hanoverian jurist, Ernst von Meier, in his massive work on Prussia and the French Revolution. Lehmann, argues his critic, disliked the nobility in every country, painted Prussia before Jena far too darkly, was strongly attracted to the French Revolution, and made Stein a mere imitator ; whereas Stein's reforms show no trace of the influence of the Revolution, except in a few trifling details. His work was purely Germanic, the result of concrete needs, and was carried out in the spirit of tradition, not of abstract reason. When Lehmann replied (*Preussische Jahrbücher*, May 1908), Meier restated his position in *Stein, die französische Revolution, und der preussische Adel*. But if Lehmann exaggerates the debt to France, his critic makes an equal mistake in contesting it. Hintze sided in the main with Meier (*Forschungen zur Brand. und Preuss. Gesch.* xxi.), while Delbrück came to the rescue of Lehmann (*Preussische Jahrbücher*, December 1908), who, he declares, proved French influence on Stein's legislation to have been stronger than had been hitherto realised. In contrasting ' the Germanic ideal ' with ' the ideas of 1789 ' Meier forgot that neither was a fixed system, if indeed the former had any real existence. The idea of reforming Prussia after French models was in the air, and Stein was wise enough to learn from the movement which he detested. Moreover, the ideas of '89 were not the creation of the States-General, but were rooted in the Aufklärung. Meier replied to Lehmann in *Forschungen zur Brand. und Preuss. Gesch.*, xxi. ; and in the biographical sketch contributed to a reprint in 1912 of Meier's earlier work, *Die Reform der Verwaltungsorganisation*, Thimme pronounces his friend to have won the victory. A middle position was taken up in Gierke's address, *Die Steinsche Städteordnung*, in which he discovers a mixture of German traditions and French ideas, or rather the new ideas which found their chief expression in the Revolution. The French inspiration of Stein and his colleagues is naturally maintained by French historians. Cavaignac's volumes, *La Formation de la Prusse Contemporaine*, are one long protest against the conspiracy of German writers to belittle or deny the debt to France. ' It needed half a century to establish throughout Germany the social principles born of the French Revolution,' writes Doniol in his book, *La Révolution et la Féodalité:* ' Prussia led the way. Stein's Edict of 1807 was the Prussian Fourth of August.'

III

The political derivation of Hardenberg gives rise to no such controversy.[1] 'While Stein swam against the stream of the time,' writes Meier, ' Hardenberg allowed himself to be borne along by it. He was filled with the ideas of the Law of Nature, of Montesquieu, and, above all, of Adam Smith. He was an adherent of the French Revolution, and he desired to imitate it.' As a subject and official of the Hanoverian Government, he was early brought into contact with English ideas and institutions, and a prolonged sojourn in England increased his familiarity with constitutional government. An enemy alike of autocracy and democracy, he greeted the Revolution and many of its early measures as making for the limited monarchy which he approved. As administrator of Anspach and Bayreuth, after the resignation of the last Margrave, he learned to detest the corrupt little principalities with which Germany swarmed. The Revolution went too fast and too far for a liberal conservative who abhorred violence ; but he never for a moment doubted that a new era had dawned, and that the task of statesmanship was to apply the lessons of the cataclysm.

In a memorandum written early in 1794, on the size of the army, Hardenberg recognises the dangerous seduction of ' French principles.' [2] ' The greatest evil would be if, under the influence of the bloodthirsty liberty-imposture, a revolt were to break out ; for in the long run it might sweep even the best subjects off their feet.' He had, however, no wish to restore the French Monarchy, nor did he think it possible ; and German statesmen would have plenty to do in warding off internal dangers. ' It would be a mistake to shut one's eyes to the existence in Germany of a class of scoundrels or impostors, who, caught by the contagion of French principles, desire their integral application. It is to be hoped that they are not very numerous ; but they raised their head now and then in the recent disasters, and they would become extremely menacing in the event of an invasion or the incautious arming of the people. There is a second class of opinion, which hates French principles and French anarchy, but desires a revolution in Germany, trusting, perhaps too generously, to German moderation. This school, which is much larger than the first, contains many men of business, and works clandestinely towards a revolution. A third variety, which, one hopes, is also numerous, sees many flaws in our constitutions, but thinks it better to change them gradually and without

---

[1] See Ranke, *Hardenberg* ; and Meier, *Preussen und die franz. Revolution.*
[2] Ranke, *Hardenberg*, i. 158–64.

making a splash, to open a career to talent, to secure an equal distribution of burdens, security of property and person, to combine true liberty with religion and civil order, and wishes for peace in order that their plans may be more speedily carried out. A fourth group, which is confined to a section of the favoured classes and some business men, frightened by the thought of losing its privileges, goes to the other extreme, is blind to the spirit of the time, and often falls into harshness, pride, and injustice.'

The writer, of course, belonged to the third school, whose ideal was to checkmate revolutionary influences by a conservative-liberal transformation. He was well aware that the old Germany was doomed. In the Memorial[1] written in the summer of 1807 at the King's request on his enforced resignation, he declared that the dominant principle of government should be the application of the ideas of the French Revolution to Prussia ; for such was their power that any State which rejected them would either collapse or be forced to accept them. There must be a revolution in the good sense, a revolution from above. The form most suited to the spirit of the age would be the combination of democratic principles with monarchical rule. A government must work in harmony with the *Zeitgeist* and with the scheme of Providence, and should not shrink from the principal demand of the time—the utmost possible liberty and equality. He even went so far as to recommend the choice of non-commissioned officers by privates, and of higher officers by their subordinates. He prescribed the same medicine for the State when he returned to power. The adoption of such principles and institutions as resulted from the progress of the human mind, he declared in a speech of 1811, was indispensable. The new system, which had come with a rush in France and which should be applied by Prussia in a peaceful manner, centred in the unfolding of all the powers of the individual and in the equality of all before the law.

Hardenberg understood by the French Revolution the legislation not of the revolutionary assemblies, but of Napoleon. In the words of Bismarck, his legislation was translated from the Bulletin of the Kingdom of Westphalia. His ideal was not democracy, but enlightened bureaucracy. ' Your Majesty, we must do from above what the French have done from below.' He was as good as his word ; for he completed the creation of a free peasantry begun by Stein, and carried forward the reform of the central and local administration. He believed more in bureaucratic control and less in local self-government than his great rival ; but it was not his fault that Prussia had to wait for a constitution till 1848.

[1] Ranke, *Hardenberg*, vol. iv.

Like Stein, he was denounced by the Prussian feudalists as a leveller ; and Marwitz passionately declared that the King had virtually abdicated in favour of his omnipotent Chancellor.[1] From his narrow standpoint he was right ; for the statesman had grasped the force latent in the idea of social equality. Throughout Europe a truceless conflict was in progress between the *ancien régime* and the ideas of '89 ; and when any State or statesman decided to break with feudalism, they were compelled to study and to some extent adopt French models. 'Hardenberg's work,' declares Cavaignac, 'is the most indubitable testimony to the action of the French Revolution on European society.' His cast of mind was rather French than German, for tradition never laid its spell upon him in the sphere either of religion or politics. Such a mind was of infinite value in the critical period following the battle of Jena ; and Ranke has justly declared that no statesman has graven his name more deeply on the brazen tablets of Prussian history.

In the little group of distinguished men who rebuilt Prussia after her unexampled humiliation, only one could boast of philosophic training and an interest in ideas. Entering Königsberg in the year before the Revolution, Schön[2] sat at the feet of Kant and Kraus. From the former he acquired the doctrine of natural right ; and he used to recall the master's utterance, 'My whole being shudders when I think of serfdom.' From the latter he learned to admire Adam Smith. While still at the University he formed a close friendship with Fichte ; and these emancipating influences fostered his tendency to probe fór the ideas that lay behind political action and institutions. His love of theory and his passion for generalisation made him welcome the Declaration of the Rights of Man. His cast of mind was indeed rather French than German, and he may be fairly described as the only doctrinaire among Prussian statesmen. He travelled through Germany to study administration, and in 1798 spent a year in England. 'Through England I became a statesman,' he wrote in his Autobiography. 'There is public life for you. In no country in Europe is there such respect for man and his rights, or such equality before the law.'[3] Returning home he worked under Struensee, whom he afterwards pronounced the greatest of Prussian Ministers, approached by Hardenberg alone.

[1] Meusel, *Marwitz*, i. 528–35. Cp. Keyserling, *Studien zu den Entwicklungsjahren der Brüder Gerlach*, ch. iv.

[2] *Aus den Papieren Schöns*, vol. i. 'Selbstbiographie.' The Memoirs were sharply attacked, on their appearance, by Maurenbrecher and Lehmann, and an angry controversy ensued. An apologia is attempted by Baumann, *Theodor v. Schön, Seine Geschichtschreibung u. seine Glaubwürdigkeit.*

[3] *Aus den Papieren Schöns*, i. 25.

Schön's chance came after Jena, when he co-operated in the emancipation of the peasantry. He was the most radical of the liberators, opposing serfdom as contrary to natural right; and his love of first principles blinded him to the transcendent merits of Stein, whose indifference to abstract ideas provoked him to exasperation. 'He had nothing of Struensee's solid, scientific culture, nor his grasp of the lofty concept of the State.' He was a typical product of Göttingen, adds the critic, lacking the philosophic, aesthetic and poetic training essential to creative statesmanship.[1] Schön was a philosophical, not an historical, head, and approached concrete tasks from the deductive, not the inductive side. This exaltation of abstract principles caused some alarm in Court circles. 'Look sharp after Schön,' wrote the Queen to Hardenberg shortly before her death; 'he is dangerous, owing to his republican principles.'[2] Schön was, of course, no republican; but Queen Luise meant that he measured the needs of the State by his own theoretical postulates. It was partly owing to his doctrinaire habits of mind and partly to the angularities of his temperament that he never attained to the highest offices, to which he deemed himself beyond all others entitled. His speculative approach to the problems of government, however, in no way interfered with his administrative capacity, which he brilliantly proved by his long service as President of East and West Prussia. Looking back in old age on the crowded years of the Prussian *risorgimento*, he painted a flattering portrait of himself as the chief architect of the reforms erroneously connected with the name of Stein; and in reading Thiers's 'History of the Revolution' he discovered, 'with astonishment and delight, the verdict that the output of the Constituent Assembly tallied with our legislation of 1807–1815.'[3]

IV

The lessons of the French Revolution were taken to heart by the reforming soldiers of Prussia no less than by the reforming civilians; and the minds of Stein and Scharnhorst were cast in the same mould. The revolt of the American Colonies earned the latter's respect, since the people were able to control themselves and had learned to enjoy freedom; but he disliked the upheaval in France, where the nation gave rein to its passions. His cool, powerful mind focussed on national strength and internal order,

---

[1] Schön, *Briefwechsel mit Pertz u. Droysen*, pp. 168, 173.
[2] Lehmann, *Stein*, iii. 68.
[3] *Aus den Papieren Schöns*, iv. 536.

and he complained that the Rights of Man dealt only with the rights of individuals, not with those of the State. He defended both monarchies and standing armies in 1792. 'Our princes are, as a rule, not inhuman despots. Injustice occurs in aristocratic and democratic governments as well as in kingdoms. Standing armies do not foster despotism, for they spring from the people and share its opinions.'[1] But his conservatism was the result of caution, not of blind satisfaction with existing conditions. 'Do not call attention to things which people will find out for themselves,' he wrote to a friend in 1793 ; 'and do not speak publicly of the injustices of the upper classes towards the lower, since most members of the former are too bad or too stupid to make any concessions, and therefore a rebellion is inevitable if the latter put forward any demand at the present time. I hope that in twenty years the upper classes will think differently ; and the Universities—above all, Göttingen—will help them. But I conceive it my duty to point out to those in a better position, whenever I meet them, their evil notions and the injustices they commit, and to convince them that things cannot go on as they are.' He approved the war of 1792 as a defensive measure against the old French spirit of aggrandisement ; but he loved the Émigrés as little as most of his fellow countrymen. 'I have had a lot to do with these revengeful folk recently,' he wrote to his wife. 'As a rule they deserve their fate. They are vain, ignorant, and superstitious.'[2]

When North Germany had withdrawn from the struggle, the great soldier discussed the causes of failure in a penetrating dissertation on 'The French Revolutionary War.'[3] His thesis is that the evil fortune of the Allies was due not to accidents or details but to much deeper causes. Accidents or ill-luck might explain the loss of a battle or a campaign but not of ten campaigns in five years. Its first cause was ignorance of the strength of the foe, due to the false reports of French opinion received by the Émigrés and blindly swallowed by the Allies, who were led to believe that the Revolution was the work of a small minority and that the invasion would be as easy as the Dutch campaign of 1787. 'It seems at first sight incredible that such a weighty enterprise could be launched on the strength of such partisan witness ; but the explanation is that men follow their predilections and their passions.' A second reason was the lack of stomach for the fight. 'When the French Revolution began, a large number of the noblest minds were fired by the ideal

---

[1] See Lehmann's great biography, i. 75–8.
[2] Scharnhorst, *Briefe*, i. 18, 26.
[3] Published as Part ii. of his *Military Memoirs of our Time*, 1797.

of a more perfect and more beneficent government, especially among young men with a generous feeling for right and for the sufferings of the less fortunate class. Those who loved reading—that is, most of the educated classes—had already grasped the idea of a better constitution, which had long been seductively preached in novels and poems ; and the ideas of liberty, equality, and independence had been thrown into circulation by the American War.' By others, whose interests were threatened, the Revolution was hated. Thus the Allies entered on the struggle without the unity and enthusiasm which they needed for victory and which were possessed by their adversaries. The Brunswick Manifesto deeply wounded the pride of a great people, and every citizen was ready for any sacrifice in order to save his territory and his independence. Necessity created a marvellous energy in the Government, the army, and the nation, whose existence and future were at stake. France employed all her material and moral resources, while the Allies only utilised a portion of their armies and were sadly lacking in morale. In their ranks, indeed, many were opposed to the war, and even certain Ministers and Generals were not convinced of its necessity. He concludes by reiterating his emphatic conviction that the main causes of the loss of the first round of the match between revolutionary France and feudal Europe were to be sought on the moral and political rather than on the material plane.

Gneisenau,[1] like Scharnhorst, was a born soldier, to whom order and obedience were more precious than liberty. His youthful experiences in the American War of Independence left no trace on his opinions and inspired no sympathy with revolutions, which, in his opinion, should be avoided by wise laws or, if they broke out, suppressed by force. He was hostile to the French experiment from the first, and he was moved by the chatter about rights to a poetical protest.[2]

> Let faithfulness to duty be proclaimed
> To all mankind, before their rights are named.

In later years he used to say that his antagonism to the Revolution dated from 1790, and it never diminished. A poem of considerable length on the deposition of Louis XVI expressed his passionate anger and pity.[3] But though he detested French ideas and spent his life fighting the forces which they had unchained, he fully recognised the strength which France had derived from them and

---

[1] The great official biography commenced by Pertz was completed by Delbrück, who subsequently published a shorter life in two volumes.

[2] See Lehmann, *Scharnhorst*, ii. 12.

[3] See Pertz, *Gneisenau*, i. 648–50.

was eager to apply the lesson to his own country. In a striking passage, written after the Jena campaign, he drew the same lesson from the Revolution as Stein. 'One cause above all has raised France to this pinnacle of greatness—the Revolution awakened all her powers and gave to every individual a suitable field for his activity. What infinite aptitudes slumber undeveloped in the bosom of a nation ! In the breast of thousands resides real genius. Why do not the Courts take steps to open up a career to it, wherever it is found, to encourage talents and virtues whatever the rank ? Why did they not seize this opportunity to multiply their powers a thousandfold, and to open to the simple bourgeois the Arc de Triomphe, through which only the noble can now pass ? The new era requires more than old names, titles, and parchments. The Revolution has set the whole strength of a nation in motion, and by the equalisation of the different classes and the equal taxation of property converted the living strength in man, and the dead strength in resources, into a productive capital, and thereby upset the old relations of States. If other States desire to restore this equilibrium, they must appropriate the results of the Revolution. Then they will reap the double advantage of being able to mobilise their whole national strength against another Power and of escaping the danger of a revolution, which threatens so long as they refuse to obviate a forcible change by a voluntary transformation.' [1] Here are the same ideas and almost the same phrases as those of Stein and Hardenberg.

The conviction that Prussia might take lessons from revolutionary France was shared in a minor degree by Clausewitz, the favourite pupil and spiritual heir of Scharnhorst. On returning from ten months' captivity in France at the close of the Jena campaign, he wrote an interesting study of the characteristics of the two nations entitled ' The Germans and the French.' [2] A survey of Germany's desperate plight, he begins, prompts the question whether it is due to character or circumstance, and whether the triumph of France results from the impetus given by the Revolution. He replies by a damaging analysis of the vanity and levity of French character. ' Their virtues and failings alike make them pliant tools of government. They are more enthusiastic, more plastic, more uniform in type than the German, and possess more *esprit de corps* and, above all, more national spirit.' The comparison of national characteristics is pursued in the ' Diary of a Journey from Soissons to Geneva,' written on his way home from captivity.[3] ' In France and Germany

---

[1] Pertz, *Gneisenau*, i. 301.
[2] See Karl Schwartz, *Clausewitz*, i. 73–88.
[3] *Ib.*, i. 104–10.

the opinion is general that owing to the Revolution, with its enthusiasm and its Terror, its victories and its despotism, France gained such an *élan* and such a warlike spirit that she is irresistible. That is an error. Its course could have been predicted. Their military successes were due not to the Revolution or to national character, but to their leaders. I find no elevation above their earlier level, except during the Terror ; and that was only a passing phase. How, indeed, could the Revolution raise the nation ? Was it not rather a moral bankruptcy ? ' Early in 1812, however, when Napoleon's power was still unbroken, Clausewitz drew up a memorandum in which he appealed to his countrymen to fight the enemy with his own weapons. France, he declares, defended herself when attacked on all sides, became a conqueror, and overthrew the old and decrepit constitutions of her foes. ' This she did without money ; and why cannot we do it without money too ? '[1] When Napoleon had fallen he once more returned to the effect of the Revolution on his countrymen. The example of France had undoubtedly excited her neighbour. Even the most law-abiding felt the need of a greater equality of classes, and desired more prosperity for the peasant and more industrial liberty. This practical need made the people as a whole approve the Revolution. Scholars and writers, moreover, were completely carried away by the Paris philosophy and plunged into the whirlpool of revolutionary doctrine. The evil rule of Frederick William II fostered the sympathy of the people with France, but danger was averted by the excesses of the French.[2] It is a grudging but none the less notable tribute to the influence of the Revolution in awakening Germany from her slumbers and quickening the demand for reform.

V

The revival of Prussia after the *débâcle* of 1806 was the joint work of statesmen and writers. In both cases the immediate impetus to action and utterance came from the stricken field, but its ultimate source was the teaching and the lessons of the Revolution. The collapse evoked all that was best and all that was worst in the country. A handful of men attacked their own State and praised France and her ruler. Their leader, Buchholz, had failed to reach the high posts in the public service which he coveted, and his contribution to the crisis was his ' Gallery of Prussians,' a series of acrid character studies of leading soldiers and civilians. He was supported by Cölln, an ex-official, whose ' Secret Letters ' were filled with invective and scandal, and by Massenbach, who, despite

[1] Pertz, *Gneisenau*, iii. 647.   [2] Schwartz, *Clausewitz*, ii. 210–15.

his own sorry military record, poured scorn on better men than himself. But these voices of discord were soon drowned by manlier accents. The political awakening, begun by the Revolution and its German interpreters, was continued by the impassioned appeal of Arndt and Jahn, by the lectures of Fichte, the sermons of Schleiermacher, and the dramas of Kleist.

When Arndt visited France in 1799 he found little to please him.[1] Education was too uniform, and was fitted to make slaves. Religion was lacking. Women had lost their modesty. The sittings of the Five Hundred were a disappointment. The site of the Bastille alone moved him to satisfaction. 'One can look at even that bloody conflict without a shudder; for it was a struggle of light against darkness.' A year later, in 'The Liberty of Ancient Republics,' he attacked the prevalent notion that republics are the best form of government. The ancient republics, he contends, did not make men happier, and Athens came to a bad end. They were only possible in small States, as Rousseau had maintained, and they required a lofty standard of virtue. While recognising Rousseau's depth of feeling, he condemns the streams that flowed from him. In an essay of 1803, 'Germany and Europe,' he expresses sympathy with a whole people fighting for liberty, despite his dislike of the French nation, and records his hope that the spirit of revolution, taught by its errors, will find its soul again. 'I have not lost these hopes; they are only disappointed.' In 'The Spirit of the Age' he once more wrote wisely and calmly of the Revolution.[2] 'The first confusion made grey-beards childish, and turned many a wise head. But fifteen years of the most wonderful changes have cooled the brain. The French cannot help this terrible drama on the Seine. It was just an accident that the sins of successive governments, the craziness of the aristocracy, and the blindest weakness combined to render a change inevitable. The spirit of ferment and movement was irrepressible, and the enthusiasm and sympathy at home and abroad were equally pronounced. How many in that stormy surge were conscious what they did? The virtues on which alone a revolution can rest have always been rare. I believe that in the first years there was really a lofty and enthusiastic spirit in the people. We must confess we were all in error. We hoped and believed too much. How could Gallic caprice turn into republican steadfastness? Republics are no good—the large ones because they are too corrupt, the small ones because they are too weak.' Yet the Revolution conferred a great

[1] See Müsebeck, *Arndt's Stellung zum fridericianischen Preussen u. zur franz. Revolution, Preussische Jahrbücher,* August 1904.
[2] *Geist der Zeit,* ed. 1877, pp. 220–35.

service on Germany, though France deserved no gratitude for the boon. ' We had become an outworn, dying people, a weak, discoloured picture set in a framework falling to pieces. We were no longer a State, a people, or an empire. We had lost all sense of high politics. And then there came a breath of wind. The rotten, worm-eaten frame fell away from its joints, and the pictures were trodden underfoot.'

The direction taken by Arndt was followed by Jahn, who as a boy had sympathised with the Revolution and the struggles of France, and had found a hero in Danton.[1] But he was proud of his birth in the Mark, and built German patriotism on a Prussian foundation. In his first book, ' The Fostering of Patriotism,' written in 1799, a hymn of praise to Frederick the Great and his paladins, he urged the study of Prussian history, the erection of monuments on battle-fields, the exhibition of busts, the celebration of anniversaries. The cultivation of patriotism, he contends, is specially necessary in these stormy times, as philosophers and other writers rail against love of princes as superstition, and against love of country as infantile. He was present at the battle of Jena, which turned his hair grey and transformed his patriotism into a flaming passion. His greatest work, ' Deutsches Volksthum,' published in 1810, was a trumpet-call to his countrymen and a declaration of war against Napoleon and his German sycophants. He blames the use of French, foretells the speedy overthrow of the tyrant, and contends that Prussia alone can serve as the nucleus of a united and powerful Germany. ' We can still be saved,' he cries, ' but only by ourselves.' He urges physical training and compulsory service—the preparation of body and mind for the coming struggle. In fighting France he employs the weapons of national self-consciousness and national pride which had released the pent-up forces of a mighty people and had carried their conquering standards over Europe.

The French Revolution was compared by Klinger to the magic work of Medea, who cast the dead limbs of old age into the boiling cauldron to emerge young and beautiful ; and Forster expressed the wish that his country would warm itself at the flame without being burned. The aspiration was destined in large measure to be fulfilled. While in England the reform movement was thrown back forty years by the earthquake and the storm, in Germany it was strengthened and accelerated. If Saxony and Mecklenburg remained unaffected by the winnowing fan of the Revolution, and the old governments of Hanover, Brunswick, and Hesse-Cassel on their return restored many of the old abuses, Prussia, the Rhineland,

[1] See Euler, *F. L. Jahn.*

and the South learned in a generation of conflict and suffering the secret of enduring advance. Even Treitschke is compelled to admit that the constitutional ideas of the Revolution everywhere struck root on German soil; and without the Revolution the famous Article xiii of the Act creating the German Federation would never have seen the light. The ringing blows of Thor's hammer awoke the nation from its slumbers, and rendered the ultimate disappearance of feudalism and autocracy inevitable. The political unification of the nation was deferred for a couple of generations; but the signal for its deliverance from the thraldom of medieval institutions and antiquated ideas was sounded by the tocsin which rang out in 1789.

INDEX

539